# BRITTON'S

# AUTO-BIOGRAPHY.

PART THE FIRST.

# John Britton, F.S.A.

VICE-PRESIDENT OF
THE SUSSEX ARCHÆOLOGICAL SOCIETY,
AND OF
THE ARCHÆOLOGICAL INSTITUTE AT SALISBURY (1849),

## HONORARY MEMBER
OF THE FOLLOWING SOCIETIES—VIZ.

THE ROYAL INSTITUTE OF BRITISH ARCHITECTS,
THE ANTIQUARIAN SOCIETY OF NEWCASTLE-UPON-TYNE,
THE CAMBRIDGE CAMDEN SOCIETY,
THE OXFORD ARCHITECTURAL SOCIETY,
THE INSTITUTE OF THE FINE ARTS,
THE BATH, THE BRISTOL, THE EXETER, AND THE
PLYMOUTH LITERARY, ETC., INSTITUTIONS,
THE NORWICH SOCIETY OF ARTISTS,
THE NORFOLK AND NORWICH ARCHÆOLOGICAL SOCIETY,
THE SOMERSETSHIRE ARCHÆOLOGICAL AND
NATURAL HISTORY SOCIETY,
THE FREEMASONS OF THE CHURCH,
THE SOCIETY OF ANTIQUARIES OF NORMANDY:
CORRESPONDING MEMBER OF THE FRENCH SOCIETY FOR
THE PRESERVATION OF HISTORICAL MONUMENTS,
AND
CHEVALIER OF THE ORDER OF MERIT OF THE
SEVEN UNITED KINGDOMS OF GERMANY.

Drawn by R.W. Satchwell & T. Uwins.  Engraved by J. Thomson.

## JOHN BRITTON,

F. S. A. &c.

London. Published in Britton's Aut Biography 1849.

THE

# Auto-Biography

OF

## John Britton,

F.S.A.

HONORARY MEMBER OF NUMEROUS ENGLISH AND FOREIGN SOCIETIES.

(VIDE BACK OF FLY TITLE.)

### In Three Parts:

VIZ.

PART I.   PERSONAL AND LITERARY MEMOIR OF THE AUTHOR.

PART II.  DESCRIPTIVE ACCOUNT OF HIS LITERARY WORKS.

PART III. (APPENDIX) BIOGRAPHICAL, TOPOGRAPHICAL, CRITICAL, AND MISCELLANEOUS ESSAYS.

### Copiously Illustrated.

"THERE IS A HISTORY IN ALL MEN'S LIVES."
SHAKSPERE, Hen. IV., Part II., Act iii., Sc. 1.

"KNOWLEDGE IS THE LIGHT OF THE WORLD: AUTHORS HAVE BEEN THE DISPENSERS OF IT, AND HAVE BEEN SUFFERED TO CONSUME THEMSELVES IN THE OPERATION."
RALPH, "Case of Authors by Profession," 1758.

### London:

PRINTED FOR THE AUTHOR, AS PRESENTS TO SUBSCRIBERS TO
"THE BRITTON TESTIMONIAL."

M.DCCC.L.

This Copy of the

# Auto-Biography of John Britton

is presented to

_J. E. Gray Esq.^r, F.R.S._

as a

Reciprocal Compliment for

the

Subscription to the Testimonial

recorded in the

List, at the End of the Appendix.

_July 7th, 1850._

_John Britton_

TO

## NATHANIEL GOULD, ESQ., F.S.A.

TREASURER,

## GEORGE GODWIN, ESQ., F.R.S.

AND

## PETER CUNNINGHAM, ESQ., F.S.A.

HONORARY SECRETARIES,

TO THE

## "Britton Testimonial,"

AND TO THOSE FRIENDS OF THE AUTHOR WHO ORIGINATED, OR HAVE AIDED IN CARRYING INTO EFFECT, THE PUBLIC SUBSCRIPTION WHICH LED TO THE PRESENT WORK.

---

MY DEAR FRIENDS,

Deeply impressed with a sense of gratitude for the kind and generous feelings which prompted you to gratify me in old age by a spontaneous Public Compliment, I am induced to inscribe the present work to you, as a more comprehensive acknowledgment of my sentiments than I could adequately convey by any private expression of them.

I flatter myself that the volume which has been produced in consequence of your friendly estimation of its Author, will tend to justify your approbation of his personal and literary conduct, and also cause his failings to be judged with charity. In the account hereafter given of Public Testimonials, will be found instances of persons who have so received, and applied to their own use, large fortunes, or valuable and splendid works of art. Unlike any of these, I have rather sought how best to make some return, of a tangible kind, to the numerous friends who proposed or promoted the Britton Testimonial, and, in furtherance of that feeling, have laboured to produce a work which may neither impeach the head nor the heart of its Author, but which, I hope, on the contrary, may satisfy the reasonable expectations and judgment of his best friends.

In exhibiting the struggles of aspiring youth, against the difficulties and hardships of adverse circumstances, my narrative may be adduced as another link in the chain already formed by those of Franklin, Gifford, Holcroft, and others, who contended with, and surmounted, many obstacles in their worldly career. Oppressed by poverty, they laboured hard under forbidding influences, but ultimately acquired honourable distinction. My progress has been marked by vicissitudes very dissimilar to either of the authors here named; although in my case, as in theirs, the ennobling "love of fame" was the main spring to exertion and perseverance. If I could command the language, and possessed the literary abilities, of a Gibbon, a Southey, a Coleridge, or a Cumberland,—or the wit and humour of a Colman, a Dibdin, or a Hutton,—the following Auto-Biography would prove more attractive and interesting to the general reader than in its present dress, and thereby do more complete justice to the writer's sentiments and feelings. But, conscious of deficiencies, and averse to every species of affectation, I have attempted to tell a simple, humble tale in my own way, influenced entirely by a wish to create a responsive sympathy in the mind of the reader. Had I indeed the fluent and vivid fancy of the author of those veracious pieces of Auto-Biography, " Cecil, a Coxcomb," and " Cecil, a Peer," I might have rendered this Memoir deeply exciting; for the times in which I have lived; the persons with whom I have associated and corresponded; the " scenes of many-coloured life," which I have beheld; the alternations of sickness and of health, of poverty and of prosperity; the occasional fits of despair, relieved and contrasted by gleams of hope, and the possession of actual happiness, if vividly and graphically described, could not fail to ensure the approval of almost every class of readers.

That you may be amused and, I hope, instructed by the following narrative, and the anecdotes therein recorded; and that your own lives may be prosperous and happy, is the earnest wish of your sincere and grateful friend,

JOHN BRITTON.

Burton Street, London,
July 7th, 1850.

# Explanatory Address;

WITH

REASONS FOR PUBLISHING THE PRESENT AUTO-BIOGRAPHY
IN AN UNFINISHED STATE.

---

For more than four years I have felt much anxiety, and made numerous efforts, to complete the present work; but repeated attacks of serious illness, added to domestic calamity and the infirmities of old age, have combined to thwart my wishes and intentions, and have occasionally paralyzed my faculties. Having now passed my seventy-ninth year, I cannot but more deeply feel the uncertainty of life, and the precarious tenure of physical and mental powers: I therefore think it advisable to present the Subscribers to my Testimonial with this tangible pledge of the exertions I have made to redeem my promises, and to satisfy, in some degree, their reasonable expectations.

I wish it had been in my power to have done so fully; but grieve to say that, far from realizing my hopes of completing the Memoir by this time, I find, on the contrary, that the task would probably occupy me continuously for some months to come, whence I am induced to believe that the readers will rather receive it in its present unfinished state, than wait indefinitely for its legitimate conclusion.

By the present arrangement I propose to ensure to myself some necessary respite and relaxation from what has now become a pressing and laborious task. The summer season, with its usually genial temperature, and the cheering influences of Creation, in the vegetable, animal, and atmospheric world, have ever been to me the greatest sources of physical enjoyment. The solace they are calculated to afford is more needed now than at any former period of life; and to derive their full advantage, I am impelled to adopt the resolution hereby announced. Relieved from the immediate prosecution of my task, I shall have leisure to deliberate upon, and likewise to mature, the portion yet to follow; which, however, it is my wish and intention to finish with all reasonable speed.

At all events, it is satisfactory to know that, in the event of death, or other casualty which may occur to prevent the final completion of this undertaking, by myself, ample materials will be left for its continuance and completion, for which I have prepared directions.

When I originally promised to write an Auto-Biography, it was my intention to limit it to about 200 moderately sized pages, with eight or ten illustrations, and to incur an expence of about £200. But the number of persons who have added their names to the Testimonial list, and the greatly increased amount subscribed, induced me to write a volume of much greater extent than first proposed; in the preparation of which upwards of £900 have already been expended; and the materials collected and arranged for the further portion are so numerous and varied, that a considerable additional cost must yet be incurred.

It is true that this has been a voluntary act of my own, unanticipated and unrequired by the majority of my friends. With a little Quixotic pride and fancied independence, though far from rich, I shrunk from the idea of receiving eleemosynary support, in old age. Having always lived with prudence and economy, I calculated that the small sum I had saved would furnish comforts, though not luxuries, for the short remainder of my life. Five years back, I little anticipated that my weak frame and constitution could possibly last to the present time; and I therefore expected that the honey which had been hived would be ample to satisfy wants and wishes. But, should life be protracted for another similar period, it is probable that the store will be wholly exhausted, and the poor, and once industrious bee may be left powerless and houseless.

The portion of the Memoir now offered to my friends extends to more than 550 full pages, and includes nearly sixty embellishments. It is divided into three parts; the first of which, under the arrangement above described, is, at present, the commencement only of the narrative of my personal life, including incidental notices of persons with whom I have been acquainted or corresponded; and allusions to such public events as have materially influenced my career and character. Of this narrative little more than one third is here printed. That portion reviews the period of boyhood and adolescence, and describes a desultory mode of life, with references to debating societies, private theatres, and some public events and persons, before my final devotion to literature, in my thirtieth year. Thenceforward, to the present time, all my energies have been devoted, most anxiously and industriously, to reading, writing, and the technical management of book-publishing. An extensive intercourse has thereby been created with artists, stationers, printers, booksellers, and publishers; with professional and amateur critics; with the ordinary purchasers and readers of books; and with the class, now almost extinct, of bibliomaniacs. My intercommunion with these, and other public persons, will furnish abundant materials for the continuation of the First Part of the Auto-Biography.

The SECOND and THIRD PARTS may fairly be considered as a separate volume, complete in themselves, and independent of the first; which, when finished, will likewise make a distinct work, but with various references to the two former; as they have numerous passages connected with the personal narrative. Annexed to them is a copious alphabetical Index, and another will be given to Part i.; for, having often lamented the want of such an essential portion of a book, I have made it a rule to give one to every published volume.

The SECOND PART is entirely occupied with a full analytical account of my various publications, and thus forms a classified and chronological view of the numerous literary works I have been engaged upon during the period of half a century. This has been mostly written by Mr. T. E. Jones, who has acted as my amanuensis and secretary for fifteen years, and who, having made himself familiar with all my publications, is peculiarly qualified to perform such a task. His preface explains the nature and materials of that portion of the work. To an introductory letter to my friend Mr. Dawson Turner, at the commencement, I beg particularly to refer the reader, as it notices one of the most remarkable men of our age and country, and also such a collection of autograph letters, with manuscript and graphic illustrations, as is, perhaps, unparalleled in the world. His repeated communications to me, with his recommendations to write an Auto-Biography (see Part ii., page xi.) may be regarded as the main incitement to the work, which is now respectfully, but hopefully, submitted to the public.

In the Appendix, or THIRD PART of the work, I have reprinted several miscellaneous Essays which have been written at different times and on various subjects; as also other papers which have not previously been published. These will be found to constitute essential portions of this Auto-Biography, and, I trust, will prove acceptable to many readers. Much has been written expressly for this portion, particularly the Shaksperian Essays, the Account of Norbury Park and its Vicinity, Notices of my own Residence, with other anecdotal matter. As portions of the Auto-Biography, I may refer to two small volumes, which were written and published since this was commenced: viz., "A Memoir of Henry Hatcher," and an "Elucidation of the Letters of Junius:" copies of each of which have been furnished to the subscribers to the Testimonial.—(See Part i., pp. 18, 19.)

The *Chronological List* of my literary works at the end of the Appendix, and a similar table attached to the "Descriptive Account," will show at once the extent and nature of those published writings, and will be found useful to future Antiquaries, Biographers, and Book-Collectors. It will be seen by these that my anxious attention has been chiefly given to Topography, Archæology, Biography, and the Fine Arts. In these pursuits I have travelled over nearly the whole of England and part of Wales; and have employed numerous draftsmen in measuring and delineating objects of antiquity, as well as in sketching landscape scenery, for the purpose of engraving and publication.

In those journeyings, it was my good fortune to be introduced to, and in some instances to form intimacies with, many Noblemen and Gentlemen at their respective country mansions, as well as with various Bishops, Deans, and other officers of Cathedrals, and with numerous Clergymen and private Gentlemen. Several of these have been eminent, either when I first knew them, or afterwards, for topographical and antiquarian attainments, and most of them have since paid the debt of nature. Numerous letters from these individuals are preserved in my collection, and contain anecdotes, opinions, descriptions, and facts, calculated to make a goodly sized volume, equal at least in variety and interest to any portion of Nichols's "Literary Anecdotes."

# BRITTON'S AUTO-BIOGRAPHY, PART I.

## Table of Contents.

FLY-TITLE, LIST OF HONORARY TITLES.

TITLE, and PRESENTATION PAGES.

DEDICATION to Nathaniel Gould, Esq., F.S.A., Treasurer; George Godwin, Esq., F.R.S., and Peter Cunningham, Esq., F.S.A., Honorary Secretaries to the "Britton Testimonial," and to the other Friends who originated, or have aided in carrying into effect, the Public Subscription which led to the present Work.

EXPLANATORY ADDRESS, with Reasons for publishing the present Auto-Biography in an unfinished state.

CHAPTER I. Origin of this Work in a Public "Testimonial" to its Author—Remarks on Biography by Dr. Johnson, Richard Cumberland, Sir E. Brydges, and Horatio Smith—Tabular View of numerous "Testimonials"—A Committee formed, and various Plans proposed, for that to the Author—A Public Dinner, and an Auto-Biography resolved on—The latter commenced in December 1846—Interrupted by repeated Illness and various Literary Avocations—Resumed, and Plan adopted for its Arrangement—Contents of the ensuing Chapters . . . page 1

CHAPTER II. Local Attachments—Miss Mitford's Description of "Our Village" contrasted with the Author's Birth-place—Natural Features and Characteristics of the Parish of Kington—John Aubrey born there—Its former and present state contrasted—Recollections of Boyhood—Traits of Village Character—Clothier's Visits—Mountebank and Merry-Andrew—Fox-hunting—The Sagacity of the Fox; with an Incident, and Wood-cut—Murderer, and a Gibbet—The Author's Parents and Relatives—Remarks on Pedigrees and Heraldry—Superstitious Faith in a Child's Caul—School-days and Pedagogues—At Foscote—At Yatton Keynel—At Draycot—At Chippenham—School-fellows: Robert Elliott, deaf and dumb; James Hewlett; Thomas Panton—Boyish Occupations—First Books—Barbarism of Rustic Life—Journey to London—Clerkenwell in 1786—Apprenticed . . page 25

CHAPTER III. Apprenticeship: its monotonous Routine—Formality of Indentures—Mode of Business described—Excise Laws—Visits of Mr. Satchwell, the Excise Officer—His Son, an able Artist—Master's Neglect of Instruction—Ineffectual Appeal for Emancipation—Gloom and Discontent—Mental and Bodily Illness—Final Release—Occasional Morning Walks—Medical and Literary Studies—Acquaintances: Mr. Essex, Mr. Brayley, Dr. Trusler, Dr. Towers . . page 63

CHAPTER IV. Emancipation—Doleful Prospects—The Pleasures and Pains of Love—A Pedestrian Tour from London to Plympton—Visit to Home, Friends, and Relations; to Bath and Wells—A rambling, boasting Youth—Disappointment at Plympton, and poignant Distress—Return to London, with empty Pockets—Employed at the London Tavern—With a Hop Merchant—Lodging with a Tinman; his Fanaticism—Account of William Huntington, "S. S."—Engagement with a

Lawyer; his Peculiarities—Studies—A Cook's Shop, and some of its Visitors described—Chevalier D'Eon—Sir John Dineley—Joseph Ritson—In the office of Parker and Wix—Notice of John Thomas Hughes—Debating Societies and Private Theatres, with Anecdotes of their Frequenters—R. A. Davenport—School of Eloquence—King George the Third's Visit to St. Paul's . . . . page 73

---

*₊* Here, for the present, the Author's Personal Narrative is suspended. The plan to be pursued for its completion is indicated at the close of Chap. I. (See page 24.)

---

## List of Illustrations.

PORTRAIT OF THE AUTHOR. Engraved by J. Thomson, from a Drawing by R. W. Satchwell and T. Uwins, R.A.

REPRESENTATIONS of the OBVERSE and REVERSE of a GOLD MEDAL of MERIT, presented by the King of Prussia to the Author. Engraved by the late A. R. Freebairn.

PORTRAITS of four of the Author's personal Friends, who will be particularly noticed in the future portion of the Memoir, viz.—

WILLIAM ALEXANDER, F.S.A., Keeper of the Prints and Drawings in the British Museum, and Draftsman to the Embassy to China under Lord Macartney. Engraved by E. Scriven from a Drawing by H. Edridge.

FRANCIS BAILY, LL.D., F.R.S., Founder and President of the Royal Astronomical Society, Author of a "Life of Flamsteed," and many valuable Scientific Papers.

HENRY NEELE, Author of "Lectures on Poetry," "Romance of English History," "Poems," &c. Drawn and Engraved by H. Meyer.

THE REV. JOHN WHITAKER, Author of the "History of Manchester," "The History of the Ancient Cathedral of Cornwall (St. Germain's)," and "Mary Queen of Scots vindicated."

INTERIOR of a COTTAGE at Kington St. Michael, Wiltshire, with the Discovery of a Fox in a Child's Cradle. Engraved on wood by J. L. Williams, from a Painting by Alfred Provis . . . . . . . . page 35

VIEW of the HOUSE, in the same Village, in which the Author was born. Engraved on wood by J. Walmsley, from a Sketch by the Author . . . 56

A ROOM in the same House. Engraved on wood by Samuel Williams, from a Painting by Alfred Provis . . . . . . . . 57

WINE-CELLAR of the Jerusalem Tavern, Clerkenwell, in which the Author was employed during his six years' apprenticeship. Engraved on wood by J. Walmsley, from a Drawing by F. W. Fairholt . . . . . 68

---

*₊* The Illustrations to the SECOND PART, and to the APPENDIX, are referred to in their respective Tables of Contents.

# NOTICE.

Of this Auto-Biography the following numbers have been printed:

Imperial Quarto, with proofs of the engravings, to class with the same sized copies of the "Architectural," and "Cathedral Antiquities."* *Twenty-five copies* only of this size are printed, for Subscribers of Ten Guineas.

Demy Quarto, with choice impressions of the engravings, to class with the same sized paper of the Works above named. Only *one hundred and twenty-five copies* of the Biography are printed of this size, for Subscribers of Three Guineas and Five Guineas.

Royal Octavo, to class with the "Architectural and Archæological Dictionary," which has been long out of print, and is known only to a very limited number of antiquarian students. *Five hundred copies* of this size are printed, with six prints less than in the quarto copies, and a different portrait of the Author, for Subscribers of One Guinea and Two Guineas. The cause for this variation has arisen from some of the plates being of quarto size, and therefore not fitted for the octavo page. It is also deemed right to offer the Subscribers of Three Guineas and upwards, a valuable consideration for such additional contribution.

The quarto copies, which have been printed after the octavos, contain some literal corrections, and a few additional paragraphs.

The printed *List of Subscribers*, I hope, will prove to be correct, as I have taken much pains to make it so. As there will be a few copies remaining after the present Subscribers are supplied, the prices of them will be £2. 2s. 8vo.; and £4. 4s. Demy 4to.

J. B.

---

* Of these works, it is believed, that more than 4000 copies have been sold, many of which have been issued (without the author's sanction) having worn-out impressions of the plates, and therefore much deteriorated in value.

## DIRECTIONS TO THE BINDER.

|  | 4to. | 8vo. |
|---|---|---|
| Medal of Merit from the King of Prussia, *to face page* | 6 | 7 |
| Portrait of Henry Neele | 86 | 107 |
| The Rev. J. Whitaker | 264 | 335 |
| Francis Baily | 372 | 474 |

The last leaf of Signature C C in 8vo. to be cancelled.

*Erratum.*—In page 184 of the 4to. copies, reference is made to p. 149; it should be p. 119.

# THE Auto-Biography OF JOHN BRITTON.

"YET HATH MY NIGHT OF LIFE SOME MEMORIE,
MY WASTING LAMPES SOME FADING GLIMMER LEFT."
*Comedy of Errors*, Act V., Sc. 1.

## CHAPTER I.

ORIGIN OF THE PRESENT WORK, IN A PUBLIC "TESTIMONIAL" TO ITS AUTHOR—REMARKS ON BIOGRAPHY BY DR. JOHNSON, CUMBERLAND, SIR E. BRYDGES, AND HORATIO SMITH—TABULAR VIEW OF NUMEROUS "TESTIMONIALS"—A COMMITTEE FORMED, AND VARIOUS PLANS PROPOSED FOR THAT TO THE AUTHOR—A PUBLIC DINNER, AND AUTO-BIOGRAPHY RESOLVED ON—THE LATTER COMMENCED IN DECEMBER 1846—INTERRUPTED BY REPEATED ILLNESS AND VARIOUS LITERARY AVOCATIONS — RESUMED, AND PLAN ADOPTED FOR ITS ARRANGEMENT—CONTENTS OF THE ENSUING CHAPTERS.

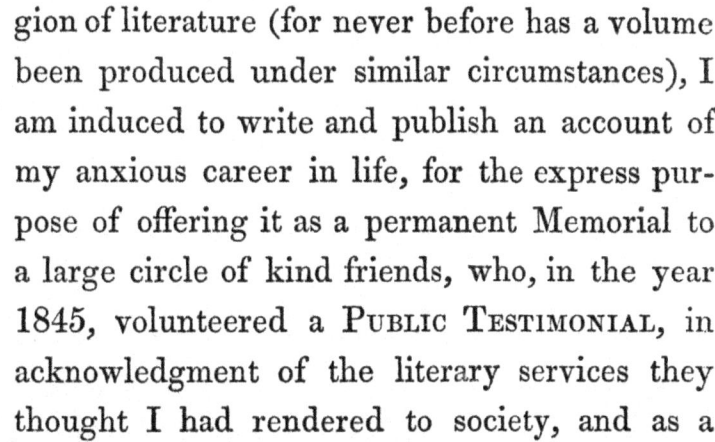

AS a complete novelty in the wide and diversified region of literature (for never before has a volume been produced under similar circumstances), I am induced to write and publish an account of my anxious career in life, for the express purpose of offering it as a permanent Memorial to a large circle of kind friends, who, in the year 1845, volunteered a PUBLIC TESTIMONIAL, in acknowledgment of the literary services they thought I had rendered to society, and as a token of their personal regard. When this suggestion was adopted, its promoters little contemplated the extent to which the Subscription would reach, the amount of exertion and solicitude which it would entail on the person whom they intended to honour, or the effect it would produce on his "night of life." At the time it was first proposed I was in my seventy-fourth year, and have now nearly completed my

---

*⁎* The above initial letter is copied from an ancient Anglo-Saxon document in the Archives of Salisbury Cathedral.

seventy-ninth, (March 1850.) In the interval I have experienced some of the severe troubles which "flesh is heir to." I have suffered from three attacks of bronchitis, each of which rendered life precarious, and completely incapacitated me from either mental or bodily exertion for some weeks; and during one of these I lost a dear wife, who had been my constant domestic companion for forty-five years. That loss seemed like the dismemberment of a part of my body, and rendered home cheerless and desolate. I believe, indeed, that life could not have been sustained during the winter of 1848-9, but for the constant watchfulness and assiduity of one who for many years, when my late wife was an invalid, had been her housekeeper and nurse. Surmounting, however, this dangerous malady, and ascribing my preservation to the unwearied devotion of that nurse; feeling, moreover, how comfortless and forlorn is a solitary fire-side; I made her my wife, from a conviction that she would not only relieve me from all the cares of domestic management, but render home the seat of comfort and enjoyment. My most sanguine wishes and expectations have been, not merely realized, but far exceeded; and I can conscientiously assert, that I have been perfectly happy since I have thus wedded a nurse, a companion, and an affectionate friend.

The following pages will contain "a round unvarnished tale" of the "whole course" of my life, from infancy to old age; and though it has been often said that memoirs of literary persons must be devoid of interest, as Authors are usually confined to a dull routine of study, abstraction, and exemption from the accidents and adventures to which men of the world and of enterprise are liable; yet, on the other hand, the Auto-Biographies of Brydges, Coleridge, Cumberland, Cobbett, Franklin, Gibbon, Hume, Holcroft, Hutton, Pemberton, Scott, and many others, are not only interesting to the general reader, but constitute valuable and important documents for the philosopher and the historian to study.* As delineations and evidences of mind, of its reve-

---

* "Why," said Dr. Johnson, "should the life of a literary man be less entertaining than the life of any other? Are there not as interesting varieties in such a life?" The question is satisfactorily answered by the Auto-Biographies above referred to, and by many others since published,—all tending to show that there have been and are literary persons whose adventures, "sayings and doings," lives and actions, are as valuable and

ries in solitude, and its workings in public life, they are at once useful and highly interesting. But for such writings, indeed, the Author of this Volume would never have undertaken and prosecuted his works on the "Architectural," and "Cathedral Antiquities" of England.

The subjoined language and opinions of Richard Cumberland, (when "full of years," in 1804, aged 72,) from his "Memoirs written by himself," are so essentially my own, that I unhesitatingly adopt them.

> "I have lived so long in the world, mixed so generally with mankind, and written so voluminously and variously, that I trust my motives cannot be greatly misunderstood, if, with strict attention to truth, and in simplicity of style, I pursue my narrative, saying nothing more of the immediate object of these Memoirs, than in honour and in conscience I am warranted to say. I shall use so little embellishment in this narrative, that if the reader is naturally candid he will not be disgusted; if he is easily amused he will not be disappointed. Of many persons with whom I have had intercourse and connexion, I shall speak freely and impartially. I know myself incapable of wantonly aspersing the characters of the living or the dead; but, though I will not indulge myself in conjectures, I will not turn aside from facts, and neither from affectation of candour nor dread of recrimination waive the privilege which I claim for myself in every page of this history, of speaking the truth from my heart: I may not always say all that I could, but I will never knowingly say of any man what I should not."

useful to the reading world, as the romances, called Travels, by explorers of foreign lands, the exaggerated fictions of novelists, or the statements and mis-statements of historians. Again, the same acute and eloquent writer, says, "Biography gives us what comes near to ourselves; what we can turn to use. A man's peculiarities should be mentioned, as they mark his character; but it is questionable whether his vices should be named—whether, for instance, it should be mentioned that Addison and Parnell drank too freely. The business of a Biographer is to give a complete account of the person whose life he is writing, and to discriminate him from all other persons by any peculiarities of character, or sentiments, he may happen to have."—(Boswell's *Life of Johnson*, by Croker, 10 vols. 18mo., Vols. iv., 72; vi., 294; and ix., 138.) An eloquent critic in the *Athenæum*, (May 2, 1846,) says, "A Biography should be, as it were, a recapitulation of whatever evidences might be adduced in justification of the person's claims to an honourable celebrity; a summing up not only of written words, but of those written, and hitherto un-written actions, traced back to the indestructible elements of childhood—themselves illustrations and proofs—which he had throughout his mission promised or performed for the good of his country; a retrospect, in fine, of those transactions of his day with which he was connected: his now deliberate judgment upon them, and the part he, himself, took therein,—his explanation of this—his extenuation, it may be, of that—his vindication, if need be, of the whole; but all meantime, treated in that temperate and dignified tone which usually characterises a chastened experience, and which so signally enhances the value of the testimony it renders."

Sir Egerton Brydges, in his "Recollections of Foreign Travel," &c. (2 vols. 8vo. 1826,) makes the following remarks:

"If Dr. Johnson's opinion be authority, no man is so obscure, or so stupid, but that he may relate something deserving to be remembered, if he will speak with truth, simplicity, and frankness; if he will describe his real feelings and undisguised opinions."—(Vol. i. p. 3.) "Among the innumerable variety of books which human ingenuity puts forth, *Auto-Biography* is one of those which has always had most interest for me; but then it must be written with sincerity and frankness. . . . I believe no one need be ashamed of confessing his mental movements, if he confesses with *naïveté* and good faith. The weaknesses of which he has been ashamed, as peculiar to himself, will be recognized by the sympathy of most minds of sensibility."—(Vol. ii. p. 179.) "Restraint and laborious effort are radical faults which destroy vitality. Extreme care to avoid censure and satisfy all, never answers its purpose. There is no escape from cavil: where one is pleased, another is sure to find fault."—(Vol. ii. p. 233.)

The following sentiments by my late estimable friend Horatio Smith, are so truly in unison with my own, and are so admirably expressed, that I cannot forbear reprinting them here.*

"The Parthian shot his arrows backwards as he fled from Death: it is my present purpose to do the same as I speed towards it; for at my advanced time of life the beneficent Power that 'rocks the cradle of declining age' must soon hush me into the long and calm sleep that knows no dreams, and fears not a disturbance. Recollections there are, fond and trivial though they may prove, which I would fain rescue from the grave, ere it closes around me. Many literary men have I known slightly, and some few intimately; but alas! out of the whole galaxy, how many have gone to join the lost Pleiade! My memory can only exercise itself by

---

* They are quoted from "A Greybeard's Gossip about his Literary Acquaintance," in the *New Monthly Magazine*, Vols. lxxix.—lxxxii. (1847-8). Though anonymous, the style and allusions are sufficient evidence of the authorship. These papers extend through thirteen numbers of the popular periodical referred to. The gossiping reminiscences of this very pleasing, prolific, and amiable writer are limited to a small circle of the literati and actors of his time, but these were "the observed of all observers." Some of them were intellectual comets in the hemisphere of genius, whose company was courted by peers and princes, and whose conversation and writings diffused not merely cheerfulness, but irrepressible mirth wherever they appeared. Among them were Campbell, Mathews, Liston, Theodore Hook, Du Bois, Leigh Hunt, J. Hunt, John Taylor, Horace Twiss, Barron Field, James Cobb, Richard Cumberland, M. G. Lewis, Sir Walter Scott, W. Stewart Rose, Thomas Hood, Wm. Godwin, Percy Bysshe Shelley, John Scott, &c. In a subsequent part of this volume, I shall have occasion to relate some particulars of James and Horatio Smith, the famed writers of the "Rejected Addresses;" and of other literary persons with whom I was personally acquainted, and occasionally corresponded.

walking through a cemetery. It must subsist, like the ghouls of oriental fable, by preying upon the dead: such is the penalty that we Greybeards pay for prolonged existence! I should have said privilege. What! shall we regret the loss of literary friends, when we ought rather to rejoice that we once enjoyed their possession? The privation we share with the whole world; the acquaintanceship was an honour and a delight wherein we find but a few select participants. Oh! if men would but fairly measure their gains against their losses, and adapt their gratitude to the graciousness of Heaven, how rare would be their discontent; how general and how cordial their thanksgivings!

'A thing of beauty is a joy for ever,'

says one of our Poets; and if this be true even of a material object, how immeasurably more joyous must be the recollection of any mental beauty that has once charmed us. As we grow older, this retrospective gratification becomes spread over a longer and more prolific period, while the prospective term for which we may have to endure vexations and annoyances is continually diminishing. So many indeed, and so various, are the advantages of senility, that I have ever considered life as a sort of tontine for the benefit of survivors. 'How then!' methinks I hear the reader exclaim, 'is it your purpose to present to us a prose Elegy in a country church yard?' No, most excusable remonstrant! We are not about to deal with the illustrious obscure, either rural or metropolitan, but with men who have attained literary celebrity in their day, although a portion of them, unentitled to the name of master spirits, may perhaps be classed among the *Dii minores* in the auctorial Pantheon."

A brief review of the origin of this Auto-Biography, with an account of circumstances and events emanating from, and connected with it, will be a proper, if not an essential, prelude to the work now offered to the public; for many persons may peruse these pages who have never seen any others of the Author's literary publications: indeed, there are probably scarcely six persons living who know the contents, or characteristics of more than half of them.*

---

* In consequence of the variety and cheapness of modern books, on those and similar subjects, the present race of Archæologists and Topographers are generally strangers even to the "Architectural Antiquities of Great Britain," the "Cathedral Antiquities," the "Architectural and Archæological Dictionary," and others of my published works. The more mature critic, however, is well aware that many compilers have made free with the literary and graphic contents of their predecessors, without remorse, and even without any sort of acknowledgment. In looking over some of these new works, I have painfully witnessed not merely single facts and circumstances, but whole pages, thus surreptitiously appropriated. Prints have been also repeatedly copied, without any reference to the artists, or to the author, who drew, engraved, and published them at very considerable expense and labour. These imitators, like the roguish Jew commemorated in song, no doubt thought it better to *steal articles ready made*, than to pilfer the separate materials.

It has been common in this rich and enterprising country to reward successful commanders, both in the Army and in the Navy, with rank and titles—with public monuments, and ample fortunes. Indeed, these two classes of society have had more than their fair proportion of national honours; as if persons who have merely done "their duty," in the horrid business of war, were more estimable and praiseworthy than those who devote their lives and talents to promote the blessings of peace, and the welfare and happiness of their species. Persons who have sufficient influence to obtain lucrative offices in Church or State, are often additionally enriched with pensions for life from the public purse. Our long and glaring list of such pensions is a reproach to the country, and may well excite the sorrow and indignation of the hard-working tradesman, the mechanic, and the author. Within the present century it has become a practice with the public generally, and with particular sections and classes, to compliment and reward persons who are considered to have rendered services to their fellow-men. These rewards have obtained the name of TESTIMONIALS,* and it will be seen by the subjoined *Tabular View*, that some fortunate individuals have received large and even extravagant rewards for heroic, and political services; whilst Authors of important works in literature, and discoverers and inventors in science and art, have experienced but trifling remuneration. The Crown, the Aristocracy, and the Church, have long exercised nearly all the prerogatives of patronage, and have too frequently exercised it with indiscriminate partiality, and merely from political or religious partizanship. The People have been taxed not only for the current age and time, but for generations yet unborn.

It cannot fail to interest many readers, and at the same time become an useful record for reference, to see clearly displayed in a condensed space, an account of some of the most remarkable Testimonials which have been conferred on persons, who have either justly, or ostensibly, earned their respective honours.

---

* In Johnson's *Dictionary*, this word is applied only to "a writing produced as evidence in behalf of the person who presents it."

J. ACHMAN F.

C. PFEUFFER F. C.

MEDAL OF MERIT.

(IN GOLD)

Presented by HIS MAJESTY

THE KING OF PRUSSIA.

TO

JOHN BRITTON.

F.S.A. &c. &c.

# A TABULAR VIEW

OF

# Testimonials and Rewards

CONFERRED ON PERSONS EMINENT IN LITERATURE, SCIENCE, ART, LEGISLATION,
RAILWAY ENTERPRISE, MILITARY AND NAVAL SERVICE, ETC., ETC.,
WITHIN THE PRESENT CENTURY.

"SEE NATIONS SLOWLY WISE, AND MEANLY JUST,
TO LIVING MERIT RAISE THE TARDY BUST."—JOHNSON.

| Name. | Nature of Testimonial. | By whom conferred. |
|---|---|---|
| | AUTHORS. | |
| Alison, Archibald | Appointment as Historiographer | The Government. |
| Anster, J. LL.D. | Pension, £150 a year (1841) | The Government. |
| Banim, John | Pension, £150 a year (1835) | The Government. |
| Barton, Bernard | Pension, £100 a year (1846) | The Government. |
| Bowles, Rev. W. L. | Canonry of Salisbury | Dean and Chapter. |
| Bowring, Dr. | Dinner at Manchester, 1838 | The Public. |
| | Consular employment, &c. | The Government. |
| Britton, John, F.S.A. | Dinner, 7th July, 1845, at Richmond. Subscription, about £1000, expended in producing his Auto-Biography | The Public. |
| | Gold Medal of Merit from | The King of Prussia. |
| | Elected Honorary Member of | Numerous Societies. |
| Brougham, Lord | Peerage and Pension | The Government. |
| | Election, 1825, as Lord Rector of | Glasgow University. |
| Bulwer, Sir E. Lytton | Baronetcy | The Government. |
| Burges, George | Pension, £100 a year (1841) | The Government. |
| Campbell, Thomas | Pension, £184 a year (1806) | The Government. |
| | Election as Lord Rector of | Glasgow University* |
| Carleton, William | Pension, £200 a year (1848) | The Government. |
| Chambers, W. & R. | Dinner at Peebles, their native place, 1841 | The Public. |
| Cobbett, William | Dinner, and subscription to pay the fine imposed on him | The Public. |
| Coleridge, S. T. | Pension, £100 a year (1824) † | { George IV., by the Roy. Soc. of Lit. |
| Coxe, Rev. William | Archdeaconry of Wilts | Dean and Chapter. |
| Crowe, Eyre Evans | Pension, £100 a year (1834) | The Government. |
| Davies, Rev. E. | Pension, £100 a year (1824) | Geo. IV., as above. |
| Dickens, Charles | Dinner at Edinburgh, 1841. Festivals, &c., in America | The Public. |
| Ellis, Sir Henry | Title, Prin. Librarian in British Museum | The Government. |
| Gurwood, Col. | Pension, £200 a year (1839) | The Government. |
| Hogg, James | Dinner, Freemasons' Tavern | The Public. |
| Hook, Theodore E. | Colonial appointment | The Government. |
| | Piece of plate | W. India Proprietors |
| | Posthumous. Subscription for his children | The Public. |
| Hunt, Leigh | Pension, £200 a year (1847) | The Government. |
| Hunter, Rev. Jos. | His Portrait to be painted by subscription for the Cutlers' Hall, Sheffield. | The Public. |
| Ivory, James | Pensions, £300 a year (1832 & 1836) | The Government. |
| Jamieson, Rev. Dr. | Pension, £100 a year | Geo. IV., as above. |
| Jeffrey, Lord | Appointment as Lord Advocate of Scotland | The Government. |
| | Election as Lord Rector of | Glasgow University. |
| Kidd, Rev. T. | Pension, £100 a year (1841) | The Government. |

* The office of Lord Rector of Glasgow University is annually conferred on some eminent public person, and is regarded as a high honorary distinction.

† The ten pensions granted in 1824, by King George IV., to literary men, through the medium of the Royal Society of Literature, are deserving of particular notice and record. These pensions were discontinued after the death of the monarch.

| Name. | Nature of Testimonial. | By whom conferred. |
|---|---|---|
| Knight, Charles | Dinner, 1841, Lord Brougham in chair | The Public. |
| Knowles, J. Sheridan | Pension, £200 a year (1848) | The Government. |
| Loudon, Mrs. | Pension, £100 a year (1846) | The Government. |
| Macaulay, T. B., M.P. | Election as Lord Rector of | Glasgow University. |
| Macintosh, Sir J. M.P. | Title, and appointments. (Annual Pension from East India Comp. £1200) | The Government. |
| Mackenzie, R. S. LL.D. | Dinner and piece of plate, Liverpool, 1838 | The Public. |
| Mc Culloch, J. R. | Appointment as Comptroller, Stationery Office; Pension, £200 a year (1846) | The Government. |
| Madden, Sir Fred. | Title, and Keeper of MSS., B. Museum | The Government. |
| Malthus, Rev. T. R. | Pension, £100, & place, Haileybury Coll. | Geo. IV., as above. |
| Martineau, Miss | Pension offered, but declined | The Government. |
| Mathias, Rev. T. J. | Pension, £100 a year | Geo. IV., as above. |
| Millingen, James | Ditto | Ditto. |
| Millman, Rev. H. H. | Deanery of St. Paul's | The Government. |
| Mitford, Miss | Pension, £100 a year (1837) | The Government. |
| Montgomery, James | Pension, £150 a year (1835) | The Government. |
| Moore, Thomas | Pension, £300 a year (1835) | The Government. |
| Morgan, Lady | Pension, £300 a year (1838) | The Government. |
| Nicolas, Sir Harris | Title, &c. | The Government. |
| Ouseley, Sir Wm. | Annual Pension, £100 | Geo. IV., as above. |
| Palgrave, Sir Francis | Title, and Deputy Keeper of Records | The Government. |
| Porter, G. R. | Appointment as Sec. to Board of Trade | The Government. |
| Roscoe, Wm. | Annual Pension, £100 (1824) | Geo. IV., as above. |
| Scott, Sir Walter | Baronetcy. Ship of war to convey him to Italy. Public appointments | The Government. |
| | Election as Lord Rector of | Glasgow University. |
| | Subscription to entail Abbotsford. Statues, &c. at Edinburgh, Glasgow, &c. | The Public. |
| Smith, Rev. John Pye | Annuity, to be converted on his death into Scholarships in his College | The Public. |
| Smith, C. R. | Piece of plate | Numismatic Soc. |
| Somerville, Mrs. | Annual Pensions, £300 (1835 & 1837) | The Government. |
| Southey, Robert | Pensions, £455 a year. Appointment as Poet Laureate, salary about £100. | The Government. |
| | Degree of D.C.L., by | Oxford University. |
| Talfourd, Sir T. N. ‡ | Appointment as a Judge | The Government. |
| | Dinner on his appointment, 1849 | The Bar. |
| Tennyson, Alfred | Pension, £200 a year (1846) | The Government. |
| Thirlwall, Rev. C. | Appointment as Bishop of St. David's | The Government. |
| Thorpe, Benjamin | Pensions, £200 a year (1835 & 1841) | The Government. |
| Todd, Rev. H. J. | Annual Pension, £100 | Geo. IV., as above. |
| Turner, Sharon | Pension, £200 a year (1835) | The Government. |
| Tytler, P. F. | Pension, £200 a year (1845) | The Government. |
| Whately, Rev. R. | Appointment as Archbishop of Dublin | The Government. |
| Wilberforce, Rev. Samuel | Appointment as Bishop of Oxford | The Government. |
| Wordsworth, W. | Pension, £300 a year (1842) | The Government. |

### ARCHITECTS.

| | | |
|---|---|---|
| Cubitt, Thomas | His Portrait painted and engraved | Architects & Builders |
| Donaldson, T. L. | A piece of plate | Architects. |
| Smirke, Sir R., R.A. | Title, and employment | The Government. |
| Soane, Sir John, R.A. | Title, and public employment | The Government. |
| | Subscription for a Gold Medal | Architects, &c. |
| Wyattville, Sir J., R.A. | Title, and employment on Windsor Castle | The Government. |

‡ The reader's memory will readily supply the names of many distinguished LAWYERS, PHYSICIANS, SURGEONS, OFFICERS of the HERALD'S COLLEGE, and others, who have been honoured with titles for *professional* merit: they are far too numerous to be included in the present list. POSTHUMOUS honours are likewise necessarily omitted: such as the statues and public monuments to Chatham, Pitt, Fox, Alderman Beckford, Dr. Johnson, John Howard, James Watt, and many others. In this class of Testimonials, Thorwaldsen's statue of Lord Byron has become conspicuous, from the pertinacious and bigoted intolerance of the Dean and Chapter of Westminster, who refused it admission into the Abbey Church.

# PUBLIC TESTIMONIALS.

| Name. | Nature of Testimonial. | By whom conferred. |
|---|---|---|
| | ARCHITECTS (NAVAL.) | |
| Bentham, Sir Saml. | Title, and Pension of £1500 a year, as late Civil Architect and Surveyor | The Government. |
| Seppings, Sir R. | Title, and annual Pension | The Government. |
| Symonds, Sir W. | Title, ditto | The Government. |
| | ARTISTS.* | |
| Allan, Sir W., R.A. | Title, &c. | The Government. |
| Beechey, Sir W., R.A. | Title, and employment | The Government. |
| Callcott, Sir A. W. R A | Title, and appointment as Keeper of the Royal Pictures | The Government. |
| Chantrey, Sir F., R.A. | Title, and Royal employment | The Government. |
| Eastlake, C. L., R.A. | Appointments as Keeper of National Gallery, & Sec. to Royal Commission | The Government. |
| Etty, W., R.A. | An Exhibition of his Paintings | The Society of Arts. |
| Haydon, B. R. | An Exhibition of his Paintings | The Public. |
| | Posthumous Appointments for his children | The Government. |
| | Pension to his widow, £50 (1846) | The Government. |
| Hayter, Sir George | Title, &c. | The Government. |
| Lawrence, Sir T. P.R.A. | Title, Royal Commissions, &c. | The Government. |
| Martin, John | Titles from | Foreign Governments |
| Mulready, W., R.A. | An Exhibition of his Paintings | The Society of Arts. |
| Newton, Sir W., R.A. | Title, &c. | The Government. |
| Pistrucci, Benedetto | Appointment as Chief Medallist, Mint | The Government. |
| Raeburn, Sir H. | Title, and Royal Portrait Painter, Scotland | The Government. |
| Robertson, Andrew | Dinner and Silver Salver | The Public. |
| Ross, Sir W. C., R.A. | Title, Royal Commissions, &c. | The Government. |
| Shee, Sir M. A. P.R.A. | Title, and Annuity, £200 to his daughters | The Government. |
| Uwins, Tho., R.A. | Appointment as Keeper of the Royal Pictures, & of the National Gallery | The Government. |
| Westmacott, Sir R., R.A. | Title, &c. | The Government. |
| | Degree as D.C.L. | University of Oxford |
| | Medal, from | The Pope. |
| Wilkie, Sir D., R.A. | Title, and appointment. His "Blind Fiddler" and "Village Festival," bought | The Government. |
| Wyon, W., R.A. | Chief Engraver to the Mint | The Government. |
| | CAPITALISTS AND COMMERCIAL MEN. | |
| Clarke, Henry | Gift of £1000 by the | Arigna Mining Co. |
| | Annuity of £400 from the | Imperial Gas Comp. |
| | Freedom and Livery of the | Clockmakers' Comp. |
| Gilbart, J. W. | Subscription, and Portrait, as Founder of | London & Wester Bank |
| | Service of plate, 1846 | Joint Stock Banks. |
| Goldsmid, Baron de | Service of plate | Portuguese Bondholders. |
| | £400 as Chairman. Given by the Baron to University College Hospital | North Kent Railway Company. |
| Joplin, T. | Annuity, as Founder of the | National Prov. Bank. |
| | DIRECTORS AND OFFICERS OF RAILWAY AND OTHER COMPANIES. | |
| Badham, J. B. | Plate, 100 guineas; purse of 1150 guineas | Raily Shareholders. |
| Booth, Henry | Subscription £2800; Plate £200 | Raily Shareholders. |
| Creed, Richard | Sec. Lond. and Birm. Railway; plate, public dinner, and sum of £2100 | London and North Western Railway. |
| Dockray, R. B. | Portrait painted and engraved; piece of plate; £500 Railway Stock | Ditto. |
| Gill, Robert | Plate, value £2000 (1849) | S. Devon Railway. |
| Gray, Thomas | Subscription: projector of Railway System | The Public. |

* Several of the distinguished artists here mentioned have enjoyed appointments as painters in ordinary and extraordinary to English monarchs, and also a large amount of royal patronage and commissions. The premiums allotted to the successful competitors in the Westminster Hall Exhibitions have greatly tended to the advancement of British Art.

| Name. | Nature of Testimonial. | By whom conferred. |
| --- | --- | --- |
| Hudson, George | Votes of Shares from | Various Rail. Co's. |
| | Subscription, £22,000 | The Public. |
| | Public Dinner as M.P. for Sunderland | Sunderland Electors. |
| | Appointment as Deputy Lieut. of Durham | The Government. |
| Huish, Captain | Silver clock, 1841; piece of Plate | Railway Officers, &c. |
| McDonnel, Sir E. | Knighted, 1849, on opening of the Great Southern & Western Rail. of Ireland | The Government. |
| Saunders, C. A. | Sec. to Great Western Railway; gift of £3000 (1844); Vote of Shares | Gt. West. Railway. |
| Tootal Edward | Plate, value £1800 (1845) | Raily Shareholders. |
| Torrington, Viscount | Service of plate, value 3000 guineas, as Chairman of the S. E. Railway Co. | The Shareholders. |

### ENGINEERS.

| | | |
| --- | --- | --- |
| Bidder, Geo. Parker | Subscription to educate him as Engineer | The Public. |
| Brunel, Sir M. J. | Title, and employment | The Government. |
| Brunel, J. K. | Plate, value £2000 | Gt. Western Railway Shareholders |
| Locke, Joseph | Titles, and gifts | Foreign Monarchs. |
| McAdam, Sir James | Title, and employment | The Government. |
| McConnell, J. E. | Gift of £3000 | Midland Railway Co. |
| McNeill, Sir John | Title, &c. | The Government. |
| Rennie, Sir John | Title, and employment | The Government. |
| Stephenson, George | 100 guineas (1817); 1000 guineas, dinner, and plate, for Safety Lamp (1818) | Coal Owners in the North of England. |
| | Premium, £500, for the best locomotive Steam-Engine, 1829 | Liverpool and Manchester Railway. |
| | Statues at Liverpool and Newcastle | Corporation and Cos. |
| Stephenson, Robert | Titles, employment, &c. | Brit. & Foreign Gov. |

### MILITARY AND NAVAL HEROES.

Field-Marshal Viscount Beresford, Lord Hill, Lord Gough, Viscount Hardinge, Lord Keane, Lord Lynedoch, General Sir Charles J. Napier, Admiral Sir Charles Napier, Earl Nelson, Lord Rodney, Sir Harry Smith, Sir Sidney Smith, and many other Officers, have received honours and distinctions from the Government, the Public, the East India Company, &c., since the year 1800. These have embraced Peerages, Titles, Appointments, Pensions, Swords, Plate, Dinners, Statues, Monuments, &c. &c. The following are amongst the honours conferred on his Grace

| | | |
| --- | --- | --- |
| The Duke of Wellington | Peerage, Honorary Titles, Pensions, Gift of Stratfieldsaye, &c. | The Government. |
| | Statues, in London, Glasgow, Dublin &c. Dinners, Civic Freedom, Plate, Swords | The Public, and Corporate Bodies. |
| | Titles, &c. | Foreign Governments |
| | Election as Chancellor of | Oxford University. |

### MUSICIANS, MANAGERS, AND ACTORS.

| | | |
| --- | --- | --- |
| Bunn, Alfred | Plate | The Public. |
| Bishop, Sir Henry R. | Title | The Government. |
| Kemble, John Philip | £1000; on rebuilding Cov. Garden Theatre | Duke of Northumb. |
| Lind, Jenny | Magnificent piece of plate | B. Lumley. |
| | A papier mâché cabinet | Queen's Coll., Birm. |
| | A silver salver | Brompton Hospital. |
| | Set of porcelain prepared, but declined | Worcester Infirmary. |
| Lumley, B. | A splendid piece of plate, 700 oz. | Subscribers to Opera. |
| Macready, W. C. | Plate, dinner, D. of Sussex in the chair | The Public. |
| Mitchell, J. | Plateau and candelabrum, value £600 | Patrons of Theatre. |
| Planche, J. R. | Service of plate | — Theatre. |
| Smart, Sir George | Title, and employment | The Government. |
| Stevenson, Sir John | Title | The Government. |

### THE PRESS.

| | | |
| --- | --- | --- |
| Baldwin, Edward, *Morning Herald* | Silver candelabrum; public dinner | Writers for the Morning Herald. |

| Name. | Nature of Testimonial. | By whom conferred. |
|---|---|---|
| Delane, W.F.A. *Times* | Appointment as Treasurer of County Court | The Government. |
| Easthope, Sir John | Baronetcy | The Government. |
| Fonblanque, A. W. | Appointment under Board of Trade | The Government. |
| Laxton, Wm. | Public dinner (for defeating Government inspection) | Steam-Ship Owners. |
| Michele, C. E., *Post* | Appointment as Consul, St. Petersburgh | The Government. |
| Times Newspaper | Subscription, for exposing a Commercial Fraud. Invested in University Scholarships for Students from Christ's Hospital, and City of London School | Commercial Men. |
| Wilson, James, M.P. | Appointment as Sec. Board of Control | The Government. |

## SCIENTIFIC PERSONS.

| | | |
|---|---|---|
| Adams, J. C. | Scholarships, founded by subscription | The Public. |
| | Pension, £200 (1848) | The Government. |
| Airy, Professor G. B. | Appointment as Astronomer Royal. Annuity, £300, to Mrs. Airey (1835) | The Government. |
| Arkwright, Sir R. | Title | The Government. |
| Babbage, Charles | Large grants towards Calculating Machine | The Government. |
| Baily, Francis | His Portrait painted and engraved | Scientific Friends. |
| Barrow, Sir John | Baronetcy, and Secretary to the Admiralty | The Government. |
| | Piece of plate | Arctic Voyagers. |
| Beaufort, Sir Francis | K.C.B., Hydrographer to Admiralty, &c. | The Government. |
| Brewster, Sir David | Title, & pensions £297 a year (1829 & 1836) | The Government. |
| | Degree of D.C.L. | Oxford University. |
| Brown, R. (Botanist) | Pension, £200 a year (1843) | The Government. |
| Buckland, Rev. Dr. | Deanery of Westminster | The Government. |
| Curtis, John | Pension, £100 a year (1842) | The Government. |
| Dalton, Dr. | Subscription for Statue, at Manchester | The Public. |
| | Pensions, £300 a year (1833 & 1836) | The Government. |
| Davy, Sir Humphrey | Title | The Government. |
| | Dinner, and £2000, for Safety Lamp | The Public. |
| De la Beche, Sir H.T. | Title, and employment, Board of Trade | The Government. |
| Faraday, M. | Pension, £300 a year (1835) | The Government. |
| Forbes, Professor | Pension, £200 a year (1846) | The Government. |
| Gray, J. E. | Keeper of the Zoological Department | British Museum. |
| Hamilton, Sir W. R. | Title. Appointment, Astronomer Royal, Dublin. Pension, 200 a year (1844) | The Government. |
| Harris, Sir W. Snow | Title. Appointment. Pension, £300 (1841) | The Government. |
| Herschel, Sir John | Baronetcy | The Government. |
| | Dinner, & vase, 1838, D. of Sussex in chair | The Public. |
| | Appointment as Lord Rector of | Marischal Coll., 1842 |
| | Prizes, and degree of D.C.L. | Camb. University. |
| Hooker, Sir Wm. J. | Title, and appointment at Kew Gardens | The Government. |
| | Degree of D.C.L. | Oxford University. |
| Kane, Sir Robert | Title, and appointment as Principal of Queen's College, Cork | The Government. |
| Lyell, Sir Charles | Title | The Government. |
| Murchison, Sir R. | Titles from | Governments. |
| Newport, Geo., F.R.S. | Pension, £100 a year (1847) | The Government. |
| Owen, Richard | Pension, £200 a year (1842) | The Government. |
| | Appointment as Hunterian Professor | College of Surgeons. |
| Sedgwick, Rev. Adam | Ecclesiastical preferment | The Government. |
| Smith, Sir Jas. E. | Title | The Government. |
| Smith, W. (Geologist) | Pension, £100 a year | The Government. |
| South, Sir James | Title. Pension, £300 a year (1831) | The Government. |

## STATESMEN AND POLITICIANS.

| | | |
|---|---|---|
| Ashley Lord | Testimonial for the "Short-Time Bill" | Factory Operatives. |
| Bright, John, M.P. | Gift of £ | Corn Law League. |
| Buckingham, Duke of | Piece of plate, the "Chandos Testimonial" | Farmers of Bucks. |
| Campbell, Lord | Title, Pension, and appointments | The Government. |
| Carlisle, the Earl of | Numerous dinners, &c. | The Public. |

| Name. | Nature of Testimonial. | By whom conferred. |
|---|---|---|
| Chandos, Marquis of | Re-purchase of the "Chandos Testimonial," at the Stowe sale | Farmers of Bucks. |
| Cobden, Richard* | Subscription, about £76,700; part invested in purchase of Farm at Dumford, near Midhurst, his native place | The Public. |
| | Dinners in London, Wakefield, Paris, Hamburgh, Florence, Turin, &c. &c. | Free Traders. |
| | Gold Box, value 100 guineas | Commerc¹ Travellers. |
| Denman, Lord | Peerage, appointment, and Pension | The Government. |
| Disraeli, Benjamin | Dinners, &c. | The Public. |
| Graham, Sir J., Bart. | Election, in 1840, as Lord Rector of | Glasgow University. |
| O'Connell, Daniel | Annual Tribute, or Rent from | The People of Ireland |
| Peel, Sir Robt., Bart. | Several dinners, especially at Glasgow, 1837; † Civic Freedoms, &c. | The Public and Corporate bodies. |
| | Election, 1836, as Lord Rector of | Glasgow University. |
| Pottinger, Sir H. | Title, Pension, Diplomatic appointmts, &c. | The Government. |
| Roebuck, J. A., M.P. | Dinners, &c. | The Public. |
| Russell, Lord John | Public dinners, Civic Freedoms, &c. | The Public & Corporations. |
| | Election as Lord Rector of | Glasgow University. |
| Stuart, Lord Dudley | Elaborate gold watch; embroidery worked by ladies; public dinner, &c. | Polish Emigrants. |
| Tennent, Sir Jas. E. | Secretary to the India Board, &c. | The Government. |
| Wilson, George | Gift of £10,000 | Corn Law League. |
| | Service of plate | Manufacturers. |

## TRAVELLERS.

| Name. | Nature of Testimonial. | By whom conferred. |
|---|---|---|
| Alexander, Sir J. E. | Title | The Government. |
| Back, Sir G. | Title | The Government. |
| Buckingham, J. S. | Subscription, and formation of British & Foreign Institute for his residence, &c. | The Public. |
| Fellows, Sir Charles | Title, &c. | The Government. |
| Belcher, Sir E. | Title, and Pension for wounds | The Government. |
| Franklin, Sir John | Title, and appointment | The Government. |
| | Subscriptions and grants to discover him in the Arctic Regions | Governments, and Individuals. |
| Grey, Sir George | Title K.C.B., and Governorship N. Zealand | The Government. |
| Lander, Richard | Subscription to enable him to travel | The Public. |
| Layard, A. H. | Appointment, & purchase of his collection | The Government. |
| | Degree of D.C.L. | Oxford University. |
| Mitchell, Sir F. | Title, and employment | The Government. |
| Parry, Sir Wm. Edw. | Title, appointments, and grant of £1000 | The Government. |
| | Degree, D.C.L. (Freedom, Bath & Winton) | Oxford University. |
| Richardson, Sir John | Title | Government. |
| | Subscription to enable him to travel | The Public. |
| Ross, Sir James C. | Title | The Government. |
| | Degree of D.C.L. | Oxford. |
| | Piece of plate, 1833 | Subscribers to Arctic Expedition. |

* In a most judicious and admirably-written letter from Mr. Cobden, acknowledging the bounty of the subscribers to this Testimonial—which had enabled him thenceforth to devote himself to public business—that gentleman expressly guarded himself against any responsibility to them for his future political career; pledging himself, however, to act on all occasions according to the dictates of a conscientious conviction, and never to become "the slave of a party, the parasite of the great, or the flatterer of the people." He adds, "I feel an inexpressible pride in owing my fortune to the spontaneous contributions of my countrymen. To be thus exalted by them, as a successful labourer in the peaceful cause of free trade, is a distinction which I would not relinquish for all the honours and rewards which have ever been bestowed upon successful conquerors."—(May, 1848.)

† Nearly 3500 persons were present at this dinner, which was given to Sir Robert by the citizens of Glasgow, in approval of his political conduct. A temporary building was erected for the purpose at a cost of £2000.

| Name. | Nature of Testimonial. | By whom conferred. |
|---|---|---|
| Ross, Sir John | Title, and Consular appointment | The Government. |
|  | Civic Freedoms, Medals, Swords, &c. | The Public & Societies |
|  | Ship for discoveries in Arctic Regions | Sir Felix Booth |
|  | Knighthoods, &c., from | Foreign Governments |
| Schomburgh Sir R.H. | Title, and employment | The Government. |
|  | Employment, and gold medal | Roy. Geog. Soc. |
|  | Titles, from | Foreign Governments |
| Wilkinson, Sir J.G. | Title, &c. | The Government. |

## MISCELLANEOUS.

| Name. | Nature of Testimonial. | By whom conferred. |
|---|---|---|
| Forbes, Sir Charles | Statue at Bombay | Natives of India. |
| Fry, Mrs. | Foundation of an Institution in her Name | The Public. |
| Hamilton, Duke of | Candelabrum, value £1200 | His Scotch Tenantry |
| Hill, Rowland * | Subscription, upwards of £15,000; Dinner at Blackwall, 1846 | The Public. |
|  | Appointment as Sec. to Post-master Gen. | The Government. |
| Jenner, Edw. M.D. | £30,000, as discoverer of Vaccination | The Legislature. |
| Jephson, Dr. | Temple, with Statue, at Leamington | Fellow Townsmen. |
| Mathew, Rev. Theob. | Annual Pension, £300. (1847) | The Government. |
|  | Subscription, Medal, Tower at Cork, &c. | The Public. |
| Montefiore, Sir M. | Plate, for services to Jews at Damascus | The Public. |
| Rutland, Duke of | Subscription for Statue at Leicester, £1400 | Gentry & Farmers |
| Thomason, Sir Edw.† | Titles, Medals, Rings, and other gifts | Foreign Sovereigns. |
| Vernon, Robert | Prize founded in his name by Subscription | The Public. |
| Waghorn, Lieut. | Annual Pension, £100 | The Government. |
|  | Subscription, 1845 | The Public. |
|  | Portrait painted, for | E. I. & China Assoc. |

\* In connection with the well-merited Testimonial to this gentleman, for his highly successful measure of Post-Office Reform, some allusion may be made to his precursors in the same path of improvement. *Ralph Allen*, of Prior Park, near Bath, the friend of Pope, Fielding, Warburton, and other literati, received from the Government a considerable sum of money for some improvements which he introduced in the conveyance of the cross mails. *John Palmer*, the Manager of the Bath and Bristol Theatres, introduced the system of mail-coaches, and thereby improved the management, and increased the revenues, of the Post-Office to a vast extent. In 1789, he was appointed Surveyor and Comptroller General of the Post-Office, with a salary of £1500; increased in 1792 to £3000. Mr. Palmer had been led to expect two and a half per cent. on the increased revenue which his plans had produced; and, after a protracted struggle with the government and the legislature, he was rewarded by a grant of £50,000, conferred by Act of Parliament in 1809. In my school-days, the mail was conveyed from Bath, Bristol, and the West of England, to London, by a mail-cart, with a single horse and man. It travelled at the rate of about four miles an hour, and, consequently, was at least thirty hours on the road between Bath and London. These carts were frequently robbed. An instance occurred when I was at school at Chippenham. The robber was apprehended, tried at Salisbury, convicted, and hanged. His body was gibbeted in chains at the place where the robbery was committed—about two miles south of Chippenham; and hundreds of country people flocked to the spot to see the appalling object. The mail-coach system, introduced by Mr. Palmer, seems to have reached almost perfection, when Mr. Rowland Hill's great and sweeping reform, and the adoption of the railway carriage instead of the coach, constituted novelties and improvements of immense advantage to the public.—(See an interesting history of this subject in the *Penny Cyclopædia*, article POST-OFFICE.)

† This gentleman was an eminent manufacturer at Birmingham, where his show-rooms and workshops were visited by all persons of distinction who went to that "toy-shop of Europe." Sir Edward presented many of his admirable productions to foreign monarchs and their ministers, and was complimented, in return, by gifts of extraordinary value. In a subsequent page I shall have occasion to advert again to my old friend and correspondent; whose "Memoirs" rank amongst the Curiosities of Literature.

The preceding List, it is hoped, will prove both useful and interesting. As "the quality of mercy blesses him that gives and him that takes," so does discriminating benevolence confer honour and pleasure on the recipient and the donor. From time immemorial the illustrious dead have been honoured by posthumous memorials: embalmment in sumptuous sarcophagi, and in pyramids; cremation, with beautiful vases; tumuli, enclosing the remains of the deceased, with numerous commemorative objects; monumental altars, and tombstones in endless diversity of form and character, have all been employed by different nations, with a view to perpetuate the memory of relations, friends, and eminent persons. Public Subscriptions and similar Testimonials to living merit, have multiplied to a great extent within the present century; and had the preceding List included *all* which have been so conferred, as well as the titles, places, and other gifts bestowed upon meritorious individuals, it must have occupied a goodly-sized volume, instead of a few well-filled pages. It may in truth be said, that many of the persons above-named have rendered, and continue to render, personal labour and mental services in return for their salaries or pecuniary rewards. On the contrary, many instances might be adduced of persons who have had rewards and honours "thrust upon them" from favouritism alone, without manifesting one particle of talent or qualification. The various departments of the State, the Church, the Army, and the Navy abound with persons who have lived for years on money which has been derived from the labour, the prudence, and the privations of the middle and lower classes of society. In the last century, as well as in the early part of the present, the greatest abuses were committed by the Government in granting pensions and places to court favourites of the most unworthy class. Fortunately, we live in times of greater liberality of sentiment and conduct, of more true philosophy and justice, and of greater wisdom, than belonged to those times, or than could have been anticipated fifty years ago. With a slight abatement for excessive "hero-worship," the most patriotic economist can hardly complain of the manner in which the special pension fund of £1,200 a year has been bestowed, since 1838; nor would they or the public regret to see further honours and rewards offered to the sons and daughters of Genius and Talent, who justly earn them.

In the winter of 1844-5 some of my friends proposed to present me with a Testimonial, and commenced a subscription for that purpose. Having formed a Committee to consider the best mode of promoting the same, and deciding on its application, several meetings were held; and in the course of a few weeks a much larger sum was collected than the Committee anticipated. A few explanatory notices were printed and sent to personal friends; and I was honoured by responsive letters from many, couched in such kind and flattering terms, that I will here indulge myself in the gratification of subjoining passages from some of them.* The Committee thought that a Public Dinner would afford

---

* On this occasion the MARQUESS OF NORTHAMPTON wrote as follows:—"As I look upon your works, especially your *Architectural Antiquities* and your *English Cathedrals*, as having contributed very much to produce the anxiety now manifested to preserve the venerable edifices of our forefathers, it will give me much pleasure to have my name among those friends who are desirous to give you a Testimonial of their regard." The letter of JOSEPH HUME, Esq., M.P., I am induced to quote more fully:—"I have much pleasure in adding my name to the list of your friends, in connection with the intended Testimonial. It is not the amount of money to be subscribed, but the proofs of sympathy from so many distinguished men, in all situations of life, that I should value, as evidence of the high respect paid to you, and your valuable and persevering labours in elucidation of the Architectural Antiquities of England; and if a long life of labour has not brought that pecuniary return which your talents deserved, you have the satisfaction of knowing, that, in the opinion of some of the best judges in the country, you have deserved a more full and ample reward than the present expression of approval can afford. I had long ago expressed my sense of your devotion to the elucidation of the Antiquities of this country, and of your claims to public attention, by examining you before a Select Committee on Public Monuments and Public Places; and it was my intention to propose that you should be employed by the Government to go round the kingdom, and place on record your opinion of all the ancient buildings which your publications had not comprehended; with a view of measures being taken by the Government to preserve those that should be considered valuable; as the French Government has done since M. Guizot's orders in 1837. I brought that subject before Parliament, and named you as the man who, of all persons I knew, could and would do justice to the confidence of such a Commission; and I shall always regret that the Government did not then adopt measures to carry out my suggestions. That you may enjoy the satisfaction during the remaining part of your life, of having done great good in your time, and of knowing that you have the good opinion of so many of your fellow-men, is the hope and wish of your's sincerely, JOSEPH HUME."

Mr. DAWSON TURNER addressed me thus:—"My dear Sir, I am delighted at the tribute about to be paid to your deserts, and hope I may be allowed to have my name inserted among the subscribers. No man living deserves such a mark of respect more richly

them an opportunity of explaining their views and wishes, and of giving certain publicity to the cause they had espoused.

The 7th of July, 1845,—the 74th anniversary of my birthday,—was accordingly named, and nearly one hundred personal friends attended at the Castle Hotel, Richmond; a favourite house of mine; when a very cheerful and cordial evening was the result. My long-tried friend and patron, the Marquess of Northampton, would have presided, but for a previous engagement. Thomas Wyse, Esq., M.P., (now the British Ambassador at Athens,) then engaged to take the chair; but on the previous day he wrote to Mr. Godwin, who, jointly with Mr. Peter Cunningham, had accepted the Honorary Secretaryship to the Committee, explaining that unexpected arrangements of particular business in the House of Commons would prevent his attending.† My old and warm-hearted friend and neighbour, Nathaniel Gould, Esq., who had taken an active and zealous part in originating and promoting the affair, then agreed to preside; and not only warmly advocated the Testimonial, but kept up the conviviality of a large party with admirable spirit

---

than yourself, and the unselfish mode in which you propose to receive it, does you the highest honour."

From T. L. DONALDSON, Esq., Professor of Architecture at University College, London:—"I concur most heartily in the idea of a Testimonial to the Father of British Antiquities; and I shall be most happy to promote it to the utmost of my power. My pen and my voice have ever concurred to assert the extent of the obligations we are all under to you; and I doubt not that the Testimonial will worthily convey the full impression of your high merits, as an antiquary and lover of the arts."

From CHARLES BARRY, Esq., R.A.:—"I shall have great pleasure in contributing to the Subscription for the Britton Testimonial, to evince my sense of the respect and admiration which are most justly due to its recipient."

† Mr. Wyse states:—"I am, *most reluctantly*, compelled to sacrifice the honour and gratification I had anticipated in presiding over the dinner to be given to my friend, Mr. Britton. I cannot tell you or him how much I feel this disappointment; I had hoped it would have afforded me the opportunity I have so long desired of expressing my own sense of the many obligations which our national antiquities owe to his zeal and intelligence, and of being the organ, in so doing, of what I believe to be the sentiment of every one acquainted with his long, and most meritorious and useful labours. Though compelled by this *mal à propos* to give up the pleasure to which I had looked, I hope you will not less believe I most warmly sympathize in the object of your meeting, and hope I may be afforded, on some future occasion, the means of enlarging these expressions of regard and respect to the object of these honours—Mr. Britton."

and tact. The sentiments expressed on this occasion convinced the Committee that the subscription would amount to a considerable sum; and they held several meetings to determine the manner of its appropriation. Amongst various suggestions, the following were recommended: A Portrait, to be painted by an eminent artist, to be engraved, and prints given to all the subscribers. A Marble Bust, of which casts might be distributed in the same manner as the Portrait. A Medal; an impression in gold to be given to the author, and others, in silver and bronze, to the subscribers, according to the amount of their subscriptions. A Literary Essay on some subject of Archæology, for which a prize of one hundred guineas was to be presented to the most successful writer, and the work to be printed and distributed to the subscribers. A Piece, or Service of Plate.—Objecting in part to all of these, and particularly to the last, I, however, preferred the Literary Essay. Many difficulties were started on this subject; the most material of which was the extent and delicacy of the labour it must entail on gentlemen, who would have to read and decide upon the papers; and also the mortification to be experienced by writers of rejected essays. The noted literary competition for fame and reward annexed to an Address for the re-opening of Drury-Lane Theatre, was referred to as a beacon to guard against. This plan being abandoned, I thought it becoming to endeavour to relieve the Committee from further loss of time, and addressed the following letter to them:

"BURTON STREET, 15th August, 1845.

"DEAR SIRS,

"When my friends first talked of presenting me with some permanent token of esteem, and tangible compliment, for my literary works, they inquired in what way I wished to have the same applied; as I had declined accepting the money as a gift. After some days' deliberation, I stated, that, as the whole of my public life and labours had been devoted to *Literature*, I should prefer having any sum they might collect appropriated to encourage and reward an Author and a Printer, in the production of a *Literary Work*, rather than a Silversmith in making a fancy piece of plate.

"This might appear to some persons affected liberality and independence. I do not, however, pretend to be rich, or to have saved enough of the lucre of this world to secure luxuries in the down-hill of life. Content with some of the usual *comforts*, I trust that my means will enable me to obtain them for a few years more; and it is not reasonable to expect that my life can be extended much longer.

"Dissatisfied with the plans which have been proposed, I am willing to entail upon myself the labour of producing a handsome *Literary Volume* for presentation to the Subscribers. In this, it is my intention to take a complete but brief review of my publications,—the character, extent, and peculiarities of each of them,—with incidental notices and anecdotes of authors, artists, publishers, patrons, and others who have been intimately connected with those works. I shall thus produce a volume calculated to interest and gratify Antiquaries, Topographers, Artists, and Bibliographers; whilst it will furnish each contributor to the Britton Testimonial with a permanent acknowledgment, or receipt, for the amount of his Subscription: a testimonial to preserve amongst his family archives. " J. BRITTON."

This proposition was readily acceded to; but, at the time of making it, I little calculated the labour and expense it would demand, or the extent of time its composition must occupy. On the contrary, I hoped that what I had to say might be comprised in about 200 pages, and completed within eighteen months, at the furthest.

The preliminaries thus settled, I prepared to proceed with a task which I felt would be not only arduous and delicate, but would require assiduous labour, and abstraction from that relaxation which I had reasonably calculated on, to smooth and soothe the last stage in the journey of life. On looking over journals and letters, I found them numerous, and of varied import: many of the last being from persons of public and literary distinction, now no more, detailing facts and opinions properly belonging to history and biography, and therefore entitled to preservation; whilst a vast mass were only fitted for the waste-basket of oblivion. The mere examination of these occupied many months.

In connection with these proceedings I was induced to publish, in January 1846, (chiefly from short-hand notes taken by Mr. Jones, my amanuensis,) a pamphlet with the following title:

"An Account of the Public Dinner given to John Britton, at the Castle Hotel, Richmond, on the 74th Anniversary of his Birth (July 7, 1845), with the Toasts and Speeches on the occasion; a List of Subscribers; and an Explanatory Preface. By T. E. Jones."

During the early part of the year 1847, I wrote and published "Memoirs of the Life, Writings, and Character of Henry Hatcher, Author of the History of Salisbury." This was commenced with a view of being made part of the present volume; but finding the materials replete with interesting matter,—not only in the biography of an old and much-valued friend, but relating to topography and archæology,—that my friend had been unjustly and ungenerously treated by a gentleman who claimed the authorship of a most elaborate and valuabl[e] folio volume which had been written by Mr. Hatcher, and that h[e] had otherwise been debarred of much of that fame to which he wa[s] fully and fairly entitled, I was impelled to vindicate his name and re[-] putation, without waiting for the present publication, and at greate[r] length than I could here have allowed to a subject personal to him rather than to myself.

After finishing this Essay, and distributing it among my subscriber[s] as an instalment and specimen of the present work, I edited and wrot[e] numerous notes to a quarto volume on "The Natural History of Wilt[-] shire, by John Aubrey, F.R.S.," which was printed for the Wiltshir[e] Topographical Society. This occupied me during several months. I[t] contains a fund of information respecting a variety of subjects in Wil[t-] shire, at the time it was written, accounts of the chief seats and ol[d] families, ancient architecture, liberal and mechanical arts, the clothin[g] trade and eminent clothiers, with particulars of "the grandeur of th[e] Earls of Pembroke," and their mansion at Wilton; and other anecdot[al] matters, illustrating the latter half of the seventeenth century.

A volume entitled "The Authorship of the Letters of Junius Elu[-] cidated," originated in memoranda intended for the present Aut[o] Biography; but in preparing them for the press, the matter was foun[d] too bulky and interesting to be thus used, and I resolved to print [it] separately. After much labour, inquiry, and correspondence, this v[o-] lume was published in 1848, and copies sent to Subscribers to th[e] Testimonial. The number of letters received in acknowledgment, fro[m] persons eminent in Parliament, the Church, and Literature, constitu[te] an interesting commentary on this long-disputed question; some co[in-] ciding with me in ascribing them to Colonel Barré, others advocatin[g] the claims of Sir Philip Francis, some regarding the authorship as st[ill] undecided, and others attaching credit to various parties whose nam[es] have been brought forward. The late learned and acute Bishop [of] Llandaff honoured me with a long and interesting letter of critic[al] opinion. On the 10th of July, 1848, he thus wrote:—

"Having read your 'Elucidation of Junius' with great interest, I can wi[th] truth say, that nothing I have ever read on that subject has equalled that Ess[ay] in unravelling the perplexities of the question, and in gaining my assent. [As] far as the means exist of solving the problem, you have, I think, succeeded.

long ago used to say, that the secret would have been discovered had not the internal evidence of rancorous malevolence threatened to lower the reputation of the author, quite as much as the display of intellectual vigour and literary talent would have adorned it. There is a fiend-like love of giving pain pervading the whole work. Deep injuries, and disappointed hopes, and mortified ambition may account for this, but cannot justify it. Hardly can they furnish matter of extenuation. Though I regard yours as a moral demonstration, yet I feel some curiosity for the production of the papers at Stowe, to which access is denied."

Since my Essay was published, and the Bishop's Letter was written, that estimable prelate has paid the debt of nature, and the splendid and valuable property at Stowe, including its extensive and choice library, has been sold by auction. The manuscripts, however, were kept separate, and disposed of privately to the Earl of Ashburnham, for £5,000; but the secret and mysterious letters by Junius were withheld by a member of the Buckingham family; whence it has been publicly inferred, that they either involve the honour of one of the Grenvilles, or contain secrets of a momentous and alarming import. I am, however, informed, by a confidential and honourable friend, who read the Junius-Stowe Letters (three in number), that they do not implicate any of the family, nor militate against my theory of their having been the productions of Barré; on the contrary, my friend states "that one of the letters alludes to the author's position in life, and appears to be perfectly in accordance with Colonel Barré's character."

This source having failed to disclose the long-hidden secret, public curiosity must be suspended till new and more demonstrative evidence be discovered. I am convinced that Barré possessed more talent, had better opportunities of knowing secrets of Statesmen and the Court, had experienced more injury and provocation from both, and was in every respect more decidedly qualified than any other person who has hitherto been referred to, to be the writer of the long-famed Letters.*

Sir David Brewster complimented my volume by a long critique in "The North British Review," in which he espoused the cause of Lachlan Maclean, a noted pamphleteer and a correspondent of Mac-

---

* A new edition of "Junius" is now printing, in 2 vols. 18mo., for Mr. H. G. Bohn's "Standard Library," to contain all the Letters and Commentaries formerly given in Woodfall and Good's Edition of 3 vols. 8vo.; together with Notes and an Essay, by John Wade.

pherson, who was Lady Brewster's father. Mr. T. B. Macaulay, Sir Robert Peel, Lord Brougham, the Archbishop of Armagh, Mr. Bancroft (the American Ambassador), Chevalier Bunsen, Lord Campbell, Mr. G. W. Cooke, Lady Francis, Mr. Joseph Hume, Sir Edw. Bulwer Lytton, Sir Francis Palgrave, Mr. Dawson Turner, Lord Amherst, Dr. Shelton Mackenzie, Mr. Cyrus Redding, Mr. G. P. R. James, the late Mr. Edward Du Bois, and several other noblemen and gentlemen favoured me with letters and opinions on the subject.

The interruptions and avocations mentioned above precluded me from fixing my undivided attention on the Auto-Biography which I had promised; and which haunted my waking, and often my sleeping mind. Though frequently prepared and resolved to commence my task, either illness or some other cause diverted me from it. The following, written at the time it bears date, shows that I had seriously begun the Memoir more than three years back.

On the 21st day of December, 1846, with the thermometer at 22°, and in the 76th year of my age, I commence writing a work which is intended to embrace a faithful and circumstantial memoir of my own public life and literary works.* As that life has been protracted beyond the period Scripturally ascribed to Man,—much longer, in fact, than that of any other member of my family,—and certainly exceeding the reasonable calculation which a life assurance Company would have

---

* Sterne was accused by Dr. Ferrier of copying, or rather stealing, not only the thoughts, but the language, of Burton's "Anatomy of Melancholy;" and I doubt not the above sentence will subject me to an impeachment for "picking and stealing" from the brains of my literary predecessors. Crabbed critics may indict me for these, amongst other offences; but I hereby assure them, as well as the confiding reader, that I never have, never did, and never will borrow from, or rob any brother Author, without giving him my "note of hand" in due and full acknowledgment of every doit received. In the above passage I perceive that there is a seeming plagiarism from Gibbon, who begins his own inimitable Memoir in nearly the same words as are here used: but I was unconscious of it when they were written; for more than twenty years had then elapsed since I had read that justly-admired piece of Auto-Biography. In April, 1847, I turned over its pages, and found much to interest my feelings, and to excite my emulation; but at the same time to make me despair of approaching its vivid and vigorous style, or of furnishing such a Biographical Essay as that produced by the learned and accomplished historian of the "Decline and Fall of the Roman Empire."

assigned to it at any given time within the last fifty years,—it may afford amusement to the student of longevity to be made acquainted with the constitutional peculiarities, as well as the vicissitudes of sickness and health, which I have encountered from infancy to old age. These will be related in the course of the present narrative; for many of the personal events in my career, and some of the literary works I have produced, have been influenced and marked by the repeated illnesses to which I have been subjected. It may be necessary, however, to premise that I am not, and never was, of a gloomy, morbid temperament; but, on the contrary, when in a fair state of health, I am, and always have been, sanguine, cheerful, hopeful, and confident. I have never sunk under ennui or despair; but, on the contrary, have looked forward and around, for relief from present ailments and difficulties, as well as for the means of guarding against others. The "Pleasures of Hope," rather than the "Pleasures of Imagination," at once reconciled me to the gloom which occasionally pervaded the present, and often presented cheering prospects in the distant landscape. In each new literary, or other enterprise, I always anticipated and contemplated its completion with ardent feelings. In prospectuses for new publications, it was my invariable practice to promise much; to announce not merely novelties, but qualities, the accomplishment of which entailed on me constant and anxious labour; and the mere promise of which had a tendency to create doubt and suspicion in the minds of readers, who had often been deceived by the florid and frothy advertisements of publishing quacks. The nature and result of my own pledges and performances will be fully explained in the following pages.

Thus far had I written on the pinchingly cold day mentioned in the preceding page; but on the following morning I was attacked by an old enemy (Bronchitis) which confined me to bed and house for some weeks, and interrupted the present Biography, as well as many other worldly affairs and duties. Once more rallying, I resumed my books and pen, and besides writing the Memoir of my friend Hatcher, I proceeded to arrange materials for this work, and had made some progress in the winter of 1847-8, when I was again assailed by severe illness.

On the 16th of April, 1848, I lost a dear wife, who had been warmly interested in all my literary undertakings, and with whom I had travelled over many English counties, and been closely domesticated for forty-five years. This was a severe shock to a weak body and nervous temperament, and rendered change of scene and society essentially necessary. The greater part of the ensuing summer was therefore occupied in visiting Bath, Bristol, Salisbury, Norwich, Yarmouth, Kent, Brighton, Richmond, Clapham, Winchmore Hill, &c.; and I cannot be too grateful to the affectionate friends who successfully devoted themselves to mitigate my mental sorrows, whereby physical health and animal spirits were eventually restored to their usual condition.

Once more I was buoyed up with the hope and confidence of being able, in the winter of 1848-9, to make material progress in writing and printing. But, alas! how deceitful, though often too seductive, is Hope. Instead of the rational and pleasing occupation of writing for the printer, and advancing my task, I was again paralysed by a renewal of the disease which had imprisoned me so many previous winters. A solitary widower, I now felt desolate and disconsolate, and therefore made provisions, by Will, for the completion of the promised work by my attached friends, Mr. Brayley and Mr. Godwin. Good medical advice, most watchful nursing, and affectionate attention from friends, once more enabled me to surmount and subdue the disease; and, in the course of the last summer, the Second Part, and the Appendix to this volume were written and printed. A renewed attack of disease assailed me in December last, and for nearly three months has debarred me from all bodily and mental exertion. In spite of old age, and the presages of my medical attendants, my enervated body has conquered this attack; another reprieve has been granted me; and I gladly and eagerly resume the pen to prosecute a Biographical narrative, which, though toilsome and arduous, will rationally occupy the mind, in reviewing and retracing a life of progress, anxiety, and vicissitude.

Instead of adopting the form of a Diary, or any strictly chronological arrangement, as has been the practice of some writers of their own memoirs, it is my intention to class and subdivide the following narrative under such heads, or chapters, as are best calculated, in my opinion, to combine personal character and incidents, with notices of literary works, persons, and subjects, connected with my career.

In this,—The First Chapter,—I have explained the origin of the present work; the proceedings of the friends who projected a subscription to present me with a public Testimonial; the public Dinner at Richmond; the works which I wrote between 1845 and 1850; several attacks of illness which have interrupted the Auto-Biography, and noticed Testimonials to more eminent public characters, &c.

The Second Chapter will necessarily advert to Boyhood, with allusions to school-days, relations, juvenile connections, country life, &c.

The Third Chapter will be devoted to the period of adolescence; with the slavery of apprenticeship; first glimpses of literature, and the difficulty of attaining knowledge; with examples of early associates.

In the Fourth Chapter will be embraced the struggles to obtain a livelihood, before I had made any attempts in Literature. It will describe the privations, studies, occupations, and amusements of an eventful period of my life.

The Fifth will relate my first crude attempts in Literature, with notices of publishers, artists, and authors.

The Sixth will explain the origin of the "Beauties of Wiltshire," and the "Beauties of England and Wales," with remarks on Topographical Literature and Illustrations, as well as on the new views of men and things which its adoption unfolded to me.

In the Seventh will be given an account of the origin, progress, and characteristics of the "Architectural Antiquities," and the associations which that work and others of the same class involved.

The Eighth will review the "Cathedral Antiquities," and notice various matters connected with Ecclesiastical Establishments, and Dignitaries of the Church.

The Ninth will refer to Publications devoted to the Fine Arts, and to my association with many distinguished Artists.

The Tenth and concluding Chapter will advert to Biographical and Miscellaneous Literature, to Public Societies and Institutions, and to the various duties and occcupations which have engaged my attention, exclusive of the subjects previously alluded to.

# CHAPTER II.

>────── "To man in every clime
>The sweetest, dearest, noblest spot below,
>Is that which gives him birth; and long it wears
>A charm unbroken, and its honored name,
>Hallowed by memory, is fondly breathed
>With his last lingering sigh."
>
>CARRINGTON'S "DARTMOOR," A Poem.

LOCAL ATTACHMENTS—MISS MITFORD'S DESCRIPTION OF "OUR VILLAGE" CONTRASTED WITH THE AUTHOR'S BIRTH-PLACE—NATURAL FEATURES AND CHARACTERISTICS OF THE PARISH OF KINGTON—JOHN AUBREY BORN THERE—ITS FORMER AND PRESENT STATE CONTRASTED—RECOLLECTIONS OF BOYHOOD—TRAITS OF VILLAGE CHARACTER—CLOTHIER'S VISITS—MOUNTEBANK AND MERRY-ANDREW—FOX-HUNTING—THE SAGACITY OF THE FOX; WITH AN INCIDENT, AND WOOD-CUT—MURDERER, AND A GIBBET—THE AUTHOR'S PARENTS AND RELATIVES—REMARKS ON PEDIGREES AND HERALDRY—SUPERSTITIOUS FAITH IN A CHILD'S CAUL—SCHOOL-DAYS AND PEDAGOGUES—AT FOSCOTE—AT YATTON KEYNEL—AT DRAYCOT—AT CHIPPENHAM—SCHOOL-FELLOWS: ROBERT ELLIOTT, DEAF AND DUMB; JAMES HEWLETT; THOMAS PANTON—BOYISH OCCUPATIONS—FIRST BOOKS—BARBARISM OF RUSTIC LIFE—JOURNEY TO LONDON—CLERKENWELL IN 1786—APPRENTICED.

THE laws and promptings of Nature are irresistibly impressive and imperative. Every living creature is attached to Home:—however driven from, or impelled to leave it, an unknown impulse renders a return to it an object of desire. The timid hare seeks security and preservation from its enemies in solitude, and in the secret form which she makes and patiently occupies during the long day; and when forced to quit it, she instinctively returns again, as to a protecting home. So Man, however enterprising and inquisitive may be his natural disposition, and however urgent his motives to travel to distant places or foreign lands, returns to his natal spot with avidity and intense gratification. The place of my birth, and residence for nearly sixteen years, in the early part of my life, became endeared to my feelings and affections; and more especially so after I had quitted it for an unknown place, and to associate with strangers. Many times have I revisited it since, and derived much gratification in the reminiscenses of those boyish sports and adventures, which, in bygone times, had been productive of pleasure and excitement.

Predilections and partialities for places, persons, and things, I am aware, invest them with undue and exaggerated importance; and I am equally aware that boys, as well as men, are variously constituted in their susceptibilities for enjoyment, or sorrow. Whilst some are devotedly attached to parents and homes, others are indifferent to both. The place of birth and childhood, of early playfulness, and of juvenile associations, has charms and fascinations which can only be duly felt and appreciated by those who have passed their early years in a rural neighbourhood.

It is with regret that I differ from Miss Mitford, the eloquent and fascinating author of "Our Village," in her florid description of rural scenery and society in the place wherein she resided for many years. That home is in the immediate vicinity of Reading, the county-town of Berkshire, having ready communication with the metropolis, and surrounded by the seats of many noblemen and gentlemen. Aided by a vivid fancy and a graphic pen, that gifted writer has painted cottage-life and cottage-inmates in such glowing colours, and with such pleasing characteristics, as to make her varied pictures full of innocence, cheerfulness, and social happiness. She describes the local scenery as fine and beautiful; the homes of the poor labourers as clean and comfortable; and their domestic manners and morals as devoid of guile and vice. A few lines from the first page of her first volume will serve to mark the power of her pen:—

"Of all situations for a constant residence, that which appears to me most delightful is a little village far in the country; a small neighbourhood, not of fine mansions finely peopled, but of cottages and cottage-like houses, 'messuages or tenements,' as a friend of mine calls such ignoble and non-descript dwellings, with inhabitants whose faces are as familiar to us as the flowers in our garden; a little world of our own, close packed and insulated like ants in an ant-hill, or bees in a hive, or sheep in a fold, or nuns in a convent, or sailors in a ship; where we know every one, are known to every one, interested in every one, and authorized to hope that every one feels an interest in us. How pleasant it is to slide into these true-hearted feelings from the kindly and unconscious influence of habit, and to learn to know and to love the people about us, with all their peculiarities, just as we learn to know and to love the nooks and turns of the shady lanes and sunny commons that we pass every day. Even in books I like a confined locality, and so do the critics when they talk of the unities. And a small neighbourhood is as good in sober waking reality, as in poetry or prose; a village neighbourhood, such as this Berkshire hamlet in which I write, a long, straggling, winding street at the bottom of a fine eminence with a road through it, always abounding in carts, horsemen, and carriages, and lately enlivened by a stage-coach, which passed through about ten days ago, and will, I suppose, return some time or other."

Not one word or idea in these lines can apply to the village in which I was "born and bred;" and where I idled away nearly sixteen years of that period of life, the greater part of which ought to have been devoted to study, and to the discipline and cultivation of mind, in order to prepare it to bear fruits and flowers in after life, and thus become useful and ornamental to its possessor and to society. "*My Village*," however, was so unlike Miss Mitford's, that it might be regarded as belonging to a different part of the world, and occupied by a distinct class of the human race. Though the street (if it may be so called) was a public road, it was rarely traversed by a post-chaise, or private carriage; a strange cart, or waggon, was seldom seen; and a stage-coach, then called a "diligence," never. Carriages of the last-mentioned kind were indeed scarcely known to the villagers; as only two or three passed through the neighbouring town of Chippenham on their way between Bath, Bristol, and London. These were clumsy, lumbering vehicles, drawn by two horses (generally very sorry, raw-shouldered animals,) and having a "basket" behind, for luggage and outside passengers. Mail-coaches were not invented; the few letters which were sent to and from the metropolis, and by cross posts, being entrusted to a mail-cart, as already noticed in p. 13. Hence I can trace scarcely any analogy between Miss Mitford's Village, and that in which I was destined to pass many precious years without the acquisition of any practical or useful knowledge. But though the parish is comparatively unimportant, and almost unnoticed in the annals of Topography, it possesses characteristics entitling it to a separate history. Such a history I would have written and published some years back, were the inhabitants within its bounds, or in the vicinity, or even within the precincts of the large and rich county of Wilts, sufficiently liberal and enlightened to encourage such a literary work: but, strange to say, the zealous efforts of John Aubrey, and Bishop Tanner, of Penruddock Wyndham, and Sir Richard Colt Hoare, have hitherto failed in their respective endeavours to obtain funds and co-operation to complete a history of the county. My topographical collections for Kington are extensive, and have cost me much time and money, but it would be improper and improvident for me to appropriate more of either, without a reasonable prospect of some reward.*

The natural features of this parish are distinguished by much variety of surface. Though neither romantic nor abounding with picturesque scenery, it presents many inequalities of hill and valley. Being the source of two streams, or rivulets, the district is evidently high ground. These streams flow through narrow, winding valleys, which skirt the northern and southern ends of the village. The southern stream has its origin in three springs immediately west of the church, which, joining at the parsonage, flow thence directly eastward for about half a mile; where they merge into another and larger brook, at the turnpike road between Chippenham and Malmesbury. The other, or northern stream, rises near a farm called Lower Easton, and passing by the Priory, where it formerly supplied a stew-pond for the use of the Nuns, it then meanders through a very pleasing, narrow valley, to the junction already named. Another perpetual spring rises near the walls of the Priory, its waters being noted in Aubrey's time, and long subsequently, for sanative qualities. From the point of junction, at the turnpike road, the united streams flow almost in a direct line to Draycot

---

* I cannot abstain from stating with feelings of gratification, that my native parish was also the birth-place of JOHN AUBREY, the first Wiltshire antiquary; and indeed the first Englishman whose researches embraced the architectural and archæological characteristics of the mediæval ages, as well as the Celtic remains of the primæval inhabitants of Britain. It has been the custom of modern writers to advert to Aubrey's literary labours in terms of disparagement and contempt; a tone of comment, doubtless based upon the partial and unjust testimony of Anthony à Wood, and on a volume of "Miscellanies" which Aubrey printed, but which merely shows that he participated largely in the common superstitions of his age. In 1813, the "Lives of Eminent Men" were published by Dr. Bliss and the Rev. J. Walker, from an original manuscript by Aubrey; and tended to correct the erroneous impression referred to. I have had peculiar satisfaction in further rectifying many errors in previous biographical notices, and in placing Aubrey before the public, as an earnest inquirer, an accurate recorder of curious and valuable information, a zealous antiquary, and an amiable and learned man. It may be thought, indeed, that I have bestowed too great an amount of care and assiduity on this author and his works; but a desire for the establishment of Truth; for the illustration of Wiltshire Biography in general; and that of my native parish in particular; impelled me onward in the task, which, though not at present duly appreciated, I feel assured, will hereafter be duly recognized and valued.

and Sutton, and join the river Avon at Christian Malford. These brooks formerly abounded with trout and eels, many of which I have assisted in catching at the end of dry summers, by laving out the water from the deeper holes of the rivulets. At the mansion-house at Kington is a fish-pond, well stocked with carp, eels, tench, &c. Many of these I have taken with rod and line, and others by fastening hooks with worms at the ends of pieces of string, and leaving them during the night. In the morning three and sometimes four large fish and eels have been caught. Another amusement, and trespass, legally called poaching, I was taught in early life to pursue; by fixing wires, with nooses, in the holes of hedges, where hares and rabbits had beaten tracks. These sports arose from idleness,—from want of good companions,—from the absence of all moral and legal authority in the parish. Without a regular clergyman to advise and admonish, or a magistrate, or private gentleman residing in the principal house of the village, the inhabitants were undisciplined, illiterate, and deprived of all good example: whilst those who were constitutionally idle and dissipated had no check on their conduct, and became too often promoters of bad habits in the young.* I can easily account for the vice of Deer-Stealing, with which Shakspere has been accused, by tracing it to want of better occupation and of good associates.

The approach to the village, either from the south, north, or west, is by a gentle declivity, succeeded by a gradual ascent. On the south side is a ridge of high ground, which in some parts forms a short but steep hill. From this ridge nearly the whole village is seen, with its gardens, fields, church, parsonage, old mansions, almshouses, &c.

---

* The following letter, by a gentleman of Kington, will verify my remarks: "I am sorry I can say nothing in favour of the habits and manners either of the farmers of this village, or the poor people. All have been neglected, and are grossly ignorant, in every way. For fifty years there was no resident gentleman or clergyman, with the exception of Mr. Coleman, who has been too quiet to interfere. Our farming is of the worst kind: a great portion of the land requires draining; but this important operation has been, and is now, sadly neglected; though I have set an example by draining all my own land. There is the less excuse for this, because a great portion of the parish consists of a stone-brash soil, which is drained at the least expense, by merely taking out the stone and putting it in again. I have taken down a few old cottages at the entrance to the village, and near the parsonage."

The parish is divided into two tithings—Kington St. Michael, and Kington Langley. The former is entirely enclosed, and the houses lie near together, forming the village, the population being in 1841, 572. In the tithing of Langley there is a common, or open green; the houses are widely scattered, and the population 601—making a total of 1173. The poor-rate in 1841 was £643. The tithing of Kington embraces 1220 acres devoted to pasture, and 1043 to arable; whilst Langley has 1030 acres of pasture and 542 of arable; the whole extent of the parish, including about 90 acres of woodland, being 3950 acres. Its length is about four miles from east to west, by two miles from north to south. The district is well wooded; the trees being mostly elms, with a few oaks in the woods and hedgerows. Beech and ash are very scarce; but the holly is luxuriant and abundant. The sign of the inn, which stands in the centre of the parish—"The Plough"—strongly and truly designates it as a purely agricultural locality; there has never, in fact, been a loom in the parish. The general character of the soil is light and dry, and of good quality in several parts, but on the whole, not rich. Its value varies considerably, the greater part being worth from thirty to forty shillings per acre. There are thirty farms in the parish; fifteen of which are under 100 acres, twelve from 100 to 200 acres, whilst three exceed the last-named quantity. These are all devoted to the dairy system; cheese (for which North Wiltshire has long been celebrated) being the great commodity produced, with a comparatively small quantity of butter.

Although the system of farming adopted here cannot be regarded as either scientific or skilful, it may not be useless to notice a few particulars respecting it; as improvements may be promoted by pointing out the errors and defects of any existing practice. Since my boyhood many and important changes have been introduced into every department of husbandry and agriculture, particularly in the country around London, and other great cities and towns of the empire; but there are still many farmers in North Wiltshire, Gloucestershire, Somersetshire, and elsewhere, who, having succeeded their fathers and grandfathers in the occupancy of their respective estates, continue the routine and practice of their predecessors with thoughtless pertinacity. I could particularize two or three instances of this kind, which would astonish the scientific farmers who frequent the London, Kent, Essex, Norfolk, or the Hertfordshire markets. In my time, the Kington farms exhibited broken and decayed gates and stiles; wide, tall, and straggling hedges, sheltering and encouraging weeds of all kinds, particularly thistles and nettles; many shords* in those hedges; undrained and foul ditches; waste and unworked pieces of land at the ends and corners of ploughed fields. The neglect to root up and destroy thistles, docks, and other weeds, was, in consequence, a punishment to the imprudent and idle farmer; whilst improper or scanty manuring was almost as bad. Many farmers failed to drain wet lands sufficiently, and neglected favourable opportunities of irrigating the surface of the dry. I believe there was not a farmer in Kington, or its vicinity, who ever kept a register, or correct record of proceedings or experiments in business; nor was there one who bestowed half the labour or expense on the land, which was requisite to make it fully productive, and proportionately profitable. The masters were poor, uninformed, and wholly unfitted to do justice to themselves, their landlords, or the public. It must be remembered that these remarks refer to the time of my boyhood; but great changes and improvements have since been made. Two or three farms have been united into one, and their occupants are a different class of persons. The neighbouring markets and fairs, and the easy and cheaper carriage by railway, have jointly produced revolutions in the agricultural as well as the commercial and manufacturing community. My late excellent and most estimable friend, Mr. W. R. Browne, of Chiselden, was a scientific and experimental agriculturalist, and not only introduced many improvements into the farming business, but induced other persons to follow his example. Mr. Atherton, the owner of the manor of Kington, has created numerous changes in the roads, walls, hedges, fields, and cottage residences of the labouring poor of his parish.

Recollections of my native home, (though I have parted from it more than sixty years,) are clear and strong: not only are the natural features of the parish and its vicinity indelibly impressed on my memory; but also the houses and other buildings, the gardens and orchards, and every living inhabitant; including dogs, horses, and other animals.

---

* This word is common in the West of England, and means broken, severed, fragmentary: as ponshords, broken earthenware; gaps or openings in hedges, &c.

The sports and pastimes of the people, as well as the singularities of those persons who exhibited any, are still retained in that wonderful storehouse, the brain: but were I to enter into detailed accounts of their personal minutiæ, (though they would tend to form a true and faithful chapter in the history of man, and his relationship to time, place, and circumstance,) my Memoir would become too bulky, and probably be deemed too prolix.

A few pen-and-ink sketches of scenery and character may not be irrelevant; as serving to mark palpable contrasts between the past and present, country and town, nature and art, illiterate and literary society—man almost in a state of semi-barbarism, and man enlightened by art, science, and refinement.

In part of my boyish days, Kington had no resident 'squire, clergyman, or person above the rank of farmer, or village tradesman. There were ten agriculturists who kept horses, cows, and sheep, and about the same number of tradesmen, or " dealers and chapmen;" but I do not think there was a newspaper or magazine purchased by one of the inhabitants before the year 1780, when the London riots were talked about, and wondered at. Five or six years afterwards, " The Lady's Magazine" was taken in by one of the farmer's daughters, and lent by her to my sister Elizabeth, who was fond of reading. One of the Bath papers was afterwards introduced to the village, and created an epoch,—food for the gossip of the whole village. Farmer Robbins, our opposite neighbour, and Thomas, *alias* Tommy Collard, an old bachelor, both of whom seemed to live upon tittle-tattle, were the bearers and special messengers of all such news as they could comprehend and talk about, through the whole extent of Kington; retailing it by pieces and scraps at the carpenter's, the tailor's, and the blacksmith's shops. At each of these houses they would devote about an hour to social converse, or rather to colloquy; for the tradesmen, if employed on work, continued their occupation, and rarely interrupted the talkers with anything beyond,—" Well, well!"—" Indeed!"—" Is it true?"—" Strange!"—" What! in foreign parts?"—" That Lunnun is a mortal queer place."—" Well! I shull never zee ut, nur any o' the papishes." Roman Catholics, papists, and devils, were synonymous at Kington, and in many other country villages. I often accompanied my old news-friends in their daily rounds, and consequently listened with intense curiosity to their narratives.* Mr. Robbins was aged, occupied a small dairy-farm, which required but a very small portion of his time; and Mr. Collard lived upon a small annuity of about £30, and was called, Gentleman.

The roads to the village, branching from those called Turnpike Roads about a mile distant, were not easy to be passed over by carriages; for, being only used by waggons and carts, they were worn into two deep ruts by the wheels, and another nearly equally deep by the horses. These roads, as well as others branching from the village, are now made level and hard, and adapted for pleasure as well as for trading carriages.

At the time alluded to, our dull village was periodically enlivened by the visits of a clothier, with one, two, or three horses, laden with bags of wool, brought from the manufacturer in Gloucestershire, and doled out to poor women, to be carded and spun for the weaver's loom. Thus several women and their daughters were employed, and derived regular payment for their labour. This was before spinning-jennies, or other machinery, were introduced. The ceremonies of distributing the wool, receiving and paying for the spun yarn, and supplying the poor with articles for domestic use, were transacted at our house, which was thronged on these occasions.

Another occasional visitant to the grassy street of the village, was a *Mountebank Doctor*, with his *Merry-Andrew* and stage caravan, or carriage. This itinerant quack was, however, a rare guest at our poor place; for the repetition of his visits to any town or village was regulated by the amount of shillings he could abstract from the pockets of his admiring auditors. He was usually clad in a scarlet coat, white

---

\* On such occasions I have witnessed scenes which would strikingly exemplify the fidelity of Shakspere's lines:

    —————— "I saw a Smith stand with his hammer (thus)
    The whilst his iron did on the anvil cool,
    With open mouth swallowing the Tailor's news;
    Who, with his shears and measure in his hand,
    Standing on slippers which his nimble haste
    Had falsely thrust upon contrary feet,
    Told of a many thousand warlike French."
              *King John*, Act IV., Sc. 2.

hat, and top boots, and always had a companion, called Merry-Andrew —a sort of clown, or buffoon, whose office and duty was to submit to the horse-whip, to tumble, leap, dance, make grotesque faces, and parley badinage and vulgar jokes with his equally accomplished master.*

During the winter season, the drowsy monotony of "Our Village" was occasionally awakened from its lethargy by the musical and stimulating cry of the Duke of Beaufort's fox-hounds, or by Sir James Tylney Long's harriers. After the latter I had many a long and tiring run in my boyish days; and on one occasion followed the pack for five hours, without a moment's rest, and was in at the death of a fourth hare. A hearty repast of bread and cheese, with a glass of ale, at a farm-house, made the most delicious meal I ever enjoyed in my life; for I had left home without breakfast, or leave, and was rewarded with a horse-whip on my return. Three events connected with this place, and the chase, may be shortly noticed, as illustrating the amazing cunning of the fox, and as facts which came under my own cognizance. On one occasion, Reynard was closely pressed by the hounds, when he

---

* In a ballad called "Sundry Trades and Callings," it is said that,—

"A Mountebank without his fool
Is in a sorrowful case."

Shakspere speaks of these wandering empirics in no equivocal language,—

"As nimble jugglers that deceive the eye,
Disguised cheaters, prating mountebanks,
And many such-like libertines of sin."

*Comedy of Errors*, Act I., Sc. 2.

Granger (in his "Biographical History of England") describes one of these mountebanks, who was noted in London in the time of James II. He was an odd figure of a man, fantastical in dress; attended by a monkey, who had been trained to act as "Jack Pudding," a part which the master had previously performed himself. In "The Spectator" is a paper on these impudent and ignorant fellows, with an account of one who gulled the poor credulous inhabitants of Hammersmith, near London, by proclaiming, from his rostrum, that from love to his native place, Hammersmith, he had come amongst them with the determination to present every inhabitant with five shillings. The gaping assembly pressed forward to accept the proffered sum, shouting their thanks and plaudits as the cunning doctor was exploring a bag. Taking out a packet of pill-boxes, gallipots, &c., he announced that each was valued at 5s. 6d., but he would distribute the whole to his fellow-natives, and to those only, at 6d. each. The contents were soon distributed, and the sixpences duly handed up to this generous medicine vendor. In a new edition of Anstey's "Bath Guide" are further remarks of the Mountebank, &c.

entered a cottage at the bottom of the hill, where all was quiet and apparently secure; and, as the only visible place of refuge, he leaped into a cradle, in which an infant was sleeping, and crept under the clothes. The mother of the child, who was in the garden, heard the hounds in full cry, near the cottage, and ran in to secure her sleeping infant, when, on lifting up the clothes, she was greeted with a snarl and display of his fine set of teeth from Reynard. The terror of the poor woman may be imagined, but cannot be described. The baby, however, was safe; the huntsman uncradled the fox; the sports were terminated for the day; and the parent's heart palpitated with joy.

On another occasion, I saw a fox approach the village, with the hounds very near to his brush. Reynard leaped on the top of a wall, and descended into a farm-*barken*.* The dogs followed within two minutes, with the huntsman and sportsmen, in close pursuit; but though there were persons very near the spot—though the scent must have been strong—though every house, stable, barn, rick, well, drain, &c. was searched, the fox remained undiscovered. The huntsman took the hounds round the village, to try if any scent could be found, but without effect.

---

* This word applies to inclosed courts, or pieces of ground, adjoining farm-houses; as cow-barken, rick-barken, &c.

A third fox, whose actions I watched from an eminence, passed through a hedge near one corner of a field, and ran on the side of another hedge, at right angles with that through which he entered, pursuing a direct line for about 200 or 300 yards, when he made a turn at right angles through a thick hedge, and thus, instead of going into a small brake or copse of underwood, which was the resort of rabbits, and occasionally the haunt of a fox, and which was only one field distant, he tricked the hounds and the huntsmen. When they had passed by, I saw him emerge from the hedge, cross his previous path, and run about a mile to a cover, called Haywood, where he found protection.

The cunning of the fox is proverbial; and the craniologists refer to the formation of its head and the capacity of its skull, as showing that the brains are larger and more capacious, in proportion to the whole animal, than those of any other brute. My grandfather kept a fox, which he had reared from a cub, had tamed it, and made it as docile and domesticated as a dog. It was generally chained to its den, or house; but was occasionally allowed to accompany its master in the fields, and to the parlour of an evening, when the old gentleman amused himself with his glass of gin-toddy, and the everlasting pipe. Reynard's company was however very alarming to me; for, having thrown stones at him in confinement, he often showed his murderous but fine teeth, which warned me against his anger and power. My grandfather was fond of a fox-hunt, and on two occasions allowed his favourite to be turned into an adjoining wood, and hunted by the Duke of Beaufort's hounds. On the first occasion, after a chase of some twenty miles, he made his escape, and returned home the next morning. The second chase was fatal: as the fox was killed after half an hour's run.

An event connected with this locality, and noticeable, as illustrating the superstitious opinions which prevailed amongst nearly the whole population of the time, may be narrated; as the relation of it made an indelible impression on my young mind, and indeed impressed me with the belief that the phenomena of lightning, thunder, and storm always accompanied human executions. When a boy, I often passed a gibbet, in Stanton field, on which a man had been hung in chains for murdering a negro in Stanton Park, a large wood so called. The two had been seen together at Malmesbury, and at the village of Stanton, and the murderer was noticed on the same day by some of the inhabitants of Kington, walking at a quick pace through that village, inquiring his way to Chippenham. He had killed his companion, rifled his pockets, and was on his road to Bristol. Within an hour after the murder was committed, the body was discovered by a woodman, who communicated the intelligence to the inhabitants of a neighbouring farm: a hue-and-cry was raised, the man was traced through Kington, and arrested at Chippenham on the same day. He was conveyed to Salisbury, tried, and condemned to be hung. According to my father, who often repeated the tale, (one story forms a staple article for retailing in a country village, for a long space of time,) he, with almost all the inhabitants of Kington and the neighbouring villages, went to see the murderer hanged on Stanton Common. As the culprit approached the place, a small black cloud was observed over the gibbet: it increased, and at the time of the execution had extended over a wide space. When the man was "turned off," there was a vivid flash of lightning, with thunder, and a violent storm arose, and continued during the remainder of the day. John Aubrey relates that he "did see Mr. Christopher Love beheaded on Tower Hill, in a delicate clear day: about half an hour after his head was struck off, the clouds gathered blacker and blacker, and such terrible claps of thunder came that I never heard greater."—(*Miscellanies*, chapter on "Omens.") Many other events connected with the locality, and calculated to depict the ignorance of the uneducated poor, and even of the farmers, might be narrated; but enough have been mentioned to show the broad and glaring contrast between the present educational age, and that in which my childhood was passed.

In the village which I have thus endeavoured to characterize I was born, on the 7th of July 1771, being the first son, and fourth child, of parents who had been settled in their own copyhold premises about eight years. Six other children were afterwards born to them, four of whom, besides myself, were destined to be successively placed in the metropolis, "to seek our fortunes," as the common phrase is. Of my family ancestry I know but little, and, as Gifford says in his own *Auto-Biography*,\* "that little is not very precise." My mother's character is

---

\* Preface to his Translation of Juvenal's "Satires."

truly marked by the same learned author and severe critic, in language which he applied to his own parent: "She was an excellent woman, bore my father's infirmities with good humour, loved her children dearly, and died at last exhausted with anxiety and grief, more on their account than her own."

My parents were differently constituted, and of dispositions and tempers entirely dissimilar to each other. My father was cold, saturnine, reserved, and phlegmatic, whilst his partner was warm-hearted, animated, sanguine, anxious, and passionate; and in these characteristics she inherited the blood of her own family, the Hilliers; whilst her husband's peculiarities appear to have been those of the Brittons. I say "appear," for I never saw, or heard more than the names of my paternal grandfather and grandmother; though I knew an elder brother of my father, and two of his sisters; each of whom displayed family tempers resembling his own. Such discordant elements as I have described, could never coalesce cordially or effectively.

For some years after their marriage the station of my parents in the village was truly respectable, and their prospects in life cheering. My father's business, or occupation, was that of baker, maltster, shop-keeper, and small farmer; and, from the earliest time of my recollection, we employed a man-servant, in the labours of making bread and malt, and attending to a few acres of land and a small stock of horses, cows, and sheep. A female servant was also part of the household, and for some time the world smiled on the family and its prospects. This, however, was attributable to the activity and good conduct of the mistress of the house, who not only attended to and managed the whole domestic arrangements, but the shop also and its customers. An increasing family naturally required more and more of her time and attention, when my father was obliged to occupy her place in personal attendance, but was entirely unfitted to be her substitute in activity, good management, and obliging conduct. The consequences were natural and inevitable. Customers contracted debts, and never paid them; the miller sent in bad flour, which made bad bread; rivals in trade secured the customers who were in debt; and ruin—complete and distressing ruin—was the result. My dear mother died broken-hearted; my father became idiotic; and my sister Mary, at the age of about sixteen, was left to hold possession of the house, with a little furniture, and to take charge of two young brothers, aged about six, and eight. I am now somewhat anticipating my personal narrative, for, at the time of these occurrences, I was immured in a London wine-cellar; two of my brothers were also apprenticed in London; my eldest sister was married and settled in Shropshire; my second sister, Elizabeth, had died at home before the catastrophe. News of these domestic troubles occasionally reached me, but were very imperfectly reported; and though deeply grieved, I felt myself helpless, and was led to lament, without the power of relieving. Often, however, was I haunted, in imagination, with visions of the privations and miseries which my poor dear mother must have suffered in her struggles against poverty, sickness, and death.

To my mother's parents and family connections I shall have occasion to advert presently; for many of my youthful days were spent with them, and my character and career in life were materially influenced by their example and association.

From the naturally taciturn disposition of my father, and the lamentable illiteracy of all his connections, I was never informed of any particulars respecting his parents, their home, or their family.* Only

---

* I will risk the charge of singularity, if I fail in originality, by abstaining from wasting my own or the reader's time in conjectural disquisition and detail about family history, ancestral pedigree, or other matters trespassing on the province of the herald. A family coat of arms I could display, fully emblazoned, from an old stone authority, and might use it as the Britton Arms; but this would subject me to taxation, and my taxes are already more weighty than pleasant. Besides, I could not reconcile myself to accept, or adopt, such an unmeaning hieroglyphic emblazonment. In an age of ignorance and semi-barbarity, when reading and writing were almost unknown, it was politic and useful to distinguish armies, clans, and followers by some visible and popular insignia, or badge; but body armour, shields of arms, and other ancient military objects are only fitted for the museum of the archæologist, where they may serve to amuse and instruct persons who are partial to such subjects. Though a devoted antiquary, I prefer a new to an old coat, whether made by a tailor or an artist. It is time that griffins, mermaids, and other monsters be exploded from modern education, and from the language of science and art; and that the rising generation be instructed in the elements of truth, nature, and pure science, rather than in fairy legends and fictitious romances. Those indeed who prefer pedigree to philosophy, and the technicalities of heraldry to the history of man, had better avoid the present volume, and everything which I have hitherto written, as utterly at variance with their partialities and prejudices, and therefore likely to hurt their feelings. At the commencement of my literary career, and at

two circumstances belonging to them were ever impressed on my memory. My grandmother, Britton, had an uncle who kept a pack of hounds in his early days, and retained a favourite one to be his companion in old age. The old man and the old dog died on the same day, and the former requested that the latter should be interred in a coffin in the same grave with him. My father's brother, Thomas, was a "back-maker," or cooper, in Bristol; whence he emigrated to Jamaica, where he acquired considerable property, and died unmarried. The property he bequeathed to his brother Henry, my father, who occasionally alluded to his landed estates in the West Indies, which he hoped his son, John, would some day go abroad to claim. This time has never arrived, and never will; nor do I know anything further of the place or nature of the property than was thus vaguely told some seventy years ago.

Within the last few years I have had some particulars forced upon my notice relating to my father's family; in consequence of which I made inquiries about them in several parishes between Bath and Bristol; particularly in North-Stoke, Beach, Weston, and Bitton,* Gloucestershire; and in Corston, Somersetshire. My esteemed friend, the Rev. H. T. Ellacombe, of Bitton, has found the names of more than a hundred of the Brittons in the registers of those parishes. On the tower of the church of North-Stoke is inscribed the name of "William Britten, Churchwarden, 1731," with an armorial shield. "The Brittens" is also the name of an estate at Beach; certain Brittons occupied the Manor Farm of Bitton two centuries ago; and the tradition of the district is that branches of the family were substantial yeomen; or

---

different times during its course, it has been my fate to read and hear much of the length and breadth of famous pedigrees—of the long lines of descent of noble families—of heraldic and genealogical trees of vast altitude and wide-spreading branches—and of the quantity and quality of quarterings in coats of arms; not one iota of which is calculated to add an inch to the stature, or one grain of merit to the moral or mental worth of their living representative.

"What can ennoble sots, or slaves, or cowards?
Alas! not all the blood of all the Howards."

"Honour and wealth from no condition rise;
Act well your part; *there* all the honour lies."

* Many etymologists and theorists would find in this name a direct connection with that of Britton, by omitting a letter in one word or adding it to the other.

persons of estate and property. Some of them were in trade in Bristol, and my old friend Robert Southey says, that his father lived as shopman with a Mr. William Britton, a linen-draper of Bristol. Some persons of the name are still residing at Corston and at Bristol, but I never had personal communication with any of them.

I was always a favourite with my poor mother, but never with my father. He preferred my brother Thomas, who, like himself, was dull, slow, and plodding. As a boy, I was devoted to every species of play, and seized all available moments to pursue it with any companion I could meet. Hence one of the attractions of school consisted in the play-hours that were allowed, and the playmates it supplied. My uncle Samuel being well and successfully settled in London, as Master Holford's chief clerk in the Court of Chancery, my mother always sought to make me fitted for similar employment. She often prognosticated that I was born to be fortunate, as I came into the world with *a Caul* over my face, which, in her opinion, and in that of many other mothers, was a sure sign of "rising in the world." The more direct and positive charm of such appendages, was the property, commonly ascribed to them, of preserving their possessors from drowning; and the wonder-working attributes, which induced captains of vessels and others to secure their possession at high prices, were occasionally subjects of comment and admiration at our winter fire-side.*

That the periods of childhood and adolescence often give indications

---

* In France, when a man is unusually fortunate in his undertakings, they say, "*il est né coëffe*,"—he was born with a caul. The Greeks always supposed that a child was predestined to good luck when it had this super-cuticle. According to Lampridius, the midwives sold these cauls at extravagant prices to advocates, who believed them capable of inspiring their wearers with supernatural eloquence. The value attached to them by our own sailors as preservatives from drowning is well known; and this superstitious notion has descended from time immemorial. My estimable and truly witty friend, Thomas Hood, has appropriated one of his exquisite poems to the subject; in which he has blended pathos and pun in his own peculiar way. Under the title of "The Sea Spell," is the story of a mariner who dares the perilous sea under the fancied security of a child's caul. Though a pathetic event, and pathetically treated, the insatiable propensity to punning could not be avoided even here:—

"The jolly boatman's drowning scream
Was smothered by the squall,
Heaven never heard his cry, nor did
The Ocean heed his *caul*."

of the future man, has been the doctrine of some biographers, philosophers, and poets; whilst others contend that the permanent conduct and character of mature age are entirely the result of adventitious circumstances. In my own case, I can safely say, from my earliest remembrances, that I was ever active, inquisitive, emulous, ambitious, and sensitive; whether in play, at school, or at work. It was my constant aim to surpass my equals, and compete with my superiors. Unfortunately I met with but little to stimulate these natural tendencies among my playmates or schoolfellows, nor had I parents, friends, or masters to direct them in a right and laudable course. Full fifteen years were wasted and frittered away in trifling miscellaneous occupation, and in learning words and things which were almost wholly useless. It is true I was placed under one schoolmistress,* and, with some intervals, under four successive masters, all of whom were wholly unfitted for the arduous and important task of instructing their youthful pupils in the principles, or elements, of scholastic, and what may be called more useful knowledge. The masters were completely ignorant of science, of literature, and of manners; and consequently could not impart either to their pupils. I cannot revert to this incipient period of life without sorrow. My first master's name was Moseley, living at Foscote, a hamlet to Grittleton, where I was boarded and lodged for about two years, between the ages of six and eight. This individual was a Baptist minister, and had a chapel, or rather a sort of shed, at Grittleton, where I regularly attended his spiritual performances. My instruction at this initiatory academy (a word, however, unknown in my connection) was so trifling that I have not the least recollection of any part of it; nor of any traits of personal character except the powdered head of my master, with large formal curls over his ears, and mane-like, close-cropt hair around the neck; together with his chilling, fanatical deportment and language, and the drawling monotony of his voice.

From this school I was often taken by my grandfather, Samuel Hillier,

---

* I mention this class of country tutors, as their ostensible business is "to teach the young idea how to shoot;" although their practice is chiefly to keep children "out of harm's way."—Here, however, I learnt the "Chris-cross-row" from a horn-book, on which were the alphabet in large and small letters, and the nine figures in Roman and Arabic numerals. The horn-book is now a rarity.

who resided at Maidford, a farm about two miles distant. There I was kept for many days and weeks at a time, without the knowledge of my parents; and there I acquired a partiality for field sports by accompanying my grandfather and his son Richard, in their hunting, coursing, and shooting excursions. When only eight years old, I was provided with a pony, and was soon afterwards taught to ride with impunity over hedges, ditches, brooks, &c. Falls from, and with the pony, were not unfrequent, but always harmless. On one occasion, however, my grandfather, as was no uncommon practice, took me behind him on his old favourite hunter, to Hullavington, a neighbouring village, where he smoked his pipe and drank his gin-toddy till evening prompted him to return home. The house was placed at the north-east angle of a large field, called the Cow-leas. The only gate of entrance to this field was at the north-west angle, whilst the road skirted its western side. To save the distance of going along the road, and to make a short cut to the house from the south-west corner of the field, he set spurs to the old horse to leap a deep ditch, with a high bank and low hedge; regardless of thus forming a breach for the access of strays and strangers. The horse cleared the fence, but left his riders, old and young, in the ditch, where I was nearly drowned; whilst my companion struggled and staggered for some time, and afterwards walked home, where the household were not a little alarmed at the appearance of the wet and dirty pair. Another adventure I encountered, when I was only four years old, with the same horse and horseman. On this occasion I was placed on a pillow in front of my grandfather, and safely taken to the dentist-apothecary, in the town of Malmesbury, about two miles distant, to have a tooth extracted. The operation over, my protector took me to the old and once-famed monastic hostel, now the White Lion Inn, where I was laid upon a sofa (then a rare article of furniture) near the window, and soon fell into the sleep of exhaustion after the pain I had endured. My grandfather took his "pipe, and his pot" of strong beer, and, I dare say, enjoyed both. In returning home over the common, where there was neither road nor track for carriage or horse, but where gorse or furze abounded, and the traveller was obliged to pick his way between thick masses and detached bushes of that prickly plant, my groggy grandfather, after several pendulous swings from side to side, fell from Old Toll (as the aged steed was called) into the midst of one of these furze bushes, carrying me also in his arms. A man might as well have been tossed into a bed of porcupines or hedgehogs. The situation was not a little alarming and perilous; for night was coming on, my companion was incapable of helping me, or even himself, and the place was but little frequented. Fortunately my thoughtful grandmother had sent one of the farming-men to meet and aid her husband in case of accident. Hearing my cries, the man was directed to the spot soon after our fall: he carried me home; led my grandfather; and the old horse followed.

Many other hair-breadth escapes I have had in childhood and school-boy days. When about three years old I fell from a bed-room window into the street, and was taken up as dead; but the injury proved trifling. Fortunately the bed-room windows in the houses at Kington are not more than eight or nine feet from the ground, and there are not more than two floors in any but the two "great houses." On another occasion I was rescued from the squire's fish-pond in a drowning state. I had leaped, head-foremost, from the flood-hatch into the deepest part of the water, and was entangled in weeds. I remember that I attempted to breathe, when I inhaled water instead of air, and felt that I must die. Thoughts of home, parents, and particularly of my sister, Ann, rushed on my mind, and I repeated the Lord's Prayer, which I had been taught as a lesson and protection "in all time of danger and tribulation." A gardener, who had seen my foolish experiment of learning to dive, came in time to rake me out, and save my life. Many falls from horses have I experienced, but none to be compared with a dangerous and expensive one which happened near Gloucester, at a comparatively recent time, and will be hereafter noticed.

Were I to detail all the little adventures and remarkable incidents of early life, which are indelibly fixed in my memory, the narrative might be regarded as too prolix, and would trench upon the space which will be required for a later period of life. It may, however, be remarked that my grandfather too often took me away from school, and thereby retarded the little education which my masters were capable of imparting. Besides which, I was injudiciously petted, and made a play-fellow by the uncle already named, who was fourteen or sixteen years my senior. Although a man when I was but a child, he was fond of all kinds of play and every sort of practical joke and mischievous frolic. He was as noted for sporting with the tempers and feelings of his playmates or inferiors, as with foxes and hares. One trick which he practised on a strange servant was nearly murderous. He directed him to raise a tall ladder against the gable end of the barn, where there was a small circular window, and through which he was told an owl, then roosting in the barn, would fly, and that if he caught it, he should have a jug of strong beer at supper. The hoaxer, in the mean time, had prepared a pail of water and taken it to the inside of the round opening, through which it was thrown on the owl-catcher. The issue was not productive of sport or mirth, for the poor man was precipitated from the ladder to the ground, a height of at least twenty feet, and was nearly killed by the fall.

When about ten years of age, I accompanied the same uncle to Sodbury, about nine miles distant from home, where he was paying his addresses to an amiable and respectable young woman, whom he afterwards married. On our return, I rode a fine hunting hackney; it was a bright moonlight night, and we reached home within an hour in perfect safety, though the dangers of the journey kept me in terror all the way. Instead of going by the usual roads, he made several short cuts across fields, and consequently was obliged to leap several hedges and gates, and three brooks. He would not allow me to dismount on either occasion, although I was much terrified, and cryingly begged to lead my horse. " Sit firm," was his reply, " keep your knees tight to the saddle, with your shoulders back; give the horse his head, and use the spurs when it comes to the leap." Thus instructed, I was compelled to follow my fearless leader. The last leap, near home, I, however, much wished to avoid, as there was a bridge within two or three hundred yards; but he led the way, and insisted on my following. This imperious lesson and experiment induced in me such a love for rough-riding, that I was afterwards often seen trespassing on the fields, and riding over the hedges, instead of keeping in the roads. One more anecdote I must relate to characterize my sporting uncle, and the instinctive sagacity of the timid, simple, hare. In a snowy day he took me, with his gun, and a young greyhound, to seek a hare. Finding the track of one, he followed it through two fields, where its leaps were clearly impressed on the snow, at nearly regular distances of about eight or nine feet apart. In the third field, puss had made a beaten track to an extent of forty or fifty yards, but there was no appearance of her having leaped from it. We traversed this path three or four times with the dog, and were prepared to return, when the hare started from the hollow stump of a tree, and had passed through a hedge before the sportsman could fire his gun, or the dog had seen it. We followed the track through several fields, when my uncle left me with directions to continue the pursuit, whilst he would proceed in another direction; saying, that after making a circuit, the hare would be sure to return to its form. My walk extended above a mile, with a distinct view of the footsteps of the game all the way. The gun was fired, one of the animal's legs was broken, and the dog soon seized the hare, which, however, by crying out and struggling, effected her escape several times, till another shot killed the broken-hearted creature. Though the fatigue of walking through the deep snow had nearly exhausted all my strength and spirits, my companion loaded me with the dead hare, which I carried for about half a mile, when my powers failed and I fell in the snow. I was indeed exhausted, and the sportsman, who had thus far enjoyed the whole sport, became alarmed, coaxed and raised me on his back. This species of tantalization he often indulged in; by placing me in dangerous situations, and coming forward to relieve me at a sort of crisis. He often won all my marbles and halfpence, and after retaining them some time, returned them when he saw me grieved to the last extremity.

Young greyhounds, I believe, are the most timid, shy, and cowardly of all the dog tribe. Soon after the event above described, I took the same animal to Didmarton, about four or five miles from my then home, where I was to spend a day or two with an old bachelor, who cultivated and made drawings of ranunculi, and was also expert in making fireworks, which he occasionally displayed to amuse his friends and neighbours. My visit was to see this exhibition, and also to learn the art of making squibs, crackers, Catharine-wheels, &c. The first cracker however that was "let off" frightened the young dog, who leaped the garden wall, and was out of sight in a moment. The next morning I and my friends made search for it, but without success, and I was advised to return home. On relating the loss to my uncle, he burst into a true *Hillier* passion, gave me a flogging, and sent me back, never to return without the dog. With smarting back, despair of ever finding the greyhound, and the intense fear of again seeing my passionate relation, I made my way through fields and lanes (now truly dismal) towards Didmarton; stopping, however, often to cry, to pray, and to look anxiously about for the lost animal. The horrors I experienced on this journey haunted me for many years, and even occasion a shudder at the present moment. My enraged relative was at Didmarton long before I reached that place, and I learned that he was gone to inquire at different farm-houses for the strayed favourite. I was put to bed in a state of fever; but was relieved in the morning by the exhilarating news that the dog was found.

Some of the incidents here related belong to the period when I was at my second school: at Yatton-Keynel, or Church-Eaton,* about three

---

* At this place JOHN AUBREY received the rudiments of education. In his manuscript reminiscences he says, "I entred into grammar in 1633, at the Latin schoole, at Yatton-Keynel, in the church; where the curate, Mr. Hart, taught the eldest boyes Virgil, Ovid, Cicero, &c. The fashion then was to save the forules of their bookes with a false cover of parchment, or old manuscript, which I was too young to understand; but I was pleased with the elegancy of the writing and the coloured initiall letters. I remember the rector (Mr. William Stump, great gr. son of Stump the cloathier of Malmesbury) had severall manuscripts of the abbey." What Aubrey wrote of himself in his communication to Anthony à Wood, for the *Athenæ Oxoniensis*, applies in many respects to myself. "When a boy, I was bred at Eston in eremetical solitude, and was very curious: my greatest delight to be with the artificers that came there; *e.g.* joyners, carpenters, cowpers, masons, and understood their trades; horis vacuis, I drew and painted. In 1634, was entered in my Latin gramar by Mr. R. Latimer, a delicate and little person, rector of Leigh-de-la-Mere, a mile, fine walk; who had an easie way of teaching; and every time we asked leave to go forth, we had a Latin word from him, w[ch] at our returne we were to tell him again: which in a little while amounted to a good number of words.—I was always enquiring of my grandfather of the old time, the rood-loft, the ceremonies of the Priory, &c. At eight, I was a kind of engineer; and I fell then to drawing, beginning first with plain outlines, then on to colours, being only my owne instructor. Copied pictures in the parlor in a table book. I was wont, I remember, much to lament with myselfe that I lived not in a city; *e. g.* Bristole; where I might have access to watchmakers, locksmiths, &c. Not very much care for grammar. Apprehensive enough, but my memorie not tenacious, so that then a boy, I was a promising morne enough, of an inventive and philosophicall head. My witt was alwaies working, but not to verse. Exceeding mild of spirit, mightily susceptible of fascination.

miles from my natal home, and the same distance from Maidford. Here I met with an instructor, Mr. Sparrow, very unlike the Baptist; for he could write a good hand, knew the common rules of arithmetic, and, I believe, could measure and calculate the acreage of a piece of land. He could also engrave cyphers and crests on silver spoons, and he even painted a White Horse, and a White Swan, for certain signboards. Seeing these wonderful performances, as they appeared to me, I made many attempts to imitate them, both on my slate and copy-book. Unfortunately for my master's works of art, they both suffered by the first shower of rain: the swan being washed away by its natural element, whilst the horse was converted into a sort of zebra, by the disappearance of portions of the white paint, in streaks. Here I was the only boarder; and under a really ingenious and encouraging preceptor, I made rapid progress; and, but for the unfortunate interruptions to study, through my grandfather's unwise partiality, should have acquired, in the two years I was with him, all the learning that master could teach me. I remember that I made myself familiar with "the Rule of Three" in one week.

After this I was called home, and remained in idleness and play for another year, when I was placed under a Mr. Stratton, at Draycot, to and from which place, about two miles distant, I had to walk every day during summer and winter. This gentleman was a dull, plodding, illiterate man, whilst his wife (a clergyman's daughter) was a woman of manners and attainments superior to the station in which marriage had placed her: yet they appeared truly domestic and happy. At the time I was with them, they had an only daughter, who was eight years old when I was ten. She became my playmate, together with a Master West, a son of the clergyman of Draycot;* whence I was treated more

---

Strong and early impulse to antiquities."—(*Memoir of John Aubrey*, by J. Britton, 4to., 1835, p. 13.) These rude, but graphic, sketches of the character of one of the earliest "searchers after antiquities" in England, irresistibly appeal to the feelings and affections of a brother antiquary, who was born in the same parish, and who in boyhood was often impressed with similar aspirations, but was precluded from all useful and rational instruction.

\* "Draycot Great House," as it was commonly called, was the seat of Sir James Tylney Long, Bart., who was the only titled person, as the house was the only gentleman's seat, I had known or heard of in my boy-days. I then viewed the mansion with

as a member of the family than as a common day-scholar. Within a year I was taken from this school, and again left to roam and play as inclination and opportunity prompted. The Strattons removed to Bath, where they established a school, and where the daughter displayed some qualification for writing verses. After I had served an apprenticeship in London, I visited Bath, where I renewed my acquaintance with them, became fascinated with the writings, conversation, and person of the young poetess, and, after some months' correspondence, offered to make her my wife. Prudently and candidly she declined the overture, but we continued friends and correspondents till her decease (unmarried), but a short time since. For many years she belonged to the Salisbury dramatic corps, and enacted successfully most of the heroines of tragedy and comedy. Her letters from several towns, describing the adventures of herself and her "vagabond" companions, as players are often uncharitably termed, are very curious and interesting.

I was once more sent to Mr. Sparrow, who had opened a day-school at Chippenham; and here I first became acquainted with town companions, who soon initiated me in new sports, created new ideas and excitements, and, consequently, made me even more attached to school and its concomitants than I was before. Here, too, I formed intimacies with boys who, in after life, became estimable and respectable members

---

wonder and awe, but when I last saw its exterior, the principal elevation appeared the most wretched piece of architecture I ever beheld. Sir James kept a pack of harriers, which I frequently followed, on foot, as already mentioned. He was strictly "the Country Gentleman," and lived a retired, domestic life. He became the parent of one son, who died a minor, and three daughters, the eldest of whom became a rich heiress, and was consequently sought, as a wife, by the Duke of Clarence, and many other young money-hunters, who hoped to obtain wealth by marriage, and thereby indulge in their dissipated habits: amongst these, one of the most noted roués of the age succeeded in carrying off the rich prize, with the young and innocent woman. This successful man was William Pole (Tylney Long) Wellesley, now Earl of Mornington, and nephew of the Duke of Wellington. He proved not only a bad husband, but a heartless, worthless man. After enduring a neglected and deplorable life for thirteen years, she died in Sept. 1825, and was buried in the family vault under Draycot church, where a monument has recently been raised to her lamented memory. Her daughter and two sons were legally taken away from their base father, and placed under the protection of the Lord Chancellor. The father resorted both to stratagems and legal means to abstract the children from that guardianship, but without success.

of society. Among these I may name *Robert Elliott,* who has been deaf and dumb from his cradle to the present time. Yet he learned to read and write, to understand figures, and to converse by signs made with the fingers, as well as by writing on a slate. After leaving school, he entered the service of James Hewlett, the eminent flower and fruit painter, of Bath, and not only became capable of assisting him in parts of his splendid productions, but also executed some very beautiful drawings, one of which I possess and greatly value. A large one, representing shells, feathers, and sea-weed, was exhibited at the Royal Academy, and praised by some of the critics. After being three years with Mr. Hewlett, he settled at Southampton, where he practised painting in oil, by which he gained a comfortable livelihood. Returning to Chippenham, he continued to paint for some years, and produced many pictures of horses, oxen, sheep, &c., which were mostly purchased by farmers.* Fond of the theatre when a boy, and being a clever mimic, he often imitated harlequin, clown, pantaloon, and other dramatic characters. In play, when provoked, he became violently passionate, and often terrified other boys, his superiors in age and strength. Many times have I played with " Bob Elliott," delighted with his intense energy, and traits of sagacity; repeatedly have I visited him in mature life, watching his manipulations in drawing; and twice have I seen him in old age, enjoying apparently the *otium,* if not with the *dignitate,* of life. His cranium and physiognomy were always strongly marked, and are particularly so in old age, affording admirable subjects for the study, analysis, and investigation of the man of science and the artist. My young friend, Alfred Provis, of Chippenham, an artist of much ability, has painted a striking portrait of him.

*James Hewlett* was likewise one of my school and play-mates. His exquisite drawings of fruit and flowers adorned the Royal Academy exhibition for many successive years, and not only obtained the praises

---

* During the formation of the Railway at Chippenham, Elliott was more than commonly interested and delighted in daily watching the operations. Its excavations, embankments, bridges, and station, with the marvellous steam-engine, and the endless variety of trains, passengers, and local objects, which seemed to revolutionize nature and art, engrossed all the curiosity and time of Elliott, as well as of many other persons. He explained to his associates that he understood the nature and objects of this new mode of travelling, as well as its vast improvements on the old.

of the periodical press, but the admiration of connoisseurs and patrons of art. They were generally sold at high prices, and the artist realized a handsome fortune, left Bath and settled at Isleworth, on the Thames, where he died in 1836, at the age of 67, and was buried in the churchyard of that parish. At Trentham, the splendid seat of the Duke of Sutherland, is one of his flower-pieces, painted on copper, which the late Marquis of Stafford purchased from the Academy Exhibition for the sum of four hundred guineas. It is described by one of my correspondents as rivalling the pictures of similar subjects by Baptiste, or Van Huysom. The Earl of Ellesmere mentions it particularly as " a very admirable flower-piece." The career and character of Mr. Hewlett rank him amongst the eminent and exemplary instances of genius, industry, and integrity, struggling against adversity and lowliness of station; and ultimately attaining wealth and high estimation. His father had been a gardener, and his widowed mother kept the toll-gate house on the north side of Chippenham, where I often spent an hour with James on my road home from school in that town. He was my senior by four years, and my schoolfellow for a short time under Mr. Sparrow. Very early he evinced a love of drawing and modelling, and often associated with Elliott to imitate or copy all the rude and common prints which they could obtain. After a heavy fall of snow he devoted nearly a whole day in attempting to model something like the figure of a man in that material; and, although his only tool was a table knife, so far succeeded as to cause many persons to visit and wonder at the crude performance, as well as the perseverance of the boy.* Meeting with an old treatise on heraldry, he resolutely and diligently endea-

---

* This reminds me of a snow adventure of my own. On the south side of the village of Kington is a field called Torhill; probably, as the parish formerly belonged to the abbey of Glastonbury, from some association with that place and its famous Tor (or tower) and hill, which are noted land-marks. On the sloping side of the Kington hill, after a snowy night, I made a snow-ball, which rapidly augmented in size by rolling. When fully as large as myself it was easily moved down the declivity, and at length rolled onwards, with increasing velocity, to the bottom; where it knocked down the garden wall of a cottage, and, lodging against the doorway, stopped all ingress and egress for some time. Indeed the poor inmates could not get out till the snow invader was removed by the labour of several neighbours. I was punished by being made to pay for rebuilding the wall.

voured to copy the shields of arms, crests, and supporters. Assisting his father in the gardens of Monkton, he seized every moment to pursue his favourite amusement, and progressively covered several pieces of board with imitations of landscapes, flowers, and fruit. Mr. Edridge, the owner of the place, instead of encouraging, scolded him for what he regarded as an idle waste of time, and turned him out of the garden. This mortified the boy, and annoyed his parents, who had received about two shillings weekly for his services. Hewlett was then apprenticed to a wheelwright, with whom he remained three years, and thence removed to Bath, where he was employed by a coachmaker, with whom he had opportunities of exercising and improving his knowledge of heraldic painting. Some time afterwards he gave lessons in the "art and mystery" of drawing. He next opened a shop to sell materials for amateurs and professional artists, at the same time prosecuting his studies and practising his art as a drawing-master. As he advanced in years he advanced also in fame, and in the arts of gaining and saving money. He at length retired from Bath; and, in order to be near the metropolis, and participate in its artistic associations and inspirations, he removed from Bath to Isleworth; where I visited, and found him not merely living in respectable independence as regarded the wants and comforts of life, but pertinaciously, though not ostentatiously, enjoying the best of all independence, that of moral and political freedom, in thought, word, and deed. Like most self-taught persons, his mind, language, and manners were original, and occasionally eccentric: for he could not speak or act according to the commonplace routine of his early associates; and when he obtained an acquaintance with some of the Bath gentry, he awkwardly endeavoured to mimic their language and manners.* Hewlett read much, and acquired considerable knowledge in science, and in the history and elements of art. With his intimate friends he was jocular, witty, and fluent in discourse; but generally assumed a Johnsonian style of language, which, though

---

* This affectation always betrays itself, and subjects the untutored actor to the contempt of supercilious pride, although true politeness views it with indulgence and a kindly smile. In early intercourse with my superiors in rank, I often saw in others, and painfully felt in myself, inferiority in matters of etiquette; and as often lamented the want of better education and association.

often strong and pungent, was as frequently ludicrous. One word I remember his using, when I last saw him, which in familiar conversation seemed truly affected. Instead of saying a certain object was oily or greasy, which every hearer would understand, he called it *oleaginous*.

One more of my school-mates I must notice, as a painfully remarkable specimen of hypocondriacism. *Thomas Panton*, about my own age, was a studious, plodding boy at school, devoted to his writing and ciphering, and excelling all his school-fellows in both. Sent early to London, he was employed in a merchant's counting-house in a humble capacity. Determined, however, to advance himself, he devoted every leisure hour to improve his penmanship and knowledge of accounts, and to the study of the French, Spanish, and German languages. After I had been in London some years, I accidentally met my old school-fellow in the street, and from that time continued on friendly and familiar terms with him till the termination of his life, which was a calamitous one. He, with my friend Mr. Brayley and myself, often met at each other's lodgings to read essays, poetry, &c., from different authors, with the view of improving, and criticising each other in the arts of reading, pronunciation, grammar, and intonation. This was a delightful and useful occupation. The *Critical Pronouncing Dictionary*, by Walker, was then new and little known, but soon became a successful rival to that by Thomas Sheridan, the father of Richard Brinsley Sheridan. In our juvenile studies we compared the two, and easily found that Walker's was much superior to the other in all its attributes. Panton manifested acuteness and discrimination, and had he lived and continued his studies, would have become an accomplished writer. Naturally of a gloomy and reserved temperature, he shunned society, confined himself to his office duties and solitary studies, and became diseased and melancholy. I advised him to visit his mother, whom he supported, at Chippenham, to try change of air, scene, and society; which, after much urging, he at length adopted. But the country had no charms for his deranged fancy; and he became worse. In a state of delirium he leaped into the river Avon to end his existence; but was extricated from a watery grave by a man who had watched him. Being placed under medical treatment, his health and spirits rallied, and he returned to London; and related to me his feelings, failings, and sufferings. My sympathy, raillery, and advice cheered him, and he continued for about a year to pursue his daily duties and evening studies. Denying himself, however, reasonable exercise, his old disease returned. He visited me often, and reiterated his gloomy thoughts and waking dreams of bodily and mental decay, and his conviction that he was a helpless, worthless wretch, an outcast from God and man, and doomed to a lingering and miserable death. I ridiculed, remonstrated, and at length became angered, at his pertinacious indulgence in misery. He again went to Chippenham, from which place I received a long doleful letter, describing a series of symptons, real and imaginary, evincing the most confirmed case of hypocondriacism I ever knew or heard of.

Without dwelling further on this melancholy case, suffice it to say, that he once more tried to drown himself; was again resuscitated, and returned to London; and shortly afterwards terminated his misery and life by cutting his throat, at his lodgings in Pentonville.

George Colman, Jun., in his *Auto-Biography*, or "Random Records," says, "I wish I could skip school altogether; but it is too material a thread in a man's Auto-Biographic web to be omitted altogether." From what I have stated, it is evident that my school-thread was often broken; and consequently was never well spun, nor made of good material. It led, however, to a succession of experiences, to new scenes, associations and reflections, eminently calculated to relieve and vary the apathetic monotony of village life.

Reviewing the circumstances here related, I cannot, without deep regret and mortification, reflect on the system, or rather want of systematic education pursued by the different schoolmasters with whom it was my lot to be placed. Instead of teaching "the young idea how to shoot;" instead of exciting emulation, and conveying, through the medium of words, useful and practical information; instead of inculcating, even in one solitary instance, the important precept, that scholastic education is intended to qualify the pupil for his future destination in life, and render him either really serviceable or absolutely useless, in proportion to his own subsequent industry and acquirements, they pursued a mechanical and routine process, employing the head and hands in writing words and making figures, but little calculated to rouse the mental energies. School, however, was always delightful to me, and its succession of tasks and duties was easily and rapidly performed. The smell of new paper, a new copy-book, and any other novelties, were always exhilarating. I do not remember to have seen a dictionary before I visited London, in my seventeenth year. Geography, history, and books of instructive amusement, were unknown in that part of the country; nor did I ever hear of such periodicals as newspapers or magazines before I was fourteen.

One event, of rather a literary nature, is however fresh in memory. About this period a sale of the household goods and effects of " 'Squire White," who occupied the "Great House," occurred. He had wasted his property in London gaiety and gambling, and was the only person, I cannot say gentleman, of landed estate in the village; and at the sale of his effects I was tempted to purchase a lot of books, nine in number, for one shilling. Among them were "Robinson Crusoe," the "Pilgrim's Progress," and the "Life of Peter, Czar of Muscovy:" all of which volumes I read with avidity, though often perplexed to understand much of their contents. The first made me long to be on a desolate island, and meet with a " man Friday," whilst the second excited a desire even to encounter some of the adventures of "Christian." That this work was an allegory, and the first fictitious, never came into my mind.

After quitting Chippenham school, at the age of thirteen, I was required by my mother to assist her in making bread, and attending to our little farm. I was now compelled to rise on baking mornings at four o'clock, and materially contribute towards converting a bag of flour into good and unadulterated bread; some of which I afterwards carried, on horseback, to villages and farm-houses.

I believe nearly the whole of my time, from my thirteenth to my sixteenth year (that is, from 1784 till 1787), was spent in my native village; either in idle play, or in thus assisting my parents in their daily labours. My clearest recollections of Kington, and of our own rustic dwelling, refer therefore to this period. The houses of the village were placed mostly on the sides of a wide street, which extends nearly a mile in length. To the east there were, however, not more than sixteen in the whole extent, most of which were insulated, and at considerable distances from their " next-door neighbours." On the west side there was a row, either attached, or with short spaces between them. Among these were a slaughter-house, a tailor's and two other shops, a public-house, a malt-house, and a group of twelve dwellings called *Alderman Lyte's Alms-houses.** A carpenter's, two blacksmiths', six farm-houses, the Squire's and the Parsonage, with some other tenements, made up the remainder of the village. A curate, with a small stipend, officiated weekly at the church; and after the deaths of Lady Forester and "Madame White," who had occupied the "Great House" in my infancy, it was shut up and deserted. The cottages and shops were of the humblest and poorest kind. With walls of rough undressed stone and mortar, thatched roofs, stone slabs from the quarries, or the bare earth for the floor, windows of varied forms and sizes, many of them papered or boarded, or with broken glass, it may be concluded that they were not calculated to form comfortable homes for labouring men on their return from a hard day's work. The house in which I was born, and which is delineated in the accompanying wood-cut, presented rather a better aspect than most of its neighbours; as the whole of the walls were "rough-cast;" having a coarse pebbly surface, which

---

* Isaac Lyte was Aubrey's grandfather. He was an alderman of London, and died in 1659, aged 83.—(See *Memoir of Aubrey*, 4to., 1845.)

was white-washed. The roof was covered with successive layers of thatch, and the external and internal finishing was rude and simple. One room "served for kitchen and parlour and hall." It was about

fourteen feet square, by six feet and a half high; with a large beam beneath the ceiling, attached to which was a bacon-rack, which served to hold two flitches, with a gun, sticks, whips, and other articles. The floor consisted of irregular slabs of stone, not more than an inch in thickness. The accompanying wood-cut will convey an idea of this apartment, with some of its inmates and furniture. The shop was about the same size as this room, and communicated with it. The premises are now occupied by two families; whilst a detached building, formerly the bake-house, is devoted to a third.

A retrospective review of my provincial life and times presents numerous other recollections which might be detailed with effect, and serve materially to characterize the boy-part of my career. Amongst these was the belief in, and continued dread of, ghosts, fairies, and spirits: of the fascinating powers of the Jack-o'-lantern, whose ignited vapour was at times seen after dark; and the misery I often endured in passing through or near the churchyard, and "the haunted house:" my eager desire to visit Chippenham and Malmesbury fairs and races:

a journey to Bath, at the age of eight, on a pony, with my sister Elizabeth on another, and two farmers' daughters on hackneys—a journey of about fourteen miles by cross roads, to escape turnpike gates (a frequent practice with farmers)—and the amazement and intense curiosity I felt on that occasion, in traversing the streets of that unique city, witnessing its gay shops, the market, the circus, and the Abbey church. I particularly remember the pastry-cooks' shops, into one of which we entered, and tasted some delicious tarts, the flavour of which seems to have dwelt on my palate to the present time; for I have ever regarded a raspberry tart as the most tempting article at the richly furnished table. The shop I allude to was built against the north wall of the Abbey church, between two buttresses, attached to one of which was the oven chimney. This house, and several other shops which abutted on the church, have very properly been removed, whereby the sacred edifice is completely insulated. A lamb was given to me when about the same age. This, at its third year, produced twin lambs; in the following year, two more; and another the next season. The whole flock, however, was sold to pay some pressing creditor; as were the ducks and fowls which I had also reared. I often accompanied my father to Chippenham market, which he attended almost weekly, and rarely returned quite sober; for he had the same unhappy failing as my grandfather. My place was to ride behind him on Jenny, a favourite hackney, and old servant. On returning home, we always halted at "The Little George," a house famed for its strong and fine beer; a pint of which was always ordered, though a superfluous quantity had been taken after the "Ordinary" dinner. Glass after glass was handed to me, which I threw to the ground, hoping thereby to save my own head and that of my parent. The old mare took us safely home; but at the door, the ceremony of dismounting, and walking, were often attended with falls. On one occasion a pig entered the kitchen in the dark, and proceeded to the fire, into which it poked its snout, squeaked most violently, but still neglected to leave the fire-place. My mother and the children, then six in number, cried loudly for assistance, for they thought the animal mad, and tried to beat it out by brush, poker, and sticks; whilst the master of the house was outside, helpless. Some neighbours came to our rescue, and by main force expelled the pig.

It was my duty to take old Jenny to a field, about a quarter of a mile from the house; but such was the fear I entertained of ghosts and Jack-o'-lanterns, that I often turned her loose in the road, whilst in sight of the houses. She sometimes leaped the hedge into the field, and sometimes was found wandering in its vicinity.

Many other anecdotes belonging to this period might be detailed; but I must forbear to narrate any occurrences that do not seem to have led to my present condition and circumstances.*

At a very early period I was induced to compare and contrast the "innocent rusticity" of the villagers,† with a certain degree of refinement in

---

* In closing these reminiscences of boyhood, and taking leave of my native village, I cannot refrain from borrowing the eloquent language of a friend already quoted, which most vividly depicts my own feelings and sentiments. "What a strange, what an anomalous thing is memory! Recent occurrences fade from an old man's remembrance, as if they had been written on sand, to be presently washed out by the tide of time: early impressions, like inscriptions cut in a rock, seem as they grow older to become more indelible. How fortunate that our youthful reminiscences, which are ever the pleasantest, should be the most enduring; while the records of that period when the contraction of time and the diminution of hope throw a browner shade upon the sunset of life, should be too superficial to wound, too evanescent to sully the mental tablet. *Fortunate*, did I say? Away with the word! Not to Thee, O blind Goddess of the blind, be the praise; but to the Great Mother, all whose arrangements have a beneficent reference to the happiness of her children."—("A Greybeard's Gossip," in *New Monthly Magazine*, by Horatio Smith.)

† Many poets and essayists have eulogized rustic life and manners, as being replete with sylvan joys, arcadian scenes, primeval innocence, and unsophisticated pleasures. Alas! these are but the closet dreams of metropolitan poets and visionary enthusiasts; for I fear that all their pleasing pictures are wholly drawn from imagination, and not from nature. The genuine rustics, I believe, in all counties, and I apprehend in all nations, have very little more sagacity than the animals with whom they associate, and of whose natures they partake: for instance, the ploughman is as dull, slow, and thoughtless as the horses he drives; but, having power over the brutes, he exerts it upon every occasion as caprice or passion sways him. The cow-herd, or dairy-man, is very similar to the other. In the shepherd we perceive a little more of humanity and inoffensiveness of character, probably derived from the natural mildness of the animals with which he is in constant society. But even the shepherd too commonly acts the tyrant and the savage, by exercising wanton and needless cruelty over his unconscious flock. Every deviation in the sheep from the direct road, or line of demarcation, is punished by the worrying of the merciless cur, who seems ever watchful and eager to obey his master's cruel orders. I have witnessed hundreds of instances where animals have been brutally beaten for faults which were wholly attributable to the neglect or stupidity of their masters.

the manners of my uncle, Samuel Hillier, and his family from London, who annually visited our part of the country. This uncle, as already mentioned, had obtained a respectable situation in the Chancery Office, had lived and moved in rather a genteel sphere of life, and was enabled to spend nearly three months—the long law vacation—in the country. I was fortunately invited to make one of his party, during his periodical sojourn in Wiltshire and Gloucestershire, and well remember to have spent four or five autumns in this way, with much enjoyment at the time, and material advantage for the future. It was this association that led me to think of, and hope to see, London; it was then I first imbibed the feeling of ambition—became enamoured of what appeared "genteel dress," educated manners, with London discourse and habits, contrasted with the clownish deportment, the uneducated and uncouth language, and the broad, prolonged pronunciation of my village companions. Kington now lost all its charms: I anxiously anticipated the annual visits of my London relatives, by whom I was received as an associate till I had reached the age of sixteen, when I was destined to visit them in a very different capacity from that I had occupied on any former occasion:—I was now to be treated and employed as a servant. This I did not consider as a hardship, or even a mortification; for it presented variety, novelty, and a source of improvement.

It was also one step on the road to London—that mysterious object of a villager's contemplation. My uncle was then residing at the old Manor-house of Weston-Birt, the seat of Master Holford, where my discipline and labours became severe and heavy, considering my age, strength, and previous habits and associations. The relation I was now

---

Yet thousands of persons reprobated Mr. Martin, M.P., for obtaining an Act to check and punish cruelty to animals. In spite of obstinacy, of vulgar intolerance, and the besotted prejudices of illiberal minds, the good and glorious work of education has made rapid advances in this intellectual and affluent country; and aided, as it is, by men of enlightened minds and ardent spirits, we may fairly anticipate that all classes of Englishmen must become wiser and better as their minds become more cultivated and expanded. The infatuated intolerance of too many of the established clergy is the greatest difficulty which the true friends of useful education have hitherto contended against, and have to encounter. Were they more sincerely intent on practising Christian charity and Christian principles, than on personal aggrandizement and power, they would be more respected and beloved by their fellow-men.

to serve was strict, harsh, and passionate.* Though prompt and active myself, it was my fate to suffer many hardships under his discipline.

After passing three months at Weston, I took leave of my parents and family on the 25th of October, 1787, to accompany my uncle to London; receiving on my departure two small tokens of remembrance from my mother,—a crown piece, and a pair of silver knee-buckles. That parting is fresh in memory, as well as the arrangements which I had made for a speedy return: my stock of marbles, and other boyish property, were carefully deposited in certain secret places; and the departure from my native village, soon after sunrise, seems as though it were an event of yesterday. So tenacious is memory of circumstances which, at certain times in life, engross all the thoughts and feelings. My parents were left, home was forsaken, and the mind was anxiously, but doubtingly, contemplating the future. The journey from Tetbury to London on a coach which travelled little more than five miles in an hour, and which reached the metropolis late at night, was fatiguing to the body; but the mind was fully occupied and amused all the way, and more peculiarly so, when passing through Hammersmith, Kensington, Knightsbridge, and Piccadilly; the last illumined by apparently endless rows of twinkling lamps. The most forcible impressions were that I should never reach Clerkenwell Close, the home of my uncle;† that London

---

* Ungovernable passion, bordering on insanity, was the characteristic affliction of nearly all the family of the Hilliers. In my boyhood, I often saw battles between my grandfather and grandmother, these with their children, and the latter with one another. Throwing missile and dangerous weapons, swearing in the most vehement and vulgar manner, and hurling hatchets, pitchforks, stones, &c., at horses, cows, calves, and other helpless animals, were incidents of almost every-day occurrence. Strange to say that, though murder seemed almost inevitable from many of these desperate freaks of passion, I do not know that it ever ensued. Such ebullitions of frenzy were fortunately of short duration, and they were always followed by equally poignant sorrow and humiliation. I was constitutionally a Hillier: in boyish days I was often a slave to such passionate excitements, and I remember to have made myself frequently ridiculous, and even contemptible, by giving way to passion. Feeling seriously the consequences of such intemperance,—by reading Watts's "Logic," his "Improvement of the Mind," "An Essay on the Conduct of the Passions and Affections," and some other books of that class, during my apprenticeship, and by reflecting much in solitude,—I successfully checked, and almost subdued, this degrading bias of my natural disposition.

† The *parish of Clerkenwell* was very different when I first visited it in 1787 to what it is at the time of writing this paragraph in 1850. The church, which now stands at

was endless; and that to live in underground-kitchens, into one of which apartments I was shown, was unnatural and inhuman.

My uncle soon apprenticed me for six years, to Mr. Mendham of the Jerusalem Tavern, Clerkenwell Green; without either consulting my inclination, or, apparently, caring about the result.* As this is a marked epoch in my life, I must devote a new chapter to its annals.

---

the junction of the Close and the Green, was not then erected; but in its place was the church of the old Monastic Priory, with parts of the Cloisters, &c. Spa-Fields, from the south end of Rosoman Street to Pentonville, and from St. John-Street Road to the Bagnigge-Wells Road were really fields, devoted to the pasturage of cows, and to a forest of elm trees; not standing and adorned with foliage in the summer, but lying on the ground to the southward of the New River Head; being destined to convey water in their hollow trunks to the northern and western parts of London, in combination with similar pipes laid under the roadways of the streets. Old Clerkenwell Prison, now replaced by "the New Prison," was comparatively a small building; and the large edifice called the "Middlesex House of Correction," in Cold-Bath Fields, was not commenced. Within Clerkenwell Close were three or four old and spacious mansions, with gardens, formerly occupied by wealthy personages. That called Newcastle-House, once belonging to the Dukes of Newcastle, was a large brick building, used as the dwelling and workshops of a cabinet-maker and upholsterer. Opposite was another spacious mansion, popularly called Cromwell-House, without any proof of its ever having been occupied by the fanatical Protector; though most likely the town-house of Sir Thomas Chaloner, one of his intimate friends. There was a Priory of Benedictine Nuns at Clerkenwell. The Priory of the Knights of St. John of Jerusalem was in St. John's Square, in the immediate vicinity. The Earls of Aylesbury, Albemarle, and Compton had mansions within the parish; Nell Gwynne resided at Bagnigge-Wells; Baron Swedenborg lived in Cold-Bath Street; Brothers, the poor deranged "Prophet," was confined in a mad-house in St. John-Street Road; a house which belonged to the Northampton family. Sadler's Wells; the Islington Spa; Merlin's Cave, and Bagnigge-Wells Tea-Gardens and Ball-room, were all places of crowded resort in my apprentice days. On Clerkenwell Green, I witnessed a man pilloried and pelted; and in Red Lion Street, another flogged at a cart's tail: both ceremonies of the most horrifying kind.

I must not omit to mention one inhabitant of this parish, whose name and fame render him interesting to me;—Thomas Britton, the musical small-coal man, who was visited by the chief nobility of London, to hear his concerts in Aylesbury Street. A good account of this extraordinary man is given in a well-written *history* of this parish, from the pen of Thomas Cromwell, published in 1828. Some idea of the increase of Clerkenwell, between the years 1801 and 1841, may be formed from the official Population Returns. In the former year there were 3427 houses in the parish, and in the latter, 7242.

* Mr. Earlom, the eminent mezzotint engraver, who lived in Rosoman Row, would have taken me with a small premium; but this opportunity was neglected.

# CHAPTER III.

"CANCEL AND TEAR TO PIECES THAT GREAT BOND
WHICH KEEPS ME PALE."
*Macbeth*, Act III. Sc. 2.

APPRENTICESHIP: ITS MONOTONOUS ROUTINE—FORMALITY OF INDENTURES—MODE OF BUSINESS DESCRIBED—EXCISE LAWS—VISITS OF MR. SATCHWELL, THE EXCISE OFFICER—HIS SON, AN ABLE ARTIST—MASTER'S NEGLECT OF INSTRUCTION—INEFFECTUAL APPEAL FOR EMANCIPATION—GLOOM AND DISCONTENT—MENTAL AND BODILY ILLNESS—FINAL RELEASE—OCCASIONAL MORNING WALKS—MEDICAL AND LITERARY STUDIES—ACQUAINTANCES: MR. ESSEX, MR. BRAYLEY, DR. TRUSLER, DR. TOWERS.

THE long, dreary, cheerless period of apprenticeship, which it was my fate to endure for nearly six years, embraced a series of privations and mortifications of a most serious and depressing nature. A few gleams of cheerful sunshine, however, broke occasionally upon my murky gloom, from the books which I sometimes obtained and read with avidity. During the last year of my legal imprisonment, I "fell in love," as it is commonly termed, with a female who attended my young mistress: an eventful incident, which will be further alluded to.

During the whole term of my apprenticeship, my physical powers were in continuous demand for business; whilst those of the mind were never called into exercise. A monotonous routine of labour was the order and practice of every succeeding day; and after a few weeks there was nothing to learn,—nothing to excite or reward curiosity. An automaton might be made to perform the work it was my duty to execute. Yet the commonplace phraseology of the legal indentures, provided that the master should instruct his apprentice in the "whole art and mystery of a wine merchant."\*

---

\* The nonsensical verbiage of these formal documents is repugnant to common sense; yet the plodding, hackneyed lawyer continues to use it in preference to clear, explicit, and expressive language. When I took articled students at a later period of my life, I was advised by my solicitor to use the old form of indenture; but I adopted one better calculated to express and explain the mutual dependance and obligations of master and pupil.

My uncle Samuel, who placed me with Mr. Mendham, was a friend and crony of the latter, and I have no doubt thought he was rendering me permanent benefit. He fancied there were many useful things to be learned in a wine cellar; and that, when out of it, I might not only be qualified to obtain good wages, but secure the friendship and assistance of my aged master. Not having paid any apprentice fee, I was never instructed in any of the "arts or mysteries" of the business, beyond forcing, or fining wines; bottling, corking, and binning the same. It was no part of the practice of Mr. Mendham's house to mix, reduce, or manufacture wines; therefore I was never initiated in the "tricks of trade," which are so common with many modern, and even with some old merchants.* Part of the legal business of the wine-cellars was the process of reducing full-proof brandies, rums, and hollands, by certain quantities of water (called "liquor" in the trade) to the strength allowed by the excise laws. The standard of strength was a capricious thing, and gave dealers in spirits many opportunities of defrauding the government, in spite of the vigilance of the officers, whose duty it was to take a strict account of the tradesman's stock every fortnight.† The periodical visits of the exciseman who attended our house were anticipated by me with delight, as his company and conversation gave variety to my dismal life, and afforded some amusement. His duty was to keep a tabular entry of wines and spirits in the vaults and house, both in cask and bottle. This occupied between two and three hours, and it was my task to attend this officer, and to give an account of full casks, the contents of those in ullage, and the particulars

---

* This word is too often basely prostituted by poor schemers, and by rogues who have no knowledge of the business they profess to follow, and who are as destitute of character as of capital. Persons of this description take an office, and inscribe their names upon it, with the imposing additions of "Wine and Brandy Merchants," or "Coal Merchants,"—these being two of the most common trades assumed by moneyless impostors.

† The excise officer, and the whole machinery of the excise laws, were moral and political evils, which disgraced and degraded the country. Whilst they created a most expensive and complicated retinue of offices and officers, they harassed and oppressed the honest tradesman; and the consumer was taxed oppressively, not only to produce a large government revenue, but to pay an innumerable gang of officers, with salaries varying from £2,000 a year to 18s. a week.

of bottles in bins, or otherwise. At the end of his labours he had always a good lunch and wine. Mr. Satchwell, the officer during my apprenticeship, was a mild, kindly-disposed man, and, therefore, never very rigid in searching holes, corners, or other parts of the premises, beyond the cellars. I visited his house, and formed an intimacy with his son, Robert William, who was about my own age. He was then a student at the Royal Academy, and in a few years became eminent as a miniature painter, as well as in making designs for the embellishment of books. In watching the practice of this truly amiable and estimable man, by his company and conversation, and from the theoretical and practical lessons which he gave me, I not only felt much gratification for the time, but derived many advantages which have lasted to the present moment. He died at an early age, at Earl Spencer's seat, at Althorpe, where he was employed to reduce and copy some of the valuable portraits in that important treasury of art and literature.

I have always regarded the apprenticeship of poor boys as a legal slavery—consigning them to continual labour, scanty food, and comfortless work-rooms and beds; all tending to degrade the intellect and vulgarize the mind. The period of human life from the age of fourteen to that of twenty-one—the usual term of apprenticeship—may be regarded as more important than any other equal space in the career of man. The mind is then eagerly curious, and capable of receiving and retaining impressions both of good and evil; whence it is of vital consequence that those of sound and useful tendency should alone be planted.

> " 'Tis education forms the youthful mind:
> Just as the twig is bent, the tree's inclined."

During my six years' training—or rather, neglect of tuition—I was never instructed in any one essential branch of the business, either in its accounts, or in the history, growth, manufacture, and qualities of wines. I was ignorant where Portugal, Lisbon, Madeira, Xeres, the Rhine, or Cognac were; and knew nothing of those places where the wine and brandy grapes are respectively grown. In like manner I was uninformed of the general nature of the trade, and the position and duties of the real *merchant*, or direct importer of wines and spirits, as the agent between the maker and the retail seller of those luxuries. I was never taken to a bonded cellar, to a merchant's stock vaults, nor to a merchant-ship; nor indeed shown or told any thing of the business beyond what I have already mentioned. It cannot be surprising that nearly six years thus employed must have proved irksome, disheartening, and doleful, to a young, active, and inquiring disposition; nor is it to be marvelled at, that bodily disease should have been the result. I certainly cannot think there was any thing reprehensible in wishing—nay, panting—for change, for emancipation from such vassalage. Yet I was fearful of complaining either to my uncle or master; knowing that the first would be likely to punish me in a burst of passion, and fearing that the other would disregard my helpless appeal. At length, however, I concocted a letter to Mr. Mendham, and after many revisals and corrections, put it into his hands. It was, however, ineffectual, and I became gloomy and disconsolate. Dodd's "Thoughts in Prison," Drelincourt " On Death," Hervey's " Meditations among the Tombs," and Young's " Night Thoughts," were books which I resorted to as being in harmony with my feelings; but they tended rather to increase than abate the morbid state of mind and body which oppressed me. I had recourse to medicine; but not having money to pay for advice or physic, I was sent to the public dispensary in St. John's Square, where I attended for many successive months, and was supplied with gallons of mixtures, and scores of pills and powders, mostly of a tonic and restorative nature. Instead of regaining health and strength, both were gradually declining, and I felt like a deserted being, bereft of hope. Believing there was not the least prospect of my restoration, my master at length gave up about half a year of my service, presented me with two guineas, instead of twenty which he had engaged to do, and sent me into the world to shift for myself.

It will be necessary to revert to several events which have been passed over in this hasty sketch; and particularly to remark, that during this confinement in a London cavern, I stole an occasional half-hour in a morning, between seven and eight o'clock, to look at the sky, breathe a little fresh air, and visit two book-stalls in the vicinity of my prison-house. The rational food and medicine obtained from these sources, not only supported life, but furnished that information which enabled me to ascertain the seat of those diseases which had long preyed on my frame, and threatened its dissolution. After purchasing and reading

Cheseldon's "Anatomy," Quincy's "Dispensatory," some "Treatises on Consumption," Buchan's "Domestic Medicine,"* Tissot's "Essay on Diseases incident to Sedentary People," Cornaro "On Health and Long Life," and several other medical and anatomical works, I was flattered with the persuasion that I knew my own constitution, with its diseases, also the regimen and medicines necessary to restore and preserve health. Dr. Dodd's "Reflections on Death," his "Thoughts in Prison," and all his other writings were familiar to me at that time; as were Ray's "Wisdom of God manifested in the Works of the Creation," Derham's "Astro-Theology," and "Physico-Theology," as well as *Benjamin Martin's* numerous and pleasing writings on Natural and Experimental Philosophy.† The miscellaneous works of Smollett, Fielding, and Sterne, were likewise perused with great avidity; but all the reading I could indulge in, during my term of legal English slavery, was by candle-light, in the cellar, and at occasional intervals only, not of leisure, but of time abstracted from systematic duties. To compensate for this time, I was compelled to labour with additional exertion, and to adopt the most rapid modes of performing my tasks. To bottle off, and cork, a certain number of dozens of wine, was required to con-

---

* This publication was then new, but had speedily obtained great popularity, by the plain and familiar style and language in which it was written, and the absence of the mongrel jargon, called Doctors' Latin, of former writers. No less than nineteen editions of the book, amounting to 80,000 copies, were sold during the author's life, whence he obtained both fame and fortune. He lived many years in Percy Street, and saw patients daily at the Chapter Coffee-house, Paternoster Row. He was born in Roxburghshire in 1729, died in London 1805, and was buried in the cloister of Westminster Abbey Church.

† Though Martin's publications are almost unknown to modern readers, they were exceedingly popular at the time referred to. Written in a fluent, familiar style, interspersed with apposite scraps of poetry, and quotations from the best authors, and illustrated by numerous diagrams, they were both amusing and instructive to the youthful student. Among the principal were, "The Philosophical Grammar," "The Young Gentleman's and Lady's Philosophy," "Biographia Philosophica," and the "Philosophical Magazine," the last extending to 14 volumes, 8vo. Martin was remarkable for the pursuit and acquirement of knowledge under difficulties. In early life he was a day labourer, became a schoolmaster at Chichester, travelled over the country as a lecturer on Experimental Philosophy, settled in Fleet Street, London, as an optician, and thence issued his numerous publications. An improvident and wicked son involved him in pecuniary bankruptcy, which affected his mind, and he attempted to cut his throat. He was born at Worplesdon, Surrey, in 1704; and died in London, in 1782.

stitute a day's work, and this I could generally accomplish in ten or eleven hours, and I then had three or four more for my favourite pur-

F. W. Fairholt, del.  
WINE CELLAR, JERUSALEM TAVERN, CLERKENWELL.  
J. Walmsley, sc.

suit of reading. Unacquainted with any literary or scientific persons before I had reached my twentieth year, my studies, or rather bookish amusements, were very desultory and miscellaneous. I regret to say they were not directed to any particular object, and were consequently unavailable to any useful end.

Towards the termination of my apprenticeship, I fortunately became acquainted, in my morning walks, with a person who was wholly employed, and obtained a very respectable livelihood by painting the figures on watch-faces. He was fond of books, had purchased many volumes, and as his business did not require any exertion of thought, he could listen to the reading of other persons, or enter into conversation, without discontinuing his usual occupation. This person was my first and principal, or indeed, my only mentor and guide. He lent and bought me books, and gave me varied useful and judicious advice. His name was Essex, and I respect his memory; for he was an industrious, intelligent, and well-informed man. He always seemed to me to be a sound philosopher, inasmuch as he practised the precepts he inculcated, and afforded a most exemplary pattern to a large family, whom he reared and educated respectably. His eldest son, William, is now the first, or amongst the most eminent, of English painters in enamel, and has executed many pictures for her present Majesty.

At Mr. Essex's shop, I became acquainted with two gentlemen who had attained considerable distinction in the literary profession; and with one who has since been a hard and successful labourer in the literary vineyard. These were the Rev. Dr. Trusler, the Rev. Dr. Towers, and Mr. Brayley. To the last gentleman I am more indebted for literary acquirements and literary practice than to any other person. He was apprenticed to a mechanical trade, as an enameller; but was neither so much nor so irksomely occupied as myself. He read much, and early evinced literary talents, both in prose and verse. It is a curious fact that we entered into "partnership" to publish a single ballad, or song, which was written by Mr. Brayley, and intituled "The Guinea Pig." Its subject was the Powder-tax, by which one guinea *per head* was levied on every person who used hair-powder. Though a ridiculous thing as poetry, and so characterized by the author, it was printed on a "fine wire-wove paper,"—a novelty in that class of literature,—and charged "one penny." Many thousand copies were sold; for, notwithstanding the "poem" was "entered at Stationers' Hall," Mr. Evans, a noted printer of ballads in Long Lane, *pirated the property*, and his itinerant retailers of poetry and music hawked and sung it all over the metropolis. Whilst the sale was yet rife, Evans declared that he had sold upwards of 70,000 copies. A choice paper impression of this ballad, which has a wood-cut, from one of Bewick's pigs, at the top, may possibly be sought for as an "extra rare" curiosity, by some confirmed bibliomaniac, at no remote time. Strange as it may seem, it can be safely affirmed, that to this partnership are to be attributed the "Beauties of Wiltshire," the "Beauties of England and Wales," the "Architectural Antiquities," the "Cathedral Antiquities," Mr. Brayley's "History of Westminster Abbey," as well as many other publications which are enumerated and described in the second part of the present volume. Of this old friend I shall have occasion to say something more hereafter; but of the other two gentlemen it cannot be regarded as irrelevant to put on record a few notices in this place.

*The Rev. John Trusler*, LL.D., and the Rev. Joseph Towers, LL.D., were the earliest literary persons I saw, and I was not a little elated to think, and to be able to say, I knew them. In their company, however, I felt as a pigmy by the side of giants—a tyro of the humblest grade, compared with masters in the literary profession. Trusler lived in Red Lion Street, Clerkenwell, a few doors from my vaulted home. He had studied and practised physic for some time; then took Orders, and occasionally officiated as a curate; but I believe never obtained preferment in the church. In 1771, he produced sermons in type imitative of manuscript.* He wrote and published a large work called "The Habitable World Displayed;" another entitled "Hogarth Moralized;" and a number of other literary works, which Dr. Watkins pronounces "too numerous and contemptible to deserve further notice." Yet, with all deference to that captious and voluminous compiler, I always considered those of Trusler's works which I had read, to be much superior in merit to his own. Dr. Trusler was born in London in 1735, and died at Bath-Easton in 1820.

*The Rev. Joseph Towers*, LL.D., like the former gentleman, was a voluminous writer and compiler of books on history, divinity, politics, biography, &c., some of which are certainly works of merit; particularly his "British Biography" (7 vols. 8vo., 1765); and "Memoirs of Frederick III., King of Prussia," (2 vols. 8vo., 1788.) His "Tracts on Political and other subjects" were collected and published in 3 vols. 8vo., 1796. At one time he kept a bookseller's shop in Fore Street, London, and afterwards joined the Unitarians, and preached at Highgate. He was born in Southwark in 1737, and died in 1799. Intimate with Dr. Kippis, he wrote many articles for the "Biographia Britannica." Unfortunately, I was too young and too illiterate to participate much in

---

* Amongst anecdotes of Trusler, in the *Gentleman's Magazine*, for August, 1820, will be found an amusing statement with reference to these Sermons. It appears they were intended to encourage the indolence of country parsons, by supplying them with ready-made discourses, abridged and altered from the *best*, but *least known* works of eminent divines, in a shape less open to detection, than the use of a volume of ordinary type would be. It is added, that the Bishop of London remonstrated with Trusler on the encouragement afforded to clerical idleness, by his highly successful speculation; to which the doctor replied, "that he gained £150 a year by his publication; but if his lordship would give him a living of that value, his *script types* should no longer be put in requisition."

the conversation, or to profit materially by occasional intercourse with these practical authors; but I ever looked up to them with respect and admiration, and refer to their memory and writings with pleasure.

My chief companions during apprenticeship were a cook, a fellow-apprentice, a porter, and a bar-woman; all subject to fluctuation, and all changed several times during my stay in the house. Though I gained but little useful knowledge, or pleasing companionship, from such unpolished associates, I acquired some insight into the dispositions and varied peculiarities of at least forty different persons, all presenting varieties of personal temperament, as much as of figure, face, and manners. In some of them the passions of envy and jealousy were predominant, and created sad and serious discord in the household; others were mean and artful; and one was a confirmed dram-drinker, addicted to the lowest slang and most indecent language, with glimpses of the "new light." She seemed, in truth, a living "Mother Cole," as delineated by Foote in the "Minor;" whilst a young woman, who was called her niece, and who occasionally visited her in flaunting dress, appeared to be one of her "chickens." The blandishments of the latter towards myself strongly reminded me of Millwood, in "George Barnwell," and but for the influence of that play on my young mind,* it is not unlikely that I might have been tempted to visit her, as often invited. Fortunately, I escaped the snare. Another cook was fond of spouting, and often made her appearance on the kitchen dresser, where, with a carving-knife for a dagger, she ranted and mouthed to the amusement of "the groundlings" below; though wofully at the expense of English orthoepy, and with sad mutilation of the author's language. More than one of these females would report the "sayings and doings" in the kitchen to Mrs. Mendham, whereby crimination and recrimination ensued, and a constant succession of suspicion, watching, and listening, was practised. The lady of the mansion, who was constitutionally jealous, and often quarrelled with her partner for being "too civil by half" to young ladies, encouraged the gossip of her servants. So strongly

---

* As it has been for many years the custom to stigmatize Lillo's Tragedy as a production of maudlin sentiment, and utterly to deny its moral influence, I have much pleasure in recording its effect in my own case; at a time when the actor had not been superseded by the lecturer, as a great public teacher.

tinctured with envy was one of these females, that she seemed to be in a state of perpetual fever. Her thin, emaciated figure, insidious looks, and ever-wrinkled brow, bespoke and indicated rancour at heart, and forcibly illustrated the sentiment of Young:

> "Base Envy withers at another's joy,
> And hates that excellence it cannot reach."

One of my fellow apprentices was a dull and plodding Welsh boy, but possessed of much good nature, and of placid temper. He became a sot, and before he left would drink two or three gallons of port wine in a week. Early one Sunday morning we escaped together from our prison-house, by a warehouse window, and went to bathe in the New River, near Newington. As we were swimming side by side, his head sunk beneath the water, and I fancied he was diving. Remaining, however, some time below the surface, I found the face to be black, and the body apparently lifeless. He was lifted to the bank, and placed on sloping ground. By friction and other means the suspended animation was restored, and we contrived to reach home before the family was up. Repeated epileptic fits were the consequence of this accident, and of the intoxicated habits he had acquired.

During the last two years of my stay at the wine-vaults a change took place in the household, the results of which were of some importance to me. The junior Mr. Mendham married a young lady from Devonshire, whose father, Mr. Rosoman, possessed the land on which Rosoman Row, Clerkenwell, was built. She brought a servant, or lady's maid with her, in whom I found a rational companion and friend, and with whom I soon became enamoured. I shall have occasion to relate some particulars of this female in the ensuing chapter.

# CHAPTER IV.

"Never did captive with a freer heart
Cast off his chains of bondage."
*Richard II.*, Act I., Scene 3.

EMANCIPATION—DOLEFUL PROSPECTS—THE PLEASURES AND PAINS OF LOVE—A PEDESTRIAN TOUR FROM LONDON TO PLYMPTON—VISIT TO HOME, FRIENDS, AND RELATIONS; TO BATH AND WELLS—A RAMBLING, BOASTING YOUTH—DISAPPOINTMENT AT PLYMPTON, AND POIGNANT DISTRESS—RETURN TO LONDON, WITH EMPTY POCKETS—EMPLOYED AT THE LONDON TAVERN—WITH A HOP MERCHANT—LODGING WITH A TINMAN; HIS FANATICISM—ACCOUNT OF WILLIAM HUNTINGTON, "S. S."—ENGAGEMENT WITH A LAWYER; HIS PECULIARITIES—STUDIES—A COOK'S SHOP, AND SOME OF ITS VISITORS DESCRIBED—CHEVALIER D'EON—SIR JOHN DINELEY—JOSEPH RITSON—IN THE OFFICE OF PARKER AND WIX—NOTICE OF JOHN THOMAS HUGHES—DEBATING SOCIETIES AND PRIVATE THEATRES, WITH ANECDOTES OF THEIR FREQUENTERS—SADLER'S WELLS—M. LONSDALE—CHARLES DIBDIN OF THE SANS-SOUCI—THOMAS, AND CHARLES DIBDIN, JUN.—DUBOIS—GRIMALDI—RITCHER—DEIGHTON—BELZONI—LYCEUM AND EGYPTIACA—GAS—BENEFIT FOR THE AUTHOR AND MR. TAPSELL—EIDOPHUSICON—CHAPMAN AND LOUTHERBOURG—WRIGHT, A MIMIC—J. O. CHAMPION—RANELAGH—VAUXHALL—BAGNIGGE WELLS—WHITE CONDUIT-HOUSE—DOG AND DUCK, ST. GEORGE'S FIELDS—TEMPLE OF FLORA—JOURNEY TO SHROPSHIRE—R. P. KNIGHT—UVEDALE PRICE—THE REV. HUGH OWEN—THE REV. J. B. BLAKEWAY—D. PARKES.

THE period between my release from the wine-cellars, and the adoption of literature as a profession, involves at least seven years of vicissitudes, privations, and hardships: though occasionally relieved by occupations which produced a bare livelihood. In very poor and obscure lodgings, at eighteen-pence per week, I indulged in study; and often read in bed during the winter evenings, because I could not afford a fire. When my finances allowed I frequented free-and-easy, odd fellows', and spouting clubs; but my expenses never exceeded sixpence a night at any of these associations of smokers, drinkers, and convivialists. Knowing the value and truth of the maxim, "a penny saved is a penny got," I abstained from laying out money on any article not absolutely wanted, particularly on beer and spirits. These associations led to debating societies, then very numerous and popular in London, to private theatres, and to lectures: but the last were very rare. Some of these pursuits and associations were not merely amusing for the time, but became ultimately of great benefit; as conducive to mental improvement, to correction of manners, language, and personal deportment, and also tending, in some degree, to cure a nervous timidity and shyness which belonged to my natural disposition.

My first and all-absorbing object, however, after leaving Mr. Mendham, was to undertake a pedestrian journey to Plympton, in Devonshire. This was to me an appalling task, and one which I contemplated at times with terror and despair, but I was again and again incited to risk it, by the all-powerful stimulant—love. This passion had been cherished for nearly two years during apprenticeship, by daily intercourse with Elizabeth Bryant, who was lady's maid to the junior Mrs. Mendham. The manners, mind, and kindly disposition of this young woman (my senior by five or six years) first engaged my respect and admiration, and very soon my most ardent affection: for, isolated as I was from all the sympathies of parents, relatives, and friends, I felt as a solitary outcast, and eagerly sought the company of a female, whom I necessarily often met, and whose language and sentiments were far superior to those of the companions it was my duty to associate with. It is not, therefore, surprising that an intense and quixotic attachment should be the result; nor that such a passion should lead to a series of troubles and difficulties. I was destined to feel most acutely that

"The course of true love never does run smooth."

The Mendhams learnt the particulars of our infatuation, and deemed a separation absolutely necessary. Absence, they thought, would give both parties leisure to reflect on the folly and danger of indulging a passion which was likely to lead to poverty and misery. I was, however, too deeply smitten, too intensely enthralled, to listen to, or heed the influence of reason; and, after the departure of the object of my affections, I addressed many letters to her, urging my suit, and explaining the misery I endured. Though of equally warm temperament with myself, and sincerely attached to me, whilst we were daily together, I received only one letter from her afterwards, in which she intreated me to forego all hopes of marriage. I could not, however, so easily subdue the passion which had occupied all my thoughts, prompted all my actions, and created a succession of those morbid visions, which youthful poets often endeavour to portray in moments of inspiration or infatuation. I pressed my master to cancel my indentures, that I might go into Wiltshire; to try if native air, change of scene, with new objects and pursuits, would restore my health. We parted; and he and my uncle left me to shift for myself, and to abide the consequences of what they regarded as an act of disobedience, and an imprudent dereliction of duty.

The world was now before me, and though in my twenty-second year, I was a child in knowledge, and as ignorant of our terrestrial world as of that of the moon. Not knowing how to replenish my purse when its contents (about six pounds) were spent, I determined first to walk into Wiltshire, solicit a few weeks' board and lodging from Mrs. Beak, an old friend at Kington-Priory, and from my uncle, Richard; and afterwards undertake my cherished project by walking to Plympton, a distance of 216 miles from London, where "my Betsy" lived. Unlike his brother Samuel, my relative gave me a kind and hearty welcome, as did also my friend, Mrs. Beak; and I passed several weeks, enjoying their society and country life with a zest to which I had long been unaccustomed. Though all the places I saw, and the persons I met, were recognised by memory, each and all presented new and striking differences since my departure, six years before. The village and priory had undergone many changes; my parents were both dead; my brothers and sisters scattered abroad; many friends of my boyhood had left their native place; those I had known as youths and girls were become men and women; and Mrs. Beak, who had befriended our orphan family in its adversity, was herself left a widow with four children. My uncle had married the female already alluded to, and some young Hilliers had come into the world. With these parties I spent the sheep-shearing, hay-making, and harvest seasons; and having derived much benefit in health and spirits, I prepared for my proposed long walk to Plympton, in the autumn of 1793. Before leaving Wiltshire, however, I spent some days at Chippenham, with my sister Mary, who had been apprenticed by Mrs. Beak to a milliner in the town; and there I became acquainted with Mr. Sadler, author of "Wanley Penson," Mr. Gaby, and other estimable persons, with whom I continued intimate till they all died. In the prosecution of my journey, I went first to Bath, where I renewed my acquaintance with the Strattons. Thence I walked to Wells, where I accidentally met a Mr.

Wright, a lieutenant in the army, who had been brought up by my uncle Samuel, his guardian. We had been playfellows together, when the London Hilliers visited Wiltshire, and during my apprenticeship he had often supplied me with clothes. On this occasion he strongly urged me to abandon, what appeared to him a wild-goose chase; and gave me a guinea at parting. From Wells I pursued the direct road towards Plympton; living in the cheapest manner, and walking every successive day till I was completely tired. At this time I was wholly unacquainted with topography and antiquities, and consequently passed through many towns of Somersetshire, Dorsetshire, and Devonshire, without visiting or seeking amusement from their fine churches, towers, castles, and monastic ruins: even the commanding beauties of nature, and the fine and interesting buildings which abounded on my route, were passed by with listless apathy. How often, since, have I regretted that my eye and imagination had not been previously tutored to appreciate the varied attractions inherent in those objects, which are replete with interest to all who can find "sermons in stones," and who delight in reading the instructive book of nature, and studying the elements of art and science!

At a public-house in Wells, I met a young man, whose fluent conversation made a strong impression on my memory. He related his adventures to a group of persons assembled in the public-room, with exultation to himself, and astonishment to his auditors. He said he was the son of rich and indulgent parents, and described his whole career as replete with marvellous incidents and "hair-breadth 'scapes." He told many anecdotes of his school-days, boyish freaks, and reckless sports; of his apprenticeship, and his determination to "see the world," before he sat down to business. He had visited different parts of England during the two preceding summers, and was returning from the Land's End towards London. Though there was some degree of dangerous temptation to me in the manners and conversation of this man, I nevertheless perceived that his only object in travelling was to seek excitement and adventures—to spend most of his time in public-houses and dissipated company—to relate his stories, sing his songs, and eventually sacrifice his health and respectability to a prurient passion for novelty, drink, and vain boasting. After many tedious days' walking I reached the famed birth-place of Sir Joshua Reynolds, whose name I had often heard, though I had not seen any of his pictures. Such, however, is the infatuating influence of true love, that it absorbs every thought, wish, and hope of its victim. I well remember the perturbed and anxious state of my mind during every succeeding day of this toilsome and fatiguing journey—the "Pleasures of Hope" which cheered me every day; the "Pleasures of Memory" which I enjoyed in reviewing the felicitous hours we had occasionally shared; and the "Pleasures of Imagination" involved in my meditations on the future. These reveries served to dispel the gloom produced by the woful, solitary state in which fortune had cast me. I found my fair but faithless Dulcinea, sought an interview, and was soon convinced that I was wrong and foolish in making such a tour, and that we must part, never to meet again. I could not argue—indeed I could not speak; but returned to my inn, disconsolate, and almost deranged. I remained mute and abstracted till the landlady told me that the family were all gone to bed, and hoped I would retire. She inquired what was the matter, trusted I was not ill, and seemed concerned to see a delicate-looking stranger in such a state of sadness; for tears trickled down my face. Her questions, tone of voice, and apparent sympathy aroused me in some degree; but my broken slumbers merely tended to relieve bodily fatigue, and failed to "minister to a mind diseased." There was now no cheering gleam in the future: I was indeed friendless and destitute; and a weak consumptive constitution strongly presaged early death. In a state of hopeless despair and misery I left Plympton early, directing my infirm steps towards London. Many times did I halt by the wayside to rest, to meditate, and to attempt to read. Pocket editions of Sterne's "Sentimental Journey," Lord Chesterfield's "Principles of Politeness," and Goldsmith's "Poems" were my companions, but I could not fix my attention on either of them. The only passage which, by a morbid feeling, occupied my mind, was the opening of the "Traveller,"—

"Remote, unfriended, melancholy, slow,
\* \* \* \* \* \*
Where'er I roam, whatever realms I see,
My thoughts, untravelled, still return to thee."

In the long, slow, and doleful walk to London, I more than once meditated self-murder; and drank many glasses of rum and milk, my only favourite beverage, in the hope that it would banish care and exhilarate the spirits. The necessity of bodily exertion, new and varied nightly lodgings, and association with strangers, whom I necessarily met, tended far more, however, to divert the mind from its unavailing gloom. Suffice it to say, that time, and the little philosophy I then possessed, gradually, but imperceptibly, cured the sad but cherished disease which had raged so long.

At Bath I endeavoured to obtain an engagement as cellar-man at the White Hart, but failed; and I returned to the metropolis almost penniless, shoeless, and shirtless. My filial affection was now severely tried; for "poverty, but not my will," compelled me to change the crown piece which my dear mother had given me at parting; and in another week I was obliged to sell the silver knee-buckles which she had also presented. Soon afterwards I obtained employ as cellar-man in the London Tavern, where I remained, however, only three months, the confinement and occupation being even more slavish and irksome than what I had experienced at the Jerusalem Tavern. From seven o'clock in the morning till eleven or twelve at night, it was my business to be in the cellar, to perform the common routine of work during the day, and afterwards to decant and supply waiters with wines for successive dinners. My sleeping place was a large room over the kitchen, where several cooks and waiters were also bedded for the night. The heat and smell of this apartment were almost suffocating.

Some weeks after quitting the London Tavern, I engaged as Clerk and Cellar-man to a widow in Smithfield, whose cajoling and bland language flattered my young vanity. She conducted her late husband's business as a hop merchant. Calling me "Sir" and "her clerk," tickled my ear. She was very inquisitive about the management of wines and spirits, and fancying that I had met with a good friend, I did not hesitate to tell her everything I knew, which was very little. There were no Histories by Henderson or Redding at that time. Instead of weekly wages, she agreed to give me £40 and breakfast, for the first year, and £50 for the second; well knowing that she would not retain me even for the first term. Indeed, after a few weeks, I perceived that she and her artful methodistic porter, had made themselves familiar with the whole art, trade, and mystery of the " wine and brandy merchant," and accordingly, in her cards, circulars, &c., assumed that title in addition to the hop business. Mrs. Lonsdale, an artful and mercenary woman, with a deformed daughter, had conducted the latter business for a few years, and employed a Mr. Sayer, as traveller, who sought by every possible means, to propitiate the friendship of one, and the affections of the other. A marriage and partnership were the result; and the names of "Lonsdale and Sayer, Wine and Brandy and Hop Merchants," were conspicuously painted on the string-course of a large house. Besides these trades, they were the receivers, or agents, for several of the market salesmen, whose practice was (as I presume it is at present), to receive money from the butchers who bought at Smithfield, take charge of the same, deposit it at the banking-house of Rogers, Towgood, and Co. This money was repaid to the salesmen or farmers as required. To assist in taking several hundreds of guineas (for the cash was mostly paid in those coins), and carrying bags of the weighty metal to the banker's, was part of my duty; and the sight of so much money, with the confidence it indicated, flattered my vanity and self-esteem. Herein, however, as in many other concerns of life, there were bitters mixed with the sweets—troubles blended with the joys; for my strict mistress made me responsible for every bad shilling or light guinea taken; whence my mind was always kept in a state of suspense and fear until the cash had passed the ordeal of "the merchant" and the banker. My hours of employ were from seven o'clock in the morning till eight at night, and, with the exception of one hour allowed for dinner, half-an-hour for breakfast, and a few moments for a cup of tea about five o'clock, every moment was actively employed, under the lynx-eyed inspection of the mistress, whose station was a counting-house, with glazed doors, overlooking the warehouse. In the cellars I was watched as closely by the confidential porter, who was always with me for the pretended purpose of assisting, but for the real object of making himself familiar with the management of wines and spirits, and to prevent my drinking a glass occasionally. This hypocritical and artful fellow never drank, was a bigoted devotee to religious words and ceremonies, and worked like a galley-slave; all these habits being quite congenial and delightful to the mistress. Such association was not calculated to last, nor was it originally intended by the newly-initiated wine merchant. I was warned to quit at the end of the first quarter; but such was the noble generosity of my sinister patron, that I was allowed to give my services for board, until I found better terms elsewhere. During this engagement, I lodged with a tinman in Smithfield-bars, having a bed-room, about nine feet by seven, for which I paid 1s. 6d. per week. He was a devoted "Huntingtonian," and seemed to employ as much time and thought to the outward forms of the religious ceremonies of his sect, as to his hammering and soldering trade. Before every meal a long tirade of words, called prayers, were rantingly and drawlingly pronounced by this sanctified tinman, to two apprentices and a female servant, the last of whom sighed and moaned in unison with her good master. It was evident that "the Spirit of Grace" was powerfully operating on these two elect people. I was a cold looker-on and listener to the verbiage and illiterate nonsense of the godly man; and was often, directly and indirectly, addressed in language of admonition, or persuasion to "become sanctified in grace, and thus become a partaker of the gifts of the Gospel."

Amongst "wolves in sheep's clothing,"—the heroes and saints of religious hypocrisy,* a countless tribe,—*William Huntington*, s. s. (or "sinner saved," as he blasphemously called himself, or, as Mathews interpreted the letters, "sad scoundrel,") was one of the most eminent in the annals of quackery and imposture. The landlord of my Smithfield-bars lodging, was one of his "servants," or disciples and followers, and eminently qualified to rank and horde with such a worthless being. Ignorant, arrogant, fanatical to frenzy and foolery, this tinman followed and imitated his spiritual master and priest in nearly all his gospel meetings, and believed in all his blasphemous stories respecting familiar and tête-à-tête converse with "the Lord." I was indulged with a seat by his fireside during the winter evenings, when I was unengaged at a club: and always further treated with relations of the wonder-working talents and preachings of the "saved sinner." Had I noted down even a small portion of these stories, they would have formed a long and

---

* "Oh for a *forty-parson power* to chant
　Thy praise, Hypocrisy!—oh for a hymn
Loud as the virtues thou dost loudly vaunt,
　Not practice!"　　　　　　BYRON.

marvellous narrative, and have rivalled the silly and disgusting romances of any saint in the Roman Catholic calendar. Though I neglected this task, enough has been preserved in the titles and pages of his own publications to characterize the man, and the gullible credulity of his followers. His works are numerous, and appear to have issued from the press between the years 1787 and 1795. The titles of one or two will be enough to make a rational reader shudder at their phraseology, —"Justification of a Sinner; and Satan's Law-suit with him," 1787. " Forty Stripes save none for Satan: or the Devil beaten with Rods," 1792. "Advocates for Devils refuted, and the Hope of the Damned demolished; or an Everlasting Task for Winchester and all his Confederates," 1794. Like the generality of religious sectarian writers, Huntington uncharitably condemned and anathematized (about as severely as Dr. Slop did) all who dissented from his own sect. The origin, life, writings, preachings, and practices of this man abound in romance, manifesting cunning and cupidity in an eminent degree on his own part, and credulity and lamentable folly in his followers. He was a natural son of a poor woman, by a farmer: he progressed through the stages of errand-boy, day-labourer, gardener, cobbler, and coal-heaver, and at last turned preacher, thinking it an easier and more profitable employment than either of the others. He struggled with poverty and privations for some time; but contrived to obtain money, food, and clothes by telling his auditors that "God would find him a horse," a pair of breeches, a suit of clothes, a ham, and various other necessaries and even luxuries, which were forthwith sent to him by his deluded followers. These presentations, or "God-sends," as vulgarly denominated, were no less remarkable than the language employed by the canting preacher to his besotted auditory and believers. In speaking of the horse, he says, "I believe it was God's gift. I have often thought, that if my horse could have spoken, he would have had more to say than Balaam's ass; as he might have said, 'I am an answer to my master's prayers.'" His congregation became so numerous, and so generous, that they built "Providence Chapel" for him, in Gray's Inn Lane, at an expense of £9000. When finished, he refused to preach, until it was settled on him in freehold. This was yielded to by his weak dupes, and he continued his rhodomontade discourses, living in a sumptuous manner at Hermes Hill, Pentonville, where he married, as a second wife, the widow of Sir James Sanderson, Bart. An interesting memoir of this singular man is recorded by my friend Cromwell, in his " History of Clerkenwell," 8vo. 1828.

My next engagement was with Mr. Simpson, an attorney, in Holborn Court (now called South Square), Gray's Inn; where, and with whom, I continued three years, at the humble wages (dignified with the name of salary) of fifteen shillings per week. With this small income I felt comfortable and happy; as it provided me with a decent lodging, clothes, and food, and with the luxury of books. Having but little writing for my master, who neither had, nor was qualified to execute, much business, I was enabled to devote time to reading; and out of two hours for dinner, I could easily appropriate more than one to booksellers' shops and stalls, by which I acquired a progressive knowledge of " the trade," as well as of the value and contents of books. In the evenings I frequented the clubs and societies already referred to, and formed connections and even friendships with many persons devoted to similar pursuits. Had the practice or study of the law been attractive to me, or had I been with a gentleman devoted to, and clever in, the profession, I might have taken pleasure in the subject, and acquired a knowledge of its technicalities and practice sufficient to qualify me to act professionally, or at least to obtain a clerkship with a handsome salary; but my master was so slow, tedious, and dull, whilst his books appeared to me to possess qualities so similar, that I could neither imitate the one, nor feel interested in the other. The drama, poetry, novels, and essays engaged nearly all my reading hours and thoughts, and detached me from serious and useful study. Mr. Simpson was a sort of human machine, that seemed to live and move by clock-work, and performed its revolutions with unchangeable order and precision. At eleven o'clock he came to the office to receive business letters, each of which he read several times, with pauses between every sentence, by which process six short letters would occupy at least an hour of his time. He devoted more than another hour to dictating equally laconic letters in reply; whilst a third was employed in reading those answers, when written. This vapid waste of time was the practice of every succeeding day, and I was subjected to the same tedious routine for three years. Almost his only practice was as agent to three or four provincial attorneys, and there was but little for me to do in copying, or in the different courts and law offices. A spouting club at Jacob's Wells, Barbican, occupied one of my evenings in every week, during the winter, the Odd Fellows' another, and Free-and-Easys one or two more. In all of these I formed many acquaintances, and secured a few real friends.

During nearly the whole of these three years, it was my custom to dine at an eating-house in Great Turnstile, Holborn, on very cheap and moderate fare; the cost of the meal, with beer, seldom exceeding ninepence.* In a humble room, the parlour, of this establishment, I became acquainted with several persons, both male and female; for some of the latter sex were occasional visitors. One, of questionable nature in this respect, excited much curiosity and speculation at the time, and for many years afterwards. This was the noted *Chevalier D'Eon*. At the time I met him, he dressed in female attire, and was respectable and respected. Though an occasional guest at this humble house of refreshment, it was evident that he had been accustomed to refined society, and was courteous, well-informed on various subjects, and communicative. I own that I always hailed the meeting with gratification, and that it induced me to prolong my dinner-time to the last moment. The history and adventures of this extraordinary person were full of romance and adventure; and it is to be regretted that they were not put on record by himself. "His story" (says Lysons' "Environs of London," Vol. ii. Pt. ii. p. 644) "has for many years excited much curiosity and interest. After distinguishing himself in the service of his native country, as a soldier and a negotiator, he assumed the habit of a female, at the requisition of the French court, and as such was appointed to a situation in the household of the Queen; but he is now known to be the son of a gentleman of an ancient and respectable family, at Tonnerré in Burgundy, where he was born, Oct. 2nd, 1728." Though subjected to many hardships and vicissitudes, he lived to attain his eighty-second year, and died at a lodging in Mill-

---

* The learned, caustic, petted Dr. Johnson, was in the habit of frequenting an eating-house, or cook's shop, in Butcher Row, Strand, where others of the literati of the age also assembled. The crazed Nat. Lee died in the street in returning from this house to his lodging.

man Street, Lamb's Conduit Street, London, May 21st, 1810, and his corpse was interred in the old parish churchyard of St. Pancras. The body was dissected by Mr. T. Copeland, in the presence of Lord Yarmouth, Sir Sidney Smith, the Hon. Mr. Littleton, and other persons, who verified that the deceased was a perfect male. The register of his baptism states the child to be a boy, though the sex appears then to have been doubtful. Throughout life the personal appearance, manners, and modest demeanour of the Chevalier were indicative of the female sex. As a man, he was noted for courage, was an officer in the army, an accomplished horseman, learned in different languages, an elegant and skilful fencer, and had fought three or four duels. In female attire, in England, he exhibited his address and skill in fencing at Ranelagh and the Opera House, and also gave lessons. As an author he wrote several works on statistics, history, politics, &c. The magazines and newspapers of London abound with anecdotes and accounts of this remarkable person; particularly the *Gentleman's* for 1810.

*Sir John Dinely, Bart.*, one of the Poor Knights of Windsor, was an occasional guest at the house above-named; and from his singular manners, person, and habiliments, attracted the gaze and wonderment of all persons who saw him. He was a large man, and dressed in a grotesque manner, with broad-brimmed hat, turned up behind, large bushy wig, loose great coat, and spacious half-boots; sometimes with pattens. The last he always wore during the winter, as a specific, according to his notions, against the gout and swelled ankles. On a print of him, now before me, is a memorandum of my having dined with him, May 25th, 1798, when he appeared about seventy years of age. His conversation was fluent and jocular, manifesting good education and select society. He said that "King George III. had given him £150 a year, and a house at Windsor," where he was living comfortably as a single, solitary man, but was very desirous of marrying a beautiful lady. This was the infatuated baronet's weak point, and it is displayed in a printed circular, with a full-length portrait of him, addressed as an appeal "To the fair Ladies of Great Britain, old and young," dated Windsor Castle, Oct. 23rd, 1799, and printed by Chas. Knight.* In

---

* This gentleman was the father of my much-esteemed friend, Charles Knight, of London, who has written, edited, and published many literary works of national utility

this he states that it is in his power "to confer on any lady who may be inclined to enter into the sacred and all-absorbing state of matrimony, the title of Lady, with a fortune of three hundred thousand

---

and influence. His productions have indeed effected more good in intellectual and moral reform than those of any author it has been my happiness to have known, in an extensive intercourse with the literary world. Mr. Chas. Knight, jun., when a youth, was permitted, as a special favour, to visit the domicile or hermitage of the gallant Lothario at Windsor, and has preserved some descriptive notices of the eccentric knight's personal characteristics:—"He constantly wore a large cloak called a roquelaure, beneath which appeared a pair of thin legs, encased in dirty silk stockings. If the morning was wet, his cloak was not his only protection from the weather. He had a formidable umbrella; and, what was most wonderful, he stalked along upon pattens. No human being, it was imagined, had for some years entered his house, except its eccentric possessor. The wise man, he held, was his own best assistant; and so he dispensed with all domestic service. In the morning he duly went forth to make his frugal purchases for the day,—a faggot, a candle, a small loaf, perhaps a herring. His income, as one of the 'Poor Knights,' was about sixty pounds. Wherever crowds were assembled, wherever royalty was to be looked upon, and the sounds of military music summoned the fair ones of Windsor and Eton to the gay parade, there was Sir John Dinely. The roquelaure was cast aside, and then were disclosed the treasures which it concealed,—the embroidered coat, the silk-flowered waistcoat, the nether garments of faded velvet, carefully meeting the dirty silk stockings, which terminated in the half-polished shoe, surmounted by the dingy silver buckle. He had dreams of ancient genealogies, and alliances with the first families in the land, and of mansions and possessions that ought to be his own. A little money expended in law proceedings was to make these dreams realities. That money was to be obtained through a wife, and to secure one, was the business of his existence. The man had not a particle of levity in his proceedings. His face had a grave and intellectual character, his deportment was staid and dignified. Perchance some buxom matron, or timid maiden, who had seen him for the first time, gazed upon the apparition with surprise and curiosity. He approached with the air of one bred in courts, he made his most profound bow, and taking a printed paper from his pocket, reverently presented it, and withdrew. Was this man mad? He had a monomania certainly, but in other matters he was the shrewdest man we ever knew. He was reserved and sarcastic to most persons, for too frequently was he insulted; but to those who were kind to him, he displayed no common mind. He was unfortunate. His misfortunes were inscribed in no less terrible a page than that book over which many a boy has wept and trembled—the 'Newgate Calendar.' In 1741, a dismal tragedy occurred at Bristol. Sir John Dinely Goodyere, Bart., and his younger brother, had become enemies on account of the entail of property. At the request of the younger, who was a captain in the navy, the brothers met again in friendship, and dined together at the house of a friend. When they separated, the baronet had to pass alone over College Green. He was there encountered by his brother and six sailors, who seized and carried him to their ship, where he was strangled. The vengeance

pounds."—"Sir John is aware," he says, "that some few, prejudiced by etiquette, may smile at his address;—let them laugh;—he has once experienced its comfortable effects. Let me intreat you, therefore," he continues, "my angelic fair, ingenuously to unbosom your sentiments, nor trust to dangerous delay, for I am resolved to give her the preference who is most explicit and most expeditious." The "poor knight" continued to print and circulate his addresses "to the fair Ladies" for several years (I have three varieties), but without success; though he referred to Nash's "History of Worcestershire," for evidence of his title and landed estates.

During my abode in Holborn Court, I occasionally visited *Joseph Ritson*, who had chambers on the opposite side to those of Mr. Simpson. He was a special pleader, or chamber counsel, and sometimes had cases submitted for his opinion from our office. He was small in person, thin, consumptive in appearance, reserved in manners; and, at the time I knew him, had but little professional practice. Attorneys, in general, though there are many laudable exceptions, have not much respect for poetry or poets, and consider that the man who devotes his time and thoughts to polite literature, can have little partiality for the dull verbiage of the Statutes at Large, or the sophisticated and delusive language too often employed in special pleading.* The sentiments and character

---

of the law was speedy, and the inhuman brother and two of his confederates were hanged within two months. Sir John Dinely, of Windsor, was the son of the murderer. That the poor man was perfectly familiar with all the circumstances of this tragedy there can be no doubt; and we have often thought that, shut up in his lonely house, with the horrible recollections of the past lingering about him, it was wonderful that he was not altogether mad. One morning Sir John was missing from his due attendance upon the service of St. George's Chapel. His door was broken open. His house was without furniture, except a table and a chair or two. The sitting-room was strewed with printing types—for he used sometimes to print his own bills after the rudest fashion: in a small room beyond was stretched the poor man upon a pallet bed. He had studied physic; and he had prescribed for himself not injudiciously, having a few medicines always at hand. He lingered a few days, and then—*all* the dream was over." He died in the month of May 1808; and, to the close of his career, indulged the expectation of forming a wealthy connubial connection.

* Literature has been worthily honoured in the elevation of Mr. Justice Talfourd to the Bench; but it is well known that his literary pursuits had for some time a very detrimental influence on his professional prospects.

of Ritson may be inferred from his published Letters, which appeared in 1833, with a Memoir, by his nephew, Sir Harris Nicolas (2 vols. small 8vo.) In one of his letters, dated in 1793 (just before I knew him) he says, "Those who die happily are certainly more to be envied than those who live otherwise." Giving directions about his sister's funeral, he remarks, "I wish the ceremony to be conducted with as much plainness and frugality as can be decently adopted. No scarfs given, nor any gloves, except to the bearers, who may be any four or half a dozen men you think proper;—I mean to carry the body to the church with napkins, and not by means of fellows concealed under a pall. Of every species of expense I abominate and detest that most which is lavished on the dead."* He goes on to enjoin "that there may not be any singing of hymns either in or out of church." In a postscript, he says, "You may give Citizen Equality a hint that I find it prudent to say as little as possible upon political subjects, in order to keep myself out of Newgate." The following paragraph from a letter to Mr. Laing, a bookseller, of Edinburgh, is curious, as characterising the writer and his times. "I wish you could hear of some careful person coming up (to London) who would take the trouble of bringing Mr. Tytler's MS. Shoals of Scotchmen are arriving here every day; the difficulty, I should imagine, would be to find one going back. Edinburgh, at the same time, is so very small a place, that you may be easily acquainted with the motions of every individual from your shop door. Formerly, I have been told, when a Scotchman intended a journey to the south, he used to ring the crier's bell for a quarter of a year beforehand, in order to indemnify himself against the enormous expenses of the Newcastle waggon, by the packets and parcels he got the charge of from his neighbours; but at present, I suppose, the neighbours go too,—not in the Newcastle waggon, I mean, but the mail-coach—*Tempora mutantur!*" His opinion of the attorneys is too strongly expressed: "I have found them not only the most ignorant and capricious, but the most insincere, unprincipled, and, in every respect, worthless of men." The state of society in August 1793 is exemplified in the following passage:—"With respect to a revolution, though I think it at no great distance, it seems to

---

* This sentiment and these expressions about funerals are in unison with my own, as recorded in my Will, and in the present volume.

defy all calculation for the present. If the increase of taxes, the decline of manufactures, the high price of provisions and the like, have no effect upon the apathy of the *sans culottes* here, one can expect little from the reasoning of philosophers or politicians."

Ritson was born at Stockton-on-Tees, 1752: he published an " Essay on Abstinence from Animal Food, as a Moral Duty," in 1803; became soon afterwards deranged, and died at Hoxton, Middlesex, in September 1803. His nephew, Sir Harris Nicolas, possessed many traits of his temper, as well as enthusiastic devotion to literature; and has left an interesting sketch of his uncle's life and character in the volumes referred to. In Nichols's *Literary Anecdotes of the Eighteenth Century*, Vol. viii., are some interesting particulars of Ritson. His affected and antiquated spelling is ridiculed with admirable effect, by my late witty friend E. Du Bois, in the *Monthly Mirror* for 1803, Vol. xvi., p. 90.

On the death of Mr. Simpson, in 1798, I was destined to seek new employment for a livelihood. After some weeks of inquiry and suspense, I had an engagement with Messrs. Parker and Wix, Solicitors, of Greville Street, Hatton Garden, where I obtained twenty shillings a week; an augmentation of income peculiarly cheering, whilst the duties of office, the connection, and the new associations it induced, were equally gratifying. My employers were bachelors of middle age, and, I believe, both continued in "single blessedness" till death. The first was active, shrewd, learned in the law, and a most honourable, honest man. The second, possessing a moderate fortune, enjoyed its advantages on a limited scale, in association with a sister and a female cousin, both spinsters. He rarely appeared in the office, but left the whole to his good partner, who lived also with a maiden sister. The firm exhibited a fine example of punctuality, system, neatness; and, for twelve months, whilst I sojourned in its office, my time was happily spent. There was not much business; whence I was enabled to pursue miscellaneous reading, and also to indulge in evening recreations at the clubs already noticed. In this establishment I secured the intimacy and confidence of a gentleman about twenty-one years of age, who was placed by his father, Admiral Sir Richard Hughes, with Mr. Parker, to study for the Bar by a course of legal reading. There could not be a sounder, a more conscientious preceptor; there could not be a pupil better qualified by talents and scholastic education to become eminent in the Courts of Law or in Parliament, than *John Thomas Hughes*. Mr. Parker was strict and persevering in advising and admonishing his young friend, whose volatility of temperament and poetical mind could not be induced to take an interest, or find amusement, in the dull technicalities and prolix verbiage of law-books. The drama and poetry, a debating society, and a private theatre, engrossed more of the thoughts of the juvenile pleader than Coke upon Littleton, Blackstone, or the Statutes at Large. My previous acquaintance with, and partialities for, the theatre, were calculated to ingratiate me in the estimation of my new and warm-hearted friend. I was often invited to his chambers in the Temple, and we both became members of a Debating Society in Coachmaker's Hall, and the Shakspearian Theatre, Tottenham Court Road. In the first he soon proved himself to be a distinguished and admirable speaker. Possessing a fine and dignified person and countenance—being well read in history and poetry, fluent in speech, and fertile in imagination—he always secured attention, and often obtained the warmest plaudits of large and critical companies. The questions proposed and discussed were on various subjects, but mostly on history and polite literature: politics and religion were generally excluded. Most of the members of this society were students for the Bar, or connected with the press: amongst these were Adolphus, Andrews, H. C. Robinson, Hughes, Kenney, Prince Smith, Wright, Storks, and several others. On one occasion, the question proposed by Mr. Hughes was "*On the Utility of Eloquence;*" and as my friend was to open the subject in the negative, he solicited Mr. H. C. Robinson, who was his senior in age and in the society, and one of its frequent speakers, to favour him with some hints on the subject. That gentleman complied; and I have now before me the letter he wrote to Mr. Hughes, from which I am induced to copy two or three sentences, indicative of the tone current among the young men of that age, as well as of the writer's turn of mind; of whom Goldsmith might have truly said, as he did of Burke, that he was represented by "tongue, garnished with brains."

"Nov. 21, 1797.—Dear Hughes, You ask me, What arguments I would use against the utility of eloquence? I will not pretend to offer you more than seeds, convinced, if their natural organization will at all allow of growth, that they will flourish; being sown in a soil well adapted to produce beautiful flowers, and rich fruit. Were *I* to follow an eloquent speaker, my exordium would consist in playing upon an obvious remark that my opponent, in defending eloquence, had been eloquent; and that I, in contending against it, should certainly not borrow its assistance: but *you*, I doubt not, will be so truly eloquent, as to render such an introduction obvious affectation and prudery. I would pursue the natural order, by asking, 'What is eloquence?' Here you might first indicate the senseless definition,—'well speaking'—which would raise Sir Isaac Newton to the character of the most excellent of orators; transfer the Grecian crown from Demosthenes to Euclid; and exalt the sublime rhapsodies of Rousseau over the incomparable orations of Edmund Burke. Having adopted Quintilian's definition,—'the art of speaking to persuade,'—I would then enter upon my grand argument, which consists in shewing that eloquence appeals to, and of course encourages and cultivates, the *Imaginations* and *Passions*, in opposition to the *Judgment;* and I would forcibly represent this by emphatically contrasting the operation of persuading with that of convincing; contending, amongst other topics, that he who reasons with another makes him his equal; but that the eloquent man plays upon his hearer as an instrument, or tool: and, being more democratic than yourself, I would affirm eloquence to have been an instrument of subjection and tyranny, tending to preserve a system of 'privileged orders,' by promoting inequality of talent; whilst the reasoning faculty is the great equalizer of mankind. To confirm these notions, I would appeal to two striking historical facts, which ought to be conclusive. Though eloquence had been cultivated in Athens and Rome more than among any other people, yet the Areopagi especially forbade the use of it before them; and Cicero tells us that in the presence of the Judges it was customary to adopt a more simple and logical style, than in addressing the people."

The above extract is calculated to show the rational and instructive amusement of the junior members of the legal profession at that time; who were only following in the laudable track which Pitt, Burke, Fox, Garrow, Erskine, and other eminent orators, lawyers, and statesmen had before pursued with advantage. In this society my friend Hughes continued for some time; and was much admired as an eloquent debater, and private gentleman. Though the class of reading required to qualify him for speaking on different subjects was amusing and instructive, and particularly so to myself, (for I participated in all his pursuits,) Mr. Parker often remonstrated with him on neglecting his professional studies; and he found still further ground for complaint, when he learnt that his volatile pupil was in the habit of attending, and occasionally performing in, the private theatre above-mentioned. Here he personated three or four different dramatic characters; and also wrote addresses, and a farce of two acts.* The rapid production of this piece was a striking manifestation of his genius and powers. Having meditated on a subject one night, he appeared at office earlier than usual on the morning, took a quire of copy, told me that he intended to write a farce for the theatre, and completed it in the course of the day. The next night he read it to me; and in a few days made copies of the different parts, which he had adapted to six of the principal performers, and at the end of a fortnight the piece was performed, according to play-bill language, " with unbounded and unmingled applause." The title was, "Eccentricity, a Farce Rehearsed;" and it contained much wit and broad humour. Amongst the scenes was one in which two characters were seated on the floor of the stage as tailors, making a coat and a waistcoat, and a short dialogue and a duet ensued; in the midst of which the leader of the band, from the orchestra, interrupted them, by saying, they must go home, practice their parts, and have lessons in singing, before they can dare to appear before a critical audience. They insist that the leader's fiddle is a mere fid., and out of tune; that he is ignorant of music, and that *they* are perfect in their parts, as well as in the tune and time of the duet; and, moreover, that they can produce, by manner, action, and expression, effects of which music is incapable; adding, that they have no bowels for cats'-guts, nor sympathy with fiddle-sticks. Here a person, from among the audience, starts up and interposes; the prompter sallies from the side wing, a warm altercation ensues, and ultimately a watchman, with rattle, blunderbuss, and lantern, enters to arrest the whole party for a riot; and here the curtain falls. Many odd scenes were exhibited at this theatre, which had previously been a cow-house. Amongst them, was a ludicrous incident in the play of Hamlet: when Mr. Young, who represented the Prince of Denmark, was saying, " It is a poison tempered by himself," a pot-boy, with two cans of porter, came into the house, and, instead of passing behind the back scene to the dressing-room, he marched across, in front, to his own and the ac-

---

* My friend, Mr. Brayley, wrote the prologue for the opening of this theatre. Besides Mr. Hughes and myself, the proprietors and performers at this house comprised Mr. Young, Mr. Noble, Mr. Farren, Mrs. Lichfield, Mrs. Baster, and Miss Simms; all of whom afterwards became eminent in the annals of the Drama. Anecdotes of some of these are recorded in the Biographies of C. Mathews, F. Reynolds, T. Dibdin, &c.

tors' dismay, but to the amusement of the audience. On another night, Mr. Parker made his first and last appearance, to reprove his unmanageable pupil, and command me to quit such pursuits and associations.

It is not surprising that a young man like Hughes, with fascinating manners and superior talents, should disrelish legal studies, and give little satisfaction to his father, who was a strict disciplinarian, or to his patron, Mr. Parker, who was a conscientious and honourable man. The pupil, therefore, forsook the law, and, through the influence of his parent, was appointed to an official post in the West Indies, where he married a rich widow. Henceforward I lost sight of a young man who, like Charles Surface in the *School for Scandal*, possessed powers and abilities qualifying him to win fame in the annals of his country; but who was wrecked for want of ballast, and became lost to the world, by allowing the promptings of his heart and imagination to govern those of a cultivated and intellectual head. Mr. Hughes was in the habit of writing songs, prologues, &c., for Mathews, when the latter was in the Swansea company of comedians, and is mentioned in the Memoirs of that extraordinary actor and mimic, by his widow. I find amongst my collections, songs, poems, and essays by my friend, manifesting much fancy, and promptitude of wit. On the Bank stopping cash payments February 27, 1797, he exclaimed on reading the news—

" Our country for greatness will ever be quoted,
For tho' we want cash we are sure to be *noted*."

Though I had co-operated with my really estimable friend in "sowing wild oats" in the fertile fields of oratory, at Coachmakers' Hall, and in dramatic personations at the Shaksperian Theatre, I was unable to take a prominent part in either of those places. " My poverty, though not my will," restrained me; but I endeavoured to make myself useful as a sort of honorary member of both societies, by prompting, and filling up occasional gaps in scenes. About the same time, I was a regular member of the Spouting Club at Jacob's Wells, where I actually became one of the leading stars, from selecting and reciting certain comic tales, prologues, and characters, written by Peter Pindar, George Colman the younger, Collins, O'Keefe, and other comic authors. These always amused, and were often received with vociferous and clamorous applause. At the " School of Eloquence," in Old Change, Cheapside, I was also a regular member, by contributing a small weekly payment towards the rent of the room. This club was of inferior grade to that at Coachmakers' Hall; but it had amongst its supporters some good as well as many very poor speakers. However, it afforded rational amusement to a mixed audience, which assembled once a week, and useful practice and instruction to young men who aspired to the honours of Demosthenes or Cicero. My old friend *Mr. R. A. Davenport,*\* who has, since that time, written a vast number of volumes on poetry, history, and biography, threatened the members of the " School of Eloquence " with a satirical exposé of their oratorical proceedings, and gave the following lines, as the motto of his Philippic :

> " *Shade of Demosthenes!* † could'st thou but view,
> This ranting, blundering, language-murdering crew,
> Much should I wonder if, in furious ire,
> Thou did'st not kick them to their sooty sire."

This announcement provoked the anger of many members, and the fear of others; but the author continued undaunted in his opposition to the society, which soon broke up.

---

\* Amongst the professional authors of my time, I cannot name one who has written more extensively, on a greater variety of subjects, or with more earnest and honest devotion to the integrity of his duties, than the gentleman here named. For Whittingham's edition of the " British Poets," in 100 volumes, he wrote all the biographical and critical prefaces; and also edited the whole work. In Rivington's " Annual Register," for the years 1792 to 1797, he wrote large portions of the history, biography, geography, and criticism. He is the author of "A History of Greece, from the Death of Agesilaus to that of Alexander," in 3 vols.; " A History of the Bastile," for the *Family Library*, 1 vol.; and a new edition of Guthrie's " Geographical Grammar," published by Tegg, and printed in the smallest type. For the same publisher he wrote " Lives of Individuals who raised themselves from Poverty to Eminence or Fortune," 1 vol. 18mo. 1841; a " Life of Ali Pasha;" a " Biographical Dictionary," 1 vol. 8vo.; and " Narratives of Peril and Suffering," 2 vols. As editor of more than 100 volumes of miscellaneous works (among which is the "Poetical Register," in 9 vols., containing contributions from eminent poets, and numerous pieces, original and translated, from his own pen) he has written innumerable articles on biography, poetry, criticism, and other subjects. Many translations of popular works are from his pen; and he has now two or three volumes of manuscripts prepared for the press. Yet this laborious, critical, and acute author is scarcely known to the public, nor even to the Literati of the present time. A devoted student and lover of books, he has lived in the midst of those fascinating companions, and has neglected to cultivate an intimacy with the active world, which owes him much.

† The speakers were in the frequent habit of invoking the " Shade of Demosthenes."

Debating Societies were prevalent and popular in London in the last five years of the eighteenth century, and indeed for some years afterwards. There were many of a similar nature to those attended by my friends Robinson and Hughes, supported by private subscriptions, managed by committees, and frequented by crowded companies, who were admitted by tickets. Political and religious subjects were prohibited in most of these bodies; but the public events of that remarkable era were great and exciting; and other societies were formed in which they were freely and critically discussed. The momentous French Revolution, of 1789, unhinged and disorganized the whole of the civilized world. Every body talked, or wrote, about politics and governments, freedom and slavery, as if those subjects had been the study of his life. Intemperate, passionate, and dogmatic declamation were of course more prevalent than cool and rational argument. Hence angry feelings were often excited, and violent animosities and antagonism provoked. England was divided into two hostile parties,—the Jacobins and Anti-Jacobins; the former rapidly increasing in number and physical force, although the latter possessed great dominion, and often employed it most tyrannically. Under the ministry of Mr. Pitt, aided by the strong party feeling of King George the Third, and a Tory Parliament, the Habeas Corpus Act was suspended, and certain Acts of Parliament, popularly known as "*Gagging Bills*," were passed, in order to curb and punish the powerful advocates of free discussion and republicanism, by suppressing "mob-meetings," by seizing the property and papers of parties suspected of treason and sedition, and by committing such individuals to prison without trial. Hence societies were formed in the metropolis and most of the large towns of the kingdom, and vast numbers of the people enrolled themselves to oppose and harass the Ministry by every possible means. One of these, the "Corresponding Society," gradually but rapidly grew to a great bulk, and presented a powerful and formidable league against the Government. Demonstrations of the extent and unity of these associations were occasionally made in the fields, at White Conduit-House, and Copenhagen House, and by large processions to the Houses of Parliament. In their endeavours to suppress these proceedings, the Government, amongst other means, resorted to a system of employing spies and informers—a class the most infamous and debased of our species, and previously but little known in England: many of the alleged traitors were tried, and subjected to arbitrary and cruel treatment by judges and law-officers; and, although several were acquitted, some were transported, and others executed. Among the most conspicuous of those who were prosecuted, were the distinguished democrats, John Horne Tooke, John Thelwall, Thomas Hardy, William Godwin, and Thomas Holcroft, who were unfairly stigmatized by the Attorney-General as the "acquitted felons."

Many of the public debating societies were formed and governed by speculating and hackneyed orators, who derived pay and profit from admission-fees paid at the doors. Their meetings were held in the city, near Charing Cross, at the east end of the town, and elsewhere. One of the most active and popular of the managers and proprietors of these societies was John Gale Jones, a noted mob-orator, of great fluency of speech, though cautious in his language: he pursued the system as a business for some years. In subsequent pages I shall have occasion to notice two or three of the persons here named, as authors, and in their personal and private capacities.

Participating, as I did, though in an humble sphere, in the political questions and excitements of the times, from the commencement of the French Revolution to the establishment of a general peace, in 1814, I became personally acquainted with many of the public authors and debaters who were then conspicuous personages, and could narrate many anecdotes illustrative of that important epoch. Instead, however, of attempting such a review, I must refer the reader to Lord Brougham's "Historical Sketches of Statesmen who flourished in the time of George III.," 3 vols. 18mo. 1845; Cooke's "History of Party" up to 1832, 3 vols. 8vo.; Long's "France and its Revolutions, a Pictorial History," 1789—1848; "The Life of John Thelwall," by his Widow, 8vo. 1837; "Memoirs of John Horne Tooke," by Alexander Stevens, 2 vols. 8vo. 1813; also to the Memoirs of Pitt, Fox, and Burke; all of which contain much information on the state of Parties, of Government, and of the times.

I have recited upwards of fifty times at the Spouting Club, at private theatres, and in friendly parties, a famous Address by George Colman the younger, called "British Loyalty, or a Squeeze for St. Paul's." This composition, in its origin and application, refers to one of the most memorable events connected with my early London life, namely, the public visit of King George the Third and the Royal Family to St. Paul's Cathedral, on his Majesty's recovery from a state of insanity. The event occurred on the 23rd of April 1789, the anniversary of England's patron saint, and of the birth of that far more estimable human being, Shakspere. I was at the time apprenticed to Mr. Mendham, and witnessed the whole cavalcade from amongst a dense crowd at the south end of the Old Bailey, on Ludgate Hill. I well remember having crept into the front rank amongst the horse-guards, and the peril I experienced from the pressure of the mob behind and from the horses in front; being sometimes forced in between those splendid animals and almost under their feet. Never before nor since has the vast metropolitan cathedral been occupied by such a congregation; never were collected in England such an assembly of royalty, nobility, and gentry, vying with each other in splendour of costume, hilarity of loyal enthusiasm, and unanimity of rejoicing, to hail the re-appearance in public of a popular monarch, and his recovery from a state of frantic derangement. From St. James's to St. Paul's every house-top and every church-roof was covered with spectators; all the windows were filled with people; galleries were erected and crowded, whilst the streets presented a dense throng of human beings collected from all quarters to gaze upon the procession. The whole interior of St. Paul's was fitted up with seats from floor to ceiling, and filled with spectators, amongst whom were at least 6000 charity children. A full account of this unique and extraordinary day's proceedings is given in the *Gentleman's Magazine* for April, 1789. In the following evening the whole of London was illuminated with unusual brilliancy. That the pens of Essayists, Chroniclers, Historians, and Poets should have been employed on such an occasion is not surprising; but whatever may have been the merits of their productions, or of the Poet-Laureate Ode by Thos. Warton, they never excited such reiterated and enthusiastic applauses as did the lines by George Colman, already mentioned. These were written for John Bannister, jun., and spoken by him, in his most effective manner, on the occasion of his benefit at Drury Lane Theatre, on the 30th of the same month. Boisterous applause burst forth at many parts of the address, and particularly at its close. The popular player was encored and was called on to repeat it many succeeding nights. My recitation of it, several years afterwards, with infinitely less experience and powers, was always rapturously received. It gives a graphic description of the humours and perils of a condensed crowd: parts of the address are put in the phraseology of an Irishman, a Scotchman, a Welshman, a Jew, an old man of 92, and a loyal Sailor.

Leaving politics and party, with the conflicting and "much vexed" questions of good and bad governments, of tyranny and freedom, I return to private life, and will endeavour to describe some of those events and scenes with which I became intimately connected. The association already referred to, naturally and imperceptibly led me to read nearly all the dramatic publications of the time, as well as those of the older writers. Partial to comedy and farce, and disposed to the *vis-comica*, I chose for singing and recitation those writings of Peter Pindar, George Colman, jun., George Alexander Stevens, Charles Dibdin, and others which seemed best calculated to amuse mixed and miscellaneous assemblies of persons, who preferred mirth to melancholy, and smiles to sighs. Hence I was generally greeted with plaudits, and my efforts to please were always cheerfully received.

In the winter of 1799, I was engaged by a Mr. Chapman, at three guineas per week, to write, recite and sing for him, at a theatre in Panton Street, Haymarket. That gentleman had assisted De Loutherbourg in preparing and exhibiting his "Eidophusikon," which had proved very effective. The scenes and machinery were purchased by Chapman, to combine with other objects for an evening entertainment. De Loutherbourg was scene painter to Covent Garden Theatre, and is well known by his many fine and interesting easel pictures. Being also a skilful and ingenious machinist, he invented several novelties for the scenic department of the theatre; and for the purpose of displaying his skill and ingenuity, he fitted up a small theatre in the street above-mentioned, and, conferring on it the mysterious name of the "Eidophusikon," he exhibited some exquisite paintings of scenery, both stationary and in motion, with the varied effects of sunshine and gloom; morn, mid-day, and night; thunder, lightning, rain, hail, and snow. My old friend

W. H. Pyne, has preserved a graphic description of this interesting exhibition in his once popular work, "Wine and Walnuts;" a few passages from which will explain the peculiarities of this ingenious and effective theatre.

"This original exhibition delighted and astonished the public and the artists, who visited it in crowds. Sir Joshua Reynolds frequently attended, and strongly recommended it. The stage was little more than six feet wide and about eight feet deep, yet such was the painter's knowledge of effect and scientific arrangement, that the space appeared to recede for many miles; and his horizon seemed as palpably distant from the eye as the extreme termination of the view would appear in nature. A view from *One-Tree Hill, Greenwich Park*, represented on one side Flamstead House, and below, Greenwich Hospital, cut out of pasteboard and painted with architectural correctness. Large groups of trees, with painted views of Greenwich and Deptford, with the metropolis beyond, from Chelsea to Poplar. The intermediate flat space represented the river crowded with shipping, each mass being cut out in pasteboard, and receding in size by the perspective of their distance. A heathy foreground was represented by miniature models, in cork;—the whole shown at morning-twilight, and under the effect of gradual daybreak, increasing to broad sunshine. The clouds in every scene had a natural motion, and they were painted in semi-transparent colours, so that they not only received light in front, but, by a greater intensity of the Argand lamps employed, were susceptible of being illuminated from behind. The linen on which they were painted was stretched on frames of twenty times the surface of the stage, which rose diagonally by a winding machine. De Loutherbourg excelled in representing the phenomena of clouds. The lamps were above the scene and hidden from the audience,—a far better plan than the *foot-lights* of a theatre. Before the line of brilliant lamps on the stage of the Eidophusikon were slips of stained glass—yellow, red, green, purple, and blue; thereby representing different times of the day, and giving a hue of cheerfulness, sublimity, or gloom, to the various scenes.

"*A Storm at Sea*, with the *Loss of the Halsewell Indiaman*, was awful and astonishing; for the conflict of the raging elements was represented with all the characteristic horrors of wind, hail, thunder, lightning, and the roaring of the waves: with such a marvellous imitation of nature that mariners have declared, whilst viewing the scene, that it seemed a reality.

"Gainsborough was so delighted with the exhibition, that he could talk of nothing else; and passed many evenings in witnessing it. De Loutherbourg tried many plans of imitating the firing of a signal of distress at sea, without success. At length he had a large piece of parchment fastened to a circular frame, forming a vast tambourine; to this was attached a compact sponge that went upon a whalebone spring, and could be regulated to produce an apparently near or distant sound, with extraordinary effect. Thunder and lightning were also marvellously imitated—the former by shaking a suspended sheet of thin copper.

"The waves of the sea were carved in soft wood, from models made in clay: they were coloured with great skill, and, being highly varnished, reflected the lightning. Each turned on its own axis towards the other in a contrary direction, throwing up the foam, now at one spot, now at another, and, diminishing in altitude as they receded in distance, were subdued by corresponding tints. One machine, of simple construction, turned the whole, and the motion was regulated according to the progress of the storm. The vessels went over the waves with a natural undulation; their sizes and motion being proportioned to their apparent distances and bulk: they were all correctly rigged, and carried only such sail as their situation would demand. The rush of the waves, loud gusts of wind, rain and hail, were imitated to perfection by mechanical means. One of the most interesting scenes was an *Italian Sea-Port*, with a calm sea. Here also shipping were seen in motion, and the rising of the moon contrasted admirably with the red light of a lofty lighthouse. The clouds were admirably painted, and, as they rolled on, the moon tinged their edges. The most impressive scene was *Satan and the Fallen Angels in the Fiery Lake*, and the rising of the *Palace of Pandemonium*. Between mountains ignited from base to summit with many-coloured flame, rose a mass which gradually assumed the form of a vast temple, seemingly composed of unconsuming and unquenchable fire: by coloured glasses, the light changed from sulphureous blue to a lurid red, or a livid light, and ultimately to a combination such as a furnace exhibits in fusing metals. To peals of thunder and all the other noises of his hollow machinery, Loutherbourg here added sounds produced by an expert assistant, who swept his thumb over the surface of the tambourine, producing groans which might easily be imagined to issue from infernal spirits."

Though the exhibition thus described was truly fascinating, and always gratified the audiences assembled, the latter were not sufficiently numerous to remunerate the skilful artist; and he sold the property to Mr. Chapman, whose wife was an actress of repute at Covent Garden Theatre. He added to the scenery, and introduced three or four other objects calculated to amuse the auditors. A learned Dog, Musical Glasses, and my Monologue, were among the heterogeneous parts of this divertisement. On the first night of my appearance, my courage and vanity were not a little damped and daunted, by a vehement volley of hisses and groans from one of the boxes, which I found proceeded from a noted *roué* Lord, who was in the habit of frequenting the minor theatres, for the express purpose of annoying performers and disturbing audiences, by vulgar and disgusting conduct. Mr. Chapman's theatre, with its contents, was consumed by fire in March, 1800.

These pursuits induced me to court the acquaintance of any person who belonged to the actor's profession. To appear on the regular stage was the height of my ambition; and to attain the recognition of the eminent professors of the "histrionic art," as Mr. Kemble pompously phrased it, was, in my estimation, the climax and fruition of hope.

From the vicinity of my lodgings, in Rosamond Street, to Sadler's Wells, I became familiar with some of the minor performers at that theatre, and even with its stage-manager, *Mark Lonsdale.* He was author of most of the burlettas, pantomimes, and songs, brought forward at that popular establishment. Amongst the last, "Abraham Newland" and "The Chapter of Kings" were received with especial favour.*

---

* The first soon became one of the most noted songs of the age. Abraham Newland had been Cashier of the Bank of England for many years, whence his name was prominent in all the bank notes. At that time forgeries were frequent, and many ingenious plans and designs were proposed to prevent them. Cash payments and the banking system were often before Parliament and the country. Hence some lines of the song were very apposite and pertinent. The following will indicate its character:

"There ne'er was a name so bandied by fame,
    Through air, through ocean, and through land,
As one that is wrote upon every bank note—
    That name it is Abraham Newland.
    Oh! rare Abraham Newland!
    Most famous Abraham Newland!
Search the world round, not a name can be found
    To surpass that of Abraham Newland."

"I've heard people say that 'sham Abraham' you may:
    But you must'nt sham Abraham Newland."

I never heard the amount of money Lonsdale received for the sale of this song, but conclude that, as it was even more popular than its contemporary, the "Tight Little Island," by T. Dibdin, it must have produced a good round sum to its author and publisher, or to both. Dibdin tells us that he sold the copyright of his song for fifteen guineas, to Longman & Co., Music-sellers, of Cheapside, who, as they declared to the author, derived a profit of nine hundred pounds from its sale.—(*T. Dibdin's Reminiscences*, Vol. i. 208.)

A memoir of "the clever, eccentric, and good-hearted MARK LONSDALE," as T. Dibdin calls him, would have proved an interesting piece of biography, had it been written immediately after his decease, or rather by himself, for he was truly a legitimate son of Genius; and, like too many of that family, was subjected to worldly vicissitudes and trials. He was a native of Carlisle, and early instructed as a designer for calico-printing, which initiated him in a knowledge of art and chemistry. Becoming acquainted with an itinerant scene-painter, he had ready access to the theatre and its interior arcana, and was induced, like myself, to commence his literary career by writing comments on the players and plays for one of the provincial journals. Introduced to the Duke of Norfolk, that nobleman gave him a letter to Mr. Kemble of Drury Lane Theatre, where his juvenile farce of "The Spanish Rivals" was produced. As manager of,

On one occasion Lonsdale invited me to dine with him at the "Sir Hugh Myddelton" (where he resided) opposite the theatre. "Tom" Dibdin and his wife, "Nance," as he called her, Joe Grimaldi, then in his teens, Dighton,* the miniature painter and caricaturist, of Charing-Cross, and other theatrical persons were present. This was my "first appearance" in the character of visitor to a stage manager, and I was not a little flattered and elated by the scene and company. Dibdin and his wife were charged with fun and *pun*, and they became famed in after life for conversational and social bye-play, which it was asserted

---

and principal author for Sadler's Wells, he gained and saved money; two-thirds of which he applied to pay off a mortgage on a family estate for the purpose of providing for certain relatives. He afterwards took the Lyceum Theatre, where he speculated on a new species of entertainment, in the hopes of realizing some little property; but was not successful. On the publication of Denon's splendid work on the Antiquities, &c. of Egypt, Lonsdale employed some of the best scene-painters to make a series of pictures from the most interesting prints. These were so adapted and applied as to produce a moving panorama for the stage, and I was engaged to write and read a short description of each successive object as it was shewn to the audience. The whole made a pleasing and rational exhibition, but was not sufficiently attractive to draw remunerating houses; indeed the unfortunate adventurer was unable to pay his creditors. Before the theatre closed I joined three friends to take a benefit, and we made up an evening's programme of the Egyptiaca, recitations, songs, &c., by which we cleared £31, after paying £10 for the use of the House. This was in the year 1802; and the event is memorable, as the house was lighted by *gas*, being, I believe, the first time that valuable light was employed within the walls of a theatre. Poor Lonsdale soon afterwards went to Ireland, and engaged as tutor in a gentleman's family, where he remained three years, with a salary too small to enable him to free himself from pecuniary difficulties. This consideration preyed on his mind, as shewn in doleful letters which he wrote to his friend, Dibdin. The latter, however, commenced a subscription, and prevailed on many of his dramatic associates to join him in a generous endeavour to "raise the wind," and enable Lonsdale to visit London, and accept an engagement at Covent Garden Theatre. He returned, but with spirits oppressed, for his heart was broken; and he died in the prime of life. In T. Dibdin's "*Reminiscences*" will be found anecdotes and letters of my once much-loved friend, Lonsdale.

* This gentleman was a favourite comic singer, and not only painted miniatures but made many designs for prints, which he published. Some of these were full-length portraits of eminent persons, similar in style and manner to those of a more recent time by the popular artist adopting the signature of H. B. One of Dighton's prints, which became very common, was a sort of Map of the Island of Great Britain, with markings on the surface, indicating the figure of a witch seated on the back of a large fish.

they were in the habit of studying at home, as they did the language of the characters they had to perform upon the public stage.*

At this dinner party I felt an exhilaration and enjoyment surpassing anything I had ever known before; for the writings and performances of my companions had not only afforded me frequent gratification, but they were praised, admired, and applauded by professional critics, and by crowded audiences. They were "the observed of all observers" within the orbit of my world. Fun, frolic, and humour were the order of the evening, and each vied with the others in performing his part with animation. On entering the dining-room Lonsdale said, "Now, ladies and gentlemen, be seated; I mean to show you *a-bun-dance* on the table to-night: but, Mrs. Barker, (to the landlady) you must let us

---

* Edward Du Bois, who was editor of the *Monthly Mirror* for many years, wrote a witty, satirical essay for that periodical (New Series, Vol. ii.) in which Mr. and Mrs. T. Dibdin are represented as keeping up a preconcerted dialogue, abounding in ready-made puns. He entitles it, "Every Man his own Punster, or Puns for all Persons and Seasons." For Sunday, he says,—"This is a day of rest for all things but women's tongues and puns: they have none. You go to church, of course, to set a good example to your family: but let *them* attend to the parson; you may be preparing puns against dinner-time, when you expect a party. The man of the house is nothing without his wife: she is your help-mate. Connive together, and let her put *leading questions*. Half an hour before dinner, company come. All very stupid, as usual. Mrs. D. observes, she fears the dinner will be rather late, as she was obliged to take *Adam*, the footman, to the park on account of the children. The husband remarks, that Adam may be the *first* of men, but he is *a dam* slow fellow. *Mrs. D.* My dear Tom, you deserve a *Cane* for that. *Mr. D.* Aye, if you were *Able* to give it me, who am a *host* to-day. Perhaps you were on the *Eve* of saying this: well, there's as much chance in these things as in a *Pair-o'-dice*. (A general laugh.) Here you end this excellent subject. N.B. Hire no man unless his name is Adam, or he will suffer you to call him so. You must not be very squeamish about delicacy. A few broad inuendoes always tell well: he who digs for diamonds must put up with a little dirt. Here Mrs. D. may say, My dear Tom, I wish the man would bring up the dinner. *Mr. D. Bring up* the dinner, my love? Heaven forbid! As we say in Latin, that's *sic-sic, so-so*. (Adam enters.) *Mrs. D.* Is dinner ready? *Mr. D.* (looking round.) The *chops* are, I'm sure. *Adam.* It's dishing now, Ma'am. (A crash is heard below.) *Mr. D. Dishing*, indeed; I fear it's *dished*. (All seated.) *Mrs. D.* Will anybody take soup? *Mr. D.* What! before grace, you *graceless* rogues. There's no parson I see, though we are not without some of *the cloth*. Well, I'll say it: *grace* at dinner is *meet*. (An universal laugh. The sight of dinner is a breeder of good humour.)" &c. &c.

Of my old friend Mr. Du Bois, with whom I continued on terms of friendship for half a century, I shall have occasion to speak again hereafter.

have candles; for good *livers* should have good *lights*." Dibdin, on looking at the young clown, remarked, "Well, Joe, as you have been *Grim-all-day*, we expect you to be *all fun* to-night." Upon which his gay and loquacious wife retorted, "Tom, Tom, attend to the good things you hear, and be thankful for them, as well as for the good things you take into your mouth, for nothing good ever came out of it yet." "This is the only *sauce*," said Dibdin, "my wife treats me with at my homely dinners." Theatrical anecdotes and adventures, mimicry and songs, with a hearty disposition to enjoy the festivities of the table, combined to make time pass with steam-engine-like velocity; and I often longed to participate in the repetition of a similar piece.

SADLER'S WELLS, at the end of the last century and beginning of the present, was truly a suburban theatre, being surrounded by fields. The New River-head, its engine-house and office; the tavern called the Sir Hugh Myddelton, and Islington Spa, formed a group in conjunction with the theatre. There were not any public lamps, and men and boys, with flambeaus, were in attendance on dark nights, to light persons across the fields to the nearest streets of Islington, Clerkenwell, and Gray's Inn Lane. Though not to be compared in number with the cavalcades crossing the Arabian deserts, the parties on these occasions collected in groups both for company and protection. I have seen ten or twelve, with two or three linkmen, thus traverse the fields from the Wells towards Queen Square, &c. At that time the theatre was a house of much repute, and was consequently a profitable concern to its proprietors. These were Mr. Siddons, husband of the justly-famed actress, who was then at the height of her fame; and Mr. Hughes, who occupied the house attached to the Wells, and possessed two or more theatres in the West of England. One of his daughters married Joseph Grimaldi, the most celebrated of English clowns; and his eldest son, Richard, joined the firm of Lackington, Allen, and Co., of the Temple of the Muses, Finsbury Square, and bought a share in Vauxhall Gardens. This connection was the origin of a novelty at the Wells Theatre, of presenting to each of the box visitors a pint of wine. Another novelty and means of attraction was the introduction of a large body of water, from the New River, to a tank beneath the floor of the stage.

This floor being taken up, a broad sheet of water was displayed to the audience, and rendered very effective in naval spectacles, pantomimes, and burlettas, which were written and adapted to exhibit aquatic scenes. Among the apparently perilous and appalling incidents thus exhibited, was that of a heroine falling from rocks into the water, and rescued by her hero-lover; a naval battle, with sailors escaping by plunging into the sea from a vessel on fire; a child thrown into the water by a nurse, who was bribed to drown it, but rescued by a Newfoundland dog. This water spectacle, with the vinous gift, continued to attract full audiences for three or four successive seasons. At that time Lonsdale's continued and unwearied exertions in producing novelties, combined with liberality in the proprietors, and by players of varied and attractive powers, gave popularity to the theatre. Changes, however, came over the scene: Mr. Siddons died, new proprietors embarked in the Wells, Mr. Lonsdale was engaged at Covent Garden, and Thomas and Charles Dibdin successively purchased shares in the theatre. Grimaldi, from boyhood to mature age, continued "a star" in this theatrical firmament; whilst Richer, a rope-dancer of distinguished excellence and graceful figure, was much admired; Dubois, Dighton, Belzoni, Mrs. Wybrow, and many other performers of varied merit, combined to give eclat to the house. It may be observed that this and the other summer theatres of London, excepting the Haymarket, were prohibited from performing plays with regular dialogue, by the law which governed the two great patent theatres. Hence, Pantomimes, Burlettas with dumb action, Melo-dramas (in which dialogue, in doggrel rhyme, with vocal accompaniments were allowed), singing, dancing, the tight and the slack rope, &c., made up the routine of the nightly amusements.

Amongst the public persons I became more especially acquainted with at Sadler's Wells, were the brothers Charles and Thomas Dibdin, Belzoni, and Richer, besides Grimaldi and Dighton whom I have already mentioned. With the two Dibdins I continued on intimate terms till their respective deaths separated us. Both were the offspring of CHARLES DIBDIN, author of the most popular naval songs in the English language, by a Mrs. Pitt, with whom he associated some years. He married Miss Ann Wyld, aged 16, who survived him, and who, in conjunction with their daughter, (Mrs. Dacre, now living,) raised a tomb to his memory in a cemetery of St. Martin's in the Fields, London, within the parish of St. Pancras. He died July 25th, 1814, aged 69, and his wife in 1835, aged 78.*

That he was a loving husband is evinced by the many songs dedicated to his wife. In ringing the changes on Ann, Anna, Nan, and Nancy, he indited and composed a variety of pleasing lyrics, which were long fashionable and admired, not only in the drawing-room and at convivial boards, but among all classes of society. His numerous songs in praise of the prowess and courage of British sailors, were especially popular amongst the "hardy tars" during the war with France; and indeed their number and variety are scarcely inferior to their intrinsic poetical and musical merits. There is not on record any instance of an author and performer enjoying an equal amount of public patronage and applause for such a lengthened period.

Some of his songs were sold by thousands, and consequently produced immense profits: but though he derived a large annual income from his publications and performances, he was so bad a manager of his domestic affairs that he was often in pecuniary difficulties. For some time he derived a pension of £200 a year from the government, as a compliment to his real talents, and for the loyalty of his songs. As an instance of his indiscretion, his son Charles told me, that on one occasion he spent his only guinea to purchase a Sunday dinner and dessert, the latter of which cost half the sum. His history is replete with romance. He was the eighteenth child of a parent, who was fifty years old when he was born. His eldest brother, Thomas, was then twenty-nine, and was the theme of the pathetic ballad "Tom Bowling." † At the

---

\* Mrs. Dacre is preparing for publication "The Life of Charles Dibdin, Esq., our National Bard and Lyrical Composer, with Anecdotes of Contemporaries, and Extracts from his Manuscripts, &c."

† The Rev. Thos. Frognall Dibdin, son of Thomas the sailor, was an eminent bibliomaniac and author, but a disreputable man, whose memoirs and conduct should occasionally be held up to the young and heedless scions of our universities, as beacons to warn them of the rocks and shoals in the ocean of human life. A complete biography of this once courted and very popular preacher, (the author of "Bibliomania," and many other literary works,) would be a romantic and valuable warning to young enthusiasts. His own "Reminiscences," (2 vols. 8vo. 1836) is a most entertaining work, detailing the leading events of his literary career up to that time, but painting only the bright lights of the picture; whereas the shadows, which marked its close, and were entirely omitted in the published narrative, were of the darkest and most heartless kind.

early age of sixteen, Dibdin wrote and composed an opera for Covent Garden Theatre, called *The Shepherd's Artifice.* A few years afterwards he produced the celebrated farce of *The Padlock,* and played Mungo, one of its characters. Soon after the age of thirty, he became musical manager of Covent Garden Theatre, at a weekly salary of ten pounds, and for some time he continued to derive a handsome income from the theatres. In 1788 he published a quarto volume, entitled *"A Musical Tour,"* and the next year commenced that series of monologue entertainments, which he continued to repeat during many successive seasons: first, at an auction-room in King Street, Covent Garden; next, near Exeter Change; and lastly, in a theatre, called the "Sans Souci," which he had built in Leicester Street, Leicester Square. At this rational, amusing, and instructive school of song and music, I spent many pleasant evenings between 1796, when the theatre was built, and 1810, about which time the proprietor withdrew into retirement. In the "Penny Cyclopædia" is a brief memoir of this once eminent song writer, concluding thus: "Had Dibdin written merely to amuse, his reputation would have been great, but it stands the higher because he is always on the side of virtue. Humanity, constancy, love of country, and courage, are the subjects of his song, and the themes of his praise."

I may also avail myself of the following remarks and opinions, which my once dear friend, Henry Neele, has recorded in his admirable *Lectures on English Poetry.*

"The value of a *Song* is a proverbial saying to express something utterly worthless; and yet it is scarcely too much to assert, that the characters of nations have been moulded and fixed by their songs and ballads, which have not unfrequently been found to be instruments of incalculable power. 'Give me,' said a great statesman, 'the making of the national ballads, and I care not who makes the laws.' History presents us with many proofs of the truth and wisdom of this remark. A minstrel, who accompanied William the Conqueror to the invasion of England, by rushing into the enemy's ranks chanting the song of Rollo, led on his countrymen to the victory of Hastings. To cite instances of a more modern date, the *Marseillaise Hymn* shook the Bourbons from their throne; and *Dibdin's* unrivalled naval songs were instrumental in quelling the mutiny at the Nore."

Such were the just and pertinent remarks of a most amiable man, a discriminating critic, and a poet of true genius. His *Lectures on Poetry* are replete with sound sense, apposite and judicious commentary, and a fine appreciation of the characteristics of our national poetry. I know not finer specimens of English prose than Neele's "Lectures."

H. Meyer. Pinx.t          H. Meyer. Sculp.t

London, Published in Britton's Autobiography, 1849.

The fates and writings of THE THREE DIBDINS may be cited as evidences of the fleeting and short-lived existence of fame. Their literary works, though voluminous, and for a period very popular, are scarcely known to the present age of readers; their songs and music rarely heard, whilst our national biographies either wholly omit their names, or pass them over with a few lines. In the zenith of prosperity their company was courted by men of wealth and worth; their writings were read and heard, not only throughout the extent of this empire but in many others; whilst they lived and moved in a sphere of respectability. Like too many others of the literary profession, they were ill-versed in the science of domestic economy, or the art of saving money. Though good stage-managers, they were bad managers of their own finances. The elder, however, was comforted and supported by a government annuity in his last days; whilst his sons were reduced to sad and lamentable poverty. Both Thomas and Charles were, late in life, so far distressed in circumstances, as to require and solicit pecuniary aid from the LITERARY FUND,* which, in its usual manner, granted at different times, between

---

* Having been an active and zealous member of this useful and valuable society for more than thirty-seven years, I can confidently and conscientiously vouch for its numerous beneficial effects. Few societies have had their origin in events more remarkable than this, whose early history exhibits a striking proof of the results which may be accomplished by the persevering energy of one mind, devoted to the attainment of its object. As early as the year 1773, Mr. David Williams, a native of Cardigan, who, early in life became the tutor of the present Lord Sudeley and Mr. Hanbury Leigh, conceived the idea of a fund for the relief of literary persons, and proposed it to a club of men of letters over which the celebrated Benjamin Franklin presided. The latter thought that a charity founded for such a purpose would be too exclusive and refined in its character to obtain the patronage of the public; and Mr. Pitt, Mr. Fox, Mr. Burke, and Sir Joseph Banks, who were afterwards consulted, treated the idea as a quixotic speculation impossible to be realized. Mr. Williams, however, persevered, and in 1790 succeeded in obtaining a sufficient number of friends to establish the institution, and commence the distribution of its bounty. Founded in this way for the express purpose of affording pecuniary relief to authors in times of distress, it has gradually acquired public confidence and respect, whilst its funds have been both well husbanded and well administered. Though, for some years after its commencement by the humane and philosophic founder, the society was small and weak, it gradually acquired strength and public patronage, and it can now boast of a funded stock of nearly £30,000, besides land and house property; a large portion of which was bequeathed to it by Mr. Thomas Newton, who, believing himself to be the last representative of Sir Isaac Newton, made the

the years 1824 and 1838, to the former the sum of £195, and to his widow £30. In about the same period, Charles had been favoured with £111, by the same noble institution. Though these donations may appear small to gentlemen who had lived and moved in what is called the genteel world, they afforded much temporary relief and comfort to their recipients; and I am assured that they were gratefully appreciated by both parties. I knew them in prosperity and in adversity—in the times of their greatest popularity and good fortune—and when reduced to the pitiable and mortifying condition of craving pecuniary boons from former convivial companions, and from the haughty rich.

Both Charles and Thomas Dibdin had been apprenticed to London citizens; the former to a pawnbroker, on Snow-hill, the latter to an upholsterer. Each manifested, in boyhood, greater love for poetry and the drama, than for the shop and business: they neglected the latter and cultivated the former, whence they imbued their minds with ro-

---

society his heir. At the present time, it distributes from £1000 to £1500 a year in benefactions to distressed authors, their widows, and orphans. Amongst the first recipients and partakers of the cheering aid it dispenses, was Mr. Williams himself, who found a home in its first house in Gerrard Street, and derived support, in old age, from the funds, for a few years previous to his decease. Sir Benjamin Hobhouse was then, and for some time afterwards, the bland and excellent chairman of the committees, and always invited Mr. Williams to attend their meetings. It was at once painful and pleasing to witness the superannuated old gentleman on these occasions. Almost "the slippered pantaloon," he was wheeled into the committee-room, where he seemed to revive from a semi-lethargy, and look around and listen to the reading of cases, and to the opinions of the members of the committee on the varied claims and miseries of applicants. At all times the amiable chairman kindly appealed to the founder for his opinion, who never differed from that expressed or implied by the former. Distressing as it was to see the last stage of poor human nature thus struggling with death, and waning away, it was gratifying to know that he had all his physical wants supplied, with a good home, and the most watchful attentions. Mr. Williams died at the house of the society, June 29, 1816, aged 78, and his remains were interred in the cemetery of St. Ann's, Soho.

The Prince of Wales had paid the annual rent of the house, and had patronized the society in order to serve its founder. After Mr. Williams's decease the committee took chambers in Lincoln's Inn Fields, and at the present time the society has apartments in Great Russell Street, in the house formerly occupied by Sir Sidney Smith. The charter by which it was incorporated was obtained in 1818, and from that time the society has gradually advanced in funds and influence. Its annals are replete with events and anecdotes illustrative of the vicissitudes of authors, and the precariousness of the literary profession, as well as the practice and management of London Charitable Societies,

mantic notions of the honours and riches which fell to the lot of successful poets and play-writers. The consequences were natural. Charles wrote and published some crude and puerile poems in his teens, and Thomas abruptly left his master to become a strolling player. In his "Reminiscences," 2 vols. 8vo. 1827, he has told his own eventful, "many-coloured" tale with candour, and honest sincerity of motive and of language, and in a style of pleasantry and playfulness eminently calculated to amuse and interest the reader. The work, indeed, contains much information relating to the annals of the stage—to the vicissitudes of a player's as well as an author's life—to the fluctuating and hazardous property of theatres, and the characters of several patrons and proprietors of such property. THOMAS DIBDIN was author of many other literary works; amongst which is "A Metrical History of England," 2 vols. 8vo. 1813—a work of considerable ingenuity and even merit, though it never attained popularity. By a summary account of his literary publications, at the end of the second volume of his "Reminiscences," it appears that he was author of eight comedies, twenty-six operas, fifteen farces, thirty-two melo-dramas, thirty-five comic panto-

---

the dispositions and influence of active persons on committees, the value of some officers and worthlessness of others, and more particularly the personal characters and pecuniary reverses of the parties who have been benefited by this most praiseworthy institution. Unlike the generality of other humane societies in this affluent and benevolent city, which generally make a public display of the objects of their charity, the principle and practice of our fund has been to administer its donations with the most delicate attention to the feelings and pride of the literary character. Many instances have formerly occurred where a suffering author has received donations without personal application, or any intimation of such a "God-send" till he received the cash. I mention this from experience, as it has been my pleasing duty, on three especial occasions, to be the medium of communication between the committee and authors, and then witnessed the mingled feelings of pride and poverty, with the conflicting struggles which agitated the distressed parties.

Besides the annual Reports published by the society, I would refer the reader to a volume entitled "Claims of Literature," 8vo. 1802, which was written and compiled by Mr. D. Williams; also to a scarce tract, entitled "A General View of the Life and Writings of the Rev. D. Williams, drawn up for the 'Chronique des Mois,' a French periodical publication, at the request of Condorset, Claviere, Mercier, Auger, Brissot, Editors of that work. By Thomas Morris, Esq.; to which the publisher hath added the first literary production of Mr. Williams." (8vo. 1792.) This is an interesting and vivid sketch of the life, character, and talents of a most worthy and estimable man.

mimes, and thirty burlettas; besides songs, essays, tales, biographies, &c. &c. "Of nearly 200 theatrical productions," he says, "ten were failures, and not acted above four or five times each on an average; sixteen were honoured with extraordinary success, and produced very great profits to Covent Garden, Drury Lane, the Haymarket, the English Opera, and three of the minor theatres; the remainder were all well received, and answered my purpose and the expectations of those who employed me. Nearly fifty of the pieces are published; and my reason for not having printed the remainder is, that I never, but in two instances, would publish on my own account." In another part of his "Reminiscences" he states, that he wrote more than 2000 Songs, Prologues, Epilogues, &c. His last production was an octavo volume, under the title of "Lays of the Last of the Dibdins," which he published a short time before his decease, chiefly with a view of "raising the wind," as Kenny expresses it, by its sale amongst friends, &c. He concludes his own "Reminiscences" by saying, "mine, in spite of good intentions, has been a very chequered and not a very fortunate life."

Of CHARLES DIBDIN, Jun., I had opportunities of knowing many personal characteristics and literary qualifications, for we were on familiar, confidential terms for many years. As a friend, a parent, a husband, and an honourable and honest man, his conduct and character were exemplary and unimpeachable. As manager of Sadler's Wells Theatre, and author of numerous dramatic pieces for several successive years, he was industrious and successful. With a good domestic wife, whom he married in her teens, and with a large family, he lived for many years in a small detached cottage, within the precincts of the theatre, and was apparently comfortably settled for life, when his brother embarked in the hazardous and ruinous speculation of renting the Surrey Theatre. This led to other speculations, one of which was to take his dramatic company, with some of the Wells performers, to Dublin. In this undertaking the two brothers joined, and, as related by Thomas, they struggled for one season against many difficulties, and returned minus nearly £2000. Poor Charles never recovered from this loss. Soon afterwards he lost his affectionate companion, in the prime of life, who is pronounced by his brother as being "one of the best of wives and mothers."—(*Reminiscences*, ii. 132.) These severe visitations overpowered him, for he was a man of great sensibility, and devotedly attached to his wife and children. A young family of eight now demanded his utmost solicitude, and were most anxiously watched and instructed. They were all well disposed and well disciplined. I never saw a group of boys and girls better conducted, or more cordial with each other, and at the same time obedient and affectionately devoted to their parents. Henceforward, however, he was doomed to encounter misfortunes and troubles, and he died at an early age. He wrote and published four volumes of Poems, a Novel, "Thinks I to Myself," in 3 volumes, besides numerous songs, a volume of which was published by myself in partnership with the author; and afterwards re-published with the title of "Mirth and Metre, consisting of Poems, Serious, Humourous, and Satirical." 18mo. 1809.

Of JOSEPH (familiarly called "Joe") GRIMALDI, the most popular and successful clown that ever belonged to the English stage, "Memoirs" have been published, "edited by Boz." It originally came out in two volumes, but a second edition, in one volume, appeared in 1846. The "Introductory Chapter" is evidently written by the unrivalled author of "Oliver Twist," "Nicholas Nickleby," and numerous other publications of surpassing merit, and of incalculable influence on the minds and feelings of the reading public. The chapter alluded to explains the origin, and part of the execution, of the "Memoirs," which were commenced by the inimitable clown himself, and then submitted to his friend, Mr. Thomas Egerton Wilks, to alter and revise, with a view to publication. Mr. Bentley purchased these materials, but deeming them too copious for the market, placed the manuscript in the hands of Mr. Dickens, (who then, 1838, lived in Doughty Street,) with full liberty to add to, abridge, or alter, at discretion. This task he performed with skill and tact, and produced a book replete with amusement. It not only gives a vivid and faithful descriptive portrait of the remarkable individual, who frequently "set the table in a roar," and convulsed many a crowded theatre with fits of laughter, but abounds with anecdote, adventure, and biographical facts of much variety and excitement. The editor says, "the book is the work of many hands, including the good right hand of GEORGE CRUIKSHANK, which has seldom been better exercised."

In the season of 1807, a remarkable incident, connected with the Wells Theatre and its extraordinary clown, created much notoriety at the time, and cannot fail to astonish even the learned physiologist of this age. A party of Sailors was stationed in the front row of the gallery to witness a pantomime in which Grimaldi performed the clown in his usual effective and grotesque manner. One of these Jack Tars was deaf and dumb, but evidently had not lost the use of his eyes, or his enjoyment of the ludicrous; for in one of Grimaldi's most eccentric scenes, the dumb man exclaimed to his comrades, in an ecstasy of laughter, "What a d—d funny fellow!"—"What, Jack," shouted the sailor at his side, starting back with astonishment—" you speak?" —"Speak," returned the new voice, "aye, and hear too?" This event not only surprised all within hearing, but was soon made known to the whole theatre, and the sailors withdrew to the "Sir Hugh Myddelton," to commemorate the event in goblets of grog. Particulars of this circumstance are detailed in "Memoirs of Joseph Grimaldi," Vol. ii. p. 12, edition 1846.

Amongst human eccentricities and singularities of character, may be mentioned one of an old friend of mine, who, as an author and artist, was accustomed to sedentary habits. James Peller Malcolm, author of "Londinum Redivivum," and other literary works, after sitting all day in the reading-room of the British Museum, or at his house in Somerstown, regularly spent his evenings in the gallery of Sadler's Wells. Purchasing a season ticket, he made it a practice to go *every night* to witness repetitions of the same burlettas, pantomimes, and other performances, by the same performers. In the same theatre, on the same seat, and witnessing the same routine of objects, I often met my plodding friend, whose conversation partook of the same monotonous character as his daily and nightly practice.

A distinguished contemporary of the dramatic corps at the Wells, about this time, was a gentleman who subsequently attained distinction in the annals of adventure and archæology. This was Signor GIOVANNI BATTISTA BELZONI, with whom I became acquainted in 1803. He then appeared under the cognomen of *The Patagonian Sampson,* and displayed muscular powers of strength which greatly astonished the public.

By the books in the Alien Office he is registered as 6 feet 6 inches. His face and the upper moiety of his figure were of fine proportions and symmetry, whilst the lower half was long, but muscular. He was an Italian, and early in life left his home "to seek his fortune." Having studied hydraulics, and invented some ingenious machines, he made an exhibition of them at different places, but they failed to excite sufficient attention to remunerate their contriver; who therefore was induced to visit London, and at Sadler's Wells, as the "Patagonian Sampson," give proofs of his amazing strength. This was displayed in a peculiar way—by affixing an iron frame to his body, weighing about 129 pounds, having steps, or branches, projecting from its sides; on which he placed eleven men, in a pyramidal form, the uppermost of whom reached to the border of the proscenium. With this immense weight he walked round the stage, to the astonishment and delight of his audience. On one occasion, a serio-comic accident occurred, which might have been fatal, not only to the mighty Hercules but to his pyramidal group. As he was walking round the stage, with the vast load attached to his body, the floor gave way, and plunged him and his companions into the water beneath. A group of assistants soon came to their rescue, and the whole party marched to the front of the stage, made their bows, and retired behind the scenes. Profiting by this exhibition of strength, he visited Bartholomew fair, Dublin, and many other places; and, having saved some money, he sailed to Egypt, to explore its pyramids, catacombs, and other antiquities. For this enterprising and hazardous task he was peculiarly qualified: being zealous, courageous, strong, and energetic. An account of his researches and discoveries, (which extended from 1815 to 1819), was published by himself, in quarto, with numerous illustrations, in folio. He also sent to London a large collection of Egyptian antiquities, which he had taken from the catacombs and temples. Some of them were sold to, and deposited in, the British Museum; whilst the most remarkable and most interesting specimen was a large sarcophagus, (or cenotaph, as Sir Gardiner Wilkinson pronounces it,) which was purchased by the late Sir John Soane, and is now preserved in Lincoln's Inn Fields. In a quarto volume, on "*The Union of Architecture, Sculpture, and Painting,*" which I published in 1827, are engraved representations of this unique and truly interesting relic of antiquity, with a particular description of its numerous hieroglyphics. I have tracings of the whole series of engravings on the interior and exterior of this alabaster coffin. Sir John Soane gave £2000 for the remarkable object, and took down part of his museum, to admit it through the walls. After giving some account of this unparalleled relic, I was induced to say, that "Scholars of different empires, and of the most acute faculties, have vainly endeavoured to translate the hieroglyphic language; and though they have apparently made some progress, and have given a meaning and interpretation to some of its figures and combinations, they have hitherto failed to produce any complete and conclusive results. The story of Belzoni,—his lamentable fate, the dispersion and, it is feared, sacrifice of his unrivalled and interesting collection, which was first exhibited at the Egyptian Hall, Piccadilly, and part of it afterwards, by his ill-treated widow, in Leicester Square,—would form a narrative of peculiar interest and pathos; and whilst it would reflect great credit on the dauntless and patriotic spirit of that enterprising and ardent traveller, it would impeach both the moral and political integrity of certain parties with whom he came in contact." The latter part of this paragraph alludes to his connection with Mr. Salt, then English Consul in Egypt, and of Belzoni's representation of that gentleman's treatment in his "Travels;" but we are presented with the Consul's version of the story, in Hall's "Life and Correspondence of Henry Salt," 2 vols. 8vo. 1834. This shows that the Italian giant was employed and paid by the Consul to make researches, and convey antiquities to London, as a profitable speculation. Belzoni, however, considered them to be his own property, particularly the sarcophagus which was bought by Mr. Soane; and these conflicting claims and assumptions led to serious disputes. The Museum hesitated to purchase the important relic under such circumstances, when the architect offered to take it at the sum demanded, but kept the vendors in suspense for many months, to obtain what he considered to be a guarantee of ownership.

Belzoni was born at Padua in 1778, and died at Gato, on his way to Timbuctoo, Dec. 3, 1823. His spirited and intrepid wife accompanied him in Egypt, but was in London at the time of his lamented decease.

A subscription was raised, and an appeal made to Government, in her behalf. Very little was then done for her; and it was reserved for Her present Majesty to confer on Mrs. Belzoni, in the year 1850, an annuity of £100. An autograph letter by Belzoni, when at Cairo, to his brother, was lately sold at Puttick and Simpson's auction-rooms, London, in which he inclosed an order for one hundred dollars, to be expended in purchasing a house and home for his aged mother.*

At the time the preceding brief notice of Belzoni was in proof, an interesting account of his career appeared in Dickens's "Household Words." This narrative places the first appearance of the adventurer in London at Astley's Amphitheatre; but this is certainly inaccurate; for he was first engaged at Sadler's Wells in 1803, when, as already mentioned, I formed his acquaintance. He performed there the whole of the season, and afterwards visited many parts of the united kingdom. The account in the "Household Words" thus closes:—"Belzoni was but forty-five years old when he died. A statue of him was erected at Padua on the 4th of July, 1827. The once starving mountebank became one of the most illustrious men in Europe!—an encouraging example to those, who have not only sound heads to project, but stout hearts to execute."

The elegant, the graceful, the much-admired RICHER, whose figure and feats on the tight rope fascinated many of the female spectators at Sadler's Wells, and in other theatres, was a distinguished *star* in his

---

* The reader will find some interesting anecdotes of Belzoni's early career, in Smith's *Book for a Rainy Day*, p. 174, &c. A full-length portrait of the "*young Hercules,*" as he was called, was engraved by Van Assen, in 1804, and a very good one is published in the *European Magazine*, for Sept. 1822, in which is a Memoir. There was another full-length portrait of him, with his pyramidal group, drawn and etched by himself. "The Life of Mr. Salt," already referred to, contains much interesting information relating to Belzoni's career in Egypt, with commendations of his zeal, skill, and unwearied exertions in exploring and removing many important objects of antiquity from that country to England. It however reproaches him for having arrogated to himself all the credit, and all the property in the antiques which were conveyed and sold to the British Museum, to Sir John Soane, and others; whereas Mr. Salt shows that Belzoni was employed and paid for his time and labours by him. This crimination and recrimination adds another tale of misunderstanding and enmity to the lamentable catalogue given in D'Israeli's "Quarrels of Authors."

hemisphere. Flattered by young, gay, and coquettish females, he became vain and fantastical: as might be reasonably expected in a young man who studied rather to cultivate the agility of the feet, than the faculties of the head. Receiving a handsome salary, he lived in an expensive style, and was profitably engaged, in town and country, for a short period. At length he married a daughter of Mr. Watson, the proprietor of the Cheltenham theatre, with whom he obtained what is usually called a good fortune. On visiting Gloucestershire for the *Beauties of England*, in 1804, I found him living at his ease, and was introduced by him to his father-in-law, and to Miss De Camp, who was then playing one of her most attractive characters in Holcroft's melo-drama, "Deaf and Dumb." Her personation of a youth who had lost the faculties of speech and hearing, was one of the most pathetic and interesting that had perhaps ever been seen on the stage.

Among the performers at Sadler's Wells was DUBOIS, who had acted as clown to the rope-dancers, Master and Miss Richer, and also in pantomimes. He was famous for dancing the egg hornpipe, which he performed with a bandage over his eyes, and a pair of wooden clogs on his feet, skipping over and amongst numerous eggs which were dispersed on the stage, and which the astonished spectators expected to see crushed every moment, by the apparently sightless dancer.

With such associates, whose company I diligently courted, and whose accomplishments I regarded as of the highest order, my time and thoughts were engrossed for some years. Though I longed to be a player, and "strut and fret my hour upon the stage," I fortunately escaped the fascination; more, perhaps, from cowardice than want of inclination, opportunity, or even qualifications for the "buskin." The accounts I had received of the struggles and privations of certain friends who had embarked as "vagabonds," in the "strolling line," alarmed my fears and damped my ambition. Miss Stratton, the only child of one of my village schoolmasters, had joined a provincial company, and gave me repeated accounts of the difficulties, hardships, rebuffs, and intense study, which she and her associates encountered, no less in regular theatres than in barns and outhouses, which were bedizened with painted paper and canvass, to represent the tented field, or the regal palace. In one of my early walking excursions from London, I met with this young lady and her strolling companions at Maidenhead, where they had fitted up a cow-house in the inn yard as a theatre, and where they enacted what the play-bill called " the most famous Tragedy of Macbeth; with the part of Lady Macbeth by a Young Lady, her first appearance in that character." It would be difficult, even for the inventive faculty of Dickens, to describe broader burlesque, or a more lamentable combination of place, scenery, dresses, and performance than were exhibited on that occasion. Instead of feeling, pathos, and horror, the audience were rather inclined to boisterous mirth, at the caricature, the ranting and mouthing, the ludicrous dresses and deportment of some of the performers, and the blunders and mishaps that were perpetually occurring. Witnessing this droll tragedy, both before and behind the scenes, I must own that my theatrical zeal was a little cooled; and the reports I afterwards received by my fair friend from other towns, from Guernsey and from Jersey, induced me to forego all thoughts of resorting to the stage as a profession.

Another of my stage-struck associates, Mr. J. O. CHAMPION, who had left a lawyer's office in Gray's Inn, and enlisted into a corps of theatrical itinerants, furnished me with anecdotes of his own adventures, with those of his associates. Though amusing to read, they did not excite a wish to participate in the pleasures of an actor's life. The following extract from one of Champion's letters (4th July, 1796) gives a vivid picture of the time and of his own hardships:

"In my passage from Portsmouth to Jersey, with 10s. 6d. in my pocket after paying my fare, I was obliged to remain on deck all night, sick, wet, and cold, as the cabin was crowded with passengers. The island is in a state of great consternation, from apprehension of a visit from the French; consequently the manager and all his train are very depressed. We can see the French army, camp, &c. on the opposite coast, and it is said that it consists of 40,000 soldiers. Numbers of flat-bottomed boats are ready. Our boats are pulled to shore, and a placard is posted this morning, offering a reward for the apprehension of Spies. Every male inhabitant is required to be prepared to act in the event of the threatened invasion. The guards are doubled; and a new tower is building in the midst of the bay.—The best French brandy is 6s. per gallon, and wine 15d. a bottle; but provisions, excepting fish, are dear. We have performed a few nights, but to miserable houses. I have been obliged to work hard, but fortunately my memory is good. At two days' notice I had to study the words and enact the two characters of *Wayford* (How to grow rich), and *Lovemore* (Barnaby Brittle.) I have now to prepare, for the night after next, *Villars* (Belle's Stratagem), with a character in the farce. My wardrobe is very scanty, and appetite very craving. I cannot recommend you to seek the actor's vocation; but rather wish you to stick to the lawyer's office, at poor 15s. a week."

A few years afterwards I received a long letter from Champion, dated Antigua, describing, in six different styles and measures of poetry, the incidents of his voyage to, and settlement in, that island. After some vicissitudes, he was engaged as clerk on one of the sugar estates of Mr. Codrington, of Gloucestershire, with a wife, a house, a horse, and servants, and a salary of £190. a year. He tempted me to become a rum merchant, as his agent in London, for the sale of that article; but I feared to embark in the responsibilities of such a speculation. At this time, however, I had no settled views, or certain occupation, but my sanguine temperament and economical habits enabled me to sustain existing privations, and anticipate better fortune.

Amongst PLACES OF PUBLIC AMUSEMENT, at that time, in and near London, besides the winter and summer theatres, were the following:—Ranelagh, and Vauxhall, being first; whilst the Tea Gardens, &c. at Bagnigge Wells, the Dog and Duck, Bermondsey Spa, and White Conduit House, ranked second. All these places were usually crowded to excess, in fine weather, by different classes of the metropolitan population. The first and second were frequented by the higher classes of society and their followers, or imitators, as the entrance-fee was half-a-crown. Singing, by popular male and female artists, was the chief amusement; whilst fireworks were often added, at Ranelagh. The company promenaded round a vast rotunda, and occasionally sought rest and refreshment in private boxes, in different parts of the gardens. Vauxhall was noted for its rural, shady walks, its illuminations, its various amusements, and its very high charges for small and thin sandwiches, and equally poor and dear wines.* Frank Hayman painted

---

* In 1843 I made arrangements to meet my much-loved friend, Thomas Hood, at Richmond, for the purpose of examining *Ham House*, on which occasion and subject he wrote one of his extraordinary poems for No. I. of *Hood's Magazine*. Not able to keep

some effective scenes and figures at the backs of the boxes. These characteristics are humorously described by a city tradesman, in the *Wits' Magazine*, who calculates each mouthful of eatables and drinkables as costing at least 2*d.*, 4*d.* or 6*d.* Vauxhall, however, has outlived all its competitors and compeers, and in spite of the caprices and changes of fashion, has attracted thousands of spectators during the summer of 1851; thus continuing its reign nearly 200 years. In 1661 they were opened under the title of "The New Spring Gardens," as contradistinguished from old Spring Gardens, at Charing Cross, where the name is still preserved in that of a fashionable street. Evelyn, Pepys, Etheridge, Addison, Walpole, and many other distinguished authors have noticed these gardens in their various works. The best account of them will be found in Brayley's *History of Surrey*, Vol. iii., p. 347, and by J. Saunders in Knight's *London*, Vol. i.

The tea-gardens and rooms at Bagnigge Wells, the Dog and Duck, Bermondsey Spa, White Conduit House, &c. were often thronged with company, particularly on Sunday evenings, during the summer, by tradesmen with their families, shopmen, clerks, and females in the same grades of society. These suburban places are all now extinct; the first was in a valley on the banks of the Fleet Brook, between Clerkenwell and the old church of St. Pancras; the second in St. George's Fields, about a mile south of the three bridges, on the site now occupied by the new Bethlehem Hospital; the third in the midst of fields and gardens between London Bridge and Rotherhithe; the fourth in the midst of fields in the parish of Islington. Each had its garden, with trees, flowers, alcoves, &c., for tea and drinking parties, with a large room for dancing, singing, and music. One of these places (the Bermondsey Spa) is entitled to especial notice, for the talents of its founder and proprietor, an artist of note in his day, and from its having been scarcely noticed in the histories of old London. Even Mr. Peter Cunningham

---

his appointment, he thus writes:—"My object in going to *Ham* was to get sketches of some of the trees, &c. by Harvey. By the bye, there must be *a Ghost*, at *Ham House*. Miss Costello once meant to inquire concerning it, and I sent her this,—

"'Never trouble Ham House, or its inmates at all,
 For a ghost, that may be but a sham,
But seek in a sandwich that's cut at Vauxhall,
 For the true *apparition of Ham*.'"

has passed it over unrecorded, in his valuable *Hand-Book of London,* though he tells us that *Bagnigge Wells* "was opened to the public in 1767, in consequence of the discovery of two mineral springs. Nell Gwynne is said to have had a country house near this spot, and her bust was here in 1789." *White Conduit House,* he says, "was once celebrated as a kind of minor Vauxhall, for the Londoners, who went for cakes and cream to Islington and Hornsey. The house was pulled down in January, 1849, to make way for a new street." White Conduit rolls were as noted as the famous Chelsea buns, at the end of the last century. Mr. Mendham, the wine-merchant, in whose cellars I was immured for nearly six years, supplied this house with port wines, which were sold in small bottles. Fourteen of these were reckoned the dozen, and were charged to the tavern at about one shilling and ninepence per bottle.

BERMONDSEY SPA tea-gardens, at the end of the last century, was a place of note, and occasionally attracted large crowds of spectators. Although, like White Conduit House, it was designated a minor Vauxhall, it presented novelties and amusements very dissimilar to any thing displayed at that more fashionable place. Its proprietor, *Thomas Keyse,* a self-taught artist, was evidently a man of genius. He painted many pictures of still-life, which not only surprised and delighted the ordinary spectator, but were even praised by some of the professional critics. The subjects he excelled in were representations of the interiors of butchers' and fishmongers' shops, with deceptive representations of some of the details of each. These were painted with so much verisimilitude that they almost deceived the eye, and consequently created wonderment to the majority of the young and uninformed visitors of the gardens, amongst whom I must candidly include myself. Mr. Keyse obtained a license in 1780, to give musical performances; and amongst other objects of attraction was an excellent representation of the Siege of Gibraltar, produced by paintings, both transparent and opaque, with fireworks. The scene, showing the famed rock fortress, occupied an area of two hundred, by fifty feet, whilst the machinery and other objects covered an area of about four acres of ground. At the time these gardens were in the zenith of their popularity (1800) the ingenious proprietor died. Then, and for some years afterwards, the whole of Bermondsey "was a region of squalor, filth, poverty, vice, and wretchedness." Dickens, in his admirable novel of *Oliver Twist*, has given a vivid, graphic description of this deleterious, appalling locality. Though now covered with houses and streets, it has many stagnant ditches, cess-pools, and undrained places.*

The TEMPLE OF FLORA was a public exhibition, in St. George's Fields, nearly opposite the Surrey theatre, and was not only a novelty, when first opened, but has not since been imitated. It was a large apartment, or covered area at the back of a house, laid out with considerable taste, with parterres of flowers, flowering shrubs, shells, grottoes, and fountains; whilst numerous gold and silver fish, singing birds, &c., added to the attractions of the scene. The whole formed a pleasing lounge for sight-seers and children.

Amongst eccentric persons I became acquainted with in my adolescent, or early career, was CHARLES O'BRIEN, who had published a volume on *Calico Printing*, and another called *The Lusorium*, a miscellany of songs, essays, dramatic scenes, &c., of broad comic humour. I first met him at Sadler's Wells, and we afterwards exchanged visits at each other's lodgings; his being on the first floor and respectably furnished, mine on the second, but scantily stocked. He was employed in making designs for calico printers, by which he could earn three guineas per week, whilst my income amounted only to fifteen shillings. I persevered, and was prudent in expenditure: he was imprudent, and neglected his regular work to make various miscellaneous drawings, write songs, frequent convivial clubs, and speculate on a variety of schemes. One of these was the adaptation of the common magic-lanthorn, to enlarge and diminish the size of objects on the wall, or screen, on which shadows were shewn. On this scheme we worked together for several weeks; painting a variety of pleasing, grotesque, horrible, and scientific objects; wrote accounts of the same, historical, descriptive, and critical, with occasional scenes and relations of the ludicrous, burlesque, and comic kind. We had so far arranged our materials that we calculated

---

* Brayley's *History of Surrey*, 4to. vol. iii. p. 200; and Knight's *London*, vol. iii. p. 24.

upon making an evening's entertainment of our novelty; but besides being doubtful of the consequences of keeping a mixed audience in total darkness for about two hours, we felt a difficulty in securing a theatre, or place in which to exhibit, not having funds or credit. On explaining the necessity of having our auditory in a dark room, our scheme was treated as too visionary and hazardous to prove successful. At this very time Monsieur Phillipstall, from Paris, fitted up a theatre in the Strand for the express purpose of showing the same sort of instrument with its striking effects. We attended the first representation of his *Phantasmagoria*, and, though pleased, were not a little mortified, to see our rival's scheme completely successful. The Frenchman cleared a large sum by his exhibition in London, and afterwards visited several towns in the kingdom. O'Brien was determined to try his own luck in the country, but failed in making money. He became a supernumerary at Sadler's Wells, and had to attend every night at the theatre, and if wanted on an emergency, was paid. Losing his connexion at the calico establishment, he made small drawings of fruit, flowers, shells, &c., and sold them at low prices to the fancy stationers, and thus gained a precarious livelihood. He also wrote philippics against Buonaparte and the French Revolution, which he *etched* on copper-plate, in imitation of manuscript, and printed and sold a few copies; and here again, as in many other speculations, he failed, and was obliged to change his lodgings to a back attic, whilst I descended to the first floor. He was always putting the question to his friends, "Does man govern circumstances, or do circumstances govern man?" He firmly believed the latter, and deemed it useless to struggle against them. Missing my improvident friend for several succeeding days, I at length received a long letter from him, dated "Pevensey Barracks," stating that he had enlisted as a common soldier, was hard worked, and almost starved; had herded with a set of reckless, hardened men and women; was acting like a machine, and was nearly broken-hearted. He lived, however, to return to London, and died in the Whitechapel workhouse.

GEORGE WRIGHT, of Tottenham Court Road, was a harmless, amiable, but odd person, with whom I became intimately acquainted at the end of the last century; and to whose morning lounges I occasionally introduced some of my friends, very much to their amusement. Wright was almost a dwarf, being only 4 feet 6 inches in height (seven inches shorter than myself); had lost his teeth, was very vain, and could gulp down a large draught of panegyric without shrinking. He played on the violin, and certainly produced extraordinary sounds from that expressive instrument, in combination with his own voice. He frequently invited ten or a dozen persons to hear and praise him, for he expected and coveted the latter with boyish avidity. He preceded my friends Mathews and Alexandre, and in many respects equalled either of them in his effects of mere mimicry; but he wanted the personifying and artistic talent of those accomplished performers. Mr. Wright was highly successful in his imitations of the sounds produced by pigs, young and old; sheep, lambs, cows, calves, dogs, cats and kittens, blue-bottle flies, and the various voices of men, women, and children. The following is a copy of a card which he handed to his friendly auditors:

"MUSICAL IMITATIONS, vocal and instrumental: in the Comic Style: performed by G. Wright, Esq." London Cries, in different voices: "Four bunches a penny primroses; Ground ivy; Hot cross-buns; Hot spiced gingerbread; Come, buy my sweet violets; and Past twelve o'clock and a cloudy morning;" accompanied with the violin and organ.—A Laughing Song; in which is introduced an imitation of the sticcato, with a violin accompaniment.—"The Highland Laddie," with a favourite Air from the overture to Oscar and Malvina; the Scotch Union Pipes, imitated on the violin.—The singing of a canary bird, accompanied with the violin. —A Song and Chorus: "Gladly may we our wealth employ; and may our duty be our joy;" with instrumental accompaniments, horns, trumpets, kettle-drums, &c. —The Vauxhall Riot; an original thought. The performer is supposed to be in Vauxhall Gardens: by some neglect of the door-keepers, the doors are left open; a number of sheep run into the gardens, which naturally occasions a confusion among the company. Some pickpockets, taking advantage of the confusion, pick the ladies' pockets; the ladies cry out "Thieves;" the thieves, to increase the confusion, cry out "Fire;" a young woman, having just begun to sing a favourite air, is forced to stop, not being able to be heard on account of the confusion; cries of "Fire," "Thieves," sheep bleating, and dogs barking, are heard for some time, and the whole ends with an instrumental concert.

On other occasions, and particularly on Sundays, Mr. Wright made up an entertainment of Sacred Music, in which he displayed his singular powers of imitation, combining the organ, the violin, &c., with his own voice. Thus he gave " a Cathedral Chant, in different voices, accompanied with the organ; a Chorus, from Handel's *Te Deum;* a Duet, in the voices of a man and a boy; finishing with the Coronation Anthem," as a full chorus, combined with the different instruments.

Among my early club associates was WM. TAPSELL, a young man, who was articled to a solicitor in Gray's Inn, and whose prospects in life were propitious. He was gay, full of animal spirits, and disposed to enjoy the pleasures of every coming day, as well as the convivialities of each succeeding night. Possessing a fine voice, and ambitious of applause, his company was courted, not only at clubs, but in private parties: and hence he wholly neglected the study of law. Playful as a child, and almost as thoughtless, it is not surprising that he became a dupe to the artful and dishonest, who continually haunted his path. He speedily exhausted his finances, and became insolvent. A married sister gave him a home, and made a great effort to reclaim him. An opportunity offered to place him in a highly respectable coffee-house, in Southampton Buildings, Chancery Lane. A house-warming, or public opening was agreed on, and I was nominated to preside at a dinner, when about thirty of our friends assembled. Unfortunately I was attacked with incipient fever on the morning of the day; but eager to serve my friend on such an occasion, I attended, exerted all the spirits I possessed, endeavoured to stimulate the party even beyond their ordinary standard, by drinking more wine than I had ever before done at one sitting, and by eleven o'clock at night was in a high fever. Taken to my lodging in Rosamond Street, I was placed in bed, to which I was confined for some weeks, and at times insensible to the cares and pleasures of life. An illiterate and unfeeling apothecary was employed, who was so stupidly ignorant both of diseases and remedial medicines, that I have often wondered my life was preserved under such circumstances. My friend Tapsell often visited me, and paid for a nurse; whilst another very warm-hearted friend, (Mr. Langhorne, of Barbican,) whose sympathy and friendship I had propitiated, rendered me many acts of kindness. Nature and youth at length conquered the fever, which had reduced me almost to a skeleton. It was some days before my strength enabled me to reach the street, and many more before I could walk into Spafields and profit by the fresh air.

During this oppressive and distressing crisis, Tapsell continued to augment his business and customers; but, after a year had elapsed, it was found that many of the latter had contracted debts, and the balance sheet showed that the expenditure exceeded the receipts by about four hundred pounds. It was therefore deemed necessary to close the concern, and the bankrupt landlord was reduced to become a clerk in a lawyer's office, at a guinea a week. Some years afterwards I found him in "shabby genteel" habiliments, gaining a few shillings occasionally by compiling and selling song-books, and exerting his vocal powers in low convivial clubs. In October, 1801, Tapsell thus wrote to me from Greenwich:—"I trust the melancholy account I have to give you will plead my apology for the seeming neglect in your business. My brother-in-law, Mr. Allen, has paid the debt of nature, and my sister is very unwell. To-morrow the funeral is to take place, and on Wednesday I shall be in town; and will then finish the Song-Book, and wait upon you with it on Friday."

My association with this person, and the contrast he afforded to myself,—flushed with youth, health, and animation, whilst my own health and prospects were alike precarious and depressing,—flits before my memory as a strange but vivid dream.

With HENRY LANGHORNE I became acquainted at the Spouting Club, in Barbican; and lived on intimate terms with him till his death. He deserves notice as combining the horse-dealer with the good and honest man. He preferred the company of men of talent to that of gamblers and black-legs; and the pages of Shakspere and Johnson to the Stud-Book, or the Racing Calendar. His father had established the famed "Repository" in Barbican, for the weekly sale of horses; which was then, I believe, a novelty. It succeeded, and he died in the prime of life, leaving a widow with one son and two daughters. The son, Henry, was well educated, of a studious turn, mild and timid disposition, and amiable in family and social intercourse. Hence he seemed but little qualified to mix and commune with horse-dealers and their clique. The business, however, was too profitable to be deserted, and he was not prepared to commence a new one, and had not sufficient property to live an idle, gentleman's life. Besides, there were a mother and two sisters to care for, and to be respectably supported. On the decease of his parent, therefore, he determined to mount the rostrum, in the yard,—to face a phalanx of cunning sharpers, and endeavour to deserve their forbearance without seeking their familiarity. Though repeatedly "quizzed," "snubbed," and bantered by some of the racing and hunting fraternity, he bore all with meekness and smiles; and, succeeding beyond the most sanguine hopes of his family and friends, he portioned off his sisters and retired with a handsome independence. He proved to me a sincere friend on different occasions; and I may mention particularly, that he furnished my lodgings, and attended my marriage, when I wedded my first wife, at the church in St. John's Square, Clerkenwell, in the year 1802.

I may close this short notice of a most estimable and exemplary man, by an extract from a letter which he wrote to me in the year 1797, as calculated to convey his estimate of my character at that time; explaining some characteristics of which I am now unconscious.

> "Your late letter, as you justly say, is unconnected and versatile; the express emblem of what you are in conversation; a mere comic extravaganza to dispel melancholy; airy, gay, volatile, and spirited; though generally, in its application, justly pertinent. In your style one thought is the foster-parent of another, which, too much like the way of the world, deserts its origin at every fresh creation, which your imagination runs wild with; and, to speak candidly, your natural character might be truly estimated by the epistle you have sent to me; so much alike is your manner in conversation and in correspondence. However, I attempt no critique; I know your plea of originality and eccentricity, and I freely allow it."

In after-life I have had the pleasure of knowing and corresponding with numerous distinguished actors and dramatic authors; and have spent many joyous moments in the company of John Bannister, John Kemble, Charles Kemble, George Frederick Cooke, Joseph Munden, Charles Mathews, sen. and jun., Charles Young, Michael Kelly, Master Betty (the "Young Roscius,") Miss Mudie (the "Female Roscius,")[*]

---

[*] Precocious genius occasionally comes before, and commands the attention and even the wonder of the public. Juvenile prodigies, like *lusus-naturæ*, though rare, sometimes occur, and are sure to be hailed with astonishment and insatiate curiosity. Master Crotch, in music; Master Bidder, in arithmetic; Master Betty and Miss Mudie, in the drama; and Chatterton, in poetry, attracted the gaze and admiration of thousands of the human race. The "Female Roscius" was not fairly treated, nor justly appreciated. She followed too soon after Master Betty, who had been petted to excess, and was

John Braham, Thomas Phillips, Charles Pemberton, Thomas Holcroft, and many others. Through the medium of those theatrical friends, I was often supplied with orders for the theatre, and then believed it was impossible to be tired or satiated by reading plays, or seeing them represented on the stage. The theatre seemed to me the most fascinating place of rational amusement in the world; and I often fancied, that if I could command leisure and funds, I should devote much of both to purchase and enjoy this pleasure. Later in life, the Literary and Scientific Institutions, which started into existence in London, presented many novelties and attractions, even surpassing those of the drama. I eagerly and zealously espoused the new cause; and successively joined the Royal, the London, and the Russell, and have continued an active member of the last up to the present time. Of these I shall have occasion to speak hereafter.

It will be seen by the foregoing sketches that, from the time of quitting the slavery of apprenticeship to the year 1800, my career was involved in doubt, perplexity, and uncertainty, for I had neither fixed income nor occupation. Though partial to reading, and eager to acquire information on every variety of subject which was presented to my attention, I had never entertained a notion of preparing myself to make literature a profession, or even of being qualified to write for the press. It is true I had ventured to pen some observations on "Bachelorship," whilst in the wine-cellar; and conveyed my first essay at seven o'clock one morning to the "letter-box of the Attic Miscellany," in Shoe Lane, from which I retreated, with hurried steps, as if I had been guilty of a crime. This being printed, I was more than commonly elated, and afterwards was tempted to write comments on plays and players, particularly relating to private theatricals, with notices of free-and-easy and odd fellows' clubs. These appeared in the "Sporting Magazine," which was published by *John Wheble*, of Warwick Square, who became

---

flattered so far beyond his merits, that the public became nauseated with the fulsome language of the press. Kemble and other members of the stage, as well as the generality of play-goers, deserted him; and as he grew in years, he was regarded as only an indifferent actor. Miss Mudie, with superior powers as an actress, was absolutely driven off the stage, and never fairly heard and appreciated.

a kind friend, and was the cause of my being ultimately and for life an author. My early career was, however, of the humblest kind, and was rather editorial than original. A sixpenny pamphlet called "The Thespian Olio," with frontispiece, was the first. Next appeared "The Odd Fellows' Song-Book," price 1s., with an engraved title-page, and a frontispiece from a drawing by my friend Mr. Satchwell. This was a daring speculation, as it involved the risk of nearly fifteen pounds, for paper, printing, engraving, &c., a sum I had never possessed at any one time. I printed 500 copies, and sold them all, with a trifling profit. At that time I became acquainted with *John Fairburn*, a print and bookseller in the Minories, a warm-hearted man, who, though diligent and laboriously industrious, was a bad manager, and consequently was always struggling with pecuniary difficulties. His connections were chiefly with seafaring persons and sea-ports. For him I compiled several annual song-books, which consisted of ballads, &c., entirely applicable to the sailor's life and pursuits. The father of the present justly eminent George Cruikshank made designs for the frontispieces, which were very unlike and very inferior to the popular and expressive designs and etchings by the latter. Fearless of prosecutions by the Dibdins for infringing their copyrights, our annual budget was made up almost entirely from their prolific and popular writings. The amount of my labour and care consisted in selecting the pieces, seeing them through the press, writing a preface, and preparing a series of toasts and sentiments adapted for convivial meetings. Believing that these annual *song-books* cannot be found in Signor Panizzi's *never-to-be-finished* Catalogue of the British Museum Library, I will venture to preserve short extracts from the prefaces of two of them, not as arrogating any claim to literary merit, but as indicative of some dramatic powers.

From the *Naval Songster*, for 1799.—"AN ADDRESS from an Old Seaman (now a Greenwich Pensioner) to all the Jack Tars in His Majesty's Fleet:—

"Hark'ee, Messmates,—I'm an old Sailor past duty, d'ye see, unfit for service as a body may say; but, thanks to His gracious Majesty, I'm provided with a snug berth on board the Greenwich, where I have laid becalmed for many a happy day. I have lost part of my rigging, though my hulk is pretty tough yet, and I fancy will weather many a hard gale in the ocean of life. As I have a kind of knack at scribbling, I sometimes write a song or two, or something of that sort, for my old friend Measter Fairburn, in the Minories.

*Naval Song-Book*, for 1800.—"AN ADDRESS from an old Greenwich Pensioner to the hearty Jack Tars:—

"Avast, d'ye see, before you overhaul my chest, suppose we have a bit of chat, just by way of renewing old acquaintance. It won't much delay your passage, and I know you will listen with patience; for patience, d'ye see, is as necessary for our comfort as a drop of grog. I should like to keep a Patience-shop, to sell it out by the quartern. But I'll tell you a story of Jack Junk. Last week Jack took a trip to London, so he weighed anchor at Deptford Dock, d'ye see, and the wind blowing so'-east by east, he made the Tower Harbour in a jiffy. Being safely landed, he bore away to the Minories, where, having taken a sup of grog with Jack Fairburn, he hailed a hackney-coach, and drove away to see his charming Nancy, as tight a little brig as ever was mann'd."

For the same worthy publisher I suggested and wrote a series of *Twelfth-Night Characters*, to be printed on cards, placed in a bag, and drawn out at parties on the memorable and merry evening of that ancient festival. They were sold in small packets to pastry-cooks, and led the way to a custom which annually grew to an extensive trade. For the second year, my pen-and-ink characters were accompanied by prints of the different personages by Cruikshank (father of the inimitable George), all of a comic or ludicrous kind. I also ventured upon a more arduous task for Fairburn, in 1799, being a volume on *The Life and Adventures of Pizarro*, which extended to 150 octavo pages, and is fully described in the second part of this Auto-Biography.

The unexampled popularity of Sheridan's Play of "Pizarro," translated and altered from one of Kotzebue's German Dramas, induced me to believe that some account of the famed Spanish hero, whose adventures and character formed its basis, would sell to a great extent amongst the thousands of persons who nightly crowded the play-house, and thus augmented its finances. In Bannister's "Memoirs" it is stated that the receipts at Drury Lane Theatre amounted, in one season, to fifteen thousand pounds, and that above thirty thousand copies of the play were sold. (I have now before me a copy of the "twenty-first edition" of the play.) For many successive nights hundreds of persons could not obtain admission to the theatre. I was present at a noted coffee-house in Broad Court, Drury Lane, on the first night of the performance, when messengers came at the end of each act to report on the progress and effect of the play. In the second act, Rolla (acted by Kemble) addresses his associates in arms, the soldiers of Peru, who assembled to repel the Spanish army, which had invaded their native land. This speech was so strikingly applicable to the threatened invasion by Buonaparte and his troops of our own shores, that the audience hailed and applauded it beyond all theatrical precedent. The player, indeed, was called to repeat it, not only a second, but a third time. The procrastinating and dilatory character of Sheridan is strikingly illustrated in connexion with this play, and the theatre. The latter was in an impoverished and almost ruinous state. It was thought that a play by Sheridan, the eloquent but disreputable lessee of the house, would tend to restore its prosperity. He undertook to write or produce one; and in a few days some passages from a recent piece by Kotzebue were sent by Sheridan for the performers to study. Further portions of the same drama were afterwards produced, when Kemble, as manager, announced its first representation; fully expecting that the author would furnish the concluding scenes in time for study and rehearsal. Strange to say, on the morning of the promised performance, the termination of the piece was not decided on, and Mrs. Siddons had not been provided with the affecting speech, which, in the character of Elvira, she was to address Alonzo, on the death of her paramour, Pizarro. Even when the performance began, the author was in his room at the theatre, meditating on, and writing the concluding sentences, and it was not till the end of the first act that he placed them in the hands of the famed actress, and Charles Kemble. The finale was, however, most triumphant; and the tragedy, which was commenced by the actors with fear and gloom, terminated in joy and exultation.

Though "the Enterprising Adventures of Pizarro" was a very humble specimen of authorship, it afforded me some useful practice in the process of compilation. Never having had any previous experience, I found it a difficult and arduous task. The exciting novel of "the Incas of Peru," by Marmontel, contained a mass of biographical, historical, and romantic matter; which, though interesting and amusing, greatly perplexed me; nor was I duly qualified to appreciate, or make a proper use of Dr. Robertson's profound and learned "History of America." These works, however, with the various translations of Kotzebue's plays, afforded abundant materials for the essay I had undertaken; which, by one of the "ready writers" of the present age, would have been prepared for the press in a week; whereas it occupied me more than six weeks of constant and anxious labour. For this, which I may consider my first literary essay, Fairburn paid me ten pounds. Mr. Thurston, a promising young artist, who had served his time with the famed Thos. Bewick, at Newcastle, was then popular with the publishers as a designer of book-illustrations. He made a clever drawing as a frontispiece to my little volume, representing the well-known scene in the play, where Kemble, as Rolla, escapes from the Spanish soldiers, with Alonzo's child in one hand and a sword in the other. This was well engraved by J. Storer, who afterwards executed several plates for the *Beauties of Wiltshire*, &c. Of the "Adventures of Pizarro," a superior edition was published, "on fine wove paper, hot-pressed, with proof impressions of the plate; price five shillings!!!"

As connected with the Lyceum theatre, I may advert to a series of Panoramic Pictures, which were exhibited in that building, from sketches by ROBERT KER PORTER, with whom I had formerly associated at the "School of Eloquence," and also in private life. The first large picture he produced was "The Storming of Seringapatam," an event which had attracted much public notice in the year 1799, and of which the talented and daring artist gave a most effective representation. His rapidity of sketching, and his vivid treatment of battle scenes, astonished all who witnessed his progress. It is stated that he painted the whole, covering a canvass of 200 feet in length, in the short space of six weeks. Horses, soldiers, artillery, baggage-waggons, and all the paraphernalia of war, were dispersed over a vast area of canvass; the walls of the fortress and the surrounding heights being represented in the distance.* Porter afterwards designed, painted, and exhibited other large pictures of similar subjects; such as the Siege of Acre, and the battles of Lodi, Alexandria, and AGINCOURT. The original finished representation of the last was found rolled up in a vault under the Guildhall of London, some years ago; having lain there in obscurity from the time of its removal from the Mansion-house. Its discovery excited much speculation and curiosity, and I was consulted about it by my friend, Mr. Fisher, of the "Caxton Press," the celebrated

---

* A series of large Etchings were executed, by Schiavionetti, from this picture.

printer and publisher. Fortunately I remembered to have seen the painter working upon it, and was enabled to furnish my civic friends with its history, which was confirmed by a letter from Miss Jane Porter, the artist's beloved sister, in 1824. She states that it "was hung up in the Egyptian Hall of the Mansion-house, where it remained for some time, but was taken down to make some alterations in that room; but it never saw the light again until *last year*, when (after about a dozen years' oblivion in—nobody knows where) it was actually found in one of the vaulted chambers under Guildhall. When disentombed, it was hastily spread out against one of the walls of the great hall itself, and announced in the newspapers as a picture of *unknown antiquity*, of some also unknown, but evidently distinguished, artist; and most probably had been deposited in those vaults for security, at the *great fire of London*, and had remained there unsuspected ever since! The hall was thronged day after day to see it; and Sir Martin Shee told me that so great was the mysterious valuation the discovery had put on it, that he heard he had been quoted as having passed his opinion on it, to the effect that it was a picture worth £15,000!"

In spite, however, of the crowds of persons flocking to Guildhall—of the fancied value of the newly-discovered prize—and in disregard of the opinions and advice of those members of the Corporation, who advocated its preservation and public display—and even in defiance of that great public censor, the press, which was then, however, very feeble and indifferent about the arts—it was again rolled up, and was committed to its former sepulchre, where it still remains. Reflecting on the fate of this picture, and of its talented but indiscreet author; and on the present state of manners and society in the City of London, as contrasted with those of 1824, I wrote to Mr. John Sewell, a respected friend, who holds a public appointment in the Guildhall, and he promptly replied, as follows: "Chamberlain's Office, 15th May, 1851.—The large picture you inquire about, is in three pieces, too large for any situation we have either in the Guildhall, or the Mansion-house, and is rolled up; but once in three or four years is unrolled and hung up to air and keep from perishing. It generally remains a week or two, and is then taken down, carefully rolled up, and returned to its old quarters, under the hall. It is a fine performance, fit to be exhibited as a panoramic painting, and I think it is a pity it should remain lost to the public." It appears, by minutes of the Court of Common Council, September 22nd, 1808, that a letter was read from Robert Ker Porter, Esq., dated Stockholm, the 19th of the previous May, addressed to Lord Mayor Ansley, requesting his Lordship to present the "large picture of the Battle of Agincourt, my last, and, I think, best work, to the City of London. The subject is so grateful to the patriotic breast of every Briton, that I need not comment on its propriety as a recommendation worthy a place either in the Mansion-house, or Guildhall. To know that the capital of my native country possesses the last of my productions will be an ample and valuable recompence for my exertions in having produced it."

Thanks were ordered by the Lord Mayor to be returned; and the Committee, for letting the city lands, was requested to " consider of the best place to display the picture." Their report is not known.

At the present momentous epoch of London and of England (June 1851) it surely would not be a subject of much difficulty to hang up and display the national picture here referred to.

My respected friend, Wm. Mulready, Esq., R.A., whom I first knew at the end of the last century, employed some of his artistic skill on this hidden and singular picture.

The life, adventures, and works of Sir Robert Ker Porter, constitute a romance of real life. From boyhood till death, his career was varied, exciting, and remarkable. He was what is commonly called, a Genius: being eccentric, actuated by strong, ardent feelings; was impetuous, quick, and acute in perception, and prompt in execution. At the age of nine he saw a picture of a battle-piece in Edinburgh, where his widowed mother and her children were residing, and was so much fascinated by the subject, that thenceforward he was constantly occupied in sketching and talking about soldiers, wars, horses, artillery, &c. That picture is said to have been shown and described to him by the celebrated Flora Macdonald, who must have been very aged at the time, but whose language was likely to have made a strong impression on the young mind. His love of art soon became so decided a passion, that his mother was advised to remove to London, where she had an introduction to Mr. West, who placed the youth in the Royal Academy.

There he made such rapid progress that, when only thirteen years old, he was commissioned to paint an altar-piece for Shoreditch church, and soon afterwards finished two other altar-pieces; one for the Roman Catholic chapel at Portsea, and another for St. John's College, Cambridge. These, though crude and slight, and evidently hasty productions, manifested thinking and talent. During his stay at Ipswich, he painted another picture to place over the communion table of the church of St. Lawrence, in that town. This he presented to the parishioners through the medium of his friend, the Rev. Dr. Lee, the incumbent. He was occasionally employed in making designs for the publishers, and continued his studies at the Academy, where his amiable disposition, great vivacity, and varied accomplishments propitiated the friendship and esteem of his fellow-students. His mother's limited income was not sufficient to support the expenditure of her establishment. The sons and daughters, as they advanced in age, and became acquainted with persons, in what is called genteel society, required more money than the parent could provide. The eldest son was an officer in the army; the two daughters, Anna Maria, and Jane, had written poetry, tales, and novels, and were consequently ranked amongst the "blue stockings" of the fashionable world; and Robert was courted and caressed in the same circles. It is not surprising that, to keep up appearances, he contracted debts, and that such debts led to money-lenders, those harpies who seduce the spendthrift into extravagance, and then prey upon his misfortunes. Our young artist, like another Charles Surface, became entangled in the meshes of those villains, and suffered most seriously and poignantly by their extortions and harassments. I have now before me a long letter which he sent to his brother, imploring the latter to raise money to protect him from ignominious disgrace, and inevitable ruin. It is a painful appeal and picture. Soon afterwards he appears to have undertaken the daring and arduous task of painting the Seringapatam, already alluded to, which, being eminently successful, proved to be the flood-tide of his career, and led to fame and fortune.

A well-written paper in "The Athenæum," March 25, 1843, gives a very interesting account of the personal and professional character of Sir Robert, under the three heads of Fine Arts, the Army, and Diplomacy. "He studied History, Heraldry, Fortification, ancient and modern, Architecture, and Geographical and Military Surveying; thus almost unconsciously fitting himself for all the subsequent changes in the pursuits of his life." He was an author as well as an artist, and wrote some early papers for Harrison's *Pocket Magazine;* also "Travelling Sketches in Russia and Sweden," 1806; "Letters from Spain and Portugal," Anonymous, 1808; "An Account of the Russian Campaign," 1813; "Travels in Georgia, Persia, &c.," 2 vols. 4to. 1821-22. Sir Robert was born at Durham in 1780, and died in Petersburgh, May 4, 1842, in the sixty-second year of his age. His effects were sold by auction in London, in March, 1843. [See *Penny Cyclopædia*, Supplement.]

The year 1798 is memorable in my own worldly and personal career, as it is in the annals of England. It may be regarded as the transition period, when I began to feel and perceive a prospect of fixing my attention and studies to a specific pursuit. Mr. Wheble, my friend and patron, who had suggested "The Beauties of Wiltshire," and had advanced me a few pounds, urged, almost goaded, me to commence that work. Conscious, however, of my own deficiencies—of my ignorance of topography, antiquities, and literary composition—I hesitated, felt reluctant and diffident, for I knew not how and where to begin. It is true, I had read some volumes on topography and archæology, but found them dull and uninviting. They seemed to trifle on trifling matters, and affected much parade of learning, where it appeared to be misemployed and misapplied. Camden's "Britannia," by Gough, the "Magna Britannia," by Cox, King's "Munimenta Antiqua," and Wyndham's "Domesday, for Wiltshire," I read, and read again, in the hopes of obtaining information, and of finding a key, or clue, to the science of topography. But, alas! I became rather bewildered than enlightened, and was more repelled, than seduced to prosecute the subject. Grose's "Antiquities" was resorted to; but that failed to awaken any sympathy, by the tasteless and trivial prints which were intended to adorn and illustrate its pages. At this time I obtained the acquaintance, I may say intimacy, of SAMUEL IRELAND, who had published his "Views on the Warwickshire Avon" (1795), besides several other works of a similar kind, all of which were printed on large, fine paper, with *pretty* aquatint prints, from the author's drawings. The letter-press, as well as the embellishments, appeared to me very indifferent, if not bad, and induced me to fancy and hope that I might, with a little study and practice, produce something equally entitled to public patronage. Mr. Walker, engraver, of Rosamond Street, who was the master of Storer and Greig, both of whom I afterwards employed to execute plates for "The Beauties of Wiltshire" and "The Beauties of England," was then publishing a periodical called "The Copper-plate Magazine," which consisted entirely of views of seats, towns, ancient buildings, &c., with a page or two of letter-press to each. I accompanied that gentleman to certain places in the vicinity of London, to see him make sketches for his work; and he persuaded me to write accounts of the subjects he had thus "taken off." The artist's and the author's qualifications were quite on a par; both were very bad, and neither would serve to contrast or depreciate the other. This association, however, proved of advantage to me, as it induced some confidence, and showed how books were then embellished and written. At that time the first "Walk through Wales," by the Rev. R. Warner, was attracting much attention and critical commendation. I read it with avidity, was pleased with it, and found that such writing did not require much recondite learning, and need not be encumbered and confused by technical terms, or dull details of genealogy, manorial and parochial history, and useless lists of rectors and vicars, with long inscriptions on tombs, in Latin, Greek, and bad English. The "Walk" was written in a fluent, familiar, and pleasant style; clear and vivid in its descriptions, entertaining in its anecdotes of persons and adventure, and calculated to excite curiosity in the reader. Gilpin's writings on the Picturesque Scenery of the Wye, the New Forest, and of the Lakes, &c., were also sought for and read by me with delight and advantage; as was also the eloquently-written work by Uvedale Price, on "The Picturesque." "The Landscape," a poem, by R. P. Knight, next afforded me a pleasurable perusal; as did the writings of Humphrey Repton, on "Landscape Gardening." A warm and spirited literary controversy was kept up for some time by those three gentlemen, respecting the elements and principles of the picturesque and beautiful, as belonging to natural and artificial scenery. Messrs. Knight and Price contended that the "picturesque"—or rough, wild, broken, and irregular—should be studied and practised in all the scenery and features of landscape around, and even close to, the country mansion; and those gentlemen exemplified and illustrated their theory and maxims at their respective homes, of Foxley, and Dowton Castle, in Herefordshire. Mr. Repton, on the contrary, pleaded the cause of "beauty" in the smooth lawn, the trim gravel path, the dressed parterre, the flowing line, and even in geometrical forms around the house, and showed their effects in his own limited cottage-garden, at Hare Street, in Essex. Taking a warm interest in this controversy and subject, which was increased by reading Burke on "The Sublime and Beautiful," the Lectures by Reynolds, and many other Essays, I was eager and curious to have a personal survey of the homes of the literary belligerents, whose hostile weapons were fortunately the pencil and pen, rather than the sword and pistol. Accordingly, I devoted several weeks, in the summer of 1798, to a long pedestrian tour, in the course of which I might be enabled to view scenery, houses, and antiquities. A dear sister, who was settled with a young family at the romantic town of Church Stretton, in Shropshire, induced me to fix upon that point for a home and station. Were I to enter into a detailed account of the places I visited, of the public persons I became acquainted with, and of my own personal adventures in a walk of several hundreds of miles, such a narrative alone would extend to a goodly-sized volume; but I must restrict myself to a few pages, and consequently be very brief. With maps, a pocket compass, a small camera-obscura (for the more portable and simple camera-lucida was not then known,) two or three portable volumes, an umbrella, and a scanty packet of body linen, &c., I commenced a walk from London on the 20th of June, and returned again to it on the 30th of September. During that excursion, I visited Windsor, Oxford, Woodstock, Stratford-upon-Avon, Warwick, Kenilworth, Birmingham, Hagley, the Leasowes, and Church Stretton. Thence I made diverging excursions to Shrewsbury, Welsh Pool, and several other places within twenty miles of my residence; and returned through Ludlow, Leominster, Hereford, Ross, down the Wye, to Chepstow, to Bristol, and Bath; thence to several different parts of Wiltshire, and back to London. This long and toilsome, but eminently interesting and attractive journey, cost me only eleven pounds, sixteen shillings, and ninepence! I was compelled to practice economy, for my finances were low, and I knew not how or where to recruit them. My sister kindly presented me with five pounds, and her good husband lent me ten more, which seemed to me a fortune. It may be reasonably supposed that I sought for and found cheap quarters for board and lodging: but often met with some of a very unpleasant kind, and occasionally put up with ungenial companions. I often reflected that Humphrey Clinker, Gil Blas, and Roderic Random had encountered and survived scenes and vicissitudes even more unpleasant and hazardous than those I occasionally endured. I may notice one adventure which occurred at Portsmouth, where I arrived between ten and eleven o'clock on a summer's night, when the town was full of troops, and sought a bed at several inns and public-houses, without success: at length, I went to a shop in a back street, where "lodgings for travellers" was placarded. Here I was shown a room where six or eight beds were placed side by side, some of which were occupied by one or by two persons. Remembering the old proverb of "honour among thieves," I chose one of these humble couches rather than go further and perhaps fare worse. In my travelling attire and unwashed, I laid myself on a sort of straw pallet, beneath a horse-cloth for counterpane, and, being over-fatigued with a long day's walk, quickly became insensible of danger and of fellow-lodgers. But I was shortly roused from slumber by a Babylonish confusion of tongues and sounds; for the room was filled with human beings: old and young, male and female, drunk and sober, rough and rude, gentle and simple. Having chosen an extreme corner of the room, and a narrow bed to carry one person, I was not intruded on by later visitants, who unceremoniously laid themselves down wherever they could see a small space unoccupied. Quarrelling, swearing, crying, intreating, mixed with a few hard blows, were heard and felt, whilst hearty prayers and curses came from other mouths. My next neighbours were an old woman, and a younger one with an infant, whose lamentations and grief were poignant and heart-felt. The first had lost a son, the second a husband, and the third a father, facts which were proclaimed by the ejaculations of the speakers, and by the cries of the child. However I might lament and pity the sufferers, and these minor horrors and calamities of war, I could not but feel disgusted at the brutal language of some of my recumbent neighbours, who cursed and anathematised the poor sufferers for disturbing their repose. This night's lodging cost me sixpence, from having the sole occupancy of one bed, whilst those who joined in partnership of two or three, were accommodated on lower terms. This incident, with others I witnessed in consequence of a congregated army of soldiers at a sea-port, tended not only to strengthen my previous antipathy to everything belonging to war, but led me to view the costume and business of the soldier with sorrow and regret; and to consider the monarchs and ministers who promoted and instigated national or intestine wars, as the most heartless and reckless of human beings—

> " One murder made a villain,
> Millions a hero : princes were privileged to kill,
> And numbers sanctified the crime."   *Bishop Porteus.*

With such sentiments and feelings, it may be readily inferred that I hail, with sincere exultation and joy, the present state of the civilized world; and particularly the conduct and humane philanthropy which my native land manifests in her monarchy, legislation, and public press.

During this tour of 1798, I was introduced to, and formed acquaintance with, many public persons, whose friendship and correspondence proved valuable in after life. At WINDSOR, I met Benjamin West, who was then painting some of his fine historical pictures for that national palace, and for the chapel of St. George. Mr. Foster was preparing his ovens and apparatus for copying some of them on glass for the same chapel; and Mr. Holloway had commenced reducing and making drawings of the justly-admired cartoons, by Raffaelle, from which he afterwards executed eight magnificent engravings.*

My next place of attraction and residence was OXFORD, where I experienced civility and kindness from the *Rev. Mr. Price,* of the Bodleian,

---

\* This first and short visit to Windsor excited a strong desire to see it again, and to obtain more information about the history and characteristics of its noble castle, chapel, halls, towers, &c., as well as of the pictures within its chambers. The connection then formed, and since acquired, has afforded me many favourable opportunities to gratify the curiosity then awakened, and to write and publish accounts of the castle and St. George's chapel, in the " Architectural Antiquities," " Beauties of England," and in a handsome folio volume, to accompany and explain a series of elaborate and beautifully-executed engravings from drawings by Gandy and Baud, two architects, who were long employed in the office of Sir Jeffrey Wyatville, the skilful renovator and improver of Windsor Castle.—See account of this work in Part II., p. 106.

and the *Rev. John Gutch,* author of the " History, &c., of the University of Oxford," 3 vols. 4to., a second edition of which had recently appeared. Mr. Price laid before me some of John Aubrey's MSS., at that time a novelty to me, parts of which I copied. At this renowned seat of learning, I also became acquainted with the Rev. Mr., afterwards Dr., Penrose, and the Rev. John Walker, of New College; the last of whom edited " Selections from the Gentleman's Magazine," which appeared in four volumes. Mr. Bliss, a respectable bookseller, was then, and continued so for the remainder of his life, a kind and useful friend. On this occasion I first met the *Rev. James Ingram,* of Trinity College, whose familiarity and kindness continued thenceforward till his decease in 1850. He subsequently rendered me useful service in the " Beauties of Wiltshire;" and presented to me a manuscript tour through some of the northern counties for the " Beauties of England," which I still possess.

I never can forget the veneration, the awe, the curiosity I experienced on approaching and perambulating this renowned seat of learning: for I had read about it, had meditated on its learned " fellows," its vast stores of literature; and had also formed romantic notions of its awful colleges, with their libraries, galleries, and cloisters. I entered it truly humble, but left it with increased humility; for I felt my own weakness and ignorance. I wished to be a sizar, or in any situation to be connected with the place; fancying that even the air and food of Oxford could not fail to impart learning, or at least would assuage the mental thirst and hunger which then created a morbid appetite. The architectural and scenic features of Oxford, the associations, the well-stocked libraries, the picture galleries, the costume and imposing air of the elder members of colleges, and the general appearance and aspect, as well as decorous air and dress, of the scholars (as they seemed to me) made not only a strong but mortifying impression on my feelings, and haunted my mind for a long time afterwards. I had read of youths who had met with stranger-friends and patrons, to place them in schools and colleges, and wished I could find such a noble benefactor and foster parent. These vain hopes and day-dreams, though they served to amuse the young mind, tended rather to oppress than foster self-respect. Further intercourse with clergymen and gentlemen, who had left college and settled in their respective country homes, exhibited them as human beings, whose converse and conduct closely resembled that of their fellows who had never sojourned in the cloister of an university, nor sacrificed years of precious time in studying useless dead languages, equally futile polemics of the fathers, and the metaphysics and theories of pagan authors.*

At *Woodstock,* I spent a day with DR. MAVOR, the voluminous author, who recommended me to visit the vast mansion and noble park of *Blenheim,* where I saw and felt the system and principles of Lancelot—commonly called "Capability," Brown—as exemplified in the grounds, the lake, and the pleasure-gardens. The architectural designs by Vanbrugh, in the mansion, made an impression which has lasted for more than half a century, and cannot be effaced whilst consciousness remains. It was the first large country-house I had ever seen, and was an object of wonder. It is true I looked at it from the park and the pleasure-garden, in its court, its hall, and galleries, and became more bewildered than instructed: for the mind was not prepared either to understand or enjoy its boldness and originality of design, and, what has since been called, its poetry of architecture.† In memorandums made at the time, I find an item of 2*s.* 6*d.* for viewing the house, a sum I could ill afford. At the same time my day's expence, with bed, at the inn, was only 2*s.* 8*d.*, and the cost of a single volume was 2*s.* 6*d.* more. This was the first "show-house" I ever visited, and, however gratifying and exciting, it was too severe a tax on *my* pocket to be repeated.

---

* Of this famed City and University I afterwards wrote a History and Description for Rees's *Cyclopædia,* occupying 39 columns of that once popular work. Afterwards I wrote and published a quarto volume on the History and Architecture of its Cathedral. The Rev. Wm. Coneybeare, now Dean of Llandaff, wrote an Account of the Church and Crypt of St. Peter's Church for my *Architectural Antiquities;* in which work is a View and Description of the Schools' Tower; and in the fifth volume are several engravings of architectural details of the old buildings, both ecclesiastical and domestic.

† Since then I have written a description of the mansion and its scenic accompaniments, with rather severe strictures on the impolicy of ministers granting such gorgeous testimonials to heroes—to honour and reward generals—for merely doing their duty—thereby encouraging the frightful and horrid game of war.—(See Havell's *Views of Seats.*)

The Rev. WM. FORDYCE MAVOR, L.L.D. In the wide range of literature, there are few authors whose pen was more active, and whose name appeared to a greater number and variety of publications, than the Rev. Rector of Woodstock. On short-hand, grammar, geography, mathematics, language, natural history, general history, topography, criticism, &c., we find the name of Dr. Mavor: from 1779, when his "Sprigs of Parnassus" appeared, till 1814, when his "Fruits of Perseverance, Three Sermons," were published. He continued to produce a succession of works in every year; and it would be a difficult task to ascertain their number and variety. Becoming connected with the notorious book-manufacturer, R. Phillips, he not only wrote original volumes for him, but is said to have lent his name, and sometimes literary revision, to others which had been written, or made by other persons. His poem on "Blenheim," and his "Blenheim Guide," went through several editions, one of which he presented to me, at the time of my visit; and which, with accounts of Hagley, Enville, and the Leasowes, were my travelling companions on the journey. They tended to excite a desire to visit and examine those then noted seats, and gave the first hints for descriptive writing. With the industrious Doctor I continued a correspondence for many years; and afterwards became familiar with his son, who was one of the partners in the monster firm of Moorfields, London: "Lackington, Allen, Hughes, Mavor, Harding, and Co." Though the literary publications of Dr. Mavor are so numerous, and many of them popular and useful, his name is scarcely noticed in the Biographical Dictionaries. Watt's "Bibliotheca Britannica," however, contains a long list of his literary works.

At the house of this new and respected friend I was introduced to Mr. S. J. PRATT, who had lately published the popular novel, called "Family Secrets, Literary and Domestic," in 5 vols.; also "a Letter to the British Soldiers;" and another to "the Tars of Old England." These, with several other works, had rendered the name of this author eminent amongst the class, and imposing to a literary novitiate. I therefore felt proud and happy to be admitted to the familiar converse of two such stars in the literary hemisphere. Thenceforward I continued on friendly terms with both, personal and by letter, as long as they lived. Pratt was then preparing his "Bread, or the Poor, a Poem," 4to., which attained much praise in the periodicals of the time, and was afterwards republished with beautiful illustrations from the effective designs of Loutherbourg. At that time he had commenced writing his "Gleanings in England," a work which was published in 3 vols. 8vo., and excited much popularity, as may be inferred by a third edition being required in little more than three years. From the time I thus met Mr. Pratt, till his decease in 1814, he continued to write for the press, and produced many volumes both in prose and verse, some of which passed through several editions. They are, however, scarcely known to the readers of the present day, and would not be tolerated, if printed; for they are so prolix and attenuated, so verbose and artificial, that the critical reader suspects the truthfulness of every statement, and the honesty and sincerity of every sentiment. The private as well as the literary character of Mr. Pratt, has been strongly drawn by Miss Seward, in a letter to the Rev. R. Polwhele, and published in the "Traditions and Recollections" of that author, 2 vols. 8vo. 1826. Her story of him shows that he was heartless, artificial, vain, false, arrogant, cruel, a cheat, and an imposter through life.* The following account of him, by Mr. A. Ramsey, in his edition of William Hutton's "Life," and another by Miss Hutton, in the same volume, manifest so much verity and impartiality, that I cannot forbear transcribing them into my own narrative. Mr. Ramsey says—

> He "was celebrated, when there were only a few mediocre poets, and no good ones. He wrote 'The Gleaner,' 'Sympathy,' two or three unreadable dramas, and many other pieces, long and short, in prose and verse, and which are all forgotten. His life was better than his writings: he is described as an amiable man. In the latter years of his life, Pratt's principal or sole means of support were derived from an annual purse made up by his Birmingham and other friends, to which

---

* There is a good portrait of Mr. Pratt in the "Harvest Home; consisting of Supplementary Gleanings," &c., 3 vols. 8vo. 1805, engraved by Caroline Watson, from a painting by Mr. Lawrence. This work contains a miscellaneous collection of the author's writings in prose and verse, with others by several of his friends, mostly complimentary of each other. In these volumes is the ninth edition of his "Sympathy, a poem, revised, corrected, and enlarged;" also poems and essays by H. J. Pye, Poet Laureat, Dr. Mavor, John Taylor, Dr. Walcot, W. Hutton, Wm. Meyler, the Rev. R. Graves, then in his 91st year, and others.

William Hutton and his family contributed. In politics, in character, and in every thing else, he was the very opposite of Hutton. He died in the year 1814, at the age of 65. He always affected great mystery as to his birth and early history, evidently wishing it to be believed that his father, at least, was a person of aristocratic distinction."—ED.

The following is by Catherine Hutton: "In early life Samuel Jackson Courtney Pratt had been attached to a young woman who had died in his arms. Grief obliged him to quit the place, and necessity obliged him to marry another. He was then under age, though the lady was considerably above it; and *she* took *him* in a post-chaise to Gretna Green. They afterwards separated, but continued to correspond as friends. In 1774, Mr. Pratt performed the characters of Philaster and Hamlet, at Covent Garden; after which time he became successively a bookseller at Bath, a stroller, and an author by profession. Pratt and Dallas (Lord Byron's friend) reviewed each others' works, and the praise bestowed by one party, was liberally repaid by the other. This is what Mr. Pratt termed the 'Jockey-ship of Author-ship,' of which, he said, my father knew nothing."—*Life of W. Hutton*, 1841.

From Woodstock I proceeded to STRATFORD-UPON-AVON, with a curiosity somewhat excited from accounts I had read by some of the commentators on Shakspere; by Ireland's "Warwickshire Avon;" by the controversy and strictures in the periodicals and pamphlets of the time, in consequence of the impudent and audacious forgeries on the name and fame of Stratford's Bard, by Wm. H. Ireland, a young man with whom I had become acquainted at his father's house in Norfolk Street, in the Strand, London. The popular acting plays of our National Bard; —Macbeth, the Merry Wives of Windsor, Richard III., Romeo and Juliet, and the Merchant of Venice;—in which Kemble, Mrs. Siddons, Cooke, Palmer, Parsons, Bannister, &c., personated some of the prominent characters—had made more impression on my young mind at that time, than either the birth-place of the poet, or even his other pre-eminent finished works. Without introduction, or any personal acquaintance, I wandered about the town, the church-yard, and the church, and even viewed the famed Bust without that admiration and emotion of sympathy, which some years afterwards I fully and deeply felt on the same spot, in the mausoleum of the Bard, and on a more close examination of his veracious stone portrait. Little could I then fancy that it would be my good fortune to be instrumental, if not the prime mover, of having a cast and engraving made from the said bust, and of causing the roof of the chancel to be new built, in a style and with ornaments more accordant with, and more creditable to the memory of the person whose ashes the last enshrined.†

My next resting-place was BIRMINGHAM, where I sojourned for a few days, and found abundance of excitement and interest. The contrast between this "toy-shop of Europe," as Burke had pronounced it, but rather "the work-shop," the smithery, and forgery,—to the vast and varied London—to Windsor and Blenheim, where architectural grandeur and picturesque scenery abounded—to Oxford, where the fine and beautiful colleges and street architecture, with the classical dress of the gownsmen, and the attraction of the libraries and galleries—and even to the clean, quiet, and rural town of Stratford—was calculated to awaken strong and anxious feelings. Besides, the name and disgrace of Birmingham had recently resounded throughout the whole civilized world, for the misdeeds and wantonness of some of its wild and infatuated inhabitants; in burning houses, furniture, and property; ruining inoffensive and peaceable people; and who continued to riot, plunder, and destroy for three successive days and nights, in July, 1791. The origin, history, and effects of these riots, have been fully detailed by Wm. Hutton, a peaceable and unoffending sufferer, whose only crime seems to have been, differing in opinion and practice on religious creeds, with some of the rabid churchmen of the town, and being opposed to the cry and watch-phrase which the rioters had assumed, of "Church and King." The reckless mob, when once collected, and incited to action by men in the higher walks of life, (who ought to have set good and peaceable example) were radically opposed both to the doctrines and conduct of the established monarchy and hierarchy, yet they eagerly and madly lent all their strength and fury to acts of plunder, and also to drunkenness, and every barbarous and wanton crime. The public mind at that time was in a state of

---

† In the Third Part, or Appendix to this volume, will be found accounts of my subsequent connection with Stratford, my pilgrimages to that shrine of genius and poetry, and many incidents of a personal and public nature. I must avail myself of this opportunity to correct an error of date in the second line of page 36: for 1790 read 1798; and instead of returning from Stratford through Oxford to London, the route of my journey was as mentioned in the preceding page.

L

frenzy and ferment. The American war and American independence led the way, and the murderous and mad French revolution followed; all the civilized and uncivilized countries in Europe were embroiled in political controvresies and contests. England was disturbed in its insulated quietude and integral monarchical government. Party spirit and religious animosities were fomented to such an excess and degree of hostility, that they led to family disunions, to personal hostilities, and frequent breaches of the public peace. The Government, under the dominion of George the Third, and his staunch, inflexible minister, William Pitt, rather irritated than conciliated the Jacobins, or Republicans, as all persons were denominated, who differed in opinion with the government authorities. Hence, newspapers, pamphlets, and other means and vehicles of literary warfare, were employed to excite prejudice and hostility against the Government; which, in return, employed spies and informers, and eventually the Attorney-General, to impeach the writers of what was considered to be sedition and treason. Many persons were sentenced to long imprisonment, or transportation, and some for execution. To these causes we may trace the riots of Birmingham, and others in London, Manchester, Newport, and Bristol.

My once respected and revered friend, Mr. William Hutton, and the amiable and estimable Dr. Priestley, were among the innocent victims who suffered by the party rancour of those times, and the recklessness of rioters. When in Birmingham, I witnessed and lamented the doleful effects of such mob-licentiousness. Houses were still in ruins, whilst new ones of novel forms and features had been raised in the places of others. But the ruined fortunes, and the oppressed hearts, of some of the unfortunate sufferers, could not so easily be reinstated. Priestley was impoverished and driven into exile; whilst Hutton, though not entirely impoverished, suffered so much in pecuniary losses as to recover from the county the sum of £5390. Though thus compensated for his worldly losses, his animal spirits, his philosophy, his admiration of Birmingham and its inhabitants, were never restored to the standard manifested in his "History of Birmingham," 1781; "The Court of Requests," in 1787; "The Hundred Court," 1788; and in his "Life," written in 1798, and published by his affectionate and talented daughter in 1816. The last work has since been re-published, in 1841, in a cheap form, with notes by the daughter, at that time in her 85th year; and with other elucidatory notes by its editor, A. Ramsey. It is one of Charles Knight's "English Miscellanies," and may be purchased for 2s. 6d. In the "Penny Cyclopædia," it is properly described as "one of the most entertaining and instructive pieces of auto-biography in the language."

When I visited the revered and estimable old man, then in his 75th year, he had recently lost his affectionate and devoted wife. His good daughter, as he writes, had also "lost her health, when she had lost that mother." He had recently sought relaxation, and amusement for himself, and health for his daughter, by visiting Caernarvon and other parts of Wales; and during the year 1797 and part of 1798, he produced twenty-one different pieces of poetry, partly to relieve the sorrows of his swollen heart. His conversation was very fascinating, and particularly so to me, then commencing not merely a country journey, but the perilous journey of life; then almost as poor and cheerless as he had been at the same age, and also, like him, eager and anxious to advance myself in the world's estimation and my own. I listened with craving ears to all he said about his own life, his adventures, and experiences; and I fear I obtruded too much on his time, for I saw him only twice, and my stay with him was not more than two hours at each visit. I had no intimation, at the time, that he had penned his autobiography, up to the very July of 1798, when I was at Birmingham; but so it appears by the "Life," as now published. Subsequently, he undertook the almost marvellous tour to, and twice along, the whole course of the famed *Roman wall*, from the north to the south coasts. The result of this tour was a very amusing and interesting account of it which he published in octavo, 1801.* He was in his 79th year, had walked, between the first of July and the seventh of August, 1800, six

---

* In 1802 I wrote a critique on, and account of this volume in *The Annual Review* for that year. "Perhaps I am the only man," says this amusing writer, "that ever travelled the whole length of this wall, and probably the last that ever will attempt it. Who then will, like me, say he has travelled it twice?" Very recently, however, the Rev. Mr. Bruce has explored and given an account of that vast Roman work; and I indulge a hope that my esteemed friend, C. Roach Smith, will favour the reading public with his account and opinions on the same military boundary between two hostile nations.

hundred and one miles, "At a loss," he writes, "on my part, of perhaps one stone of animal weight in perspiration, and a lapse of thirty-five days." Miss Hutton, in the life of her father, has published an interesting account of the journey.

I will only add, "*The Life of* WILLIAM HUTTON, *Stationer, of Birmingham*, written by himself," may justly rank with that of Benjamin Franklin, as of commanding interest to young readers, in the class of auto-biographies. It details the rise, progress, fluctuations, privations, vicissitudes, and ultimate prosperity of a man, who, in youth, suffered and endured the most abject poverty, but who progressively acquired honour, knowledge, distinction, and wealth; whose assiduity, perseverance, fortitude, and amiability of character furnish a most exemplary model for youths, who may be animated with laudable ambition to attain distinction in this vast world of trial and vicissitude.

Having become acquainted with MR. J. BISSET, who had a museum of curiosities, and was author of some songs and other poems, I was introduced by him to some of the great manufacturers of the town. Buckles, buttons, guns, and other warlike weapons, were made in greater quantities than almost any other articles. Of the buckle, now rarely seen, Sir Edward Thomason says, in his "Memoirs," that his father "completed one thousand pairs of buckles per diem, when in full work." Mr. Bisset afterwards published "A Poetic Survey round Birmingham," and several other works, and removed thence to Leamington, where he had an interesting museum, and published a Guide to that watering-place. He also took charge of, and brought into notice, a girl, named Shakspere, who, he contended, was a lineal descendant of the Stratford Bard. Sir Richard Phillips gave publicity to this opinion by statements in the *Monthly Magazine*.

Though not in chronological sequence, I may reasonably introduce, in this place, a short notice of my subsequent intercourse and connection with Birmingham, as essentially belonging to my literary life. In the year 1832 I was invited, by the Committee of the Birmingham Athenæum, to give a course of *Six Lectures on Architectural Antiquities*, parts of which I had previously read at the London Institution. On this occasion, however, I found it necessary, not only to vary my matter, but to re-write much of it; for the audience was very different to that I had addressed in London, and I felt that a mixed and miscellaneous auditory required to be instructed and amused by a style and treatment more adapted to the tyro than to the advanced student. My company was numerous and attentive: seemed to take an interest in the subject, and greeted me with smiles and plaudits every succeeding night. At the conclusion, the treasurer handed me £73 for the course. On this occasion I was honoured and gratified with courteous and friendly attentions from the Committee, and from many of the gentry and manufacturers of the town. Indeed, a month passed pleasantly and quickly away. Amongst these gentlemen, I venture to name, with feelings of respect and gratitude, the following :—

SIR EDWARD THOMASON, in whose museum and shops I was gratified by the sight of numerous works of art and science, which he had invented, patented, and sold to a great extent. From that time till his death, which occurred in 1849, we continued on friendly terms. I visited him in Bath, where he resided some years, in the largest house in Pulteney Street, which was adorned with numerous splendid works of art, of high value, presented to him by several of the monarchs of Europe. Engravings of these, with copies of the letters, and their accompanying autograph signatures, are printed in his "Memoirs during Half a Century," 2 vols. 8vo. 1844. A pleasing engraved portrait is also in the first volume, representing the author adorned with a galaxy of foreign orders attached to his coat. This publication contains a very flattering letter from my much-esteemed friend, Dr. Birkbeck, in which he speaks of Sir Edward as "one of the noblest spirits, in regard to manufacturing enterprize, he has ever encountered." *

---

\* In the same work is an engraving of a *French Medal*, which was struck at Paris in 1804, for Buonaparte, when he projected and threatened to invade England, with a flotilla of 2000 small vessels, which he had ordered to be built at Boulogne. It is a great curiosity and rarity, plainly showing that the Emperor was sincere in his vain boast of intending a descent on this country, though the fact has been doubted by many historians and politicians. Bourrienne, in his "Mémoires," decidedly asserts, that Napoleon never intended it; but Comte Las Casas, who was on equally familiar terms with the Emperor, declares that the invasion was fully intended, and the medal was to be struck on the conquest of London. The Emperor had adopted a similar plan on the invasion of Austria, having prepared a medal, in Paris, with the inscription as being struck in

Of all the published specimens of Testimonial honours—many of which have been fully noticed in the early part of the present volume—I know of nothing to equal the Memoirs of Sir Edward Thomason; as it contains such a galaxy of autographs, of royal, noble, and other eminent persons; besides copies of their letters to the author, and a profusion of prints. I am aware of a very extraordinary book, of large size and extent, published in Paris, by *Monsieur Alexandre Vattemare*, who was celebrated in London, in 1826, as a ventriloquist and actor, where he entertained large audiences in the style and manner of our famed countryman, Charles Mathews. The French book contains not only autograph complimentary letters from kings, queens, emperors, ministers, generals, nobles, and other eminent personages, but the signatures of others, and many lithograph prints from designs of celebrated artists of different countries. During one of his visits to London he indulged me with his company, one morning, to a *déjeûner*, when I invited several friends to meet him, and witness some of his wonderful specimens of ventriloquism, mimicry, and personation of various characters. At the same time we were amused with looking over his mass of letters and works of art, which had been presented to him by the parties above-named.

From the family of THOMAS WRIGHT HILL, of Edgbaston, I experienced marked attention and courtesies. He kept a large school, whose excellent system has been manifested to the world by pupils who have attained distinction; and by the eminence which the following Sons have acquired in their respective spheres of usefulness. He died at

---

Vienna. Sir Edward has given a particular accouut of the history and mystery of this medal, which had been executed from designs by Denon, who had charge of the two dies, and had taken a few impressions, when the Emperor and his immense army had assembled on the coast. On the obverse was a finely-engraved head of the Emperor; and on the reverse, figures of Antæus strangling Hercules, with the legend, DESCENTE . EN . ANGLETERRE. On the exergue, FRAPPÉ . À . LONDRES . EN . 1804. Denon had orders to strike off many impressions in the event of London being thus conquered. A friend of mine, the Rev. T. S. Turnbull, made particular inquiries, some years ago, for impressions of the French medal, both in Paris, London, and other cities, and found the account in Sir Edward's volume correct, and that the original medal is very rare. He could trace only eleven, of which four were in England. In Paris, it is said, there is only Thomason's copy.

the advanced age of 88, in June, 1851. *Matthew D. Hill*, is Queen's Counsel, Recorder of his native town, Birmingham, Commissioner of Bankrupts for the Bristol district, and is justly esteemed for integrity of conduct as well as professional ability. His strenuous endeavours to promote a radical reform in the education and early training of the working population of the country is entitled to the praise of all philanthropists. To prevent crime and superinduce habits of industry and honesty is more to be wished and encouraged than the punishment of vice. Mr. M. D. Hill's eldest brother, *Edwin*, is Controller of the Machinery of Postage Stamps, in Somerset-House, and is the principal inventor and joint patentee of the Envelope Folding Machine, which attracted so much attention at the late Great Exhibition. The laudable and successful exertions of *Rowland Hill*, to improve the Postage system, has won for him not only " golden opinions " but a golden harvest; whilst a fourth son of the Birmingham family, *Arthur Hill*, was distinguished when a youth by learning and diligence; as evinced by lectures which he gave whilst I was at Birmingham. He conducts the eminent school at Bruce Castle, Tottenham, on principles similar to those of his father. *Frederick Hill*, was twelve years Inspector of Prisons for Scotland, and devised a system for their management which has been pursued to the present time. He is now Assistant Secretary to the Post Office, in London.

At the time I gave my lectures, the new *Music Hall* was creating much speculation and wonder; for the buidling was a daring novelty in design, and manifested more daring and temerity in the architects who engaged to erect it at such a low sum that other builders and architects were alarmed, either for the fate of the reckless contractors, if they failed, or for their own, if they succeeded. Though much skill and activity were employed, and the early part of the work proceeded rapidly, it was found that the estimated sum would not pay for much more than half. The contractors were ruined, and their sureties called on to pay their bonds.

Requested by my auditory to devote one Lecture to Modern Architecture, I was induced to write a few remarks on, and descriptions of, some of the public buildings which had been raised since the dissolution of the monasteries by Henry VIII. For the new Music Hall could not well pass unnoticed; and the architects provided me with a large plan and view of the proposed finished building, which I briefly described. This circumstance, however, produced a bad feeling in, and an intemperate letter from, Mr. Rickman, an architect of the town, with whom I had formerly corresponded, before he had published, or commenced his "Attempt to discriminate the Styles of Architecture."* This was the only unpleasant event that occurred during a month's sojourn at Birmingham; and the Quaker architect never forgave me for complimenting a rival.

Mr. Barry's new building, "Edward the Sixth's Grammar School," in New Street, not only attracted my attention, but admiration, because the architect had dared to apply an imitation of the genuine style and character of the mediæval buildings to one of modern date. In the practical execution of this work we may trace the origin of the designs of the new Houses of Parliament.

Among the eminent manufacturers of this great town, I cannot forget, nor omit to acknowledge, my obligations to *Wm. Phipson, Esq.*, whose workshops, with their contents, in the simple article of Pins, cannot be viewed by strangers without astonishment and gratification. Here, men, women, and children, aided by machinery, are actively and assiduously occupied daily and yearly in producing that single article; but making pins by millions in number, and tons in weight, per year. Mr. Babbage, in the Introduction to his volume on Mechanics, has alluded to the pin-manufacture, to exemplify the principle and value of "division of labour." An interesting article on this subject, is given in the *Penny Cyclopædia*.

The *Glass Manufacturers* of Birmingham are justly famed for the quantity, variety, and beauty of articles they annually produce in this truly elegant material. In the works of *Mr. Follet Osler*, I was delighted and equally pleased by the artistic and scientific skill that gentleman exhibited, in the designs and execution of his numerous works.

---

* This was originally written for, and published in Smith's *Panorama of Science and Art*; but the author wrote me word that he had a few copies struck off, separately. One of these, of 56 octavo pages, he presented to me in 1815, with a note. It is a literary curiosity, as showing the slight and superficial foundation of a work, which has since grown to a large volume, with numerous illustrations, and extended to several editions.

At the great Cosmopolite Exhibition of 1851, some specimens of his novel and splendid works attracted the admiration of millions of persons.

From the following gentlemen connected with the Athenæum I experienced much courteous attention: the Rev. Dr. Corrie, the president; — Parsons, the secretary; Joseph Wickenden, who, on a subsequent visit to Birmingham, preserved my life, by skilful and prompt professional advice and medicine in a case of cholera; Francis Clark, who had married one of Mr. Hill's daughters, and Timothy Smith.

In the year 1839, I spent another week in Birmingham, with " *The British Association* for the Advancement of Science," when I had opportunities of renewing my acquaintance, not only with most of the persons already enumerated, and their varied interesting manufactories and museums, but I was also introduced to many others. In spite of unpropitious times, depression in trade, dearness of provisions, and a spirit of insubordination and turbulence amongst the working classes of society in the town and district, the assemblage of scientific strangers was very great; and everything went off with harmony and satisfaction. Within a month of the meeting, it was, however, doubtful whether it would be safe to assemble at Birmingham, and it was deemed advisable to consult the Minister on the subject. The magistrates and authorities of the town announced to the scientific committee that every precaution should be used to protect the public. The Society held its first meeting on the 26th of August, and a week was devoted to scientific readings, discussions, and inspection of numerous objects of local manufacture and art. A journey to Dudley coal and iron-works and caves occupied one day: an immense dinner party assembled in the great hall on another. This association was an imposing fête for Birmingham; and it may be presumed was more beneficial to its future prosperity and fame, than all the musical festivals that have since occurred at its spacious Town-hall. It may not be irrelevant to remark, that " The Times," and certain other periodicals, commenced a literary warfare against the " Association," by accusing it of irreligion, profanity, &c.; but we now find that the Society has outlived and confuted this tirade of petty and silly hostility.*

---

\* Instead of waning by age, and growing stale by use, the British Association evidently increases in vigour and usefulness as it increases in years. I have now before me

I wrote a short account of Birmingham, for Rees's *Cyclopædia;* and in 1838-9, a Description of the "*London and Birmingham Railway,*" to accompany a series of elaborate and beautiful lithographic drawings by J. Bourne. This is described in the Second Part of the present work, page 95.

Of this unique and extraordinary town, now a borough, I may safely say, in the language of its first historian, Hutton, "I approached her with reluctance," (or rather with intense curiosity, blended with some apprehension,) "because *I did not* know her: I shall leave her with reluctance, because I do."

I may venture to quote from the conclusion of my lectures in 1836, the following remarks on Birmingham, expressive of opinions formed after sojourning some weeks in the town, and associating with many of its best-informed inhabitants.

"*Birmingham* may be fairly and truly compared to the *Bee-hive*, in which perpetual activity pervades every part—in which unwearying industry is in constant operation, to construct repositories, and lay up stores for future wants; in which also wax is employed to produce a comb, or house—a piece of instinct-mechanism, of wondrous beauty and perfect symmetry. When perfected, and stored with honey, it is assailed, and plundered by the drones and other foes of industry and skill. It is then taken from its persevering and accomplished artists and artizans and applied to the luxuries and indulgences of man. So in the ever-active, ever-enterprising hive of Birmingham, multitudes of human beings are incessantly occupied, in conjunction with machinery, to make numerous beautiful and exquisite works of art and utility to administer to the wants, and indulge the fancies, of mankind. The interior economy and workmanship of this hive, unlike that of the bee, however, has been gradually advancing towards perfection: its complicated operations have been simplified, and rendered apparently complete. I say apparently: for the mind of man can never rest; is never satisfied; and as naturally seeks for improved novelties and additional knowledge as the appetite for its requisite food. The present state of the Birmingham manufactures, compared with that of the last half century—indeed the last ten years—will verify this remark. The cursory observer would fancy that everything had now attained its climax of excellence; not only in the process of workmanship, but in the execution and effect of each article. Until very lately, however, very little has been done to adorn the exterior of this hive. Houses, churches, chapels, and public buildings have been raised one after another, without

---

a most eloquent and well-written address by Sir David Brewster, which he delivered at the twentieth anniversary meeting of the Society, at Edinburgh, in 1850, and which not only points out the many and vast advantages effected by that Society, but manifests the quantity and quality of science and zeal which there animated its members, and seemed to be diffused throughout the learned world.

much regard to the principles, the beauties, or the excellencies of architecture. A new era, however, has commenced: the spirit of improvement has visited the town, and it may be fairly presumed that it will impart a due portion of influence to the buildings, as to the manufactories, for competition and emulation lead to excellence; but the road is long, devious, and intricate. A short review of the progress in architectural works in this town, would show, that from the time of building St. Martin's Church, in the twelfth century, to that of St. Philip's, in the eighteenth, scarcely one step, one palpable advance, had been made in public edifices. Of the former building, in its original character, we know nothing; but may infer that it accorded with the style and spirit of the age when erected. Its present materials and appearance have little analogy to its ancient state; for it may be compared to the *old* knife, which had been repeatedly sent to the makers to have new handles and new blades. Adjoining St. Martin's, on the north, is a mass of bricks, or stones, piled together *à-la-Pyramid*, and called an Egyptian design. Were it a *Gipsy* work we should not complain.

"On the Bull Ring we find two old *timber-houses* still remaining, indicating the style of buildings, when the *moated* manor-house, and the adjoining parsonage were standing.

"If the topographers of Warwickshire, and of its towns, have not been very discriminate and critical in their descriptions and remarks on architecture, they have been abundantly panegyrical. Almost every public building is described as beautiful, elegant, grand, fine, tasteful, splendid, chaste, &c.; and sometimes with the superlative, *very* beautiful, *very* fine, &c. Foreigners and other strangers, on reading such works, may infer, that the county is another Italy, and Birmingham another Rome. With such impressions I penned the Account of this town for Rees's *Cyclopædia*, many years ago, having no other knowledge of it than what was to be derived from the amusing history by Mr. Hutton, a trifling pamphlet, and Mr. Bisset's poetical panegyrics. Were I to write a new account of it now, my language as well as matter would be very different to my former essay, to Hutton's History, or to any of the guides. I am persuaded, also, that it would be still more complimentary, because it would be more just and discriminating. False praise and inappropriate epithets will never confer merit on man or his works."

To one of the inhabitants of Birmingham I am more obliged and indebted, in my archæological and topographical works and pursuits, than to any other person in the world—WILLIAM HAMPER. With that estimable and well-informed antiquary I continued on intimate terms from the year 1812, when he first addressed a letter to me, till the time of his lamented death in May, 1831. A mass of his beautifully-written letters, now before me, is replete with sound information on various subjects of topography, antiquities, biography, &c., always couched in terms of kindness and playfulness. Thus, in one of his notes (April, 1830), after receiving a copy of the "Memoirs of the Tower of London," which I had presented to him, he writes—

> "'How doth the little busy B-ee
> Improve each shining hour,
> And gather honey all day long,'
> From Castle, Church, and Tower.

"To write *seriously* (which I very seldom do in my familiar epistles.") \*

Mr. Hamper was a partner in one of the large manufactories of the town, and was accustomed to travel to various parts of the country, on account of business. On those occasions he was in the habit of exploring and making notes and sketches of churches, castles, abbeys, and other antiquities; and he occasionally communicated such notes and sketches to the *Gentleman's Magazine*. In later life, and after being made a magistrate, he became acquainted with some of the noble and eminent families of his county and the neighbouring district; and thereby obtained free access to family and public documents, from which he made many interesting and useful extracts. Hence he ultimately collected a large mass of valuable materials to illustrate the History and Antiquities of the Counties of Warwick and Stafford. Those relating to the former county were intended to be used for a new edition of Dugdale's *History*, which was required by the public, and particularly urged by certain booksellers, when Ormerod's "Cheshire," Clutterbuck's "Hertfordshire," and the "Monasticon," were in course of publication, and the last proved to be a most successful speculation. At that time I visited Birmingham and Coventry, to see and consult Mr. Hamper, at the former, and Mr. Sharp, of the latter, about what co-operation and assistance they would be willing to render me towards a new history of their county. After due deliberation, both offered the use of their collections, with advice and cordial assistance; but Mr. Harding, the managing proprietor of the new "Monasticon," wished to engage another person as editor, with whom neither of the

---

\* In a note to me, with a copy of his Essay on "Hoar-stones," in March, 1820, he thus playfully writes :—" My health is much improved, though I am still very delicate and unable to give attention to any one subject long together. Mr. Pipe Wolferston, however, visits me to-morrow to nurse his brother antiquary. He is a prodigious Whig, and I am a stupendous Tory, but happily Literature is of no party, and his disciples are "' followers after Peace.'"

above-named gentlemen, nor myself were satisfied. Hence the relinquishment of the proposed new work, which has not since been undertaken; and the valuable collections by Hamper and Sharp have been dispersed by public auction. The materials by the former were numerous for the history of Birmingham, and were purchased by Beilby, Knott, & Beilby, of the town, probably for publication, but I have not learnt that they have been given to the public.*

A well-written, discriminating memoir of my once much-beloved companion, W. Hamper, is preserved in "the Gentleman's Magazine," for June, 1831, written by his old and confidential friend, Thomas Sharp, who tells us that he was born in Birmingham, Dec. 12th, 1776, where he died, May 3rd, 1831, at the age of fifty-four—in the prime of life. He may be referred to as one amongst many other instances of the advantages of industry, zeal, and integrity, in a person who possessed natural genius. His biographer states, that he "raised himself in society by the cultivation of his superior talents and taste: he had the distinguished merit of self-education, and was the simple architect of his own reputation and station in the republic of letters." Very early in life, he displayed the natural tendency of his mind, by some comic poetical compositions, which Mr. Sharp says were noticed " for felicity of expression, and occasionally strong marks of original humour." One of these, re-printed in Taylor's "Sussex Garland," is " a clever versification of the silly legend relating to the Devil's Dyke, on the Sussex Downs."

As a topographer and antiquary, Mr. Hamper evinced an intimate acquaintance; and not only prosecuted those studies through the medium of the best published works, but by deep researches amongst the family archives and ancient documents of the country.

Fully coinciding with the sentiments and opinions of Mr. Sharp, I will reiterate the language he has used in pourtraying the character of our mutual friend: " Mr. Hamper was a kind and sincere friend, an excellent husband and parent, and a most devout but unpretending Christian. His amiable disposition and pleasing manners gained the

---

* To show the extraordinary caprices and fluctuation in the names of places, the late Wm. Hamper found no less than *one hundred and forty* variations in spelling the word Birmingham in old and modern writings.

esteem of all who knew him; and even those who differed from him in political opinions could not avoid admiring and respecting his candour and disinterested sincerity. Such was the range of his talents, and so agreeable his society, that, whether condescending to sport with children, or to delight and inform superior minds, he has left recollections that will not easily be obliterated. Such was the irresistible charm of his conversation, that he was the centre of attraction in every society he joined. His letter-writing was the very beau-ideal of perfection; easy, elegant, clearly expressed; and, whether grave or gay, couched in language as remote from common-place, as it was evidently unstudied."

His published writings are in the *Gentleman's Magazine*, from the year 1804 to 1812; in the *Archæologia;* in a quarto volume, entitled "Kenilworth Illustrated;" a tract "On certain Ancient Pillars, called Hoar-stones, 1820;" and in the "Life, Diary, and Correspondence of Sir Wm. Dugdale," a handsome 4to. volume, 1827. The last is a truly interesting work, not only as unfolding the memoirs and character of the eminent Warwickshire antiquary and herald, but as containing a fund of amusing anecdote of his contemporaries, and various local topics. In 1822, Mr. Hamper printed a few specimens of a singular tract: "Two copies of Verses on the Meeting of King Charles the First and Queen Henrietta Maria, in the Valley of Kineton, below Edge Hill, in Warwickshire, July 11th, 1643."

Very shortly after the decease of Mr. Hamper, his interesting collection of Books, MSS., Seals, &c., was sold by auction, by Mr. Evans, of Pall Mall, London; amongst which were the following lots.

> Mr. Hamper's MS. Collections—Ancient Seals, with Deeds—County Histories, interleaved and illustrated, amongst which was Dugdale's "Warwickshire," in 4 large folio volumes, replete with valuable and important information. This work was fully described in the Catalogue, and was knocked down to Sir John Eardley Wilmot for £300. It has since been resold.
>
> Britton's "Life of Shakspere, with Remarks on his Writings, Bust, &c.," privately printed, interleaved, 8vo. 1818.—Sold for 22s.
>
> Britton's Memoirs of his own Life, privately printed, with Autograph Letter from the author to Mr. Hamper, 8vo. 1825.—Sold for 11s.
>
> Nash's "Worcestershire," interleaved, in 4 vols. folio, illustrated and enriched with numerous MS. notes, abstracts from deeds and public records, and an extensive mass of original materials, drawings, prints, &c.—Sold for £10. 5s.
>
> Webbe's "Rare and most Wonderfull Things which he hath Seene in his Trou-

blesome Travailes in Jerusalem, Damasks, Bethelem, Russia," &c., &c., VERY RARE, *cuts*, 1590.—Sold for £5. 18s.

Sharp's "Dissertation on the Coventry Pageants, or Mysteries," largest paper. Only three copies printed on this size, 1825.—Sold for £6. 10s.

Shaw's Fragment of a History of Staffordshire, abounding with MS. additions and corrections by the author, Mr. Hamper, and others; also thirty unpublished pages, and proof prints, &c.—Sold to Sir Thomas Phillips, Bart. for £27. 6s.

Kenilworth Illustrated, *largest paper, only two copies printed.*—Sold for £10. 5s.

The literary fame of HAGLEY, and of the LEASOWES, induced me to make an excursion from Birmingham to see them: the first, from the style and character of the house and grounds; and the second, from the descriptions which Shenstone had written about his native home. Lord Lyttleton's "Monody on his Wife's Death," speaks of the "well-known ground," the "fountain's side," the "waters gliding along the valley," the "wide-stretch'd prospect, and the verdant lawns," all allusive to his home. The park and pleasure-grounds were justly admired and noted for variety of scenery, and combination of fine old forest woods, undulating lawns, distant prospects, streamlets with cascades, and devious walks and drives; whilst the large, old, rich mansion was well stored with works of art, which were then regarded of great value. George Lord Lyttleton's "History of the Reign of Henry the Second," has remained a standard book in English History; whilst several others of his published writings were formerly popular. He was brother of the Rev. Dr. Lyttleton, Dean of Exeter, and Bishop of Carlisle, who wrote several papers on archæology, and was President of the Society of Antiquaries for some years.

I cannot sketch the character of Hagley better than in the language of Warner: "The land rises majestically behind the house, but is spoiled by those artificial decorations, which the fashion of the day, sixty years ago, considered as additions the most elegant and appropriate; and which attached to Hagley Park almost the exclusive character of taste in the design, disposition, and ornament of pleasure-grounds. These decorations are, a temple; a gothic ruin; an obelisk; a pillar; a palladian bridge; two or three trumpery grottoes; and as many *bits* of water, of diminutive size and accurate mathematical forms. Quotations painted on tablets of wood, culled from poets, ancient and modern, with the most artful care, in order that every word may have its appropriate feature in the scene to which it applies, complete the list of ornaments in the famed Hagley grounds. An urn, with an inscription, is dedicated to Pope; and a pavilion, with another inscription, to Thomson, both of whom were visitors to Hagley." The same author has enumerated some of the works of art within the mansion, amongst which are busts of Milton, Shakspere, Spenser, and Dryden, bequeathed by Pope to George Lord Lyttleton. The portraits are numerous and interesting.—[Warner's *Northern Tour*, Vol. i., p. 69. "Topographical Works," edition 1802.]

The Leasowes had attained celebrity, a century ago, by the writings of its proprietor, Wm. Shenstone, and the encomiums of Dr. Johnson, who relates that the poet "began to point his prospects, to diversify his surface, to entangle his walks, and to wind his waters; which he did with so much judgment and fancy, as made his little domain the envy of the great, and the admiration of the skilful: a place to be visited by travellers, and copied by designers." Thus, under the care of the poetic owner, it "became a perfect fairy-land," says another accomplished critic and successful commentator on and illustrator of the Fine Arts—S. C. Hall, in *The Book of the Poets*. Following the example of Dr. Johnson, several writers on the picturesque and beautiful in nature bepraised the Leasowes: hence my curiosity was excited to see and admire it; but I must own that disappointment was the result. The author had been dead some years, and the place had been neglected. The house was a poor, mean-looking building; and the bedizenment and decorations of the poet, in his grounds, had been taken away, or materially altered; but the natural features of the place, in undulation of ground, flow of water, with its cascades, and the woods, with distant views, could not fail to gratify every lover of the picturesque and beautiful. Shenstone having but a slender annual income, and being imprudent in its management, became impoverished in the latter part of life, and died in debt. Dr. Johnson, in his brief Diary of a "Welsh Tour," in 1774, has only this slight remark on the Leasowes: "We visited all the waterfalls. In one place there are fourteen in a short line."

From Birmingham to Wolverhampton, a distance of thirteen miles, the country was curious and amusing; though not very pleasing to eyes, ears, or taste; for part of it seemed a sort of pandemonium on earth—a region of smoke and fire filling the whole area between earth and heaven: amongst which certain figures of human shape—"if shape they had"—were seen occasionally to glide from one cauldron of curling-flame to another. The eye could not descry any form or colour indicative of country—of the hues and aspect of nature, or anything human or divine. Although nearly mid-day, in summer, the sun and sky were obscured and discoloured: something like horses, men, women, and children occasionally seemed to move in the midst of the black and yellow smoke and flashes of fire; but were again lost in obscurity. A straggling boy or girl was at times seen in the road, with uncombed and uncut hair, unwashed skin, and naked limbs, which appeared as if smoke-dried, and encased with a compound of that element and soot. This scene, however, is confined to a small portion of the road near Bilston: in other places, green fields, trees, and hedges appear, with houses, or substitutes for houses, in almost endless succession. The surface of the earth is covered and loaded with its own entrails, which afford employment and livelihood for thousands of the human race. Men, women, and children—indeed the whole population—are workers in iron and coal, the latter of which is used to convert the former into useful and ornamental articles. My friend, the Rev. R. Warner, who walked over this district soon after I had visited it, writes thus, in the second volume of his *Northern Tour* :—" This country is quite a land of Cyclopses; spotted in all directions with vast works for the preparation of iron; founderies, slitting-mills, and steam-engines, pouring out flames and smoke, and forming a sight tremendous to those unaccustomed to such manufactories. Add to this, the appearance of a *soil of fire,* where the earth literally burns to the eye, and the no less fearful sight of vast heaps of red-hot coke, on all sides; the fiend-like look of the dingy workmen managing the liquid flaming metal; and the horrible din of engines and bellows, the rushing of the steam, and the roaring of the flame,—and nothing carried on in the haunts of men can give so complete an idea of the appearance which we conceive those places would represent, where ' the worm dieth not, and the fire is not quenched.' "

The poet Cowper tells us that "GOD made the country, and MAN made the town:" but as the district I have noticed is neither country nor town, it may be regarded as out of the category of the poet's assertion. Certainly, the contrast between the sweet, clear, cheerful country, and the smoky, dirty, noisome town, is palpable to all our senses. The first evinces the skill and wisdom of an incomparable Maker and Master; the second, the hand of a poor apprentice. One is full of beauty, utility, and fitness; whilst the other abounds with uglinesses, defects, and incongruities. One was made perfect, and never needed repair, nor alteration; the other was commenced by its first builder without foresight, and without due consideration of ulterior and lasting effects. Incapable of amendment, the one has lasted for unnumbered ages, without the slightest decay; whilst the other is perpetually altered and changed, and still is full of faults. It is true that there are weeds, poisons, fungi, parasitical plants, storms, blights, and tempests; but these necessary evils are essential to man's welfare and to his happiness. He was made to gain his livelihood; to preserve his health by "the sweat of his brow"—by the labour of his own hand and mind; and therefore it is necessary to the healthfulness of that body as well as mind, that he should toil to subdue weeds, as well as apply antidotes to poisons. If man could content himself by striving to imitate nature, and obey her dictates and promptings, he might become more happy and skilful than he is at present; but, too full of self-conceit and arrogance, he vainly endeavours to excel her, and thereby subjects himself to the sneering reproaches of the captious, and the just castigation of the profound moralist and critic.

At WOLVERHAMPTON, I was advised to examine the fine old church of St. Peter's and its commanding site, with the monuments, and a singular pillar, in the adjoining cemetery. The ancient carved-wood screens, octagonal font, curious stone pulpit, brass statue, in armour, of Sir Richard Leveson, and certain old tombs, with inscriptions, excited my curiosity, though they tantalized my archæological knowledge. The ancient pillar in the churchyard, induced me to sketch it with pencil, from which I perceive that its shaft has various sculptured figures of animals and birds in basso-relievo, with scrolls, commonly called Runic knots. This is probably the shaft of a sepulchral cross, intended at once to commemorate a public person and some legendary event connected with the place. Several stones of a similar sort are found in Scotland, and there is one in Bakewell churchyard. The font and the pulpit are certainly objects of curiosity and interest, and are probably works of the beginning of the 15th century. The parish of Wolverhampton occupies an area of about thirty miles in circumference; within the town are four churches, subordinate to the Dean, who has paramount ecclesiastical jurisdiction, and is also Dean of Windsor.

On proceeding from Wolverhampton to Shrewsbury, the county-town of Shropshire, new, fruitful, picturesque, and grand features of country are successively presented to the eye of the traveller. Amongst these, the celebrated demi-mountain—*the Wrekin*—forms a conspicuous and exciting object. It is an insulated pyramidical hill, rising out of a flat, to the altitude of 1320 feet above the level of the sea. Though in the neighbourhood of certain mountainous ridges and chains, which enter into, and mostly terminate in Shropshire, the peculiarity of form, the height and character of the Wrekin, tend to render it remarkable amongst the eminences of the country. In popular phraseology it is marked as the centre of the world: " All round the Wrekin," is a toast and proverbial expression. It may be regarded as one of the outposts of the mountainous district of Wales; and from its apex may be traced the more lofty ranges of the Caradoc, the Breidden, the Longmynd, and the Clun-forest. It may naturally be inferred that this new class and feature in the phenomena of nature excited intense desire in me to be amongst them, and to explore their craggy and steep sides, their varied and romantic summits and ridges, their defiles, streams, waterfalls, lakes, and entrenched summits. I was therefore eager to reach my proposed temporary home, and resting-place—CHURCH STRETTON. Here I was affectionately received and welcomed by my eldest sister, and her good husband, John Meredith, with whom I sojourned for some weeks. My brother-in-law was master of a large school in this small town, and was much-respected by his neighbours, and by the parents of his pupils, most of the latter being his boarders. The house was large, and the foundation was an endowed grammar school for a certain number of boys, to which the master added others on his private establishment.

At the time I visited, there were about forty pupils, ranging from the age of six to fourteen years. Some of these required and were provided with tuition from masters who came once or twice a week from the neighbouring town of Shrewsbury. This fact is more particularly impressed on my mind from the gratification and benefits I derived by being indulged to attend the classes of the drawing, dancing, and French masters. Not having ever experienced the advantages of such instruction in my school-days, I listened to, and noted most attentively, every lesson, and every maxim, of these different professors; and have often regretted that I was not then enabled to devote one or more years to the education which was then and there inculcated. To this association—to the language and manners of the gentlemen I met there, in Shrewsbury, and the neighbourhood—I may fairly date my *début* on the stage of life, and the benefit of deporting myself with some degree of ease and respectability, in the company of noblemen and gentlemen, to whom it was my good fortune to be afterwards introduced in my native county of Wilts. At Church Stretton I experienced much courtesy and condescending kindness from the Rev. John Mainwaring, Rector of that parish, and the Rev. Richard Wilding, Curate, who resided at All Stretton, at the base of the Caer Caradoc mountain. The latter gentleman gave me much useful and exciting information about the castrametation on the summit of that famed hill. He was the first person from whom I derived any oral hints and plain suggestions respecting the distinctions and varieties of form and construction in the British, Anglo-Roman, and other fortresses, which abound on the borders of Wales and England, as well as of Roman roads and fixed stations. The Watling Street, from Uriconium to Braminium, supposed to have passed through Church Stretton, was often alluded to, and its traces pointed out.

Church Stretton consists only of one street, which is a public roadway between Shrewsbury to the north, and Ludlow to the south: being nearly joined to the two other Strettons, called *All*, and *Little*, the whole seems one large straggling town. The houses are placed in a narrow valley, bounded by the lofty hills or mountains of Caradoc to the east, and the Longmynd to the west, whose sides are abrupt in some places, producing a spare, scanty herbage for poor sheep; and in others, with rocks coming to, and forming the surface. In some parts narrow defiles or "dingles" run up from the vale, into and amongst these hills.

Reflecting on the numerous and formidable mountain-fortresses of this district, it is not surprising that such an important battle as that in which the famed Caractacus was conquered, and this part of Britain finally subjected to the Roman legions, should be a subject of dispute with antiquaries and historians; for the descriptions of Tacitus are not sufficiently precise and specific to identify localities. Hence the site of the last desperate struggle of the Britons for their independence and freedom has necessarily become a matter of importance, not only with topographers, but with the best-informed historians. General Roy wrote a dissertation to show that Coxwell Knoll, north of Ludlow, was the site of the fortress occupied by Caractacus previous to the engagement, and that Brandon, or Braminium, a steep hill on the opposite side of the river Teme, was fortified and possessed by Ostorius and his army. Other authors name different places in this part of the island, but the real site is still doubtful, and consequently a point for further investigation and controversy. It is, however, generally admitted, that the gallant and noble British prince and general was conquered and obliged to retreat for personal safety, and that he was traitorously betrayed by Cartismandua, Queen of the Brigantes. He, his wife, and his daughters, were made prisoners and sent to Rome, where it seems that he propitiated the reigning emperor to spare his life. His subsequent career is unknown, though Tacitus is copious on previous matters.

After deriving incalculable profit from the rational converse and company I fortunately met, it became necessary to resume my travels towards the south, and I took leave of my dear relatives, with their young family and large group of pupils, with a heavy but anxious heart. Here was displayed a home and harmony, with every prospect of success and advancement in life, whilst my situation was that of a wanderer—an adventurer at sea, without chart or compass, and ignorant of a port wherein to cast anchor with security and confidence.

It was during this journey, and in this part of the country, I became acquainted with two eminent and learned topographers and antiquaries, with whom I continued to correspond for many years—

*the Rev. J. B. Blakeway* and *the Rev. Hugh Owen,* both of Shrewsbury. These gentlemen co-operated in literature, in a pleasing and useful way; the former devoting his studies and writings to history and genealogy, whilst the latter made architectural antiquities the more essential part of his inquiries and elucidation. Thus united and thus employed, they produced "A History of Shrewsbury," in two volumes, 4to. 1826, of acknowledged merit and value. To these gentlemen I was indebted for interesting historical and descriptive Essays on the fine ruins of Wenlock Priory; also of Ludlow and Stoke-say Castles, in Shropshire; the former writing the history, and the latter the description of those ruinated and deserted edifices. I now refer to those Essays with great pleasure, as I do to the very kind and friendly conduct which those gentlemen evinced towards an unknown but anxious juvenile author. Unfortunately, I was not sufficiently versed in topography and antiquities to profit fully by their learning and judgment.

In the Rev. Dr. Butler, then Master of the famed Grammar School, of Shrewsbury, and afterwards Bishop of Lichfield, I met a valuable friend and adviser. Mr. David Parkes, who was master of a large school in this old town, I found to be "a man after my own heart," who, being self-educated, and having worked his way up in the world, from poverty and obscurity to a respectable station in society, felt a sort of instinctive sympathy for a young man whose commencement seemed somewhat analogous to his own. Mr. Parkes was partial to drawing, topography, and antiquities, and had begun a correspondence with the *Gentleman's Magazine,* which he continued for many years, accompanied by many drawings of churches and antiquities. Mr. Dovaston, a barrister, whose admiration of Shakspere, and poetical talents, I have noticed in the *Appendix* to this work, p. 45, has recorded in the Gentleman's Magazine for June, 1833, a pleasing tribute of literary respect and affection to the memory and worth of this gentleman. He describes him as having exercised, for "more than half a century, the useful calling of an intellectual and assiduous schoolmaster;" and further, that "his manners were mild, gentle, and affectionate; his industry intense, and his integrity inflexible. He enjoyed the friendship, correspondence, and familiar acquaintance of very many literary characters." His topographical collections for Shropshire were of large extent, carefully classed, and arranged in several quarto volumes, which were dispersed at the sale of his effects. It is but just to the memory of this amiable and much-respected person, to ascribe the preservation and substantial renovation of St. Mary's Church, in Shrewsbury, to him. He was born in the parish of Hales-Owen, February 21, 1763; and died at Shrewsbury, May 8, 1833.

In the ancient, half-English, half-Welsh, town of SHREWSBURY, I could not fail to be much and diversely interested: first, with the gentlemen whom I met, as strangers, and parted with, as friends; and by the peculiarity of site, external appearance, and interior arrangement of streets; and also with the style and character of the public and private buildings. The old town is singularly spread over a small peninsular tract of ground, formed by the winding course of the river Severn, which borders three-fourths of the land, in a sort of horse-shoe shape; the other part being an eminence on which the first settlers raised a fortress, to guard that entrance to the town. That fort progressively became a large, formidable, and strong castle. Soon after the Norman conquest, it is stated that the new monarch gave the town to his kinsman, Roger de Montgomery, who cleared away fifty-one houses to enlarge the area for new castellated works. Hence we may infer that Shrewsbury was an important post for the chieftain of the district; and that its strong walls and powerful garrison would attract and afford something like protection to the people who congregated within their precincts. Some of the churches, the Market-house, the ruins of the Abbey, and several old timber houses were calculated to awaken and gratify my curiosity; but I was not sufficiently initiated in archæology to appreciate their intrinsic merits and history, or discriminate the variety of styles and peculiarities which belong to and contradistinguish one building from the others. At two later visits to the town, and after commencing *The Architectural Antiquities,* I was better enabled to enjoy the advantages and pleasures to be derived from educating the eye to see and understand forms, proportions, and details of those old edifices which belong to our country, and which serve as indexes and land-marks to many important events, and epochs in our national history.

My first place to visit, after leaving Stretton, was DOWNTON, or DOWNTON CASTLE, the seat of RICHARD PAYNE KNIGHT, ESQ., then M.P. for Ludlow, a second edition of whose poem, entitled "The Landscape," with copious notes and comments, had appeared in 1795. This seat had excited my curiosity, and induced a longing desire to see grounds, a house, and a man, which had become celebrated in the annals of poetry and literary controversy. Meeting with the author, and lord of the domain, at home, I was received with courtesy and cordiality. He showed me his new demi-castellated mansion, and his more interesting grounds; the last of which are so truly romantic and picturesque, that they would be likely to excite a fastidiousness of feeling in their possessor. In front of the house the park slopes rapidly to a narrow valley, through which the river Teme rushes over a rocky bed. This vale and water extend nearly three miles through the grounds, and afford, with their well-wooded sides, variety of land and rock, and diversified effects upon the eye and ear, a fund of pleasure to the artist and the poet. Hence it is not surprising that the former should endeavour to transfer some of these scenes to canvass and paper, whilst the latter would be equally inclined to make efforts to describe them in harmonious language, to please the ear and imagination of the reader. Alas! how weak, how inadequate are the powers of either,—even both,—to do justice to such grand and diversified features, incidents, and ever-changing scenes of nature! Not only the vicissitudes of seasons, of sunshine, and of gloom—of the grey morn, yellow mid-day, and sombre evening—but the glitter and varied music of the gurgling rill and the rattling torrent produce effects which human art has not yet acquired the skill and felicity to imitate. Hearne made drawings of some of these scenes, and faithfully delineated the permanent objects— ground, trees, rocks;—but the ripple and glitter, the music and motion of the bright and restless waters, were beyond the art of a Ruysdael or a Turner to define on canvass. One of these Downton drawings, with the copper-plate engraved from it, Mr. Knight presented to me, for the *Beauties of England*, in which publication it may be seen, with some account of the seat. In the latter, it is stated that, "with the advantage of a fine mountain river, a profusion of wood, some bold rocks, and a variety of distances, Downton may be justly considered as one of the most picturesque seats in England." The scenery about the Mill, at some distance from the house, is peculiarly wild and romantic. This mill may be regarded as a main feature in the accumulated fortune of the Knight family; the grandfather of Richard Payne and Thomas Andrew Knight having amassed it as an iron-master, before steam-engines were constructed. The house of Downton, which was built between 1774 and 1778, after its wealthy proprietor had come into possession of a large income, and had returned from Italy, is thus described, by himself, in his " Enquiry into the Principles of Taste." It is " ornamented with what are called Gothic towers and battlements, without, and with Grecian ceilings, columns, and entablatures, within; and, though his example has not been much followed, he has every reason to congratulate himself upon the success of the experiment: he having at once the advantage of a picturesque object and of an elegant and convenient dwelling, though less perfect in both respects than if it had been executed at a maturer age. It has, however, the advantage of receiving alterations and additions in almost every direction, without injury to its original and genuine character." Though evidently the design of an amateur, the house has that variety of outline and form which the author intended to harmonize with the scene; and which also, in its interior, would be in keeping with those antiquities and works of art which he had collected. The lawn and grounds, immediately adjoining the mansion, when I saw them, presented more of the wildness and ruggedness of nature than the dress and decoration of the landscape garden; for large heaps of stones, with briers, thorns, and even thistles, were to be seen in many places.

Besides " The Landscape " and his volume on " Taste," the last of which has passed through several editions, Mr. Knight was author of " The Progress of Civil Society," a didactic poem in six books, 4to. 1796; a work, says " The Penny Cyclopædia," now only known by the witty parody in " The Anti-jacobin," supposed to have been written by Mr. Canning. This remark, however, is neither generous nor just; for it may be safely asserted that the former is as well known, and much more respected than the latter. It is not customary with readers of our times to seek either amusement or information in the poetry, and what is called "light reading" of the last century. Mr. Knight was, however, a poet, learned in the Greek language, also in the history and fine arts of Athens, as his numerous writings on those subjects amply testify. With wealth, and love for the works of the best Grecian artists and authors, he purchased large collections of their productions, which were displayed in his town-house, in Soho Square, London. The whole, valued at £50,000, he bequeathed to the British Museum; to legalize which gift an Act of Parliament was passed in June, 1824, two months before which event the generous donor died at his town mansion. His corpse was removed to Wormesby church, Herefordshire. An interesting memoir of Mr. Knight, with notices of all his publications, will be found in " The Penny Cyclopædia," and a very good portrait of him, engraved by E. Scriven, from a picture by Sir Thomas Lawrence, is in " The British Gallery of Contemporary Portraits," Vol. ii. 1822.

Quitting the eminently interesting locality of Downton, with its fascinating scenery, and the prepossessing society of its truly classical and enlightened proprietor, I directed my slow steps to LUDLOW, a town replete with objects and matter of the first importance to the English historian and antiquary. I had read about it, and its associations, as a place much frequented and admired by artists—of being the fortified palace and residence of Princes, "Lords Marches," or guardians of the district—the border land of England and Wales—of the importance and power of their baronial residence, at different and successive epochs from the Norman conquest to the civil wars of the seventeenth century. These matters, however, belong to the studies and evidences of the library; whereas my object, like that of most travellers, was to see tangible remains in *statu-quo,* or at least as portions of buildings which were once great, probably beautiful, at all events that had belonged to former races of our ancestors. In the ruined castle, the fine church and tower, the old houses, and the varied scenery of the whole, as presented in the streets and from different stations, I was assured of finding abundant matter to gratify the eye of the artist and the antiquary. A sojourn of two days enabled me to see these, however, superficially, though quite enough to show that every part and separate portion of the buildings, and each spot, were connected with some memorable events or persons, or both, belonging to national history. Since I first visited Ludlow, much has been written and published about it; but the castle, the church and its monuments, as well as some of the old houses, remain to gratify and reward an artist who can faithfully and skilfully delineate them, and the reader who will encourage their publication. In *The Architectural Antiquities*, Vol. iv., will be found two views of that portion of the inner ballium of the castle, called the Round Tower, with a ground-plan of the same; and the Rev. J. B. Blakeway, of Shrewsbury, wrote a short history to accompany the prints; whilst the Rev. Hugh Owen obliged me by a satisfactory description of the castle buildings. Since that time (1814) Mr. Blakeway has extended and improved his "Early History of Ludlow," for a very interesting volume which has been printed at the expense of R. H. Clive, Esq., M.P., a Shropshire gentleman. It is entitled "Documents connected with the History of Ludlow and the Lords Marches," imp. 8vo. 1841, pp. 361, and contains some important papers and materials relating to the town. The topographical reader will find a more detailed and ample history of Ludlow and its vicinity, written by my respected friend, Thomas Wright, who is a native of this part of the country, and who has evidently performed his task *con amore*. It is clearly the production of an experienced, learned, and discriminating author; and I cannot help regretting that its illustrations were not more numerous and better executed. The Rev. Mr. Owen describes Ludlow as "seated on an eminence, commanding views on every side of great beauty. On the summit is a handsome market-cross, from whence the streets, which are generally spacious and well built, branch off in easy declivities. The church is a stately cathedral-like structure, with a light and lofty central tower. In the choir and chapels are very large remains of painted glass, and there are many fine tombs of the vice-presidents, chief-justices, and other principal officers of the Council of Wales." He next gives a very particular description of the castle, which consisted of numerous towers, with intermediate buildings, and extended around two balliæ, or courts. Within the area of the inner court is a tower of peculiar form and architectural character, and, I believe, unique in design. Its exterior and interior, with ground-plan, are represented in the *Architectural Antiquities*. It is described by Mr. Owen as the nave, or outer portion of a *Chapel*, which, in its perfect state, appears to have been similar in general design to the famed "round churches" of Cambridge, London, and Northampton. At present the tower only remains, which, from the semi-circular shape of the doorway, of the windows, of the arcade extending round the interior, of the style of mouldings and capitals, was evidently raised soon after the Norman Conquest. In Dr. Stukeley's "Itinerarium Curiosum," are prints of the castle, which, though slightly and badly drawn, show the plan of the building when he visited it in 1721. The prints are particularly valuable, as indicating the whole "ground plot" of the chapel, and its junction with the private apartments, on the north side. By these it appears that the four sides of the inner court were occupied by buildings, and detached from the outer ballium by a deep and wide fosse, cut out of the rock. The same valuable, but too often visionary antiquary, states that "the present inhabitants of the castle live upon the sale of the timber, stone, iron, and other materials and furniture, which dwindle away insensibly."

That Ludlow Castle was a place of importance in the seventeenth century, is evinced by the circumstance of Charles the First's coronation having been solemnized here, with great pomp and festivity.

The lovers of poetry will not fail to associate the names of *Milton* and *Butler* with the castle of Ludlow; as the *Comus* of the former was acted here in 1634, when the Earl of Bridgewater was appointed Lord President of the Marches. On that occasion some of the junior members of the Earl's family were performers in the mask; and it is known that the *Arcades*, by the same author, was enacted by the Countess of Derby's grand-children, about the same time, at Harefield-place, in Middlesex. It is singular that neither Dr. Symonds, nor the Rev. H. J. Todd, in their respective lives of Milton, has noticed the acting of *Comus*, at Ludlow. In the large and elaborate edition of Milton's Works, 3 vols. 4to. 1777, by Dr. Newton, Bishop of Bristol, is an account of its first performance, when the author was in the 26th year of his age; also copious notes of commentary, and numerous tasteless illustrations, from the designs by F. Hayman. In this poem the following lines evidently apply to Ludlow castle:—

> ——— "All this tract that fronts the falling sun,
> A noble Peer of mickle trust and power
> Has in his charge, with tempered awe to guide
> An old and haughty nation proud in arms:

> Where his fair offspring nursed in princely love
> Are coming to attend their father's state,
> And new entrusted scepter."

The once very popular and truly-original poet, *Samuel Butler*, author of "Hudibras," was more identified with Ludlow castle than even Milton; as he was steward and secretary to Richard, Earl of Carbury, whilst Lord President of the Marches, and had apartments in the tower-gate-house, between the outer and inner court. This was after he had lived in the service of Sir Samuel Luke, of Bedfordshire, one of Cromwell's commanders, and who is supposed to be the caricatured Knight, Hudibras. It is believed that parts of Butler's famed poem were written in the castle, now referred to.—But I must check my pen, as the best descriptive language can convey but very imperfect information without the aid of illustration.

A personal incident connected with Ludlow may be introduced here, as showing an adventure which my veteran friend, the celebrated *Walker* through Wales, could have made a lengthened and amusing tale of. My account is only worthy of record as one of the romances of real life, and therefore calculated to "point a moral, if not adorn a tale."

At Tunbridge Wells, in days before it became a popular though fashionable watering-place, and even for some time afterwards, it was customary for persons to way-lay visitors on the road, soliciting their company, at certain inns and lodgings. This practice was called "Touting." At many of our modern sea-bathing and other towns and villages of public resort, strangers are accosted by waiters with cards, and invitations to different houses and places where refreshments and accommodations are offered "of the best quality" and on "the most reasonable terms." Though I have travelled over many hundreds of miles of English and Welsh ground, and visited many different hotels, inns, and public-houses, I never was invited, or "*touted*," but once—by a pretty girl, about eighteen, to take up my travelling quarters at her residence. This was at Ludlow, at the time of the walking excursion now alluded to. Standing near the middle of the town, at the junction of four streets, and where some picturesque old timber houses attracted my attention, the said young lady accosted me with, "Pray, Sir, are you looking for an inn?" Though I could not say yes, she proceeded, "We can accommodate you with comfortable lodgings at our house." The comfort, or rather discomfort of the Portsmouth "lodgings" (noticed in p. 138, *ante*) came across my mind; but all alarm was removed by my inquirer pointing to an interesting old timber hostel, which she said was kept by her aunt, to whom I was soon introduced. She was seated in a large armed-chair, in front of a very capacious fire-place, whose mantel-piece was adorned with a shining display of polished-iron spits, tongs, shovels, pokers, and candlesticks; also others of brass, with warming-pan and a few minor articles. A gun, a blunderbuss, and a sword constituted part of the group. At the sides of the fire-place were two alcoved recesses for seats, whilst flitches of bacon were hung up, within the chimney. Attached to the ceiling, or rather to the rafters and beams of the chamber floor, was a large bacon rack, well stored with various articles of food, or for use and ornament; whilst a broad wood settle, chairs, tables, &c., to match, were distributed about the room. The floor was flag-stones, with two or three patches of brick-tile, and slate, and the whole was sprinkled with sand. Four or five persons were seated, with mugs of cider, ale, and pipes, whose converse partook of a mixture of English and Welsh. In such a place, and such company, I felt quite at ease; had a glass of ale and a Welsh-rabbit, with the intention of going early to bed. My loquacious and officious waiter told me, however, that "the players" were at Ludlow, and were to perform *Pizarro*, with *Crotchet Lodge*, that very night, put a bill into my hand, and asked if I should like to go to the theatre, and she had an order for two. I did not require to be coaxed, and only wished to be behind rather than before the curtain. The niece could talk about plays and players, and she soon found that I knew something of the Kemble, the Siddons, and other shining stars in the London firmament. "Birds of a feather flock together." Boys and girls—for I was truly young in experience and worldly knowledge, whilst my new acquaintance was much younger in years, but evidently more "forward," being a real hoyden—we soon became familiar: she discoursed glibly on acting, whilst I told her stories of London heroes and heroines:—planets of the "dramatic hemisphere." She often wished to be on the stage, but her aunt never went to a play, and did not think players good customers or good men. In a previous page (see *ante*, p. 117) I have given the reader some notion of the stroller's life and difficulties, and therefore will not again bring it on the stage by describing the "house," and the performers, with their dresses and acting, but merely say that I was amused if not instructed by the Ludlow "theatricals." I was also pleased with the vivacity and intelligence of my companion, who, I found, before the end of the performance, had a sweetheart amongst the young heroes of the sock and buskin. Two years afterwards I met with the same company at Newtown, in Wales, with my young waiter enlisted into the dramatic corps, and made an actress, a wife, and a mother.

In my road from Ludlow to Hereford, I paid short visits to LEOMINSTER, an interesting old town, and to Hampton Court, the equally attractive ancient seat of the Earl of Essex. At the former, the old timber houses, with the town-hall, or Butter Close (as there called) of corresponding material and character, induced a longing desire to have good drawings of them; and when I arrived in London, I found that my young friend, John Varley, had made elaborate sketches of the latter. Like the old shire-hall of Hereford, this building consists almost entirely of wood, having twelve oak pillars resting on a paved floor and supporting a large, heavy superstructure: the brackets and spandrils of the arches, springing from pillars, and the upper part of the building, display much carving of grotesque figures, coats of arms, foliage, &c. This edifice was constructed—I will not say built—about 1633, by John Abel, who made the shire-hall at Hereford a few years afterwards, resembling his previous work. Parts of the church are evidently of the Anglo-Norman age, and exhibit some fine specimens of the architecture then prevalent; particularly in the great western doorway: on the north side is another of corresponding character, whilst there are other parts of similar architecture in the old parts of the church. This originally formed a portion of a priory, of ancient date, and of much historical note.

I called at HAMPTON COURT, in my way from Leominster to Hereford, having understood that its noble proprietor was a lover and patron of art and literature. As his Lordship was not at home, I only examined the outside of the castellated mansion, and the fine scenery in which it is placed. Two years afterwards, I had the pleasure and advantage of spending two days at this interesting seat. I cannot, however, resist directing the reader's attention to a few lines from Stukeley's work, already referred to. He tells us that he and his companion, Roger Gale, were entertained by Lord Coningsby at dinner, when " one of the ancient bards, in an adjacent room, play'd to us upon the harp, and at proper intervals threw in many notes of his voice, with a swelling thrill, after a surprising manner, much in the tone of a flute. This fine seat was built by our countryman (Lincolnshire) Harry of Bolinbroke, afterwards H. IV. 'Tis castle-like, the gardens very pleasant, terminated by vast woods, covering all the sloping side of the hill; a verdant theatric concavity. Here is a great command of water for all sides of the house, for fountains, basons, canals. Within are excellent pictures of the Earl's ancestors, by Holbein, Dobson, Vandyke, Sir P. Lely, &c. There is an original of the founder, H. IV.; of Queen Elizabeth, the Dutchess of Portsmouth, &c. After dinner, my Lord did us the honor to ride out with us into the park, which for beauty, diversity, and use is very fine: eight miles in circumference. There is a new river cut quite through the park, hewn out of the rock. Here are new gardens and canals laid out, and new plantations to compleat its pleasures. Warrens, decoys, sheep-walks, pastures for cattle, and the like, supply the house without recourse to a mercut. His Lordship show'd us four or five vast books in MS., transcripts from record offices, relating to his manors, royalties, estates, and muniments, which cost him £500."

The CITY OF HEREFORD, being the first ancient Cathedral-town I had ever visited (for Oxford is a modern city) excited a new species of curiosity, with new trains of thinking and speculation. Though I had not read much on cathedral history, nor had opportunities of seeing even one of those interesting edifices of our country, excepting, indeed, that of St. Paul's, London, which only excited wonder at its magnitude, and vast cupola; I had learnt something about them in different topographical works, and particularly in the pages of the *Gentleman's Magazine*, in which my captiously critical friend, John Carter, had been long waging war against James Wyatt, for his innovations on the genuine style and character of what has been, and still is, popularly, but absurdly, called Gothic Architecture. The Cathedral of Hereford had, for some ten or twelve years, been rendered an object of general lament from the circumstance of the decay and fall of its western front, with parts of the nave and its aisle, in 1786. Such an event was a novelty in cathedrals; and the exaggerated stories that went abroad to the world, " of the destruction of this fine and ancient edifice, from the negligence and parsimony of its guardians," excited no small amount of popular clamour. Mr. Gough, the most zealous topographer and antiquary of his age, says, " My heart bleeds at the sacrifices already made to the caprices of our modern architects:—partly through the neglect of the Chapters, and partly by the ill-management of the architects they employ, the cathedrals are falling about their ears. The lives of sixteen men were placed in danger, and some were killed, by the negligence of the influential persons at Hereford, in placing the scaffolding within the nave."—[*Gent.'s Mag.*, 1790.]

The dangerous situation of the whole church, after the catastrophe alluded to, induced the Dean and Chapter to solicit the professional advice of James Wyatt, who was then a fashionable, and consequently favoured, architect. He made designs, which were approved, and the works were commenced, to form a western front, and inclose that part of the church. Instead of making the new harmonize with the old Norman circular architecture, which prevailed throughout the nave, his design showed large pointed-arched windows, with mullions and tracery, crocketted pinnacles, &c. Unfortunately, all these parts and features were not merely out of character with the adjoining building, but were poor, meagre, and tasteless. At that time, as in the preceding age, from the dissolution of monasteries till the commencement of the present century, it was not deemed a matter of the slightest consequence, in the reparation or alteration of cathedrals, or of parish churches, to make the new correspond with the older and good work. Public taste, as well as knowledge, were in a lamentable state of debasement. The higher classes of society were not merely uneducated in art, but wholly ignorant of the science and history of architecture; and many professional men were equally uninformed. Hence it was never thought requisite to imitate the numerous beauties which are now known to belong to the cathedrals, and even to parish churches of the middle ages. Suffice to say, that, at Hereford, new walls, with new windows, arches, pillars, and details, were built at an expenditure of nearly £20,000; and that the cathedral officers, the architect, and the many artificers employed, appear to have been well satisfied with their performances. Strange, however, though it be, a learned clergyman, the Rev. T. Garbett (who favoured me with some interesting information on the cathedral, when I was writing its history, and illustrating its architecture, in 1831) wrote and published an octavo volume, to vindicate, and even to praise, most of Mr. Wyatt's alterations and additions to this cathedral. In summing up his arguments on the effects of these changes and novelties, the author says, "the spectator is irresistibly struck with the magnitude of the work, the *chastity of its style, and the harmony and proportion of its several parts.*"—[*Brief Inquiry,* p. 23.] In my volume on the Cathedral, I was induced not only to reprove such comments, but to write some severe strictures on the architect and his employers.—[See *History,* pp. 45—47.] In that volume is an engraving, from a beautiful drawing by Hearne, showing the ruins of the west end and the nave, as they appeared soon after the fall thus alluded to.

The year 1842 is memorable in the history of this cathedral. The late zealous and enthusiastic Dean (Merewether) was then apprised by Mr. Hardwick, architect, that the large central tower, as well as the Lady Chapel, were in danger. The Dean, who had been attached to the church for about ten years, and who had previously noticed cracks and defects, immediately ordered the walls to be shored up, and summoned the Chapter as speedily as practicable, who resolved to adopt prompt and efficient measures to preserve and restore the building. Plans, drawings, and estimates were obtained from Mr. L. N. Cottingham, who had been strongly recommended; whilst Professor Willis, of Cambridge, had made a careful survey, and as careful a report on the state of the fabric, and its peculiarities of architecture. Thus provided, the Dean and Chapter agreed to appropriate £2000 from their joint funds, which were already burthened with a debt of £9244, for the Wyatt alterations. The Dean, from a zeal more ardent than prudent, pledged himself for £500; the Bishop, £500; and other officers of the cathedral made further subscriptions to the amount of

£4771. A public meeting was called, in January 1842, to raise additional funds; for the architect's estimate was £17,674. The principal nobility, gentry, and clergy of the diocese attended; the Dean read a long and impressive appeal, and several subscriptions of £200, and of £100 were made. At another public meeting, in the same month, further funds were promised: the architect was soon instructed to proceed with the works, which were continued up to the time of his decease in 1850. The architect had a most difficult task, as the walls and piers were very unsound. The Dean published a very interesting volume on the subject, with prints illustrative of the defects in the building. In consequence of opposing the present Bishop of the Diocese, in 1848, the Dean had involved himself in lamentable disputes and controversy with that respected prelate and his friends. This preyed on his mind, and affected his health, and he sunk under a weight of anxiety, oppression, and disease, in April, 1850. I had enjoyed his friendship for many years, and knew that he was sincere, ardent, conscientious, warm-hearted, and an enthusiastic antiquary. Had he been at Hereford when I commenced my History of its Cathedral in 1830, that volume would, most likely, have been more circumstantial in its historical materials, better in its illustrations, and consequently more complete than it now is.

A short account of my connection with the city is given in the Preface to the History referred to, wherein the reader will find ample illustrations of the architecture of that remarkable church, and of some of its monuments. One of the latter, to Bishop Cantelupe, is as singular for its design as for the romance and irrational legends belonging to the saint it commemorates.*

---

\* I must venture to direct the attention of the antiquary to a very *ancient Map of the World* preserved in this Cathedral, of which a particular account is given in an early volume of *The Transactions of the Royal Geographical Society*.

In *The Picturesque Antiquities of English Cities*, I have given representations and accounts of three objects of antiquity, connected with Hereford: an *old timber house*, being part of a series of the same kind called Butcher Row, and adjoining the Shirehall, likewise formed almost wholly of timber. The last consists of twenty-seven wooden pillars, ranged in three lines, on the ground plan, with capitals, bases, and ornamented arches. Above is a wooden floor, which was originally divided into apartments for fourteen of the trading companies of the city. As already noticed, p. 175, these premises

Whilst staying at Hereford I was tempted to visit *Kenchester*, where the Romans had a station called *Magna-Castra*, during their residence in this part of the island. There is a small arch against a blank wall, and numerous relics of pavements, masonry, urns, and coins have been disinterred, distributed, and mostly lost. At *Bishopstone*, north of Kenchester, was a tesselated *Roman pavement*, in the garden of the parsonage, which was carefully preserved by the *Rev. A. J. Walker*, when I last visited it in 1830. In that amiable and well-informed clergyman I found an interesting companion, and equally interesting correspondent. He left a widow and an only daughter, who settled in Hereford, after the decease of the good husband and father. I have seen some literary essays by Miss Walker, which evince talent of a superior kind.

I cannot reconcile myself to quit Hereford without briefly noticing two gentlemen, whose names and characters have been fixed in my memory from the end of the last century to the present time—JOHN THELWALL, and JAMES WATHEN. The latter was a native of this city, and intimately associated with the place of his birth and death: whilst the first was strictly " a citizen of the world," though born in 1764, and nurtured in the British metropolis. He was a person whose name and deeds were repeatedly proclaimed to the reading world, through the columns of newspapers, magazines, and reviews, both foreign and domestic; whose talents and courage impelled him to impugn the character of monarchs, princes, and the mighty of the land, and also to brave their authority and power. It is difficult, if not impossible, for Englishmen of the present quiet and peaceable times to picture to their imaginations the state of society in London, and in the great manufacturing towns of England, for the last ten years of the past century. During that period Thelwall was almost constantly before

---

appear to have been made by John Abel. The date of 1621 appears on one of the gables of the Butcher-row houses.

In the garden of Coningsby's Hospital, in the northern suburbs of the city, are the chief remains of a *preaching, or pulpit Cross*, which belonged to a Priory of Friars-Preachers, founded in the time of Edward II.

About one mile west of Hereford, by the side of a turnpike road, is a stone Cross, elevated on seven steps, which is said to have been erected by Bp. Charlton about 1350. A singular history is attached to this ancient relic, as set forth in Duncomb's "Hereford," and in the first volume of *The Architectural Antiquities*, where it is represented.

the public—in lecture-rooms, mob-meetings in the open fields, and in debating societies; before the Privy Council of the State, and in public courts of justice. In each, and on all those occasions he manifested great command of language, extensive knowledge of the English laws, constitution, and history, and a degree of fortitude and intrepidity which enabled him to stand unabashed and unintimidated in the presence of a harsh Lord Chancellor (Thurlow), and almost equally severe Prime Minister (Pitt), with other officers of State, at the Privy Council board; to bear up against cruel treatment and privations in the Tower, and in Newgate; and afterwards before a bench of judges,[*] and a crowded court of lawyers; finally, to repel a press-gang of sailors, at Yarmouth, which, it was stated, had been employed to seize him in the lecture-room, and bear him off to sea. I have heard him relate, in vivid language, all these events in his worldly career; and most, if not all of them, with others, will be found fully described in the fragment of his "Life," which was published, after his decease, by his devoted but bereaved widow, in 1837. Thelwall's career from his first "coming out," before he was twenty, till his death at Bath, in 1834, in the 70th year of his age, was for many successive years full of excitement and anxiety. Harsh treatment at school, and likewise at home, under a widowed mother and capricious elder brother, with the conflicting hopes, and fears, and studies—for business, for the arts, for the bar, and for the medical profession, for all of which he was successively intended—were ordeals enough to overpower and subdue even hardy and vigorous constitutions; whereas our young hero was from childhood of a weak and tender frame, and was therefore nearly reduced to the verge of life, when he was advised to seek relaxation from mental distress and bodily decline by visiting some relations in Rutlandshire, in 1789, the 25th year of his age. Here he remained some time, gaining strength and spirits; became attached to a young female aged only fifteen, whose

---

[*] At the memorable trial in the old Bailey, when Tooke, Hardy, Godwin, Holcroft, Thelwall, &c., were impeached for high treason, the eloquent Erskine was counsel for the defendants, and was materially instrumental in obtaining their acquittal. During his own trial, Thelwall handed a pencilled note to the counsel, saying, it was his "wish to plead his own cause;" to which Erskine replied, "If you do you will be hung." Thelwall immediately returned the rejoinder, "Then I'll be hanged if I do."

parents were in humble circumstances, and whose education he paid for, for two years, and then made her his spouse. This most interesting and amiable female proved to be an exemplary wife and mother, and also a substantial friend and adviser in his future troubles and dangers. Returning to London, with a renovated frame and ardent spirits, with a resolution to attain distinction and property, and thereby provide for a young wife, and probably a family, he published two volumes of poems, which led to the editorship of a magazine, to literary connection, and to diligent studies. He had previously distinguished himself at a debating society in Coachmakers' Hall, and had devoted some time to the law. Afterwards he attended the hospitals, in the Borough, but left both for general literature, and particularly for oratory. Joining the Corresponding Society he soon became popular; and was induced to give public lectures on the politics and history of the times, which were attended by crowded audiences. Though naturally enthusiastic, bold, and free in comments on public men and measures, he was singularly circumspect in his public writings and speaking. He often trenched on the boundaries of what was by some politicians deemed sedition and treason; yet he employed only the speech of a true-born Englishman, by advocating liberty without licentiousness, and freedom of discussion within the boundary of common sense and the laws of the land. Unlike many of the unprincipled and reckless demagogues of the time, who by fluency of speech and unscrupulous language produced exciting effects on the idle, the dissolute, and the dishonest, Thelwall, even in the midst of his most eloquent speeches and writings, was select and cautious in his phraseology. Hence all the spies, informers, and suborned witnesses, who were arrayed against him at the memorable trial for high treason (1794), could not substantiate any one act, any written or oral sentence, to prove his guilt. This extraordinary trial, which lasted five days, and which ended in the prisoner's acquittal, is detailed at length in the "State Trials," and also in "The Tribune," a periodical published by Thelwall; whilst its origin, progress, and some of its effects are described in the Author's "Life," by his widow. Though the Judge, in summing up, could not entirely disguise his prejudices against the prisoner, he was courteous enough to remark that " the gentleman of the bar had produced such testimony, as to character, as was seldom heard in that court." In one part of his address the Judge made a mistake, when Thelwall ventured to interrupt his Lordship, and respectfully, but firmly, pointed out the error. On referring to his notes, the Judge found the prisoner to be correct, and acknowledged the mistake. I have frequently heard my friend declare, that he did not derive so much pleasure and exultation in the fiat of acquittal as in having an opportunity of amply vindicating his character, by such full and unequivocal testimony as was given by witnesses of the first respectability on that occasion.

A verdict of "*not guilty*," from the jury, electrified the crowded and excited auditory, as well as thousands of persons who were assembled on the outside. It also produced visible effects on the judges, counsel, and even the prisoner. The last, however, after a few moments' pause, arose calmly and collectedly, and thus addressed the court: "My Lords and Gentlemen of the Jury: If anything could increase the affection I bear my country, it certainly must be the circumstance of this acquittal. If a plain, simple, unconnected man, with neither fortune, rank, nor connections to recommend him, after having laboured twelve months under all the calumny which a particular set of party writers could pour upon his head—after lying seven months in prison without any opportunity to vindicate himself, and whose friends could not dare to vindicate him for fear of falling under similar predicaments themselves—if, under all these circumstances, after the diligent collection of the mass of evidence, (a great part of which, I own, appeared to me not connected with my case, but I submitted to the judgment of the Court)—if, under all these circumstances, the accumulated weight and pressure laid upon me was not sufficient to bear down and crush so isolated and unprotected a man, there must be something in the dispositions of the people of Great Britain—something eminently virtuous in this country, which every Briton must reflect on with pride, and which must render every individual still more anxious to promote its happiness and prosperity. I protest, in the sight of my country, and call upon that posterity whose applause I hope to obtain, and whose happiness I have anxiously laboured to procure, to bear witness for me, that I never was actuated by one vicious motive in any part of my political conduct, however provoked by the insults and indignities that may have stimulated a too-irritable disposition."—These words, and more of the same kind, spoken in a tone and manner, so extraordinary in that Court, produced such an effect on the judges, that "they actually forgot to go through the customary forms of liberating the prisoner, until reminded of it by the gaoler."—[*Life,* page 261.]

At this memorable epoch Mr. Thelwall was only in the 30th year of his age—merely commencing his career of usefulness, for it continued through two other equal cycles, or periods of time, with increased energy, zeal, and devotion to the united causes of literature, science, and political reform. After making strenuous endeavours to regain his books, manuscripts, and property, which had been ruthlessly seized by government officers, and many of which were either stolen or destroyed, he resorted to debating societies, lecture-rooms, and the press, to procure a livelihood for himself and family. He was, however, still pursued and harassed by spies and officers, who tried various modes to provoke him to actionable language, or breaches of the peace. On some occasions the parties, who let the rooms for debates or for lectures, were threatened by the Lord Mayor, and magistrates, and constables; at other times some of these attended in groups, interrupted the proceedings, and occasioned riots. Irritated by a continuance of such proceedings, Thelwall left the metropolis, and gave lectures in some of the provincial towns; but the rancour and vehemence of party spirit were more rabid there than even in London. At Yarmouth, he had obtained the use of the theatre to give his lectures in, but, on the first night, had nearly lost his life, by a press-gang. One of these sailors attempted to seize him at the stage door, when Thelwall, taking a pistol from an inside pocket (he carried a brace, loaded, for some years), placed it against the face of his enemy, and with resolute voice said, " Leave me immediately, or I'll blow your brains out." The man stept back, terror stricken, not merely with the words and pistol, but the piercing look of the orator. Thelwall bolted the door, made his escape through back premises, and left the town. This event I have heard him relate in his usual graphic style, but he published a particular description of it, 8vo. 1796.

This, and many other dangerous annoyances which he successively encountered, induced him, and principally at the urgent entreaty of his good wife, to adopt some new course of life—to seek personal security, and some degree of repose, in a distant part of the country. Chance induced them to settle in a farm (Llyswen) in Wales, some miles west of Hereford, where they resided four years, almost estranged from society, and the busy world. Without attempting to give an account of the changed condition, habits, and altered state of my rustic friend and his family, in this sort of antipodes to London, I have merely to remark that I accidentally met him at the shop of Mr. Allen, a respectable bookseller of Hereford,—that we spent an hour together in friendly, retrospective chat,—that I expressed myself much astonished at his altered dress and pursuits, and that he referred me to the *Monthly Magazine* for 1797, for a paper he had lately written, descriptive of a remarkable winter scene on the river Wye,—that he frequently contributed to that respectable periodical, and was diligently studying for future proceedings, and a new course of life.

After a kind of exile, or voluntary transportation, he returned to London, hired a large, handsome house (No. 40, Bedford-place), issued prospectuses announcing his plans for a new institution, or school, for the cure of impediments of speech, for instructions in elocution, and other branches of useful learning; and particularly to qualify students for the bar, the pulpit, and the stage. This bold and daring scheme alarmed some of Mr. Thelwall's friends, astonished and mortified his political enemies, and created no small speculation in literary and scientific circles. He commenced, persevered, and obtained several pupils, in his house, at very light terms. Amongst them were sons of noblemen, and gentlemen of rank, who have since distinguished themselves in Parliament; others who have attained eminence at the bar and in the church; some on the stage, and many in private life. Henceforward he eschewed politics; but gave frequent courses of lectures on elocution, history, the classics, polite literature, impediments of speech, &c. At these lectures, and at his Historical Society meetings, I was not only a frequent visitor and admiring listener, but often joined his private dinner and evening parties, where I met Godwin, Holcroft, Dr. Wolcot, Major Cartwright, Kenney, Robinson, Lamb, Quin, Cline, Taylor, and many other eminent authors as well as artists, and also men of science, whose works have enshrined their names amongst the

"Worthies of Great Britain." In Watts's "Bibliotheca Britannica," is a list of the orator's publications. Besides the "Life," referred to, I can recommend the notice in the "Penny Cyclopædia," as a well-written Memoir; and will avail myself of a few lines from it, in corroboration of what is here stated. "Thelwall was of a mild and amiable disposition, of domestic habits, open-hearted and generous, of high moral feeling, and of inflexible integrity. His sentiments were exalted by public feeling, and he was buoyed up by hope." S. T. Coleridge, in a letter to his substantial friend, Mr. Joseph Cottle, of Bristol, gives this opinion, in 1797, of a man who was called a "traitor," and an "acquitted felon," by anti-jaocbin orators and writers: "John Thelwall is a very warm-hearted, honest man, and we like each other uncommonly well. Energetic activity of mind and of heart is his master-feature. He is prompt to conceive, and still prompter to execute. He is intrepid, eloquent, and honest; perhaps the only acting democrat that is honest."

JAMES WATHEN.—As a traveller to foreign lands, and author of a quarto volume, describing and illustrating the scenery, &c., of some of the places he visited; as a pedestrian, who traversed many thousands of miles, over England, Wales, Ireland, and Scotland; and as being sought and respected by nearly every artist and author who made Hereford a resting-place in journeying to or from the Principality, the gentleman above-named, claims a passing notice and compliment from me. He was one of those kind-hearted, social persons, who seem destined "by nature, and their stars," to oblige and attend to the wants and wishes of all who appeal to them. With a moderate income, which he inherited from his father, who was a leather breeches maker—for at that time, and for many previous years, the making of that human garment constituted a separate and distinct branch of business, in every country town—James's moderate wants were well supplied, without the necessity of working for his daily bread; and he sought amusement, and rational employment, in perambulating and "seeing the world;" whence he became known, and rendered little services to many persons, who thenceforward were the admitted friends and acquaintances of Mr. Wathen, of Hereford. He "had the nack" of making sketches of all remarkable scenes and buildings; and, believing that a few hieroglyphic traces would serve to delineate all such places and objects, and that perspective, horizontal and perpendicular lines, were unnecessary restraints on the free use of the pencil, his buildings were always shewn in sloping forms, and of such sketches he accumulated a countless number. With a liberality quite in harmony with such rapidity of execution, he presented one or more of these drawings to any stranger who would " honour him by accepting his testimonials of friendship." In return, he expected to receive some token, either of art or literature, from his stranger friends. Hence he became possessed of numerous sketches and drawings, by Rooker, Hearne, Dayes, Girtin, Turner, Varley, Nicholson, Christal, Munn, Cotman, and many other artists; and also volumes of Tours, Walks, and Travels, by authors. When I first met him he was a middle-aged bachelor, but he lived to be an old one; for his florid, unwrinkled, unthinking countenance, prudent habits, and love of air and exercise, all seemed calculated to prolong life equal to that of the respectable and intellectual William Hutton, previously noticed and praised. He frequently walked to London, generally at the time of the annual exhibition, and there and then saw and conversed with the artists whom he had met, either at Hereford, or in his country strolls, and I was generally gratified with " a friendly call." I say gratified, for he always had news to impart—of, where he had been, what and whom he had seen, and what was doing, had been done, or was preparing by the artists. In one of these visits to the metropolis, which was then comparatively a small town, and had only one regular annual exhibition, Mr. Wathen started on an excursion to the continent, during the short peace of 1802; and after spending a few days at Calais was proceeding to Paris, when the news of his mother's death induced him to return home. This event probably saved him from the miserable detention, imprisonment, and rough treatment which many of his countrymen subjected themselves to by their too great eagerness to see merry Paris, and its merciless, murdering Emperor, at that memorable epoch. Disappointed of this pleasure-trip, my wandering friend, some years afterwards, accepted the offer of a friend, Captain Pendergrass, to sail with him to the East Indies and China. This was accordingly performed between January 1811, and July 1812; and a detailed account of his voyage was published in 1814, in a handsome quarto volume, with twenty-four coloured prints, executed in aquatinta, from the author's sketches and memoranda, or, as described in the title page, "Drawings." I must own, however, that the execution of the literary and graphic parts of this work surprise me at the present time (1852), as I do not remember to have seen it before; for the writing is not only respectable, but creditable to a practised author, and the prints appear to be as satisfactory as such illustrations generally were in books of travels, at that time. The names of persons, places, and things, with the incidents that occurred during the voyage, and the facts related, may be trusted; but it requires more faith than I possess to believe in the truthfulness of the drawings. Amongst other evidence, may be adduced the statement that Mr. Wathen made "thirteen drawings, in less than three days," of various scenes in the island of St. Helena, besides visiting the most remarkable places in that mass of rock and land. Short-hand marks and hieroglyphics convey specific language to those who have studied and understand them; but I do not believe that even Mr. Bartlett, who is the most rapid sketcher I ever saw, could make the number of drawings here named, with tolerable accuracy of detail, and traverse the island also, in the time specified. Hence we cannot be fully satisfied with the "Series of Views illustrative of the Island of St. Helena, drawn on the spot by James Wathen, Esq.," which were published in quarto, with a portrait of the author, in 1821, seven years after his "Voyage" was manufactured in London. These prints were published at the price of £1. 11s. 6d., with six pages of letter-press. Though Mr. Wathen lived a bachelor to the age of seventy-six, he vainly sought to wed a lady whose fortune and connections were far above his own. He continued to visit her once a week, for many successive years, and at his decease bequeathed to her some drawings, amongst which was one by Girtin. He died in August 1848, and was buried in the cathedral.

From Hereford I made an excursion to FOXLEY, the seat of Uvedale Price, Esq., to view the practical exemplification of his principles on the picturesque in the decoration of ground around the house. The learned author received me, after a little explanation, with courtesy; but though

I had the passport of a note from his friend, Mr. Knight, he did not manifest so much affability and blandness of manners, as I found in the author of "Principles of Taste." I spent a few hours in the house and about the grounds, with much gratification. The mansion is a large, brick building, without any pretension to architectural ornament. Its interior, however, compensates for any exterior insipidity, by the fine works of art and the library it contains. In the bold and grand features of the park scenery and country around, there is so much to engage the eye and attention, that a hasty traveller will not have time to examine or appreciate the artificial works of the landscape-gardener, in what he has done to the ground and plantations immediately around the house. Suffice it to say, that all seemed formed, disposed, clustered, and laid out with due regard to the picturesque. Certainly, the whole presented a palpable contrast to the pretty flower-garden of my friend, Mr. Repton, at Hare-Street, as well as to many other pleasure-grounds which that gentleman had professionally formed and adorned. At the entrance to the park, in the village of Mansel Lacy, was a timber lodge, with rustic gate, and on the sides of the roadway were several wild thickets and clumps of stones. From the house and different elevated parts of the grounds, many fine, even grand, views are obtained over a vast extent of country, in which the windings of the river Wye, the black mountains of Wales, with some of the border castrametations, are descried. Mr. Price's " Essays on the Picturesque " first appeared in a single octavo volume, 1795 ; but were afterwards extended to three goodly-sized volumes, in 1799. Another edition of the whole, with much additional matter, was produced under the editorship of Sir Thomas Dick Lauder, Bart., in the year 1842, in one large volume. Mr. Price's writings occasioned much criticism and commentary by different authors, in the Edinburgh and other reviews, and also by separate essayists. I have now before me a learned and interesting volume, " On the Elements of Picturesque Scenery, considered with reference to Landscape Painting. By Henry Twining, Esq.," 8vo., 1846, pp. 375. The work is privately printed.

The RIVER WYE.—There are few rivers in Europe—perhaps none —which have been so much and so often described as the river Wye.

In its course, from the mountain of Plinlimmon, in Wales, to its junction with the Bristol Channel, near Chepstow, a distance of 130 miles, it passes the city of Hereford, and is navigable for large craft up to that place. The popular and graphic "Observations" of Gilpin, which were made in 1770, gave the first impulse to public curiosity. Having been patronized by the Duchess Dowager of Portland, with a subscription of one hundred pounds, and afterwards praised by Mason and Gray, the Reverend author's peculiarity of comment and criticism were much noticed in the literary coteries of the time, and he was induced to publish them in 1784. They immediately attracted so much public commendation, that several successive editions of his volume were afterwards printed. Coxe, Williams, Warner, Ireland, and other popular authors, progressively visited and published their accounts and praises of the diversified, bold, romantic, picturesque, and beautiful scenes which belong to this "Vaga," or mountain-torrent of the Wye. Its most remarkable and most impressive features are to be found between the town of Ross and the junction with the Bristol Channel. I must limit my pen and attention to a very brief notice of some of these, and refer the reader to publications which have made their appearance long after I wandered by its craggy shores, and over the adjoining eminences, first in the year 1798, and subsequently at different times. The last work that has come under my notice, is "The Book of South Wales, the Bristol Channel, Monmouthshire, and the Wye," by C. F. Cliffe, with maps and engravings, small 8vo., 1847.* This comprehensive, well-written, well-printed, and skilfully-illustrated volume, constitutes a most interesting and, I believe, faithful guide to the country it pro-

---

* Mr. Cliffe was for some years editor of "The Kentish Mercury," a weekly paper, published at Greenwich, and for which he wrote many interesting literary articles. Whilst there, he contributed several others, on antiquities, &c., for a periodical, which my old friend, Mr. Brayley, edited, called "The Graphic Illustrator." From Greenwich, Mr. Cliffe moved to Gloucester, to take charge of, and a share in, "The Gloucestershire Chronicle," a "family newspaper, conducted with much talent and energy." The incessant labour and confinement which he devoted to this weekly periodical, to the volume above referred to (which attained a third edition within four years), and to another of corresponding size, quality, and merit, on "North Wales," in 1851, subdued and prostrated his physical powers, and his weakened frame sunk beneath the burden, in the forty-second year of his age, in November 1851.

fesses to describe. Its amiable and talented author has lately died, at Clifton, in the prime of life; and, like too many other literary men, shortened that life by eschewing air, exercise, and that rational amusement, which is essential to promote healthfulness; and in devoting nearly all his time and energies to literary studies and labour.

The name and fame of Ross had been so forcibly impressed on my fancy and memory by the poetical encomiums of Pope, and the descriptive writings of Gilpin, and other authors, that I was tempted to proceed directly to that town, after leaving Hereford.

> —— "But all our praises why should lords engross?
> Rise, honest Muse! and sing THE MAN OF ROSS."—POPE's *Essays*.

The poet did sing his praises, and posterity has duly honoured and revered the name of *John Kyrle*, who spent a long life, and nearly all his property, in acts of judicious benevolence to his native place, to its inhabitants, and to the public, who visited Ross, either for business or for pleasure. Kyrle lived many years at a house in the town, now the King's Arms, and died there in 1724, at the age of 84. A monument was raised to his memory in the church; but more lasting and effective mementoes were formed by himself, in acts of charity, of improvement, of substantial utility in the town, and by the lines of Pope, in his "Moral Essays," Epistle iii., which have made indelible impressions on the memories and hearts of thousands of persons who are in the habit of reading, and who also "mark, learn, and inwardly digest." The poet asks,

> "Who taught that heav'n-directed Spire to rise?
> 'The Man of Ross,' each lisping babe replies.
> Behold the market-place with poor o'erspread!
> The man of Ross divides the weekly bread;
> He feeds yon alms-house, neat, but void of state,
> Where age and want sit smiling at the gate;
> Him, portion'd maids, apprentic'd orphans blest,
> The young who labour, and the old who rest.
> Is any sick? the Man of Ross relieves,
> Prescribes, attends, the med'cine makes and gives.
> Despairing quacks with curses fled the place,
> And vile attorneys, now an useless race."
> &c. &c. &c.

The human being who can read these lines, who can tread the ground which gave life and disposition to the exemplary and ever-estimable person who deserved them; and whose soul is not warmed and improved by the contemplation of such a character, is to be pitied and despised by every philanthropist.

The situation of the town of Ross, and its spire-crowned church, cannot fail to arrest the attention and demand the admiration of every stranger. On the brow of a lofty eminence, which rises abruptly from a broad plain, to the west, in which the meandering Wye winds its stream, is obtained a grand and glorious prospect; whilst the summit of this hill is adorned with a row of fine trees, shading a long walk, planted and formed by the amiable man whose praises we have once more repeated. One visit to Ross, as here noticed, served only to excite a longing desire to renew my acquaintance with it, on some future occasion. Accordingly, when I journeyed to Hereford, to survey its cathedral (in 1830), I devoted a day and night to this place. At that time I wrote a line to my respected friend and correspondent, the *Rev. T. D. Fosbroke*, who was living at Walford, a short distance from the town, to spend an hour with me "at mine inn." He promptly obeyed the summons, came whilst we were at dinner, partook of the same, with a few glasses of *old* port—lingered, and talked, and drank, whilst time glided on imperceptibly to friends who had thus met for the first time, and whose hearts were warmed, and enthusiasm not a little excited, by converse on the glories of "hoar antiquity;" on the fascinations of the Wye; the intense interest of the many important ruined buildings on its banks; on poetry—for my friend was a poet as well as an antiquary; topography, and other branches of literature. Tea-time came, supper-hour also, and bed-time arrived; but my friend seemed fixed to his seat, and at the hour of eleven Mrs. Britton retired to bed: a succession of glasses of rum-toddy made my loquacious friend still more voluble in speech, as well as more firmly seated in his chair! The clock struck twelve—an unreasonable hour for a country clergyman, and a young antiquary to be "tippling in the tavern,"—when I claimed the privilege of retiring, though I could not feel quite at ease to send my friend across the fields and through bye-lanes at that "witching time of night." He therefore willingly accepted a bed, and a breakfast the next morning, when he pressed me to visit Walford, and his church. My duty and inclination impelled me to pursue my journey. Mr.

Fosbroke was a rapid and prolific writer, and favoured me with several sheets of manuscript on antiquities and topography; but on comparing them with printed publications, I found his extracts so copious, and his own compositions so blended and confused with the former, that I was afraid of using much of his communication. He published, however, many works: the first of which, I believe, was, "The Economy of Monastic Life in England; a Poem, with Philosophical and Archæological Illustrations," 4to. 1795. This publication provoked the hostility of the Roman Catholic writers; but, in spite of these, and even of some Protestant critics, Mr. Fosbrooke (as he then spelt his name) soon afterwards continued his lucubrations on the same subject, and further impeached the doctrines and practices of the same religionists, in "British Monachism; or, Manners and Customs of the Monks and Nuns of England," 2 vols. 8vo. 1802. This work was referred to me, for comment and criticism, by the editor of the first volume of "The Annual Review," 1803, in which I ventured to find fault with the author. "It is an unpleasant part of our task"—I truly said—" to censure, where we wish to praise: in the present instance we are certainly compelled to this disagreeable duty, for it is not easy to find another such an undigested mass of materials in any published book. It seems as if the author had sent the result of his readings to the press as they occurred in his memoranda, without attempting to put them in any order; as irregularity and careless inattention are everywhere conspicuous. This is the more to be regretted, from the curious and valuable information which the work contains."

In the third, and posthumous, edition of "British Monachism," 1843, is a short auto-biography of the author, who was born in London, 1770, and died at Walford in 1842, leaving a widow and seven surviving children.—[See *Gentleman's Magazine* for February, 1842.]

That I traversed the banks and eminences of the Wye with pleasure and intense curiosity, may be reasonably inferred; and that I met with persons and objects calculated to make strong and even lasting impressions, is not surprising. The bold and romantic scenes in the neighbourhood of, and at *Goodrich Castle*, were the first to rivet my attention; and whilst the natural objects delighted the eye and mind, the ruins, and their peculiarity of position and war-features, induced at once sympathy for their builders and occupants, with self-exultation, in feeling ourselves relieved from the terrors and miseries of foreign and domestic warfare. Between the time of my first visit to Goodrich castle, in 1798, and last, in 1831, a modern building of note and interest has been raised in its immediate vicinity—i. e. GOODRICH COURT. This edifice, of castellated-monastic appearance, was designed by Edward Blore, Esq., architect, for Sir Samuel Rush Meyrick, to contain and display his valuable collection of ancient armour and other relics of antiquity, and furnishes a most impressive text and lesson for the historian and antiquary. Of *Mr. Blore* I may have occasion, hereafter, to make a few remarks; for he has attained fame and fortune as an architect, by diligence and skill as an artist, and the result of favourable events. I believe that he dates the commencement of his architectural knowledge to the year 1816, when he made an elaborate section of the east-end of Winchester cathedral, and also other very beautiful and accurate drawings of views, sections, and details of that very interesting ancient church. These may be seen, skilfully engraved by J. and Henry Le Keux, in my History of that edifice. For some years afterwards he was mostly engaged on the same class of drawings, and studies for the "Cathedral Antiquities;" for Baker's "Northamptonshire;" Surtees's "Durham;" and other similar publications. *Sir S. R. Meyrick* was a Proctor in Doctors' Commons; but he appears to have devoted more time and study to ancient armour than to his profession; and having made a large collection, he was induced to publish a fine and expensive work under the title of "A Critical Inquiry into Ancient Armour," in 3 vols. folio, 1824, with nearly 100 engravings. After his settlement at Goodrich Court, he aided in another work, in 2 vols. folio, with 154 highly-finished etchings, by Jos. Skelton, an artist, of Oxford.

Early in life Sir Samuel was left a widower, with an only son, who became the heir of his grandfather's fortune, in consequence of his parent having offended his father by marrying in opposition to his wishes. It appears, however, that Sir Samuel made use of the property in purchasing the collection, and afterwards in building the mansion alluded to, to contain it. Both father and son have paid the debt of nature, and Goodrich Court, with its valuable contents, remains, as a show-house for the Wye-wanderers, at the entrance-fee of one shilling for each person. This house and its collection were visited and admired by a large party of "The Archæological Association," in the summer of 1847, when the proprietor displayed the whole to the greatest advantage, having engaged Welsh bards and minstrels to perform, during the repast of the party, in the banqueting hall. The proprietor did not live long to enjoy his Museum, as he died on the 2nd of April, 1848, in the 65th year of his age. An account of him and his writings appears in the *Gentleman's Magazine*, for July, of that year.

Between Ross and MONMOUTH, the Wye presents some of the most romantic, and also the finest, scenes and objects in its course; whilst the latter town may be regarded as a convenient station for a traveller to select, whence to make excursions to the fine castles of Raglan, Skenfrith, Pembridge, and others of less note; also to various eminences near the rivers Wye and Monnow, which unite their streams at this town. Monmouth has objects to interest the antiquary: viz., ruins of a castle in which King Henry V. was born; the Welsh gate-house, on the Monnow bridge; and a very old church, pronounced, by most of the tour-writers, to be a Saxon building. The walks and views around the town are much praised by the same travellers. These, however, I was precluded from examining on two different occasions when I visited Monmouth for that purpose; first by bad weather, and secondly by an incident, which may be called a tantalizing adventure, as it impelled me to proceed on my journey sooner than was intended.

After ordering our dinner, I called on the principal bookseller of the town, according to long habit, and not finding him at home, left my card; for he was not only the noted Cicerone of Monmouth, but its literary guide, and also of the famed river, to which it may be said to owe most of its fame and consequence. This gentleman returned my call, whilst we were dining. He had just come from the market-table, where it seemed that he had indulged in Welsh ale, as well as cheese; for his cheeks were flushed, and we soon found that his tongue was sensibly affected by the cause which tinged his cheeks. He was exceedingly voluble, as well as superabundantly good-natured. He would accompany us after our repast, and his tea, to "the lions" of the town, —the eminences, the river, &c.—and we should return in the evening to supper with him. Such overpowering civility, such physical and mental treats, so far alarmed our nerves and politeness, that we pleaded an engagement to meet friends at Tintern Abbey, and packed up our luggage to travel immediately after dinner.

"Too civil by half," is become a proverbial axiom: though it seems unnatural and unreasonable to fancy that courtesies and kindnesses can ever be offensive. From experience, I must allow that they may become annoyances and troubles. In the present instance it was eminently so; for rather than endure the company and talk—not conversation—of such a visitor, and under such circumstances, I chose rather to risk a journey over the hills, in the evening, with the chance of accommodation at a village inn, and other events. This alternative, however, led to vexations; for we did not arrive at *Trelech* till after it was dark, and when the blackened sky gave presages of a thunder-storm. The country inn afforded but miserable "entertainment for man and horse." The latter was put into a shed, which was promiscuously devoted to cows, pigs, poultry, &c., and seemed not to have been cleansed oftener than the Augean stable. Like the equestrian Cantabs, I was placed in their situation with Hobson—"this or none." The "entertainment for man" and woman, or household accommodation and provender, was some degrees better than those for the quadruped; and like old travellers we endeavoured to reconcile ourselves to "the ills we have, than fly to others which we know not of." A tempestuous thunder-storm came on: our bed-room was ill furnished, and a night-light was unknown to the inmates—

> "No curtained sleep had we,—
> Because we had no curtains to the bed."—G. COLMAN.

We sought in vain for a bell; we tried our newly-invented phosphoric instantaneous light, but it refused to kindle the match, though it showed its blue flame on our hands and night-clothes. The rain poured, the lightning flashed, the thunder seemed to shake the crazy walls and timbers, whilst some of the water ventured to pay us a visit through the roof, and down the chimney. I must own, that our uncomfortable situation, compared with good-tempered inebriety, in a good inn, seemed something like "out of the frying-pan into the fire." However, the morning brought day-light, and sun-shine, and cheerfulness: we had passed the ordeal; and new objects, tinged with hope, were anticipated. Before leaving this place, I examined and sketched a view of three *large stones*, which are raised upright, and are commonly said to have been of Celtic or Druidic origin and appropriation. There are not any indications of a circle, or temple.

TINTERN ABBEY.—One of the most beautiful, and perhaps the most attractive, ruins on the banks of the Wye, is the ancient monastic building in the narrow and romantic glen of Tintern. Singular in situation, —peculiarly picturesque in architectural form, as a whole, and beautiful in many of its separate parts—with a rapid mountain-torrent, in continued action, and sending forth liquid sounds of natural music, passing by its walls—woods, in abundance, climbing up, and starting from, abrupt acclivities, interspersed with rocks, rustic cottages, mills, and factories—all unite, at this place, to attract and fascinate the artist, the antiquary, and almost every class and variety of travellers. Though I have visited Tintern thrice, I have been peculiarly unfortunate in weather. Rain has not only damped my ardour, but my clothes and umbrellas, and also destroyed all the charms of colouring, of distances, and effects of light and shadow. On my first introduction to Tintern, in 1798, it was my lot to meet with another adventure, at the Beaufort Arms, which Mr. Warner had bepraised in his first "Walk," and where I had taken up my quarters for the night, hoping to be blessed with a little sun-shine on the following day. Like many other houses built against rocks, or the steep sides of hills, the small public-house of the last century—now probably a flaunting hotel—was humble in aspect, and moderate in accommodation and charges. My bed-room was on the first floor, as seen from the front, but from the garden was approached by one or two descending steps; and there was a door-way from that garden to the chamber, as if the latter was a common passage of ingress and egress. In the midst of the night I was aroused from a sound sleep by remarkable sounds of water rushing through the room, and leaping from stair to stair in its descent to the lower floor. Mr. and Mrs. Gethin, the landlord and landlady, bringing lights, relieved me from all doubts and alarm, by showing that the water from the sloping garden at the back had forced a passage through the door-way, across the room, and down the stairs in a new sort of cascade. In the morning, the waters of the Wye were seen and heard rushing over their rocky bed in torrents; and a scene of much grandeur was presented to a person who had only known the Thames, the Medway, the Loddon, and the Avon.

Though the ruins of Tintern Abbey have been repeatedly exhibited to the public by views in various styles of drawing and engraving, I am not aware that the whole design of the church and its monastic buildings have ever been correctly and well delineated.

From Tintern to Chepstow there was only one road, when I first saw the district; and that was not of the most pleasant kind for carriage passengers, as it was very narrow, and rough, ragged, and rather alarming to nervous travellers. But great improvements have since been made there. Amongst these, is a drive through the fine woods which overhang the Wye, and leads to a grand and impressive view from an eminence called the *Wyndcliffe*. This is the most popular, and most remarkable feature in the course of the river, and has been very vividly described by the " German Prince," who published a *Tour in England*, in 1826. It is considered as superior to that of Ehrenbreitstein, on the Rhine; and, "in its way," says Mr. Cliffe, "not equalled in Europe. A vast group of views, of different and opposite character, here seem to blend and unite in one." The height of the rock is 970 feet. From this eminence are descried parts of nine counties.—But I must refer to Coxe's " Monmouthshire," and other publications, for descriptions of this fascinating locality,—also for the Wyndcliffe, the Wye, Tintern, Chepstow, and PIERCEFIELD. The last is the name of a celebrated gentleman's seat, between the Wyndcliffe and Chepstow, whose inequality of ground, devious walks, and varied picturesque scenes, cannot fail to gratify all travellers. To save time, and the distance of a long circuitous walk, I ventured, with some qualms of conscience, to trespass through a hedge, and by an unbeaten track, across the Park, and thus followed the course of the river, for nearly three miles, to the Chepstow Lodge. According to the printed Guide, this park contains the following points and objects of attraction: the Lover's Leap; a Seat on the edge of a precipice; the Giant's Cave; the Halfway Seat; the Double View; the View above the Pierce Wood; the Grotto; the Platform; and the Alcove. The house has no particular architectural pretensions : but the name and history of *Valentine Morris* are intimately associated with this place, as he first gave it celebrity, by expending large sums of money in embellishing the park, &c. Compelled, however, to leave it in debt and difficulties, he went to the West Indies, where he acquired a new fortune, which he lost whilst Governor of St. Vincent's; returned to England, where he languished some years in prison, during which time his good wife was bereft of her senses. Mr. Morris, however, regained his liberty, and some of his property ; but never that tranquillity of mind, and human enjoyment, which belonged to him in the days of Piercefield's prosperity.

CHEPSTOW, with its magnificent castellated ruins, scenic features, and its ancient priory church, is calculated to afford the antiquary and lover of the picturesque abundant matter for study and inspection. In Coxe's and Williams's respective books on "Monmouthshire," the reader will find these objects fully elucidated, though not so well illustrated.

From Chepstow I proceeded to Bristol, by crossing the Severn, at the old passage, before a steam-boat had been seen ; and when passengers, cattle, horses, carriages, &c., were conveyed in flat, common boats and barges: whence this, as well as the new passage, was always regarded as dangerous. In one of my tours I experienced a serious loss at this passage, as well as had a narrow escape from a watery grave. On arriving at the passage-house, with a horse and carriage, the usual barge was put in for repair, and a small boat, with two men, was provided for temporary purposes. I was alarmed, and intended to take up my quarters at the inn; but the boatmen assured me there was not any danger, and that they had been across four or five times during the day. Eager to reach Bristol, I ventured on board, and was proceeding smoothly over the water, under two sails, when a gust of wind came up the channel, nearly capsized the boat, and tossed my writing desk, which was loose on the seat of the gig, into the sea. We were not a little alarmed for personal safety, concluding that a repetition of the gust, perhaps a little augmented in force, with horse and carriage and ourselves on the lower side, would inevitably upset the boat. The two human brutes were as senseless and reckless of peril as their oars, which they refused to handle, and also refused to ease or lower their sails. Fortunately, we reached the opposite shore, minus twenty pounds in notes, and other property, some palpitations and ejaculations; but thankful to gain terra-firma and escape from passage-perils, and the heartless stolidity of animals, miscalled men.

BRISTOL, at the time I first became acquainted with it (1798), was very dissimilar to Bristol of the year 1852. In its commerce, trade, art, science, literature, population, and domestic economy, the transitions and changes have been numerous and various. Still, though much advancement has been made, in almost every one of those branches, she remains in arrear of some of her rivals. Old laws, customs, and habits seem to have clung to the corporation and government of Bristol, more closely than to any other great commercial town in England. The march of intellect, and the progress of knowledge have, however, within the last few years, invaded and taken possession of the place. New docks, with connecting works; new regulations and laws respecting the port, with reduced duties; and material improvements in the manufactures, have been established; whilst the vast and marvellous changes effected by the introduction of gas, of steam-vessels, and of rail-roads, have co-operated to elevate Bristol in the commercial and intellectual scale of civic ports. Corresponding improvements in public and private buildings—in widening streets, formation of institutions and societies for the advancement of science, art, and literature; founding of hospitals, schools, and other public establishments; a new guildhall, council-house, custom-house, with modern churches and chapels; are among the tangible public works, which have been progressively and rapidly produced during the present century. It may be reasonably inferred that such novelties—such radical changes—must have effected corresponding alterations in the customs and condition of the permanent inhabitants. Increase of the population in Bristol and Clifton, the last of which being only a suburb to the former, has been commensurate to the other changes. In 1700, it was calculated at 80,000; in 1800, at 100,000; and in 1850, at least 150,000.

A philosophical and candid review of the past and present condition of Bristol—of its commerce, trade, political economy, manners, and in the mental and moral condition of the people—would be not only interesting to the general reader, but of great benefit to the emulous inhabitants. It would be worthy of an enlightened corporation, or a patriotic Bristolian, to offer a handsome prize for a literary essay of this kind.

As stated in the Preface to my History of its Cathedral (1830), "this city has peculiar claims on my feelings, both from early associations, and from partialities. Though not my natal home, I consider my paternal ancestors were connected with the city and its immediate vicinity. In boyish days I heard much of the Bristol merchants and tradesmen, and of peculiar privileges and customs of the freemen." This Preface contains other remarks on Bristol, in its civic, ecclesiastical, and domestic attributes; whilst its commerce and trade, with the geographical and geological peculiarities of the surrounding country, are commented on in a "Lecture on the Great Western Railway," which I gave at the Bristol Institution, in the year 1833.

Of Bristol, previous to my first visit, I had read accounts; and some of the literary works of Miss Hannah More; of Ann Yearsley, the Bristol Milk-maid; of William Barrett, and his History of Bristol; of Thomas Chatterton, the "marvellous boy;" of Catcott, and his exploration of Pen-park-hole; of Robert Southey, S. T. Coleridge, C. Lloyd, and their wild, visionary scheme of "Pantisocracy;" * of Joseph Cottle, and his poetry, as well as of his generous conduct towards the young poets and literary aspirants of his time and sphere of usefulness. Besides, I was not wholly unacquainted with the names, and far-spread fame, of Sebastian Cabot, of William Cannynges, of Admiral Penn, of Colson, Whitson, and other commercial worthies of the city.

These names, with their associations, could not fail to awaken my curiosity and stimulate inquiry. Some days were therefore devoted to

---

* See a good account of this in Cottle's interesting volume of "Reminiscences of S. T. Coleridge and R. Southey," 8vo., 1847, with portraits. This interesting volume is well calculated to exhibit the mental and moral characteristics of the two eminent persons named in the title; also of Robert Lovel, who, with Coleridge, had projected the chimerical notion of forming a social colony in America, exempt from all political and civil laws. The volume contains also interesting letters by, and anecdotes of Charles Lloyd, George Catcott, Dr. Beddoes, Humphry Davy, Ann Yearsley, Hannah More, Charles Lamb, Thomas Poole, Robert Hall, John Forster, Wm. Wordsworth, the Wedgewoods, and other "Worthies."

Bristol, with more than common avidity. Though not prepared to understand and enjoy the beauties of Redcliffe church, I could not forbear to inquire after and examine the old chests over the north porch of it; the house and chapel of Cannynges, in the adjoining street; the leaning tower of Temple Church; the old timber houses in different parts of the city; and also the Cathedral, and its monuments. But I must frankly acknowledge that the scenery about Clifton and Blaize Castle, with King's Weston, and a walk to Dundry Tower, gave me more pleasure, on my first visit to this district, and made a stronger impression on my memory, than any of the works of man.

Reminiscences of Bristol and its locality, and of the public and estimable persons with whom I have been personally acquainted and corresponded, would extend to a goodly-sized volume, were I to write down all that belong to them as public objects and persons. I must therefore limit my pen to personal connections with the city.

In 1812, I was tempted by Charles Joseph Harford, Esq., to devote some weeks to Bristol, for the purpose of examining and describing the church of St. Mary Redcliffe, which had continued to excite much public curiosity, from the lamentable fate of poor Chatterton; the intimate connection of his story with the edifice alluded to, as well as the remarkable architectural beauties and peculiarities of the building. Several essays had been written about the boy-poet, and of certain manuscripts and poems which he pretended to have discovered in old chests of the church. Southey, and his friend, Joseph Cottle, had lately published three volumes of Chatterton's Poems, with a conviction that the "presumed ancient documents" were written by that "phenomenon of nature, and enigma of genius." *

The result of my researches in Bristol, Oxford, the British Museum, and other places, was "*An Historical and Architectural Essay on Redcliffe Church,*" with prints illustrative of the building and its

---

* A new edition of the poet's writings was published at Cambridge in the year 1842, with the title of "The Poetical Works of Thomas Chatterton, with Notices of his Life, History of the Rowley Controversy, a Selection of his Letters, and Notes, Critical and Explanatory:" 2 vols. small 8vo. This very interesting edition contains most of the author's admitted writings, and an ably-penned biographical essay, with a commentary.

monuments; also anecdotes of eminent persons interred in the church, with a brief biography of Chatterton. The publication of this volume introduced me to the popular poets just named; to the vicar, the *Rev. M. R. Whish;* to *Thomas Eagles, Esq.*, who had written a pamphlet entitled "Sir Charles Bawden," and who then strongly contended for the genuineness of the Rowley MSS., as *Dr. Sherwin*, of Bath, did afterwards in the *Gentleman's Magazine*, and in long letters to myself; the *Rev. Samuel Seyer*,* who had lately published a quarto volume of the Bristol charters, with translations, and was then preparing a history of his native city. *Granville Penn*, whose ancestor, the Admiral, was buried in Redcliffe church, furnished me with original memoranda relating to that officer. To Thomas Park, Lady Millman, Philip Bliss, the Rev. B. Bandinell,

*Thompson, del.*        *Mason, Sc.*
DESIGN FOR A MEDAL,
to be presented as a Receipt to Subscribers for the proposed Restoration of the Church of St. Mary Redcliffe, Bristol.

---

* This amiable and learned gentleman became a little jealous and captious, after I had announced my volume on Redcliffe Church; and wrote to me an angry letter, complaining of my trespassing on his pre-occupied ground, and interfering with his proposed history. I have explained this "quarrel of authors," in the Preface to *History of Bristol Cathedral*, p. vii., wherein I also state, that the liberal patronage of the Corporation in presenting Mr. Seyer two hundred guineas, is unparalleled, I believe, in the annals of topographical literature. It is gratifying to record another instance of similar patronage of literature connected with this city. By the exertions and energy of Lord Brougham, an Act of Parliament was passed, some years back, to inquire into and report on the Public Charities of England and Wales. The effect has been of great benefit to Society. Bristol is remarkable for the extent and number of its Charitable Institutions. A full account of these has been printed and laid before the public, in two volumes 4to., 1831, by Thomas J. Manche, who was encouraged to undertake the work by twenty-eight gentlemen of the city, &c., who subscribed three hundred guineas towards the expense of printing. By this publication it appears that no less than forty-three of the charities are under the management of the corporation.

Joseph Hazlewood, the Rev. John Eden, and the Rev. T. D. Fosbrooke, I was indebted for literary communications. A circumstance of recent date, but unusual nature, grew out of the volume here alluded to. In the year 1840, I received a letter from Bristol, with the signature of Thomas Proctor, directed to "J. Britton, Esq., Architect, London." This inquired if I was an architect, and had written a history of Redcliffe church many years ago; to which I promptly replied, Yes, to the last, and No, to the first, query. Another letter soon followed, stating that T. P. was churchwarden of the parish; that the Vestry desired advice about the condition of, and repairs to, their church; and asked if I could give such advice. This led to further correspondence; to a long Report from myself and my professional friend, W. Hosking, architect, with elaborate drawings; and to a final arrangement that we should superintend a complete and extensive repair and restoration of the whole edifice. The Report and Estimate, with an address from the Vestry to the public, and also a descriptive letter from myself, were printed, and circulated extensively. The Estimate was given, in a round sum, at about £40,000., which alarmed the Bristolians, and even surprised the public. I always considered it unwise to put down such a total: from a conviction that I should not have lived to see Waterloo Bridge, or the Great Western Railway completed, had the engineers in the first proposal plainly and honestly told subscribers the full amount of their liabilities. The parish funds guaranteed a large sum to begin; many of the parishioners put their names down for further aid; some of the citizens likewise came forward, and urgent appeals were made to the public. The time was, however, inauspicious, from a depressed state of trade; but the Vestry have persevered from 1843 to the present time, and much good and substantial work has been done to protect the building from further dilapidation, and in restoring some of its walls, windows, buttresses, parapets, &c. Early in the proceedings, my coadjutor, receiving a government appointment, was unable to attend to this work, and I recommended George Godwin, F.R.S., to supply his place. Being engaged, he soon made himself well acquainted with the style and peculiarities of the building, both in construction and in detail. The work has been prosecuted for some years, with entire satisfaction to all parties concerned; and the church might have been finished, ere this time, had the architect been provided with funds. These "sinews of war," as well as of peace, are often tardy in their march. A remarkable incident has occurred relating to this restoration. A person, unknown, under the signature of "Nil Desperandum," has promised funds to restore the whole of the singular north porch, and has paid up at least £1000 towards the full expense, which is estimated at £2000. This is a noble trait of generosity, which derives its reward from silent and secret gratulation, and the pleasure of watching the progress and effect of a tangible and public act, without the usual stimulus and reward of popular applause. It is barely justice to my respected friend, Mr. Godwin, to state here, (perhaps the last opportunity I may ever have) that, for promptitude in action, integrity of principle, extensive knowledge of science and art, and zeal in every cause he embarks in, the authorities of Redcliffe cannot be better served than by the architect who has gained and justly secured my esteem.

I cannot satisfy myself to quit Redcliffe church, without alluding to, and complimenting, the Vestry of that parish, whom I have met in conclave several times, and always found them united and zealous in promoting the plans and recommendations placed before them, respecting the preservation and pure restoration of every part of the glorious church which is bequeathed to their custody. To one of their body, Thomas Proctor, who I believe originated the recent new and important works, and to whose zeal, good sense, and good temper much is due, I shall continue to entertain the greatest respect and affection.

BRISTOL CATHEDRAL.—As a portion of the *Cathedral Antiquities*, I produced the history of that of Bristol, in the year 1830. Occupying respectable lodgings for six weeks, on the College Green, I was close to the edifice which I had to visit daily, to make notes, and direct and advise the three artists* employed in making elevations, sections, and

---

* These pupils were W. H. Bartlett, T. H. Clarke, and C. Hacker; the first of whom has since visited the four quarters of the globe, and made an immense number of drawings for publication. He has lately produced some volumes on Egypt and the Holy Land, which have justly earned him distinction as an author, as well as artist. The third is now in a most respectable and confidential station, in the service of the Duke of Bedford, at Woburn.

details of that fragment of one of the modern cathedrals which Henry the Eighth created when he dissolved the monasteries. The Dean, Dr. Beeke, was courteous, and desirous of affording every facility and attention, and favoured me with several letters respecting the history of the edifice. Other officers of the church rendered me and my artists civilities which made our residence here very pleasant.

The church here alluded to has some peculiarities deserving the especial notice and study of the architectural antiquary: viz., the unique Anglo-Norman chapter-room, which has recently been restored to its original style of finish. Nearly the whole surface of the walls of the interior is covered with circular-headed niches, interlacing arcades, diapered mouldings, ornamented columns, and ribs; and thus exhibits a galaxy of architectural adornment. At the west end is a doorway, and two windows of corresponding ornament, communicating with a vestibule of the same architectural members, but less decorated. This is remarkable in design, being an apartment vaulted over, and supported by four clustered short pillars, with semi-circular and pointed arches.*

Unlike any other church that has come under my notice, this at Bristol has ailes to the choir, of corresponding height with the central division, separated from each other by five lofty arches on each side, and lighted by tall windows reaching to the apex of the vaulted roof. This vaulting, and the peculiarity of design and construction of the roofing of the ailes, are worthy the especial study of the architect. They are fully delineated, and explained, in the prints of the volume referred to; as are the several parts and members of this singular portion of the edifice. The whole of the west end, from the central tower and transept, has been destroyed. In the south wall of the church, immediately above the stone seat, is a series of remarkable recesses, containing recumbent effigies of different persons of the Berkeley family, with framed ornamental mouldings of inverted arches, with crockets, and finials.

---

* This vestibule and the interior of the chapter-room are carefully and correctly represented and explained in two prints, in the volume referred to. At the meeting of the Archæological Institute, in the summer of 1851, one of the Sections assembled in the chapter-room, where the reverberation of sound, from speaking, was so strong, that it was impossible for auditors to hear words and sentences with distinctness.

Within the church are memorials to the following persons, whom I once loved, and whose memory and talents I often reflect on with delight, viz.: *Edward Bird, Esq.*, R.A., a native of this city, who died in the prime of life, and at a time when his professional talents were rising high in public estimation. My friend, Allan Cunningham, has written a brief memoir of him, in his " Lives of Eminent British Painters," to which I can add a few facts and traits of character, if opportunity should hereafter occur. Another memorial of an old departed friend is the bust of *Robert Southey*, D.C.L., whose name and personal features are thus preserved within these walls, to show that he belonged to Bristol, and was honoured, to this extent, by certain inhabitants who wished to pay him a posthumous compliment. Much was published in the provincial papers of the time respecting a *Bristol Testimonial to Southey;* and something of consequence and truly effective was expected: but, alas! the result is unworthy of the natal home of the poet, and of his mental and moral worth. I was strongly excited in the cause at the time, and wrote letters and paragraphs, urging the desirableness of raising a large sum, and of producing a cenotaph commensurate to the merits of the man, and to the estimation in which he was generally held.*

My next intercourse with Bristol was in the year 1833, when I gave a course of *Lectures on Architectural Antiquities,* at the Institution in Park Street. These were delivered twice in one day, and three days in the week. On concluding the course, I read another Lecture, or Essay, on the proposed *Great Western Railway*, its desirableness and utility; and the peculiarities of the port of Bristol, in regard to geology, and facilities of land and water carriage to the interior of our own island, and to foreign shores. At that time the Bristolians were not sanguine in the projected railway, and did not come forward eagerly

---

* An event connected with the name of Southey and Redcliffe, not generally known, may be referred to in this place, with propriety. He had made arrangements to sail to Spain, with his uncle, on a certain day, by a vessel from this port, and immediately afterwards agreed to marry on the morning of that very day. In the Register of Redcliffe Church is this entry: "*Robert Southey* and *Edith Fricher* were married in this church, Nov. 1, 1795." An account of this is given in Cottle's "Reminiscences," p. 189, with an explanatory letter from Southey to his friend.

to support it. I may therefore venture to state, without arrogance, that its cause and success were promoted by the remarks then made, by their repetition in the public papers, and by the distribution of many thousand copies by the Directors of the Railroad. I must, however, complain of the conduct of those Directors. Though I pleaded their cause with more than common zeal; gave them the Lecture to print, and of which, I learnt, they circulated many thousands of copies; and we may reasonably conclude that they ultimately benefited; yet they failed to make the author the slightest compliment. For the facts and data in this Essay, I was indebted to my friend, Mr. John Provis, of Chippenham, who is familiar with the geology and statistics of Bristol, and the surrounding country.

Connected with these Lectures and the time, was the death of *Rajah Rammohun Roy*, which event occurred at the house of his friend, the Rev. Dr. Lant Carpenter, 27th September, 1833; and caused not only that amiable and learned author to be absent from my exhibitions, but also many of his friends. The decease of that extraordinary Christianized Bramin was a source of great lament in Bristol, and in various parts of England; for he was a sincere radical reformer of political and religious abuses in pagan India, and had conciliated the friendship and affections of many kind-hearted persons in this country. At Bristol, and particularly amongst the class of persons which took an interest in literature, art, and science, the event was more than depression—it was melancholy. It was only three days before I commenced my course; and I had calculated more on the influence of Dr. Carpenter, and his friends, to whom I was strongly recommended, than on any other persons. In spite of such an inauspicious cloud, I was met and cheered by a large and truly respectable auditory, which continued during the whole course.

I cannot advert to the subjects of these Lectures, but with mingled emotions of gratitude, pleasure, and pain: the last arising from a lamentable incident that occurred at the time; and the sad conviction that nearly the whole of the kindly-disposed friends, who then honoured and cheered me are passed away. The first arises from the cordial and very kind treatment I received from the managers of the Institution, several influential gentlemen of the city and its vicinity, and from the periodical press, both of Bristol and of Bath. Nearly all the newspapers (there were no fewer than eight) gave copious reports, with praises of each Lecture. To Mr. William Tyson, one of the writers, I was indebted for particular attention and care in the matter and manner of imparting to the public, not merely the spirit of my discourses, but the peculiarities of language sometimes used.*

In concluding my task at the Institution, I was tempted to allude to, and compliment, the female part of my auditors, by saying, that "it gave me sincere pleasure to be honoured with so many ladies, whose attention, and marked inspection of drawings, showed that they took an interest in the subject. Besides, in bringing their pupils and families, they adopted a good and laudable course to expand and improve the minds, and excite curiosity, in that class of society which was destined to be the mothers and teachers of future legislators, artists, and benefactors to their species."

The reporter thus concludes his review of the Course, which I may venture to repeat as a public testimony and complimentary reward for the zeal and the exertions then made: "These Lectures have been well attended throughout; and although they might, on their first announcement, have been considered as a dry matter of detail, they were diversified, by the ingenuity and information of the lecturer, with many pleasing anecdotes. Mr. Britton evidently knows how to address and delight a mixed audience. We hope to see him again, and hear him inculcating that sound architectural taste which he himself has so deeply imbibed by travel, study, and evident research."

For this Course I received sixty pounds; whilst the Institution derived a profit of twenty pounds more.

Since that time I have made several visits to Bristol, in consequence of my connection with the restoration of Redcliffe church, and of friendly attentions from Mr. Proctor, a gentleman already referred to. In the summer of 1851 I spent a week there with the Archæological Institute, and felt it a sort of duty to prepare a short paper to direct the attention

---

* This once amiable man, devoted antiquary, and Bristolian topographer, died at his native city in the autumn of 1851, after an intimate connection with the *Bristol Mirror* for many years. I knew and esteemed him, for his simplicity of manners, kindness of heart, and warm attachment to archæology.

of members, who were not familiar with the district, to the best authorities for information on those objects of interest in the city and its vicinity which are most calculated to gratify curiosity. These are so numerous, so various, and of such remote dates and characteristics, that volumes have been, and still may be, devoted to their history and elucidation without becoming tedious or unimportant. Within an area of twenty miles in extent from the centre of the city, may be seen tangible works of the ancient Britons, Romans, Saxons, Normans, and later dynasties of the English, in different degrees of identity and importance to the antiquary and historian. Besides, the scenery, geology, and natural history of the district are all peculiar, and present so many varieties of subject for study and investigation to persons partial to these branches of inquiry, that they may find rational occupation for months instead of a few weeks.—I must not, however, linger more at this city, for I have still a long journey to accomplish, and numerous attractive objects demanding attention. My next place of sojourn is remarkably dissimilar to that just noticed.

There are three roads between Bristol and Bath, all of which are hilly, and thus, though pleasing to the traveller, are not so to those who are desirous of expedition, or have any sympathy for horses. Hence the lower, or new, road, south of the Avon, was the only one used after it was completed. This presents some interesting views on its course, of steep acclivities, narrow dells, the windings of the sluggish Avon, and fine specimens of church architecture. On the side of the road, about one mile from Bristol, is a place called *Arno's Vale*, where a handsome modern house was built at the end of the last century, with large offices on the opposite side of the way: the latter, having an embattled parapet, and towers at the angles, also embattled, assumed a more imposing appearance than the house itself. In this locality my esteemed friend, Mr. Thomas Eagles, resided, when I was writing the History of Redcliffe Church, and from whom I derived some valuable information. It is traditionally related that Addison wrote some of his "Spectator" at this place.

A retrospective view of the former city, from *Brislington*, is very striking, and gives palpable intimations of the characteristics of that place, by numerous lofty kiln-towers and chimney-shafts, pouring out dense clouds of black and grey smoke; by several towers and spires rising above a compact mass of houses, and backed by a high hill, called Kingsdown, whose acclivities are covered with other houses, rising row above row, and street above street, to the summit. To the west of this range is descried part of the modern and rich suburb of Clifton, with the remarkable chasm in its rocks, through which the tidal Avon passes in its progress to sea. Near the foreground is a bend of the river, with mud-lined banks, beyond which, and forming the middle distance, is seen the truncated spire, and grand tower, of Redcliffe church; also numerous masts and flags of the shipping, which are admitted into the midst of the crowded streets and quays. The whole of this scene, with its picturesque accessories, is more particularly impressed on my memory by a clever sketch which Bartlett took from this point. At the same time he made a series of beautiful drawings of *Broomwell House*, in the parish of Brislington, the seat of G. W. Braikenridge, Esq., who possesses a valuable and interesting collection of drawings, fragments of antiquity, manuscripts, and prints, relating to Bristol. To that amiable gentleman I dedicated my volume on the Cathedral. The small tower of the church of Brislington ranks amongst the beautiful specimens of the Somersetshire buildings. In this parish resided, for some years, my respected and learned friend, the *Rev. Wm. C. Conybeare*, previous to his removal to the Deanery of Llandaff; and at this retired place, I believe, he wrote some of his interesting geological works.

In the town of KEYNSHAM, my attention was arrested by a baywindow to a small common house in the street, which was supported by two grotesque sculptured figures; and also by some large specimens of *Ammonites*, or "snake stones," inserted in the walls of houses, and others lying amongst heaps of stones by the road-side. On inquiry, I learnt that they abounded in the vicinity. This remarkable phenomenon was represented by the legends, or fables of the Roman Catholic biographers of saints, as supernaturally formed. The silly story of St. Keyna, who is said to have been surrounded by serpents in a wood near Keynsham, and protected against their poison by praying that they might be converted into stone, and deprived of their heads, can only be regarded as the invention of a fool or a knave. See a rational geological account of these fossils in Phillips's "Guide to Geology," and also in Dr. Buckland's "Bridgewater Treatise." The lofty tower, with its attached church, I found to contain some good architectural details.

About two miles east of Keynsham, is the village of BITTON, which I have repeatedly visited on account of its fine church and lofty tower; and of two inhabitants whom I mention in this place, with feelings of esteem, bordering on affection, viz.: HENRY ASHTON BARKER, and the REV. HENRY THOMAS ELLACOMBE. The former, now nearly my own age, I became acquainted with on the opening of the first *Panorama*, in Leicester Square, which originated with his father, at the end of the last century. That gentleman was a portrait-painter at Glasgow, where his son was born in 1774, and was educated as an artist. In his thirteenth year, he was sent by his father to make sketches of Edinburgh, from the Calton Hill. These gave the parent so much satisfaction, that he instructed the boy to make large studies of some of the parts. Hence originated the earliest Panorama ever exhibited in London. Mr. Robert Mitchell, of Newman Street, was employed to make designs for a circular building, with spacious sky-light, and stairs of approach to a platform, in the centre of the room. It was successful, and became very popular. Mitchell published delineations and an account of the building in a folio volume in 1801. From that year to the present time, the Leicester-fields Panorama has continued to exhibit a succession of very interesting views of various cities and remarkable places in different parts of the world. Mr. Barker has long retired from the excitement of London art and society, and settled in the quiet, retired village of Bitton, respected and beloved by all who know him. In his next-door neighbour, the Rev. Mr. Ellacombe, the vicar of Bitton, he has found a learned and excellent acquaintance, who, to an active disposition unites the amiable and estimable parish pastor, the inquisitive topographer and antiquary, the geologist, botanist, friend, and instructor of the poor. His house, gardens, cemetery and church give evident proofs of his watchfulness, good sense, and good taste, in rendering the whole conducive to the comforts and pleasures of his own united family, and also to the benefit of his parishioners.

The church, immediately adjoining his garden, is a large and fine edifice, with a lofty decorated tower; all of which have been carefully preserved and really beautified by and under the direction of the good vicar. To this gentleman I am indebted for numerous searches in the registers of Bitton and several adjoining parishes for the baptisms, marriages, and interments of the Britton families. In a previous part of this volume (p. 40, &c.) will be found references to this place, to my friend, and to the Brittons, who appear to have abounded in this part of Somersetshire and Gloucestershire. Amongst a list of more than one hundred names, I am unable to ascertain those of my father's parents; and have only recently found the registry of the marriage of my own father and mother. The last was born at a farmhouse in the very small parish of Norton, near Malmesbury, surrounded by its own fields, at some distance from the village church. In the summer of 1851, the Rev. J. E. Jackson, who resides at another living about three miles distant, was in attendance on a dying female in one of the cottages, where he accidentally met with one of the old parish registers, and thought it right to take it away: amongst other entries in it, he discovered that of the marriage of my parents, which I had vainly sought after for years.

At Newton St. Loe, about three miles west of Bath, the excavators, in forming the line of the Great Western Railway, laid bare the foundations, pavements, &c., of a Roman Villa; the central part of one pavement of which has been preserved in the station, at Keynsham.* The *Rev. Richard Warner*, the historian of Bath, and author of many other interesting literary works, resided at a pretty ivy-bound cottage in this parish for some years before he removed to his present Rectory of Chelwood, where I saw him, serene and happy, in August 1851, in the eighty-ninth year of his age.

Meditating on this interview, as I returned to the once gay city of the healing springs, I was naturally and forcibly impressed with strong emotions, as well as reflections, on the changes and contrasts which man and his finest works exhibit in their progress from maturity and beauty

---

* An account of this Villa, with illustrations, was communicated to the Society of Antiquaries by H. E. Goodridge, Esq., architect, of Bath, and has been published in the *Archæologia*.

to decline and decay. Like myself, Mr. Warner has attained very old age, has passed through a long career of authorship, and has been the theme of flattering commendation by some, and of severe censure by other professional critics, as well as by real and pretended friends; for to such conflicting tribunals is every public person subjected. He has likewise mixed in varied society, courted by many, but envied by others; and is now disqualified, by the wear and tear of natural causes, to carry to the festive board that amount of intellectual converse and anecdote, which seems to be a necessary passport to social life. Thus circumstanced, he is, however, enabled to amuse himself in reviewing his past "walks" through the "high-ways and bye-ways" of his world, by perusing the history and philosophy of mankind in their works; and, with confidence in that Omnipotence, which is apparent in all created matter, and inherent in mysterious mind, he awaits the final close of his career, with calmness and equanimity. Let it not be said, or thought, that old age must be peevish and unhappy; but, on the contrary, that, to the sincere Christian and the sound philosopher, it has its own, and many enjoyments. Mr. Warner has at once manifested his good feelings, as well as poetical powers, in the following lines, lately written on

### THE FADED LEAVES, IN THE GARDEN OF CHELWOOD PARSONAGE.

"Man that is born of a Woman, hath but a short time to live—
He cometh up, and is cut down, like a flower."—*Burial Service.*

Sweetly "the Swan of Avon" sings;
How NATURE'S GOD INSTRUCTION gives,
By murm'ring brooks and bubbling springs;
By all that DIES, and all that LIVES.

The "FADED LEAVES" that strew my path,
(As oft I tread the yielding sod)
Tho' silent—seem to tell—of DEATH!
Of JUDGMENT—and, the LIVING GOD!

"'Gainst THEE"—they say—"the WORD'S gone forth,"
"That—'when thou'st lived thy little day'—
"THOU, too, shalt FADE, and sink to earth,
"To mingle with thy fellow-clay."

"Then, cease the chace of WITHERING toys;
"And UPWARD turn thy roving eyes,
"To those IMPERISHABLE joys—
"The EVER-GREENS of PARADISE!"

Dec. 21, 1849.

In many respects the cases and circumstances of Mr. Warner and myself have been widely dissimilar. Though the son of a shopkeeper, he had the advantage of a learned education; was placed early in life in a respectable station; became a favourite and fashionable preacher, as well as an attractive companion in the gay, and then rich, circle of Bath society; attained deserved popularity as an author; and is now the Rector of two livings, which, however, I fear, do not produce a large income. On the contrary, I never enjoyed, what may be called, any education; was cramped and oppressed with poverty, and failed to meet with any patronage, unless the wages of publishers, for "work done and performed," be brought under that denomination; and have been necessitated to continue labouring at the literary oar from the time I took it first in hand, when youth and enthusiasm were buoyant and ardent, till the present time, when old age and consequent decrepitude combine to enervate the physical and mental powers.

More than half a century's familiar acquaintance with an author's writings and his personal character, affords ample time to estimate his intellectual and social qualifications. Besides this evidence, Mr. Warner has furnished me and other readers with "Literary Recollections" of his career in life, and of his published works, which present such a vivid, graphic, full-length picture of the Historian of Bath, that I cannot render him better justice, or the reader a greater favour, than by referring to the volumes published under the above title, in 1830. He was then in his sixty-seventh year: ardent and enthusiastic, with fertile fancy, a fine memory, and wielded the pen of a ready writer. These powers are shown in relating his own adventures, in the biographical sketches, which he has therein preserved, of several public persons with whom he became connected. Many of those belonged to Bath, where the author was domiciliated for many years. His two "Walks in Wales" had acquired great celebrity, and consequently the author was "the lion" of Bath coteries. Rather beauish in dress and manners, and with well-curled hair, as shown in the portrait to his "History of Bath," he was severely reprimanded by "The Anti-Jacobin Review," which pronounced him a coxcomb. The article was written by the *Rev. John Whitaker,* who was a frequent contributor to that periodical, and also to "The British Critic," two publications of extreme loyal principles.

The reverend critic had been ordered by his physician to visit Bath, and particularly advised to abstain from studies and writing. It seems that the latter was almost impossible; for the new History of the City had recently made its appearance, and attracted the attention of the new visitor; and such was the natural effect of habit, that he could not read without writing, and could not write without finding fault in strong terms of reprobation. The author's person, his style of writing, his matter, and his manner, were all subjects of censure and vituperation. A sentiment, a liberal or approving term of any political or religious person, or subject, not in unison with those of the reviewer, were pronounced to be Jacobinical, and consequently vile and bad. The book and the matters it embraced became so exciting and interesting to the infatuated critic, that he continued his review through two or three numbers of his periodical. Indeed, it seemed to have revived his early speculations and theories, contained in his antiquarian romance, "The History of Manchester," that he wished to reprint it in a separate volume: as he had done in a review of Gibbon's " Decline;" but at length he yielded to the entreaties of his good wife and some kind friends, to forego this plan. A few months after the review was finished, I spent some pleasant days with the learned and splenetic critic, at his isolated rectory, Ruan Lanyhorne, in Cornwall, and never was more gratified by the intellectual and conversational powers of any man. My esteemed friend, Warner, treated the matter with great forbearance and fortitude; and passed it over with slight notice in his "Literary Recollections." To that work I refer the reader for detailed and honest accounts of the author's numerous publications, on topography, antiquities, and miscellaneous literature.

BATH.—With this favourite, unique, and truly picturesque and architectural city, I have had much intercourse, from the days of boyhood up to the year 1850; and have written to some extent on its topography, antiquities, and memorable "Worthies." At page 58 of this volume, I have alluded to a visit to this place, when only eight years old.

About twenty years afterwards, I saw it with new eyes, and under very different circumstances; thenceforward I paid it many visits, from having a beloved sister settled in the city, and having formed intimacies with different families, particularly with Drs. Parry, father and son, Dr. Falconer, Messrs. Crutwell, Barrett, Upham, Godwin, Hewlett, Meyler, Dr. Harington, the Rev. R. Graves, the Rev. R. Warner, the Barkers, and many others. In 1803-4, I was commissioned to write an account of Bath for Rees's *Cyclopedia;* to qualify myself for which task, I was induced to collect and study all that had been previously published on the subject. About the same time, a "*Bath Guide*," abridged from "the History of the City," by the Rev. R. Warner, and Lysons's account, and illustrations of " Remains of two Roman Temples, &c., discovered at Bath," were placed in my hands, for comment and criticism in the *Annual Review.* My learned and acute friend, the Rev. John Whitaker, had recently published severe strictures in the Review alluded to, on Mr. Warner's history; all tending to direct public attention to this then fashionable city, to its annals, and to its literature. Such reading and writings, with associations naturally emanating therefrom, led me to look at, and admire, the architecture of the most prominent edifice of the city. Hence originated " *The History and Antiquities of Bath Abbey Church*," which was published in 1825, in three different sizes, two of which, in quarto, were to match my Cathedral and Architectural Antiquities, whilst the third, in royal octavo, was adapted for more general perusal. Indeed, this work was addressed rather to the general reader, than to the antiquary and architect.—See Part II. p. 148.

I will brave the charge of vanity, in saying that it is calculated to afford much amusement and information to various classes of students, as it contains biographies of several public personages; some criticism on architecture and sculpture, and particularly on the fabulous legends of monastic writers; with something about the provincial annals of the Romans. It also includes a learned and truly interesting *Essay on the History and Characteristics of Epitaphs.* This was written expressly for the volume by my much-beloved friend, the *Rev. John Josias Conybeare, M.A.*, formerly of Christ-Church College, Oxford, but who had settled in the living of Bath-Easton when I commenced the volume now referred to. He was carried off in the prime of life, when he appeared to be fixed for many years in a happy home, and with every prospect of a long and joyous sojourn on earth. His amiable manners, kindly disposition, love of literature and art, and Christian conduct in professional duties and intercourse with the world, caused him to be beloved by all who knew him whilst living, and sincerely deplored in death. As he had rendered me such a gratifying favour, in the Essay alluded to, which I believe was amongst the latest of his writings, I was prompted to express my gratitude to, and esteem for, him, by inscribing the volume " to his memory."

The Abbey Church, popularly, but improperly, called *the* Abbey, exhibits in its architecture the last and weakest specimen of that really interesting and beautiful class of edifices which the Christian architects of the middle ages designed and erected to adorn this country. There is little to admire in its design, as a whole, or in its details; but it affords an instructive lesson to the historian, as a tangible evidence of the decline and fall of a system of national religion and art, which had passed through a long period of political dominion and moral tyranny, in a country where new lights and new opinions were starting into operation. Appropriated to parochial purposes, and to the simple ceremonies of the reformed religion, it had only one communion table instead of several altars, with chantries, piscinas, &c. Though divested of these, of shrines, and mortuary chapels, it was soon occupied by sepulchral monuments; and, from the increase of population in the city, was destined to become a sort of museum of sculptured memorials; for the waters of Bath being much resorted to and used by invalids, they flocked to this place from various parts of the country, where many of them died, and were very improperly interred within the walls of the church. The late Dr. Harington, in allusion to these circumstances, made the following epigrammatic distich:

> "These walls, adorned with monument and bust,
> Show how Bath-waters serve to lay the dust."

See *History, &c. of Bath Abbey*, p. 64, 4to. edition, for comments on this epigram; and for remarks on the peculiarities of this church, and that of Westminster, being over-crowded with monuments.

Anstey's *New Bath Guide* had long been a popular work, having passed through several editions, in 1829, when my friend, Mr. Thomas Hurst, of St. Paul's Churchyard, put a copy into my hands and asked me to prepare another edition, with a biographical preface and notes. The justly-admired Mr. George Cruikshank was to adorn its pages with five of his original and witty designs, whilst Mr. S. Williams was to make two others, which proved to be equally effective and original. This congenial task was undertaken and executed *con-amore*. I dedicated it "To the Respectable Booksellers of Bath," being personally acquainted with six, at that time, who, for integrity of character, general information, and friendly conduct, were not surpassed by any bibliopolists of the kingdom.* Besides, I had found Publishers to be not only my best, but only patrons, and could therefore truly and conscientiously speak of their merits as tradesmen and friends.† I told them, "Authors never praise *you;* for they say, you live on their brains, and that your profits are derived from the vital current of their life-blood. But, from long experience, I repudiate these invidious charges, and am prepared to shew, that you are the author's best friends, best advisers, and best patrons. The age of patronage is gone by; the days of Shakspere and Southampton, of Dryden, and of patron Princes, Dukes and Earls; of Sterne,‡ and of Pitt and Halifax, are past, and only to be found recorded in your libraries and in your memories." I told them likewise much more in the same strain.

Anstey's Poetical Guide appears to have passed the ordeal of public and private criticism with more than common success. In the volume referred to, I have endeavoured to point out and discriminate the writer's qualifications as a poet and a satirist; and also show that many of the Bath visitors were proper and palpable subjects for literary castigation and ridicule. We cannot read the accounts by Smollett, in his "Humphrey Clinker;" by Graves, in his "Spiritual Quixote;" and of many other novelists, essayists, dramatists, and periodicals of the middle of the last century, without some degree of surprise and pity

---

* These were Barrett, Godwin, Meyler, Upham, Simms, and Collings.

† On a subsequent occasion, I was tempted to compliment the London publishers under similar feelings, and in sincere terms of approbation; for I knew three or four of them who duly appreciated literary merit. This address is prefixed to "The Pleasures of Human Life," which is described in the Second Part of this Auto-Biography, p. 188.

‡ Sterne's dedication in his inimitable *Tristram Shandy*, "to be let, or sold for fifty guineas," is poignantly satirical; as are most of his writings. Dr. Johnson, speaking of one of Dryden's Dedications, says, "It is in a strain of flattery which disgraces genius, and which it is wonderful that any man that knew the meaning of his own words could use without self-detestation."

at the sottish, illiterate manners and language of even the fashionables of that time, and must derive self-gratulation in contrasting them with the mental and moral condition of society in our own age. There were, certainly, a few brilliant planets in the intellectual hemisphere at that epoch, which derived additional lustre from the dulness of the other stars in the system. Smollett, Fielding, Warburton, and Garrick; afterwards, Sheridan, the Lindleys, Anstey, Graves, Harington, the Lees; whilst a third group consisted of Warner, Hunter, the Drs. Parry, father and son; Drs. Sherwen, Falconer, and Gibbes; the Rev. T. Leman, Wilson, Gainsborough, Meyler, the Barkers, Conybeare, Mangin, and several others, may be named as belonging to the city.

The Rev. Joseph Hunter, the learned author of some valuable topographical works on parts of Yorkshire, resided in Bath for several years, and in 1826 read an Essay, at the commencement of the second session of the Literary Institution, on "*The Connection of Bath with the Literature and Science of England.*" A few copies of this small brochure were printed, and I cannot help regretting that it has not been published in a popular form, or in one of the best Guides, for general information, and for the gratification of a numerous class of readers. The author proves "that Bath has ever had, and deserved to have, a name in the literature and science of England;" and notices the following names, with comments on their writings, to verify his theorem: " Ralph Allen, Christopher Anstey, the Bowdler family, Thos. Carte, Dr. Samuel Chandler, Chapman, Dr. Cheyne, S. Daniel, John Davies, Dr. Falconer, H. Fielding, Gainsborough, Gildas, Guidot, Hales, Sir John Harington, Sir Wm. Herschel, the Rev. Thos. Leman, C. Luders, S. Lysons, Mrs. Macauley, Dr. Mayow, Wm. Melmoth, Lady Miller, Drs. Oliver, sen. and jun., Drs. Parry, sen. and jun., Governor Pownall, Prynne, Dr. Sherwen, Mrs. Siddons, Dr. Smith, the Rev. Joseph Townshend, the Rev. Dr. Warburton, Sir W. Watson, and Wood, the architect."

The building of the Bath Institution was designed and erected for assembly-rooms, on the site of an older edifice which had been devoted to the same gay purposes. Cheltenham, Brighthelmstone, Tunbridge Wells, and even the sea-coast watering-places, were at that time but little frequented. Bath, however, has undergone a vast change, by the ascendancy of the other towns surpassing it in fashionable estimation; and its assemblies have so much declined that a second house is not required: indeed one is not sufficiently patronized to support its requisite style of splendour. The Institution, though at first fairly encouraged by the influential inhabitants of the city and its vicinity, is not flourishing equal to its deserts, and to the benefit it is capable of affording to a reading and thinking public. The rooms are commodious and handsome; the library is well stocked; the museum abounds with interesting and valuable objects; whilst the situation, and the views from the windows, are singularly delightful. Amongst other valuable objects in the library, I may mention the following as of importance for their local and general value:

> The *Rev. J. Skinner*, of Camerton, near Bath, presented to the Institution, copperplates of a *Roman pavement*, at Wellow; also, a volume of Autograph Letters by himself, Sir R. C. Hoare, the Rev. J. Douglas, and Samuel Lysons.
>
> *Captain J. J. Chapman* has left in charge of the Institution, about 150 volumes of printed and manuscript materials, relating to Bath, &c.
>
> The *Rev. Thomas Leman*, who, in company with the Bishop of Cloyne,* devoted many summers in traversing and investigating the courses of the Roman roads of England, left his numerous manuscript collections on the subject, with maps and printed books to this establishment; also several volumes of pedigrees of families in the counties of Berks, Bucks, Cambridge, Cornwall, Devon, Gloucester, Norfolk, Somerset, Suffolk, Warwick, and York.
>
> *Dr. Sherwen* presented to the Institution his Manuscripts on the Chatterton Controversy, in which he advocates the cause of Rowley, and the genuineness of certain papers which were exhibited as ancient; also other manuscript annotations on Shakspere's writings.

At this same Institution, in December, 1832, and January, 1833, I read eight *Lectures on the Architectural Antiquities of Nations*, being nearly a repetition of the course I had delivered at Bristol. Here,

---

* It is rather a curious circumstance in topographic literature, that whilst these two learned antiquaries were thus rationally occupying their time, and seeking amusement in hunting after the vias, or roads of the Anglo-Romans, they also contributed information to two publications which were then printing, on the general topography and antiquities of the island. Messrs. Samuel and Daniel Lysons were writing and printing a valuable work, called "Magna Britannia, a general account of the English Counties," for which the Bishop of Cloyne contributed descriptions of the Roman roads. At the same time, J. Britton and E. W. Brayley were publishing "The British Atlas," for which Mr. Leman wrote his commentary on the same lines of road-way, in each county.

however, the theatre was very different to that, as was also the company, to those of the mercantile city I had recently left. There was a holiday-air in the manners and deportment of my auditors, and the school classes presented a variety, both in genera and species. The lectures, as at Bristol, were to be given twice in one day, at half-past two and at half-past seven—the first, for the class called the fashionable; the second, for the next descending grade, the professional and the trading part of the community. Amongst the latter were the artists, the architects, builders, &c.: and though there were trifling varieties in the manner and expression of the two classes, they treated me with marked cordiality and kindness. I never felt more at ease, or more gratified with an auditory than at Bath. The whole presented a remarkable contrast in place, persons, scenery, and association with Manchester, where I seemed to have passed a month of purgatory, whilst this was a sort of Elysian field.

The receipts for the Lectures amounted to £51. 11s. 6d.

Though the cities of Bath and Bristol are within twelve miles of each other—i. e. about two hours as performed in the days of stage-coaches, and now only twenty minutes by rail—they are singularly dissimilar in all their characteristics. It cannot fail to amuse the stranger to be informed, that in buildings, inhabitants, and local scenery they are as dissimilar as if belonging to different nations, and a different race of people. Bath seems to be adapted for, and occupied by, the gay and the idle, the old and the invalid, the valetudinarian and the lassitudinarian; and has nothing of sea-port, or factory, or trade in its whole area. Its shops and markets, as well as their occupants, present features, customs, and manners which exclusively belong to the place, seem to have grown with it, and are strictly indigenous. The whole of the houses and other buildings are constructed with the light, fine freestone of the district, whilst those of the better class have architectural pretensions. All the orders, and some of the *dis*-orders, of architecture are exhibited in its Circus, Crescents, Squares, and Streets. Smollett, in " Humphrey Clinker," is severe in his strictures on the architecture of the Circus; and very just in representing the form of that and the crescents as objectionable. Though the nucleus of Bath occupies the site of, and is raised on, the ruins of an ancient

Roman town, or station, it is strictly of modern character; for there is not any building which can be referred to a date before the beginning of the sixteenth century. As a place of public note, it must date its origin and fame to the reign of Richard Nash, popularly designated "Beau Nash," who attained a sort of sovereignty here for some years, after his first appointment as Master of the Ceremonies, in 1704.

As Madame D'Arblay exclaims in one of her letters, (*Diary*, Vol. v., p. 249), "I must not, however, write a literal Bath Guide, and will only tell you, in brief, yet in truth, it looks a city of palaces, a town of hills, and a hill of towns. It is beautiful and wonderful throughout. The hills are built up and down, and the vales so stocked with streets that, in some places, from the ground-floor on one side of the street you cross over to the attic of your neighbour. The white stone, where clean, has a beautiful effect, and even where worn, a grand one."

This account was written in August, 1791, and refers to a former visit to the same place, with remarks on some of the changes which had occurred in the interim, by births and deaths, by vicissitudes in life, and the alterations which fashion and improvements had made. She tells us, "Its circumference is perhaps trebled; but its buildings are so unfinished, so spread, so everywhere beginning, and nowhere ending, that it looks rather like a piece of ground lately fixed upon for erecting a town, than a town itself of so many years' duration. O how have I thought of my poor Mrs. Thrale! almost every old place brings to my mind some scene in which we were engaged. How are most of the families altered and dispersed within the last ten years! No acquaintance here, except Dr. Harington, who is ill. Well! we live but to die, and are led but to follow." Such were my own feelings and experiences, in connection with this city, between my early and late visits.

In addition to the public persons already named, and with whom I had secured varied degrees of intimacy, there were several others, who properly belong to the class of *Bath Worthies*, though they have hitherto been overlooked, or slighted by the topographers and biographers of Bath. Amongst these, were the brothers, *Thomas, and Benjamin Barker*, both artists of acknowledged talent, and well entitled to be enrolled and fully described in the biographies of English painters. The first was hailed as a prodigy, a precocious genius, who, in boyhood, almost in childhood, produced pictures which astonished the cognoscenti of the city. His full-length picture, when a youth, size of life, of an old Woodman with his Dog, excited the highest encomiums in the provincial press, and even by Sir Edward Harington, son of the witty Doctor of the same name, who published a volume expressly in its praise. This was entitled " A Schizzo on the Genius of Man," 8vo. 1793. In Mr. Spackman, a coach-builder of Bath, the youth found a substantial and kind friend, who not only received him as apprentice to his own business, but furnished him with education and instructed him in the elements of painting, in which he was practically, though not professionally familiar. The patron did not rest here, but sent his accomplished *protégé* to Rome, where he distinguished himself by diligently studying the native manners, &c., of that capital, and also by examining and copying some of the famed pictures contained in its churches.

Before Mr. Barker left his home, he had sold his picture of " the Woodman " to Mr. Thomas Macklin, a noted print-seller and publisher, of Fleet Street, London, in whose " Poet's Gallery " it formed a popular exhibition for some time. An engraving was published from it, and Mr. Alderman Boydell afterwards purchased the picture for seven hundred guineas.*

On returning from Italy, the young artist settled at Bath, where, having married, and attained the fairest prospect of success, he obtained a commodious and handsome house on the romantic slope of Sion-hill. To this he built a beautiful picture-gallery, and adorned one of its walls with a fresco painting of "the Massacre of the Sciotes," a composition and picture of much originality, force, vigour, and effect.

I forbear further remarks on this once amiable man, and highly accomplished artist, as I perceive from a well-written Prospectus, now

---

* In the interesting life of Sir Thomas Lawrence, by D. E. Williams, it is stated that he rented a house, No. 2, Alfred Place, Bath, in 1782, at an annual rent of one hundred pounds, when he was in his thirteenth year. At that time his portraits in crayons were from two to three guineas each; and it appears that before he was eighteen he supported his parents and family from his professional gains. In Warner's " Recollections " are copies of four of Sir Thomas's Letters, allusive to his connections with Bath, his prices of pictures, &c.; also an account of Mr. Barker giving the future President of the Royal Academy his first instructions for *setting his palette*.

before me, that a large volume is preparing on the professional life and works of Mr. Barker, by his son, Thomas Jones, and George V. Irving, Esqrs. This work cannot fail to be interesting to every lover of art. Mr. Charles Empson, of Bath, an old and intimate friend of the late Mr. Barker, is to be the publisher. The son, I observe, has settled in London, and has painted pictures of a high class.

*Benjamin Barker*, the brother of Thomas, painted numerous small landscapes, which were very popular, and readily sold at the exhibitions of the British Institution. He saved money, purchased and possessed a very delightful villa, on the west side of Claverton Down, where his hanging gardens, trout stream, woods, and paintings were calculated to command the admiration, and almost the envy, of his visitors. At this delectable retreat I spent many happy hours, in company with some of the Bath "Worthies," amongst whom was James Hewlett, already referred to. See *ante*, p. 50.

*Thomas Gainsborough*, R.A., though he had quitted Bath before I became acquainted with the place, had so identified himself and his works with the scenery and persons of the district, that we may fairly class him with its superior artists. In Mr. Wiltshire, of Shockerwick, he found a substantial patron: in that house there are three or four of his eminent pictures. One of them, a waggon and horses, with human figures, is well known to, and duly admired by, artists and amateurs. There is also a portrait of an old man, commonly called the Parish-Clerk of Bradford, which ranks with Rembrandt's portraits, for colour, effect, and character. Gainsborough resided at Bath from 1758 to 1774, and left many of his paintings and sketches there, and in the neighbourhood. At a house in the Circus I saw more than fifty, in 1801. In Cunningham's "Lives of English Artists" will be found a good account of this eccentric man and talented painter. Jackson, of Exeter, published some interesting anecdotes of him in his "Four Ages and other Essays." He was born in 1727 and died 1788.

*William Hoare*, R.A., and *Prince Hoare* were natives of this city, both of whom conferred honour on the place of their birth, and on their own names. I knew the latter intimately, loved him for his many amiable qualities, and admired him for his talents. Though educated for an artist, he did not pursue the profession for a livelihood. Possessing a handsome fortune, he indulged his predilections for literature and the fine arts; and continued his connection with the Royal Academy by acting as Honorary Foreign Secretary for many years. In addition to about twenty dramatic pieces, in tragedy, comedy, and farce, he was author of some volumes on the Fine Arts, and also Essays in different periodicals. Two of the last he wrote for "The Fine Arts of the English School"—one, on the celebrated picture by Sir Joshua Reynolds of "Garrick between Tragedy and Comedy;" and the other, on a historical picture by Northcote, representing "The Earl of Argyle in Prison." This work ranks amongst the best of the artist's paintings: its subject is awfully impressive and grand.

Mr. Prince Hoare has left a memorial of his own filial gratitude and goodness, and of his father's worth, by a sepulchral monument, placed in the Abbey church of Bath. This was designed and executed by his friend, Sir F. Chantrey. Prince Hoare died at his house in Brighton, in 1834, in his eightieth year.

Intimately associated with the modern history of Bath, with the west of England, and the civil annals of the country, is the name and actions of the late WILLIAM BECKFORD, ESQ., who, in the latter part of his life, had made this city his home for full twenty years. His residence here was a singular contrast, and sort of antipodes, to his previous habits and mode of living. For a long period of time he had led a kind of hermetical life within the barricaded walls of Fonthill Abbey, where he seemed shut out, and estranged from the civilized world; and where he could luxuriate within the sumptuous apartments of a vast and splendid mansion, or ride for miles in extent on the smooth lawns of his own estate, in the midst of forest and mountain trees, flowering shrubs, the dressed parterres of the pleasure-garden, or wild scenery of nature. This garden, with vast woods and a wild lake, abounded with game of all kinds, and all the choristers of the forest, which were not only left undisturbed by the licensed sportsman, but were fed and encouraged by the lord of the soil and all his domestics. Within, the mansion was furnished and adorned with all the luxuries of upholstery, as well as the choicest works of art and literature. A widower, and without any family, at home, Mr. Beckford resided at the Abbey for more than twenty years, ever active, and constantly occupied in reading, music, and the converse of a choice and select circle of friends, or in directing workmen in continuing the erection of the building, which had been in progress between the years 1798 and 1821. About the latter date his restless spirit required a change; whilst his finances became inadequate to support the expensive establishment he had formed, and the habits in which he had long indulged. To the astonishment of his friends and the public, he purchased two houses, in Lansdown Crescent, Bath, with a large tract of land in connection with them, and removed from the solitude of a sort of country forest, to the gay, the idle, the gossipping, the scandalizing city. Here he not only became "the observed of all observers," but the target at which folly, spleen, and envy levelled their bitter but pointless shafts. The property at Fonthill was placed at the disposal of the amiable and learned Mr. Christie, who speedily prepared a Catalogue for the sale of the estate and the house with its splendid, and even gorgeous, contents. The auctioneer first made an Exhibition of the place in the summer of 1822, fixing the price of admission at one guinea for each person. Thousands flocked to see, admire, and wonder; and Fonthill-fair continued "the rage" for some months. During this gala I was a resident in the Abbey, with my wife and an artist, for nearly a month, for the purpose of writing and publishing a volume illustrative and descriptive of the place.* Mr. Beckford had frequent communications with his confidential agent and friend, the Chevalier Franchi, who had charge of the property at Fonthill. Towards the end of the summer, instead of a sale on the premises, the whole was bought, in one lot, for a very large sum, by Mr. Farquahar, an old miser, who had amassed an immense fortune in India. He was advised to do this by Mr. H. Phillips, an eminent auctioneer of Bond Street, who, in the following year, made a new exhibition of Fonthill, and sold its contents, with numerous other articles sent from London, and foisted upon the public as the genuine property of the renowned builder of "the Abbey." The whole tale forms a sort of romance of real life and actuality. During these singular transactions, Mr. Beckford was storing his twin houses at Bath with some of the choicest

---

* In a subsequent part of this Memoir I shall have occasion to advert to this seat, and to my early acquaintance with its accomplished and extraordinary possessor.

articles from his old libraries and cabinets; was forming and creating new gardens, with hot-houses and conservatories, on the steep and rocky slope of Lansdown; and also built a lofty and handsome tower on the summit of that hill. From the top of that building the eye, naturally, and by aid of telescope, commanded a vast extent of country, in every direction—east, west, north, and south—in which were to be seen the Bristol Channel and the Welsh Mountains, towards the west, and the two towers of Stourhead and Fonthill, towards the south. Thus seated, and thus circumstanced, it is not surprising that such a person, with such a mind, would exult and even enjoy the change, the novelty, and the contrast presented in the new creation, in which he was now actively and constantly occupied, with that which had grown beyond his means to support and improve, and the ruin of which he had anticipated when he left the place. It was not long after the property was sold, and the old India-miser had occupied it, that Mr. Beckford's telescope, on Lansdown tower, failed to present within its field of vision the Tower of Fonthill, for it had fallen upon, and crushed, other parts of the building during a stormy night.

Decidedly domiciliated in Bath, the two houses and their annexed grounds afforded ample scope for speculation and occupation to their new and eccentric possessor. A street or carriage-way intervened between the dwellings; but they were soon united by a flying-gallery, or aerial corridor, which formed a passage of communication between them. One of these houses was fitted up, filled, and decorated in accordance with the master's own peculiar notions of beauty, fitness, and elegance. Large mirrors, rich carpets, choice and fine pictures, bijouterie, objects of vertu, books in every room, and works of the most rare and valuable kind, combined to fascinate the eye and charm the senses. His daily meals, whether alone or in company, were always served up in rare and fine china, whilst all the appendages were silver, gold, or gilt. The wines and desserts were in character and harmony, being rich and costly, and cooked by the most skilful professors.—On one occasion, whilst in old Fonthill House, which had been built by his father, the celebrated Lord Mayor Beckford, he bought nineteen pipes of peculiar Malmsey Madeira. The merchant, who imported them, offered the whole or part to Queen Charlotte, who could take only one, as the price was too great. The Fonthill Crœsus, however, purchased the whole cargo, and I was treated with a glass every day after dinner, during my abode in the Abbey.

In converting a large tract of comparatively sterile land to gardens, lawns, and ornamental plantations, he was intensely occupied; and in the course of three or four years, large timber trees, fertile gardens, and many sylvan beauties were brought to vigour. His old and skilful gardener, Vincent, from Fonthill, and an army of assistants and labourers, were employed for some time in these operations, whilst the idle Bathonians were constantly amused and astonished by the novelties which were perpetually brought forth. A lofty and long extent of wall was raised between the road-way and the grounds to shut out the gaze of the vulgar, but served rather to excite more intense curiosity. The lofty and commanding tower, rapidly built from the working drawings of Mr. Goodrich, an eminent architect of Bath, rose high and vauntingly above all other objects, and it still remains to perpetuate the sneering appellation which has long been annexed to tall and prominent buildings—*Beckford's Folly*. Of this unique building an elaborate and splendid volume has been published by Mr. Edmund F. English, a gentleman of the city, who, with his father, was employed by Mr. Beckford to furnish and decorate the fancy apartments in the base of the tower. Twenty coloured engravings, resembling drawings, represent the architectural, artistic, and upholstery characteristics of the apartments, whilst several pages of well-written matter are devoted to describe " an object so unique, and a bijou so exquisite."

The following passage of a letter from Mr. Beckford to Mr. English, in remarking on the fitting up one of the rooms, is characteristic of the epistles and language used by the celebrated author of *Vathek*:—

" The little book-gallery may be moreened, as proposed, but I shall defer performing that operation upon the dining parlour till another season, so that the moths may enjoy themselves to next April, and then come forth in hundreds, or tens of thousands, if they please."

During Mr. Beckford's abode at Fonthill, he was regarded as the richest, the proudest, the shyest, and most haughty man in England. He was envied and traduced by many of his wealthy, narrow-minded neighbours, feared and avoided by those of lower station, and regarded with awe and respectful deference by the literati and artists of our own country, as well as by many distinguished foreigners. On settling at Bath, where he was frequently seen on horseback in the streets, with his groom, he appeared as the plain, unostentatious country gentleman, though his person always excited the gaze and speculation of the idlers and gossips. A dwarf, an Italian, named Piero, of very short stature, large head, with stunted arms and legs, was occasionally seen on a pretty grey pony, with the groom. Such an object, in such company, became a theme of intense speculation and commentary; and very strange and very wild conjectures were hazarded on the history, destination, and functions of this human phenomenon. The fact is, his master had taken charge of him in Italy, where he was deserted by his parents, and was homeless and houseless. He was brought to England by a humane patron, who supported him for life.

In the "New Monthly Magazine," for 1844, are two papers by Cyrus Redding, who had been sub-editor to Mr. Campbell for some years, and who was residing at Bath in that year. He describes, in graphic language, interviews and conversations with the author of *Vathek*, characterizing the writer and the man, from which I quote two or three sentences. "Mr. Beckford's literary career was protracted—no less than fifty-eight years between the appearance of the 'Memoirs of Extraordinary Painters' and the 'Visit to Alcobaça.' His mind was vigorous, his spirits were good, and he displayed his wonted activity of body nearly to the last. He declared to the present writer, in his seventy-sixth year, that he never felt a minute's *ennui* in his life. To this the great variety of his mental resources, as well as his bodily temperament, which would never permit him to remain inactive, greatly contributed. He was the most accomplished man of his time: his reading was perhaps the most extensive.* Besides the classical languages of antiquity, he spoke four modern European tongues, writing three of them with great elegance. He read the Persian and

---

* His faculty for, and mode of, reading were remarkable. When I attempted to read part of some writing of my own, and was pausing, he instantly repeated the complete sentence, and then told me, he could easily read and understand a goodly-sized octavo volume during his breakfast. He caught a sentence at a look; did not recognize and dwell on a word, or words, but embraced the whole at a glance.

Arabic, was an excellent designer with the pencil,* and perfect master of the science of music.† The last he was taught by Mozart, to whom he was so much attached, that when that great musician settled in Vienna, Mr. Beckford made a visit to that capital, as he said himself, 'that he might once more see his old master.' "

Wishing to view the Lansdown tower, and the proprietor's choice libraries and pictures, Mr. Redding sought that indulgence through the medium of Mr. Beckford's architect: the wish was granted, not in a cold and common-place way, but by the use of the owner's private carriage for the morning,‡ and by the personal company and conversation of the enthusiastic owner, whose originality of comment, description, and criticism, astonished the " Ex-Editor " of several periodicals, who has put on record many opinions and remarks made by that gentleman on a variety of topics.§

Mr. Beckford's custom, says Mr. Redding, "in fine weather, was to rise early, ride to the tower, or about the grounds, walk back, and breakfast, and then read until a little before noon, generally making pencil notes in the margin of every book; transact business with his steward; afterwards, until two o'clock, continue to read and write, and then ride out two or three hours afterwards. He was never idle. When planting or building, he passed the larger part of the day where the work was

---

\* In this opinion my friend must err, as I have seen, and possess, three or four pencil sketches by Mr. Beckford, which are very puerile and defective. He could describe and design better in words than by drawing.

† That he could play well and with much skill on the piano-forte, I have had opportunities of witnessing, both at Fonthill and at Bath; but he was far surpassed by the Chevalier Franchi, whose execution was so remarkably fine, that his master's seemed flat and insipid by comparison.

‡ Mr. Beckford frequently sent his carriage into the city, to escort a friend, or friends, to his house; for his horses and coachman, &c., were rarely employed by their master, who preferred riding on horseback. The descent from Lansdown to the lower town was long and steep, but his horses were accustomed to trot both ways, to the terror of some nervous persons and astonishment of strangers. I and my wife have been thus honoured four or five times, for we were always invited when we were at Bath at the time of Mr. Beckford's residence there.

§ In several successive numbers of Douglas Jerrold's " Weekly News," for 1847, is a series of interesting Essays, by Mr. Redding, detailing his experience and opinions as " an Ex-Editor."

proceeding. He sometimes expressed contempt by a sarcastic look peculiar to himself. Few could utter more cutting things than the author of *Vathek:* the utterance was accompanied with a caustic expression of countenance that made them tell with double effect."

Mr. Redding ventured to remark, "It must have cost you much pain to quit Fonthill."—"Not so much as you might think. I can bend to fortune. I have philosophy enough not to cry like a child about a plaything. The Chancellor took away from me, by a decree, in the course of what lawyers call justice, two large estates that had been sixty years in my family. You may imagine their importance when I tell you that there were fifteen hundred slaves upon them. This decree, too, the Chancellor accompanied with the reflection that, 'Mr. Beckford had plenty of property left.' That was my reason for quitting Fonthill."

Had the late Mr. Beckford been accompanied in the greater part of his long life by such a friend as Johnson found in Boswell, the records of his " Sayings and Doings " would have formed a literary work calculated to compete with, if not decidedly surpass, that which the obsequious, but veritable Scotchman produced, relating to the stern and uncompromising lexicographer. Beckford's life afforded a much broader and more diversified scope and sphere than that of Johnson: his reading was even more extensive, his conversational powers were more poignant, witty, original, and occasionally eccentric ; his accomplishments were still more pre-eminent, and his extensive intercourse with varied society was remarkable; whence a faithful and graphic record of them would have formed a literary work, not only of greater extent than that lastly augmented by Croker, but one calculated to amuse and astonish readers of all ages and countries. The very brief notices by Mr. Redding afford some glimpses of his conversation ; but the remarks and opinions, which pervade the novels of " Cecil, a Coxcomb," and " Cecil, a Peer," said to be from the pen of the justly popular novelist, Mrs. Gore, and mostly written by that lady, when on a visit to Mr. Beckford, at Bath, afford the nearest approach to the language, the ideas, the peculiar sentiments, of the author of *Vathek,* than any thing I have seen in print. I venture to offer these remarks in this place, from having repeatedly been honoured and delighted with the converse of that gentleman at my own house, at the two houses of Fonthill, and at Bath: not only "*tête-à-tête,*" but in the company of foreigners, artists, and men of letters.

Mr. Beckford continued to reside at Bath (excepting his annual visits to the metropolis, when he lived in Park Lane, and in Gloucester Place, New Road) for about twenty years, and died there in 1844, in the eighty-fourth year of his age. His intention was to make the ground attached to the Lansdown tower his place of sepulture, and had prepared and placed a granite sarcophagus on the spot; but, strange to say, the ecclesiastical authorities refused to consecrate the ground, and the executors had not moral courage enough to resist this tyranny of custom. The body was embalmed and placed in the said sarcophagus in the cemetery of Lyncomb, to the south of Bath. Here it formed a beautiful and original object; but it has since been removed to the ground adjoining the tower, and which the ceremonious clergy have recently thought right to consecrate. Alas! what a tyrant is custom, and what a slave is prejudice! When I first saw the tomb, newly raised, with its polished granite, emblazoned shields, bronzed and gilt posts and rails of novel form and beauty surrounding and enclosing an area of lawn, with the truly beautiful scenery, I regarded the whole as calculated to fascinate the eye and soothe the mind of every reflecting spectator. The changed situation of the sarcophagus, and its neglected state, when I viewed it in 1850, exhibited a lamentable contrast and aspect.

*Sir Edward Thomason,* who has been noticed in a preceding page, (p. 149) retired to Bath, in old age, and rented, for a few years, the largest house on the south side of Pulteney Street. At this handsome mansion he arranged and displayed the choice articles of art and vertu, which had been presented to him by monarchs, princes, and nobles, in return for objects which the spirited Birmingham manufacturer had designed and made as specimens of the skill and workmanship of the provincial artists. Retirement from active life, and comparative idleness, were incompatible with this gentleman's nature. Old age and bodily infirmities failed to derive relief from jewels, trinkets, and other valuable objects. When almost helpless, he desired to be removed to his native county, and died very shortly afterwards in the town of Warwick. His lady went to Malvern for change of scene and air, but was soon destined to follow her deceased husband.

I cannot reconcile myself to take a sort of "French leave" of an old friend, who has selected and fixed on Bath, as a resting-place and domicile for the latter part of an active life. *James Heywood Markland, Esq.* was a youth when I travelled over Lancashire for the *Beauties of England,* in the year 1806, and was residing with his parents on Ardwick Green, Manchester. I was introduced to him, and found that he was enthusiastically devoted to the study of topography and antiquities, and proffered his services to visit and write accounts of certain places and old buildings in that county. This was thankfully accepted, and some of his early writings were inserted both in the *Beauties of England* and in the *Architectural Antiquities.* He also favoured me by purchasing large-paper copies of those works; also the *Cathedral Antiquities,* and other similar publications. Coming to and settling in London, he practised as a solicitor for some years, became an active member of the Society of Antiquaries and the Royal Society, and wrote occasionally some learned essays for the former. Marrying a daughter of the amiable, learned, and liberal Sir Francis Freeling, he retired from his profession, and fixed on a house in Lansdown Crescent, where he is possessed of a splendid and choice library, and where I hope he enjoys not only every domestic happiness, but that *otium cum dignitate,* which is essential towards promoting it.

About two miles east of Bath is the village of CLAVERTON, in whose church is a tablet commemorative of the once amiable, cheerful, and aged Rector, the *Rev. Richard Graves,* who died there at the age of 89, in 1804. His happy temper, ready wit, and benevolent heart, made him respected and loved by all who had the pleasure of his acquaintance. During the summer and fine weather, he was almost a daily visitor at Bath, where, in the library of Mr. Meylor, editor and proprietor of the *Bath Herald,* he met and enjoyed the company of some of the most accomplished inhabitants of the city. Of the village, church, and old mansion of Claverton, much might be written; for each was peculiar, and all were and are replete with interesting associations. The scene is truly romantic, wild, and picturesque. An abrupt declivity from the table-land of the Down descends to a narrow, ever-green valley, through which the river Avon meanders silently and sluggishly towards the west. This steep hill consists of rocks and woods, interspersed with natural terraces, on one of which the present lord of the manor, *George Vivian, Esq.*, has built a handsome modern mansion, which is adorned with a few good pictures, and also a very choice library. This gentleman was one of the Commissioners to whom the designs for the new Houses of Parliament were referred for selection. He is author of some well-written pamphlets on the architectural improvements of London, which it is much to be regretted were not duly appreciated and followed by public officers and responsible persons. He has also written able articles for the *Quarterly Review*, and published two large volumes of lithographic Drawings of Views in Portugal and Spain.

The following truthful and vivid sketch of the talents of Mr. Graves, by Mr. Warner, (*Literary Recollections*, ii. 18) is worthy of repetition and admiration in this place. "It is a 'retrospection' affording me much pleasure to look back upon the hours which I have spent with the ingenious, cheerful, and amiable author of 'The Spiritual Quixote.' Never did the hand of advanced age lie lighter upon a human being, or less exert its withering influence on the intellect, the genius and the feelings of a nonagenarian, than on Mr. Graves. When in his 88th year, I attended with him at a visitation; sat near to him at table; and listened with astonishment to his uninterrupted flow of neat and epigrammatic impromptus, lively *jeux-d'esprit*, and entertaining anecdotes. Most of his works, and they were numerous, are instinct with the same spirit of wit and poignancy; though others, more serious, vindicate his claim to sterling and diversified erudition. The literary production, however, with which Mr. Graves's name is principally associated, and which will probably survive his other works, is 'The Spiritual Quixote,' a novel entirely *sui generis*, as far as English literature extends."

At the celebrated BATH-EASTON VILLA, where LADY MILLER assembled occasionally, not only the fashionables, but men of science, art, and wit, Mr. Graves was a regular visitor, and for whose Vase he contributed many smart and jocular poems, which have been printed, with numerous other pieces, in the three volumes of "Poetical Amusements at a Villa near Bath," 1775—77. Though this villa had lost its fascinating mistress, and was merely noticed and spoken of as what it had been, when I first became acquainted with Bath, I was familiar with the published "Amusements" referred to, and never passed the famed secluded lawns without reflecting on their palmy days of joyous greetings, and gay soirées. It was no small pleasure and honour to me, at a later time, to meet the group of provincial literary gossips and quidnuncs, at the house of our mutual friend, Mr. Meylor, in the Grove. Here daily assembled Dr. Harington, Mr. Graves, Mr. Warner, Dr. Parry, Dr. Falconer, and a few other "Worthies" of congenial minds and manners. Here also I became acquainted with *John Feltham*, a native of Salisbury, who had lately published "*A Tour in the Isle of Man*," one volume 8vo. He afterwards visited the Islands, called *The Holmes's*, in the Bristol Channel, for the purpose of writing accounts of those two insular masses of rock and earth, for the *Beauties of England*. One of Mr. Feltham's sisters married Mr. Hawes, of Southwark, and another wedded Wm. Hazlitt.*

---

At this place it will be expedient to make a pause: to advert to the previous part of this Biography, and anticipate the matter and manner of the future; for it is evident, by the former, that I have been inadvertently, almost unconsciously, led into an extent and scope of narrative and comment, which, if continued, would extend the work to a length and bulk calculated to injure my own pecuniary interest, and perhaps over-tax the patience and philosophy of the reader. I cannot, however, persuade myself that any portion of it has been, or is, incompatible with the legitimate object and end of an Auto-Biography. The year 1798 (as already stated, *ante* p. 135) was an important era in the history of my own life; as it opened new views of men and manners —new scenes, places, and connections, and led almost to a re-formation of personal character, feeling, and opinions. After emancipation from the gloom and privations of murky vaults, with almost estrangement from human society, I struggled for four or five years to obtain a bare subsistence, and also sought in vain to secure the company and advice of persons competent to instruct, or willing to associate with, one so

---

* In my volume on "Wiltshire," part of the *Beauties of England*, p. 199, I have related a few particulars of my once-respected friend, Mr. Feltham.

humble as I then was. An anticipated walk through a wide extent of country to visit places of note, whose histories I had read imperfect accounts of, and of which I had formed crude and visionary notions,—to see and converse with authors and other eminent persons, who were living at, and belonged to places, which were honoured by their names,—not only stimulated my curiosity and ambition to a high degree of excitement, but seemed almost to change my nature, and create new impulses to latent energies. The result more than realized my most sanguine anticipations: as may be inferred by the following places which were visited, and the public persons, named, who were for the first time seen, and united to my friendly connection:—*Windsor*, with Benjamin West, P.R.A.; Thomas Holloway, engraver; Mr. Forest, painter on glass; the Dean of Windsor:—*Oxford*, the Rev. W. Crowe, public orator; the Rev. J. Gutch, Mr. R. Bliss :—*Woodstock and Blenheim*, the Rev. Dr. Mavor, and Mr. Pratt:—*Stratford-upon-Avon*:—*Birmingham*, Wm. Hutton, and J. Bisset:—*Shrewsbury*, the Rev. Hugh Owen, the Rev. J. B. Blakeway, David Parkes :—*Church Stretton*, the Rev. J. Mainwaring, and the Rev. R. Wilding :—*Downton*, R. P. Knight :—*The Shropshire and Welsh Mountains* :—*Hereford*, John Allen, James Wathen, John Thelwall, Uvedale Price:—*Ross*, the Rev. T. D. Fosbrooke :—*The River Wye*, with the castles of Goodrich, Wilton, Monmouth, Chepstow, and Raglan :—*Monmouth*, and its historian :—*Tintern Abbey* :—*Chepstow* :—*Bristol, and Bath*, with several of their distinguished inhabitants.

From the last city I proceeded to visit many parts of *Wiltshire*, particularly the western and southern sides of the county, where I was introduced to, and laid the foundation of friendly intimacy with, several of the nobility, gentry, clergy, and others. On that occasion I travelled in the capacity of an intended author, who was collecting materials for a work in two volumes, to be called " *The Beauties of Wiltshire.*" This title was adopted by Mr. Wheble, my patron, who had projected the publication some years previously, when stationed at Salisbury, and had received a few subscriptions, of five shillings, from some ten or twenty persons. Settling in London, and there fully occupied on a newspaper, he could not devote either time or thoughts to a book which he had engaged to publish, and which, indeed, he was desirous of producing. This task I undertook; though, at the time, unqualified for it. To attain that qualification, I found it essentially necessary to read a variety of books which were previously unknown to me; and whose language, style, and matter, frequently were almost as unintelligible as if couched in Greek. Embarked in the undertaking, I studied diligently; sought the company, conversation, and advice of authors, particularly such as had written on topography and antiquities; and embraced the earliest opportunity to travel to different places, and obtain introductions to persons likely to enlighten and aid me. The journey, already referred to, proved of great importance, of incalculable advantage; and another more extensive walking Tour, in the year 1800, in company with my friend, Mr. Brayley, was still more beneficial in its results.

This walk extended over a wide range of country, and presented such variety and diversity of objects to be viewed and admired—so many persons in different stations of life, and of such varied qualifications, with whom we were to become acquainted—that we derived not merely temporary amusement and gratification, but great permanent advantage. Previous to leaving London, we had engaged with Vernor and Hood, publishers in the Poultry, to write a new topographical work, to be intituled " *The Beauties of England and Wales*," to be comprised in about six volumes. Having at that time read and thought more about the scenery and antiquities of the Welsh Principality than of English counties, we calculated that the former would afford more gratification than the latter, at the commencement of our career. Indeed, we were both uninformed, as to the amount and extent of knowledge which would be required to execute the new undertaking, with even tolerable success. Our publishers were still less informed, and unfortunately had very vague and prejudiced notions of the best mode of making their speculation permanently respectable and profitable. They—that is, Mr. Hood, for he was the acting person in the firm— considered that six volumes would be sufficient to embrace " The Beauties " of the country to be comprehended; that it was necessary only to abridge the matter, and vary the language which was to be found already printed; and that it would be a very easy and profitable work for two authors, or rather compilers (in his view of the case) to produce five octavo sheets per month. Without settled notions, or plan, we left London June 8th, 1800; and returned about the 20th of September, after walking above 1350 miles. The following list of places visited, and persons introduced to, will give the reader some intimation on these topics. The most remarkable are marked in italics: Fulham; Richmond; *Hounslow Heath*, with the devastation of the Powder Mills, which had been blown up the preceding night; Weybridge; *Oatlands*, with its famed grotto, and the canine-cemetery adjoining; Chertsey; *St. Ann's Hill*, and its very popular and almost idolized proprietor, Chas. James Fox; Staines and *Runnymead*, the memorable scene of the signature of Magna Charta, by King John and the English Barons; *Cooper's Hill*, renowned by Denham's once popular descriptive poem. At Bishop's-Gate on the eastern extremity of *Windsor Forest*, we spent some hours with *George Cumberland*, who had recently returned from Italy, and had produced "The Life of Julio Romano," a poem on the "Landscapes of Great Britain," "Thoughts on Sculpture," and several other literary works. Mr. Cumberland removed to Bristol, where he died in 1850, at the advanced age of 86. The noble Forest of Windsor is honoured by one of Pope's epistles, devoted to its name and grand features; and since that poet's time, by the writings of various other authors, and the pencils of many painters. *Windsor:* At this royal home of English Kings—this castellated country palace of all her monarchs from William the First to her present Majesty Victoria—we sojourned some time to examine that vast edifice and its pictures, its splendid chapel, its park and forest scenery; and here we met and became acquainted with Benjamin West, President of the Royal Academy; Thomas Holloway, who was then employed in reducing Raffaelle's Cartoon of Paul preaching at Athens, the first of his series, which he lived to copy and engrave, to the honour of his own name and that of the famed Italian master, whom he almost worshipped. We saw Eton college and chapel, and the vast telescope which Herschel had lately made and raised at Slough. At Eton, we also examined the stained-glass works of Mr. Forest, who was employed to execute the painted-glass windows in Saint George's Chapel. *Stoke-Pogeis:* at a short distance to the north of Slough, is the parish churchyard in which *Gray*, the poet, was interred; also the old mansion, noticed in his "Long Story," and a modern house, which was inhabited at that time by John Penn, a descendant of Admiral Penn.

From Windsor we proceeded through some of the finest parts of the Forest to view *Virginia Water*, and its fine, artificial cascade, which had been lately completed from the designs, and under the direction, of Paul Sandby, who had recently made numerous drawings of scenes in the Forest; also at and about Windsor. Many of these were engraved for the "Virtuoso's Museum," containing 150 select views in England, &c., 2 vols. 4to. 1781. Oakingham, the *Rev. C. Cruttwell*, author of numerous publications, amongst which is "A Tour through the whole Island of Great Britain," in 6 vols. 8vo., which he was writing when we called on him. Reading, *John Mann*, who was preparing a History of his native town, and who afterwards proved a valuable correspondent to the "Beauties." Newbury, *Donnington Castle*, of which I made a sketch, that was engraved as a vignette for the title of the first volume of our work. *Marlborough*, Savernake Forest, and Tottenham Park, the seat of the Marquess of Aylesbury. The vast and mysterious remains of the antique Celtic Temple at *Avebury* were visited; also several earth-works, barrows, and cromlechs, scattered over Marlborough Downs. Our route next led us to the south, through cross roads over Salisbury Plain, to *Stonehenge, Amesbury, Old Sarum, Salisbury*, and thence to several other places in Wiltshire; turning to the north from Frome, to *Bath, Wells, Glastonbury, Wokey-hole, Chedder*, over the Mendip Hills, to *Bristol, Thornbury, Berkeley Castle, Gloucester, Ross, Hampton Court* (where we met the *Earl of Essex*,) *Holm-Lacy, Hereford, Ludlow*, and *Church-Stretton*.

At the last town we sojourned some days, to explore the neighbouring mountains and castrametations. Here I and my fellow-traveller parted, with the agreement of meeting again at *Welshpool*, at a time and inn named. That did not occur: Mr. Brayley, after crossing Wenlock Edge, and visiting Much-Wenlock, Brosely, Coalbrook-Dale, and other places in the neighbourhood, was detained nine or ten days at my brother's house by illness, whilst I proceeded on my pre-arranged *Walk round North Wales*, after visiting *Newtown, Llanydloes, Aberystwith*, the *Devil's-Bridge*, Mr. Johns's, of *Havod*, &c. The castles, the mountains, the rivers, with their cascades, the Celtic monuments, and other prominent natural and artificial objects which were presented in such a tour, with the public persons to whom I was favourably introduced, and incidentally met; as also the amusing and the tantalizing adventures encountered, were sufficient to keep the mind in continued excitement, and afford abundant materials for subsequent reflection, for conversation, and for graphic narrative. Had not our previous engagements and plans, after returning to London, demanded and engrossed all our thoughts and solicitude, we might have been tempted to "print our notes," and make a book, in imitation of some of our predecessors and contemporaries. For we had a superabundance of materials descriptive of objects of antiquity, of beauty, of art, and of nature: of *Man*, as a rich, haughty despot; of him, a philosopher, a patriot, a friend to his fellows; of man, an idler and drone, living and luxuriating on the honeyed produce of the poor labourer, who, though working like a slave, was almost penniless and foodless; of the good and active parish priests, who watched their human flocks, gave them kind looks, useful advice, and comfort in sickness; of others, who not only neglected their own offspring and homes, but wasted their substance in besotting and gambling habits; of another class, fortunately a large one, who united the good husband, the discreet parent, the beloved neighbour and friend to the poor, and also the patron of art, of literature, and science; and who therefore found home the happiest place on earth, and all his fellow-men his friends and admirers. Of *Antiquity* we had opportunities of seeing and studying some of the wonder-working, mystical Celtic temples and sepulchral monuments; of castrametations, and other earth-works of the earliest colonists of our island; of *Anglo-Roman* buildings, and other vestigia of a horde of national plunderers, who, after subjugating the country and making its inhabitants vassals and slaves, occupied their property four hundred years: of the finest ecclesiastical and castellated edifices of the island, its cathedrals, churches, and chapels; of castles, in varied stages of ruin and of different ages: three of which are still occupied (Windsor, Warwick, and Berkeley) and present many fine and interesting features of feudal and semi-civilized architecture and domestic economy: of old domestic buildings, which showed indications of an improved condition of society and of manners; of new domestic mansions, which manifested the dawn, and even advanced daylight of art, science, and taste. To these subjects and topics might have been added the many and commanding features of Nature, which attracted attention and admiration, in forest and plain; in hill and valley; in lake, river, and brook; in the broad, fertile vale; in the rocky glen; in the boggy, wild common; in the lofty and craggy mountain, and in the boundless sea. Again, our own personal adventures and "incidents of travel," though not in a foreign, or savage country, were not devoid of occurrences and scenes, which a Warner, a Scott, or a Washington Irving could have narrated in language calculated to amuse and interest a numerous class of readers. The accommodation, or want of accommodation, at "the hotels" we frequented; the company we were occasionally subjected to keep, such as quack doctors, itinerant " merchants "—i. e. hawkers and pedlers—strolling players, farmers, small tradesmen, gamblers, and smugglers, certainly furnished variety of character, but not such as was calculated to delight or instruct the young topographer and antiquary.

In the following chapters, intended to exhibit and explain my decided devotion to a particular subject, and to a professional class of studies and occupation, I intend to adopt the classification and arrangement marked out in the second part of this Memoir, as calculated to exhibit and explain the various publications I have produced, and the connexions which emanated from them, interspersed with a few incidental personal circumstances which belong to the literature and the times they respectively involve.

# CHAPTER V.

"GREAT IS THE DIGNITY OF AUTHORSHIP: I MAGNIFY MINE OFFICE;
ALBEIT IN MUCH FEEBLENESS I HOLD IT THUS UNWORTHILY.
FOR IT IS TO BE ONE OF A NOBLE BAND, THE WELFARE OF THE WORLD,
WHOSE HAUNT IS ON THE LIPS OF MEN, WHOSE DWELLING IN THEIR HEARTS,
WHO ARE PRECIOUS IN THE RETROSPECT OF MEMORY, AND WALK AMONG THE VISIONS OF HOPE,
WHO COMMUNE WITH THE GOOD FOR EVERLASTING, AND CALL THE WISEST BROTHER,
WHOSE VOICE HATH BURST THE SILENCE, AND WHOSE LIGHT IS FLUNG UPON THE DARKNESS,
—FLASHING JEWELS ON A ROBE OF BLACK, AND HARMONY BOUNDING OUT OF CHAOS,—
WHO GLADDEN EMPIRES WITH THEIR WISDOM, AND BLESS TO THE FARTHEST GENERATION;
DOERS OF ILLIMITABLE GOOD, GAINERS OF INESTIMABLE GLORY!"

M. F. TUPPER: *Proverbial Philosophy*, 9th edit., 1849, p. 275.

AUTHORSHIP, AND THE WRITER'S EXPERIENCE—MR. TUPPER PRAISED—AUTHORS HONOURED, BUT OFTEN DISTRESSED—LITERARY FUND, AND ITS BENEFITS—PUBLISHERS AND AUTHORS, MUTUAL DEPENDENCE AND OBLIGATIONS ON EACH OTHER: NAMES OF SEVERAL—CHATEAUBRIAND (NOTE)—RIGHTS AND POWERS OF LITERATURE—THE AUTHOR'S EXTENSIVE CONNEXIONS—UNITED WITH LONGMAN'S HOUSE AND JOSIAH TAYLOR—SOUTHEY'S OPINION AND ADVICE—PATERNOSTER ROW: THE AUTHOR'S VISITS TO IT IN EARLY LIFE—NOTICES AND ANECDOTES OF SOME OF THE PRINCIPAL PUBLISHERS AND BOOKSELLERS; ALSO OF AUTHORS AND BOOKS, BY THE REV. DR. THOMAS REES, WITH NOTES BIOGRAPHICAL AND DESCRIPTIVE BY THE AUTHOR.

THE above eloquent, and eminently poetical, lines from one of the most original and profound volumes of its class of our age, are calculated to excite in young minds exalted and almost chimerical notions of the pleasures, the honours, and the dignity of Authorship. An experience of more than half a century, and extensive intercourse with many contemporary Authors in all grades of society, from the noble to the plebeian, from the wealthy and learned writers of history, poetry, science, and the *belles-lettres*, to the poor "hack-writer," who laboured daily, almost hourly, to obtain a precarious subsistence, enable me to state that Mr. Tupper's views and opinions have been verified in many instances within the sphere of my own knowledge. Authors of probity and talent have been and are honoured and rewarded in our times; but whether the honours and rewards have been always proportionate to their deserts and merits, is not so clearly and fully defined and understood, as could be wished. All the published evidence on this subject comes from interested, partial witnesses, who have rather argued and asserted from their own personal cases and constitutional temperaments than from a general and impartial inquiry and deduction. As an active and diligent member of the committee of the *Literary Fund* for nearly forty years, I have had opportunities of ascertaining the circumstances of more than twelve hundred persons, male and female, who have appealed to that noble institution for pecuniary aid in times of severe distress; and who have derived temporary relief and consolation from its grants. An inquiry into the causes of their respective calamities has shown that a large portion of the applicants have been improvident persons, heedless of accounts, negligent of money, and of that property which they have honestly and laudably earned, but imprudently expended. Some of the unfortunate individuals, who had lived and moved in, what is regarded, high society,—i. e. the church, the magistracy, the army, the navy—have been amongst the applicants, and even four or five of them been subscribers to the fund, and associated in committees to dispense pecuniary aid to their necessitous brethren.* Such events and facts are truly lamentable and appalling; but vicissitudes and fluctuations, in the affairs of human life, are inevitable to, and uncontrollable by man. Fortune and misfortune seem to pervade and attach themselves to every station and rank in society, and occasionally visit and cling to persons without any assignable or recognized cause.

I could name several authors, who have derived not only fair remuneration and incomes from their literary works, but have been better paid than many other industrious and learned professional persons; and yet have querulously complained, and even reprobated their calling. They seem to live and act under some mental hallucination; and to make assertions and statements irreconcilable to palpable facts and truth-

---

* One person may be named as the recipient of the funds, who made a public acknowledgment of his obligations at an anniversary festival. The celebrated *Viscount Chateaubriand* was amongst the sufferers in the great conflict of the French Revolution; and then derived essential aid from our literary fund. In after years, he was the accredited Ambassador from his own court to ours, and at an anniversary dinner, when the Duke of York presided, he candidly and magnanimously acknowledged his obligation and gratitude to the society, for the favour he had received in the hour of adversity, and then presented sixty pounds to the fund.

ful convictions. They not only impeach the liberality and even honesty of publishers, but also upbraid and reproach the public—the buyers of books—for want of liberality and sound judgment; whereas I have witnessed many cases, and heard of more, where the former have paid freely for a bad, unsaleable article, and the latter have been imposed on by the same goods. It is notorious among the trade—in the conclaves of Paternoster Row—that the clever, well-informed publisher will give large, even extravagant sums, for the copyright of manuscripts adapted to the popular requirement of the times; and expend other sums in embellishment and advertisements, to enhance the attractiveness and permanent interests of such works. It should also be borne in mind by the eager and infatuated author, that the publisher is a man of business—an adventurer who often risks a large amount of capital on an article which may be successful and profitable, or be quite the reverse. Many instances might be adduced where firms and individuals have purchased the copyrights of books, at very high prices, and expended further money in producing them, but ultimately lost more than half of their outlay, after "wasting" a mass of dead stock.* It is both the duty and the interest of publishers to pay liberally for good materials; whilst it can never be advantageous or creditable to publish defective and inefficient works. It is true that there have been occasions where some of the latter kind have proved successful, for a time, and where the former have failed. That many authors have been fairly and even generously remunerated by publishers, is proved in the cases of Gibbon, Robertson, the Rev. Dr. A. Rees, the Lords Byron and Jeffrey, Sir Walter Scott, the Rev. G. Crabbe, the Rev. W. Coxe, Southey, T. Moore, W. Gifford, Pratt, Mavor, Theodore Hook, Horace Smith, Lockhart, C. Dickens, Thackeray, Macaulay, Charles Knight, Miss Martineau, Douglas Jerrold, Dr. Charles Mackay, W. H. Ainsworth, Leigh Hunt, Mac Culloch, and many others; whilst it is equally well known that all those authors have been caressed and honoured by the

---

* My friend, Mr. Wodderspoon of Norwich, has a large collection of letters by the liberal and truly honourable publishers, Cadell and Davies, and Dr. Drake, Archdeacon Coxe, Messrs Lysons, and other authors, which amply verify these remarks, by proving the liberality of the former, and the erroneous views and unreasonable demands of the latter.

courtesies of the wealthy of the land, as well as by the public.* It has not been a fashion with the Government of Great Britain to confer titles, employment, or pecuniary benefits on literary persons, though foreign countries, with inferior resources and lower claims, have set laudable examples. †

Let it not be inferred from what is here said that I include the entire phalanx of authors and of publishers in these remarks. I am well aware that there are many of the latter who have fattened on the former, without compunction or sympathy. In a volume which I printed and distributed, gratuitously, in the year 1814, under the title of "*The Rights of Literature,*" ‡ I vindicated and espoused the cause of Authors; who, "of all other persons," according to the *Quarterly Review*, of that time, "confer upon the country the most *lasting honour* and the *most permanent benefit*, but who are the only ones to whom the State denies a fee-simple in the produce of their own industry." "To *Literature*," I further said, "we are indebted for many and truly valuable blessings: it is the safeguard and bulwark of liberty, and the main-spring of moral and intellectual excellence. Through its influence man is elevated high in the scale of mental dignity; is qualified to trace the progress and revolutions of the vast and marvellous planetary system, and to estimate the properties, contents, and countless phenomena of the terrestrial globe. It is the storehouse of wisdom, and from its exhaustless treasures he is enriched, delighted, improved, and made 'the paragon of animals.'" These sentiments are confirmed by nearly forty years' further acquaintance with books and men; whence I cannot too strongly urge on the attention of young students the invaluable attributes of literature, the

---

* The relative duties and qualifications of authors and publishers have been fairly and justly discriminated by Mr. Thackeray, in *Fraser's Magazine*.

† I cannot neglect this opportunity to pay a passing compliment to the late Sir Robert Peel, who, on several occasions, when in power, manifested proper sympathy for, and judicious appreciation of the literary character, and of literature in its best features. In an address he read at the Tamworth Library, January 1841, are remarks and opinions which reflect honour on his heart and head; and which might be beneficially printed and circulated in all the literary societies of the country.

‡ See Account of this work in Part II., p. 190, of the present Auto-Biography.

pleasures and rewards that attend its honest and talented professors, as well as the benefits they confer on the present and future generations. My own experience in the publishing trade has been extensive, and amongst different branches of booksellers, printsellers, and mapsellers; but chiefly with the first. For almost half a century I was connected with the large and respectable firm of Longman and Co., who held shares in "The Beauties of Wiltshire," "The Beauties of England," "The Architectural," and the "Cathedral Antiquities," and several others of my publications. During the whole of that connection, and in the expenditure and settlement of large annual sums of money, we continued on friendly and amicable terms. They kept the accounts, and rendered to me, and to Mr. Josiah Taylor, a detailed statement, which, being examined and vouched, was regularly balanced, and the profits, when any, divided into three portions and promptly paid. As part of the expenses on each work, I charged a fair price for authorship and management; for it was my duty to direct every department of each publication; whence I obtained an acquaintance with draftsmen, engravers, stationers, printers, copperplate printers, and private gentlemen, in town and country.

The list of publications named at the end of the *Appendix*, furnishes the reader with the extent not only of my literary works, but with the progressive and successive times of their production and completion, the moneys expended on each, and other bibliographical particulars. In the history of literature and the bookselling trade this list cannot fail of being useful; whilst it will probably surprise persons whose knowledge of the world and its trades has been obtained merely in closet studies. I may quote a few words from Southey's article, in *The Quarterly Review* for 1826, on my publications and a brief memoir then written, to show his opinion of me, and of the faculties that induced the accomplishment of such an aggregate of literary and active labour. "The author," he writes, "commenced his career with hope, ardour, and perseverance, the best qualifications for acquiring wealth, independence, and contentment." Again, speaking of the Biography then published, he says, " the fear of being thought trifling or egotistical has withheld Mr. Britton from entering into the details of his early struggles in life; but we may remind him that details of this kind carry with them an interest to which no fiction can attain; and that the memoirs of a man, who, from such circumstances, and under such difficulties, has made his way to a station of comfort and respectability, is one of the most useful lessons that could be put into the hands of the young." This opinion and these remarks, from such a profound and accredited writer, not only gave me consolation, and afforded a reward for past privations and labours, but awakened renewed energies to prosecute the career in which I had embarked.*

The period of time in which I lived, and during the greater part of which I have been a public performer, was replete with stirring and memorable facts and events, which have produced vast and almost marvellous effects on civilized society. Not only in the political, but in the moral and intellectual world, have these been rendered palpable to all who had eyes to see, and minds to appreciate them.

---

* The student and lover of literature will derive much amusement and information relating to literature, its professors, and amateurs, by consulting D'Israeli's " Curiosities of Literature;" " Amenities of Literature;" " Quarrels of Authors;" and on " the Literary Character, illustrated by the History of Men of Genius;" Corney's "New Curiosities of Literature;" " Life of Sir Walter Scott," by Lockhart; the following publications by Southey, " The Doctor;" " Lives of Uneducated Poets;" " Omniana;" " Progress and Prospects of Society;"—"The Rights of Literature," by J. Britton, 8vo. 1814; Boswell's " Life of Dr. Johnson," edited by Croker, 10 vols. 18mo. 1835; Dr. Dibdin's " Reminiscences of a Literary Life," 2 vols. 8vo. 1836; " Memoirs of the Forty-five First Years of James Lackington;" Davenport's " Lives of Individuals who raised themselves from Poverty to Eminence;" " The Life of William Cobbett;" " Exposition of the False Medium and Barriers excluding Men of Genius from the Public," by R. H. Horne, Esq., 12mo. 1833;—"The Auto-Biography of Benjamin Franklin;" " The Auto-Biography of Richard Cumberland," 2 vols.; " The Auto-Biography of William Hutton;" " A Memoir of the Life and Writings of William Taylor, containing many years' Correspondence with Robert Southey," 2 vols. 1843. This work abounds with literary information. " The Life and Literary Remains of C. F. Pemberton: with Remarks by W. J. Fox," 8vo. 1843; Polwhele's " Traditions and Recollections," 2 vols. 8vo. 1826; Warner's " Literary Recollections," 2 vols. 8vo. 1830; Sir Egerton Brydges's " Recollections of Foreign Travel, of Life, Literature, and Self-Knowledge," 2 vols. 12mo. 1825; " The Pursuit of Knowledge under Difficulties," 2 vols. 18mo. 1831; " The Auto-Biography of Leigh Hunt," 3 vols. 8vo. 1850; " The Auto-Biography of William Jerdan," 1852; " Sketches of English Literature, from the fourteenth to the present Century. By Clara Lucas Balfour." 18mo. 1852, pp. 404,—a well-written, discriminating volume.

Though personally restricted to a narrow sphere, my own intercourse with public characters has enabled me to observe much of the spirit of the times, as manifested in the British Metropolis; and it cannot surprise modern readers to be told that I imperceptibly imbibed some of the popular democratic opinions prevalent at the end of the last century; particularly amongst persons who frequented debating societies, and who read the cheap publications then disseminated.

"Time makes more converts than reason." The vast changes produced by "the progress of knowledge," have not passed unobserved by me; nor have I continued to entertain and maintain opinions which were formed in days of comparative ignorance, and cherished from want of understanding the laws and etiquette of society, and the duties which Christian charity and philosophy inculcate in the minds of those who covet and deserve the respect and esteem of honest and good men. The books I read in the murky and dark wine-vaults—Watts's "Logic," "Improvement of the Mind," Derham's "Astro" and "Physico-Theology," Ray "On the Creation," and others of similar tendencies—served as antidotes to atheism, to intolerance, to the dogmas of bad men, who espoused the tyranny either of creeds, of governments, or of partizans. The brawlers in politics, and in pulpits, the declaimers and sophists with the pen and the tongue, though they amused and decived me for a time, have long ceased to excite any other feeling than pity and regret. "By the French Revolution," wrote my friend Southey, at one time, "the minds of men throughout all Europe were thrown into such feverish excitement, that more than an usual degree of tolerance should be exercised towards the errors and extremes into which all parties were hurried during the paroxysm." Had the learned and estimable writer of this sentiment continued to act up to it in after life, he would have secured the respect and approbation of the whole reading world; but his intolerance of, and severity of censure on those who differed from him in political and religious opinion, provoked the hostility and sorrow of many who had been formerly his friends and admirers.

In former parts of this Biography I have had occasion to refer to the times and parties now alluded to. For vivid and interesting views of the *eventful period* in which it has been my destiny to be placed, and called into literary exertion, I can refer with confidence and commendation to Harriet Martineau's " Introduction to the History of the Peace, from 1800 to 1815," 1 vol. large 8vo. 1851; to Charles Knight and H. Martineau's " History of England during the Thirty Years' Peace." These are historical works, which cannot be perused without producing decidedly beneficial effects on the minds and hearts of readers. In the annals of English historical literature, I do not think there is any portion so fully, impartially, and discriminatingly developed and elucidated as that embraced by the copious volumes referred to; not merely as regards the proceedings of governments and of parties, but as descriptive of the elements of society—the customs, the manners, the tone and temper of public men, and public measures. In writing an account of self, and of the various literary works I have produced, I cannot help feeling humbled and mortified in contrasting them with those of such gigantic compass and power as exercised by the unflinching philosophic historians here commended.*

It cannot be regarded as irrelevant to this Memoir, and to the author's literary life, to say something about

### PATERNOSTER ROW,

*St. Paul's Churchyard, Ave-Maria Lane,* and *Amen Corner,* all of which were familiar names to the eye and mind in my boy-days; but I had no more notion of the features and character of the places than of the interior of a man-of-war, or of Robinson Crusoe's island. After reading numerous magazines, and taking in several of the sixpenny numbers, published by Harrison, Cooke, Parsons, &c., and thereby ascertaining something about authors, artists, printers, and booksellers, I became curious and anxious to see such gifted personages, their homes, or haunts; and also where the manufacturers of literature

---

* There is a small, cheap work recently published, which I can recommend to the student in English history and literature, as calculated to afford clear and explicit information concerning the period between the years 1800 and 1850. It is of humble pretensions, being printed on thin paper, crowded pages, and vended at 4s.; but it is ably written, and contains accounts of the essential body, spirit, and features of a half century, which, for eventful and momentous changes, and improvements in art, science, literature, and all that concerns the welfare of man and of society, has not had a parallel in the history of the world. The title of the volume is—" The Half-Century: its History, Political and Social. By Washington Wilks." Small 8vo. 1852, pp. 368.

resided, what were their peculiarities, and who and what sort of beings they were. I also coveted to see and read more books than I could afford to purchase. During the apprenticeship, I do not remember to have had an opportunity of satisfying this curiosity, except early in a morning, before shops were opened, or on Sundays, when they were all closed, and "The Row," with its appendages, as dull and silent as many village churchyards; but after being relieved from my apprentice-bondage, I found my way to the famed book-mart; traversed the narrow, dark street, miscalled *Row;* stopped to gaze at every shop window, and even stealthily looked in at every opened doorway, to see if a Harrison, a Cooke, a Hogg, or even one of their Grub-street workmen, or a rich author, could be descried. The names of Peter Pindar, Thomas Holcroft, Dr. Buchan, Wm. Godwin, Dr. A. Rees, Mr. Howard, Mr. Hall, Thos. Paine, the Misses Porter, Hannah More, Mrs. Radcliffe, and many others were familiar to me, and I longed to see such super-human beings, as I then regarded them. At length I ventured to enter some of the houses, and thus obtain a sight of labelled numbers, and volumes of new publications, and also the persons and faces of some of their proprietors. At that time most of the tradesmen attended in their respective shops, and dwelt in the upper parts of their houses: now, the heads of many of the large establishments visit their counting-houses only for a few hours in the day, and leave the working part to junior partners, clerks, and apprentices. Vast and numerous changes have taken place in the publishing and bookselling business since I first haunted Paternoster Row, and book-stalls; and many and important improvements have been introduced into all the essentials of book-making. Paper, type, ink, compositorship, and press-work, have advanced from almost the lowest to nearly the highest degree of perfection. The number and qualifications of authors have progressed in nearly an equal ratio. This assertion, I believe, will be fully verified, by referring to, and comparing, the books and periodicals which were published at the end of the last century with those of the year 1852. It would not be a difficult task to exemplify this by explaining the varieties and dissimilarities between the material and mental characteristics of literature at the two epochs; but I must limit myself to a brief account of Paternoster Row.

This far-famed thoroughfare is commonly said to derive its name from the stationers, or text-writers, who formerly dwelt there, and dealt mostly in religious books, horn-books, and others, which were marketable before the Reformation. It more probably had its appellation from the rosary, or pater-noster makers, a more thriving trade than bookselling, before Henry the Eighth, of revolutionary memory, commanded the books of Luther to be burnt in the Churchyard.

Strype, in his edition of Stow's "Survey of London," 1720, says, "This street, before the fire of London (1666), was taken up by eminent mercers, silkmen, and lacemen; and their shops were so resorted to by the nobility and gentry, in their coaches, that oft-times the street was so stopped up that there was no room for foot passengers." Soon after that conflagration most of these moved to the vicinity of Covent Garden. Some of the mercers and silkmen renewed their residences in this spot in new houses; but near the east end there were "stationers and large warehouses for booksellers; well situated for learned and studious men's access thither, being more retired and private." St. Paul's Churchyard appears to have been the chief mart of the bookselling trade at the time of the great fire. Dugdale told Pepys that more than £150,000 worth of books were destroyed on that fatal occasion. Previous to this epoch, Little Britain, and Duke Street adjoining, seem to have been the most noted site for booksellers.

However sanguine my young imagination may have been, I did not dare to anticipate the possibility of ever writing or publishing a book; still less of being on friendly terms with the many partners of the largest publishing establishment in the world. Yet such has been my lot; and having indulged the habit of continually visiting *Paternoster Row*, on the last day of every month for more than forty years, it has become identified with many and various associations and connexions of deep and exciting interest; and I have often meditated on writing an account of this literary emporium. But I have thought it advisable to solicit my old and esteemed friend, Dr. Thomas Rees, to indulge me with his opinions and recollections on this subject. With his usual kindness and courtesy he promptly favoured me with the following letter, to which I have subjoined a few memoranda of my own, in the form of notes:—

My dear Britton,

You ask me to furnish some reminiscenses of Paternoster Row, in the earlier period of my acquaintance with it, towards the conclusion of the last, and the commencement of the present, century. Our long and intimate connection, our kindred pursuits, and our joint labours on some occasions, in the same field of literary research, render it difficult for me to meet your wishes with a denial; at the same time I feel very sensibly that in recurring to a period so long past, between which and the present, half a century has intervened, important matters relating both to events and persons may have escaped my recollection, or may be recalled too indistinctly and imperfectly to be of real value for a practical object. I will, however, endeavour to revive the image of this locality, as it appeared to my view at the period alluded to; and to awaken the memory of such facts and incidents relating to the character and enterprises of its inhabitants, as may be likely to afford some interest or amusement to your readers.

Near the close of the eighteenth century, "The Row," as it is now popularly called, contained two or more printing establishments, one of which was conducted by the late *George Woodfall*, who had succeeded his father, Henry Sampson Woodfall, well known as the printer and publisher of the "Public Advertiser," in which appeared the far-famed "Letters of Junius." The latter was still living, and I had the pleasure of seeing him in the enjoyment of a "green old age," when I first visited London. Those daring epistles, with the newspaper in which they were published, excited intense curiosity during the course of their publication. There were also two houses of wholesale stationers; one belonging to the family of Key, and the other to Peter Wynn. The University of Oxford had, under the management of Mr. Gardner, a depôt to supply the London trade with their editions of Bibles and Prayer-books. But with these, and a few other exceptions, the majority of the houses were tenanted by persons who were strictly, in the ordinary sense, *Booksellers*. The varieties of these may be classed under three divisions. The first comprehends publishers only, whose sale of books was confined to their own property. The second might be designated book-merchants, who were chiefly wholesale dealers, and carried on an extensive and important trade with country booksellers: they were also publishers upon a large scale, both of periodicals, under the designation of magazines, and reviews; and likewise works on general literature and science, of the larger and more important and costly descriptions. The third were chiefly retail traders, mostly in old books, but in some instances were publishers of pamphlets, and books of comparatively small expense.

In the first class, at the time under consideration, three persons were conspicuous, viz.: HARRISON, COOKE, and HOGG. The first, on many accounts, is entitled to pre-eminence, as he took the lead in a class of publications which deserve great praise for valuable improvements in their editorial qualities, and particularly in pictorial illustrations.

It is not easy to pronounce decidedly the exact time when books of magnitude were first divided into small portions and issued periodically in numbers; but Harrison may be said to be one of the first persons who embarked, with much spirit and upon an extensive scale, in such a mode of publication. His first speculation of the sort was "The Novelist's Magazine," which embraced several of the larger standard and popular English novels then known. They were printed in octavo, in double columns, stitched up in small numbers, and published weekly, at sixpence each. The most striking feature of this publication, and one of its chief attractions, consisted of engraved embellishments. Harrison had the judgment to select artists of acknowledged merit, who afterwards rose to distinguished eminence; including Stothard, R. Corbould, Smirke, and Burney; whilst the engravings bear the names of Heath, Sharpe, Grignion, Smith, Milton, Neagle, &c. The "Novelist's Magazine," commenced by him in 1779, extended to twenty-three good-sized volumes. Its popularity may be estimated by the fact that, at one time 12,000 copies of each number were sold, weekly. The success of this work encouraged Harrison to publish, on the same plan, with embellishments by the same eminent artists, "The New Novelist's Magazine," a series of short tales; which was followed by "The British Classics," embracing the Spectator, Tatler, Guardian, Connoisseur, &c., of which a very large edition was sold. These publications still maintain their credit; and clean copies, with good impressions of the plates, are purchased at fair prices. He also produced a corresponding work, intituled "The Sacred Classics."

The same publisher embarked in another literary speculation, somewhat singular in its plan: a "General Geography," upon a large scale, extending to forty numbers, in quarto, closely printed. He engaged to supply its purchasers, without additional charge, with a pair of twelve-inch globes. Harrison published "The British Magazine," in 3 vols., with beautiful engravings of portraits, views, and prints of historical and fancy subjects. These included also a large portion of Biographical, Historical, and Critical Essays, with Poetry. His next publication was "The Musical Magazine," which, in an octavo size, gave a selection of the works of the most eminent and popular composers, arranged for the piano-forte. The purchaser of the entire work was entitled to receive a square piano-forte. *Dr. Busby*, at that time a popular musical professor, was employed as editor, and the instruments were examined and attested by him.*

Amongst the periodicals of this publisher was "The Wit's Maga-

---

* This gentleman was much employed by Sir Richard Phillips, in writing for the *Monthly Magazine*, &c., and later in life made himself very conspicuous, and amenable to severe public criticism, by translating *Lucretius*, and "giving living recitations of the translation, with tea and bread and butter," at his house in Queen Anne Street, to select parties of friends, who were invited to endure the one and relish the other. I was among the number, and must own that the display of poetry, oratory, and coxcombry was lamentably ludicrous. Never did I behold a young man more vain, impudent, and heartless, than the juvenile Busby, and rarely, perhaps, has the diploma of *Mus. Doc.* appeared more ridiculous and degraded than by the conduct and appearances of the musical professor with his finical son. These gentlemen made a finishing exhibition of themselves on the re-opening of the famed Drury Lane Theatre, after its memorable rebuilding. It is very generally known that an Address was sought for amongst the authors of the age, and that in the mass presented was one from Lord Byron, accepted, and another from Dr. Busby, rejected. The mortified and vain Doctor fancied that he could bring the committee to shame, if not repentance, by publishing his own poetry and prose, in a truly novel manner. Accordingly, he and his accomplished son were seen in the stage box of the theatre soon after its opening. At the end of the play the young gentleman leaped upon the stage, with his father's rejected address in one hand, and an opera hat in the other, and repeated the following lines.

"When energizing objects men pursue,
What are the miracles they cannot do?"

Here, however, the juvenile spouter was stopped by Mr. Raymond, the stage manager, and a constable, who handed the young gentleman off the stage. The "Rejected Addresses," by James and Horace Smith, contain a good burlesque imitation of the Busby address.

zine," edited by Thos. Holcroft, and containing a variety of amusing articles both in prose and verse, written by the editor, by Mr. Harrison, and by other authors of talent. It was embellished with large prints, folded. His "Biographical Magazine," an 8vo. volume, contains small engraved portraits, with short notices of each subject, well executed.

Harrison issued two periodicals of smaller size, the "Pocket Magazine" and the "Lady's Pocket Magazine,"* which were published monthly, and embellished with portraits and views. These works contained writings of several young authors, some of whom afterwards attained eminence; amongst them were my esteemed friends, the Misses Porter, and their brother, the poet, artist, and traveller. A frequent writer in these magazines was R. A. Davenport, who sometimes officiated as editor. Both Charles and Thomas Dibdin contributed many well-written and amusing papers; as did also Peter Courtier.

Contemporary with, and a near neighbour to Harrison, was JOHN COOKE, who for many years carried on a large and successful business as publisher of periodical works. He was probably one of the earliest of the Paternoster Row booksellers who applied himself to this branch of trade, upon a large scale. The subjects and form of his books and their illustrations were, however, very different from those of Harrison. Cooke confined himself, for some time, to religious publications, the principal and most popular of which was Southwell's "Commentary on the Bible:" it had a large sale, and produced a profit of many thousand pounds. After the appearance, in numbers, of Chambers' "Cyclopædia," under the editorial care of Dr. Abraham Rees, Cooke published an imitation, with the name of Hall, as editor, of some merit, but inferior to its predecessor. All Cooke's publications were in folio, divided into small portions, and issued weekly, at sixpence each number: they were "adorned with cuts," which were of the old school, both as to drawings and engravings.

At an advanced age Mr. Cooke retired to the country, with a handsome fortune, and died, in 1810, at the age of 79. His son, Charles,

---

* In this periodical was a series of small engraved views of places, from drawings by the late J. M. W. TURNER, R.A., who eventually became the most eminent landscape painter in the world. He was a pupil of Edw. Dayes, and will be again noticed in a subsequent page.—J. B.

continued for some time his father's principal publications; but he soon commenced a new course, which was attended with great success. The copyright of Hume's "History of England," belonging to Cadell and Longman, having expired, Cooke availed himself of the circumstance to publish an edition, with Smollett's Continuation, in weekly numbers, at sixpence each. It was neatly printed, and embellished with portraits and vignettes tolerably executed. Contemporaneously with this, he also published a series of the older popular English Novels, with attractive embellishments. The original drawings and paintings, from which the prints were taken, were exhibited in a picture gallery, at the rear of his shop. At a later time Cooke published an edition of Bell's "British Theatre," under the editorship of Richard Cumberland. Besides inheriting a handsome fortune from his father, he acquired a considerable increase by his own speculations. He built a new house in Epping Forest, where he lived a short time, and died, in the prime of life, after a painful operation performed by Sir Astley Cooper.*

ALEXANDER HOGG, who lived next door to Cooke, formed his literary schemes on the model of his neighbour. His publications were chiefly religious, and issued in weekly sixpenny numbers. The principal were, a *Bible with Annotations*, by the Rev. Timothy Priestley, the

---

* Although my finances would not allow me to purchase the whole of Harrison's and Cooke's publications, I bought some of them, at what is technically called "trade price," and must own that they not only afforded me much amusement and instruction, on repeated perusal and examination, but, I believe, created that love of literature and art which progressively rose to a confirmed passion. The periodicals, by the publishers above noticed, were sought for and hailed with intense curiosity as they made their appearance; and I may safely aver that the embellished works, which I have since produced, sprang from the seeds which the Cookes and Harrisons sowed, at the end of the last century. The very beautiful and effective drawings and engravings by Stothard and Heath were eminently calculated to fascinate the young eye, as they gratified also that of the learned professor of art. Harrison's "British Magazine," of which three volumes were published in 1782, 3 and 4, contained several very highly-finished plates by Heath, from Stothard's designs. A short time before his decease I spent a day with Charles Cooke, at his rural villa, which had attained the cognomen of Cooke's Folly. Though expensively fitted up and furnished, it was wholly devoid of the elegancies of high life, and exhibited more ostentatious finery and show than classical or simple beauty. Its walls were, however, amply covered with paintings, drawings, and prints.—J. B.

brother of the eminent philosopher of that name. Like Cooke, Hogg brought out an "Encyclopædia," with the name of Howard, as editor. All his publications were in folio; with a profusion of most wretched prints. Miserable as these works were, both as to literary and artistic execution, their proprietor contrived to derive from them a handsome fortune.* At the period under consideration, his publishing business was conducted by a young man, familiarly known in the trade by the name of "Thomas," who was much liked by the booksellers' collectors. He served his master many years, and was with him when the latter died. He declined to serve in the same capacity under the son, who had previously been a stranger to the business; and therefore, after some demur, was admitted by the latter into partnership. The union did not last long. Hogg retired, and the business devolved on "Thomas," who introduced important changes into it, by which he raised the character of the house and improved his own fortune. He rose gradually in the esteem of his neighbours, and the shopman of Mr. Hogg is now deservedly respected as Mr. Alderman Thomas Kelly.

My next Class comprises the greater wholesale booksellers and publishers, inhabitants of the Row. The first of these, at the sign of the

---

* Amongst the books published by Hogg, was a large folio volume, called *Antiquities of England and Wales*, with the name of Henry Boswell, as author, or editor. It has a great number of prints wofully executed, both as to drawing and engraving, and copied from any and every source that was accessible. For pirating one or more from Grose's "Antiquities," the publisher was sued, and sentenced to pay damages, with costs. The letter-press was quite in harmony with the prints, and equally valueless, being taken from any book or books that could be obtained, without acknowledgment. The editor is said to have been a servant of Hogg's, who was paid by the week for his services, in cutting up books for the printer, and reading the proofs. That there was not much congeniality of sentiment, or friendly feeling between Harrison and Hogg, may be inferred by an epigram which the former wrote for and inserted in the *Lady's Pocket Magazine*, July 1795.—J. B.

ON A STUPID BOOKSELLER.

*By Peter Pindar, Esq. (James Harrison.)*

Thou Beast! amid the sons of WISDOM plac'd,
Who, times of old, as well as modern, grac'd,
Couldst thou not catch a portion of their fire?
Rolls not thine eye upon their works each day,
And canst thou, from them, nothing bear away,
To lift thy HOG-like soul above the *mire?*

"Bible and Crown,"* were the RIVINGTONS. They constitute an old and highly-respectable firm, with premises extending from the front to St. Paul's Church-yard. The earliest of this family, whom I have been able to trace, was Charles, whose name appears in the beginning of the eighteenth century. It is certain he carried on business here as early as 1710. In 1730 his name is joined with that of Thomas Longman and some others, as publishers of Thuanus's great historical work. He died in 1742, and was succeeded by his son, John. This family has always been distinguished for its zealous attachment to the Church of England, and has consequently enjoyed an intimate connexion with the established clergy. It is related of John Rivington, that he was a very assiduous attendant on the services in St. Paul's Church, and was seldom absent from the early morning prayers, at six or seven o'clock. If surprised by the bell before he had quitted his bed, he has been known to put on his clothes hastily, and finish dressing in the church, during the service. He died in 1792, at the age of 73, and was succeeded by his two sons, Francis, and Charles, who constituted the firm when I first became acquainted with the Metropolis. The first died in 1822, and the second some time in 1831. The Rivingtons engaged largely in the publishing trade, but chiefly in books relating to the Established Church. In 1791, during the political and religious excitement produced by the French Revolution, they commenced the "British Critic," a monthly review of literature, professedly intended to uphold the tenets of the Established Church, and the Tory politics of the ruling government.†

---

* Almost all the booksellers' houses of London, as well as those of other trades, were formerly contra-distinguished from each other by Signs, either over the doors, or projecting into the streets. The latter becoming a nuisance were prohibited by Act of Parliament; but the former are still continued, in many places. The following are some of those Signs: Bible and Ball; Anchor; Black Swan; Black Boy; Golden Anchor; Cicero's Head; Shakspere's Head; Red Lion; Ship and Black Swan; Raven; Sun; Bible and Crown; the Dunciad; and the Star.—J. B.

† The principal and most influential periodical of this class was the *Monthly Review*, which was ably conducted by Dr. Griffiths, who had the assistance of several eminent writers. The first number was published in May 1749, when he carried on the trade of a bookseller at the "*Dunciad*," in Ludgate Street. In 1754 he removed to a new shop in Paternoster Row, afterwards occupied by H. D. Symonds, and in 1759 to the

Another periodical, published by the Rivingtons, was the *Annual Register,* originally brought out by Dodsley, with the literary aid of Edmund Burke. The Rivingtons purchased the copyright, and continued the work on its original Tory principles. It was for some years edited by Mr. R. A. Davenport. The principal books of the ornamental class published by the Rivingtons were those written by the late MR. DONOVAN, on several subjects of natural history. He was an excellent naturalist, and an accurate and skilful draughtsman.

On the south side of the Row, near the premises described, was located *Robert Baldwin,* at the time of which I am writing. He was greatly esteemed as an upright and honourable tradesman. For many years he published the "*London Magazine,*" which commenced almost as early as the "Gentleman's," the first number bearing the date of 1732. This was for many years a very popular periodical. Mr. Baldwin died in 1810. His nephew and successor commenced a new magazine in

---

Strand, where he continued his original sign of the *Dunciad*. On relinquishing business in 1764, he committed the publication of the Review to Mr. Becket. Dr. Griffiths died at Turnham Green, in 1803. After his death the Review was conducted by his son, Colonel Griffiths. At his decease the copyright was sold, but the publication was not long continued. At the time of which I am writing, there were two other reviews, published monthly—the "Critical" and "Analytical"—both of which, as well as the "Monthly," were the property of the liberal dissenters. Under these circumstances it was thought desirable to bring out another Review, which should counteract and neutralize their principles as much as possible; and, at the same time, develop and sustain the religious and political opinions of the party who were attached to the Established Church. Hence originated the "*British Critic,*" as an antagonistic publication. It was projected and conducted by two learned and able clergymen, the Rev. Richard Nares, and the Rev. Wm. Beloe, the translator of Herodotus, who were aided and supported in the undertaking by Dr. Parr and other eminent writers. It may well be supposed the articles contributed by such men were distinguished by erudition and general literary merits; and yet the Review was never, I believe, a popular or profitable work. Of late years it has been changed from a monthly to a quarterly publication.—T. R.

In association with Mr. Nares, was my old and much-respected friend, the *Rev. John Whitaker,* author of a Life of Mary, Queen of Scots, and of many other learned and "party-coloured" works. He was very severe in his criticisms on those authors whose religious and political opinions differed from his own prejudices. In a subsequent part of this work I shall have occasion to notice him again, as I spent some days at his house in Cornwall in 1802, when on a tour through that interesting county for the *Beauties of England.*—J. B.

1820, with the same title, under the avowed editorship of *John Scott*, a young author of excellent character and considerable literary talents. The work was proceeding very satisfactorily, and rising into popularity, when the editor was unhappily involved in a quarrel, which ended in a duel. The meeting was conducted by young men wholly unaccustomed to such affairs of " honour," and the fatal result of the rashness and inexperience of his second was the cause of the death of Mr. Scott.* Charles Baldwin, brother of Robert, had an extensive printing business in Bridge Street, Blackfriars, and realized much profit by printing the " St. James's Chronicle," a newspaper which at one time attained great popularity. It is still conducted by his son, Charles, who is also its printer, and it is said he is joint proprietor of the "Morning Herald," and the " Standard." He is a gentleman of the highest respectability, and of extensive knowledge.

THE ROBINSONS, at the end of the eighteenth and beginning of the nineteenth centuries, when I first became acquainted with the firm, carried on the largest business of any house in London, as general publishers, and also as wholesale and retail booksellers. George, the head and founder of the house, had been an assistant to John Rivington, and about 1763 embarked in business in partnership with John Robinson, at whose death, in 1776, he was left alone in the concern. His rising reputation for personal integrity and steady habits of business recommended him to the friendly notice of Thomas Longman, the

---

* In traversing Lincolnshire for the *Beauties of England*, in the year 1810, I met Mr. Scott, at Stamford, where he was engaged by Mr. Drakard, to edit a new weekly newspaper, which the latter had started. The high tone of politics and powerful writing of Mr. Scott soon attracted popularity, and the writer was invited to contribute articles to some of the London periodicals. These also excited both the admiration and envy of many readers and authors. A controversy arose in the *London Magazine* and in *Blackwood's Edinburgh*, which became sarcastic, vindictive, and personal, and ended as above stated, in a manner which created a mingled sensation of sorrow and horror in many minds. The magazines and newspapers of the time were much occupied, afterwards, with a succession of papers on the ceremonies, folly, and unhallowed practices of duelling. At the time of penning this note (June 1852) " an affair of honour," as a duel is misnamed, has occurred between two "honourable gentlemen" of the House of Commons, which has fortunately turned the event into ridicule, and will be likely to produce good moral effects.—J. B.

second publisher of that name, who, well knowing the difficulties which young tradesmen had to encounter with a deficient capital, voluntarily offered to give him any credit he might require for books of his publication. By unremitting attention, and the judicious application of strong natural talents, his business steadily and rapidly increased, so that by the year 1780 his wholesale trade had become the largest in London. About that time, the necessity for assistants in the management of the concern, led him to take into partnership his son, George, also the two brothers, John and James, the firm being then designated that of G., G., J. and J. Robinson. They published largely, books of considerable size and of great value. The head of the firm was considered to have an excellent judgment in the difficult and often critical undertaking of the superintendence and management of the literary concerns of a publishing establishment. He greatly respected meritorious authors, and acted with singular liberality in his pecuniary dealings with them. Besides the works of which they were the sole proprietors, they were engaged jointly with several of the principal houses in numerous works of great extent, such as Kippis's "Biographia Britannica."

In 1780 they commenced the "*Annual Register,*" following the plan of Dodsley's, but advocating a different system of politics. They engaged in the preparation and conducting of this work gentlemen of high character and established literary reputation, by which it soon acquired great popularity. The current sale of each volume, for many years, exceeded 7000 copies. They were also the publishers of the "Town and Country Magazine," of which there were sold about 14,000 copies, monthly; and of the "Ladies' Magazine," a publication for a long period of equal popularity and emolument. For many years the confidential friend and literary adviser of the house was the late *Alexander Chalmers,* who possessed many qualifications for that delicate and difficult office. He is said to have contributed largely to their several periodicals, and had a prominent share in the editorial direction of the "Biographical Dictionary," which extended to 32 volumes 8vo., and was in progress of publication from 1812 to 1817.* George Robinson

---

\* Having often had occasion to refer to this work, in the expectation of finding full and accurate information, with discriminating comments on the writings and merits of the authors, whose memoirs it professes to narrate, I have too often been disappointed

died in 1801. Though he had succeeded in creating and sustaining the largest bookselling and publishing trade of his time, he failed to provide for his successors that mental organization and machinery which were indispensable for continuing it: conscious that the concern was of his own creating, he seems to have thought that he could not keep the management too exclusively to himself. His son and his brothers he admitted, indeed, into partnership, and assigned to each his place and duties; but they were treated by him rather as agents than principals. He was king and autocrat; and whilst he conceded to them, nominally, the position of equals, in rank, he carefully retained the supreme and ruling power. The consequence became painfully manifest, immediately after his death. The surviving partners found themselves engaged in a large and intricate business, of which neither of them knew much beyond the particular department to which his attention had been almost exclusively devoted. Ignorant of the pecuniary position of the house, of the money capital at their disposal for sustaining it, and equally so of the means and method of its proper application, they saw no hope of relief but by a friendly commission of bankruptcy.

---

and mortified. A good Biographia Britannica is a literary desideratum. I cannot conscientiously praise the execution of this Dictionary, yet I feel sincere respect for the man, and admiration of many of his literary works. He was a truly estimable professional literary character, and it is said that "no man conducted so many works for the booksellers of London; and his attention to accuracy of collation; his depth and research as to facts, and his discrimination as to the character of the authors under his review, cannot be too highly praised." Such is the remark of Mr. Timperley, in his "Dictionary of Printing and Printers," 1839. Besides writing for several periodical works, Mr. Chalmers edited "The British Essayists," in 48 vols. 18mo. 1803; an edition of Steevens's Shakspeare, with Life and Notes, 9 vols. 8vo. 1803—1805; A History of the Colleges, &c., of Oxford, 2 vols. 8vo. 1810; an edition of "The English Poets, from Chaucer to Cowper," 21 vols. royal 18mo. 1810. He was also author of an original work, in 3 vols. second edition, 1815, which had previously appeared in the *Gentleman's Magazine*, intituled "The Projector," a periodical paper, originally published between January 1802 and November 1809. Of this work Mr. Timperley fairly writes that "it successfully seized on the follies and vices of the day; and has displayed in their exposure a large fund of wit, humour, and delicate irony." Mr. Chalmers was a pleasant, convivial companion, which, with his conversational talents, and intimacy with the principal London publishers, secured him a seat at the Hall Dinners of the Stationers' Company at all their public meetings. I met Mr. Chalmers frequently, and ever found him cheerful, communicative, and friendly. He died Dec. 10, 1834, aged 75.—J. B.

The affairs were wound up, the property sold, and, to their surprise, it was found that there was enough to satisfy every creditor, in full, with a surplus of £20,000. The surviving partners arose from this painful investigation with their personal credit and honour untarnished, but their commercial importance had departed.

It remains that I now give some account of the LONGMANS—the first of whom was *Thomas*, at the sign of "the Ship and Black Swan," whose name appeared to books in 1726, joined with Thomas and John Osborne. He appears to have realized a good fortune, and, dying in 1755, left the property to his widow. She, with the nephew of her first husband, Thomas Longman, conducted the business for some time. They possessed valuable copyrights, in Greek and Latin school-books of the higher class, which, at that time, had a large sale. This nephew was esteemed a tradesman of correct judgment, of great integrity in his dealings, and of kindly disposition. I had opportunities of seeing him occasionally towards the close of his life. He retired from business about 1793, retaining only so much of it as was connected with the sale of the stock belonging to his copyrights, and died at his house at Hampstead in 1797, at the age of 60, greatly esteemed by all who knew him. His eldest son, Thomas Norton Longman, succeeded to the father's business as wholesale and retail bookseller and publisher, on the same plan and scale, his principal assistant being Christopher Brown, the father of my excellent friend, Thomas Brown, who served his apprenticeship to Mr. Longman, and now deservedly occupies the honourable post of a principal partner in the house. In 1797, my eldest brother, *Owen Rees*,[*] who had been thoroughly trained to business in one of the prin-

---

[*] My brother, finding his health declining, determined to close his connexion with the house at Midsummer, 1837, and arrangements were made with this view. Before they were concluded, he went to Wales for the removal of what was deemed a temporary indisposition, and on the 5th of September, died, in the 67th year of his age, upon the estate (then his own property) on which he had been born, and where he had hoped to pass some years in tranquil retirement, after the anxieties and fatigues of a long life of arduous and unremitting application to business.—T. R.

Of this once-amiable and estimable person, I avail myself of the present opportunity to put on record an expression of my own warm feelings of attachment and sincere friendship. Intimately acquainted with him for nearly forty years, and often associated in the

cipal bookselling houses in Bristol, joined Mr. Longman, when the firm was briefly designated, "Longman & Rees." In 1804, Thomas Hurst*

---

counting-house, on committees, at the social board, and in other pursuits, I knew him well, and not only respected him for generosity of conduct and sentiment, but for that friendly and kindly disposition he manifested on all occasions. Never was there a man who more fully and truly acted the character of "Harmony" on the great stage of the world, than Owen Rees. In an extensive intercourse with authors and artists, with booksellers and other tradesmen, indeed, with all classes of society, he was bland, courteous, candid, and sincere. In the numerous meetings of the partners in the *Beauties of England*, when I was but little known to or by Mr. Rees, and when there were often angry contentions between the booksellers and the authors, I always found him eager and anxious to reconcile differences, to sooth irritated feelings, and endeavour to urge the authors to industry and perseverance, and his colleagues to forbearance and generosity. Such conduct and such manners could not fail to create a friendly feeling in my heart, and, from a more intimate connexion with him afterwards, in consequence of the firm having a share in the *Beauties of Wiltshire*, the *Architectural*, and the *Cathedral Antiquities*, and in others of my literary works, I invariably found a sincere friend in Mr. Rees. Many happy hours have I spent in his company, in Paternoster Row and at my own humble home, and never saw him with a frown on his benignant countenance, nor heard a harsh, ungenerous sentiment from his lips—I loved him, whilst living, and have often lamented his loss, since death has parted us.—J. B.

* The story of THOMAS HURST may afford a lesson and warning to speculators, and also to generous-hearted persons, who are susceptible of being imposed on by the seductions of the cunning and crafty. I knew him some years before he joined the firm of Longman and Co., and found him then, as I did in his days of prosperity, kind, friendly, and generous. At first he conducted a business nearly opposite Longman's, and supplied several country booksellers with the London publications. By diligence, devotion to his customers, and obliging manners, he soon augmented his property and profits, and was doing well when he joined the new firm. In this he managed the country department, and was highly esteemed by all who knew him. He was living in an elegant, but unostentatious style, with a carriage and good establishment, on the brow of Highgate Hill, where I have spent many joyful hours in the company of cordial friends. In an evil moment he became connected with an artful and unprincipled man, who was engaged in a good bookselling business in Yorkshire, and who afterwards embarked in a large and daring undertaking in London. John, the elder brother of Thomas Hurst, who was a man of retiring disposition, of unassuming manners, and of punctilious honesty of principle, was partner with the person alluded to, but wholly unfitted for the hazardous game in which he became involved. He was quiescent, whilst his partner was artful and ostentatious. Their capital was soon sunk, and credit was then obtained to a vast extent; for the partner, not satisfied with a large business in books and prints, embarked in building houses, and speculated in hops. The elder Mr. Hurst saw and felt the imminent danger in which he was embarked, and prevailed

and Cosmo Orme were added to the firm. In consequence of some subsequent changes occasioned by the death of my brother, and later by that of T. N. Longman, the retirement of Hurst and Orme, and the introduction of other persons, to take their places, the firm has assumed its present form of "Longman, Brown, Green, and Longmans." After the introduction of these new partners, of excellent business habits, various new schemes for the enlargement and extension of the trade were carried into execution. Hence, within a short period, the house rose to an importance and reputation which had never before been attained by any similar establishment in the world. To the retail branch they devoted a distinct department, to which was joined a choice and extensive library of old books.* The general wholesale trade, for the

---

on his brother to sign accommodation bills to a great amount. He had not courage to refuse, but drew in the name of the firm, of the Row, as he had been accustomed to do in the regular routine of business. Some of these bills were duly paid, but they became so numerous and to such large amounts, that Longman and Co. required an explanation, dissolved the partnership, and bound Mr. T. Hurst to be personally responsible for all further outstanding bills. They also paid to their retiring partner more than forty thousand pounds, his valued share in the house. But even this sum was not enough to meet all the liabilities: whence he became a ruined man. He made two or three efforts to regain credit and business; but these were not to be obtained. The elder brother, John, died broken-hearted; and Thomas was reduced to the mortifying state of seeking an asylum for old age, as an inmate to, and dependant on the charity of the Charter House, in which he died in the year 1850.—J. B.

* This was a novelty in a publishing house, and I believe that it originated in obtaining a large collection of scarce and curious books, on old Poetry and the Drama, which the partners had purchased, for a very large sum, from Thomas Hill. The event was at a time when Bibliomania was raging in London,—when certain noblemen and gentlemen were in the habit of attending sales, and competing for large and tall-paper books, and for rare copies, many of which had become so from their worthlessness. A remarkable Catalogue, called "*Bibliotheca Anglo-Poetica*," of the Hill library, was prepared in 1816 by — Griffiths, a clerk in Longman's house, and secured much praise from the book-buyers, and the learned in black-letter lore, for the knowledge and tact it manifested. Thenceforward, for many years, the house continued to purchase largely at sales, and from individuals, either libraries or collections of books, and occasionally issued catalogues. After the death of Mr. Griffiths, his place was supplied by Mr. Reader; but within the last few years the whole collection was sold by public auction. I am not a little surprised and mortified to look over the pages, and meagre Index, of the Rev. Dr. Dibdin's "Reminiscences," in vain, for some notice of T. Hill, and Mr. Griffiths's "Bibliotheca."—J. B.

supply of country booksellers in the British Isles, and for the foreign markets, surpassed that of all preceding establishments; whilst the publishing business, if it cannot be said to have gone beyond that of any other British house, was unquestionably inferior to none.

In adverting to the publications of this firm, it is curious to observe one name of some eminence in literature and science, which has been in association with Longman and Co. for more than 120 years. This is *Ephraim Chambers*, the author, or editor, of the original "Cyclopædia," which work was first published by subscription in 1728, in two volumes, folio. It soon acquired great popularity, and attained a second edition in 1738. The author, finding his health impaired by literary labours, went to France, in hopes of recruiting his mental and bodily strength, and at the same time collecting materials for his projected book. I have in my possession some interesting letters written by him during this tour, addressed to his publisher. The "Cyclopædia" was reprinted under his superintendence in 1739, and was his last literary effort. His constitution gave way, and he died in May, 1740. The work was again reprinted in 1741, and also in 1746, when it was thought desirable to add a Supplement, to embrace the more modern discoveries in science and in the arts. This Supplement, prepared by Dr. Hill, and Mr. G. L. Scott, was published in 1753, in two folio volumes. After an interval of some years, the work still maintaining a high reputation, the proprietors projected a new edition, incorporating the Supplement, together with new matter of importance. Some difficulty was experienced in finding a suitable editor. At last *Dr. Abraham Rees* was chosen, who was then mathematical tutor at a dissenting college in London, and had acquired considerable reputation for his scientific knowledge and literary talents. The first number, in folio, was published in 1778, and the work was continued weekly till completed, in 418 numbers, forming four large volumes, with numerous prints. The current sale for many years amounted to 5000 numbers weekly, and there was a large demand for the work, in this form, for a long time after its completion. At length it was found expedient to publish another edition, or rather an entirely new work, under the same title, and under the same learned and laborious editor, who called to his aid a number of writers holding high rank in the several important departments of science. The work received the designation of the "NEW CYCLOPÆDIA." It was published periodically, in parts, or half volumes, and appeared regularly till completed in 40 volumes. The publication, which commenced in 1802, occupied about sixteen years; but the labour of the indefatigable editor, including the period of preparation, extended over twenty years, measured, as he said, not by fragments of time, but by whole days, of twelve and fourteen hours each. In the general preface, the editor has given the names of his principal coadjutors, and I find your name recorded in the list, in connexion with the subjects of antiquities, topography, &c., upon which you furnished many valuable articles.*

---

* Respecting the extent and character of my own contributions to this once valuable and popular work from the year 1802, when I wrote the account of "Avebury," to 1819—"Wiltshire,"—the reader will find full particulars in the Second Part of this work: vide Index. I had the gratification of introducing the following gentlemen to the firm, to write articles on subjects connected with their professional studies: E. W. Brayley, who wrote on Enamelling; T. Phillips, R.A., on Painting; and Sharon Turner, on English History. The last gentleman became intimate with the partners, was employed by them for many years afterwards, and attained great popularity and handsome remuneration for his historical works, through the medium of such publishers.

Reminiscences respecting this once important work, and its phalanx of contributors, in art, literature, and science—of their frequent intercourse at the *Soirées* which the publishers established at their great book manufactory and mart, No. 39, &c., Paternoster Row—are impressed on my memory and feelings with intense pleasure, mixed with some painful emotions of having for ever lost the converse and excitement which emanated from the friendly and intellectual collision, then and there produced. The respectable firm of Longman and Co. not only invited and assembled nearly all the contributors to the *Cyclopædia*, periodically for several successive winters, but were in the habit of calling many of them together around the social and splendid dining table, where the acknowledged professors of literature and art met, on equal and friendly terms, eminent amateurs of both. Such unions were novelties in England, and, I believe, in Europe; and were eminently calculated to foster good feelings, and promote harmony and intimacy between persons in different gradations of trade, literature, art, and science. Hence friendships were made; new discoveries were proclaimed; opinions, public measures, and the conduct of public men, canvassed; courtesies and civilities were exchanged between persons whose studies and pursuits were often in rivalry, and human amenities were cultivated. In such company, and under such influences, I own that I not only felt elated and proud, but substantially benefited, both mentally and morally. The amiable and benignant editor of the *Cyclopædia*, who often formed one of these parties, seemed, to my fancy, something above humanity: for never was there a man more deservedly beloved and respected than the *Rev. Dr. Abraham Rees*.—J. B.

Besides giving to the editor the assistance and co-operation of eminent writers in literature and science, the proprietors spared no expense to provide artists of the first talents for its illustrations. Among those who furnished drawings, were Howard, Landseer, Donovan, Russell, Opie, Ottley, Phillips, and Farey; while among the engravers, were Milton, Lowry, and Scott. The " New Cyclopædia" was in all respects a great and important undertaking. It embodied writings by some of the most distinguished scientific men of the age, on subjects of primary consequence, and it involved an expense almost unexampled in the history of literature: the pecuniary outlay could not have been less than 300,000 pounds sterling.

Another literary speculation of considerable importance, undertaken in 1803, was the *Annual Review*, intended to comprise, in one large volume, an account of the entire English literature of each year.* The editorship was committed to Arthur Aikin, whose scientific and literary attainments eminently fitted him for such an office. He was ably assisted by the distinguished members of his own family, and by many persons of note in the literary world: among whom may be mentioned, in theology, the Rev. Chas. Wellbeloved, of York; in natural history, the late Rev. Wm. Wood, of Leeds; and in general literature, Robert Southey, and William Taylor, of Norwich.† I must add, besides many others, your own name; for to you the editor was indebted for some valuable articles on topography and antiquity. The work was conducted by Mr. Aikin for six years, when, in consequence of new arrangements in the management of the literary concern of the house, I undertook to prepare the seventh volume. In this arduous task I was materially aided by most of the gentlemen who had lent

---

* See the Second Part of this work, pp. 66-76.

† The numerous letters by Taylor and Southey, in "A Memoir of the Life and Writings" of the former, 2 vols. 8vo., by J. W. Robberds, are truly interesting, as calculated to unfold some of the mysteries and fascinations of authorship and reviewing, as well as characterising two writers, whose works produced many and great effects in the world of literature, between the years 1793 and 1836. Though not much known to the reading community, Mr. Taylor was an extraordinary writer; and from the number and variety of his criticisms and essays, in the *Monthly Magazine*, the *Monthly Review*, the *Annual Review*, the *Athenæum*, in magazines, and other periodicals, he must have produced strong and important results on the readers of his works.—J. B.

their services to my esteemed predecessor, and I had the gratification of receiving a valuable contribution from Walter Scott, on a subject, for the treatment of which he was perhaps the fittest writer of the age;—Ancient Romance. With the seventh volume the work ceased.

In the year 1807, Longman and Co. entered on the publication of a new periodical, called *The Athenæum*, under the editorship of Dr. Aikin, in competition with the "Monthly Magazine," which had been commenced a few years before by Mr. R. Phillips, of St. Paul's Churchyard.* This publication consisted of monthly numbers, at one shilling each, and was continued to the close of the seventh half-yearly volume. The work included contributions by Dr. Falconer, of Bath, and Mr. Dewhurst, of London; Robert Southey, — Bland, Elton, and many others. On this periodical I had the pleasure of acting as sub-editor, and furnished for it most of the larger articles of obituary. But the sale did not yield an adequate return to compensate the publishers, and the work was on that account relinquished.

Not long after the discontinuance of the "Athenæum," the house embarked in an undertaking of great magnitude and expense, entitled "*The British Gallery of Pictures;*" which was intended to consist of fine engravings from the best works of the old masters, in the private collections of English noblemen, &c.; some of the prints being coloured in imitation of the originals. In the plan of this work two objects were embraced:—firstly, small prints, including *all* the pictures in certain celebrated collections; and, secondly, copies of a selected number only of the more important and admired works. The latter prints were on a

---

* The *Monthly Magazine*, under the able editorship of Dr. Aikin, assisted by the contributions of various members of his own family, with Dr. Enfield, and other persons of distinction in literature, had acquired great popularity. The projector was at the time regarded as a sufferer from his political principles; and Dr. Aikin, with other friends to liberal opinions in politics, readily espoused his cause, and lent their talents to assist him. No sooner, however, had the magazine obtained an extensive circulation, than Phillips took the entire management, and dispensed with the services of his first friend. The magazine, however, if it lost from this cause much of the literary excellence and refinement which had characterized the earlier numbers, retained, by his judicious selection of miscellaneous matters of general interest, its hold of the popular mind, and commanded a very extensive sale. It occurred to Longmans that a magazine, which should be devoted to topics of a higher literary character, might be successful; and under this conviction they projected the periodical above-mentioned, under the title of *The Athenæum*.—T. R.

larger scale than the former, some being of the actual size of the original pictures. Each series was accompanied by appropriate letter-press, and the prints in both cases were coloured. Eminent artists were employed to copy the pictures for engraving, as well as to colour the prints. Among the engravers were Cardon, Schiavonetti, and other able artists; and, whilst the artistic arrangements were entrusted to Tomkins, the literary department was confided to Henry Tresham, R.A., and W. Y. Ottley; both gentlemen being well qualified for their respective duties. An immense outlay was incurred upon this work, which was carried on for some years with great spirit; but it proved to be a very unprofitable speculation, and was brought to a premature close, when the only portion really finished was the Cleveland-house collection, in one volume, folio. The water-colour drawings from the original pictures had been exhibited to the public in a gallery specially appropriated to them in Bond Street; and, on the termination of the work, the proprietors obtained an Act of Parliament to dispose of the pictures, with the engravings, by lottery.

But whilst the house thus employed a large capital, in the production of what may be termed periodical works, it was liberal in the appropriation of other portions to standard books, on important literary subjects, by authors of the most distinguished reputation. Amongst these were the Aikins, Scott, Moore, and Southey. Complaints have often been made of the sordid spirit of booksellers, and their inadequate remuneration of authors. No doubt writers are often very badly paid for works upon which they have bestowed much time, labour, and talent; and the cause of literature has, it may be believed, suffered on this account. But I am quite sure the evil has not always originated with publishers, who, like other tradesmen, give for the material the amount which they deem it to be worth in respect to the profit it is likely to yield. Generally, I believe—and I speak from a long experience—the booksellers act with commendable liberality. A reference to a list of prices given by Lintot to authors, early in the last century— a curious document, printed by Nichols, and now in my possession— shows that authors, at that time, were handsomely paid. In well-known instances, booksellers of a later date,—the Robinsons, the Dillys, the Johnsons, the Cadells, the Murrays, and lastly the Longmans,—have dealt most liberally by authors, and on some occasions have given sums of large, not to say exorbitant amount, for manuscripts, on the bare supposition that the returns might justify the expenditure, and yield a fair trading profit. In my personal knowledge, I can say that the firm, now alluded to, always acted in such transactions with great and generous spirit.

At a later period, Oct. 1802, Longman and Co. became part-proprietors and London publishers of the "*Edinburgh Review.*" This produced them an important accession of literary friends of eminent abilities, among whom were Walter Scott, Rev. Sidney Smith, Francis Jeffrey, Henry Brougham, Francis Horner, James Mill, and others.

About this time they became connected also with JOHN PINKERTON,* the author of " General Geography," which appeared first in three, and afterwards in two quarto volumes. It was a work of great labour, being written and compiled from the best authorities in the European languages, and illustrated by numerous maps, engraved by Lowry. Pinkerton also prepared a large " General Atlas," a well-executed folio volume; and, more especially, a "Collection of Voyages and Travels," in sixteen quarto volumes, with prints by the Cookes and others. These large and costly works were the joint property of Longman

---

* With this singular and degraded man, I was made too well acquainted, for his own reputation and for my own domestic comforts. He rented, and occupied, for a short time, a house, No. 9, Tavistock Place, next door to my own. His home was frequently a place of popular disturbance, by females whom he had married, or cohabited with, and deserted. When in want of money, or over-excited by drink, they knocked at his door, broke the windows, and otherwise behaved riotously. He was a disreputable character; and though he had been most liberally paid by Longman's house, he went to Paris in the latter part of his life, and died in poverty in 1826. He was author of several works, in poetry, history, geography, criticism; all of which, says the writer in *The Penny Cyclopædia*, " with all their faults, not only overflow with curious learning and research, but bear upon them the impression of a vigorous, an ingenious, and even an original mind. His violence and dogmatism, his arrogance and self-conceit, his pugnacity and contempt for all who dissented from his views, but above all, his shallow and petulant attacks upon the common creed in religion and morals, have raised a general prejudice against Pinkerton, which has prevented justice being done to his acquirements and talents." Mr. Dawson Turner possesses a large collection of his correspondence, from which two octavo volumes have been published, but not much to the credit of the Scotchman.—J. B.

and Co. and Cadell and Davies. A later speculation, on a large scale, published by Longman's house, was "*Lardner's Cabinet Cyclopædia,*" in small 12mo., extending to 133 volumes; for which many distinguished writers were engaged, and heavy expenses were incurrred.

For several years it was the custom of the firm to give Dinners at certain intervals, when the partners assembled around their hospitable board a number of authors and artists of high reputation; and, besides these more limited *réunions*, they opened the house in Paternoster Row, one evening in the week, during several seasons, for a *Soirée;* which was rendered easily accessible to persons of literary tastes, and from all countries.

I come now to the third Class of booksellers who chiefly dealt in retail; whose traffic was mostly with their brother tradesmen, whom they supplied with a single copy, or several copies of books, at what was called the trade price, which produced them only a small profit. Paternoster Row contained, at that time, several respectable booksellers of this class. *Mr. Bladon's* shop was the well-known depository of old plays. You may remember to have seen, some years ago, in Leadenhall Street, a large hardware warehouse, which attracted the notice of all passengers by its filthy appearance, both on the outside and the inside. The proprietor was scarcely less notorious on account of his dingy aspect, which obtained for him the designation of *Dirty Dick.* Bladon was greatly respected as a tradesman, but his shop might have rivalled the Leadenhall Street repository for its affluence in dust and soot. The next to be noticed is *Symonds,* who carried on a large business in the sale of periodicals, which he purchased in quantities, as they were published, and sold singly, or in small numbers to booksellers' collectors, at the wholesale prices. By this plan the trade was greatly accommodated, and his own interest promoted. He pursued the same course with respect to the more popular pamphlets of the day. In times of great political agitation, such as those in which he lived, this practice of publishing for authors was not without danger, as Symonds had the misfortune to experience. One tract, to which he had permitted his name to be attached, was pronounced a libel; and he had to endure the penalty by an imprisonment of some months in Newgate, where I once visited him. He died in middle life, greatly respected. The business of this house was aftewards conducted on the same scale and plan, by *Mr. Sherwood*, who had been Mr. Symonds' active and valuable assistant. Contiguous to this shop was that of *Parsons*, who sold books and pamphlets upon the same plan, but on a less extensive scale. He was occasionally a publisher, on his own account. His chief speculation was an edition of Hume and Smollett's "History of England," in 18mo., which, like that by Cooke, was embellished with prints and portraits.

*Thomas Evans*, though advanced in age, ranked among the retail booksellers of the Row. He was originally a porter to Johnson, a bookseller of Ludgate Street, and succeeded to the business of Howes, Clarke, and Collins, by which he obtained respectability and a good fortune. The bulk of his property he bequeathed to Charles, father of the present T. Brown, already noticed. In his will, he directs that his funeral expenses do not exceed forty shillings. In early life he acted as the publisher of the *Morning Chronicle*, which first appeared in 1770, and in that capacity had the misfortune to offend Oliver Goldsmith, who went to the office and unceremoniously assailed Evans with a stick. The sturdy Welshman, however, soon recovered from his surprise, and with one blow laid the poet prostrate on the floor. Another of the retail booksellers of this period was *John Walker*, who for some time officiated as (what was called) the *Trade Auctioneer*.*

---

* It is a common adage that there are "secrets in all trades;" and it is well known that every craft and calling has its peculiar customs, privileges, and technicalities of language. A few of the large wholesale publishers of London are in the habit of making up, either annually or occasionally, what are called "trade sales;" when they prepare a catalogue of their large stock books, and distribute it to a select number of retail dealers, who are invited to meet the publisher and his auctioneer at a certain tavern, where, after partaking of an early dinner, the "trade auctioneer" proceeds to dispose of the works named in the catalogue, to the parties present. The various lots comprise many copies of recently-published works, and are offered and sold at rather less than the usual trade prices; the purchasers being moreover allowed to give bills, at three, at four, eight, twelve, and sixteen months, according to the amount they buy, or take a moderate discount for cash. Hence have originated two great evils in the bookselling business; namely, the encouragement to print large editions of books, from the facility of disposing of them at reduced prices, and the depreciation of those works in the public market, by copies being offered at such sales much below their original prices. Mr. Walker, I believe, was amongst the first trade auctioneers, and was followed by Mr.

He was greatly respected by his neighbours. In the latter part of his life his name was familiar to the public as publisher of Dr. Wolcot's, alias Peter Pindar's, works.*

Saunders, a prompt, off-hand man, whose language and peculiarity of manners are humorously burlesqued in "Chalcographiomania." The celebrated *William Hone* was for a short time auctioneer to the trade, but was irregular in his accounts, whence arose many embarrassments in after life. Two large stock-holders of books have since become their own salesmen, on these occasions: both eminently qualified, from promptitude of thought and action, and extensive knowledge of business. The late *Thomas Tegg*, of the Poultry, when I first knew him, kept a small shop in St. John's Street, for pamphlets, songs, &c. Thence he removed to Cheapside, where he accumulated a large stock of books, and established an evening auction. He afterwards took the old Mansion-house in the Poultry, and progressively published numerous books. Having settled one of his sons in Australia, he thereby obtained a channel for the sale of large editions of cheap books, and deemed it expedient to adopt the practice of some of the great publishing firms, by making up an annual sale, and acting as auctioneer. My friend, *Mr. H. G. Bohn*, has followed the same track, and has astonished the Metropolitan traders in literature by the stock brought forward, the rapidity of dispatch, and the novelties he has introduced into this branch of London business. Mr. Hodgson, of Fleet Street, is at present the confidential and respected agent of the London publishers.—J. B.

* The Poems of this once noted and powerful satirist were extensively read at the end of the last century. They were, however, very dear to the purchaser, being printed in thin quarto pamphlets at 2s. 6d. each, and containing only a very small portion of letter-press. His first attacks, in 1782, were the Royal Academicians, some of whom he assailed with bitter satire, sarcasm, and irony. King George the Third was next vituperated, in a poem called "The Lousiad," descriptive of the circumstance of an animal, unnameable to "ears polite," being seen on the plate of the monarch at a royal dinner. For some years the author continued to publish his philippics against artists, royal and noble personages, and also on some authors; one of whom, Wm. Gifford, who had written the "Baviad and Mæviad," a poem, in which many of the authors of the time were severely castigated, also wielded his galled pen against the morals and poetry of Dr. Wolcot. This castigation was so stringent and caustic that the Doctor was provoked to seek his lampooner in the shop of Mr. Wright, a political publisher, of Piccadilly. Thither Peter repaired, with a stout cudgel in hand, determined to inflict a summary and severe chastisement on his literary opponent. Gifford was a small and weak person; Wolcot was large, and strengthened by passion, but he was a coward, and after a short personal struggle was turned into the street by two or three persons, then in the shop. Gifford afterwards wrote and printed an "Epistle to Peter Pindar," with an "Introduction and Postscript," 1800, in which he dealt out a most virulent and unqualified tirade against the Doctor. It acquired great popularity, and in a few weeks attained a third edition. The pamphlet has not any publisher's name. This was the second victory which Gifford had achieved over literary opponents; a former being Anthony

*Mr. Bent* was a bookseller of long standing in the Row, but he was chiefly known as the publisher of that very useful work, the "London Catalogue of Books," first printed in 1799, which is still continued

---

Pasquin, alias John Williams, a man notoriously acrimonious and severe in his poetical and prose criticisms on actors, actresses, and authors. Gifford was amongst the number, who smarted from his lashes, and who retaliated by lines more caustic and personal. For these Williams brought an action for libel, but was driven out of the Court of King's Bench by the unanimous reprobation of judge, jury, and the auditors assembled. I was present at that memorable trial; and can never forget the severity of sarcasm and irony exerted by Garrow, counsel for the defendant, against the notorious libeller, who had the effrontery and impudence to ask for damages, in a court of law, for what he called injury to private and public character. Notorious, and despised for his long career of literary vituperation and scandal, the Judge interrupted Mr. Garrow, and asked the Jury if they thought it desirable to proceed further with the trial, or non-suit the plaintiff. The latter was pronounced instanter. In the wide and diversified annals of literature, the reader will seek in vain for three more notorious and unprincipled satirists than the triumvirate here alluded to.

Wolcot's connection with Paternoster Row and John Walker arose from the latter becoming the publisher of some of the former's writings, and ultimately proprietor of the whole. I have heard Peter boast, he was the only author that ever outwitted, or "took in" a publisher. His works had attained great popularity, and produced for the writer a large annual income; and many of them were often out of print. Walker was disposed to purchase the copyrights, and print a collected edition. He first made the author a handsome offer in cash, and then an annuity. The poet drove a hard bargain for the latter, and said that "as he was very old and in a dangerous state of health, with a d—d asthma, and stone in the bladder, he could not last long." The bookseller offered £200 a year, the poet required £400; and every time the Doctor visited the Row he coughed, breathed apparently in much pain, and acted the incurable and dangerous invalid so effectively, that the publisher at last agreed to pay him £250 annually for life. A fine edition of his works was published in three volumes, 8vo., 1794, with a portrait and engraved title-pages; other editions have since appeared. Another portrait of him was published, as a separate print, which did not sell to any extent; but its proprietor derived a great profit by taking out the name of Peter Pindar and substituting that of "Renwick Williams, the Monster," who was notorious for stabbing ladies in the streets. This event was related to me by the Poet. A good account of his life is given in the "Penny Cyclopædia." Mr. Cyrus Redding, who had been familiar with Wolcot for many years, gave some interesting anecdotes of him in the "New Monthly Magazine," vols. 17 and 19; and has recently written further notices in "The Athenæum" for May and June 1852, to correct certain mis-statements in Jerdan's "Auto-Biography." In another part of this Biography will be found a notice of this eminent satirist: vide *Appendix*, p. 179. Wolcot died in Somers-Town, Jan. 13, 1807, in the 81st year of his age, and was buried at St. Paul's, Covent Garden.—J. B.

monthly by Mr. T. Hodgson.* Bent also published "The Universal Magazine," a periodical which at one time had an extensive sale.

I may conclude my list of retail booksellers with the names of the *Wilkies*, brothers, who were long respected inhabitants of the Row. With their retail business they carried on a wholesale trade of some extent in supplying country booksellers. One of the brothers, Thomas Wilkie, trafficked also in the public securities, and kept an office for the sale of lottery tickets. †

[Thus far my old and much-esteemed friend, Dr. Rees, has committed to paper a series of anecdotes and notices of Paternoster Row and its Bibliopolists, which cannot fail to amuse and interest the general lover of literature. He has, however, omitted to explain the extent of his own literary occupation, as it arose out of his connexion with the publishing establishment here alluded to. A detailed narrative of it, if written in the style and manner of an article by Sir Francis Head, on the large printing-house of Clowes and Sons, in the *Quarterly Review* (Vol. lxv. 1839) would be eagerly and profitably read by thousands of persons. It would unfold much curious and interesting information on the principles of commercial partnerships; on the best systems of wholesale and retail business; on the variety of practices in debtor and creditor accounts; on profit and loss, discount and ready money; with numerous other particulars on the different branches of trade and manufacture, in which the house must have had constant intercourse; and lastly, many characteristics and peculiarities of authors, artists, traders in literature, and of its patrons, or consumers. I am aware that this firm, as well as all others on a large scale, has secrets—particular practices, or modes

---

* This gentleman is also editor of "The London Catalogue of Books published in Great Britain, with their Sizes, Prices, and Publishers' Names, from 1814 to 1846," 8vo. 1846; and "Bibliotheca Londinensis: a Classified Index to the Literature of Great Britain during Thirty Years," 8vo. 1848.—J. B.

† He removed to Salisbury, where I became acquainted with him, 1798, and found him obliging and kindly disposed. Amongst other things, he told me that on the first performance of Sheridan's play of "The Rivals," which the Wilkies published, the author was so scantily supplied with wardrobe, that he borrowed a shirt of Mr. W.'s father to witness the first acting of his own play, but forgot to return the said shirt; as he did also a few guineas, which he had borrowed of the same party.—J. B.

of transacting business—which it would not be expedient to impart to every impertinent and loquacious reader; but such might be withheld, and still leave abundant material to gratify and delight every person of laudable and generous curiosity. From the long intimacy and experience which Dr. T. Rees had in that house, for nearly half a century, the extent of its literary business, the number and celebrity of authors, men of science, art, and commerce, who were connected with it, I consider that he possesses ample funds for such an essay. Let us briefly consider what were his situation and duties for many years. As brother of the second partner in the firm, when he settled in London in the year 1806, he was received and treated as a confidential friend, and was progressively engaged to write, translate, abridge, and advise generally on the merits of manuscripts, and occasionally adapt some of them for the press. For *Rees's Cyclopædia* he wrote many articles; and towards the close of that valuable work, it was his laborious duty to read over the whole, for the purpose of ascertaining if references to prints, pages, and articles had been properly made; if subjects referred to in one part had been printed, and corresponded with announcements, in another; if figures and letters in prints were true to those in the letter-press; to supply deficiencies, correct errors, and indeed make the work as complete and perfect as practicable. It may be remarked that he had been placed in Longman's house some years before the time here mentioned, to qualify himself for business; but during that servitude his love for literature induced him to read so much during the night, that he injured his health, whence his father thought it necessary to remove him from the shop to college, to prepare for the ministry. As travelling tutor, he afterwards made the tour of France and Italy. Soon after his return, he was engaged, in 1806, as sub-editor and assistant to Dr. Aikin, on "*The Athenæum*," a magazine which the Doctor had projected as an improvement on Phillips's "Monthly Magazine," which he had previously edited and advanced to great popularity. Thenceforward my friend continued attached to the firm for many years; indeed, I believe, until his brother retired from it. His duties involved much solicitude, as well as mental labour. Though great circumspection was employed to preserve secrecy, and incognito, he progressively became known to nearly all the literati and artists who were connected with the house. In addition to the varied and numerous literary labours arising from this engagement, he wrote a large volume on the *Topography and Antiquities of South Wales*, for the "Beauties of England and Wales," and also edited, and wrote several articles for the seventh volume of the *Annual Review*. I resume the narrative by Dr. Rees relating to "the Row."—J. B.]

---

In AVE MARIA LANE, the firm of *Scatcherd and Letterman* carried on a large wholesale country business.* In the same lane, the house of *Law* was chiefly noted for school-books. An apprentice, and afterwards managing clerk, in that business, was *Peter Courtier*, whose partiality for poetry induced him to write and publish a volume of "Verses," some of which had appeared in periodicals. He was the first mover in, and an active supporter of "the School of Eloquence," which has been referred to, (*ante*, p. 92.) The Laws were succeeded by the *Whittakers*, whose active exertions and skill in business speedily increased it to a great extent. Amongst many of their publications, was one in five volumes, by MISS MITFORD, called "*Our Village*," which has passed through several editions, and is justly admired for the vivid fancy, the pathos, and amiable sympathy which pervade its pages. This work is now brought into two volumes by Mr. H. G. Bohn, and issued in his popular series of books. She first appeared as a poet in 1810.—[See *ante*, p. 26.] The reader will find some pleasing, and justly complimentary, remarks on Miss Mitford's writings, in a recently published and interesting volume, "A Journal of Summer-time in the Country," by the Rev. R. A. Willmott. Second edition, 1832.

[WILLIAM PINNOCK was author of a long list of books, which, though little known in the literary world, have been of great value in the advancement of education and knowledge. All his writings have been adapted and addressed to the juvenile age, and have been peculiarly calculated to "teach the young idea how to shoot," and tempt it to

---

* Amongst other works they published, was "*London and its Environs, or the General Ambulator*." The 12th edition, 1820, greatly enlarged and improved by my coadjutor, Mr. Brayley, is now before me, and is a very useful work, though supplanted by the justly-popular publications by Charles Knight: "Pictorial London," 6 vols. 1841.—J. B.

pursue the path of learning with pleasantry and even fascination. By "The London Catalogue from 1814 to 1846," I see that Pinnock has produced twelve volumes of Catechisms, eight of Histories, and twenty-two others on Grammar, Languages, Arithmetic, Geography, Poetry, &c. These books have all been very popular and profitable to the publishers, though the author has, like too many other improvident ones, known the galling pressure of indigence.—J. B.]

Near Mr. Law's house, was the printing and publishing establishment of J. WILKES, who became well known by the "*Encyclopædia Londinensis*," with numerous engravings, a work which extended to twenty-six quarto volumes, at £63., and had a considerable sale.*

In STATIONERS' COURT was the warehouse of B. CROSBY,† who had a very extensive country business, which has for some years been conducted by *Simpkin and Marshall.* ‡

[This paved COURT is associated with my own personal and topographical reminiscences too memorably to be passed unnoticed. In this central part of London, resided John, Duke of Bretagne and Earl of Richmond, during the reigns of Edwards II. and III., in a large

---

* The names of Wilkes, Ave-Maria Lane, and Encyclopædia Londinensis, are indelibly impressed on my memory. On my first visit to Salisbury in 1798, I assumed the title, or rather it was forced upon me, of Artist; and Mr. Easton, a bookseller and printer of the city, asked me to make a drawing of Salisbury Cathedral, to be engraved for, and published in, the great "national work" above-named. My ambition was aroused, but I was terrified; for I knew not how or where to begin, nor how or in what manner I was to proceed, even if I dared undertake such a herculean task. I was impelled to try: had pencils, rulers, and a table placed opposite the middle of the North chief transept. With the print from Price's "Survey," from the same point, before me, I sketched, and scratched, and rubbed out; and continued thus occupied for three successive days, with several persons looking on, and wondering at my temerity and incompetency. Often have I reflected on this scene and event; and more than once have I heard friends, who were there, remark on the exhibition, and their astonishment at seeing afterwards a tolerably-executed engraving from the sketch then made.—J. B.

† One of the original partners in the *Beauties of England and Wales.*—J. B.

‡ Though not distinguished as publishers, this firm carries on the largest business in the book-trade of any house in Europe, and is only rivalled perhaps by the Harpers, of New York. The only daughter of the late Mr. Simpkin is the wife of the most enterprising and energetic publisher and bookseller of this metropolis, Henry G. Bohn, whose Catalogue of Books of 1841 is unprecedented for the number, value, and variety of its articles. It extends to no less than 1948 octavo pages.—J. B.

mansion which was afterwards occupied by an Earl of Pembroke, and called Pembroke's Inn. It was afterwards possessed by the Company of Stationers, who rebuilt it of wood.* That was burnt in the great fire of London, after which the present plain, tasteless Hall was erected. According to Clarendon, the stationers' property then destroyed was valued at £200,000. Here the Company of Stationers hold their courts, transact their business, register and deposit books, and assemble frequently at the festive board. At two of the Master's feasts I have been a guest, and enjoyed the company, conversation, and civic repasts with much zest. The Portraits preserved here remind us of names and literary works which have excited our curiosity and gratified our feelings in early reading days. These are of Richardson, Prior, Steele, Hoadly, Nelson, Dryden, Alderman Boydell, and others. The first was one of the Masters of the Company, and had his wife painted for the place, to keep him company. Leigh Hunt, speaking of these portraits, says, that representing the author of *Clarissa Harlowe* represents him as a "sensitive, enduring man—a heap of bad nerves." He further remarks, that Hoadly, "looks at once jovial and decided, like a good-natured controversialist." Concerts, as well as dinners, were frequently performed in this hall. Odes and other pieces were written for such occasions. Amongst these, Dryden's "Song for Saint Cecilia's Day," was produced in 1687; and, ten years afterwards, "Alexander's Feast" was written, composed, and performed: the composer being Jeremiah Clarke, who shot himself "for love." Though the Hall and Company of Stationers are associated with pleasant memories, persons, and events, there are others which tend to lower both in my own estimation. From the commencement of my literary career to the present time, I have been obliged (by Act of Parliament) to present one copy of every book which I have written and published to this company. For many years the said Stationers assumed the exclusive privilege of publishing all the almanacs of the country, and produced many which were frivolous and illiterate in style and matter. To counteract these, Charles Knight projected and published, for

---

* This is the only London Company whose members are restricted to their own craft. It is called, "The Mystery or Art of the Stationers."—See Cunningham's "Hand-Book of London," 2nd edit., 1850.—J. B.

"The Society for the Diffusion of Useful Knowledge," in 1828, "The British Almanac," which has become eminently and justly popular, and has also superseded most of the almanacs which disseminated astrological nonsense and literary absurdity. The reader will find a very interesting paper on the history and characteristics of almanacs in "The Companion to the British Almanac," for 1829; also in "The London Magazine," for December, 1828.—J. B.]

Proceeding to the north-west corner of St. Paul's Church-yard, we recognize a name associated with the earliest recollections of youthful readers,—that of Newberry, who, after Carnan, furnished the largest and most interesting contributions to the juvenile libraries of the country. On the death of Newberry, his widow continued the business, aided by John Harris,* who afterwards became her successor. He was in turn succeeded by his son, who soon transferred the business to the present firm of Grant and Griffiths.

Francis Newberry, a member of the above-mentioned family, had a house on the east side of the Church-yard, near Cheapside, where he sold Dr. James's celebrated fever powder, as a patent medicine. He was also proprietor of Paterson's "Road-Book," which, by judicious management and progressive improvement, he rendered a very lucrative property. The editing and publication of that volume was a favourite occupation of Francis Newberry, and he pursued it to the end of his life. The stock and copyright were afterwards possessed by Mr. Mogg, who made further improvements. The volume is now extinct: railways have superseded stage coaches, and steam-power that of horses.

Joseph Johnson long occupied a prominent station in St. Paul's Church-yard. He held the same position amongst the liberal Protestant dissenters that the Rivingtons did with the members of the Church of England. He was truly generous in dealing with authors, by frequently adding to the price originally agreed on for a successful manuscript; and in this manner he is said to have paid as much as £10,000 for Hayley's "Life of Cowper." Johnson issued the works of Price, Priestley, Belsham, and many others; together with "The Analytical Review." Having published a libellous pamphlet, by Gilbert Wakefield, reflecting on Dr. Watson, Bishop of Llandaff, the author was

---

* See a notice of this gentleman in Part II. of this Auto-Biography, p. 56.—J. B.

imprisoned for two years, and Johnson, as the publisher, for six months.* At stated periods his house was open to literary men; and his parties derived great interest from the presence of such persons as Doctors Price, Priestley, Geddes, and Aikin; Bonnycastle, Fuseli, Gilbert Wakefield, Mary Wolstoncraft, and many others.

SIR RICHARD, then Mr., PHILLIPS, commenced business in St. Paul's Church-yard, by publishing "*The Monthly Magazine,*" in 1796. He had previously been settled at Leicester, first as a schoolmaster, and afterwards as a bookseller; but political causes obliged him to quit that town. His case met with much sympathy in London, as he had incurred heavy losses by his removal. He was a man of strong mind and varied attainments, and, with a view to repair his injured fortunes, he projected the magazine above-mentioned. Dr. Aikin, who was much interested in Phillips's success, edited this periodical, and was aided by his sister, Mrs. Barbauld, by his friend, Dr. Wm. Enfield, also by Godwin, Holcroft, and many other writers. Johnson at first published this periodical, as agent for Phillips; and his extensive connexion enabled him to promote its success. The speculative proprietor was, however, soon induced to open a small shop for himself, and about the same time he also undertook the task of editing his magazine; thus dispensing with the services of two of his best friends. The "Monthly" rapidly increased in popularity and profit, and for many years continued to be a valuable property. Phillips published numerous other works, chiefly educational, many of which were written by himself, but appeared under the names of popular authors; who probably revised the proofs, and allowed their names to be attached, for a pecuniary consideration. Like his competitors, Phillips published an "Encyclopædia," professedly under the editorship of Dr. Gregory; but which was in fact mostly written by *Jeremiah Joyce,*† whose varied

---

* This incarceration appears to have produced beneficial effects to the warm-hearted publisher. Instead of enjoying the converse and social company of his talented authors, he studied his ledger, which had been neglected; and by sending notices of its unsettled contents to different debtors, he realized a large amount of income on being released from prison.—J. B.

† This gentleman was an industrious, punctilious, and valuable coadjutor to the *Encyclopædia,* and was author of several elementary and useful works on science and philosophy.—J. B.

scientific attainments were most inadequately appreciated. In the year 1807, this enterprising publisher served as one of the Sheriffs of London, and discharged the duties of that important office with zeal, energy, and great credit. During this period he was knighted, on presenting an address on behalf of the ministers. In the latter part of his career he suffered severely by the panic, and was obliged to surrender his business to his creditors.*

[The name and house of *Carington Bowles,* on the north side of St. Paul's Church-yard, were noted for the number and variety of popular Prints which were distributed thence all over the country at the end of the last and beginning of the present century. "Death and the Lady," a figure half skeleton, half female—"Keep within compass," a beau

---

* Besides numerous original papers in "The Monthly Magazine," Sir Richard was also author of the following literary works : " A Letter to the Livery of London, on the Office of Sheriff," 8vo. 1808; " On the Powers and Duties of Juries, and on the Criminal Laws of England," 8vo. 1811; " A Morning's Walk from London to Kew," 8vo. 1817; " Golden Rules of Social Philosophy, or a New System of Practical Ethics," 8vo. 1826; " A Personal Tour through the United Kingdom," 8vo. 1828. It is also stated that he originated and published numerous treatises on "The Interrogatory System," in school education, which has proved eminently successful. He was likewise author of "Twelve Essays on the Proximate Causes of the Universe," being a reformed system of natural philosophy; substituting matter and motion for what he called " the silly superstitions and fancies" of attraction, repulsion, &c. These works abound with originality of thought, expressed in terse and pungent language. Though the " Walk to Kew" and the " Personal Tour" do not contain much topographical and antiquarian information, they tempt the reader to accompany and sympathize with the writer, by the fund of anecdote, vivid description, and shrewdness of commentary, which pervade every page. In reading these works, the young student cannot fail to regard the author amongst the philosophers and moralists of his age and country. Sir Richard was a native of London, where he was born in 1767, and died at Brighton, April 1st, 1840. He thus writes to me from Brighton in April 1838, two years before his decease: "Your friendly letter was a ray of sunshine on a very dull day. You struck out for yourself a path of literary renown, and I am quite sure you have reached the summit. For my own part, my pursuits have been so diversified for the last twenty years, that I had almost forgotten one of my youngest literary children—'The Walk to Kew.' Your approbation I value, because on such a subject you are a first-rate judge. You must have read fifty such works: I never read one; and therefore, in my mind, there is no element of comparison. I had no design of the book when I took the walk; and my notes were very scanty. Had it been republished with a dozen good engravings, it might have become popular. Another volume might have been devoted to Hampton Court, and a third to Windsor."—J. B.

with cocked hat, scarlet coat, &c., standing between the two legs of a pair of compasses, and other showy, admonitory pictures were to be seen in the farm-houses and cottages in Wiltshire, in my youth-days, whence the names of publisher and place were impressed on the young mind. The late Mr. C. Bowles, on retiring from business with a handsome fortune, built a large villa or mansion at Enfield, on the bank of the New River, and called it *Myddleton House,* in compliment to the adventurous speculator in that important undertaking. Mr. Bowles's ancestor possessed shares in the New River Company, which were bequeathed to the son, who for many years was an active member of that company. He was a Fellow of the Society of Antiquaries and took great interest in its weekly meetings.—J. B.]

CHARLES DILLY, of the Poultry, was the survivor of two brothers, who published largely, and accumulated handsome fortunes. On relinquishing business, he was succeeded by JOSEPH MAWMAN, of York, who afterwards removed to Ludgate Street, where he was succeeded by MR. FELLOWS.*

The firm of VERNOR AND HOOD had removed the business from Birchin Lane to the Poultry, where they published many literary works, and with whom, if I remember rightly, you commenced your literary career as a Topographer.†

---

\* Mr. Mawman published "An Excursion to the Highlands of Scotland," &c. 8vo. 1805, which contains two prints from drawings by Turner. In the *Annual Review* is my notice of the volume.—J. B.

† My business and personal connections with that House, involve reminiscences of persons, books, and events, which would afford matter for a moderately sized volume. From the year 1799 to 1810, I was in almost constant communication with Mr. Hood, who was the managing partner, and who was an active, persevering, punctilious man of business. The House attained considerable distinction in the literary world by the publication of Bloomfield's "Farmer's Boy," and other volumes of poems by the rustic, self-educated author—by the exuberant praises of Capel Lofft—by the publication of "The Monthly Mirror," under the editorship of Edward Dubois and Thomas Hill—by "The Poetical Magazine," edited by David Carey, who had published "The Pleasures of Nature," with other poetry, novels, &c. Among many works which issued from this firm, was "The Beauties of Wiltshire" and "The Beauties of England and Wales," with the accompanying "British Atlas."—[Vide the *Second Part* of this work, p. 48.] —In 1808 the House acquired much notoriety by a trial in the Court of King's Bench,

[C. FORSTER of 91, Poultry, published, amongst other works, "The Literary Magazine and British Review," which extended from 1788 to 1794. It is distinguished for a series of well-engraved portraits, mostly by T. Holloway, accompanied by original memoirs; also other prints and essays on literary and scientific subjects.—J. B.]

Under the Royal Exchange, JOHN RICHARDSON, who was a highly respected tradesman, carried on an extensive trade amongst the city merchants. He was one of the original proprietors of "The Beauties of England," and was assisted by a nephew of the same name.

In the same street, MR. J. SEWELL, a worthy but eccentric man, published the "*European Magazine;*" the biographical articles in which, especially those connected with the drama, were written by *Isaac Reed*, who edited the work for many years, and was succeeded by Stephen Jones. *Mr. Moser* was a prolific writer in this popular periodical, which contained many well-engraved portraits.*

[At the north-east corner of Bishopsgate Street, MESSRS. ARCH, two Quaker brothers, enjoyed an excellent retail trade. They had shares in "The Beauties of England," and were the publishers of Turner

---

when *Sir John Carr* brought an action-at-law against these publishers for a libel on himself and his literary works. This author had obtained much reputation for his Tours in France, in the North, in Holland, in Ireland, &c., and had been rewarded by different publishers with nearly two thousand pounds for copyrights. His "Tour in Holland," one volume 4to. 1807, which was purchased and published by Sir Richard Phillips, was turned into ridicule by Edward Dubois, in a sportive, ironical, and satirical small volume, entitled "My Pocket Book," written in a fluent, anecdotical, gossipping style. The "Tours" were much read and abundantly commented on by the regular reviews and by daily journals. The author obtained fame and fortune, when the witty and caustic satire alluded to provoked him and the publisher to prosecute the writer of "My Pocket Book." A verdict was given, in behalf of the liberty of the press, against the plaintiff, who was non-suited, and driven from the court in disgrace. A full account of the trial was published, with several letters from the Earl of Mountnorris, Sir Richard Phillips, and the author of "My Pocket Book"—Edward Dubois. See account of this publication and of the Pocket Book, in "The Annual Review," vol. vii. 1808. Of Mr. Hood and his Son, the justly-famed and much-lamented Thomas, I shall have occasion to offer a few remarks, hereafter.—J. B.

* Amongst them was one of Dr. Joseph Priestley, in profile, drawn by myself, from life, when the reverend philosopher was reading a farewell discourse to a crowded congregation in Hackney Church, in March 1794.—J. B.

and Cooke's "Southern Coast," which contains many fine specimens of the skill of the respective artists.*—J. B.]

[The *Minerva Press*, by Wm. Lane, in Leadenhall Street, must not be omitted in this short retrospect of the older metropolitan publishers. It was noted for the number and variety of books, called novels, which were continually produced and distributed to all the circulating libraries in the country. From ten to twenty pounds were the sums usually paid to authors for those novels of three volumes. The Colburns and Bentleys drove this trash out of the market.—J. B.]

---

[*Fleet Street* and its immediate vicinage are noted in the annals of Literature for the number and estimation of authors, printers, and publishers who have been located here, in addition to those already named. Amongst these may be specified, JOHN M'CREERY, an eminent printer, who had distinguished himself at Liverpool by writing and publishing a poem, called "*The Press*." This was reprinted, and a second part added, on his settling in the metropolis. He was strongly recommended to the London publishers by Mr. Roscoe. In his employ were *Ralph Rylance* and *John Nightingale*, two young men, who were afterwards engaged in writing and editing several literary works for London publishers. Three volumes on *London*, part of "The Beauties of England," were compiled by the latter, in a very heedless manner. He was author of two octavo volumes, "Portraitures of Methodism" and of "Catholicism." His friend and associate, Rylance, was a learned, diligent, and trustworthy author, and was much employed by the house of Longman and Co. in translations, preparing the manuscripts of inexperienced authors for the press, and on miscellaneous literature. He was a most worthy and honourable man. He became deranged in intellect, and died in the prime of life, respected by all who knew him.

BENJAMIN MARTIN, an optician and author already referred to

---

* This work, somewhat like "The Beauties," was the cause of repeated disputes between the publishers and the artists and authors. The late amiable William Alexander, then one of the curators of the British Museum, wrote an urgent and kindly-expressed letter to Messrs. Arch, advising them to pay more liberal prices to the engravers. I have a copy of that letter, from the original in possession of Dawson Turner, Esq.—J. B.

(page 67), had a shop and lived many years in this street. The long list of his publications—more than sixty volumes, all of which were eminently useful, and many of them popular, specified in Watts's *Bibliotheca Britannica*—shew that he must have been industrious and scientific; but also prove how fleeting and evanescent is literary fame.

JOHN MAJOR lived on the south side of Fleet Street, for some years, having removed from No. 71, Great Russell Street, Bloomsbury. He was much respected by a numerous circle of book-lovers and book-buyers, and particularly by the followers and disciples of *Isaac Walton:* by artists, poets, and the friends of the three. A poet, himself, and fond of books, not only as articles of profit, but as friends that were never capricious, but ever ready to impart good counsel, and the most disinterested and wholesome advice, he was constantly in their company. His shop was well stocked with some of the choicest, and he successively published, with useful and discriminating notation and fine embellishments, *Walton and Cotton on Angling;** the *Physiognomical Portraits*, 100 heads beautifully engraved with Biographical Sketches, 2 vols. large 8vo., and large 4to. 1824; *Robinson Crusoe*, designs by Stothard; *Hogarth Moralized*, by *the Rev.* Dr. Mavor; Walpole's *Anecdotes of Painting*, in 5 vols. imp. 8vo., 1835; " *The Cabinet Gallery of Pictures,*" with Critical Dissertations by Allan Cunningham, 2 vols. imp. 8vo., 1833. This interesting publication contains 72 prints, from the engravings of several of the most eminent artists, and a series of essays on the respective subjects and their authors, by one of the most honest and discriminating writers on such matters.

Walpole's "Anecdotes," from the manuscript collections of Virtue, was a work in much estimation by readers in the fine arts, for some time after its publication; but thence to the time Major produced his new edition, there were various sources opened, and further information easily obtainable, for correcting and greatly enlarging the book. Had Major engaged Allan Cunningham instead of the Rev. James Dallaway, he would have benefited himself and have satisfied his critical customers. But, alas! this was not the case: an unsatisfactory

---

* The Rev. Dr. Dibdin refers to "a copious and excellent review of this enchantingly-decorated and got-up little volume in *Blackwood's Magazine* for Oct. 1823."

and erroneous book was produced, though lavishly embellished with 150 prints of portraits, &c., also good paper and printing. Some of the portraits were skilfully engraved by Robinson, Scriven, Worthington, and Finden. From printing too many copies, a large remainder was sold off after the bankruptcy of its publisher, and Mr. Bohn disposed of them at the reduced prices of £4. for the small, and five guineas the large paper, with India proofs; instead of ten guineas for the former, and fifteen for the latter.

Some of these publications obtained the unqualified encomiums of the Rev. Dr. T. F. Dibdin, in his "Reminiscences of a Literary Life," 1836; but it was unfortunate for the honest bookseller to be too familiar and confiding in the unprincipled parson. The former accepted bills to a large amount drawn by the latter, who failed to honour them, and the consequence was bankruptcy and total ruin. Major sunk never to rise again : for his mind became deranged, and he was placed under restraint. Recovering, in some measure, he was released from the asylum, and found a retreat and comparative comfort in the Charter-house, London, where three other respectable booksellers were then sheltered and maintained in old age.

MR. KEARSLEY, of the same street, published the "English Review;" also the "English Encyclopædia," in several quarto volumes: the last publication possessed considerable merit. He also produced many other works, which became exceedingly popular and profitable—the *Beauties* of different authors. Those of Sterne, Johnson, Shakspeare; of the Spectator, Tatler, and Rambler, and other periodicals, were selling for many years, and reprinted in several editions. These, with Adams's "Flowers of Ancient and Modern History," "Flowers of Modern Travels," "English Parnassus," "Curious Thoughts on the History of Man," constituted a large portion of my early library. I have now before me "the eleventh edition" of Sterne's "Beauties," 1790.

In Fleet Street originated "THE QUARTERLY REVIEW," which was commenced in February, 1809, by JOHN MURRAY. This gentleman, in a respectable line of business, evidently possessed strong religious and political opinions, and was annoyed at the popularity and signal effects which the "*Edinburgh Review*" was producing in the republic of literature. To oppose, and endeavour to counteract its "*virus*," as called by Mr. Canning, he addressed a letter to that gentleman,—then Chancellor of the Exchequer,—suggesting and urging the necessity of printing a periodical, the joint production of some of the most eminent Tories of the time, in opposition to the famed Northern Review. He tells Mr. Canning that "he is no adventurer, but a man of some property, inheriting a business that has been established for nearly a century." This led to a correspondence, and to communications with William Gifford, Walter Scott, George Ellis, Hookham Frere, George Rose, Robert Southey, and some others of name and note, and very speedily to the publication of the first number. The high and rancorous spirit of Tory party, which then prevailed, thus obtained a dauntless champion, who has combated vigorously and intrepidly four times in the year up to the present age of peace, and a comparative truce in the war-field of politics.* Both reviews have produced decided and important effects on the literature and politics of the country; and it cannot fail to interest and instruct the lover of books to look over and compare the early writings in these periodicals with the *Monthly*, the *Critical*, the *Anti-jacobin*, and other Reviews which had long occupied the critical market. Mr. Murray removed from Fleet Street to Albemarle Street in 1812, to premises that had been occupied by WILLIAM MILLER, who had published some fine and expensive books.† Here

---

* A brief account of the origin of the Quarterly Review, with remarks on its politics and general character, and a list of articles written for it by Sir John Barrow, are given in the "Auto-Biographical Memoir," 8vo. 1847, of that remarkable gentleman.

† Amongst these were Forster's "British Gallery of Engravings," folio; Blomefield's "History, &c. of Norfolk," 10 vols. 4to. and imp. 8vo.; "The Itinerary of Archbishop Baldwin through Wales," 2 vols. 4to. 1806. The last work is peculiarly impressed on my mind, by a circumstance which gave me much annoyance at the time of its publication. Mr. Miller, knowing that I was acquainted with many book collectors and antiquaries, tempted me to subscribe for six copies, by allowing a discount of thirty per cent. under the publishing price, and payment by bill at three months after delivery. This induced me to speculate: I gave the bill, and was prepared to pay on the day it became due. The banker's clerk, however, failed to present it, and on the next day I had a notice that the bill was at a banker's, and there was 3s. 6d. due for noting the same. Unacquainted with bill transactions, but sensitive to everything that might impeach my credit, I hastened to Albemarle Street and paid the money, explaining that I had remained at home all the preceding day. The clerk's excuse was that Burton Street was too far out of town, and he had not time.

he became popular, successful, and much respected, not only by some of the most talented and eminent authors of his time, but by many of the nobility. His liberality to the literati, his tact in business and general information, were frequently exhibited in his correspondence with the parties above named, and many other distinguished writers. At the social and friendly board, both at home and abroad, he manifested engaging conversational powers; and it has been my good fortune to have been repeatedly amused and informed by him, in company with some of the bright literary planets which have appeared in, but have left, our hemisphere. In my library I often refer to some of those beautiful and valuable books which he has published, and honoured me with as presents.

At No. 55, Fleet Street, WILLIAM HONE had a small shop, in 1815, where he published "The Traveller," a newspaper; also "*The Life of Elizabeth Fenning*," who was hung for attempting to poison an idiot, though Hone's account of her life shows she was guiltless of the act. At this house appeared the first of his famed political pamphlets, which was graphically and effectively illustrated by his young and talented friend, the now eminent literary artist, George Cruikshank.* These two continued in association for many years, and had the bookseller fully profited by the counsels of the artist, he might have escaped State prosecutions, become a respectable and successful tradesman, and have lived to witness his friend's pre-eminence. Though they often differed in opinion on religious and even political subjects, they remained in friendly attachment during the chequered life of Hone. I have often wished that the artist had given to the world a graphic and literary review of his own career and connections, and still hope he may be incited to execute it; for his pen and pencil are competent to produce one or two volumes of surpassing and unparalleled interest.

Hone very soon moved from Fleet Street to the Old Bailey, where,

---

* Of this most witty, poignant, morally satiric and talented artist, an interesting biographical essay has been preserved in "The London Journal," November 20th, 1847, from the fluent and discriminating pen of *Dr. R. Shelton Mackenzie*, with a clever woodcut portrait. This paper not only shows the reader the peculiar graphic merits of the highly-gifted artist, but gives a vivid review of the political and moral character of the age in which he lived and worked, and points out the merits and demerits of some of the most prominent actors on the stage.

in conjunction with Cruikshank, he produced successively and successfully, "The Political House that Jack Built," "A Slap at Slop," and three "Parodies on the Book of Common Prayer." The first of these publications became so popular, that more than fifty editions were published, as appears by a volume now before me, entitled "Hone's Popular Political Tracts: containing The House that Jack Built; Queen's Matrimonial Ladder; Right Divine of Kings to Govern Wrong; Political Showman; Man in the Moon; The Queen's Form of Prayer; A Slap at Slop," 8vo. with numerous cuts, for William Hone. 1820. The last pamphlet was a smart and smarting attack on Dr. Stoddart, and his daily paper, called "The New Times." But Hone's Parodies were the most noted, and the most successful in their results, though productive of cruel and vindictive persecution and prosecution to the author. For printing and publishing these, three several indictments for libels were tried against him, in the Court of King's Bench, on the 19th, 20th, and 21st of December, 1817. Justice Abbott presided on the first, and Lord Ellenborough on the second and third days. The strong political prejudices of the latter judge were well known, and became apparent on the trials; but Hone conducted his own defence, with a firmness, fortitude, and talent which astonished both his friends and foes. His addresses to the jury, as stated in a note in the printed report of the trials, lasted, "on the first day, six hours, on the second, seven, and on the third, upwards of eight hours;" yet he was in a bad state of health, oppressed and depressed, and manifested much physical exhaustion. Still he was clear, close, resolute, and self-confident, and was listened to with intense interest by the court, but with evident signs of mortification by the judge. The result was an acquittal upon each indictment. Rarely have there been criminal trials which excited more popular sympathy and curiosity during their progress, or more general rejoicing in their termination.* The accused returned to his home in triumph, and a large public subscription was raised on his behalf. He had removed from his small shop in the Old Bailey to a large and expensive house on Ludgate Hill. Here he was followed, caressed, and praised by a succession of visitors—real, or affected friends,—amongst whom

---

* A cheap edition of these trials has been published, from the originals, which were first issued by the "acquitted felon," as termed by some of the Tory writers.

were some of the most popular members of opposition in the two Houses. A sum of nearly £4,000 was raised for him by voluntary subscription. With such a vast fortune, to him, and living and faring sumptuously every day, he had neither time nor incentive to write, or attend to shop business. The consequence was natural. The down-hill road from affluence to poverty is often travelled with special-train velocity, and terminates in the "slough of despond." Such was the case with our once-fortunate, but many times unfortunate, political and poetical hero; for in a short time his affairs were involved in the labyrinth of bankruptcy; and ruin, irretrievable ruin, ensued, from which he never became released. In February, 1834, he appealed to the Literary Fund for aid, when he intreated my intercession in his behalf, in a letter, wherein he says: "I am too much enfeebled to move about, and my family is in great distress, and I am worried out by little claims upon me, and have not a shilling." The Committee of that noble institution inquired into his case and character, and finding the first to be urgent, and the second to be more "sinned against than sinning," awarded him a handsome grant. I knew him well, and respected him for warmth of heart, kindness of disposition, and strength of head; but he was most improvident and indiscreet in the management of money affairs. Had these been placed in the charge of an honest, good accountant, William Hone might have lived to be a rich man, and died a happy one. His later publications were useful and valuable, as calculated to combine amusing, with good historical, topographical, and antiquarian information. They were "The Every-Day Book," "The Year Book," "The Table Book," and "Ancient Mysteries." Never, perhaps, was political and personal satire, irony, ridicule, burlesque, caricature, sarcasm, and unflinching temerity of language and graphic representation carried to such a pitch as in his once-popular pamphlets, which, with the exalted and illustrious personages represented and ridiculed, are now scarcely to be descried in the haze of distance. Had there not been gross delinquency and bad conduct in the parties satirized, and also palpable originality and talent in the author and the artist, these publications would not have attained their surprising and unprecedented popularity. —[See *Gentleman's Magazine*, January, 1843.]

The POETS' GALLERY, 192, Fleet Street, was a place of much distinction at the end of the last century and beginning of the present. *Thomas Macklin,* its proprietor, was a publisher and printseller, and besides using the Gallery for temporary exhibitions, continued to keep on view a succession of works of art; amongst which was the popular picture of *The Woodman,* by Thomas Barker, of Bath: (already referred to, p. 224 *ante*). Many of these were painted by the most eminent English artists for the splendid *Bible,* which he published. This was produced in rivalry of Boydell's magnificent "Shakspeare" and Bowyer's "England." These contemporary publications surpassed all literary works either of this or any other country; as comprising and displaying the finest examples of paper and typography, with the highest specimens of the fine arts of England. Herein Bowyer, Boydell, and Macklin did more to benefit art, and the sciences connected with printing, than had ever before been done, or perhaps will be effected, by any triumvirate of tradesmen. Macklin died at the early age of 43, in Oct. 1800. The Gallery has since been occupied as an auction-room.

The old-established bookselling firm of BENJAMIN and JOHN WHITE, at No. 63, Fleet Street, was amongst the most respectable of the class in London fifty years ago. Its stock was large and of the best books. They published some fine works in Natural History; amongst which were those of Pennant, Latham, and White, of Selborne. The last was a relation to the booksellers, as acknowledged by John, who edited the collected edition of his works in 2 vols. 8vo. 1802, in which is a very brief notice of that most amusing and amiable author.* The last of the Whites of Fleet Street joined in partnership with J. G. Cochrane.

The once-noted and eminently-notorious WILLIAM COBBETT issued many of his remarkable *Weekly Registers* from an office in this street, and, for several years afterwards, from his printing establishment in Bolt Court, where most of his voluminous publications on history, politics, travels, grammar, &c. were produced. In the annals of the human race, and particularly amongst its remarkable men, Cobbett appears conspicuous, if not pre-eminent. Emerging from the humblest of peasant society, without education, and struggling against many difficulties and

---

* Editions of White's "Selborne" have been published under the editorship of Bennet, 1837; by Jenyns, sm. 8vo. 1843; and another, with additions, &c., by Sir Wm. Jardine, in 1832.

privations, he advanced himself to high political and national distinction, obtaining a seat in the British Parliament, and writing several volumes, which secured great celebrity for some years, and which will be read with surprise and gratification in future ages. His works are numerous, very voluminous, and on various subjects. Amongst them is a copious, and apparently very candid Auto-Biography, which details a pretty faithful account of his public career and writings. But I would more particularly direct the young reader to "The Life of William Cobbett," a small thick volume in 18mo., of which the third edition appeared in 1835, extending to 422 pages. This is dedicated "To the Sons of William Cobbett," and contains apparently a fair, discriminating account of the man, the author, and the politician. It also reprints the opinions and criticisms of Wm. Hazlitt, Gifford in the *Standard,* and others from the *Morning Chronicle,* the *Times,* and the *Atlas.* Charles Knight has recorded his opinions and remarks on Cobbett, in the "History of England during the Thirty Years' Peace," vol. i. p. 48.

At 186, Fleet Street, was the shop of the *Eton School Books,* for many years conducted by EDWARD WILLIAMS, grandson of Joseph Pote, the historian of Windsor. He was one of the Court Assistants of the Stationers' Company for the last five or six years of his life, and proved himself an active and zealous member of that famed corporation. He was also active in the committee of the Literary Fund, and there, as well as in public and private life, manifested general benevolence, suavity of manners, true philanthropy, and those social, amiable traits of disposition, which conciliate all associates. Hence his company was generally courted. To a natural cheerfulness of temper he added the happy qualification of writing and singing songs, appropriate to times, persons, and places. In Jan. 1838, as he was walking in one of the streets of London, near the Haymarket, he fell on an ice slide, and received such serious injury as occasioned his speedy death. His eldest son, Edward Pote Williams, has succeeded him both in London and at Eton.

"THE JOHN BULL," weekly newspaper, has been printed and published at No. 40, Fleet Street, ever since its commencement in Dec. 1820. If not projected and edited at first by the celebrated THEODORE HOOK, it is generally known that he was intimately connected with it for many years, and that he wrote many of its highly poignant articles. Conservative and of high church principles, it has continued an unflinching course of advocating these two branches of the government, and to censure and ridicule all classes of society, and all departments of politicians of opposite opinions. The eminently witty, and as eminently reckless, editor soon rendered it popular and profitable to the proprietors, and to himself, by the severity of its political articles, and by the poignant wit and satire of its personal and literary essays. It is said that he derived at least £2000 a year from writings in this journal; at the same time he was in receipt of nearly as much more for novels, farces, &c.: yet he was often in debt and embarrassment. Never, perhaps, was there a man of such precocious and versatile talents. "As a wit, confessed without rival to shine," his company was courted, and he was incessantly flattered by princes, nobles, and the most noted in the world of fashion and of fame. As a writer of novels, farces, songs, and particularly in improvisation, he was, perhaps, unrivalled in the world of genius. Having been several times in his fascinating company, I can bear witness to these qualifications: when in contact and competition with the famed authors of "The Rejected Addresses," he seemed to shine with additional brilliancy. Yet this man, this accomplished wit and novelist, was imprisoned and degraded for disreputable neglect of his duties in a public government office, in which he was misplaced by political friends. His story and his leading characteristics are well described in the last volume of Knight's "Penny Cyclopædia."

"THE DISPATCH," of 139, Fleet Street, a weekly newspaper diametrically opposed to the *John Bull*, has continued to have a popular and prosperous career from 1818 to the present time. Besides a copious amount of political matter and general news, this journal has long been noted for its smart reviews of literary works, the fine arts, the drama, and the theatres. For some years my respected friend, Edward Dubois, contributed numerous witty articles on those subjects.

At No. 93 in this street, "*The London Magazine*"* was published, by TAYLOR AND HESSEY, from Midsummer 1821 to the same month

---

\* It is to be regretted that authors, and even publishers, who ought to know better, affix titles to books and periodicals which have already been used. It occasions deception and error. There are now three, if not more, named "London."

in 1825. It was edited by Mr. Taylor, who made the work highly popular, with the aid of such men as Henry Southern (now our Ambassador at Brazil), J. H. Reynolds, Thos. Hood, Chas. Lamb, the Rev. H. F. Cary, Allan Cunningham, Barry Cornwall, Charles Phillips, Horace Smith, Charles A. Elton, Thomas De Quincey, Wm. Hazlitt, Bernard Barton, J. Clare, the Rev. G. Croly, Hartley Coleridge, Dr. Bowring, Thomas Carlyle, and other similar writers. With such a phalanx of wits and literati (now nearly all dead), it is not surprising that this periodical was very popular. In 1827, these publishers sold the magazine to a new editor and proprietor. They published some works of older and eminent authors, under careful editorial superintendence, and embellished from clever designs by Hilton, who was then coming into notice, and who attained just honours as an artist of the higher class. Taylor and Hessey brought out several successful books by the amiable moral writers, Mrs. and Miss Jane Taylor, of Ongar (no relatives of the publisher), and also other works. They afterwards removed to Waterloo Place, and on the establishment of the London University, Mr. Taylor was appointed its bookseller, which induced him to settle in Upper Gower Street, where he has continued in co-operation with Mr. Walton to the present time. He is author of a well-written volume on the controverted and never-ending dispute as to the authorship of Junius's Letters, in which he endeavours to prove that Sir Philip Francis was the writer; but of which evidence I cannot admit the validity. In a learned volume, "The Emphatic New Testament," and other works on scriptural criticism, and in several pamphlets on currency, Mr. Taylor displays much erudition and acute logical argument.

ARTHUR COLLINS, called by Watt (*Bib. Brit.*) "the laborious antiquary and heraldic writer," who was editor and publisher, if not author, of the first edition of the English Peerage, in 1700, then lived at the Black Boy, in Fleet Street. EDWARD CURLL published several books "at the Dial and Bible, St. Dunstan's Church." BERNARD LINTOT was living here at the beginning of the last century; and the amiable Izaak Walton was a denizen of this district. The first edition of his "Angler" was published in 1653, in St. Dunstan's Church-yard, price 1s. 6d.—[A copy sold at Haworth's sale for thirteen guineas.]

*Michael Drayton*, the poet, died in a house near Saint Dunstan's Church, according to Aubrey. The same authority tells us that *Cowley*, the more voluminous author, was the son of a grocer in this street. *T. Snelling*, who drew, engraved, and published numerous plates on *English Coins*, had a shop in this street, where he dealt in those, in medals, &c.

Branching off from Fleet Street, to the south, is Bouverie Street, at the bottom of which my once much-esteemed and confidential friend JAMES MOYES, built large premises for a printing establishment, after the destruction, by fire, of his former offices in Greville Street. Here he produced numerous literary works for different publishers, also some for private friends, and was in an extended and respectable way of business, when the severe commercial panic of 1826 involved him, with several of his friends, in bankruptcy. The shock was much more severe to his susceptible nerves, and high sense of honour, than the former calamity. His mental and coporeal faculties seemed paralyzed for some weeks, and his friends were alarmed; but rallying, and aided by a few gentlemen who knew his integrity of principle and moral worth, he took new premises in Castle Street, Leicester Square, where he progressively obtained a large amount of business, and was prosperous and happy, until death arrested his career in 1838, at the age of 59. He was interred in a vault in the cemetery of Kensal Green, where a marble slab is placed to his memory. Intimately acquainted with this honourable tradesman for a quarter of a century, I can conscientiously assert that he fully deserved the encomium Pope applies to "the noblest work of God"—an honest man. I never knew a person more widely and uniformly esteemed. In business, he actively and zealously endeavoured to secure the confidence and good opinion of every employer; and, I believe, was always successful. As a man, he was well informed, upright, kind-hearted, and generous both in word and deed, and as completely exempt from the infirmities of poor human nature as any of his species. With such qualities, and a thorough knowledge of business, he must have attained a good fortune in a few years.

He printed different literary works for me, entirely to my satisfaction and to his own credit. Besides being employed by many respectable publishers, he printed "The Literary Gazette" and "Fraser's Magazine" for many years; also several successive volumes of "The Gems of Beauty," "Friendship's Offering," and other works, under the editorship of Lady Blessington. He also worked for the Admiralty and for other public offices; and produced two handsome and beautifully printed books for J. H. WIFFIN, of "Jerusalem Delivered," and "Historical Memoirs of the House of Russell," in two vols. royal octavo. This led to a connection with John, Duke of Bedford,* for whom Mr. Moyes printed different works, on the pictures, statues, grasses, ferns, &c. at Woburn Abbey. I have now before me letters from this truly generous nobleman, also from Lady Blessington, Mr. Wiffin,† and others, expressing approbation of his works, and thanking him for skill and kind attentions.

In *Bolt Court* was the printing-office of THOMAS BENSLEY, which attained marked distinction at the end of the last century and beginning of the present. It was here that Mr. Konig's *printing machinery* was first employed, and advanced towards perfection; and from this office issued, in 1797, a magnificent royal folio edition of Thomson's "Seasons." Here also were printed Macklin's Bible and many other fine books; likewise my fourth volume of Architectural Antiquities, and the History of Redcliffe Church. These premises, like too many

---

\* Of this truly estimable and generous Nobleman, I shall be induced, in a subsequent page, to relate a few particulars of his devotion to literature, art, and science.

† Though I have been acquainted with several Quakers, I never met with one who was more sincere, candid, warm-hearted, and unsophisticated, and who united with these qualifications the susceptibility of the poet with the perseverance and discrimination of the faithful historian. His "Memoirs of the House of Russell," which were printed by Mr. Moyes in 1832, will justify these remarks, and will derive further confirmation by his translation of Tasso's "Jerusalem Delivered," with a series of beautifully-executed engravings in wood, also in two smaller volumes. He produced a volume of Miscellaneous Poems, under the title of "Aonian Hours," and other poetry. Mr. Wiffin was Librarian to John, Duke of Bedford, in which honourable office he died, in May 1836, in the prime of life, much beloved by all who knew him. A well-written account of his personal and literary character is preserved in the *Literary Gazette*, May 1836. He has been succeeded by John Martin, formerly in partnership with Mr. Rodwell, of Bond Street, and who, in 1834, published "A Bibliographical Catalogue of Privately-printed Books," a handsome and curious volume.

other printing-offices of London, suffered by fire: first, on the fifth of November, 1807, when they were much damaged, with several works, by a fire supposed to have been occasioned by careless boys. Again, June 1819, the whole, with their valuable contents, were consumed in or materially injured by another conflagration.

RED LION PASSAGE, at the end of the last century and beginning of the present, was familiar to a large class of readers of the *Gentleman's Magazine*,* and to every topographer and antiquary in England, by the spacious printing-office of *John Nichols*; and the many publications issuing therefrom. I was indulged by my venerated and kind friend, the "Deputy of Farringdon Ward," with the use of any books in his valuable topographical library, but none were to be taken away; for he justly remarked, these were his working-tools almost in daily demand. I found them invaluable to me at a time when my own stock was very small—when the reading-room of the British Museum was not easily accessible, and when I had engaged to write and print "The Beauties of Wiltshire;" and also, in conjunction with my literary coadjutor, Mr. Brayley, Topographical Accounts of Bedfordshire, Berkshire, and Buckinghamshire, for the first volume of "The Beauties of England." This courtesy, however, proved of great benefit, as was also the personal intercourse and converse with the author of the "History of Leicestershire," in eight folio volumes, his valuable "Literary Anecdotes," in nine volumes, with two of indexes, and of other similar works. Here I occasionally saw Richard Gough, who was a frequent visitor; and here I also had glances of other eminent topographers and antiquaries, who employed the same respected printer and author. Some years afterwards, I was honoured and gratified by friendly intimacy with most of the personages to whom I then looked up with awful respect and admiration. They are all removed from this

---

* This veteran, respectable, and truly valuable periodical has continued its monthly course from 1731 to the present time; and it is a singular part of its history that it was commenced by a journeyman printer, and for ninety-six years continued under the editorship of three. In accordance with the spirit of the times, this venerable journal has now all the freshness, vigour, beauty and interest, which good writing, paper, and typography can impart.

terrestrial sphere, but have left their names, and varied qualifications, indelibly recorded in the lasting pages of their respective publications. With Mr. Nichols, I continued on friendly terms from the end of the last century to the time of his death, Nov. 26, 1826.* By a fall in Red Lion Passage, in January 1807, he fractured a thigh-bone, by which he was lamed for life; and in February of the following year he suffered severely from a calamitous fire, which destroyed his premises, and a large stock of paper, printed books, manuscripts, &c. At the time of my early communion with Mr. Nichols, his son *John Bowyer*, was taken into partnership, and continued so for nearly a quarter of a century. In such an office and its associations, it is not surprising that he became an antiquary and topographer as well as printer; and that his son, *John Gough*, should be one of the most devoted, zealous, and learned amongst the present numerous class of archæologists.

A. J. VALPY, M.A., a son of the learned Dr. Valpy of Reading School, after being a short time in Tooke's Court, removed to the more spacious offices vacated by Mr. Nichols, in which he executed, besides many other works, the "*The Delphin Classics*," with the Variorum Notes. These extended to 141 volumes, which were charged 18*s.* each, and in large paper, £1. 16*s.* He also printed, for different publishers, many other books both in Greek and Latin, and not only employed some of the most learned compositors that could be obtained, but several scholars from the Universities, to read and correct the proof-sheets. Hence the Valpy office and press obtained high distinction in the learned world. Mr. Valpy retired from business in the prime of life, to enjoy "otium cum dignitate."

Nearly opposite to the printing-office last referred to was a small house occupied by STEPHEN JONES, a gentleman with whom I was on familiar terms for many years. He was Secretary to a Freemasons' lodge, and was occasionally employed by some of the publishers to edit and arrange miscellaneous papers, make indexes, &c. He first

---

* From feelings of respect and the sincerest regard, I solicited my friend, John Jackson, R.A., in April, 1831, to make one of his beautifully-accurate portraits of this veteran topographer for me, to be engraved, and employed Charles Heath to translate the same, and perpetuate it on copper, for publication. This is a most faithful, expressive representation of the full, but cheerful, and spectacled features of a truly good man.

appeared, in 1791, as abridging Burke's "Reflections;" and two years afterwards his name was attached to an Abridgment of Ward's "Natural History," in 3 vols. In 1796 he produced "A Biographical Dictionary in Miniature," a copy of which he presented me, with his autograph: the first literary work I had then received, though I can now enumerate more than sixty volumes. He produced several other publications, which are specified in Watt's *Bibliotheca Britannica*, the last of which is "A Pronouncing Dictionary of the English Language," a large octavo volume. The third edition of the work, now before me, has the author's autograph, with the date of 1798. He also edited a new edition of the "Biographia Dramatica:" this was harshly criticised, when he published a pamphlet, entitled "Hypercriticism Exposed, in a Letter to the Readers of the Quarterly Review," 8vo. 1812.

Towards the end of life, my respected friend, a man of mild disposition, strict honesty, great industry, and unblemished character, was embarrassed in circumstances, applied to, and derived pecuniary aid from, the Literary Fund. Dr. N. Drake, in a letter to Cadell and Davies, respecting his large work, "Shakspeare and His Times," says, "S. Jones was the compositor to my Essays on Periodical Literature, and I was perfectly satisfied with his accuracy and attention;" whence he strongly recommended him to those publishers to make the index to his two quarto volumes. It extends to six quarto sheets.

In *New Street* and *New Street Square* are the large and famed printing-offices of STRAHAN, "the King's Printer," who obtained great wealth, and at whose presses an immense number of books have been printed. Among these was the *Cyclopædia*, edited by my early and much-loved friend, Dr. A. Rees, and for which I wrote many a closely-packed page. Besides accounts of nearly all the cities, towns, and counties of England, Wales, and Scotland, I wrote separate articles on Avebury and Stonehenge, with illustrative prints, and a memoir of Shakspeare. With copy and proofs I had frequent communication with one of the offices, for there were several, and witnessed the order, discipline, and admirable system which prevailed. The liberality and riches of Andrew Strahan, Esq., who died in August 1831, render his name illustrious in the annals of man. In 1822, he presented £1000 to the Literary Fund, and bequeathed a similar sum after his decease, in the year 1831. He also gave other large sums to different charitable societies. He died, in the 83rd year of his age, at his house in New Street, leaving property to the amount of above one million of money; and presented his great printing establishment to his nephew, Andrew Spottiswoode, who married one of the daughters of Mr. T. N. Longman, of Paternoster Row.

In Chancery Lane, north of Fleet Street, was a shop which WILLIAM PICKERING gave name and note to by publishing many valuable volumes under the titles of "Aldine Edition of the Poets;" "Walton and Cotton's Angler," and other books on the subject; Richardson's Dictionaries of the English Language; Greek, Latin, Italian, and Diamond Classics; and several works on Ecclesiastical, Biblical, and Polemical History; on Anglo-Saxon and Anglo-Norman Literature; "Small Books on Great Subjects, by Well-Wishers to Knowledge;" and last, though not least in merit and popularity, the novel, unique, and original *Bridgewater Treatises*, in 12 volumes. These were by *Sir Charles Bell*, on the Hand; *the Rev. William Buckland, D.D.*, on Geology and Mineralogy; *the Rev. Thomas Chalmers, D.D.*, on the Moral and Intellectual Constitution of Man; *John Kidd, M.D.*, on the Physical Condition of Man; *the Rev. William Kirby*, on the History, Habits, and Instincts of Animals; *William Prout, M.D.*, on Chemistry, Meteorology, and the Function of Digestion; *P. M. Roget, M.D.*, on Animal and Vegetable Physiology; and *the Rev. W. Whewell*, on Astronomy and General Physics.

These Essays were written by the respective learned authors, in compliance with a bequest of *Francis Henry, Earl of Bridgewater*, in February 1829, of £8000. to be paid for eight Treatises "On the Power, Wisdom, and Goodness of God, as manifested in the Creation." Never, perhaps, in the annals of the human race, and of testamentary generosity and rightful application, was a legacy more wisely and laudably given. It was Mr. Pickering's good fortune to be selected as the publisher of the series, whence his house and character were prominently brought under the notice of the reading world. In 1843 he removed to 177, Piccadilly, where may be seen a house full of rare and valuable books, and where may be obtained many of those he had printed and published, under the editorial care, learning, and ability of Sir Harris Nicolas, Basil Montagu, the Rev. W. L. Bowles, S. W. Singer, the Rev. Alexander Dyce, the Rev. J. Mitford, J. H. Marsden, Thomas Wright, Robert Roscoe, George Daniel, W. Tooke, the Rev. Dr. T. F. Dibdin, and many other authors of eminence.

Let us look at a "Pen and Ink Sketch" of Mr. Pickering by the last-named reverend gentleman, in his own peculiar style of touch and effect. "How does Mr. Pickering this morning? and where are the Caxtons, and Wynkyns, and Pynsons—his Alduses, Elzevirs, and Michel Le Noirs? But Mr. Pickering has a note of louder triumph to sound, in being publisher of the BRIDGEWATER TREATISES, which bid fair to traverse the whole civilized portion of the globe."—[*Reminiscences*, p. 904.]

From Chancery Lane to High Holborn is a mere step, and there, at No. 59, is a house, which was built by JOSIAH TAYLOR, *the Architectural Bookseller*, with whom I became acquainted at the early part of my literary career, and with whom I fortunately continued on intimate terms to the time of his lamented death, January, 1834. In 1805, I showed him some drawings of ancient buildings which Mr. Hood thought were not calculated to adorn the pages, and come under the title, of "The Beauties of England." After a little consultation and deliberation, it was agreed to publish a new quarto work, entitled "*The Architectural Antiquities of Great Britain*." A plan was digested, a prospectus was written, Longman and Co. engaged to take a third share in the work, and be the publishers. Hence originated a publication, which not only extended to five quarto volumes, and brought before the public 360 engravings, representing a great variety of old buildings of the country, but many of historical, descriptive, and critical essays. These were not by my own pen only, but by those of several gentlemen, who thus laid before the reading world much original and interesting information. This work, indeed, gave origin to a new school of artists, both draftsmen and engravers, and to many competing and rival publications. It obtained great popularity, and was consequently profitable to the publishers and to the author. Had the latter been a little more the man of business, and more anxious to obtain wealth than fame, he might have been enabled to retire from the labours and anxieties of authorship at the age of eighty, with competence to provide all the comforts, and even some of the luxuries of life. His chief solicitude and ambition, throughout the whole extent of that and other publications, have been to render them truthful, original, correct, and replete with the best artistic illustrations and literary information which he could obtain and impart to the reader. His partners were confiding and kind, upon most occasions; and Mr. Taylor evinced his friendship by a posthumous bequest. Mr. O. Rees proved himself a warm and even affectionate friend throughout life.— See *ante*, p. 264, for a notice of his character.

Mr. Taylor was a punctilious, persevering, and honourable man of business, and confined his attention, and publications almost exclusively to those devoted to architecture and engineering. Hence he became acquainted with most of the professional gentlemen of the kingdom, published for many of them, and was connected in business with nearly all. Thus we find that his catalogue of works contains the following, amongst other, names: Stuart and Revett, Soane, Malton, G. Richardson, Peter Nicholson, Lugars, Gwilt, Pocock, Dearn, Gandy, Aikin, Plaw; and the following on *Gothic Architecture*, the Rev. G. D. Whittington, the *Rev. J. Milner*, the Rev. James Dallaway, the *Rev. Joseph Warton, James Bentham, Captain Grose*, the Rev. J. Gunn, the Rev. George Millers, and J. S. Hawkins. The Essays, by those whose names are in italics, were published by Mr. Taylor in a separate volume, which went through three editions.

Towards the latter part of his life he purchased a good house at Stockwell, where he was in the habit of assembling frequently a succession of friends around his social board; and there I have often met, and enjoyed the converse of, some of the most eminent architects and engineers of London. On those occasions it was his practice to send a carriage to and from London to convey two, three, or four gentlemen who did not keep carriages. In the year 1822 the house and shop, in Holborn, with their contents, were consumed by an accidental fire, whereby I sustained a considerable loss. Mr. Taylor died at the age of 73, in the year 1834, and was buried in Bunhill Fields cemetery.

THE STRAND, at the end of the last century and beginning of the present, when a much narrower street than it is now, and when Exeter 'Change occupied a large area of the road-way between the present Lyceum Theatre and Exeter Street, contained several booksellers and publishers of distinction. Amongst these was the house of Alderman THOMAS CADELL, which occupied the site of old Jacob Tonson's, (the Shakspeare Head). Andrew Miller, a friend of Thomson, Fielding, Hume, Robertson, was the master of Alderman Cadell.—I, again, avail myself of the following notice by my friend Dr. Thomas Rees.

[At the period to which my notes chiefly relate, Alderman Thomas Cadell was living in the Strand, and I had the pleasure of being occasionally in his society. He resigned the business to his Son and to William Davies, jointly, who long traded under the well-known firm of "Cadell and Davies." The Alderman was accustomed to say that he was chiefly indebted for his prosperity to the works of four *Bees*, alluding to four popular publications: "Blair's Sermons," "Blackstone's Commentaries," "Burn's Justice of the Peace," and "Buchan's Domestic Medicine." Johnson's "Dictionary," and Hume and Smollett's "History of England," were also amongst the valuable copyrights belonging to this firm. In reference to the two publications last-mentioned, this establishment, in conjunction with Longman and Co., who were part proprietors with them in those and other works, had to encounter a vigorous opposition from other booksellers when the copyrights expired; but their operations were so judiciously and promptly conducted that they effectually maintained their ground. The "Dictionary" had been published in two costly volumes, folio; and when the copyright was about to expire, an edition in one folio volume was prepared, with great secrecy, by a bookseller in Paternoster Row. The proprietors of the book hearing of that scheme, prepared an edition in two quarto volumes, which, being of a more commodious form, at once became a popular work, and obtained a rapid sale: whereas the rival undertaking involved the speculator in a serious loss.*

---

* The quarto edition, being published at £5. 5s., produced a considerable profit to the shareholders, who were proportionably tenacious of maintaining its integrity. One of them, however, the managing partner, happening to say vauntingly in the presence of Mr. Childs, an energetic printer at Bungay, that the partners would ruin any one

The standard octavo edition of the "History of England" was issued by Cadell and the Longmans, in anticipation of opposition, in periodical numbers, embellished with portraits. Both Cooke and Parsons, nevertheless, entertained the project of duodecimo editions, without prints; but the proprietors forestalled them by a similar edition, with reduced copies of the engravings. The rival publishers proceeded, however, with their respective undertakings, and so great was the sale of the works, that each edition reimbursed its expenses.]*

Near the middle part of the ever-crowded, noisy, tumultuous thoroughfare called the STRAND, is the very focus—the hot-bed, the forcing-house—of the *Newspaper-Press*, now emphatically called "*The Fourth Estate.*" † This literary manufactory and news-mart may be almost regarded as exemplifying the perpetual motion. From dawn to night, and thence to dawn again, here is a continued, never-ceasing succession of editors and sub-editors, reporters of various topics, correspondents from foreign states, and from the provinces, merchants and

---

who set up a rival edition, he forthwith stereotyped and reprinted the entire work in a single volume, imperial 8vo. (now currently sold for 18s.) and employing that indefatigable and unscrupulous agent, the late John Ogle Robinson, (formerly of the firm Robinson, Hurst, and Co.) a large and remunerative sale was speedily obtained, and the quarto was consequently much depreciated.—J. B.

* By a volume of Autograph Letters and Papers, one of a series now before me, belonging to my friend, Mr. John Wodderspoon, I find that the above-named firm embarked a large capital, at great risk, on Dr. Drake's "Shakspeare and his Times;" Lysons's "Magna Britannia," and Samuels' "Britannia Romana;" G. Chalmers's "Caledonia;" Alexander Chalmers's "British Poets," 21 vols. royal 8vo.; Coxe's Works, (mostly written by Henry Hatcher) Dr. Clarke's Travels, and several other expensive publications. By memoranda amongst this correspondence, it is also evident that they acted with much courtesy and liberality to those authors. Dr. Drake was paid £800. for his two volumes; and in a statement of accounts it seems that the losses were above £900. The works by the Lysonses entailed a great loss on the respectable publishers. Hence we learn that, after their decease, a large stock of unsold books came into the market, and were dispersed at very low prices.—J. B.

† A very interesting work, in two volumes, made its appearance, with this title, in 1851, by F. Knight Hunt, containing "Contributions towards a History of Newspapers, and of the Liberty of the Press." The reader is also referred to the third edition of a small, but fully charged volume, "The Newspaper-press Directory, containing full Particulars relative to each Journal published in the United Kingdom and the British Isles," by Charles Mitchell, 1851, pp. 534.

manufacturers, politicians and players, compositors, pressmen, and engineers; also crowds of news-vendors and letter-carriers, with carts and horses to convey loads of wet Papers to railway stations. Could an inquiring and acute foreigner see and appreciate the whole working of this complicated machine, he would marvel, and vainly attempt to give a full and vivid account of it to his distant friends and countrymen. During the sitting of Parliament, and when warmly-contested party questions are under discussion, the activity and excitement in this region are only to be compared to a hive of bees, at the time of swarming. Unlike the generality of London business, that of the News-press is generally conducted during the night, and whilst most people are reposing in bed. Hence we see the windows of the offices fully lighted up, and hear the continued rattle and noise of steam machines and presses in ceaseless operation. I cannot reflect on the comparative and contrasted state of the Newspaper-press, in its mechanical and literary characteristics, as it was at the beginning of the century, when I was occasionally admitted into the editor's "sanctum," and as it is now, when such important reforms have been produced in all departments of paper, type, ink, and particularly in machinery; but still more in the independence and integrity, the vigour and comprehensiveness of editorial writings, without feeling astonished and delighted. It is these improvements and powers which have conspired to gain for the English Press the political title above-named. To the late James Perry, John Walter,[*] Thomas

---

[*] Mr. Walter's career, opinions, and intense perseverance in advancing "The Times" from a journal of common-place influence to that of staunch independence and irresistible power, have been recorded in a copy of that paper which was published immediately after his decease (28th July, 1847). I have been informed that the matter was mostly written before his death, put in type, "kept standing," the concluding part inserted and the sheet worked after his death. Mr. Walter's courage and resolute determination in resisting ministerial influence, and in establishing the press machinery to work 8000 copies in an hour, in opposition to the tyranny of the one, and the combination of workmen connected with the press, of the other, is among the glorious achievements of private heroism and patriotism, which cannot fail to obtain the sympathy and admiration of all persons in all times. I must again refer to "The Fourth Estate," vol. ii., p. 165, &c., for particulars of Mr. Walter's character and indomitable energies in the cause of English literature. In that work the reader will find a detailed account of the weekly expenses of a daily paper, and many interesting particulars of the life and career of my much-respected friend, James Perry.

Barnes, and a few other talented and honest men, much of these effects are to be ascribed; and I indulge the hope that others of like powers may continue in the same ranks, and act as substantial checks against every species of tyranny and dishonesty in church and state, in law and commerce, and, indeed, in all gradations of civilized society.*

At No. 15, back of St. Clement's, Strand, "*The British Press*" and "*The Globe*" first made their public appearance in 1803, "with new and high pretensions," and were ostensibly started by, and intended to promote the views and trading speculations of, the publishing booksellers. These had justly complained of the capricious charges made by the Newspaper proprietors for advertisements, and also for the heedless manner in which notices of fine and expensive literary publications were associated with vile and disgusting quack puffs. To remedy such evils, and obtain a medium between themselves and the public, they procured premises, type, an editor, and the combined establishment for conducting a newspaper. George Lane was engaged as editor, who had been on the Morning Post, and the Courier, under Daniel Stuart.† By examining some early numbers of the "British Press," I cannot wonder that it failed to secure purchasers, and consequently did not answer the requirements of the speculators. Poor paper, bad printing, tasteless display, and inefficiency of editorship, are conspicuous. Mr. Lane acknowledges that "the actual sale did not exceed two hundred." The "British Press" proved a complete failure, and it was given up.

---

* For further remarks and opinions on this subject see my volume on Junius's Letters; also another I published in the year 1814, entitled "The Rights of Literature."

† This gentleman wrote an explanation of the dispute between the publishers and newspaper proprietors in the Gentleman's Magazine (Sept. 1838) to vindicate himself and his brothers of the periodical press, and impeach the former. Mr. George Lane, in the same magazine, published a reply and justification of the booksellers. Among the reforms and improvements which the present denizens of London have cause to rejoice in, when compared with their predecessors, who lived amidst and under numerous annoyances of savage warfare, may be specified the relief from ruthless gangs of street news-vendors, who infested the peaceable and nervous inhabitants with noises that surpassed bedlamites broke loose. Tin horns, of different calibre and sounds, mixed with yells and bawling of men and boys, in troops, who paraded the quiet streets proclaiming, "News! Great news! Bloody news! Armies slaughtered by thousands and tens of thousands:—*Currior!* Extraordinary *Currior!!* Sixth edition of *The Currior!!!* &c. &c.

The *Globe* was however continued, under new proprietary management, and is still among the diurnal journals. As already noticed, I wrote several articles for "The British Press."—[See Part II., p. 175.]

JOHN BELL, of the Strand.—Not only as an enterprising and spirited publisher, but as an author, this gentleman continued before the public many years, and brought forward a succession of literary and embellished works which gratified and gave profitable employ to numerous writers, artists, printers, stationers, &c. His "British Poets," "British Theatre," part of which includes the plays of Shakspeare; his "Weekly Messenger," commenced May, 1796; the "New Weekly Messenger," a paper of unprecedented quantity and varied literary matter, commenced in 1832; his "New Pantheon, or Historical Dictionary of Heathen Gods, Demi-Gods, Goddesses, &c.," which Lowndes calls "an excellent and useful compilation;" and his "Classical Arrangement of Fugitive Poetry," in 18 vols., were each and all variously popular, and calculated to gratify and improve the minds and taste of readers by their literary and graphic contents. In embellishments, he employed the best artists of the age, both for designs and for engravings. He also produced a monthly periodical called "La Belle Assemblée."

RUDOLPH ACKERMANN, from Germany, settled in the Strand, opposite old Exeter 'Change, at the latter part of the last century, as a Printseller; and by perseverance, industry, and skill in business, with some knowledge of art, progressively advanced himself and his establishment to the highest degree of prosperity and credit. When I first became acquainted with him, in 1800, his shop was small, and his first floor was let to my friend, *George Holmes*, an artist, who was induced by my suggestion to publish, in 1801, an octavo volume, "Sketches of a Tour through the South Part of Ireland." The artist, though possessed of abilities and of very engaging manners, did not advance in life so fast as his landlord, who soon required and occupied the whole house, and increased his business, family, and fortune. He then moved to larger premises, at No. 101, Strand, which occupied part of the site of the old Fountain Tavern, celebrated in the days of Steele, Addison, Pope, &c. Here was also a famed drawing academy, in which Richard Cosway, F. Wheatley, Shipley, and others, afterwards men of fame, were pupils. The more noted lecture-room of

John Thelwall was also here. In 1825, Mr. Ackermann built the present large and commodious "Repository," at the corner of Beaufort Buildings, from the designs of Mr. Papworth. This building occupies the site of five previous houses. The new edifice was provided with a fine and spacious gallery, at the rear, in which were constantly on view a vast number and variety of works of art. The architect also made many designs, and wrote essays for Ackermann's Magazine. The shop, the staircases, the gallery, &c., were not only lighted but brilliantly illuminated by night, with gas, which was manufactured on the premises, from apparatus which Mr. Ackermann had invented, and which was supplied with Canal, or Kennel coal, producing the most vivid light. During the first winter, after these works were completed, crowds of the nobility, gentry, and artists, were in the habit of visiting the place every night, to see the splendid novelties. Once a week the proprietor opened his galleries for a Soirée, where I often met many of the most eminent artists and men of science of our own and of foreign countries. Amongst numerous interesting articles displayed on these occasions was a copy of the spirited proprietor's work on Westminster Abbey, printed on vellum and bound in two large volumes; one containing the letter-press, printed in Bensley's best manner, the other comprising proofs of the plates and the original drawings, also skilfully mounted. The binding, of the most sumptuous kind, alone cost Mr. Ackermann nearly three hundred pounds! This very splendid work is now in the possession of *John Allnut, Esq.*, of Clapham, whose gallery of pictures by English Artists not only reflects honour on his taste and liberality, but on his patriotism.

This article alone serves to give some notion of the liberal and enterprising disposition of the amiable and estimable German, who manifested a corresponding liberality and enthusiasm in all his business speculations and intercourse with artists and literati. Mr. Shoberl tells me that he paid *William Combe* at least £400. a year for many successive years, and that he was often a guest at his table; that he proved a friend to him during his last illness, and not only contributed towards, but waited on several of his rich friends to solicit aid in the expenses for the funeral, tomb, &c.

To this improvident, indiscreet man, to T. Rowlandson, to W. H.

Pyne, and to several other persons, he was the warm and generous patron. Indeed in all his public dealings, as well as in private life, he displayed generosity, courtesy, frankness, sincerity, and unostentatious benevolence. After the disastrous, murderous, and devastating wars of the French Revolution, the Germans were reduced to the most distressing condition. Poverty and privation pervaded their towns, their villages, and their entire provinces. The English, as usual, afforded many of the emigrants homes and sustenance. To Mr. Ackermann they were indebted for a vast amount of aid and comfort. He took a most active and zealous part in obtaining subscriptions and remitting money to his countrymen. No less than £250,000. were collected for the sufferers in Great Britain, £100,000. of which were voted by Parliament; and as a proof of the effective service of my friend on this occasion, he was rewarded and honoured by the King of Saxony with the Cross of Civil Merit; whilst the King of Prussia, and several of the reigning Dukes of Germany, presented him with handsome testimonials in token of his valuable services.

As Cicerone to Mr. Ackermann's Gallery, my friend, *William Henry Pyne,** was engaged, and in that capacity was respectably and profitably employed, both for himself and for his worthy master. The former had published, and progressively produced numerous works, both graphic and literary, in all of which, from partialities and experience, Pyne became eminently useful. Hence the artist and the printseller worked in harmony and unison for some years, and jointly completed several publications on the fine arts, topography, and poetry. Besides several lessons, elementary books and prints, for the instruction of young artists, they brought forward a large and expensive work, entitled " The Microcosm of London," 3 vols. royal 4to. with 120 illustrative prints. To Mr. Ackermann we are indebted for the introduction into England, and for effecting many improvements in the new art, of *Lithography*, by translating and giving publicity to Senefelder's Treatise on the subject; a work that excited much curiosity, specula-

---

* Of this artist and author I possess letters and memoranda sufficient to make a goodly-sized volume; and one calculated to exhibit some of the eccentricities and fallacies of genius—which would " point a moral and adorn a tale." I must, however, defer them to another time and page.

tion, and experiments among the artists. He also imported stones for that novel process, and by adapting presses and paper, and by the employment of competent artists to make drawings, progressively, but slowly, advanced lithography to distinction.* He was the first publisher of a class of books, called *Annuals*, by his "Forget-me-Not,"† which became exceedingly popular, and was a source of employ to numerous artists, authors, and different tradesmen. His large and handsome volumes, with illustrations, of Westminster Abbey, of Cambridge, Oxford, and of Public Schools, were amongst the most beautiful topographical works of their class, in paper, typography, and embellishments. The writing, though anonymous, was by WILLIAM COMBE, one of the most extraordinary men of his age, and who ranks amongst the most prolific of authors.‡ The engravings were in aqua-

---

* The following lines were written by Mr. Combe on the first lithograph stone which Mr. Ackermann printed, when he had prepared every thing for working:

"I have been told of one
Who, being ask'd for bread,
In its stead
Return'd a Stone:

"But here we manage better;
The Stone, we ask
To do its task,
And it returns us every letter."
"Wm. Combe, January 23, 1817."

† This was edited, from its commencement in 1823, to its last volume in 1834, by F. SHOBERL, one of the most industrious, persevering, and honourable of the literary fraternity, who has been solely, or mostly, dependant on his profession for a livelihood. Watt, in *Bibliotheca Britannica*, has given a long list of his publications, in translations from the French and German, original and compilations, from 1800 to 1814, since which year he has written a further and longer list of works: amongst others I perceive that his name is attached to the histories of the counties of Suffolk, Surrey, and Sussex, forming one of the volumes of "The Beauties of England."

A history of this literary family—"the Annuals"—would embrace much curious anecdote, biography, and exposition of art and artists; of professional and amateur authors; of trade, manufactures, and commerce; of fashion, fame, and frivolity; and last, though not the least, the fluctuation and caprices of taste and *ton*. The Annuals, which were so popular and profitable to a Heath, and a Fisher, twenty years ago, are now superseded, and a totally different and new species has been introduced by Messrs. Longman and Co. and by Virtue; in which topography, history, travels, and substantial literature are the basis.

‡ Though I was never on intimate terms with this talented and eccentric person, I knew him personally by meeting him often at the houses of my friends, the Ackermanns, and James Lonsdale, portrait-painter of Berners Street. Combe was of good family connection, had received a classical education at Eton and Oxford, and very

tint, and coloured in imitation of the original drawings, by Mackenzie, Pugin, W. Westall, F. Nash, W. Turner, and others: many of them represent interior views of the principal public buildings. There are

---

early came into the possession of a large fortune, in ready money. To dash at once into high life, and enact the fashionable gentleman, he (according to his own narration) took a large mansion at "the West End" of London, furnished and filled it with gorgeous articles, and also hired servants, bought carriages, &c., and successively assembled around him a crowd of sycophants and the "beau-monde." This comedy, or rather farce, lasted only for a short time, and it is said that from the commencement to the drop-scene of the ridiculous drama, was not more than one year. Though he fancied this gave him an insight into high life, it is quite evident that the company thus assembled, and thus held together, could only be of a class which ought to rank below the low —gamblers, swindlers, tricksters, imposters, &c. The consequence was ruin—complete, disgraceful ruin, and Combe fled from his creditors and from society. We next hear of him as a common soldier, and recognized at a public-house with a volume of Greek poetry in his hand. He was relieved from this degrading situation, and henceforward, for a long period, the annals of his life have been pretty fully detailed. The walls of the King's Bench Prison, and "the Rules" of that famed establishment, were the limits and sphere of his locomotion; and from his conduct, manners, and general deportment in society, they do not appear to have proved causes of much punishment or lamentation. Horace Smith, in the Memoirs of his witty and much-caressed brother, James, says, that Colonel Greville, with several of his friends, established a Pic-nic club for theatrical amusements, &c., and published a newspaper to vindicate their association from severe strictures that appeared in the daily papers against them. Our imprisoned hero was appointed the paid editor, and, to suit his peculiarity of situation, the weekly meetings of the writers of articles were held after dark. Horace Smith, who knew Combe, justly remarks, that "a faithful biography of this singular character might justly be entitled a romance of real life; so strange were the adventures and the freaks of fortune of which he had been a participator and a victim. A ready writer of all-work for the booksellers, he passed all the latter portion of his time within "the Rules," to which suburban retreat the present writer was occasionally invited, and never left him without admiring his various acquirements, and the philosophical equanimity with which he endured his reverses." Mr. Smith further asserts, that if there was a lack of matter occasionally to fill up the columns of their paper, "Combe would sit down in the publisher's back room and extemporize a letter from Sterne at Coxwold, a forgery so well executed that it never excited suspicion." I cannot but regret that my witty friend had not favoured us with more anecdotes of, and remarks on, the character and literary talents of Combe; but I can easily excuse him when I reflect on the superabundance of material which his memory and his memoranda must have afforded for the two amusing volumes he had planned of his brother's memorable "sayings and doings." Were I disposed to dwell on the character of Combe, I could extend the present note to several pages. He was born in 1741, and died in June 1814. Sub-

also several prints of full-length portraits from drawings by T. Uwins, and etchings by J. Agar, representing the official costume of all the different orders of Officers of the Universities. Mr. Ackermann also brought out a Poetical Magazine, which became the parent of a race of novel publications of unprecedented notoriety. These were a sort of hybrid twins of poetry and art, in the illustrated, or rhyming, rambling, ricketty, and ridiculous poems, "DR. SYNTAX's Tour in Search of the Picturesque." The work not only passed through several editions, of three Tours, but extended to three volumes; and within the last few years they have been again brought before the public at reduced prices by Mr. H. G. Bohn. "Dr. Syntax" was a lucky and large prize in the lottery of publication, and was also a novelty in origin and writing. Instead of the composition and designs for the illustrations growing out of, and serving to ornament and give tangible forms, figures, colours, effects, &c., to the language and imaginings of the poet, or other writer; the artist, in the work referred to, preceded the author by making a series of drawings; in each of which he exhibited his hero in a succession of places, and in various associations, calculated to exemplify his hobby-horsical search for the picturesque. Some of these drawings, by the versatile and ingenious artist, Rowlandson, were shown at a dinner-party, at John Bannister's, in Gower Street, when it was agreed they should be recommended to Ackermann for publication. That gentleman readily purchased, and handed them by two or three at a time to Combe, when the latter was in the King's Bench. He fitted them with rhymes, and they made their first appearance in the magazine alluded to. Exciting much popularity, the publisher reproduced them in separate volumes, and found demand keep pace with his supply. Hence Syntax was succeeded by "The Dance of Life,"

---

sequent to his death, a small volume was published, entitled "Letters to Marianne," said to have been written by him after the age of seventy to a young girl, and, according to the *Literary Gazette*, are trivial, silly, puerile. However eventful and amusing may be the adventures and vicissitudes of such a man as Combe, if narrated by a Dickens, a Thackeray, or a Douglas Jerrold, I must resign the task to such vivid writers, or their followers, and merely refer to the *Gentleman's Magazine*, for May 1852, for a communication from my friend, Mr. R. Cole, who has a large collection of Autograph Letters and Manuscripts, amongst which is a detailed list of the literary works of, and numerous interesting letters from and to Combe.

"The Dance of Death," "Johnny Quæ Genus," and "Tom Raw the Griffin," all of the same class and character, and ultimately extending to two hundred and ninety-five prints, with annotatory poetical letter-press.

Without adverting further, in this place, to the periodical press and publishers, generally, I cannot forbear to notice two weekly journals which had their birth in this locality, and which have proved themselves resolute and powerful advocates of moral, political, and literary reforms: viz., THE EXAMINER, and the Literary Gazette. The former was projected and undertaken by two enthusiastic young men, almost boys, JOHN and LEIGH HUNT, who thought patriotism and literature were the only things worth living for; and believing themselves not only slighted, but oppressed by the rulers of the land, thought that it would be glorious, either to obtain emancipation, or suffer martyrdom in the attempt. They paid dearly for their rashness and courage, as may be seen fully set forth, with honest candour and truthfulness, by the latter, in his Auto-Biography, in 3 vols., published in 1850, to which work I can refer the reader, with an assurance that he will find much amusing as well as eloquent and exciting commentary on the popular events and persons of the half-century after the year 1800.

Amongst the literary persons of the present century, that voluminous author ranks in the first class. From boyhood (for he was a precocious poet), up to the present time (1853), his whole time and mental energies appear to have been employed in literature; and the amount, variety, and merits of his numerous published writings are at once manifestations of industry, enthusiasm, zeal, an ardent love of liberty, and of the better productions of genius and talent. His first volume, intituled "Juvenilia," was a series of poems written between the ages of twelve and sixteen. It appeared in the year 1801, when, I believe, he was in "The Blue-Coat School," and a contemporary with the two brilliant intellectual planets in the hemisphere of talent, Coleridge and Lamb. The times when his first volume made its public appearance, when its author sought the approval of crictics and patrons, were rife with political excitement and contention. Party spirit was violent and rancorous; and every person who possessed warm feelings and thinking powers became imperceptibly a jacobin, or an anti-jacobin: i.e. a Reformer, or a Tory opposed to all changes. Mr. Leigh Hunt and his brother John avowed themselves of the former class, and started their "Examiner," as a medium to promulgate their sentiments, and oppose both the opinions and principles of the other party.

The consequence was, State prosecutions and consequent heavy fines, as well as cruel imprisonment. Unintimidated and unflinching, they continued to publish the *Examiner*, and also continued to occupy its weekly columns with severe and caustic writings on the malpractices of ministers, and on the vices and follies of those princes, nobles, and commoners, who lived and luxuriated on the revenues of the State.

One department of their paper was devoted to the *Fine Arts*, the criticisms and comments on which were mostly written by ROBERT HUNT, brother of the two partners. Related to Benjamin West, the President of the Royal Academy, and having been educated as an artist, this gentleman rendered his critical articles popular and influential. He wrote two or three Essays for me, which appeared in "The Fine Arts of the English School;" and also produced others for different publications.

THE LITERARY GAZETTE, which made its first appearance on the 25th of January, 1817, has proved eminently serviceable in promoting the national literature, as well as its fine arts. It was at first the property of *Mr. Colburn*, an active and enterprising publisher, who possessed "The New Monthly Magazine," and other works of popularity, and who eagerly availed himself of every channel to attract the notice, and excite the curiosity, of readers. A new medium was found in this Gazette, which not merely professed to advocate, but to bring forward the better specimens of literature, and scout and expose its quackery. It is generally admitted that it was almost constantly kind, generous, and complimentary to young aspirants for fame—in authorship, art, and the drama. I cannot, however, forget, or palliate the severity it manifested towards a youthful Poet of real genius and equal modesty, who ventured to launch a small volume on the "sea of troubles," and which was assailed by the Literary Gazette in unqualified terms of reprobation. The principal poem was "*Richmond Hill*," a site calculated to arouse the most intense admiration in every lover of the fine and beautiful scenery of nature. In his verses on this fascinating prospect,

I may safely assert that Charles Ellis evinced ardent feelings as well as genuine sympathies for the beauties of the scene, and also genuine, if not the highest, poetical powers to depict them.

The new periodical ultimately proved a large prize in the lottery of book-speculation, as it progressively rose high in the thermometer of fashion and fame. Its progress and fluctuating annals would afford abundance of interest to the general reader, were they fully and faithfully narrated. *Mr. William Jerdan,* who tells us in his Auto-Biography that he was its "sole editor and part-proprietor, from its commencement to August 14, 1841," has narrated many particulars of its contents, contributors, proprietors, and changes. To that work I must refer my reader, as well as for an account of the literary career and worldly vicissitudes of an old friend, with whom I have continued in occasional correspondence and personal intercourse for nearly forty years: I cannot, however, help deeply regretting to read his account of the profession of authorship; it being so much at variance with my own experience and opinions. These I have partly explained in the present work, also in "The Rights of Literature," in "The Authorship of the Letters of Junius Elucidated," and in other parts of my numerous publications. On referring to past volumes of the Literary Gazette, I always find them replete with valuable and interesting information on the contemporary literature, the fine arts, science, and the drama; also on the manners and customs of the constantly changing times from 1817 to 1850. The recent numbers of this weekly periodical show it to be conducted by an editor of science, candour, and literary talents.

The *Strand* has long been known as the place of congress of certain learned and eminent national societies, whose "Transactions" have travelled to, and been located and studied in, all the civilized cities of the globe. Those of the Royal, the Antiquaries, and the Astronomical, have free quarters within the government edifice of Somerset House; whilst the Society of Arts, in a noble mansion of its own, has taken root and prospered, in John Street, close to the Strand. The history of each and all of these societies is replete with interesting matter, not merely for the archæologist and scientific, but for the historian of man, in developing the progress of his intellectual qualifications. Mr. Weld has given to the public a well-digested history of that of the Royal, and it is hoped that other authors will shortly produce similar publications on their respective societies.

No. 32 in the Strand was a large print-shop, belonging to *Mr. Richardson*, whose extensive collection was noted for portraits, topographical and antiquarian prints, and for public sales of that class of property. In February and March, 1800, he sold an amazing collection of British portraits, which continued for thirty-one days, and which appears to have been accumulating for forty years. He was also employed on many other similar occasions to dispose of graphic works. During the winter he frequently had sales in the evening, which I often attended, and as often purchased "lots." Here I met several gentlemen, with whom I became intimate, from congeniality of attachments. Amongst these were Mr. Alexander, of the British Museum, Mr. Baker, of St. Paul's Church-yard, Mr. R. Holford, Mr. Bentham, Mr. Bindley, Dr. Gossett, Mr. Molteno, and several others, whose hoards have since been again brought to the hammer, and distributed to amuse other illustrators. Richardson published several portraits, fac-similes of scarce prints, and also three different-sized prints of the "Felton Shakspeare," as it is usually named. At his rooms were sold by auction the famed collections of Musgrave and of Tighe.

In the Strand were the shops of *Mr. Faden,*[*] *Mr. Cary*, and *Mr. Smith*, who entirely devoted themselves to Geography, by publishing Maps, Charts, Globes, &c. I often visited them to obtain and communicate information. The most important topographical surveys were published by Mr. Faden, but they were too expensive for my pocket. I always travelled with the best small map I could obtain, and marked in such alterations and corrections as I met with. These were handed

---

[*] This gentleman has been succeeded by *James Wyld*, *Esq.*, M.P., who has brought into the business more energy and enterprise than his predecessor, and has consequently produced great changes and improvements in his published works. As a feature of the times in which we live, we find that Mr. Wyld is a member of the Legislature, and a bold competitor with the daring and unparalleled Crystal Palace of 1851, by designing and constructing a building, with an exhibition to display the geographical surface of the terrestrial Globe. The invention and the execution are honourable to his name and country; and it is hoped that it will reward his enterprise.

over to the publishers above-named, and consequently inserted in new impressions of their respective plates. The Trigonometrical and the Ordnance Surveys were not published when I walked round Wales, into Cornwall, and through some other districts. These truly important national works are now produced, and, being sold at very low prices, are of incalculable value to modern antiquaries and topographers.

Near the western end of the Strand, on the North side, was the house of a Mr. Baxter, having in the rear a large Room, which he let out for private theatricals, for debates, and for readings and music. His wife possessed a fine soprano voice, played well on the piano-forte, and occasionally performed on the stage. At this place I became acquainted with *George Saville Carey*, who published a small volume called "Balnea, or Sketches of Watering-places," 1799, which, I believe, was the first work that gave a general account of those famed places of fashionable resort; and it would be interesting to show the extent, population, &c., of Bath, Brighton, Leamington, Margate, and Buxton, as they were when that volume was published, and as they now are. Carey wrote a volume on "Mimicry," and was famed for his Imitations of Garrick, Henderson, Kemble, Mrs. Siddons, and others. I have a vivid recollection of the mellow, flexible voice, and expressive intonations of Garrick, as well as the dull, phlegmatic, monotonous tones of Kemble, as Carey displayed them: one was mellifluous to the ear, the other grating and discordant, though not quite so bad as Coleman describes it in his famed Preface to *The Iron Chest* —"a crow in a quinsey." Carey contended that his father wrote "God Save the King;" but his statement is confuted by the Rev. Richard Clark, of Westminster Abbey, who asserts, and has produced authority to show, that it was composed by Dr. John Bull, who wrote it for, and that it was performed at, a public concert at Merchant Tailors' School, London, on the 16th of July, 1607.* In Mr. Baxter's room, I occasionally appeared in the reading-desk, and also as one of the speakers, or rather talkers, on some debated question; and I well remember that Mr. Gale Jones, who was the founder and manager of the society,

---

* In "The Musical World; a Magazine of Essays, &c., on Musical Science," for Dec. 5 and 19, 1839, and Feb. 13, 1840, are letters from Mr. Clark on the subject.

praised me for the matter and manner of my remarks.* "Readings and Music" were popular sources of amusement in London, about fifty years back; and I not only exhibited myself at the place described, but at a large room in Foster Lane, in another at the Globe, Fleet Street, and, lastly, in two others at the Freemasons' Hall, and in the Argyle Rooms.†

---

* It was on the subject of the *Slave Trade*, then much discussed both in Parliament and in public. I had read a good deal about it, and consequently was ardently prejudiced in the cause. Sermons, Essays, Poetry, History, Debate, were variously and numerously employed to rouse the passions and judgment of the public against the barbarous and horrible traffic. The letters of Sterne and of Ignatius Sancho were familiar to me, and warmed my enthusiasm. The history, amiable character, and literary tact of the latter excited my warmest sympathy, and prepossessed me in behalf of black skin and the ever-curled hair. I longed to know and love such a man as Sancho. Experience is the only correction of prejudice. In 1815, I was introduced, at a Freemasons' Lodge, to PRINCE SANDERS, a complete negro, who was said to be an agent from Christophe, King of Hayti, and who had obtained access to, and the patronage of the Duke of Sussex, W. Wilberforce, and other persons of note. This was a passport even to Freemasons and to fashionable society. The "Prince" became popular, was lionized in the metropolis, lived in a gay style, told artists and authors that he was commissioned by "his royal master" to engage several of both classes to emigrate and settle in Hayti, where the King would confer fortune and fame on them. Some were tempted to send specimens of their respective works; and I became one of Mr. "Prince" Sanders's dupes, by confiding to his *friendly* charge fine-paper copies of three volumes, valued at £25. Of these I never heard more; but found that my new friend, in whom I had no suspicion of roguery, continued to visit and be visited by several distinguished persons, from the West End of London. He resided in the vicinity of Tavistock Square, and one night assembled, at a Soirée, a large party of nobles, gentry, and ladies, amongst whom were the Duke of Sussex, Mr. Wilberforce, and other personages of rank. Before he quitted London, he published an octavo volume, with his portrait engraved by Charles Turner. Its title is: "By Authority. Haytian Papers: A Collection of the very Interesting Proclamations, and other Official Documents; together with some Account of the Rise, Progress, and Present State of the Kingdom of Hayti. With a Preface by Prince Sanders, Esq., Agent for the Haytian Government. London: printed for W. Reed, 17, Fleet Street." 8vo. 1816. This volume is a curiosity. I never heard what became of its editor, after he left London; but I learnt that several other persons, as well as myself, had been imposed on by him.

† These societies assumed pompous Greek names—"Museodeans," and "Odechorologeans,"—with parade and much etiquette, in aping the operatic customs and manners of theatric and ball-room concerts. The large rooms at both places were crowded with company, every night of performing; and amongst the performers were Miss Brunton, Miss F. Kelly, Miss S. Booth, Miss Bolton, &c.

Connected with the Strand are reminiscences of the Lyceum Theatre, with my public appearance on its stage, and in the stage-box; of Robert Ker Porter's exhibition of Seringapatam and other pictures; of the wonderful mimicry, ventriloquism, and transformations of *Monsieur Alexandre*,* the rival of Mathews; of Phillipstall's Phantasmagoria; and also of the "Sans Pareil Theatre," as it was called in 1806, when Mr. Scott, a colour-maker, built and fitted it up for his daughter, who made her first public appearance there, and gained much applause for songs and recitations. This lady's performances, united with mechanical and optical illusions, gave character to the house, and made the fortune of its proprietor. "Tom and Jerry," by Pierce Egan, afterwards attracted immense crowds, when the name of "Little Adelphi" was given to the theatre. In 1825 Terry and Yates became lessees, but lost money. *Charles Mathews* joined the latter, and continued to give his popular and profitable "At Home" here for three successive years. It was at this house I first became acquainted with that extraordinary actor, mimic, and man, and continued to meet him frequently afterwards. He was born in 1776, at No. 18 in the Strand, and died in 1835, after a long career of theatrical adventure, vicissitude, and fame. Among the numerous volumes of biography and auto-biography of the heroes and heroines of the sock and buskin, there is not one surpassing in variety, wit, and amusement, that of the eccentric and much-admired Charles Mathews. It is written jointly by the player and his widow, and extends to four volumes. A few pages only of the first are by the pen of the former, and the remainder is admirably executed by the latter.

At No. 145, Strand, were the book-shop and auction-rooms of Messrs. Leigh and Sotheby, at the beginning of the present century, in which many choice and costly books were transferred from one collector to another. After the decease of the first gentleman, the second continued the business for some years in the same street, and disposed of many celebrated libraries.† He has been succeeded by

---

* This gentleman has been noticed in a preceding part of this volume, page 150.

† Mr. Leigh was established as an auctioneer in King Street, Covent Garden, in 1744; and from that time to the present, the Catalogues, with prices and purchasers' names, are preserved by the present respectable firm in Wellington Street.

his worthy Son, who inherits many of the good points of his much-respected parent, and equally respected partner, retaining the names of both. Since the retirement of Mr. Evans, of Pall Mall, *Mr. Samuel Leigh Sotheby* has been most extensively occupied in selling distinguished libraries, and, I believe, with credit to himself and advantage to his employers. On comparing one of his recent catalogues, for Samuel Prout, with another printed for his godfather and father, in 1806, of nine days' sale of the library of one of my earliest literary friends, the Rev. Jonathan Boucher, the contrast is remarkable. The last exhibits bad type, bad ink, bad paper, and heedless editorship; whilst the former is the reverse in all these qualities: yet the Boucher Catalogue is charged 3s. 6d., and that of Prout's Collection was given away. Mr. Sotheby's partner (John Wilkinson) conducts the selling department with as much zeal and promptitude as the former manifests in arrangement, catalogueing, and in other parts of the business. Their rooms are now in Wellington Street.

In alluding to the *Auction-rooms* of the western part of London, it would seem negligent or invidious were I to omit two which have been justly eminent in credit and respectability for many years in the early part of the present century: those of ROBERT H. EVANS, No. 93, Pall Mall, and JAMES CHRISTIE, first in Pall Mall, and afterwards in King Street, St. James's. Brief notices of the numerous and various sales of books, MSS. and prints which have been distributed over the world by the first auctioneer, would extend to a large volume, and might be made particularly interesting to the lovers of literature. It would embrace accounts of a vast variety of valuable and important books, whose histories involve not merely their own intrinsic merits and peculiarities, but the fluctuations of prices and caprices of purchasers. Some have been highly prized and hoarded for their scarcity, (a lamentable criterion, as many of these "extremely rare" articles are worthless); others for being a trifle larger in the margin than another copy which has been pronounced the tallest; whilst a third quality is the possession of some cancelled leaf or print, which was originally deemed useless, or objectionable. I have often seen the large sale-room crowded by real lovers of literature, by collectors, by bibliographers, and by bibliomaniacs, and witnessed the enormous prices given for books, both of intrinsic beauty and merit, and of capricious worth. The Roxburgh, the Sykes, the Spencer, the Hibbert, the Dent, the Hoare, and the Broadley libraries were noted for their extent, value, scarcity, and for other peculiarities: some of these have been sold and resold by auction since their first appearance in a sale-room. Dibdin's "Library Companion," his "Bibliomania," and his "Reminiscences," contain much curious information on the subjects here referred to: and I must not omit to notice my respected friend Mr. Clarke's "Repertorium Bibliographicum," a large royal octavo volume of 1819, which contains much valuable and curious information on celebrated British libraries, and their choicest book-treasures.

*Mr. Christie's Sale-rooms*, in Pall Mall and in King Street, have been noted for more than half a century, as well for the high respectability and qualifications of the auctioneers, as for the vast amount and nature of the property they have exhibited. I have known three generations of the family, and had reason to esteem each and all. Though I saw but little of the first, who was famed for his bland and engaging manners and voice, as well as for his florid, spontaneous addresses, or panegyrics, yet I never see the exquisite portrait of him, in the counting-house of King Street, without emotions of admiration of the artist, and the auctioneer.* With the late *James Christie* I was familiarly acquainted, in his public and private characteristics; and though I occasionally lamented to see him in his auction-rostrum, surrounded by

---

* On referring to a Catalogue of "a most capital and precious assemblage of pictures" by Mr. Christie, Sen., whose "Great Room" was in Pall Mall, June 13th, 1807, I see a flourishing, and rather a Robins-like account of a small collection of only 44 pictures, each of which is highly eulogised. One of them, by Rembrandt, is described as "the finest picture, without exception, ever painted by that master." The Catalogue is marked 2s. 6d. George H. Christie succeeded his parent in 1831, in the same premises, and in the same career of high character, and in costly sales of works of art and vertu. In the same year Peter Coxe, author of "The Social Day," a poem, sold a small gallery of "original paintings, the property of Mr. Andrew Wilson," the Catalogue of which, marked 2s. 6d., contains a highly coloured advertisement, with comments on each "painting," also praised. He was brother of Archdeacon Coxe, and a popular auctioneer for some years. Amongst other sales was one of the Bowood collection of pictures, out of which I purchased three, by Sir Joshua Reynolds, Romney, and Wright, of Derby. The first and second were transferred to the Marquis of Stafford, and the third, half-length of the Marquis of Granby, to a gentleman of Devonshire.

unshaven and rude brokers, and sometimes subjected to the cant language of such "gents," I also saw him in the company of nobles of the land, and commoners of equally noble character.* With the latter, my amiable friend seemed " at home," and addressed them in language and manners which could not fail to propitiate their confidence and respect. More than once I have attended his sales, for the purpose of seeing certain fine pictures, and also to bid for some on account of friends. The celebrated series of Hogarth's " Election " I bought for Sir John Soane, at what was thought to be a large sum. The lot excited competition, and the auctioneer made occasional pauses and a few apposite and judicious remarks between the biddings. On knocking it down, he pronounced as neat and pointed an address to the successful candidate as ever was heard at any electioneering contest in the united kingdom.†

In King Street, Covent Garden, were the Auction-rooms of *King and Lochee*, chiefly devoted to books, in which I was first tempted to compete for a few topographical articles in 1800. It was the library of *Philip Luckombe*, who had published a small " History of Printing," in 1771; "A Tour in Ireland, in 1783;" and " England's Gazetteer," in 1790, in 3 volumes, 12mo.; also some other works; whence it appears that he had been connected with the press. His library, though small, contained Camden's *Britannia*, interleaved and illustrated; his own Gazetteer, interleaved, with MS. Notes; also other Topographical books. There being but little competition, I laid out about £20., and carried away a hackney coach load of literary materials for future reference and application.

At the same rooms, the Rev. Dr. Richard Farmer's large library had been sold in 1798; extending over thirty-six days.

---

The preceding notices of booksellers and publishers, with incidental anecdotes of authors and auctioneers, may, by some critical readers,

---

* Mr. Christie, Sen., died in 1805; and James Chistie, his Son, in 1831, aged 57.

† In my volume on "The Union of Architecture, Sculpture, and Painting" I have given some account of these four pictures; also a brief notice of Mr. Christie's learned volume, "Disquisitions upon the Painted Greek Vases," 4to. London, 1825. The latter evinces much classical discrimination and taste.

be deemed almost beyond the pale—the legitimate scope—of Auto-Biography. I reply, that my earliest aspirations, after engaging to write on Topography, were to cultivate the acquaintance of those persons, who either sold or collected books, prints, or other articles in that class of literature; and that I progressively and ultimately became familiar with most of the bibliopolists, print-sellers, and auction-rooms in the metropolis. My limited funds, however, precluded me from purchasing to a great extent; but I may safely aver that, from the year 1800 to 1850, there was not one olympic cycle passed without an increase of my library, in books, prints, and drawings. As already remarked, my fit of Bibliomania was first caught at the sale of the library of Philip Luckombe, when I obtained the " Britannia," with printed, manuscript, and graphic acccompaniments.

Thenceforward the disease increased in strength, and I continued to frequent nearly all the book sales of London, in which topography and antiquities constituted any distinguished portion. On these occasions, I not only became acquainted with eminent collectors, but also obtained some knowledge of the relative merits and value of books. Unlike many of my associates at these competing marts, I never sought to possess works which were valued and purchased merely from rarity, or dimensions of margin. Fine paper and good prints I coveted, and sometimes bought. Under these influences, and of warm temperament, it is not surprising that my own collection increased to an unwieldly and inconvenient extent. My rooms, boxes, closets, &c., were crowded, whilst the purse collapsed, and I deemed it prudent to commission Mr. Southgate to sell some of the books at his rooms. In June, 1832, I sent enough to make up six days' sale; and subsequently, at different times, have sold a sufficient number to occupy ten more days. Every sale, however, furnished cause of mortification and sorrow; for books, drawings, prints, and objects of vertu, were sold at very low prices.

The following Address was written and printed by me in June, 1832, to accompany Catalogues sent to particular persons ; and is reprinted, in this place, as expressive of the feelings and opinions I then experienced and entertained on such a subject.

## BOOKS: READING: STUDY.

A MAN who has been actively engaged for forty years in collecting, and in using Books,—who during that space of time has been economical in all his other expences for the purpose of indulging this "hobby," and who has also been much occupied in the pleasure of writing, and penalties of publishing, will be likely to find the said hobby grow rather too large for his stable, and demand more than common care and labour in "looking after." Though thus overgrown and incommodious, I can truly re-echo the sentiment of Cumberland, who in his "Memoirs" asserts, that his "books and pen have been his never-failing comforters and friends."

From these, and all other earthly ties, a time of parting must arrive; and Books will have failed in one of their important duties, or qualities, if they have not inculcated the lesson of submitting to inevitable events, without unavailing murmur. Philosophy has many pretty maxims, but it has not one among the number to render sensibility insensible. It certainly teaches us "to bear the ills we have," and guard against, or ward off others, which may assail us. Dr. Kitchener instructed "every man to make his own Will"—and he might have taught him, also, to be his own Executor. This would tend to shorten lawyers' bills, and lengthen legacies; would benefit widows and orphans, and abridge posthumous taxation. If there were no other reasons for a man's looking beyond the grave, than a desire of saving litigation, and mulcts to the tax office, these were sufficient; but how often and how effectually can he apply his superfluous property—if he has any—towards the end of his life, if he has resolution and good feelings, to bequeath it to deserving relatives and friends.

Let us hear what PETRARCH said of BOOKS, about five hundred years ago, when there were neither Magazines nor Reviews, and when printing and engraving were alike unknown, and let us endeavour to appreciate and profit by his just and philosophical remarks.

"Some people consider the pleasures of the world as their supreme good, and not to be renounced. But I have friends of a very different description (MY BOOKS), whose society is far more agreeable to me: they are of all countries, and of all ages; they are distinguished in war, in politics, and in the sciences. It is very easy to see them; they are always at my service. I call for their company, or send them away, whenever I please: they are never troublesome, and immediately answer all my questions. Some relate the events of ages past, others reveal the secrets of nature; these teach me how to live in comfort, those how to die in quiet. In return for all these services, they only require a chamber of me in one corner of my mansion, where they may repose in peace."

If, however, instead of one corner of his mansion, Petrarch had found every room and every closet of his house filled with these dear friends, he might have experienced some inconvenience from their company, and been induced, like myself and many others, to turn some of them out of doors, for the purpose of seeing and enjoying the selected few.

A short account of the rise and progress of the Library, of which a part is now to be disposed of, will "point a moral," if not "adorn a tale." In boyhood I attended the sale of a country 'squire's furniture, &c. and bought a lot of nine books for 1s. One of them was Robinson Crusoe, which I read with avidity, and longed to be cast on a desert island, with a "Man Friday." This library travelled with me to London, and occupied—with Bailey's Dictionary, a few magazines, some anatomical and medical books, &c.—a small deal box, during six years of miserable apprenticeship, the greater part of which was spent in a murky, damp, and dirty cellar. Sanguine in hopes, and ardently looking forward to emancipation from a sad state of legal slavery, my health gave way, and I became weak, emaciated, and desponding. But for the "little knowledge" obtained even from my small library, I should have sunk into an early grave; from books I acquired some knowledge of my own constitution, frame of body, and the latent disease which exhibited evident symptoms of consumption. Thus, I attribute prolongation of life to reading. At the end of apprenticeship my boy-library contained twenty-five volumes, and my purse five guineas. For the ensuing ten years my stock increased but very slowly; a small nest of shelves held the whole. Commencing with Mr. Brayley the Beauties of England in 1800, it became necessary to have nearly every printed book relating to the counties described; but as these were expensive, they were retained only as long as wanted, and then sold to purchase others. This class of reading and writing excited a desire to possess a library, and every new year not only increased the desire, but it also augmented the collection.

In Tavistock Place it occupied three sides of a small room nine feet square, and I then thought myself truly rich and happy. Infected with the *Bibliomania*, which raged for some time in London, I was impelled to attend the sale rooms of King and Lochee—Richardson—Leigh and Sotheby—Evans, and other famed "contagionists"—where I continued to purchase, as if "increase of appetite grew with what it fed on." Many "curious, choice, and rare articles" have thus come into my possession, which I have seen pass through the hands of three or four "famous" collectors. Here the retrospect is painful, and melancholy; for it brings before imagination the Names, Tales, and varied Characters of the indefatigable and zealous *Strutt*—the eccentric and enthusiastic *Carter*—the magnificent *Lansdowne*—the amiable and learned *Boucher*—the plodding and laborious *Reed*—the talented but splenetic *Steevens* and *Ritson*—the universally esteemed *Alexander*—the ostentatious *Dent*—the historical *Coxe, cum multis aliis.*         J. B.

# CHAPTER VI.

"It is most worthy of observation with what diligence he (Camden) inquired after ancient places, making hue-and-cry after many a city which was run away, and by certain marks and tokens pursuing to find it; as by the situation on the Roman highways, by just distance from other ancient cities, by some affinity of name, by tradition of inhabitants, by Roman coins digged up, and by some appearance of ruins. A broken urn is a whole evidence; or an old gate still surviving out of which the city is run out. Besides commonly some new spruce town, not far off, is grown out of the ashes thereof, which has yet so much natural affection, as dutifully to own those reverend ruins for her mother."
Thomas Fuller.

"O, books! ye monuments of mind, concrete wisdom of the wisest;
Sweet solace of daily life; proofs and results of immortality;
Trees yielding all fruits, whose leaves are for the healing of the nations;
Groves of knowledge where all may eat, nor fear a flaming sword:
Gentle comrades, kind advisers, friends, comforts, treasures:
Helps, governments, diversities of tongues; who can weigh your worth?"
M. F. Tupper: *Proverbial Philosophy.*

Topography: its capabilities and attributes; Warton's and Sir R. C. Hoare's opinions on; my essay on, in 1843; Joseph Hunter's, and Richard Gough's—Hoar Antiquity—Society of Antiquaries of London—Archæological Attractions of Wiltshire—Rev. J. Whitaker—Edward King—G. Chambers—Rev. Dr. Whitaker—Rev. W. Gilpin—Thos. Pennant—Francis Grose—Chippenham—Robert Sadler—J. Provis—R. Gaby—Elliot—Sparrow—Intoxication—Corsham—Castle Combe—Grittleton—Malmesbury—Charlton House—Bowood: the Marquesses of Lansdowne—Devizes—Earl Stoke—Longleat—Stourhead—Heytesbury: Mr. Cunnington—Fonthill: Mr. Beckford—Wardour Castle—Salisbury—Wilton House—Longford Castle—Old Sarum—Stonehenge—Salisbury Plain—Avebury—Marlborough—Hungerford—Tottenham Park—Littlecot, &c., &c.

The present chapter will be devoted to my first initiation into the mysteries and labours of *Topography,* and to my progress and experiences in traversing through, and connection with my native county. In other parts of this work the subject has been alluded to; but for the sake of coherency and perspicuity, I may be excused for repeating a few particulars. In consequence of writing some crude remarks on private theatricals for the Sporting Magazine, in 1796, I became acquainted with *John Wheble,* its proprietor, who was also owner of two weekly county newspapers, published in London. For the magazine, I also wrote an account of a remarkable incident in a fox-hunt, which occurred at my birth-place, when a boy. This led to conversation about *Wiltshire*, when Mr. Wheble told me he had proposed, some years before, to publish a work, in two volumes, to be called " The Beauties of Wiltshire," but was prevented continuing it. He urged me to undertake the task, and offered pecuniary and other assistance. Without any tie, engagement, or profitable occupation, I eagerly caught at his suggestion, as it would lead me again and again to visit and even explore my native county. Not having studied or scarcely read any works or essays on topography, I could not form a notion of the laborious task it involved, nor of the varied information which the writer ought to possess. I felt, however, that I was much better qualified than my friend and patron, who had undertaken a literary work for which he was unqualified. In a prospectus which he issued in 1784, he asserted that three hundred subscribers had engaged to patronize the work. The price of the two volumes was to be ten shillings, half of which was solicited to be paid in advance: a common practice then, and often since. The work, however, never proceeded beyond the first prospectus, and only a few subscriptions were paid. Mr. Wheble had obtained some notoriety as publisher of " The Middlesex Journal," in which he reported certain speeches in Parliament, when such a proceeding was contrary to the practice of the House of Commons. He was arrested by a messenger from the House, and taken before Alderman Wilkes, who denied the authority of such messenger and of his employers, and discharged Wheble. This event, and the times are memorable and important in the annals of English history.*

The preceding pages furnish the reader with several intimations of the pursuits and profession in which I embarked early in life, and prosecuted the latter diligently and zealously for a period of more than half a century. The result of my literary labours is pretty fully detailed in the first half of the second volume. It is my intention now

---

* See Wade's edition of "Junius's Letters," 2 vols. 1850, vol. ii., p. 348. I refer to this edition of these once celebrated epistles as the most comprehensive and complete of any published. My own volume on "The Authorship of the Letters of Junius," will be found to contain much information on public men, and the political and literary characteristics of the æra.

to relate some events and circumstances descriptive of my first embarkation and progressive movements in Topography.

In the year 1840 I penned and printed the following, on the capabilities and essential requisites of this class of literature.

TOPOGRAPHY, according to popular phraseology and dictionary explanation (as used in an age when the full latitude of the word and the science were not understood) meant description of a place, or, according to the Greek compound, "place-description;" i. e. local history. It is now become as much a science as any other department of literature, though there are not many of its professors, or rather amateurs, who are well skilled in its principles and technicalities. As Geography is general, Biography personal, so Topography is strictly confined to special accounts of particular districts, or places. Though thus comparatively of limited scope and powers, it is evident, from what has been already produced by men of learning and talent, that it is susceptible of varied and commanding interest, as well as conducive to the public welfare. The matter and the manner of this species of writing constitute its excellence or its defects. By furnishing full, vivid, and authentic accounts of all the essential features of a country, a parish, a district, or other place—of its natural products, both beneath and on the surface of the earth—the artificial objects which are truly indigenous, with such biographical anecdotes of eminent and remarkable persons, and notices of the phenomena, which belong to the place—the Topographer will have fulfilled his duty as to *matter;* but he must also, to be eminently useful and attractive, narrate and illustrate the whole, in a *manner* calculated to attract the uninitiated, and to please and satisfy the veteran critic. This will test both the taste and ability of the writer. In the History of Kiddington, by T. Warton—of Selborne, by the Rev. Gilbert White—of Whalley and of Craven, by the Rev. Dr. Whitaker—of South Yorkshire, and of Hallamshire, by the Rev. Joseph Hunter—of Northamptonshire, by George Baker—and of Ashridge, by the Rev. H. J. Todd—we have truly valuable specimens of what has been accomplished by the abilities of the respective authors, and at the same time have manifestations of the capabilities of Topography. Warton tells us, that—

"Histories of Counties have been condemned as the dullest of compilations. They are commonly supposed to contain only materials of a circumscribed and particular nature, and consequently to be incapable of acquiring any large share of the public attention. But Histories of Counties, if properly written, become works of entertainment, of importance, and universality. They may be made the vehicles of much general intelligence, and of such as is interesting to every reader of liberal curiosity. What is local is often national.

"There are indeed many Topographers who think nothing tedious or superfluous; and it must be confessed that books of this kind are too frequently encumbered with the pedantries of Heraldry, fantastic Pedigrees, Catalogues of Incumbents, and ostentatious Epitaphs of obscure individuals. But in the hands of a judicious and sensible examiner they are the *Histories* of *Ancient Manners, Arts,* and *Customs.*"
—WARTON'S *History, &c. of Kiddington,* 4to. 3rd edition, 1815.

"The literary annals of the present age," says Sir R. C. Hoare, "proclaim *Topography* as one of its most favourite subjects, as very justly may it be considered as worthy of general attention; for what information can be more useful, or desirable, than the knowledge of our own country, of its inhabitants, its property, and its antiquities?

"I am fully aware of the many difficulties which will occur to any person who may attempt the *General History of a County*: I am also aware of the great length of time and the heavy expenses which would be incurred in collecting the necessary documents for a general *County History*; but a SOCIETY might accomplish what an individual would not venture to begin, or hope to complete."

Again, in 1843, I wrote and published, for a Wiltshire Society, "An Essay on Topographical Literature: its Province, Attributes, and varied Utility; with Accounts of the Sources, Objects, and Uses of National and Local Records and Glossaries of Words used in Ancient Writings." To this Essay I devoted sixty-six quarto pages, closely printed in small letter; but the Society having "died a natural death," by the inactivity or lethargy of the majority of its members, and only a very small number of its Transactions being published, the Essay here referred to has been scarcely known to the general readers of Topography and Archæology.—(See *Index* to vol. ii. of this Biography.)

In 1847, *The Rev. Joseph Hunter*, Sub-Commissioner of Public Records, and author of several learned and interesting publications on the Topography and Antiquities of Yorkshire, wrote a paper for "The Archæological Institute," which he modestly entitles "Hints on the Nature, Purpose, and Resources of Topography." This is printed in "Memoirs Illustrative of the History and Antiquities of Norfolk and the City of Norwich," 8vo. 1851. From such a profound, zealous, and indefatigable "searcher after antiquities," and practical expositor of their uses and value, the reader may be sure to find much valuable information in the Essay here referred to.

*Richard Gough*, a learned and enthusiastic, but not very discriminating Topographer and Antiquary, thus speaks of, and characterizes his predecessors, in the preface to his valuable "British Topography:" "Those who hitherto have treated our topographical antiquities seem to have trodden only in mazes overgrown with thorns, neglecting the flowery paths with which the wilderness of obscurity is diversified.

Incorrect pedigrees, futile etymologies, verbose disquisitions, crowds of epitaphs, list of landholders, and such farrago, thrown together without method, unanimated by reflections, and delivered in the most uncouth horrid style, make up the bulk of our county histories. Such works bring the study of antiquities into disgrace with the generality, and disgust the most candid curiosity."

Writings such as those here described by a gentleman of fortune, who studied, wrote, and published many volumes on the subjects he thus harshly reproves, were not calculated to excite the curiosity, or propitiate the sympathies of a reader whose favourite authors had been Fielding, Smollett, Sterne, Goldsmith, Moore, Ray, Watts, Thomson, Akenside, Reynolds, and others of similar powers, with magazines, reviews, and plays. When accident, therefore, directed my attention to the Topography of my native county, I was necessitated to commence a new career of reading and thinking, and at first found it rather dull and forbidding. "Appetite," however, "grew with what it fed on," and progressively and ultimately, I found the food not only palatable and savory, but often luxurious. Indeed, I fully estimated the poetical sentiment of " Tom " Warton, who wrote thus about a century past,—

> " Nor dull nor barren are the winding ways
> Of *hoar Antiquity*, but strewn with flowers."

Having traversed those paths for more than fifty years,—explored their " highways and by-ways," on mountain and dingle, on the widespread plain, in the secluded dell, in the " busy haunts of men," and in deep recesses, now almost deserted by the human race, and only occupied by the owl, the bat, the toad, and the fox,—I can confidently assert that objects of the deepest interest may be found in all those devious tracks. It is true, the flowers of the parterre, referred to by the poet, have not much similitude or analogy to the relics of by-gone ages; but it is equally true, that " hoar Antiquity " has many charms and fascinations to persons who can appreciate it. As the florist and the botanist have their *hortus siccus*, to preserve, and renew, to the eye and mind, the forms and hues of flowers and plants, so has the archæologist his casts, models, drawings, and engravings, of rare and interesting antiquities. If one studies the living world and its beauties, the other admires things that have been. One looks " through

Nature up to Nature's God," whilst the other studies the progress and history of man through his works, and therein traces the omnipotence and omniscience of Deity. Let us, therefore, pursue our favourite studies with zeal and with discrimination; deriving, as we must, a great amount of useful knowledge, by comparing and contrasting the memorials of former ages with the arts and customs of the wondrous epoch in which we live.

Throughout the regions of England's Antiquities, from the rude Celtic monuments of Wiltshire, Cornwall, Wales, and other parts of our island, to the elaborate and truly florid architecture of King's College Chapel, and the still more gorgeous monumental mausoleum of Henry the Seventh, at Westminster, it has been both my duty and pleasure to examine, study, and direct the delineation of every class and variety of those national works. When I commenced my Topographical career, at the end of the last century, it should be remembered, that most of the books I could refer to, or regard as models, were of the class described by Mr. Gough; and that the great mass of the people were besotted in ignorance and consequent superstition, whilst the higher orders were generally immersed in partizanship and political ambition. The rich kept aloof from and shunned the poor, whilst the latter regarded the former as severe and cruel taskmasters. Hence discord and contention ensued, and hence arose those hatreds and animosities which became manifested in the insurrections and rebellions of America, France, and Ireland. Though these national convulsions were terrific and lamentable at their respective epochs, we may derive from them the consolation of knowing and enjoying the enlightenment and amenity of sentiment which belong to the present philosophical age. In the current state of Topography and Archæology, we witness the effects of this spirit—this progress of mind and sentiment. The old, and once apparently superannuated, *Society of Antiquaries* has lately made a desperate plunge to reform itself, to awake from a state of lethargy and sloth, and to make an effort to compete with, if not surpass, the young societies which have sprung up in strength and in numbers which threatened extinction to the parent. With the vast advantages of a " local habitation and a name," and also privileges and wealth, which no rival society can obtain, it

Engraved by S.F. Stenns from a Miniature by Henry Bone Esq.r R.A.

THE LATE JOHN WHITAKER,

AUTHOR OF "HISTORY OF MANCHESTER"

has only to pursue the course it has lately adopted to secure ascendancy above all competition in this and every other country.

*Archæology* is an important if not the most essential part of Topography; and I can safely assert that but for the attractiveness, the fascinations of the remarkable and very important *Antiquities of Wiltshire*, I never should have been a confirmed, almost an enthusiastic, topographer. After seeing, reading, and thinking about such objects as Stonehenge, Avebury, Salisbury Cathedral, and Malmesbury Abbey Church, I should have been apathetic and heartless, had I not felt my curiosity excited—my love of knowledge aroused—my ambition stimulated, and all my latent energies called forth and directed to the comprehensive but previously unattractive study of Topography. This will be amply shown in the course of the ensuing narrative, as it is pretty fully exemplified by the list of publications at the end of the second volume of this work.

As some apology for the defects of my earliest publications, I must entreat the reader to bear in mind the evidences of Warton and of Gough on the characteristics of the writings I had to refer to as exemplars and incitements to study. They do not notice such works as "The History of Manchester" and "The Life of St. Neot," by my learned and eloquent, but romancing friend, the *Rev. John Whitaker*, or another learned, but visionary author, my kindly-disposed, early friend, *Edward King*, in his "Munimenta Antiqua" in four folio volumes, a work now rarely seen and never quoted.* Contrasted with

---

* This gentleman was a very early and a kindly-disposed friend, at the commencement of the *Beauties of England;* and was the first carriage-visitor to my humble home in Wilderness Row, Clerkenwell. This row, or line of houses, faces a tall old brick wall, bounding one side of the inclosed grounds of the Charter-House. Mr. King came in his family coach to my door; but, the roadway between the houses and the wall being very narrow, not affording room to turn a carriage and pair of horses, the coachman was puzzled to make a retreat. A crowd collected, as usual in London, when street accidents or difficulties occur; the horses were taken out, and some men dragged the carriage into Sutton Street. Mr. King—a proud man—was sadly annoyed; and the following day I received a letter from him, saying he could never visit me again, in such a place and neighbourhood; but advised me to move towards the west. Soon afterwards I shifted from No. 21, Wilderness Row, to 10, Tavistock Place; the former

such as these, we may adduce the names and writings of *George Chalmers,* the erudite author of "Caledonia," and other works. The *Rev. Dr. Whitaker,* though no relation, either by family or ability, to the historian of Manchester, has manifested incomparable tact and talent in his histories of Whalley, Craven, and other places of Yorkshire. I might refer to other commendable topographical authors, whose style of writing, varied information, and vivid pictures, cannot fail to engage and interest almost every class of readers. The *Rev. William Gilpin* was among the first who not only pleased but often fascinated the students, by vivid language, and the poetical and graphic accounts with which he invested scenery, buildings, works of art, and persons of note. *Thomas Pennant,* his contemporory, wrote and published several popular quarto volumes on Wales, Scotland, and parts of England, all of which tended to give value and importance to such works. His travelling servant-man, *Moses Griffith,* made the drawings for his various tours, and they were far superior in accuracy to those by *Francis Grose,* whose "Antiquities of England, Scotland, and Ireland," however, obtained great popularity, and continued to secure it for many years; though, like many other literary and graphic works, they are now rendered almost worthless by superior competitors.

## CHIPPENHAM.

Since I wrote and published an account of this town in 1837, it has participated in the changes and improvements of modern times. Boy associations and schooling endear the place to memory: but nearly every one of my early acquaintance has paid the debt of nature, and

---

house rented at twenty guineas a year, and the latter, at seventy-four pounds. Mr. King continued his friendly civilities during life; gave me the four volumes of his biblical, archæological work; and patronized all my publications. The reader is referred to Nichols's "Literary Anecdotes," vol. viii., for an interesting account of this eccentric gentleman, who is there called "a learned and philosophical antiquary;" but which is not exemplified by his writings and conduct in life. Philosophy and fanaticism; "Morsels of Criticism," a large quarto volume, the greater part of which sold for waste paper, devoid of good sense and common sense; with four large folio volumes on the History of Nations and of Castellated Architecture, in which round arches and pointed arches are misdescribed and misrepresented, cannot be regarded as very philosophical, or soundly critical.

reposes among the silent dead. Hence a new race and a different class of persons have settled here; built a young town, which has grown to considerable magnitude in connection with the railway station. An iron manufactory is formed and worked, with a gang of men amounting to more than one hundred, aided by a steam-engine. A new district church is to be built forthwith. Chippenham, in my juvenile days, abounded with clothiers, their manufactories, shops, and work-people. These gradually gave way, and were dispersed when machinery was introduced, and revolutionized the business with all its human hands and heads. Recently, however, the firm of Everett, Pocock, and Rawlins, have established works upon a larger scale, which, by machinery and hand-labour, produce a large supply of cloth of the finest and best quality. Instead of stage-coaches, chaises, waggons, and horses, giving employ and activity to trades-people and the working classes, the Great Western Railway, with its numerous trains, has introduced much variety with striking changes in the features, business, and general character of Chippenham. A new Hall and Market-house has been built, and a large monthly market established, within a few years; but, strange to say, the old and ruinous Town Hall, and more ruinous Shambles, or covered sheds, are allowed to remain in nearly the centre of the town, to disgrace and degrade its appearance. In paving, lighting, cleansing, and draining the place, great improvements have been made within the last few years; but a sufficient supply of good water is still to be desired. There are two public pumps for hard water; but the soft is obtained from the river Avon, at the southern extremity of the town. It is conveyed from the river in casks, on wheels, to all persons requiring it, and sold by pailsful; whence it becomes an expensive article. Amongst the novelties in the new town, are six pretty, small houses built at the expense of *Charles Bailey, Esq.*, a retired medical practitioner of this place, and intended to afford comfortable homes for so many old professional persons, who from misfortune may be reduced to pecuniary distress in the decline of life.

In the early part of this Memoir (*ante*, p. 50) I have adverted to Chippenham in boy-days, and given accounts of certain school-fellows, who, in after life, attained some distinction. With its history, politics, and other characteristics I became more familiar, at later periods, in consequence of having resided occasionally in the town, and having a beloved sister settled there. Besides, being engaged by Mr. Wheble to write a work on my native county, I was naturally and irresistibly impelled to establish a starting point where I had some connection, and where there seemed to be a prospect of acquiring friendly aid and information. Topography and Archæology, at that time, were, however, more strange and foreign, even to the better-informed inhabitants, than they were to myself.* On referring to letters, which passed between the clergyman, the best-read persons of the town, and myself, I am surprised at their contents, at the language used, and of the absence of all technical phraseology on local history. I must own that my spirits and ambitious aspirations sunk low in the scale of hope, and I often felt the nightmare of despair haunt not only my sleep-dreams, but waking reveries. Fortunately, I was tempted to persevere, and slowly, but progressively, was excited by the encouragement I experienced from gentlemen in Wiltshire. Amongst these were the Rev. Josiah Allport, Ralph Hale Gaby, a solicitor; James Coombs, a printer, and professor of music; Robert Sadler, a tradesman, and author of some publications in prose and verse, and John Provis,—all of Chippenham. Several other gentlemen, particularly in the southern part of the county, subsequently rendered me essential aid and advice.

With Mr. SADLER I continued on intimate terms till the time of his death in 1839, when I learnt that he had bequeathed one hundred pounds to me, "in testimony of many years' friendship." During more than forty years' correspondence, we exchanged a large mass of letters; mostly on the current literature of the times, on party politics, and particularly on the deplorable vassalage and corruption of certain Wiltshire boroughs. Those of Chippenham and Malmesbury were

---

* Although there was not any topographer at Chippenham, or in its vicinity, when I commenced "The Beauties of Wiltshire," it should be known to the reader, that JOHN THORPE, author of some works on the Antiquities of Rochester, &c., had settled in the town, where he died in 1792, and was buried in the church-yard of Hardenhuish, near the place of his decease.—(Vide " *Beauties*," &c., vol. iii. p. 162.)

more particularly mentioned and reprobated.* Though of a poetical temperament, and naturally partial to writings of fancy and fiction, my friend was discreet and generally discriminating in his opinions and language, on those, and on all topics, whether religious, moral, political, or "polite literature." Hence I coveted and profited by his epistles, and hence I was induced to preserve and value them. If my limits permitted I might adduce several passages, or whole letters, to justify and elucidate these remarks. I cannot resist the opportunity of giving one specimen of my own, and another of his writing, in 1837. On December 19th of that year I wrote to him as follows, chiefly for the purpose of obtaining his opinion and sentiments on a subject which then and since has often occupied my thoughts.

THE MACHINERY—THE PHYSICAL AND METAPHYSICAL ECONOMY OF MAN.

Among the marvels of this marvellous globe, what is there more wondrous and admirable than the mind and machinery of Man? "How noble in reason! how infinite in faculties! in form and moving how express and admirable! in action how like an angel! in apprehension how like a God!"—"Who can paint like Nature?" and who can describe like Shakspere? He was the "Paragon of Animals," but when did he ever see an angel? and how does he reconcile his Christian doctrine with " *a* God?" Surely there cannot be two or more gods. The exquisite mechanism of the human frame, with the wondrous faculties of sight, hearing, *thinking*, bewilders the brain. Is thinking a faculty? what is it? where is its seat? how is it acted on, and by what process does it perform its manifold operations? What thinking and language can explain thought?—These, and many other reveries, often amuse and perplex me? Can you—can the wisest of men—explain and anatomise mind?

This convivial, social, frolicksome, romping, and it may be called childish season, (Christmas) has called up recollections of boyish home, and boyish practices. How distant and dim is the scene! What "seas of troubles" have I passed over since! and what variety of men, events, and worldly changes, have I seen during the last half century?

This is an odd epistle; but I wanted to shake hands with you,—in imagination,—to ask you how you and yours are?—to provoke you to say something to me; because I well know that whatever you say, will be at once out of the common-place way, therefore gratifying and useful to your old and sincere friend,

JOHN BRITTON.

---

* I have his manuscript comments on those places and subjects; which will be deposited, with my other Topographical Collections for Wiltshire, in the Library of the Wiltshire Archæological Society at Devizes. (May 1853.)

To this challenge, he thus replies on February 6th, 1838:—

My dear Britton,

Whether the compliments you paid to *old Wanley Penson* [a novel by Mr. Sadler], in the letter previous to your last, were merited or unmerited, it would seem affectation in me to question. Permit me, however, to say, that though I waive the question, I feel its import against me. Wanley Penson is not *now* what he was [allusive to himself]; his mind certainly retains the same *Die* which imprest his heretofore lucubrations; but the machinery which once gave effect to this *Die* has now lost its wonted energy. This defect may have escaped the eye of a friend; and I will suppose it has, as you seem to wish more of those "Ponderings" which, even forty years ago, Penson's editor, "the Curate," characterized as "unprofitable." Also, why question the enfeebled octogenarian on the subject of "*Thinking?*" Bless me! Why may you not as well ask a *clock* why its wheels move,—why it points the time, and strikes the hour,—as ask a *man* why he thinks, or why he reasons?—both which, together with memory, are the results of the machinery which its Omniscient Framer undoubtedly calculated on. Man, therefore, has nothing to do with them; they are not acts of volition, more than the beating of the heart, or the heaving of the diaphragm. Thought will obtrude, whether we will or no; so will memory and reason, and that often painfully. This subject, however, to pursue, would lead me into a wide field, both of exemplification and argument; I therefore dismiss it for the introduction of one less liable to be questioned, though perhaps not wholly so:—I mean your Picture of *Man*, as drawn by the immortal Shakspere, whose talent for portraying both the mental and personal make of human-kind I admire fully as much as yourself; yet the sample you have sent me of his skill in taking a likeness appears to me to be only a profile. Not but that I am sure he was capable of sketching, and even of drawing, and has left striking likenesses of both sides of the human face,—or rather say a full-faced portrait. These sketches, though admirable, being unconnected, it occurred to me, as a reply to your Shaksperean portrait, to hand you a double-sided, or full-faced likeness of *Man*, as delineated by another poet, of admitted and admired abilities, and inferior *only to Shakspere*, for the brilliancy, force, and aptitude of tropes, similes, and metaphors. This, perhaps, I should say, with the exception of those who think his subject an unworthy one. But why is a poet's subject to be weighed against his merit as *a poet?* What, in the eye of reason, can be more ridiculous than Ovid's subjects? yet, as a poet, his merits are not denied. But enough by way of prelude,—I will not say apology, for I cannot think the poet in need of one;—whether you may think his subject is or is not in such necessity, I leave as a point to be mooted.

### A FULL-FEATURED PORTRAIT OF MAN.

"How great! how mean! how abject! how august!
How complicate, how wonderful is Man!
How passing wonder He, who made him such!
Who center'd in his make such strange extremes,
From different Natures, marvellously mix'd;
Connection exquisite of distant Worlds!—
Distinguish'd link in Being's endless Chain,

> Midway from Nothing to the Deity!—
> A Beam ethereal sullied, and absorpt!
> Dim Miniature of Greatness absolute!
> An Heir of Glory! a frail Child of Dust!
> *Helpless* Immortal! Insect *Infinite!*
> Though sullied, and dishonour'd, still Divine!
> A Worm! a God!—I tremble at myself,
> And in myself am lost! At home a Stranger.
> Thought wanders up and down, surprised, aghast,
> And wond'ring at her *own*. How Reason reels!
> O what a Miracle to man is man!
> Triumphantly distress'd—what Joy! what Dread!
> Alternately transported and alarm'd.
> What can preserve my Life, or what destroy?
> An Angel's arm can't snatch me from the Grave—
> Legions of Angels can't confine me There!"
>
> YOUNG's *Night Thoughts.*

The writer of the preceding letter was a man of singular person, manners, and abilities: the first was natural, but disfigured by costume; the second arose from the station and connection wherein he was placed; and the third, like the first, was formed by nature, and developed by associations and self-culture. Had the same mind been well instructed and disciplined in early life, it might have become eminent in art, in literature, or in science; for it manifested, on many occasions, the rudiments and principles, as well as the union of philosophy and poetry, whilst the disposition was philanthropic and generous. Unfortunately, he seems to have been a victim to circumstances and connections. He was born at Swindon, a town near the northern boundary of Wiltshire, in 1754, but soon removed to and settled at Malmesbury. His father was a glover and breeches-maker, and being one of the Moravians, a sect of religionists then in its infancy, young Sadler was initiated into their opinions and doctrines, and also into the elements of school-learning by their minister. Of this peculiar sect he has detailed many curious particulars in the novel of "Wanley Penson, or the Melancholy Man;" and again, for my account of the parish of Tytherton, in "Beauties of Wiltshire," vol. iii. p. 168. Mr. Sadler, after marrying in 1775, settled in Chippenham, as a draper, but from bad health, and an ardent love of reading, was not calculated to manage and attend to the trifling details of a retail shop. His wife soon died, and in 1779 he wedded another, with whom he lived in harmony and unity for more than half a century. When we have read many of his hearty, generous letters, and the sentiments inculcated in his " Wanley Penson," we feel surprised at the contrasted theories and practices of the man and the author; for my friend often exhibited singularities, bordering on eccentricities, in dress, habits, and manners. Like most sedentary, studious persons, his whole frame was morbid, and the animal secretions being irregular, the muscles relaxed, and, the nervous system deranged, his physical powers were always weak and languid. In person he was tall, thin, and apparently in a state of consumption. The face was narrow and pale, the cheeks were collapsed, and his general physiognomy was that of an abstracted and melancholy, but highly intellectual man. It was generally said, that the imaginary "Wanley Penson" was drawn from, and exhibited the leading characteristics of, Robert Sadler; and these, as exemplified in the now obsolete but interesting novel, were calculated to win the affections of all who best knew the one, and had read the other. His countenance very much resembled that of the amiable and highly intellectual Dr. Priestley, and from the memoirs and letters of the latter, I should infer that there were striking similarities of mental faculties in the two. He is thus described by a mutual friend, who was familiar with him for nearly half a century. " His countenance was that of a deep thinking man; his manners were mild and bland, as usually shown in the tones of his voice, and in the remarks and sentiments he expressed. His conversation displayed varied and extensive knowledge, conveyed, generally, in appropriate, often terse and eloquent language, with an earnestness and impressiveness indicative of conviction and sincerity." With such qualifications and attributes, it is not surprising that his company, advice, and opinions were much coveted and courted by intimate and familiar friends. With one or more of these he passed many hours in his shop, the usual scene of converse and consultation; for he rarely invited them into his simple, humble parlour. I have spent many hours thus in his company, but was never invited to dine or partake of refreshment with him until the very latter end of his life, and after he had converted the shop into a sitting room. In one of his letters to me, dated 1802, he says, " It is a misfortune, my friend, for a man to be supposed to possess talents, for (like property) if once the supposition takes place, he is sure not only to be heavily taxed, but surcharged beyond his real amount. Hence I am scarcely ever alone, have but little time for reading or writing, or any species of personal amusement. My visitors are not merely private friends, but persons of the town, many unknown to or by me; and others, from villages in the neighbourhood, who, in difficulties or troubles of any kind, and often imaginary, break in upon me, take up my time, and sometimes try my philosophy and equanimity. I have often made wills, marriage settlements, contracts, indentures, and agreements; even written love-letters, and other confidential epistles, communicating good and bad news to relations and friends. Indeed, I have been solicited to 'tell the fortunes' of some sighing maidens; and even to discover thieves, murderers, highwaymen, &c. On one occasion I was nominated, and required to act as 'Overseer of the Poor' of this large parish, which proved a heart-rending, distressing occupation. Real suffering and affected misery were constantly preferring claims and petitions for relief."

Besides the novel already referred to, Mr. Sadler published three small poems, on local persons and events, under the titles of "The Discarded Spinster, or a Plea for the Poor;" allusive to the time and effects of introducing machinery into the manufacture of cloth. The others were, "True Patriotism, an Apostrophe inspired by the Public Loss of Sir James Tilney Long, Bart., M.P. for Wilts;"—"An Elegy on the Death of an Esteemed Friend, Wm. Colbourne, Esq." Amongst manuscripts in his possession, at the time of his decease, and which he bequeathed to John Lewis, of Malmesbury, a nephew, with legacies to pay for their revisal, printing, &c., were two novels, "The Pupil of Experience," and "The Proselyte of Principle," which I have reason to believe possessed considerable merit, and therefore calculated to be popular. The party to whom they were given is dead, and the present state and even existence of the manuscripts are alike unknown; both probably are lost to the public, as much other valuable property has been, by that disreputable den, the Court of Chancery.

Although Mr. Sadler is known to have written many Wills for friends, and which it is said have never been litigated, he was not courageous enough to make one for himself. This was unfortunately entrusted to a professional adviser, and extends over nineteen sheets. Two solicitors and one medical gentleman are named as executors. The will is dated April 2, 1838, and Mr. Sadler died the 23rd of August, 1839. His personal property is sworn at £4000., which, with various leasehold, copyhold, and freehold estates, canal shares, and securities for moneys lent, he bequeathed to relatives, friends, and the poor. It will not surprise the reader to be told that such property and such a will became a subject of Chancery litigation, which was continued for many years; that some of the legatees died in the interim, and that others (poor relations) were kept out of their money during the legal ordeal. My legacy of one hundred pounds was for a piece of plate, and, strange to say, one or more of the executors ordered it to be made by a workman of Chippenham, without apprizing me, or asking my opinion. This I protested against, as such a *thing* would, in my opinion, be an useless bauble. A correspondence ensued, and the result was, that the silversmith agreed to forego his commission on my paying him ten pounds!! This, with the same sum for legacy duty, reduced my hundred to eighty. "Hence," as writes the friend who negociated the business for me, "one-fifth of your legacy has been abstracted (not pilferred) by the State, the Lawyers, and a Jew Silversmith. What would R. S. say to this, were he living?"

RALPH HALE GABY, Esq., a solicitor of Chippenham, I must class amongst my early and stanch friends, not only at the beginning of my topographical career, but for many years afterwards, to the time of his death: he is therefore deemed worthy of respectful notice.

As a long resident in, and a zealous member of the borough; as a respectable and honourable solicitor, and a despiser of the conduct and practices of those who entered the profession merely to aggrandize themselves at the cost, often ruin, of persons they pretended to serve; as having taken a warm interest in promoting the humble topographical work on my native county, he is entitled to my gratitude and esteem. He was a native of the parish of Bromham, near Devizes; the domestic home for many years, and last resting-place, of Thomas Moore, (the eminent poet, biographer, and amateur musician). Born there in 1748, he was buried in Chippenham church in 1829, at the respectable age of 81. Articled to a solicitor, he pursued that *business* for many years; but, from constitutional dilatoriness, and a sort of natural repugnance to the technicalities and routine of common law, he never derived much employ or profit from its "bills of costs." He is justly characterized by one of his intimate friends, who had known him for nearly fifty years, and who generally co-operated with him in many public objects relating to the town and district, though they were directly opposed to each other in all the manœuvring and practices of Borough-mongering. "Mr. Gaby," he writes, "was an eccentric character,—a lover of science, with but little knowledge of it. Fond of classical learning, yet too indolent to study it, or scarcely to read its records. Desirous of having a knowledge of all things—for his mind was naturally inquisitive—but so prone to procrastination, that he was for ever postponing till the morrow what ought and might have been done to-day. As 'the battle is not always for the strong, nor the race to the swift,' so he acquired a large fortune, not by industry and activity, 'not by rising early, and taking little rest,' but by lucky purchases of land, and by the knowledge, which arose from professional connections, where and when 'good bargains' were to be made. His company was much courted by those who loved conviviality and the social evening circle: whence it was often said of him, that he was most awake and alive at midnight; or, like Milton's Philomela, was then 'most musical' but not 'most melancholy.'"

After marrying a second time, late in life, Mr. Gaby retired to Bath, and in one of the handsome houses of Queen's Square he lived "at his ease" for a few years; where, at Chippenham, and at my own humble home, I have spent many cheerful, happy hours in his company. I have several letters from him, with topographical accounts of Bromham, Chippenham, and other places, and with biographical anecdotes of some of their public characters.

In previous parts of this volume (p. 50, &c.) the reader will find references to Chippenham, with notices of two or three of its natives. *Robert Elliott* has since died, at the advanced age of 80, and, I believe, the last years of his life were passed in great serenity and comparative comfort. Shut out, as it seemed, from the most attractive and exciting stimulus in human life—personal intercourse and converse with his dearest relatives and friends, and with his fellow-creatures—his long-lived journey must have been occasionally irksome and cheerless. It is evident, however, from his expressive manifestations of joy and sorrow, that he often viewed, with a sort of gusto, many scenes and incidents which would be either disregarded, or seen with indifference, by persons having good ears and eloquent tongues. I have often wished that my friend Sadler, or some other person of equal talents, had given a full and discriminating account of the life, thoughts, actions, and mental peculiarities of Mr. Elliott. It might have been made additionally interesting, had a minute and scientific dissection of the organs of the ear and of the voice been made, and well illustrated. [A good portrait is preserved in the Wiltshire Archæological Library at Devizes.]

I cannot quit Chippenham on this occasion (and perhaps for ever) without expressing my obligation to the only schoolfellow, now living, who has passed a long and enterprising period in his native place. JOHN PROVIS, as a boy, and through life, has been studiously devoted to science in general and to mechanics in particular. Geology, however, was, for many years, a favorite study; and of the numerous varieties of fossils which abound in the northern part of the county, he made a large collection. For my *Beauties of Wiltshire*, he wrote a short geological essay; and again, when I was reading a course of lectures on " Architectural Antiquities," at the Institution in Bristol, he furnished me with a series of observations and facts calculated to show the geographical and geological peculiarities of that district, and the eligibility of its port as a great and popular depot for the western coasting trade and for general commerce. The " Great Western Railway " was then struggling against prejudice and opposition, and was purchasing partizans and friends to combat enemies and parliamentary influence. Though both my friend and myself advocated its cause, not only zealously but beneficially in many cases, we failed to secure any profit or advantage from the company. On the contrary, Mr. Provis lost a large sum of money by joining in contracts for some of the works, and supplying materials. Instead of being paid promptly, he was involved in tedious and vexatious lawsuits, which entailed on him very serious losses. For many years he has devoted much time, and displayed considerable scientific skill, in making designs to improve the naval architecture of our wealthy marine nation. The appalling shipwrecks which are continually occurring, and which involve the sweeping loss of so many human lives and the destruction of such vast amount of property, must astonish and distress every humane person. To provide a remedy, or even to mitigate these calamities, is much to be desired; and although the Trinity House and the Government of the country are continually introducing improvements and novelties intended to remedy the evil, there is still much to do, and much that ought to be done. The inventions of Mr. Provis therefore deserve the due and careful examination of the Admiralty Board. I understand that they have been submitted not only to that department of Government, but to merchants, ship-builders, and other persons of science and general knowledge. He has made 250 drawings to illustrate his various schemes of naval improvement, and has written 1150 quarto pages to explain and describe them. It is his wish to publish the whole; but, from the long experience I have had in literature, I intreat him not to incur the imminent risk and expense which such a work would necessarily involve. If practical gentlemen of the Admiralty, of the navy, and of the ship-building craft decline to adopt any of the inventions which the sanguine author may regard as infallibly good, it is not likely there will be a sufficient number of purchasers and readers to repay him for a large outlay of money in publication.

The Schoolmaster, who first instructed me to use a pen for writing letters and figures, but who never "taught the young idea how to shoot," and who, I remember, was rather over-fond of Wiltshire strong beer, which "frequently did steal away his brains," and occasioned debts and disgrace, to cancel both, threw himself into a pond, and was drowned, at Hardenhuish, one mile north of Chippenham. In the church-yard of that small parish, the present respectable and learned Rector writes me word, "there is a little grave-stone with the initials of W. S., and date 1790, which have often excited my curiosity;" but of its meaning he had failed to ascertain any explanation until my inquiry led him to conclude it must have referred to the poor, deranged suicide, William Sparrow.

The vice, the folly, the weakness, and the wretchedness of INTOXICATION cannot be too often, nor too strongly, reprobated, and exhibited to the gaze and consequent pity and contempt of the rising generation. I have unfortunately and distressingly known many lamentable instances, where this destructive habit has led, not only to the personal degradation and ruin of the infatuated drunkard, but to that of wedded partners and their offspring. It has also often occasioned mental derangement and led to the murder of their dearest relatives; as well as to suicide. When I was struggling for a poor subsistence, after the termination of a miserable apprenticeship, I was harassed and distressed by a younger brother, who, having contracted this disgusting habit, by unfortunate association in an attorney's office where he was articled, and where his prospects were propitious, became so inveterate a drinker of ardent spirits, that he was haunted with ever-craving thirst. Hence he became heedless of food and raiment, and regardless of all the decencies and respectabilities of social life. I gave him home and shelter for some time, but was compelled to force him from that home, and place him in a humble lodging, where he soon sunk a victim to that slow poison, which he voluntarily swallowed, though fully conscious of its deleterious quality.

This one example created such a horror in my mind, that I never saw a person either slightly or fully intoxicated without shuddering, and being oppressed with the most painful sensations. It has been my misfortune to see other and very distressing instances of the same kind, in persons immediately connected with, and even dearly related to me. No less than four young men employed by me, as clerks or amanuenses, were victims to this "besotting sin," who, otherwise, were men of talents and probity. One was a clergyman who had produced three respectable literary works, from whom I had anticipated valuable assistance at a time when I was oppressed with the periodical production of part of the Beauties of England, the Architectural Antiquities, and other engagements. He was invited to my house, and expected to render me daily aid in my library. Unfortunately, I had a nine-gallon cask of fine "Kennet ale" just tapped at the time. He was delighted with its quality and flavour, praised it as the most wholesome and nutritious of all liquors; said that it excelled the nectar, the hippocras, the metheglin of the gods and men of former times, and that his talents would be called forth by its salubrious and animating powers. In the mornings he seemed attentive to his task, and busy and zealously employed in studying books, writing notes, &c. A fortnight passed in this way: very little was written, and that little useless. The nine gallons of ale were gone, and I found it necessary to part with my clerical friend. He then took lodgings in Kentish Town; was often seen going into and coming out of a certain public-house. In a few months afterwards he was discovered a corpse in the street.

Another of those gentlemen came to me with the most flattering testimonials of qualification and character. He had been well schooled in ancient lore, in records, in general literature, and I anticipated from him valuable and useful aid. For some time he was steady, humble, obliging, industrious, and ingratiated himself in my esteem and confidence. Tempted to spend an hour occasionally with a friend at a noted ale-house in Pentonville, he became a lover of the beverage, and insensibly and progressively was a confirmed sot. Not satisfied with an occasional hour at the "private parlour," he visited it every night, and was often sent home by the landlord, who required rest and respite from company. Writing was neglected, and what was attempted was erroneous and useless. I was obliged to part with him also; and he closed his sottish career, in the prime of life, in a parish workhouse.

A third was a native of the Emerald Island, who came to London, with a good education and intense love of reading, particularly history, languages, and archæology. He was with me only a few months, as higher salary and more influential connection tempted him to engage on one of the daily newspapers. This brought him in contact with other young men who frequented a noted tavern in the purlieus of Covent Garden, where they often spent the greater part of the night. Drinking, smoking, debating, and singing constituted their chief amusement and occupation. Having joined them myself, on some particular occasions for a few nights, I felt that the danger and expense were too much for my prudence and principle, and I ceased to belong to that, or any other convivial club. Not so my young friend, who, being fascinated with the varied talents of the members, and becoming more and more attached to insidious liquor, and its provocative, the cigar, became a constant visitor. Fortunately, the managers of the paper dispatched him to a foreign city, where a congress was held, and of whose proceedings it was his province to furnish reports. These were punctually and well executed; and he was employed for a long time on the continent to furnish political and other news for the English reader. The task was easy, and the pay good; but the habits of the London eccentrics had corrupted his system, and led him to wine and liquor-houses; whence he neglected his duties, and was summoned to London. He was soon dismissed from the paper, entreated employ from myself and other acquaintances, became a confirmed sot and a vagabond, and died in a miserable lodging in Drury Lane.

A fourth young man, of gentlemanly address and manners, was introduced to me by a friend at Paris, and I gave him temporary employ. He wrote a beautiful hand, was a good accountant, was a scholar, and had been confidentially employed in a mercantile house in Liverpool. At the time of his coming to me I was engaged in one of the speculating societies of London, at the solicitation of three wealthy and honourable friends. In consequence of the negligence and roguery of its solicitor, who acted as secretary, it was found necessary to break up the said company. I was requested to take charge of the books and papers, balance the accounts and return the surplus money to different subscribers. The task was neither pleasant nor easy; but I was induced to undertake it from a persuasion that my new amanuensis was peculiarly fitted to execute such work. It proceeded smoothly for some weeks; the accounts were made out, examined by a committee, and allowed to be correct: drafts were drawn and signed by members of the said committee to return the subscriptions (deducting for expenses) to parties who had taken shares, and the business seemed to approach a close, when I found that a draft for £50. had not been paid to the right party. On examination, it was ascertained that my clerk had received the money. Inquiry was made at his lodging in Somers Town, and I found that he rarely went to bed sober, and that he spent every evening at a public-house with a group of drinkers. Though we neglected to prosecute the miserable man (the money having been advanced by one of the committee), he became an outcast from society, as unfitted to work; and, undeserving of commiseration, he died in the parish hospital, a lamentable victim of the worst of all human vices—drunkenness.

I could enumerate many other instances of similar persons; but if those described do not serve as effective beacons to warn others against the perilous gulph of intoxication, neither language nor facts can be of any avail. In man, inebriety is bad; in *Woman*, it is a

> "Vice of such an hideous mien,
> That to be shunn'd need only to be seen."

It has been my misfortune to witness several examples of such aberrations and weaknesses in a sex that I have ever admired, and whose amiable qualities are calculated to fascinate and rationalize man. Three instances of this sad infirmity, this deplorable vice, have occurred under my immediate and painful cognizance, the parties having been endeared to me by intimate association and relationship. It is scripturally said, that "the sins of the fathers will be visited upon the children to the third and fourth generation;" and it is also related by medical writers that gout and many other disorders are hereditary. I can affirm, from the examples alluded to, that the disease of inebriety descended to the females referred to from their parents, and was accompanied by great irritability of temperament, hysteric affections, poetical genius; with strong emotions of remorse and sorrow on mornings of sober reflection, and a large amount of good sense and intelligence on other subjects, and other parts of mental and social discipline. In the indulgence of, and ready yielding to, their favourite vice, they were slaves and vassals; in other acts and deeds they often manifested acuteness and philosophy that surprised and delighted their friends. All died in the prime of life, and all, towards the end, suffered much from deranged intellects, or brain fever. On this subject I venture to recommend to the reader's attention, Dr. Trotter's "Essay on Drunkenness," 8vo. 1804, fourth edition; and Cruikshank's acute satire, "The Bottle."

The lamentable and notorious case and history of GEORGE FREDERICK COOKE, must be strongly fixed in the memory of persons who were accustomed to frequent the theatres in the palmy days of that eminent actor and of his compeers, John P. Kemble, Mrs. Siddons, John Bannister, and other "stars." With histrionic talents calculated to command the admiration and praises of the most able critics, but too often eclipsed and degraded by the vice of intoxication, Cooke might have secured riches, as well as the friendship of the first classes of society. An infatuated love of ardent spirits, however, often led him to drink to such excess, even on the days he was to perform some of his principal characters, that he was sometimes carried off the stage. He indulged me with orders for the theatre, and I invited him and Thomas Dibdin to dine with me, in Wilderness Row, in 1802, on a Saturday. He drank freely of port and brandy, and consequently was not only very loquacious, but vociferous in reciting passages of his most favourite characters. Dibdin made many efforts to restrain his excitement, and induce him to go home. Soon after twelve o'clock they left the house, with the intention of taking a hackney-coach in Smithfield. In that famed arena, and under the beams of a bright moon and twinkling lamps, Cooke spouted forth one of his fine soliloquies, to an audience of hackney-coachmen, &c. On the Monday following my small dinner-party, my landlord, my next-door neighbour, called and gave me notice to quit the house as soon as possible; for he could not rest in peace and security with such a riotous and wicked person separated from him only by a few bricks. This landlord was a fanatical Huntingtonian, whose nasal hymns, and boisterous extempore prayers, often grated upon my ears and discomposed the nervous system. Cooke's public life and character have been amply described by W. Dunlop, his biographer, in two volumes, octavo, 1815; and by Charles Mathews, in the Life, &c., of that extraordinary player.

## BOWOOD,

#### COMPARED AND CONTRASTED, AT THE END OF THE LAST AND MIDDLE OF THE PRESENT CENTURY.

The history of eminent places, as of eminent persons, cannot fail to engage the laudable curiosity of intellectual readers. Each has its infancy, progressive growth, maturity, decline, and fall; and both involve events and vicissitudes which render the topography of one and the biography of the other eminently interesting to the philosopher and the philologist. Bowood belongs to this category, as I hope to exemplify by a few brief notices. Had I the fluent and vivid pen of

Mrs. Jameson, or Sir Walter Scott, I might render this more apparent than will be manifested by the following comments on the place, as it has appeared to me at different times between the years 1798 and 1853, my first and last visits.

My reminiscences and memoranda respecting this eminently historical, political, scientific and literary Seat involve matter and materials calculated to make a goodly-sized volume; but I must restrict my pen to a few pages. Intimately connected, as Bowood is, with my own literary annals, I cannot revert to my first visit to it but with astonishment and feelings of exultation. It seems as a dream—a reverie of fancy—a vision—an unreasonable event in human life. Up to the age of twenty-six, I had never conversed with a nobleman, or scarcely with a gentleman in the higher ranks of society, and had never visited any of the wealthy mansions of the great personages of the land. I certainly had been admitted into the studios of a few artists, and also into the wine-cellars of Sir William Chambers, in Berners Street and at Whitton Park; and I had spent two days with Mr. Scrope, and his aged mother, at Castle Combe, as will be noticed hereafter; but the last event occurred immediately after my emancipation from the wine-cellar, and before I undertook my Quixotic journey to Plympton, already noticed, or had any notion of literature as a profession. Otherwise my intercourse with aristocracy and intellectual beings was as "rare as snow in June, or wheat in chaff." It is true that I was from boyhood ambitious to be in the company of my elders, and superiors in knowledge; and a little of the rust and rudeness of village life and menial manners had been rubbed down, if not polished, by partiality for debating societies and private theatricals, which were popular in London at the beginning of the present century. I must frankly acknowledge that I was as unfitted for communion, and unqualified to converse, with princes or nobles of the land, as with utopian autocrats or celestial monarchs. I approached the house, through a lodge and park, which inspired awe and wonder; I rang the bell to the domestic part of the premises with hesitation and doubt; I asked incoherent questions about the Marquess, the house, &c.: the porter was perplexed and called the footman, who consulted the valet, and he appealed to the butler, who good-naturedly construed my meaning and wishes, and introduced me to his noble master, who was seated in a well-filled and spacious library, and who appeared to my dizzy vision like something superhuman. Without a card, or prospectus of the work which was the ostensible object of my visit, I was requested to explain who I was, and what was the nature of my inquiry and intentions. Unprepared to explain what I had no distinct notion of, myself, I related something of my short and uneventful career, and the reasons for attempting to write about my native county; told of my friendless and forlorn circumstances, love of reading, and the arts; desire to acquire knowledge, and qualify myself to accomplish the task I had undertaken with some degree of credit to myself, and not discredit my friends. From persons at Chippenham and from public report, I had been led to consider the Marquess as naturally high, stern, and haughty to strangers, and with this impression I approached him with a full recognition of the embarrassed situation of poor dear Goldsmith, in his interview with the Duke of Newcastle. Fortunately I found him very different from anticipation; for he was bland, courteous, and affable. Hence I was soon relieved from all painful restraint, and told my "round unvarnished tale" of birth-place, near Bowood, of being parentless, friendless, and almost homeless, but ambitious to do something to mitigate those misfortunes. After I had been indulged and honoured with nearly an hour's most exciting converse, his lordship called his librarian, Mr. Mathews, directed him to provide me with such books and maps as might be useful, allot me a bed-room, and send a person to show me the house, the pleasure-grounds, the cascade, the park, and other objects. Relieved from the painful suspense of doubt, anxiety, and alarm, my heart expanded, my mind was exhilarated, and every thing, scene, and person, seemed supernaturally exquisite and charmed. Had his lordship repulsed my first overtures, and sent me from his house with cold pride, or indifference, it is probable that "The Beauties of Wiltshire" would never have appeared before the public, nor its author ever become known in the annals of literature. To Lord Lansdowne, therefore, am I indebted for the condescension and kindness he manifested towards an unknown and very humble person; who has laboured hard from that time to the present in the fields of literature and art to produce a succession and amount of books, which may be considered to equal, if not surpass, those of any other English author, in quantity and quality of embellishment, typography, and in the varied matter and manner of their miscellaneous contents.—(See *List* at the end of vol. ii.)

At Bowood I remained four days, and revelled not only in the luxurious scenery of the park, pleasure-grounds, and general features of the locality, but in the well-stored library, and in examining the many fine pictures which adorned the house and reflected honour on its possessor. These, indeed, were peculiarly attractive to me, as my associations and reading, at that time, had been mainly with artists and their works, and consequently I had imperceptibly become the friend and advocate of both. In the Beauties of Wiltshire, already alluded to, and in a small volume devoted to the pictures at Corsham, and in several other publications, I have employed my pen in the cause of art, as well as in reprobation of the injudicious fashion which before then, and since, has prevailed amongst connoisseurs and patrons of art in expending money on pictures of the old schools, or for bad copies, or imitations, to the aggrandizement of picture dealers, and picture manufacturers. With such sentiments and expressed opinions, it gave me no small amount of pleasure to learn from the noble Marquess that he had purchased many English pictures, with a view of forming a *Gallery of Modern Art,* and that he had advocated the adornment of the interior of St. Paul's Cathedral Church, London, with appropriate sculpture by native masters. His Lordship's opinions on this subject are put on record in the second volume of Pettigrew's "Memoirs of John Coakley Lettsom, M.D." and are highly honourable to his liberality of opinion and good taste. These views, indeed, were on many occasions, and in different places, brought forward by his lordship; and had the age been qualified to appreciate and encourage them, they would have sprouted and blossomed. But they were not then understood at the fountain-head of fashion, and were consequently left to run to waste. Besides making great additions and improvements to the mansion at Bowood, the Marquess built a handsome *Mausoleum,* at the south-western extremity of the park, in the midst of forest trees. In this, are marble monuments to John Petty, Earl of Shelburne (grandfather to the present Marquess), and to William Petty, first Marquess.

It will not be expedient to make further comments on his lordship's public character, as it is developed in some of the best annals of our country; for he was an historical personage of an exalted and important class. That his views on the patronage of English Art were of the best kind, was evinced by the pictures and sculptures he possessed at Bowood, and in Shelburne House, London. The last, indeed, was singularly rich in *ancient* statues, busts, and bassi-relievi, which competed with the famed Arundelian collection, in value and celebrity. It is fortunately preserved entire by the present noble proprietor of Shelburne House, who purchased the whole from the widow of his brother, the late Marquess, to prevent its dispersion, by sale. The former had bought them of the executors of his father for the sum of £6000., and it is known that their present possessor has increased their number and value by purchasing other antique specimens.* Amongst Pictures of the English School, I mention the following, as indicating the best artists of the time: sea-beach by Barrett, with figures by Gilpin and Cipriani; a sea-piece with vessels in danger, by N. Pocock; a landscape with a winding road, woods and a group of carrier's horses, cows in water, &c., by Gainsborough; landscape, with figures, representing Apollo and the Seasons, by Wilson, engraved by Woollett.

Amongst a large collection of Portraits, the following were particularly interesting, and some of them very fine: Sir Wm. Petty, by Closterman; Oliver Cromwell, by Walker; Dean Swift, full length, by Jervas; John, Earl of Grenville; Sir Robert Walpole, who asserted that every man has his price, i. e., politically, and as borough-mongery was then practised; Wm. Pitt, Earl of Chatham, the wise and patriotic minister; John Dunning, afterwards Lord Ashburton;† the Marquess of Granby, by Sir Joshua Reynolds;† General Washington; Colonel

---

* In Mrs. Jameson's interesting "Companion to the most celebrated private Galleries of Art," 8vo. 1840, is a List of the Sculptures, and a Catalogue of the principal Pictures at Bowood and in Lansdowne House, with able descriptions and criticisms.

† These two pictures I purchased, in 1809, at a sale of the Bowood collection, by Peter Coxe: the first I sold to the Marquess of Stafford, and the second to a gentleman of Plymouth. An engraved print from the last may be seen in "The Fine Arts of the English School." 4to. 1812.

Barré, when young;* Doctors Mead, Sydenham, Mayherne, and Boerhaave; Edmund Waller; Richard Gibson, commonly called the Dwarf Artist, by Sir Peter Lely; Peg Woffington, by Hogarth.

---

* The once-remarkable COLONEL BARRÉ, who was one of Lord Shelburne's nominee members for Calne, had been a distinguished officer in the disgraceful American war, and had signalized himself in the skilful siege and conquest of Quebec. He had been the confidential secretary to the courageous general who lost his life in that memorable victory, and had been a "soldier of fortune," but failed to attain it in the battle-field, or by the English ministry; was patronized, befriended, and brought into Parliament by Lord Shelburne, whose confidential companion he appears to have been for the remainder of life. In the House of Commons he was noted for unflinching courage, for terseness and vehemence of language, which often cowed the corrupt partizans of a corrupt administration, and rendered him an object of malicious animadversion by the party pamphleteers and political critics of the day, who were equally hostile and caustic against the Colonel's patron and friend. Hence, whilst one was pronounced "the Bull-dog," the other was stigmatized as "the Malagrida," of Parliament. That Barré was author of a remarkable "Letter to a Brigadier-General," published in London in 1760, and re-published in 1841, I have endeavoured to show, in "The Letters of Junius Elucidated," 1848, and have also taken some pains to prove that Barré was their author, and that William Greatrakes was his amanuensis. For the last ten years I have read much and thought more on that mystical subject; and, whilst I am convinced that not one of the persons since named as the author, was truly so, I am the more confirmed in opinion that the Colonel "was the man." Were I twenty years younger, and possessed the learning and varied talents of a Brougham, a Macaulay, or a Hallam, I am convinced that there is sufficient circumstantial evidence to trace the authorship to Barré and Greatrakes. The labour is, however, too much for me to undertake at my age, and I bequeath it to some younger, and equally zealous person to pursue and accomplish the task. To the two justly-eminent authors above named, and to my learned and acute friend, Sir David Brewster, I venture to appeal, by intreating them to examine the evidence which has been published since they last reviewed the question; and I feel persuaded they will decide against the claims of either Sir Philip Francis or Maclean to the authorship of the Junius Letters. The late profound Bishop of Llandaff, Coplestone, believed in Francis until he had perused my volume, which, he said, he had "read with great interest; and I can with truth say that nothing I have before examined on that subject has equalled your essay in unravelling the perplexities of the question: as far as the means exist of solving the problem, you have, I think, succeeded."

The only, or principal, circumstance that serves to invalidate the evidence against Colonel Barré, is the long and confidential intimacy that subsisted between him and Lord Shelburne, with the severity of language used by Junius, or the presumed Junius, against that nobleman. But this, I think, may be explained: the writings signed Junius, Philo-Junius, C., and by other words or marks, both praise and vilify the same persons, and cannot be trusted as evidence for, or against, particular parties. I

As essentially connected with the Lansdowne family and its history, the famed MANUSCRIPTS, now forming part of the National Library in the British Museum, constitute an important fact and feature. These were purchased by Parliament in 1807 for the sum of £4925. They had been originally collected by James West and Philip Carteret Wheble, two gentlemen who had signalized themselves in the last century by their industry and liberality in purchasing manuscripts. They consist of papers which had belonged to Lord Burghley; the Earl of Salisbury; Strype, the historian and topographer; Bishops Kennett and Warburton; Anstis and Le Neve, heralds; Sir Julius Cæsar's copies of the most important documents amongst the Tower and Cottonian Records; also Royal Autograph Letters, and other similar materials. From such persons, and on important national topics, we may fairly infer that the whole collection was and is of much importance. Fortunately, the whole was obtained, in one lot, from the executors of William, Marquess of Lansdowne, for the gratification of readers who take an interest in such matters, and for the benefit of historical literature in particular. Two volumes of Catalogue were printed in 1807 previous to the sale; and in 1812 another copious Catalogue was printed from the MSS. of F. Douce and Sir Henry Ellis, in folio.*

---

could adduce the opinions of many other good authorities in ascribing the Letters of Junius to Barré. Let us state the evidence of an acute, profound witness, who must have seen much of the Colonel, at Bowood, in 1781: "*Barré* (says Bentham) loves to sit over his claret, pushes it about pretty briskly, and abounds in stories that are well told, and very entertaining. He really seems to have a great command of language; he states clearly and forcibly, and upon all points his words are fluent and well chosen."—(*Bentham's Works,* by Dr. Bowring, vol. x. p. 104.) I may venture to insert a few lines from my own publication on this subject: "The character and mental qualifications of Colonel Barré have been fully elucidated in the course of the preceding narrative; and it must be allowed that his powers of sarcasm and invective, the boldness of his language, the intrepidity and patriotism of his conduct, apart from those peculiar circumstances of his position and connection which I have now endeavoured to illustrate, present an extraordinary resemblance to the characteristics of Junius, and render it surprising that such claims have not been previously, and more carefully, examined and elucidated."—(*Junius Elucidated,* p. 86.)

* This Catalogue may now be purchased for eleven shillings. A careful account of the collection of manuscripts, with much other interesting information, is published in "A Hand-book to the Library in the British Museum," by R. Sims, 12mo. 1854.

From the attainment and possession of such a manuscript library, alone, something of the character of its noble possessor may be inferred; and when combined with his patriotic exertions in the national councils, he must be entitled to the gratitude and admiration of every "true-born Briton." I avail myself of a few lines from a letter to me by my once-esteemed friend the Rev. Dr. Popham, dated April, 1814, who says, that he was often a guest at Bowood, when Dunning, Barré, the Rev. Joseph Townsend, Jeremy Bentham, and many other eminent persons, were also visitors.

> "My information respecting the birth, life, and character of Lord Lansdowne may be comprised in a small compass. I never knew the place of his nativity, [Dublin, 1737. J. B.] or the early part of his education, which I guess was under a private tutor at home, from his having lamented to me, more than once, that the Earl of Shelburne, his father, would not permit him to go to a public school, which, he said, would have given him more confidence and a greater fluency of language, when he spoke in the House of Lords. My first acquaintance with his lordship was when he was at Christ Church, Oxford. He was then remarkable for his regular conduct, and strict attendance at daily prayers. When he left the University, his lordship entered the army, and soon went abroad. Returning to England after the death of his father, he married, if I recollect aright, one of the Grenvilles. She dying in 1771, he next espoused a sister of the Earl of Upper Ossory, in 1779. In 1765 I became possessed of the living of Lacock (about three miles west of Bowood), which preferment I resigned in February, 1814. My frequent visits to Bowood gave me opportunities of seeing and conversing with persons of high rank in this as well as in other kingdoms; with men of learning and artists of the first eminence; in short, with everything that could conduce to render the table of an English nobleman elegant, polite, easy, and instructive. Politics were seldom the subject of conversation; religion, never; though I have often met there, not only clergymen of the Established Church, but Doctors Price, Priestley, Franklin, &c. The only allusion I ever heard from his lordship was a remark made on the death of Bishop —— 'Then,' said his lordship, 'we shall have a rookery at St. James's.'"

The preceding affords a glimpse into the interior of Bowood, as it was more than half a century back: we obtain, however, other and further evidence of the same period in the writings of a multifarious author, whose literary works extend to twenty-two crowded volumes, as edited by *John Bowring, LL.D.* These abound in original and acute comments on various subjects—ethics, politics, law, history, morals, biography, mathematics, &c.,—and cannot be perused without affording instruction to every impartial reader. He proceeds thus:

"In 1781 the Earl of Shelburne visited me, and touched one of my cheeks with his." In a letter dated July, 1781, his lordship says, "I am ambitious of your friendship." In another epistle he writes, "By Lord Mansfield I was disappointed: at Lord Shelburne's I was indemnified: at Kenwood, I should have been mortified and disgusted: at Bowood, I was caressed and delighted. A novel, and that altogether not an uninteresting one, might be made out of a correct unvarnished picture of the incidents to which that visit to a garret at Lincoln's Inn gave birth. Of esteem, not to speak of affection, marks more unequivocal one man could not receive of another, than in the course of about twelve years I received from Lord Shelburne."

Dr. Bowring writes:—"A few weeks after the visit of the lord to the lawyer, the latter had an interview with the former in Berkeley Square, and an invitation to Bowood, where he remained for some weeks. From this place, which he describes as a home of elegant hospitality and intellectual fascination, he addressed many letters to his friends, containing anecdotes of, and descriptive comments on, the characters of his noble host and the visitors. Many of these are printed in the collected works of the author, and will afford much curious and interesting information, conveyed in original language and comment." The following warrants this remark:—

"Lord Shelburne had been the making of Judge Blackstone; having been in personal favour with George III., he introduced the lecturer (the 'Commentaries' were first brought forward thus) and made the monarch sit to be lectured, as he himself told me. The lecturer, as anybody may see, showed the king how majesty is God upon earth. Majesty could do no less than make him a Judge for it. Blasphemy is, saying anything a judge may gratify himself by punishing a man for. If tailoring a man out with God's *Attributes*, and under that very name, is blasphemy, none was ever so rank as Blackstone's. The Commentaries remain unprosecuted; the poison still unto all eyes: piety is never offended by it: it may be, perhaps, should party in high places ever cease to be a tool of despotism." From these letters we learn that Bentham urged Lord Shelburne not to send his son and heir to college, as it was a place "where perjury was daily practised." Attending the family service one Sunday, in the hall, he says, "the parson was a sleek young curate of the parish, and our saints were a naked Mercury, an Apollo, and a Venus, in the same dress; the congregation, two ladies, my Lord and Lady, and your humble servant, upon the carpet; whilst the domestics were placed below with poor Mathews, the librarian."

"There seems to be no want of money here. The grounds are laying out and plantations making upon a large scale. A gate (lodge) is going to be made with a pyramid on each side of it, for an approach to the house, at six miles distance: the pyramid to be at least 150 feet high. I call it Egypt."

## VISITORS TO BOWOOD: END OF EIGHTEENTH CENTURY.

From these letters it appears that "Capability Brown" had been employed in advising about laying out the grounds, forming the fine lake, the cascade, &c.; that Mr. Hamilton, of Pains Hill, whose seat at that time was famed for its beautiful grounds, furnished much valuable advice; and that Josiah Lane, of Tisbury, executed the rock-work and the caves at the *Cascade*. The last was, and, I believe, is, the best, the most picturesque and least artificial, in effect, of any made work of the kind in Great Britain.

From Bentham's testimony we learn that Colonel Barré had been Lord Shelburne's confidential adviser for many years; but that late in the life of the former a rupture had occurred, and Bentham was chosen to be his successor in that delicate office. The following list of *Visitors to Bowood*, during Bentham's residence in that distinguished mansion, will furnish some notion of the company the noble proprietor kept and courted: Sir Edward Baynton, Bart.; the Earl and Countess of Pembroke; Alderman Beckford and his noted Son; Lord Maldon; the Duke and Duchess of Bedford; Lord Bristol, the eccentric Bishop of Derry, who derived £7000. a year from his see; Lord Elliot; the Earl of Radnor, said to have a rent-roll of £20,000. a year; Paul Cobb Methuen, £16,000. a year; Lord and Lady Holland; Lord Dartrey; the two Ladies Waldegrave, daughters of the Duchess of Gloucester; Sir Benjamin Hobhouse, Bart. (of this aimable and most estimable gentleman, I shall have occasion to say something hereafter); Lord and Lady Tracton, whom Bentham (x. 104) describes as "the queerist jigs you ever saw: my Lord wears his bob-wig, black coat, and coloured worsted stockings; and looks like a plain, stout, thick-set country parson. My Lady is a little shrivelled figure of about 60, with a hook-nose and ferret-eyes, a long white beard and a mahogany-coloured skin, in a grey riding-habit, with black hat and feather."

In one of his letters he characterizes Lord Lansdowne "for discernment as eminent, for quickness of comprehension not less so. I met him one night on the stairs, when I was retiring to bed and when his lordship was coming to the supper table, for I usually resorted to one whilst the company was at the other. He then said, in his usual hurried manner, 'Mr. Bentham, what is it I can do for you?' I told him, nothing; and he found this so different to the unequivocal spirit of those around him, as to endear me to him thenceforward." On another occasion, and after decided intimacy, Bentham thus writes to his noble friend: "In the name of God, my Lord, what are those shadows for which you are sacrificing every thing and every body? What in the scale of politics can be the weight of a parliamentary interest, so far as mere members are concerned, of which the sole constitutional elements are so many votes, neither more nor less, as three seats can purchase? for Lord Wycombe's is not yet at market; he is not yet called up, or chosen for a county." After remarking on personal reputation, borough influence, and party, the writer thus characterizes his lordship's members; "*Dunning*, I think I have understood from you, you had an affection for: *Townsend*, at any rate: and I suppose *Barré*, at one time. Dunning, though a narrow-minded man and mere lawyer, was a most able advocate, and, I dare say, drew a considerable *stirps* after him. Townsend was of use to you in the city. I believe, at one time, he governed it. Barré, though he knew nothing, was a good party bull-dog, barked well, and with great imposition and effect, where nothing was necessary to be known. To the herd of statesmen, power is its own end; by the dignified few it is regarded as the means to an end. There have been times when I have had the pleasure of seeing your lordship ranking yourself amongst those few; I wish I could say always..... Put *Jekyl* in Parliament! it is quite a burlesque upon Parliament, the very idea of it!...... When the beginning of the French Revolution was on the carpet at Bowood, you scarce durst own your good wishes on its behalf; whilst Jekyl, who has so many good jokes, was exhausting himself in bad ones to endeavour to make it look ridiculous." [*Bentham's Works*, vol. x., p. 235.]

These contemporary notices of the first Marquess of Lansdowne and of Bowood, furnish hints for imagination to make a picture which cannot fail to amuse and gratify the reader, who wishes to be informed of public persons, events, and a place, which belong to English history. On taking my reluctant leave of Bowood, his lordship increased my gratitude by his kindness, and tested my personal strength (for I was a poor pedestrian) with five volumes of books, and a copy of Andrews and Drury's large "Survey of Wiltshire," in eighteen folio sheets.

Exultingly and proudly I wended my steps towards Chippenham, to gladden the heart of my sister and some good friends, who anxiously awaited the report of my adventures and long absence. Whilst my story gratified some, I learnt afterwards that it had a very different effect on others, who from that sad, moral disease, envy, combined with another severe malady called party-spirit, both vilified the Marquess and his humble visitor.*

Since my first acquaintance with Bowood, I have witnessed both the "decline and fall," with something like a revolution, in that noble Seat. The second Marquess, to whom it descended, preferred the town of Southampton, and a private Yacht on the sea, to the splendid home and fine domain of his illustrious parent; and hence not only neglected both, but let out the park for grazing, and even endeavoured to denude the land of its forest timber and fine woods. The powers of the Lord

---

* Chippenham at that time and for many years afterwards was a hot-bed of political animosity and rancour. Friendships were turned into enmities, and families were separated from, and divided against each other; discord and enmity pervaded the whole population, and it was painful for a peace-loving person to visit any of their houses, and to hear nothing but backbiting and scandal. Amongst Mr. Sadler's writings I find the following lines, which at once exhibit his poetical genius and the times when they were penned.

WAR. ON THE RENEWAL OF HOSTILITIES. THE PEACE OF AMIENS, 1803.
BY ROBERT SADLER.

Hark! again the storms of war
Burst upon the dusky world,
Thunder, from its iron car,
Speaks again the death-bolt hurl'd.

Flying wide, in sheets of fire,
Blood and smoke stain deep the sod;
Far and wide a dreadful pyre,
Kindled to the horrid god.

Nature starts! and, all aghast,
Lifts her apprehensive eye,
Shudders, and amidst the blast,
Thus for succour heaves a sigh.

"Author of my injured frame,
See around me ruin rave;
Still shall devils mock thy name,
Prince of Peace? Oh! save. Oh! save."

Chancellor were employed to check his waste and heartless desecration. Fortunately for Bowood, for its environs, and for the country, Lord Henry Petty, second son of the first Marquess, came into possession of the property, the title, and the family seat, on the death of his elder brother, in 1809. A change came over the whole scene; and from that memorable epoch to the present time, Bowood has progressively and regularly advanced to its present state of beauty, utility, and importance. In the completeness, spaciousness, and luxury of the mansion, it is entitled to admiration and commendation; in its pictorial and sculptured works of art and literary treasures, it cannot fail to gratify every genuine lover of intellectual productions; for whilst it tends to adorn the locality, it becomes one of the great features of our extraordinary country. I could pleasingly dilate on the peculiar characteristics and beauties of Bowood, for they are strongly impressed on my memory and feelings; but must rather refer my readers to the *Beauties of Wiltshire;* to *Beauties of England:* "Wiltshire;" to Mrs. Jameson's volume, already noticed; and to Moore's *Memoirs,* for anecdotes and miscellaneous memoranda, than attempt a systematic and copious account of a Seat which has grown under the fostering judgment, and good taste, of its present much-respected possessor. His political and parliamentary character has been subjected to public recognition and commentary for nearly half a century, and has borne the ordeal with unimpeachable credit. His private and personal character, those only can duly and fairly appreciate who have been honoured with his friendly confidence. In the *Memoirs and Diary* of the late intellectual Thomas Moore we are indulged with so many anecdotes of his lordship's sentiments and domestic habits, that we cannot fail to honour the man, who has passed through such changes in the political world amidst the violent conflicts of party, with feelings of more than common respect—of admiration, almost approaching to idolatry.

Having noticed the principal distinguished visitors to Bowood at the time of the residence of the first Marquess, it may serve to indicate at once the social and intellectual character and habits of the present nobleman, by giving a list of the most eminent of his guests. Sir James Macintosh; the Reverends Sidney Smith, W. Lisle Bowles, Geo. Crabbe, Wm. Crowe, Joseph Townsend, and Dr. Popham; the

Earls of Malmesbury, Essex, Albemarle, Aberdeen, Suffolk, Pembroke; Lords Holland, John Russell, Brougham, Grenville, Arundel; Messrs. S. Rogers, Tierney, W. Allan, O'Connell, Jekyl, Luttrell, Canning, Abercrombie, Agar-Ellis, Hallam, T. Moore: also many titled Ladies, and eminent Artists of the English School; likewise Architects and Literati, both British and foreign.

We have already seen that the first Marquess of Lansdowne was justly noted as an admirer and patron of English Art, and its professors: we shall now find that his favourite son inherits the same spirit, as shown by more extensive purchases and even more zeal in the cause. Bowood and Shelburne House are profusely adorned by choice works of the most distinguished British artists. When Mrs. Jameson wrote her Catalogue in 1813, there were 160 pictures, besides many fine pieces of sculpture. Since that date several additional works have been purchased. "I have never known," says Mrs. Jameson, "any possessor of rare and beautiful things who seemed so really and habitually to enjoy all the pleasures they can impart, except perhaps Mr. Rogers and Sir George Beaumont, nor one who more kindly imparted a gratification of which he felt the full value." It should be remarked and understood that the Lansdowne collection is strictly a private one, and dispersed over the whole extent of the principal apartments in the two houses referred to. It contains specimens of almost "every school, every style, every age, and every country." But those by English masters are the most numerous, and by far the most interesting; for they come before the eye of the impartial critic with the warranty of truth and authenticity: they are divested of all mystery and trickery, tell their own tales, and they appeal to the hearts and heads of unprejudiced British minds. It would occupy more space than I can spare to enumerate all that adorn and enrich this collection; but the names of the artists will intimate to the connoisseur the character and merits of some of their best works:—Reynolds,* Hogarth, Jervas, Wilson, Gainsborough, Romney, Morland, of the last century; whilst the following belong to the present: Boddington,

---

\* Of this fascinating artist and aimable man Lord Lansdowne has seven specimens at Bowood, besides others in London. Mrs. Jameson's Biographical Criticism on him and his works is a most flattering and just commentary.

Barker, of Bath; E. Calcott, Collins, W. Cooke, Cope, Sir Charles Eastlake, Harlow, Howard, T. E. Hurlestone, Inskipp, John Jackson, Sir Edwin Landseer, Chas. Landseer, Sir Thos. Lawrence, Chas. R. Leslie, Linnel, Maclise, Newton, H. W. Pickersgill, E. Parris, D. Roberts, Severn, W. Simson, F. Stone, Sir D. Wilkie, and Stanfield: the last has nine pictures fitted to panels in the dining-room. Of *Modern Sculpture*, the collection includes fine specimens by Thorwalsden, Canova, Flaxman, Chantrey, Gibson, Bailey, and Sir R. Westmacott.

The Demesne, or Liberty of Bowood is extra-parochial, but within the boundary of the parish of Calne, and extends over an area of more than 1000 acres. Of these, 81 acres are appropriated to the deer-park, with a home-farm; 62 acres to pleasure-grounds; and 50 acres to the lake. The grounds may be described as consisting of undulating surface, in which eight small valleys converge to a ninth of greater extent, nearly the whole of which is occupied by a broad and finely-formed lake, whose collected waters are conveyed through openings in, and over, a walled embankment, and thus form a very picturesque cascade.

My last cursory visit to this domain was in the autumn of 1853, when the park, the woods, the mansion, the new flower-garden, the lake, were all resplendent, and the whole *coup-d'œil* full of beauty and harmony: the vast woods tinted with those vivid and pleasing colours which mark the intermediate stage between summer and winter—between strong and florid youthful health, and drooping, depressed old age. On that occasion I penned the following remarks to a friend, with which I conclude these few desultory pen-sketches.

Bowood may—nay, must—be regarded as classic ground,—as the home and haunt of genius and talent, of liberality and learning, of worth and of wisdom. It seems now to have attained its zenith: the beauties of nature are various and eminent; whilst art—fine art—abounds in all its internal adornment, and even in its gardens, glades, and park-lodges. Hence the stranger, whether foreign or English, who first visits this noble house, is favourably, pleasingly prepossessed with notions of dignity and elegance by the gate-houses which are raised at the different entrances to the park. The last is on a grand scale, abounds with much variety of surface,—of hill and dale, of narrow valleys, of high grounds commanding distant scenery, of a large extent of forest, of copse, of lawn, and of water. The whole consists of a wide area of table land, bounded to the south by a bold ridge of the Marlborough and Cherril Downs, whose precipitous northern slope, like a vast ocean wave, seems as if it were suddenly arrested in its career, and solidified into a terrestrial mass. Formed of chalk, and covered with a fine herbage, with undulating outline opposed to the sky, and alternate concavities and projections on the surface, it forms an imposing boundary to the scenery of the park and pleasure-grounds. Under the ever-varying effects of sunshine and of cloud—of morning, mid-day, and evening—I have witnessed scenes which would have delighted, but defied the fascinating pencil of, a Claude, or a Turner, to portray, or even approach: for "who can paint like Nature?"

It would be ungrateful in me, and unjust to the memory of the late amiable and estimable MARCHIONESS OF LANSDOWNE, were I to take final leave of the home, which she loved and adorned for so many years, without recording my humble tribute of thankfulness and praise to her memory. In the memories and hearts of all the cottage inhabitants of the neighbourhood of Bowood, her urbanity, generosity, and good counsel, were deeply implanted; and I have often heard, with delight, their fervent, but uncouth expressions of gratitude and admiration. There are few things to be more admired, in country life, at least to my eye, than the good, clean, neat, and carefully-adorned cottage of the villager; and the more particularly, when contrasted and compared with the filthy, ruinous, noisome lodgings and houses of the poor inhabitants of London, Manchester, Birmingham, and many other crowded towns: whilst one bespeaks the prudence and domestic comforts of their occupants, the others are palpable evidences of vice, wreckless folly, and depravity. In the legislative councils and sound politics of Lord Lansdowne, we perceive that Parliament has adopted laws and regulations calculated to cure some of the evils here named, by educating, rationalizing, the ignorant population of the country. Lady Lansdowne generously and humanely employed herself in administering instruction with good advice to mothers of families, and their growing offspring, who were tenants of, or in any way connected with her provincial home. I have seen her carriage at the comfort-looking cottages at Derry Hill, and two other places, adjoining Bowood, and learnt from some of their inhabitants that her ladyship was happily employed in comforting the sick, instructing the young, and feeding the hungry. Yet, though thus beneficently and humanely occupied abroad, she was the accomplished, the elegant, the intellectual companion at the festive board and in the drawing-room. Moore, in his *Diary*, has related many traits of her amiable and endearing characteristics, and he had ample opportunities of knowing something of the heart and mind of her ladyship. In the *Gentleman's Magazine* for July, 1851, is a brief account of the late lamented Marchioness, in harmony with, and corroborative of, the preceding testimony. She died April 3, 1851, and was deposited in the family mausoleum in the park of Bowood. The obituary notice says, " Of Lord Lansdowne's refined and intellectual household the Marchioness was the animating spirit. It may seem strange that the *prestige* of being the acknowledged friend and patron of literature and art, should not be more largely coveted in the upper orders of society. It is possible that the ambition is more extensively entertained than the success of the aspirants would imply. However that may be, the triumph of that true Mecenatian hospitality which places wit on the level with wealth and prefers mind to pedigree, appears to have been reserved for our days, for the brilliant receptions of Holland and Lansdowne Houses. Their days are now past: whilst those who have partaken of the splendid hospitalities of Bowood, will be equally conscious of a vacancy not to be supplied in that more limited circle; and hundreds of poor families spread over the many thousand acres of that princely demesne have sustained a loss such as it is no derogation to those who shall succeed her to pronounce irreparable. The lively interest which this excellent lady took in everything that related to the comfort and moral habits, the well-being and well-doing of the poor on the estate, has passed into a proverb."

The following admirable tribute to the memory of the late Marchioness, by an author whose praise is precious, is worthy of repetition. Lord John Russell, in a brief Preface to the sixth volume of " Moore's Diary," says, her ladyship " diffused an air of holiness, of peace, and purity over the house of Bowood which neither rich nor poor can ever forget."

## ANECDOTES OF THE REV. W. L. BOWLES, THOMAS MOORE, AND THE REV. G. CRABBE.

In the immediate vicinity of Bowood are three places which have attained distinction in the annals of English poetry, as the "homes and haunts" of a trio of authors whose names and fame have been echoed throughout the realms of the reading world. Hence they demand especial notice here, not only as belonging to the locality, but from my own personal intimacy and correspondence with them. These were the REV. WILLIAM LISLE BOWLES, of Bremhill; Thomas Moore, of Sloperton Cottage; and the Rev. George Crabbe, of Trowbridge: the elder of the three, first and from long residence in Wiltshire, claims precedence. He was placed as Curate in the parish of Donhead, near the south-western end of that county, as early as 1796, and after being Vicar of Dumbleton, Gloucestershire, for a short period, was advanced to Bremhill, in 1804, the vicarage of which parish he held for forty-six years, to the time of his decease. From the number and character of his various publications, his name was often before the public, and whilst his Sonnets obtained for him the admiration and praises of most of the lovers of poetry and its critics, his prose writings led him into much angry controversy, not only with anonymous reviewers, but with such authors as Byron and Roscoe. His personal eccentricities attracted the notice and smiles of all who knew him. It is not my intention to attempt a Biography of my once-loved and respected friend, though I hope it may be soon written by a person well qualified for the task; for the man and his works are worthy of elucidation and record.*

Mr. Bowles was the son of a clergyman of King's Norton, Northamptonshire, where he was born September 24, 1762; he was educated at the famed collegiate school of Winchester, under the Rev. Joseph Warton, and thence advanced to Trinity College, Oxford, where he

---

* Soon after Mr. Bowles's death, I urged my friend, the Rev. John Mitford, to undertake the task; but on inquiry I found publishers unwilling to speculate on an edition of his poems, with a memoir. I am pleased to hear that the Rev. Dr. Bowles, of Staunton Lacy, is likely to undertake this very pleasing task, whence we may calculate on justice being done to the poet and the man.

met and became acquainted with Thomas Warton, the historian of English Poetry. To this education and association may be ascribed, if not the original bias, at least, the early cultivation and ripeness of the poetical talent in young Bowles; for I have often heard him speak in the highest terms of the judgment and abilities of those two men. Destined for the church, we find that he was early placed in the Curacy already named, adjoining the fine seat of Wardour Castle, the residence of Lord Arundell, a Roman Catholic, whose private chapel, in that mansion, excited my wonder and admiration after I left Bowood in 1798. It was in that year I first met Mr. Bowles, a gay and handsome young man, then flushed with the fame arising from praises by Coleridge and by many other poets and professed critics. Thence he was promoted to the vicarage of Dumbleton, Gloucestershire, by the patronage of the Earl of Somers. Good fortune or favouritism soon advanced him in the scale of promotion to the better living of *Bremhill*, where he resided for many years, beloved by the rich and honoured by all. To the emoluments from this parish he was enabled to add those of a Canonry, and afterwards of an Archdeaconry, in the Cathedral of Salisbury. Thus he became amply provided with a handsome clerical income, and also with professional occupation. Though diligent, attentive, and conscientiously devoted to his pastoral duties, he had much leisure to cultivate literature; and there is scarcely any species of poetry which he did not write about, nor any modes of composition, then fashionable, which he did not practice: sonnets, elegies, monodies, ballads, and descriptive lays; from the fourteen-line sonnet to the more extensive poem of many pages. The extent of his literary productions, in prose and verse, it is difficult, if not impracticable, to specify; for, besides four volumes of poetry, he wrote and published numerous pamphlets, with miscellaneous letters and poems, in magazines, and in newspapers. Amongst these, I have heard that he wrote and printed an Auto-Biographical Sketch; but which I have vainly sought to obtain. Like the generality of poets, my good friend was very sensitive, and easily led into literary controversy and contention. I have now before me a thick volume of pamphlets, mostly of this kind, which he wrote and printed between the years 1800 and 1830, amounting to nearly 2000 pages.

His poems, sermons, and pamphlets were numerous. He edited an edition of *Pope's Works* in 10 vols. 1807, which was criticised in the tenth volume of the "Edinburgh Review." In this popular work his "gentleness to the living was pointedly contrasted with his severe treatment of the dead." He rashly ventured to "take up arms against a sea of troubles," in hostility even to Lord Byron, and the amiable author of the life of Lorenzo de Medici, and other justly popular authors. It would be a long and tedious task to bring under review all his poetical and prose works, for they were numerous, both acknowledged and anonymous.

Moore, in his "Diary," September 1, 1818, says of Bowles that he "never comes amiss: the mixture of talent and simplicity in him is delightful. His parsonage house at Bremhill is beautifully situated; but he has frittered away its beauty with grottos, hermitages, and Shenstonian inscriptions." My early friend (1796) and valuable correspondent, Dr. Robert Southey, calls Bowles, "Byron's antagonist, and Coleridge's preceptor in poetry;" and thus praises *Bremhill*: "The garden is ornamented, in his way, with a jet fountain, something like a hermitage, an obelisk, a cross, and some inscriptions. Two swans, who answer to the names of Snowdrop and Lily, have a pond to themselves, and if not duly fed they march to Mrs. Bowles's window. The view from the house extends over a rich country to the distant Downs, and the White Horse may be distinctly seen. Much as I had heard of Bowles's peculiarities, I should very imperfectly have understood his character had I not passed some time under his roof. He has indulged his natural timidity to a degree little short of insanity, yet he laughs, himself, at follies which he is nevertheless continually committing. He is literally afraid of every thing. His oddity, his untidiness, his simplicity, his benevolence, his fear, and his good nature, make him one of the most entertaining and extraordinary characters I ever met with. He is in his 73rd year, (1837) and for that age is certainly a *fine old man:* in full possession of all his faculties, though so afraid of being deaf, when a slight cold affects his hearing, that he puts his watch to his ear twenty times in the course of the day."—(*Life, &c., of Southey,* vol. vi.)

Our poet has given an ample description of his parsonage house and garden in "The Parochial History of Bremhill," which he published in the year 1828, in a goodly-sized octavo volume; and says he does it "to exhibit the clergyman and his abode in their proper moral position in English society, at the present age of clerical obloquy. With respect to the description, it will be considered that in a very few years every vestige of the house, as it now stands, and the garden, as it appears, may be swept away." This garden consists of upwards of two acres of land laid out in lawn, gravel and green walks, flower-beds, terraces, &c. The house itself has no architectural beauties, though it has gables, tall chimney shafts, open parapets and pinnacles, which were intended by the mason-builder to harmonize with the village church. "By parapetting the whole," the poet says, "with a simple Gothic ornamental railing, a unity has been given to the exterior, and the long low roofs have put on ecclesiastical appearance." I wish it were in my power to compliment the parson, or the builder, for the manifestation of either taste or judgment in their weak attempt to imitate the forms, proportions, or character of any one of the varieties of genuine Christian, miscalled Gothic, architecture.

Having referred to eccentricities in my friend, and Dr. Southey having specified one or two, it cannot be irrelevant to notice others; for they belong to and are marking features of the poet's character. His pathetic and simple Sonnets must be known to general readers, but his personal peculiarities could only be ascertained by intimate association, or from repeated interviews. Devoid of guile, as harmless as the dimpled infant, as bland and affable as courtesy and kindness in union, he gained the love and excited the sympathy of all who knew him; but he often aroused the pity and the fears of those who had witnessed or heard of the negligences and hair-breadth scrapes in which he was occasionally involved. Mr. Bowles was noted for absence of mind, abstraction from the affairs of every-day reality, whence the temper and stoicism of his good and truly philosophic wife were often tested, and, fortunately for her, were efficaciously exerted. When I was at Wells, surveying the Cathedral, for my Antiquities, I dined and spent an evening with him at the Bishop's palace, where he engaged me to breakfast with him the next morning, and afterwards visit Glastonbury, Wokey, and Cheddar. At the appointed time I was at the White Hart Inn, and was not a little surprised and mortified to learn, from the waiter, that Mr. Bowles had ordered his carriage at seven o'clock, and was gone to Bath. In an early part of his life, it has been related that he came to London for the express purpose of waiting on the Archbishop of Canterbury, to solicit a vacant living, but omitted to leave his address, and quitting London abruptly, could not be found when the prelate sought him a few days afterwards. At another time, I am assured that he started from Bremhill, on horseback, to ride to Chippenham, dismounted to walk down a steep hill, leading the horse by the bridle slung across his arm, and continued to the turnpike gate, where he offered to pay the toll, and was not a little surprised when the man said, "We doont charge nothing for your honor, as you beant on osback." On turning round, he perceived the bridle dangling on his arm, but could not descry his horse. Many anecdotes of this kind, and others, far from being merely whimsical, have I heard of my once dear friend, and such as would have made wives of nervous irritability miserable, were borne by Mrs. Bowles with exemplary equanimity, and almost without a murmur. Hence she proved to be an invaluable wife and companion; and it is believed that she not only prolonged his life, but guarded him against many accidents that might have been fatal. After living together many years, she died in 1844, aged 72, leaving the bereaved poet disconsolate, forlorn, and almost helpless. He, however, lived, or rather existed, some years afterwards, at his official home, in the Cathedral Close of Salisbury, but was deprived of mental consciousness: his existence was a blank, a sort of mechanical routine of motion and action, devoid of all those sympathies and enjoyments which distinguish man from the lower race of animals. He continued in this deplorable condition for six years, and was relieved by death in April 1850, at the patriarchal age of 89. He was interred in the Cathedral of Salisbury, with his wife; and a handsome monument has been raised to commemorate both, from the designs of Osmond and Son, of that city.

THOMAS MOORE may be named as the domestic chronicler of the "sayings and doings" at Bowood, for a succession of years. These chronicles having recently been published to the world, excited a vast amount of commentary by readers and critical writers; whence it seems a part of my duty, in this place, to relate a few particulars of such an author and man. During the greater part of his life he might be strictly called "the observed of all observers," in the hemisphere of English fashion. Courted and caressed by nearly all the magnates of aristocracy, his name and fame pervaded their whole region, as well as the more expanded one of periodical and other literature. It was the latter, indeed, which led to the former; for his early poetry became eminently popular, and their author was sought for, courted and petted by all the rival houses of the gay, and the illustrious world. A prolific author, he progressively wrote and published many works on various subjects, nearly the whole of which were eminently successful, consequently, profitable to the author and to his publishers. He was liberally paid for all, and was applauded throughout the vast republic of literary criticism. The last few years of life he was lost to the world, by mental infirmity, and during that time the public heard but little of its once "bright particular Star." Towards the middle of 1853, two volumes of "Memoirs, Journal, and Correspondence of Thomas Moore, edited by the Right Honourable Lord John Russell, M.P.," made their appearance. At two different times four other volumes have been published, and two more are promised, by the editor. This publication has excited more of popular commentary and criticism than attended any of his former publications. Such excess of publicity is to be attributed to the combined circumstances of his early fame; to the copiousness of his journal; to the style and criticism of its entries; to the distinguished eminence and celebrity of persons it notices, describes, and criticises; to the literary and political character of the learned editor; and still further to the universality of commentary and criticism which have now been spread over the broad and almost boundless fields of literature. To enhance the zest of this popularity, and furnish stimuli for the craving thirst of gossip, a tart and cutting correspondence has just appeared (Feb. 1854) in *The Times* newspaper, between the noble editor and a noted critic of the *Quarterly Review*. This critic has also been criticised, in language almost equally pungent to any of his own, in the *Gentleman's Magazine* for the same month. The controversy and commentary on Mr. Moore and his writings, do not, cannot, end here; for it may be fairly presumed and expected that Lord John, who has written a short prefatory address to the sixth volume, and has also appeared as champion for the poet, in the public arena above-named, must once more, if not finally, wield the pen in vindication of himself and his friend from obloquy and every impeachment of character. As the famed gladiators of classic antiquity were wont to try strength of arm and cunning of action before and in presence of congregated spectators, so modern disputants resort to the steel pen and paper-field, in order to display courage in rhetoric, or cowardice in evasion, or in artful vituperation. This sort of conflict is often harmless and even amusing to spectators, whilst the silly and heartless duels of a former age, and the murderous rencontres of chivalrous times were opprobrious to the perpetrators, and disgraceful to their patrons and admirers.

Of all the Auto-Biographers who have bequeathed memoirs to the world, there is not one, I believe, who has more minutely and honestly fulfilled his task than the late Thomas Moore. His full-length Portrait of himself, in his "Memoir, Diary, and Correspondence," is so faithfully painted, so completely delineated in every form and lineament, that "he who runs may read," and may also, with moderate sagacity, recognize and discriminate every outward and visible feature, as well as the inward operations of mind, of the person portrayed. In the copious Journal, which he penned at different and progressive stages of life, and with the intention of its future publication, whereby friends might review the whole amount of his "Sayings and Doings," and enemies (who are without them?) might see and exult over those weaknesses and frailties which belonged to him, as to all his fellow-mortals, we cannot help feeling surprise and sorrow at the insertion of many personal trivialities. These, with certain comments on the characters and singularities of persons with whom he came in contact, have materially depreciated the fair fame of the voluminous writer, and afforded matter for persons envious of his talents and unexampled popularity, or who were diametrically opposed to him in politics and religious creeds, to pour forth their spleen and ill feelings in bitter language. I can easily suppose that Mr. Moore always intended to revise and amend the first copy of his Diary; for it seems evident that the greater part, if not the whole, was written *currente calamo*, in the midst of that continued excitement and distraction in which his life was daily, and almost nightly involved.

When the number, variety, and popularity of the publications of this author were known and duly estimated, it could not be surprising that he attained high distinction in the literary annals of his country. But these were not the only sources and causes of that almost boundless celebrity which attaches to his name. His personal faculties and attainments delighted nearly every class of persons with whom he associated. His ready and pregnant wit, untiring vivacity, courtesy and true politeness of manners, sweetly modulated voice and vocal talents, rendered him always pleasant, and generally fascinating. Poets praised him, the fair sex admired him, and even the princes, nobles, and the legislators of the land courted his company and his friendship. If not an Adonis, he might be called "the glass of fashion and the mould of form." From boyhood onwards, he continued to write and publish, often anonymously, under assumed names, or his own, whence Lord Byron thus apostrophises him:—

> "Oh, you, who in all things can tickle the town,
> Anacreon, Tom Little, Tom Moore, or Tom Brown,
> For, hang me, if I know of which to most brag,
> Your Quarto two pounds, or your Two-penny Post Bag." \*

It will be seen by several entries in Moore's "Diary," that he found a kind friend and confidential adviser in MR. OWEN REES, of the firm of Longman and Co., not only as affecting the publication of his literary works, but in many private transactions. In a former part

---

\* These are the names to some of his publications. His first appears to have been published in 1800, being "The Odes of Anacreon, translated into English verse," 4to., 21s., the eighth edition of which was issued in 1813, in 2 vols., 8vo. In 1801 appeared his "Poetical Works," under the name of Thomas Little, the eleventh edition of which came out in 1813. His next were "Political Pamphlets;" and in 1812 he issued "The Two-penny Post Bag," by Thomas Brown the younger; of this work a fourteenth edition was issued in a few years. "Irish Melodies, Songs, Glees, &c.," both in verse and with the music, followed for many years; whilst several volumes of poetry and prose, amatory, romantic, historical, biographical, political, and miscellaneous, continued to be produced in rapid succession; though from his *Diary* it would appear that he was almost constantly visiting and feasting and *fêting* in town and in the country.

of this Biography (*ante* p. 264) I have spoken of the generous disposition of that gentleman, and may here notice that I often heard him commend the learning, general knowledge, and varied abilities of Moore. I know that his earnest desire was to serve and befriend him at the time of his pecuniary liabilities to Government; and on all occasions, indeed, he was eager to promote the success of his publications. In Mr. Rees, Moore found a sincere, warm-hearted friend; whilst in the respectable firm of Longman and Co. he experienced substantial patrons. At that house I often met some of the most respectable authors of my time, and it was there I first became acquainted with Mr. Moore. Afterwards I joined him at dinners of the Literary Fund; the Wiltshire Society, at the Albion, in Aldersgate Street; at London Soirées; at his own delightful cottage; at Mr. Bowles's, Bremhill; and at Bowood. In his *Diary,* he has alluded to some of these events; and particularly noticed the remarkable circumstance of three Wiltshire Poets assembling at the above-named Tavern, under the presidency of the Marquess of Lansdowne, who was not only witty himself, but, as usual, courteous and most felicitous in his short addresses to the company, and in calling up the poetical trio to speak to, and gratify a large party of Wiltshire gentlemen, who there assembled in the cause of charity and good fellowship. I wish it were in my power to recal and repeat the language used by Mr. Moore on that occasion, and display the hilarity and " flow of soul" which prevailed amongst a party of real provincials, and others, of Wiltshire birth, then settled in London. This retrospection carries memory over a wide extent of time; embraces facts, incidents, and reflections relating to public places and persons. Most of the last, however, after " strutting and fretting their hour" on the stage of life, have made their exits, and will never appear again. But, as Shee poetically and truly remarks, in speaking of " The Commemoration of Sir Joshua Reynolds," they

> " Have left their best image in their works enshrined,
> And made a Mausoleum of mankind."

Moore was one of these, and I must venture to notice two or three other traits of his character and eventful life, even at the risk of being thought too prolix. It is asserted by some of his posthumous critics that he neglected, and thereby illused his amiable and estimable wife.

But before this impeachment be admitted and sentence passed, it is but justice that evidence should be heard, and in my estimation abundance will be found in the posthumous "Memoirs" now published. These show that he was fond of company, and that his pleasing person and manners, his ready wit, his poetical fancy and talents, his sweet voice and musical accomplishments, rendered him an object to be courted and caressed; whilst the splendour, eclat, blandishments and fascinations of highly-polished society, were eminently calculated to seduce him from the plain and simple path of common-place, every-day life. Instead of tying him to her apron-string, and demanding from him undivided attention and devotion, his wife advised him to mix, occasionally, in the gay and fashionable world, but not require her company, as she preferred home and economy. Prudence and true love prompted this advice and conduct, for it is evident that her dominant wish was to administer to his happiness,—to love, honour, and obey him in all things. Finding her own comfortable but humble home not sufficiently spacious and diversified to satisfy his vivid fancy and highly-wrought aspirations, she philosophically submitted to that frequent separation which is mentioned in the Journal. His return to home, however, was always hailed and reciprocated with joy; but the manifestation of that feeling was a subdued tempered emotion in one, and an ardent, hearty, indulgence of joyfulness in the other.* His

---

* Familiar with a very analagous case, I may notice it to show that Mr. Moore's conduct was neither unnatural nor unique. A gentleman far advanced in life, whom I have known many years, married a young woman of domestic habits, great humility and prudence, practical philosophy, and divested of every taint of jealousy and envy. She soon found that her husband was partial to company, and particularly that of his superiors, both in station and intellectual powers, and that he wished for variety and amusement by country excursions, and by frequent attendances at London Societies, soirées, theatres, exhibitions, and dinner parties. These partialities and habits she rather encouraged than checked, though at the expense of a solitary home. That home, however, was never gloomy, nor haunted by suspicion, or the dread of evil doings abroad. On the return of her husband, whether after hours or days, she received him with smiles and manifestations that she had often thought of him during absence, by trying to make home more attractive, by numerous little improvements and domestic attractions. As time moved on and the old husband advanced in years, and consequent infirmities, he was compelled to relinquish his wanderings, to forego some of his former amusements, and during the severities of winter to confine himself

fine intellectual qualifications were felt and appreciated by those who were indulged with his company, and as the number rapidly increased he imperceptibly became involved in a vortex of engagements, some of which may be called idling occupations. Hence it is evident that he was too much from home, neglected his literary engagements and duties, and was thereby often harassed by creditors, and oppressed by obligations. Perhaps the most distressing event of his active and over-excited life was an indiscreet appointment to a place of business and trust in the Island of Bermuda. Unfitted for such a duty and occupation, he became involved in liabilities to a large amount, by the dishonesty of an assistant officer; the Government lawyers were directed to sue him for the defalcation: he was distressed almost to madness, and his friends, particularly the Marquess of Lansdowne, and the firm of Longman & Co., proffered him money to liquidate the debt. This generosity he courageously declined to avail himself of, and left the country to avoid the moral and legal fetters of confinement for life, within the rules of the King's Bench. This anticipated incarceration haunted his waking fancy and sleeping dreams for a lengthened period, and he retreated to France to escape arrest. His numerous letters to friends, and the entries in his journals, furnish painful pictures of the protracted misery he endured; but he ultimately weathered the storm, returned to his home, and was seen in the gay and fashionable world, giving and receiving pleasure. From this time to the lamentable epoch of mental aberration, Moore was, as heretofore, fully and intensely occupied in flirtations with the gay world, mental intercourse with the most learned and distinguished persons, of all sects and parties, though chiefly the Whigs, and in various literary works. Bowood, Holland House, and his own flowered cottage, were, however, the chief places of his resort and residence. About the year 1847, his mind became " clouded by loss of memory,

---

to home, and here, fortunately for him, he found a companion, a friend, and a nurse, in that wife whom he had too often deserted, or rather neglected. Like Moore also, he loved and respected her, and, when absent, almost daily communed with her by letter, to afford her some amusement, and likewise to direct his own thoughts to that home which ultimately became a haven for security, and a sort of terrestrial heaven for conjugal happiness.

and a helplessness almost childish," as expressed by his noble editor. He was visited by Lord John, and the Marquess of Lansdowne, on the 20th of December, 1849, "when he spoke rationally, agreeably, and kindly." He continued thus under the ever-watchful and over-anxious care of a beloved wife till the month of February, 1852, when the physical frame ceased to act.

On reverting to, and reflecting on the lives, attributes, and mental powers of four of the most popular and voluminous authors of my time, and with all of whom I became personally acquainted and corresponded, I cannot but admire the brilliant mental powers of Bowles, Southey, Scott, and Moore, whilst the lamentable condition to which each was reduced at the decline of life, excite the most poignant sorrow. The contrast and opposition is painful to contemplate: minds of such compass and powers seem to exalt man almost above his species, and render him in "apprehension like a God"; but bereft of this faculty, what object is more deplorable to sight and painful to the heart than the living frame of humanity, deprived of its animating spirit? The four eminent authors above named conferred honour on human nature and their native land, by their writings. They were all courted and admired in their generation; they disseminated pleasure and information around them; and, like the far-famed comet now known as Halley's, attracted the gaze and wonderment of thousands of spectators. Their courses have been traced and defined; their appearances and mental attributes have been investigated and described; and although they can never return to gladden and delight the planet they once belonged to and adorned, their effects are lasting and permanent. Of the elements—the phenomena, of the comet referred to, and of all comets, man knows scarcely anything: they are beyond and above the grasp of human intellect to comprehend. Their course, in the vast path they travel, seems to have been ascertained by the profound astronomer referred to; but he and all others have failed to discriminate their analogy, or dissimilarities to the terrestrial globe we inhabit: whence we are left to admire, wonder at, and hope that further and more comprehensive knowledge may be acquired by man to ascertain the laws of Providence in physical science, and in the bodily and mental formation and functions of the human machine.

THE REV. GEORGE CRABBE, BORN AT ALBOROUGH, SUFFOLK, 24TH DEC., 1751;
DIED AT TROWBRIDGE, WILTSHIRE, 3RD FEB., 1832.

When we become acquainted with the extent of the poetical works of this once very popular author, and also with his amiable characteristics as a friend, a husband, a father, and a parish priest, we must reverence and admire him in all those capacities. One of his sons has furnished the reading world with a rational and gratifying account of his father's career in life, of his habits, his manners, his "sayings and doings;" also testimonies to his talents from some of his most eminent contemporaries: Byron, Moore, Scott, Bowles, Lockhart, Joanna Baillie, and others. Byron thus compliments him as a poet, being

"The first in point of power and of genius."

Mr. Duncan, of Bath and Oxford, thus writes of Mr. Crabbe, in a letter to the author of the poet's life. "I was much struck, as I think every one who was ever in his company must have been, by his peculiar suavity, courtesy, and even humility of manner. His conversation was easy, fluent, and abundant in correct information; but distinguished chiefly by good sense and good feeling." Bowles characterizes him "as an amiable, gentle, and affectionate man." In a letter dated 1833, Lockhart, the son-in-law and biographer of Scott, after being associated some days with Crabbe in Edinburgh, thus marks his opinion of the author of so much popular poetry: "His noble forehead, his bright beaming eye, without any mark of old age about it,—though he was then, I believe, above seventy,—his sweet, and I would say innocent, smile, and the calm, mellow tones of his voice—all are reproduced the moment I open any page of his poetry: and how much better have I understood and enjoyed the poetry since I was thus able to connect with it the living presence of the man!"—[*Life of Crabbe*, p. 78, large 8vo. edition of 1851.] Such opinions, from such authorities, cannot fail to excite a desire in the reader to be made better acquainted with the man, and with his numerous poetical productions.

The remarkable, though uneventful, career of Crabbe's life and writings should be studied by all the sons and daughters of Genius; particularly at the early part of their own career. His case and example give pith and moment to the hopeful moral maxim and proverb of *Nil desperandum*. Nature and family circumstances planted him in a most unpropitious and forbidding soil. He seemed destined to mix with the most reckless species of the human genus—poachers, smugglers, pirates, wreckers: men who appear to live by rapine and murder. What a contrast to the young poet, the lover and worshipper of Nature and her harmonious beauties, and of the mildnesses and amenities of his fellow-creatures! We must infer, however, that he had but little personal intercourse with such inhuman beings; that his time and thoughts were occupied by reading books obtainable within his sphere; and that the wide and ever-varying ocean, which was daily before his eyes, with countless vessels on its surface, and the wild, open heath, with its natural inhabitants, would both engage and gradually expand his mind. That these objects were indelibly impressed thereon is evidenced by many passages in his writings. "The opening picture of 'The Village' was copied in every touch from the scene of the Poet's nativity and boyish days," says his son, in the biography referred to:—

> "Lo! where the heath, with withering brake grown o'er,
> Lends the light turf that warms the neighbouring poor;
> From thence a length of burning sand appears,
> Where the thin harvest waves its wither'd ears;
> Rank weeds, that every art and care defy,
> Reign o'er the land, and rob the blighted rye;
> There thistles spread their prickly arms afar,
> *And to the ragged infant threaten war.*"

This descriptive scene strongly reminds me of the drear and infertile district I travelled over with my much-loved friend, the Rev. John Mitford, some years back, when he kindly conducted me to the birth-place of the poet, and, at the same time, to the fine ruins of Orford Castle.

Up to the epoch of manhood, Crabbe's life was almost as cheerless and inauspicious as my own. He, fortunately, had a firm foundation laid in better education; had a home to reside in, and parents to resort to for counsel and subsistence. His apprenticeship, however, after leaving that home, was like my own, ungenial to his mind; and his masters—country apothecaries—seem to have been ill calculated to afford him domestic comfort or instruction. Still he had time and opportunities to read,—that never-tiring solace, and ever-cheering occupation,—and thus improve and ripen his mental faculties. Not only dissatisfied, but disgusted with the business in which he had wasted so much time, he left it at the termination of apprenticeship, and, after "lingering hopelessly about his native place, he at last resolved to cast himself on the wide ocean of London, and tempt the fearful dangers that belong to the career of a literary adventurer. Here he struggled, and starved, for a year. During the first three months of his London life he sent manuscript poems to the booksellers, Dodsley and Becket, which they civilly declined. He addressed verses to Lord Chancellor Thurlow, who informed him that 'his avocations did not leave him leisure to read verses.' He sold his clothes and his books, and pawned his watch and his surgical instruments. His one coat was torn, and he mended it himself. He was reduced at last to eightpence, but the brave man never despaired. He had a strong sense of religion, and was deeply attached to one who became his wife after thirteen years of untiring constancy. His faith and his love held him up, and kept him out of degradation. At last he wrote a letter to Edmund Burke. It contained this passage: 'In April last [1781, aged 30] I came to London with three pounds, and flattered myself this would be sufficient to supply me with the common necessaries of life till my abilities should procure me more; of these I had the highest opinion, and a poetical fancy contributed to my delusion.' Burke saved Crabbe from the fate of many a one who perished in those days when patronage was dying out, and the various resources for the literary labourer that now belong to the extension of reading had scarcely began to exist. Burke persuaded Dodsley to publish 'The Library,' and the Bishop of Norwich to ordain the author without a degree. His lot in life was fixed. Thurlow invited him to dinner, and, telling him he was as 'like Parson Adams as twelve to a dozen,' gave him two small livings. He published 'The Village' in 1783, and 'The Newspaper' in 1785. From that time to 1807 the world had forgotten that a real poet of very original talents had appeared for a short time and was no more heard of. When Crabbe was fifty-three years of age he published 'The Parish Register.' 'The Borough' speedily followed. His 'Tales' were in the same vein. Their success was triumphant. The author, whose worldly means were reduced to eightpence in 1780, sold the copyright of his poems in 1807, to Mr. Murray, for three thousand pounds."

This exquisite graphic sketch is from the prolific pen of Charles Knight, an old friend of some fifty years' standing, who during that long period has been zealously occupied in writing and publishing to inform and improve the juvenile, and even aged, generation. It must gratify him to feel, as it does me to relate, these facts. The above account appears in two volumes lately issued by him under the title of "*Once Upon a Time,*" and I may venture to say that they contain a series of most amusing, instructive, and luminous essays; and therefore cannot fail to produce lasting, as well as beneficial effects on the mind and heart of every person who reads them. The writings and character of Crabbe are amply and vividly illustrated in the essay from which I have culled the above passage. Burke's patronage and friendship not only rescued the poet from dire poverty and gloom, but introduced him into the broad sun-light of fame and favour. The Duke of Rutland made him his domestic chaplain, provided him a home in his splendid mansions of Belvoir Castle and in London, and successively gave him livings, whereby he was enabled to wed his long-betrothed wife, live in a respectable style, and bring up a most exemplary family.

My first introduction to Mr. Crabbe was in the year 1819, at a public dinner in the Albion Hotel, London, at which the Marquess of Lansdowne presided. The purport of the meeting was to promote "The Wiltshire Society in London," to apprentice the sons of poor Wiltshire parents settled in the metropolis. It is rather a curious event in the history of this society that the first apprentice by its funds was Job Austin, brother of the noted "Billy Austin," whose connection with the ill-used Queen, Caroline, was often before the public during the wedded career of that personage. The said Job had not much of the patience or character of his scriptural namesake, for he often came before the committee to complain of the hardships of apprenticeship, and the committee soon found out that the mother with this son had imbibed such wild notions of Royalty that they fancied themselves entitled to distinction and luxuries in imitation of the favourite of a Queen. Though the Committee experienced much vexation in their first move, they have continued their useful and laudable career up to the present time, by apprenticing and aiding no less than 213 persons. Of the anniversary meeting referred to, Mr. Moore states, that "Lord Lansdowne made a very tasteful speech in giving the health of 'the three Wiltshire Poets.' I was called on to return thanks, and succeeded marvellously. Among other things, I said that as far as a Union by acts of friendship,—which after all was a more binding thing than a union by Acts of Parliament,—could convert an Irishman into a Wiltshire-man, I was in as fair a train of transformation as they could desire. Of Crabbe I said, that the *musa severior* which he worships has had no influence whatever on the kindly dispositions of his heart; but that while, with the eye of a sage and a poet, he looks into the darker region of human nature, he stands in its most genial sunshine himself."—(*Moore's Diary*, vol. ii., p. 308.) Mr. Moore should also have alluded to the short but neat and apposite remarks of his poetical friends, which, if not equally sparkling and vivid to his own, were appropriate, kindly, and good. Though I have attended many public dinners, particularly those of the said Wiltshire Society, of the Literary Fund Society, the Society of Antiquaries, and others, I never witnessed such display of cordial good humour, with " the feast of reason and flow of soul," as on the occasion referred to. Having been chiefly instrumental in founding the Society, by soliciting the much-respected and beloved Sir Benjamin Hobhouse to take the chair at its inaugural meeting in 1817, and being more than commonly ardent in promoting its welfare as Honorary Secretary, I hailed with exultation the eclat it attained and would derive by such a gala day as that of the 12th of May, 1819.

The career and conduct of Mr. Crabbe, during his residence at Trowbridge, form an admirable lesson and example to his brethren of the cloth, in their introduction to, and residence amongst large and heterogeneous flocks of parishioners. Trowbridge, at the time of the new Rector's first introduction to it (1814) was a populous manufacturing town, and consequently contained many Dissenters. It was also infested and demoralized by intemperate political partizans, though not a borough; also opponents to the church, and to rational and national reform; whence he experienced, for some time, much rancorous contention and hostility. With admirable presence of mind, unflinching moral courage, great courtesy, and benevolence of conduct, he progressively " won his way," and ultimately conciliated all parties. " Those who came to scoff, remained to pray;" whilst his intolerant opponents in politics could not refuse to respect, and even admire the Protestant clergyman, who administered comfort to the unhappy, fed the hungry, clothed the naked, and preached peace and good-will to all who would listen to his discourses. We cannot, therefore, be surprised that when he departed this life there was much grieving, not only amongst his own immediate congregation, but by all the inhabitants of the town. He died at Trowbridge, in the 78th year of his age; and at his funeral the inhabitants testified their attachment and respect, by closing their shops, and by other demonstrations of sorrow. They also raised a handsome subscription for a Monument, by E. H. Baily, R.A., which is placed in the church. It consists of a group of figures, in which is one representing the late poet apparently looking at the Sacred Volume, and two others of allegorical character, indicative of angels, or genii, prepared to escort the body, or departed spirit to its heavenly home. A simple inscription, rationally, in English, describes his abode as Rector of the parish for nineteen years, " discharging his duties as a minister, and a magistrate, to acquire the respect and esteem of all his neighbours."

As a writer, he is well described in the language of Byron as

"Nature's sternest painter, and her best."

The following lines were written by the once amiable and most estimable *John S. Duncan, Esq.*, of Bath, and of New College, Oxford, after the death of Mr. Crabbe. The author, like his generous and benevolent brother, Philip B. Duncan, of the same city and college, was beloved by all who knew him: his manners were gentle, kindly, bland; whilst his fine and fertile mind produced certain writings which evidenced talents of high order; whence it is to be regretted that his publications had not been more numerous. In the year 1831 he published a few copies of a very interesting volume, entitled " Analogies of Organized Beings," which he calls a " Speculative Essay;" and dedicated it to three of the most estimable as well as the most usefully learned members of Oxford University; Edward, Bishop of Llandaff, the Rev. R. Whately, now Archbishop of Dublin, and to his dear brother, P. B. Duncan.

### LINES TO THE MEMORY OF THE REV. GEORGE CRABBE.

"Farewell, Dear Crabbe! thou meekest of mankind,
With heart all fervour, and all strength of mind;
With tenderest sympathies for others' woes,
Fearless, all guilt and folly to expose:
Steadfast of purpose in pursuit of right,
To drag forth hypocrisy to light,
To brand th' oppressor, and to shame the proud,
To shield the righteous from the slanderous crowd:
To error lenient and to frailty mild,
Repentance ever was thy welcome child;
In every state, as husband, parent, friend,
Scholar or bard, thou couldst the Christian blend.
Thy verse from Nature's face each feature drew,
Each lovely charm, each mole and wrinkle too.
No dreamy incidents of wild romance,
With whirling shadows, wilder'd minds entrance;
But plain realities the mind engage,
With pictur'd warnings through each polish'd page.
Hogarth of Song! be this thy perfect praise:
Truth prompted, and Truth purified thy lays;
The God of Truth has given thy verse and thee
Truth's holy palm—His Immortality."

### CASTLE COMBE,

a romantic village, once a market-town, is strongly impressed on my memory by many circumstances and incidents belonging to boyhood, almost childhood, of more than seventy years' retrospection. Hence it may be said to appertain to my personal annals; and I must own that it affords me high gratification to identify myself, in any way, with a place whose History has been so amply and judiciously elucidated as that of Castle Combe by its present learned and patriotic Lord of the Manor. During my first school-days at Foscote, and at Church-Eaton, and residence afterwards at a solitary house, in the midst of fields, marked in maps, and noted in local tradition as "The

Small-pox House," where I and many other children were doomed to endure a sort of quarantine at the period of sickening and cure,* I often heard much of the old castle, the mill, the mansion, the church, and the "pretty village" of Castle Combe, and the Scropes. One of them, the Rev. Dr. John Scrope, possessed the living of my native parish when I came into the world; and my father often related personal anecdotes of that gentleman, who was partial to music, or rather to the violin, on which instrument my parent was said to be expert, in the early part of his domestic career; and the baker and the parson often met to talk over tunes, try them on their fiddles, and spend an hour in social chat.

In the year 1796, after my emancipation from subterranean slavery, I spent some weeks with relations and friends near to my native home. At that time I visited Castle Combe, and ventured to call at "the great house," where MR. WILLIAM SCROPE, and his aged mother, then called by her neighbours, Madam Scrope, received and treated me with much kindness. As already related, I had read much during my legal servitude, and afterwards had associated with artists, from whose converse and study I obtained some knowledge of the technicalities and merits of pictures. Price on "The Picturesque," Gilpin's "Tours," Burke on "The Sublime and Beautiful," had been perused by me in solitude, and excited a desire to look for illustrations and exemplifications of their theories and principles in the more instructive and practical book of Nature. The romantic and diversified scenery of Castle Combe, therefore, excited my curiosity, and gave me much pleasure; and I may safely assert, that it awakened to life and

---

* That *Vaccine Inoculation* had not been adopted many years before Dr. Jenner's time is amongst the marvels of history. It was well known in the dairy district of Gloucestershire and North Wiltshire, when I was a boy, that persons who were in the habit of milking cows were frequently affected with a disease called the "Cow-pox," and were thereby exempt from the more perilous "Small-pox." Dr. Jenner was some years engaged in contending against the prejudices and dogmatism of the most famed practitioners of the age, from 1780 to 1798, before he obtained their approval and co-operation. He was at last, however, handsomely rewarded by national grants of £10,000 and £20,000. See an interesting "Memoir of Dr. Jenner," by my much-respected friend, and estimable man, Dr. Baron, of Gloucester, whose professional kindnesses to me, at the time of a fractured leg in that city, cannot be forgotten.

action a hitherto slumbering love for picturesque scenery. Three days' sojourn at the village mansion seemed all felicity; for every sense was gratified, and each succeeding day afforded new scenes and new matter for exultation and enjoyment. Before I left, I learnt from my prim, but courteous, hostess that the circumstance of my being christened John by her brother-in-law, John, had prepossessed her in my behalf. Mr. Scrope's conversation and talents rivetted my attention and created admiration; for he manifested genius of no common order —had travelled, and had read much, was skilled as an amateur artist, and was a sportsman of high repute in the country. He unrolled, to my astonishment, a picture of brilliant colours, and of mysterious composition and expression. This was an heraldic, emblazoned pedigree of the Scrope family, as furnished by the Heralds' College, and, I conclude, is still preserved amongst the archives of the Manor-house. A similar pedigree, with additions and corrections, impaling the Scropes and Pouletts, most elaborately emblazoned with proper colours on forty-two shields of arms, and three crests, is given in the history above referred to.

As an amateur, Mr. Wm. Scrope's pictures were mostly of Landscapes with figures, in the style and manner of Loutherbourg, and of Ibbetson, two academicians and popular artists of the time. The first I was personally acquainted with, admired his works, and knew something of his versatile talents and habits. On coming of age, Mr. Scrope possessed the Wiltshire and Lincolnshire family estates; his father having died about six years previously. Of ardent temperament; enthusiastic, intrepid, and almost uncontrolled, he became a devoted sportsman, and was known to excel all his associates in the chase, on the turf, in mountain streams, in lake, and in the ocean-bay. At the time I first met him he was in his twenty-fourth year, in the hey-day of youthful spirits, vigour, and reckless daring; but in the library, and at the dining-table, he was the scholar, the accomplished man, and the wit. I have heard it remarked by a gentleman, his intimate acquaintance, that "he excelled in everything he undertook." He was of small stature, and known as a pugilist, a bold rider, and a certain shot. He kept racers, and hunters, and, in conjunction with a neighbouring 'squire, a pack of hounds. As a fisherman, however, he was regarded as pre-eminent amongst his countrymen; and has left behind him ample evidences of his skill and qualifications in two volumes which surpass all other literary works of the class in this or any other country. These are on "Salmon Fishing," and on "Deer Stalking," which have rendered his name eminent in the annals of the scientific and sporting world. In enthusiastically pursuing, and in writing on these subjects, Mr. Scrope has evinced a resolution and genius of rare occurrence, and certainly never surpassed. From childhood to old age—for his volumes constitute an auto-biography—he tells us that he was an infatuated follower of field and aquatic sports. His own narratives of adventure and successful capture, when even a child, a boy, and in manhood, may rank among the romances of real life. Not only eminent as a sportsman of the first grade, but as an author, Mr. Scrope has acquired the unqualified praises of critics who have brought his literary volumes under review. They are not addressed merely to the professional sportsman, but may be examined with pleasure and advantage by all lovers of natural history, and by almost every class of readers.

The "*Days of Deer Stalking*" attained so much celebrity that the publisher issued a third edition in 1846. Like a well-penned romance, or novel, it irresistibly arrests the attention and excites the curiosity of every reader who once enters its leafy defiles, and catches glimpses of the pleasing scenes and incidents represented by the skilful artists, whose designs and engravings adorn the pages. In following—i. e., *stalking*—the deer through the forest of Athol, over the craggy and wild mountain, the equally wild glen with its mountain torrent, and through the heathy and boggy moor, the sportsman's muscles and nerves must have been constantly exerted and excited; whilst the perilous situations into which he was irresistibly enticed, must occasionally have aroused the strongest emotions of alarm and terror. The author has described some of these in forcible and thrilling language. *Salmon Fishing* is strongly contrasted with Deer Stalking: the latter being on terra firma, with the object of sport sometimes seen at a great distance and to be approached only by bodily exertion and cunning, and finally killed by the skilful use of the gun. Unlike this object of sport, the beautiful Salmon occupies a different element: is dissimilar to the noble antlered deer of the mountain in all its natural characteristics. To effect its capture by the hook or the spear, requires other operations and aptitudes, as well as different studies and knowledge, and it naturally leads to scenes and situations entirely dissimilar to those connected with the wild forest deer. It is also unlike anything which was ever witnessed by, or known to, the meek and placid Isaac Walton. Mr. Scrope has given vivid descriptive sketches of the sporting belonging to the Salmon Fishery of Scotland and the north of England; and has also presented the reader with many pictorial scenes and incidents, by the aid of artists who have furnished illustrations for the two volumes. Herein also, as in literary contents, these productions are of a high class, as may be readily inferred by persons who are familiar with the engravings after Sir Edwin and Thomas Landseer, Sir D. Wilkie, J. D. Harding, Edw. W. Cooke, L. Haghe, S. Williams, Wm. Simpson, and also by the talented author, himself.

The Reviewer in the *Quarterly* (Dec. 1838) has devoted a long and encomiastic paper to the volume on "Deer Stalking," in which he says that "Mr. Scrope does not follow any formal, didactic method, but has made his book, no doubt unconsciously, a picturesque image of his life; the practical everywhere intermixed with the theoretical. We are introduced, partly by dialogue, partly by narrative and description, to a familiar acquaintance with his faithful and attached foresters—his favourite dogs; those used for this sport being a cross between the tall northern wire-haired greyhound and the bloodhound —his sure-footed indefatigable little ponies—the natural history and habits of the deer, themselves; and the majestic beauties of the wide region over which he has traced them so often 'from dawn to dewy eve.' His book has all the charms of an Auto-Biography (a most modest one) combined with that of a series of unaffected lectures on the science of the chace. Playful interludes of poachers arrested, and cockney and *muscadine* interlopers mystified, are not wanting; but all is touched with the same light hand; everywhere the same instinctive observance of the limits of becoming mirth; the fun everywhere *shot* with good breeding."

At the time this review and compliment were published, the veteran author was capable of pursuing and enjoying his long-accustomed sports, and rational home amusements; but age advanced and brought with it some of its natural concomitants — gout and other infirmities. With occasional fits of these, and abridged visits to his favourite haunts, he passed some years, till he approached his eighty-first anniversary, when he expired in Belgrave Square, London, in July 1852. His remains were interred in the church of Castle Combe, where a monument has been raised to his memory.

Mr. William Scrope married early in life the only daughter and child of Charles Long, Esq., brother of Sir James Long, Bart., of Draycot; and as the latter continued without an heir till late in life, his niece was led to expect that she would become possessed of her uncle's large estates in Wiltshire. The Baronet, however, married at the age of seventy, became the father of three daughters, the eldest of whom was the rich heiress, and ultimately the unhappy and ill-treated wife of the notorious William Pole Tylney Long Wellesley, as already noticed in page 49 of this memoir.

It appears that Mr. Scrope's marriage was so far from being a happy union, that the couple separated after a few years' association. An only daughter was the issue of the union, and she was married to GEORGE POULETT THOMSON, ESQ., who took the surname of SCROPE, by royal grant, in 1821. This gentleman has been Member of Parliament for Stroud for some years, is fellow of the Royal, Geological, and other scientific societies, and has produced numerous volumes, pamphlets, and essays, on geology, political economy, topography, and other subjects, all manifesting industry and zeal, as well as the enlarged and enlightened views of a highly cultivated mind. In the latest production of his pen, an Inaugural Address to a large assembly at Devizes, on the 12th day of October last, on founding an "Archæological and Natural History Society for Wiltshire," the reader will be gratified by the knowledge and sentiments expressed, and will readily infer that they must emanate from a head fully imbued with sound information, and a heart well and finely organized.* We are well assured that the same

---

* This Address is printed in the first number of "The Wiltshire Archæological and Natural History Magazine," March, 1854; in which is another very interesting Essay on the Utility, Benefits, and varied Attributes of Topographical Publications, by the

feeling, and a corresponding patriotism, prompted him to write and print a small number of copies of a handsome quarto volume, entitled, "*History of the Manor and Ancient Barony of Castle Combe,*" which, I must own, ought to have been *published,* and thereby made easily accessible to all classes of readers who take an interest in this species of literature; whereas, now, only a few volumes are "printed for private distribution;" hence its utility is limited, as is its information, whilst the author's labours and merits are circumscribed to a small sphere of private friends. Of books like this referred to, containing such a fund of sound and useful information, a number should be printed adapted to the demand, whence local history would become an essential and valuable auxiliary to national history. But for the diligent labours and generous conduct of Mr. Scrope in producing the present work, the dormant annals of this "Manor and Barony" might have remained torpid and valueless to the end of time. Now they are not only called into life and light, but rendered permanent, useful, and accessible to any and every person who may require the information they embrace. I must own that the execution of the volume as well as its handsome aspect and literary contents astonished me on its first appearance, but still more on a careful examination of the varied and recondite contents; for it is evident that the author has devoted much time and labour to this as well as to other branches of literature. Topography has too generally been pursued by the mere genealogist, the amateur antiquary, the solitary bookworm who feeds only on old leaves, black-letter, and parchment; whence it has been commonly regarded as dull and insipid to the more enlarged and enlightened reader and critic. When, however, the public is treated with such a local history as that under consideration, or Admiral Smyth's "Ædes Hartwellianæ;" the Rev. Archdeacon Todd's "History of Ashridge;" the Rev. Dr. Whitaker's "History of Whalley," or Warton's "Kiddington," it will be enabled to see what learning and genius and taste can accomplish, and the general critic will be better disposed to appreciate and do justice to Topography and to its

---

Rev. J. E. Jackson, M.A., one of the Honorary Secretaries of the Society, and author of a "History of Grittleton," 4to. 1843, and of "A Guide to Farleigh-Hungerford, co. Somerset," 8vo. 1853.

authors.* The "Quarterly Review," for March 1853, contains an interesting essay on Mr. Scrope's "Castle Combe." I may quote a few lines from the said Review in corroboration of the preceding opinion, and at the same time observe that the critic bestows unqualified praise on the volume. "Nothing could be more true or philosophical than certain remarks of Sir Francis Palgrave in his Preface to the Parliamentary Writs; and nothing in better taste, or more indicative of his knowing what he was undertaking, than Mr. Scrope's adopting them as the first paragraph of his own Preface.

> "'The genuine history of a country can never be well understood without a complete and searching analysis of the component parts of the community as well as the country. Genealogical inquiries and local topography, so far from being unworthy the attention of the philosophical inquirer, are amongst the best materials he can use; and the fortunes and changes of one family, or the events of one upland township, may explain the darkest and most dubious portion of the annals of a realm.'

"There is no doubt of this; and no need of any thing like an apology for any gentleman, who, possessing 'a large collection of well-preserved documents' relating to a 'manor and ancient barony,'

---

* A splendid book of this class has recently made its appearance, with the title of "*Apsley House and Walmer Castle*," illustrated by Plates and Descriptions: the former from drawings by Jos. Nash, T. Boys, T. Dibdin, and M. and N. Hanhart; the latter by Richard Ford. Large folio. 1853. Amongst the illustrations is a beautifully executed view of Stothard's "Wellington Shield," which cost £10,000.

Having devoted more than half a century to the study of, and writing on, Topography and Archæology; and having examined almost every publication, with many manuscripts; diligently investigated most of the ancient edifices and ruins of England and Wales; and having also associated and corresponded with nearly every modern author on those subjects; it is not surprising, and, I hope, not unreasonable, that I should have acquired some knowledge as well as partiality for the science, and for all the tangible objects which it involves, and which it is intended to elucidate. In the year 1843, I wrote and published a small quarto of 66 closely-printed pages, with the following title, explaining the result of my own experience, and the opinions therefrom superinduced:—"An Essay on Topographical Literature: its Province, Attributes, and varied Utility; with Accounts of the Sources, Objects, and Uses of National and Local Records, and Glossaries of Words used in Ancient Writings."

My much-respected and learned friend, the Rev. Joseph Hunter, wrote a valuable paper "On the Nature, Purpose, and Resources of Topography," which was read to the members of "The Archæological Institute," at Norwich, in 1847, and is published in the volume of their "Memoirs," for 1851.

conceives an idea that a narrative compiled from such materials may be 'not devoid of value as a contribution to the topography of the country.' He will have a right to consider it something higher; or a contribution—if not a great, a genuine one—to the materials which, if such a fabric is ever to be raised, must lie at the foundation of the History of England."

The following list of separate publications from the pen of Mr. Scrope are at once evidences of his industry and zeal, as well as of his varied literary acquirements.

"Considerations on Volcanoes." 8vo. 1825.

"A Memoir on the Geology of Central France; including the Volcanic Formations of Auvergne, the Velay, and the Vivarais." 4to. With Maps and Plans in folio. By G. P. Scrope. 1827.

"The Elements of Political Economy." By G. Poulett Scrope. 8vo. 1833.

"A Memoir of the Life of Charles, Lord Sydenham; with a Narrative of his Administration in Canada." Edited by his Brother, G. Poulett Scrope. 8vo. 1843.

In the years 1825-6 he acted as Secretary to the Geological Society, after having devoted previous years in examining the volcanic districts of central France, Italy, and Sicily; whence he returned with a mind stored with practical information on those wonderful phenomena; and hence the very important works which he afterwards published. Before their appearance, the two classes of geologists—Neptunists and Vulcanists—had been puzzling themselves and their readers by disputes about the igneous or aqueous origin of trap-rocks, &c. But a new and more rational school of geologists was founded, or commenced by Mr. Scrope, his companion and friend, Sir C. Lyell, and a few other active and scientific persons, by whose researches and deductions the active forces now seen in operation on the globe's surface are applied to explain its past history, to the exclusion of the imaginary revolutions, deluges, comets, &c., of the old schools of hypothetical geology.

Since Mr. Scrope entered parliament in 1833, he has honestly and zealously devoted his zeal and best judgment to the onerous and honourable duties of a British Senator. The public are aware of most of his labours in the cause of improving the physical and moral condition of the working classes. On this subject, both in the House of Commons, and in publications, Mr. Scrope has effected substantial good; and more particularly in obtaining an extension and practical operation of the English Poor Laws, both to Scotland and Ireland.

No. I.

MARKET CROSS.

The Village and Parish of Castle Combe are singular in geographical, geological, and manorial characteristics. Three narrow vales, or dells, diverge from a centre and extend by gradual, or steep, acclivities to a tract of table land which surrounds the whole. Through two of these combs, or gorges, a rivulet winds its course, over masses of rock in some places, and in others fine sand. In this stream the late Mr. W. Scrope exercised his boyish skill in trout-fishing, which probably led to the more daring and exciting pursuit of salmon-fishing, in which he became renowned. One of the vales forms a small home-park to the family mansion, and, by its ever-green turf, wooded hills, verdant slopes, and transparent waters, must be always pleasing to the eye during the spring, summer, and autumn, and also be sheltered in the winter. The manor-house, a gabled and turretted edifice, is placed at the base of a steep hill on the north side of the principal valley, and, with its garden, lofty flights of balustraded steps, ever-green hedges, interspersed with vases, fountains, conservatory, &c., constitute a group of objects peculiarly gratifying to the lover of the picturesque. About 200 yards south-east of the house, embosomed in trees, is the *Parish Church*, whose lofty tower forms an interesting feature in the scenery. At the first time I examined this church, about thirty years back, it was in a neglected, almost ruinous condition. I was therefore both surprised and gratified, in the autumn of 1853, to find that it had been renovated, indeed, for the most part rebuilt; and also ornamented with skill and taste. Walls, roof, flooring, and timbers were rendered sound and good; windows were re-glazed, and adorned with stained glass; and the furniture of the chancel, and the pulpit, desk, font, seats, were all new, and made in appropriate and harmonious style and character; whilst old and modern tombs had been placed with some regard to position and character.

The annexed *Wood-Cuts* have been kindly lent to me by the present lord of the manor and patron of the living. No. II. represents an ornamented niche in the north wall, inclosing an *Altar-Tomb* sus-

No. II.

NICHE AND MONUMENT.

taining the effigy of a warrior, supposed to be for a Dunstanville, one of the Barons of the Castle.

### No. III.

FONT AND BASE OF A COLUMN.

No. III. represents a picturesque *Octagonal Font*, against the base of a clustered column, indicating two of the oldest architectural objects of the church: they are evidently of the thirteenth century.

The houses of the village agreeably harmonize with, and give interest to the scenery. They are all of stone, covered with thin stone tiles, and most of them have gables, with good chimney shafts. At the junction of three streets, which form almost an equilateral triangle, is the *Market Cross*, a covered building resting on four posts at the angles, and having a central shaft of a stone cross, as represented in a print on a preceding page. (No. I.)

At the south-west extremity of the village, is a new *Rectory House*, which Mr. Scrope has built for the present respected incumbent, the Rev. Richard Cooper Christie, M.A.

Of WILLIAM SCROPE, ESQ., an interesting and graphic memoir might be written; for he was a distinguished "Worthy" of my native county.

GRITTLETON HOUSE: IMPROVEMENTS: LEIGH-DELAMERE, AND ANECDOTES: THE HUNGERFORDS: THE REV. J. E. JACKSON: STANTON ST. QUINTIN: SIR THOMAS GORE: LUCKINGTON CAVES: NORTON: MAIDFORD: THE HILLIER FAMILY: AGRICULTURAL CONTRASTS.

Abutting on the eastern boundary of Castle Combe is the parish of GRITTLETON, which is entitled to especial notice in this place, as well from personal recollection as from the revolutions which this district has undergone within the present century. Perhaps there is no thoroughly rural part of England that exhibits more distinctly than this how much public and social improvement depends upon the actual residence and direct interference of proprietors themselves. When I first knew this neighbourhood, and even at a later period, when I have occasionally visited it, the general appearance with respect both to human dwellings, to roads, hedges, and walls, was such as may always be expected, whenever, from accidental circumstances, the eye and purse of influential landlords have not been upon the spot to superintend and civilize. During winter and wet weather, some of the highways were almost impassable, and indeed there were but few carriages on four wheels, and not often even upon two, to make the attempt.* Now, on the contrary, roads of approach, from the east, west, north, and south, are sound and good; but the turnpike tolls are unreasonably high: boundary hedges and walls are not merely useful, but ornamental; whilst lodges, gates, and fine plantations, afford demonstrative evidence of the wealth and rational economy of the resident lord of the soil. This is still more strikingly exhibited in the comfortable-looking cottages, spacious farm-houses, new churches, school-houses, and other buildings distributed through the whole district. These important and commendable improvements have been gradually made within the last twenty-seven years, by Mr. Neeld, one of the members for the borough of Chippenham, who purchased the manorial estates of Grittleton from

---

* I have vivid recollection of passing through one of these roads, on horseback, in continued terror, from the apprehension that the horse would be fixed in the moist clay, as at every step it sunk above the knees; yet this was the only public way to one of the largest farm-houses in the neighbourhood. In after years, the same farm was occupied by a family who kept hunters, hackneys, and even a pleasure carriage.

Colonel Houlton in 1828. Since that year he has bought other land in the same parish, with lands, manors, and advowsons in adjoining parishes, and thus created a domain of large extent, and placed the whole under one system of general amelioration and good cultivation. It is generally known that Mr. Neeld came into possession of great wealth on the demise of his maternal great-uncle, the late PHILIP RUNDELL, ESQ., of Ludgate Street, London, an eminent goldsmith, who died at the advanced age of 81, on the 17th of February, 1827. After many munificent presents, during his long and money-saving life, he bequeathed, by will, the very large sum of five hundred thousand pounds and upwards to be distributed to his nephews and nieces, to personal friends, and to public charities. The residue of his fortune was given to his "great nephew and esteemed friend, Joseph Neeld, Esq., the younger." This item was presumed to amount to at least eight hundred and ninety thousand pounds. The personal effects were sworn to exceed one million of money, the utmost limit to which the scale of probate duty extends.*

It may be remarked that Mr. Neeld had been on intimate terms with Colonel Houlton before he came into possession of his princely fortune, and as the latter gentleman was disposed to settle at Farleigh Castle, after the death of his uncle, Rear-Admiral John Houlton, he met with a liberal purchaser of the Grittleton manorial estate in the gentleman who has created such vast beneficial improvements in this district.

Since his purchase of the estate, Mr. Neeld has generally resided at Grittleton; but the old manor-house, though suitable in point of size to the property formerly attached to it, and not a bad specimen of its kind, as a country residence, was inadequate to the position of its new owner. Taking, therefore, the opportunity of some injury done by a fire, Mr. Neeld added a few larger apartments, from the designs of Mr. James Thomson, architect, of London.

The more spacious mansion on the same site, now in progress of

---

* Amongst numerous relatives of this affluent gentleman was my friend John Bannister, the eminent comedian, who received some liberal donations from the rich bachelor. Mrs. Bannister was one of Mr. Rundell's nieces, and was a favourite with the rich uncle, who presented to her son ten thousand pounds on coming of age.

erection at Grittleton, is on a large scale, and intended to present, in architectural design, finishing, and adornment, a house fitting for a wide and rich domain. The ground-plan covers an area of 160 feet from N. to S., by 120 feet from E. to W., exclusive of a fine Conservatory, of original design, occupying the south front, and with extensive offices at the other extremity. The halls, staircases, and vestibules, rise to the summit of the building, and are to be appropriated to pictures, sculpture, &c. From what I know of the art and literary treasures in the town and country houses of Mr. Neeld, it may be reasonably inferred that the mansion at Grittleton will be entitled to rank, in its finished state, with the noble and historical seats of the county. It is gratifying to find that the proprietor has directed his attention and patronage chiefly to British art and artists, whereby the genuineness, quality, and real meaning of such works may be fairly understood and appreciated; and not come before the possessor and his friends with suspicion and falsehood. The works consist almost entirely of paintings and sculpture by British artists: viz., Chantrey, Gibson, Baily, Wyatt, Papworth, Constable, Gainsborough, Etty, Roberts, Stanfield, Wilson, Ward, West, and many others; whence it may be presumed that Grittleton House will become a gallery of fine art, and a mansion of splendour. Its spacious library will also contain a large collection of books, amongst which it cannot fail to gratify my literary, as well as provincial vanity—I will say pride, home feelings—to know that an unique copy of my *Architectural Antiquities*, large paper, with proofs, etchings, and the *Original Drawings*, will be preserved here. This set was originally purchased by my very good friend, and most substantial patron, John Broadley, Esq., of South Ella, Yorkshire, for the sum of 650 guineas, and was resold, at the sale of that gentleman's very fine library, to Mr. Neeld. Mr. Thomson likewise designed and directed several other buildings on different parts of his patron's estates: at Grittleton, Leigh-Delamere, Alderton, and Chippenham.

The farm-houses are respectable and comfortable edifices, with appendages to correspond; whilst the villages, school-houses, and cottages, are calculated to make the homes of labourers and their families places of shelter from inclement weather, and afford them inducements to prefer home to the demoralizing beer-shop and public-house.

In the new churches the architect has introduced novelties of form and ornament to distinguish them from domestic buildings.

A "History of the Parish of Grittleton," including pedigrees of its former chief proprietors, the White and Houlton Families, was published in 1843, by "The Wiltshire Topographical Society," from the manuscript of the Rev. J. E. Jackson, at that time curate of Farleigh-Hungerford, near Bath. Of that gentleman and of the late Lieut.-Col. Houlton, of Farleigh, I shall have occasion to speak again in a subsequent part of this Memoir. The volume contains also "An Essay on Topographical Literature; its Province, Attributes, and varied Utility," by J. Britton.

The whole southern boundary of Grittleton parish joins that of LEIGH-DELAMERE, or SEVINGTON, which belongs to Mr. Neeld, who has carried his improvements through its whole extent by erecting a new church, a new parsonage-house, a group of alms-houses, also a school, farm-house, and cottages. This parish was noted in Aubrey's time for its clerical schoolmaster, the Rev. Robert Latimer, who had been preceptor to the famous *Thomas Hobbes* of Malmesbury. Of that daring, original philosopher, in an age when science and toleration were rare and scarcely known, Aubrey thus writes, "This summer, 1634, (I remember it was in venison season, July or August,) Mr. T. H. came into his native county to visit his friends, and amongst others he came to see his old schoolmaster (who died in November of that year) when I was then a little youth at school, in the church, newly entered into my grammar by him. Here was the first place and time that I ever had the honour to see this worthy, learned man, who was then pleased to take notice of me, and the next day came to visit my relations. He was a proper man, briske, and in very good equipage; his haire was then quite black. He stayed at Malmesbury and in the neighbourhood a week or better: 'twas the last time he ever was in Wiltshire." Aubrey continued on intimate terms with Hobbes till the death of the latter in 1679, and wrote a Memoir of him, which will be found in "Letters from the Bodleian Library," vol. ii., p. 604. In my own Memoir of Aubrey, 4to., 1845, are many anecdotes of both, with notices of places and persons belonging to this vicinity. Before I was ten years of age, I was accustomed to convey four three-penny loaves every Saturday to Mrs. Comely, of the farmhouse. On these visits I was always treated with two slices of the new bread with new butter and new milk, thus constituting a memorable treat, and considered most delicious. In one of these visits I rode a three-years-old blood colt, which had been recently "broken in," but which was literally "as playful as a colt," though mild as a lamb. At that time the road, or rather approach, to the house was through three fields, and there were three gates to open: these occasioned difficulty and labour, even with an old horse which I generally rode on occasions of bread delivery. On returning, I had passed two of the gates, and was at a gentle canter by the side of a hedge, when a blackbird flew near the colt's head, and made one of those sharp, half-singing, half-screaming noises which the male generally does when frightened from its perch. The colt threw down its head, kicked up behind, plunged, and gallopped off across the field; had a fine piece of frolic for itself, but great terror to its young rider. My hat and wallet fell off at the first start, the bridle was pulled out of my hand, and I was entirely at the mercy of the playful animal—clinging something like the monkey; for I never had a lesson in the art of sitting, holding the rein, or managing a horse. She stood still at the gate, and I felt more difficulty and alarm in regaining the hat and wallet, remounting and riding home, afterwards, than I had done before in retaining my seat. Holcroft, in his very interesting "Auto-Biography," has related two or three cases of blood horses running away, and playing vicious tricks with him, when a boy, on Newmarket Heath. His account of the tempers, habits, discipline, and characters of famed racers is very interesting.

Connected with Leigh-Delamere, and its domestic annals, was an event which created almost as much local gossip and scandal as that of the murder of the poor negro in Stanton Park, described in a previous part of this volume (p. 37.) One of the young Mr. Comelys had been too familiar with the female servant, and bastardy was the consequence. The poor girl continued her work in the house till she was painfully warned that certain effects were ripe; and, in the night, she left the house, with the intention of going home to her parents, who lived at Stanton, an adjoining parish. The shortest path led through the large wood, and she chose it—as bodily pains overcame the terrors of fancy—but she had not proceeded far when nature compelled her to lie down. A child was born in this much-dreaded place: she wrapped it in a piece of flannel, and carried it to the alarmed home of its grandmother. Though the heartless father was required to pay half-a-crown per week towards the support of the innocent and helpless infant, there was no provision made to restore character and comfort to the seduced and ruined mother, nor to her distressed and oppressed parents. The event has often occurred to my memory, on reading of numerous similar instances, at parochial boards, and in law-courts, and by reflecting on the pitiless and cruel conduct of officers, and other young men, in boasting of conquests, and seductions of innocent females. I was once at a mess-table of officers at Winchester, where a prince was present, whose vain and disgusting language and anecdotes were of this kind. Goldsmith, in his inimitable " Vicar of Wakefield," and Dr. Dodd, in " The Sisters," have given distressing pictures of this infamous libertinism.

The author of the "History of Grittleton," already referred to, now occupies the new and pleasant parsonage of Leigh-Delamere, having been presented to that rectory, as well as to the vicarage of the neighbouring parish of Norton, by the patron, Joseph Neeld, Esq., M.P. Since his residence there, he has written "A Guide to Farleigh-Hungerford," in 1853; and several Topographical Essays, in "The Wiltshire Archæological and Natural History Magazine," 1854-5. He is one of the honorary secretaries of that Society, of which I propose to give some account in a later part of this work. In the first volume of its publications is an "Address" on Wiltshire Topography, which was read by him to a large county meeting at Devizes, October 12, 1853, when the *Marquess of Lansdowne* presided, supported by a large assembly of ladies and gentlemen from different parts of the county. It is hoped that the author may be tempted to reprint it, for more extensive circulation through the county; as it is well calculated to promote inquiry, create, or call into action, other lovers of topography, and bring forth in time the ripened fruit of a yet unfinished County History. The paper shows Mr. Jackson's notions of this desideratum, his willingness to co-operate, and the nature and character of the materials which he has already collected. Of these a considerable portion relates to the genealogical, manorial, and civil history of the HUNGERFORD FAMILIES, who possessed numerous estates, manors, and mansions in the counties of Wilts, Berks, Somerset, Gloucester, &c. Of the origin of Mr. Jackson's manuscript collections on this subject, their progressive augmentation and present extent, he gave a vivid account in the magazine referred to. Though, at the zenith of its prosperity, the Hungerford genealogical tree spread its branches over a wide tract of territory, it had dwindled almost to nothing in my boyish days, and was said to have had one of its last distant female representatives in Chippenham near the end of the last century; and though its history may be worthy of being preserved in the county, I can hardly expect to see it perpetuated in print; for few readers, and a smaller number of purchasers, of dissertations on a bye-gone age of persons, places, and things, will be likely to patronize such a work. I hope, however, that Mr. Jackson may continue to give his attention to subjects of local history, and thereby set an example to his clerical brethren and to provincial gentlemen to do likewise.*

I have alluded to STANTON ST. QUINTIN as in the vicinity of the parish last noticed. The ancient Manor-house of this place combined the lay and ecclesiastical characters. At the end of the last century, a square tower, of castellated appearance, was standing, and is represented in the "Beauties of England," vol. xv. There were also some pointed arched windows, indicative of a domestic chapel, or a hall; whilst the adjoining church exhibited arches, columns, and a south porch, characterising an Anglo-Norman origin. A small, plain, square tower was placed over what may be called the choir (between the nave and chancel,) whilst an aile, on the south side, appears to have been added to the nave, and separated from it by Norman arches. At the north side of the tower was a small square room forming a kind of cell. When I last visited this church, about forty years back, it was in a

---

* A paper from this gentleman's pen, on the Connection of the Hungerfords with Salisbury, is published in the second volume of the *Wiltshire Magazine*, containing more particularly an account of two chapels founded by them in the cathedral of that city.

dilapidated state, but it has since been repaired and rendered fit for its sacred purposes. I remember a pond, near the house, was well stocked with fish. A large wood of about 250 acres still retains the name of Stanton Park. This is subjected to annual cuttings and loppings, to supply bakers, carpenters, hurdle-makers, tanners, and others, with fire-wood, timber, bark, &c. The estate belongs to the lords of Longford Castle, near Salisbury. The late Earl of Radnor was vexed that his steward had ordered, or allowed, the old tower of the mansion to be taken down rather than expend a few pounds in repairs to preserve it.*

Between Upper and Lower Stanton, there was a large, open common (since enclosed.) Here I occasionally saw *Pewits*, or lapwings, which were rare in this part of the county, and often attracted my admiration by their plumage, rapidity of running, and varied evolutions. Seeing one of these apparently wounded, and fluttering on the ground, I eagerly sought to catch it; but whenever I stooped to place my hat over it, it made efforts to fly and elude me: its cries indicated pain, or terror. Having thus seduced me from its nest, it mounted in the air, where it flew in circles around me, and was joined by its mate. This ruse—or cunning trick of the pewit to seduce a person from its nest —I have since learnt is a peculiar stratagem or instinct of the bird, to deceive its enemies and plunderers.

An interesting account of the pewit, with a very beautiful representation, is given in Yarrell's interesting *History of British Birds*, 3 vols. 8vo. second edition, 1848.

The north-western boundary of Grittleton parish is formed by the still-remaining ancient trackway, called the *Foss-road*, being one of the great Roman " vias " across the island from east to west; having the permanent stations of *Corinium*, Cirencester, to the east, and *Aquæ-Solis*, Bath, to the west. A little beyond the northern extremity of this parish, where a parish cross-road intersects that of the Romans, is a place of historic and legendary note, called the *Elm-and-Ash*, from two trees, which, united at the stool, or root, ascended, distinct and

---

* Aubrey tells us, that in his time the parish consisted of only twenty-three houses, and that eight of its inhabitants were eighty years of age. His mother's grandfather had attained the age of ninety-six at his death in 1626.—(*Nat. Hist. Wilts.* p. 69.)

separate, to large and healthy specimens of their species. It was traditionally related that they were two stakes transfixed to the body of a suicide, interred at the junction of these roads, in conformity to a barbarous law, which entailed this stigma on a self-murderer. It is not surprising that such an act, such a spot, and the natural superstition of an illiterate age, should invest the scene with tales of ghosts and midnight spirits. As a boy, I had to traverse this road occasionally, but never without palpitating fears and imaginings; and similar apprehensions haunted older, and even aged persons. The two trees dying more than twenty-seven years ago, others were planted on their site. Young plantations have been made in the vicinity, and, according to Mr. Neeld's report, seven human skeletons were discovered, but again committed to the ground. Probably these were persons killed during the civil, or rather savage and merciless, Wars of the seventeenth century, when several battles and skirmishings occurred in this part of the island. Sherston is a noted site, and Lansdowne, near Bath, is still more distinguished; but nearly the whole of the gentry and yeomen of Wiltshire were then kept in a state of war-conflicts and fearful watchings.

To the north of the foss-road are the parishes of ALDERTON and LUCKINGTON, both of which are of historic and archæological note. The former, as far back as the time of Henry IV., was the property of the GORE FAMILY: some of whom were knighted, and one has been described as an antiquary and herald of distinction. He joined with Aubrey, Bishop Tanner, and a few other gentry of Wiltshire, in a small local society to promote a history of the county; but there were not two Aubreys amongst them, and the times were not sufficiently calm and genial to foster and rear such works. *Thomas Gore* was a native of this place, where he was born in 1611; was of Magdalen College, Oxford; removed thence to Lincoln's Inn, London, where he qualified for the bar; but, preferring the country to a town life, settled in his manorial home, and devoted his time almost entirely to antiquarian and heraldic studies and writings. On the latter subject he published "A Catalogue of Antient English Families," 8vo. 1667; and another, "Of all the Writers on Heraldry in all Languages,

1668—1674."* He likewise printed, "Nomenclator Geographicus; Latino-Anglicus and Anglico-Latinus Alphabeticè Digestus," &c., 12mo. 1667. He also produced the following very humble, but useful, "Book of the Names of all the Parishes, Market-towns, Villages, Hamlets, and Smallest Places in England and Wales," &c., 4to. 1657. Another edition was published in 1668, with Norden's *Tables*. The titles of these works are lasting evidences of Mr. Gore's partialities and qualifications, and it is to be regretted that he and Aubrey had not been on more familiar and confidential terms than is recorded in any of the latter's numerous writings. From his respectability of station and character, Gore was made High Sheriff of Wiltshire in 1680, an office which he executed with such unusual impartiality and integrity of conduct as to incur the censure and hostility of the rank royalists, who fancied and represented Charles II. as immaculate. Gore deemed it necessary to write and publish, in 1681, some account of his opinions and conduct, in "Loyalty Displayed and Falsehood Unmasked, in a Letter to a Friend." From his early death, in the 53rd year of his age, it may be inferred that the temper and manners of his compeers were not much in unison with his own, as he died in 1674, and was interred with many of his ancestors in the parish church of Alderton. This edifice, as well as the ancient manor-house, which Aubrey classes with the "old English gentleman's houses, especially in Wiltshire and thereabouts," is entirely taken down, and, I believe, there are not any representations of it preserved. A new church (the base of the old tower being retained) has been erected, from the designs of Mr. Thomson, the architect of Grittleton House; also new farm-houses and cottages, whence the parish presents an air of domestic comfort and respectability. It is, indeed, a continuation and appendage to the Grittleton estate. Mr. Gore, at his death, left a large folio volume of manuscripts, with numerous genealogies, coats of arms, &c., which was possessed by James Montagu, Esq., of Lackham, in Wiltshire. I believe it is now in the safe possession of Mr. Scrope of Castle Combe, where it will be duly appreciated by the learned historian of that interesting baronial manor. In the same library are preserved many valuable and curious manuscripts by William of Worcester, the

---

* Gough's "British Topography," vol. i., p. 50: edition 1780.

Fastolfs, and the Scropes; also a large quarto volume of copies of John Aubrey's collections in the Ashmolean Museum at Oxford.

At LUCKINGTON, adjoining Alderton, is a large mound of earth called *The Long-Barrow*, or *The Caves*, of which the earliest account, by Childrey, in "Britannica Baronica," (1661) and some other old authors, say it was "the graves of Saxon or Danish heroes, or it may be Roman, slain in battle," &c. These caves were opened before Childrey wrote; but it is not said that any sepulchral remains were found. It is intimated that the cavities were formed by upright stones, with others placed horizontally on the upper ends of the former. From the slight notice hitherto given, I should infer that it was a kist-væen, or series of cells formed with large stones, similar to Wayland-Smith, another near Uley, Gloucestershire, and many of the like class in England, Wales, Ireland, Jersey, &c.

MAIDFORE, or MADEFORD, a farm-house in the parish of Norton, near the northern extremity of Wiltshire, was the birth-place of my mother, and where I was much petted by her family in my early boy-days. It was and is a solitary house, in the midst of fields, with two woods near it; also a large, uncultivated, and unproductive common, nearly covered with gorse or furze, and almost impassable for horse or man in wet weather. Some hundred years back it must have been almost as dreary and cheerless as some of the new settlements in newly-discovered countries. It is true, the place was not infested by the wild carnivorous beasts of Africa or America, or the mighty and poisonous snakes of the East, or the treacherous and perilous volcano of Italy, but it abounded with vipers, polecats, weazels, foxes, and other mischievous if not dangerous animals. Seeing the masses of the woods waving and beaten about by high winds and storms, in my early days and nights, I fancied that the said winds were created by trees, and often wished to be at Kington at such times to escape the effects of bad weather. I feared to traverse alone the said woods, as the fancied haunts of witches, spirits, or sprites, and other supernatural nothings. Being what is called a dairy farm, its land was mostly appropriated to pasture a herd of cows and a flock of sheep. Thus I became familiar with all the processes of milking, cheese and butter-making, and other operations of the dairy. I also knew the processes of sheep-breeding, rearing, fatting, and killing, and was particularly amused and interested with the sheep-washing, shearing, and final feasting after the last operation. This season, being the beginning of summer, and having strangers and novelties, was always hailed and enjoyed by me more than any other event of the year. The final harvest-home, however, when the hay and corn were safely barned and ricked, was the next memorable epoch of the year. Then the master and mistress, with sons, daughters, servants, and strangers, were occupied, and usually merry on the occasion; and, indeed, during the whole season of harvest, through the processes of cutting, making, and securing the hay and corn in well-thatched ricks. The system, or rather the management, of farming by my maternal relations, was a sort of common-place routine, some seventy or eighty years back.* The farmer then had little intercourse with the world; there were no experimentalists, or they were rare; there was scarcely a book or a pamphlet printed on the subject; there was but little competition or rivalry in the public market; and the conveyance of cattle, sheep, corn, cheese, &c., to the large markets or fairs of Reading, London, Bristol, Winchester, Weyhill, Tan, or St. Ann's Hill, &c., prior to the construction of turnpike roads, or canals, or railroads, was only effected by long and expensive journeys. I remember that a waggon with five horses was sent once a year from Maidford to Reading by cross country roads, and occupied about a week on the journey. Now, a large and well-stocked public market

---

* It is worthy of note that the first systematic and efficient English Agricultural Society was "The Bath and West of England," founded in 1777. It grew in strength and importance, published several volumes of valuable *Transactions*, and may be referred to as the parent of "The London Board of Agriculture," founded by Act of Parliament in 1793, which fortunately had the indefatigable and zealous Sir John Sinclair for its President, and Arthur Young for its active and devoted Secretary. To those two gentlemen I was much indebted in the early part of my Topographical career for introductions, the use of books, and other advantages. That Board gave instructions and authority for THOMAS DAVIS, Esq., Steward to the Marquess of Bath, to write his "General View of the Agriculture of Wiltshire," which was published in 4to. in 1794, and was reprinted, with additions, corrections, &c., by a son of the author, in 8vo. 1811, and which may be read with advantage by the modern agriculturists of the county. Mr. Davis was a shrewd, well-informed, and strictly honourable man. In my first visits to Longleat, 1798, he proved himself my good adviser and friend.

is established at Chippenham, about seven miles from this farm, a good turnpike road nearly all the way, and a fair price paid for the farm produce. I believe there was but little skill, no science exercised, and rarely any records or journals kept by the plodding farmers of that age. Until Sir John Sinclair established the "Board of Agriculture" in London, already referred to, it may be said that the mind of the agriculturist was as steril and unproductive as the soil, which he practically ploughed and sowed with corn, but never manured with skill, nor drained with care, nor cleared of those weeds and insidious plants which became poison to the valuable corn. I never can forget the impressions made on my mind when I visited the much-famed sheep-shearing at Woburn Abbey, in 1800, when I first saw that seat, with its ducal lord surrounded by a vast crowd of gentry and farmers, to witness the improved stock and lands which that nobleman had patronized and produced. I cannot neglect to notice, as in unison with the subject now under consideration, a volume lately published entitled "Talpa, or Chronicles of a Clay Farm." It is a sort of romance of science, of experiments, of thinking, and therefore calculated to cause reflection, inquiry, and beneficial results. Nor can it be irrelevant to refer to a person and place of agricultural note at the present time, *Mr. Mechi*, of London, and of Tiptree Hall in Essex. This gentleman has devoted much labour and skill, as well as courage, in a daring speculation of making a large tract of poor, almost steril land, not only commonly productive, but even fertile and prolific. It is glorious and gratifying to witness such patriotism and such results; for even should the experimentalist fail in realizing the full amount of anticipated pecuniary profit, he derives the gratification of knowing that mentally and morally he has excited rivalry, competition, and public national benefits. Mr. Mechi has laid before the public the accounts and operations of four years' practice at his farm, from which the inquirer may ascertain what has been done, and the results.

Connected with Maidford are two events indelibly impressed on my memory, though occurring so long back as nearly eighty years. A small spring rises in the parish of Norton, crosses the road between the church and the farm-house, and at that point forms a pool in wet seasons. My uncle, and myself when about six years old, passing this pool one evening near dusk, saw the edge of the water, which was very low and muddy, strewed with the heads of an immense number of eels, mostly with their mouths open. The first move of my companion was an endeavour to catch some of them with the hands; but the moment he disturbed the water and had secured one eel, all the others vanished—were immersed in the mud in an instant. It was then thought advisable to return to the pool early in the morning, with two or three companions, all with rakes, and with a pail to hold the captured prey. Rain came on in the night, and the eels had an abundant supply of fresh water and fresh air, and thereby avoided the onslaught which had been meditated on their lives. Another small stream runs through the two farm barkens, in front of the house, but is bayed back, and forms a pool, or receptacle, for the liquid manure from the cow-sheds, stables, pigstyes, &c. Hence the water was always foul at the time alluded to, and the essence of manure was wasted. One end of this pool was five or six feet deep, to which a fine and valuable young stallion had gone to drink. In attempting to return, it fell into the said hole, for its head was tied to its fore leg, and it was dragged under water. It plunged, reared, and made a struggle for life, but was drowned before assistance could be obtained for its rescue.

Though Maidford was even much worse than here described at the time referred to, the Hilliers occupied it for nearly a century, and were ranked with the respectable yeomen and farmers of the surrounding district. My grandfather kept his hunter, and frequently joined the Duke of Beaufort's sportsmen in the fox-chase. He was consequently one of his blue and buff partizans in county elections. His eldest son, Samuel, who had settled in London as clerk to Mr. Holford, one of the Masters in Chancery, and who had the unreasonable indulgence of nearly three months holidays, from August to the beginning of November, made the fox-hunt twice a-week the chief amusement and occupation of his time. My uncle, Richard, already referred to (p. 45) succeeded his father in the farm, as well as in his hunting career; and, I suspect, was more devoted to the sports of the latter than to the cultivation and profitable production of the former; for I remember he made three or four changes of farm and home after I had escaped from apprentice slavery.

I have seen Maidford only once since that epoch of my life, when numerous changes and improvements were apparent in the house and all its appendages—in the roads, hedges, aspect of the fields, and in the manners and habits of its inhabitants. It is now the property of John Daniel Garlick Bennet, Esq., who also rents an adjoining farm, the whole of which consists of 300 acres. On these he grazes about 200 sheep and sixteen cows. From the latter, nearly two tons of cheese are annually made, which are conveyed to Chippenham market, about seven miles distant, instead of Reading, between forty and fifty. Hence the producer has a ready market near his home, has always competitors for his goods, and obtains prices proportionate to their quality and value. Besides, Chippenham has a railroad, and thus readily and cheaply has intercourse with London and the eastern parts of the island, as well as with Bristol, Liverpool, &c.

I have noticed that Maidford has a WOOD near the house, and so has Bradfield, a large, old mansion, adjoining; so have the Priory, Stanton St. Quintin, Leigh-Delamere, Easton Pearce, and other ancient manor-houses of the same character and class: all originally intended and used to provide fuel where coal was unknown, or rare.

I have already (see *ante*, p. 40) made remarks on pedigrees, genealogies, &c., and alluded to ancestors of my father's family. I have now to say something about those on my mother's side. Since the publication of the first portion of this work, my old and much-respected friend, Charles Henry Parry, Esq., formerly of Bath, now of Brighton, writes me word that his father derived his Christian names from those of his mother, whose parents and ancestors were seated at Upcott, Minety, and other places on the southern borders of Gloucestershire, adjoining the north boundary of Wiltshire. This information induced me to make some inquiry respecting my maternal grandfather; and although I have not ascertained his Christian name and birth-place, I cannot doubt, from having visited and kept up acquaintance with some of the Hilliers of Skipton Moyne, near Tetbury, when I was on visits to my uncle Samuel, at Weston Birt, that they were of the same branch as my grandfather, and Dr. Parry's mother. I must own, that for the first time in my life, I should feel a certain amount of pride and pleasure in ascertaining some consanguinity with the Parrys of Bath.

Dr. Caleb Hillier Parry was amongst my early and kindest friends, when I frequented that city at the end of the last century, and his son and heir above-named has observed the same friendly courtesies on several subsequent occasions. Were I younger and stronger, I should be tempted to institute inquiries to settle this question.*

It is only within the last four years that I have ascertained the place and time of my parents' marriage. Mr. Jackson, the Vicar of Norton, was officiating at the bedside of an old man, one of his parishioners, and having finished his duties, while casting his antiquarian eyes round the room, espied a box of unusual material for such a place, and asked the nurse what it contained: "Lor zur," says she, "unly two or dree ould raggid buks that beant gud vor nuthin." Whilst these words were drawled out in the broad Wiltshire tone and twang, the antiquary had opened the lid of the box and discovered certain long-lost parish registers. On taking them home, as the rightful guardian of such strays, he found amongst other entries the following, which I must own surprised and gratified me when transmitted to London:—

"HENRY BRITTON, of Kington St. Michael's, and ANNE HILLIER, of this parish, were married in this Church by Licence, with consent of Parents, this tenth day of January in the year of our Lord Seventeen hundred and sixty-five, by me, Thos. Hornidge, Vicar.

"This marriage was solemnized between us, HENRY BRITTON, ANNE HILLIER, in the presence of SAML. HILLIER, JOHN SMITHIES. Extracted by me, J. E. Jackson, Vicar of Norton, 27th March, 1851."

---

During my abode at Maidford, I visited the town of *Tetbury* with my grandmother, and, on another occasion, with one of my uncles. Both required farm servants; one for the dairy, to milk the cows, make butter, cheese, &c.; the other, for a man to perform the work of the fields, attend the horses, assist in milking, and also look after

---

* A very interesting brief biographical account of Dr. Caleb Hillier Parry, written by his accomplished son and heir, will be found in my volume on "Bath Abbey Church," in which are several other short biographies of eminent persons, as well as topographical anecdotes relating to this part of the county.

the pigstyes (the word piggeries not then in use). These servants were hired by the year, and subject to the law of old customs. The meeting, or human market, was and is called "a mop."* The servants congregated in groups, or rows, on the sides of a public street, dressed in their best, or Sunday clothes, whilst the masters and mistresses walked in front of the said rows, inspecting and questioning the servants whose appearances seemed most prepossessing to the chooser. These meetings constituted a sort of fair, as perambulating dealers in gingerbread and toys, shows, &c., usually attended them. At most of these "mops" it was, and may yet be, the custom to roast an ox, or a couple of sheep, and retail the same at sixpence the plate to numerous visitors who came from miles around to seek pleasure in a holiday. At night the public-houses were full of company; drinking, dancing, and singing were kept up to a late hour; peace and order either winked or slept, whilst the shepherd and dairy-maid enjoyed their annual saturnalia. A graphic as well as dramatic notice of a Gloucestershire mop is related by my respected friend, J. Y. Akerman, in his volume of "Wiltshire Tales," in which he has given vivid pictures of persons in the humbler walks of life, whose provincial phraseology, ideas, or rather routine of common-place phrases, with their figures and physiognomy, are characterized with striking effects and truthfulness. There are villages between Gloucester and Chippenham where many of their inhabitants continue as uninformed as they were in my boyish days, and where they are true descendants of their parents, not only in name, but in superstition, credulity, and language, or rather gibberish.

## MALMESBURY.

Within two miles of the farm-house here noticed, is the above-named picturesque and remarkable town; which, though impressed on my youthful mind by monastic tales and miracles, and by the frightful death of a poor person afflicted with hydrophobia, has been still more firmly and pleasingly associated with personal, archæological,

---

* "*Mop*," *Statute;* or, as pronounced, *Statie-Fair*.—(See Miss Baker's valuable "Northamptonshire Glossary" for particulars of this provincial custom.)

and picturesque facts and features. Among the most appalling modes of human decease is that of canine madness: to be smothered by suffocation between beds, and under paroxysms of bodily convulsion, is awful to contemplate, even in imagination.

John Aubrey—the memorable "worthy of Wiltshire"—has transmitted to our and to future times some amusing anecdotes of Malmesbury and its inhabitants. When at school at Yatton-Keynel, he says, "it was the fashion to cover copy-books, &c., with parchment manuscripts," which, though he did not understand, he admired for "the elegancy of the writing and the coloured initial letters. Mr. William Stump, great grandson of the rich clothier of Malmesbury, had several MSS. of the abbey. Being a proper and good fellow, when he brewed a barrell of special ale, he stop't the bung-hole, under the clay, with a sheet of manuscript; and said nothing did it so well: which methought did grieve me then to see. In my grandfather's dayes the manuscripts flew about like butterflies. All musick bookes, account bookes, and copie bookes, were covered with old manuscripts, as wee cover them now with blew or marbled paper. The glovers made great havoc of them; and gloves were wrapt up no doubt in many good pieces of antiquity. Before the late warres a world of rare manuscripts perished hereabouts. Within half a dozen miles of this place (Leigh-Delamere) was the Abbey of Malmesbury, where it may be presumed the library was as well furnished with choice copies as most libraries of England: there were Broadstoke Priory, Stoneleigh Abbey, Farleigh Abbey, Bath Abbey, eight miles, and Cirencester Abbey, twelve miles.—Anno 1647, I went to Parson Stump, out of curiosity, to see his MSS., whereof I had seen some in my childhood; but at that time they were lost or disperst. His sons were gunners and souldiers, and scoured their gunnes with them, but he showed me several old deedes granted by the Lord Abbotts, with their seals annexed, which I suppose his son, Capt. Thos. Stump of Malmesbury, hath still."—(*Natural History of Wiltshire*, p. 79.) In another page of the same volume is a sketchy notice of the extraordinary adventures of the said Captain, which, had it come into the possession of Daniel De Foe, he might have been tempted to write "The Life and romantic Adventures of Thomas Stump, of Yatton-Keynel; his Captivity by Savages, and, after long Residence amongst them, his Return to his Native Home," &c. This Thomas Stump, at the time of Aubrey's writing, was captain in King Charles the First's army; but of his career, deeds, and death we are not informed. Aubrey tells us that he was a native of Yatton-Keynel, where his father was Rector; that he "was a boy of most daring spirit; would climb towers and trees, and walk on the battlements of the former. He had too much spirit to be a scholar, and about 16** went in a voyage with his uncle, Sir Thos. Ivy, to Guyana, in anno 1633 or 1632." Amongst the sailors who left the vessel to explore the country, were young Stump and another boy, and all were made prisoners by the wild natives. Those with beards were barbarously murdered and eaten, whilst the two boys were saved by the queen. Stump tried to drown himself, but did not succeed: he appears to have remained for about four years, when he made his escape by swimming to a Portugeuse vessel that was passing near the shore, from which he also made his exit in the same manner, on passing Cornwall. Thence he wandered to his home, where, from altered appearance and language he was treated as an imposter for some time, but was at length recognized and made welcome. "His narrations," says Aubrey, "are very strange and pleasant, but so many years since, have made me almost forget all. He taught them to build hovels, and to thatch and wattle. I wish I had a good account of his abode there."—(*Nat. Hist. Wilts.*, p. 81.)

Aubrey has preserved many other biographical particulars of persons, places, and local circumstances belonging to Malmesbury, which constitute materials of its history. Leland, in his *Itinerary*, has also given publicity to certain facts and anecdotes, between the years 1540-42.—(See interesting accounts of his journeys through Wiltshire, in the first volume of *The Wiltshire Magazine*, with copious notes by the Rev. J. E Jackson.)*

Malmesbury involves reminiscences of various, many, and different personal events in association with archæology, history, biography, and also that long-established vice, borough depravity. At the end of

---

* At the time this note is penned, (February, 1856) two of the descendants of the Stumps are in the Poor-house of Malmesbury. Such are among the vicissitudes of human life.

the last century I spent a few days with a clergyman of the town; and then commenced my acquaintance, not only with its ruined castle, abbey church and house, nunnery, cross, pilgrim's inn, &c., but with J. M. Moffatt, a schoolmaster, and future historian of the town; with Mr. Thomas, a solicitor, who was then, like myself, a dabbler in topography; with Mr. J. Hanks, a breeches-maker, a trade then flourishing, but now extinct, who had recently published four large aquatinted views of the church. At the same time I visited Charlton House, in the vicinity, and saw a farmer Stump, of the parish, and descendant of a person of the name who had purchased the fragments of the abbey buildings of Malmesbury to convert them into a parish church, the old edifice having become ruinous. At Mr. Stump's, of Charlton, I was surprised to find many old folio volumes deposited in a substantial and large chest in a bed-room, and apparently unread, or unfingered, for a long time. They were old Chronicles, Speed's *History*, Camden's *Britannia*, Bibles in black letter, &c. I regret that I did not take a list of them, and ascertain something of their history. Of my host at Malmesbury, I painfully found him so lamentably fond of strong Wiltshire ale that he rarely went to bed sober: his amiable wife and a young family were neglected and impoverished; and, when I visited the town, two or three years afterwards, with eyes better qualified to see the peculiarities of architectural antiquities, and a mind to understand and appreciate their historic and artistic characteristics, my clerical friend had died, in the prime of life, and left a young widow and four orphan children as oppressive legacies to relatives and friends. *Mr. Moffatt*, whose school adjoined the west end of the Abbey Church, had published a small octavo volume, entitled "A History of Malmesbury," &c., 1805. His son was apprenticed to an apothecary, and afterwards settled in London, where for some years he gained a limited income by writing for the press. Both Mr. Brayley and myself gave him frequent employ in making searches, abstracts, translations, &c., at the British Museum, and in other public libraries. I often regretted that I had not been placed with such a master as Mr. Moffatt, as his school-room abounded with books, maps, prints, chronological charts, and other mental food, calculated to excite the curiosity and arouse the fancy of young and susceptible minds.

Malmesbury is singularly placed on the sides and summit of a sort of small geological peninsula extending between two brooks winding through narrow valleys, which unite at the south-western extremity of the town. On the apex of this ridge, and overtopping all other objects, are large and imposing masses of the once-famed Abbey Church, which must have vied with the more noted monastic church of Glastonbury. Only about one-third of the original edifice remains. It contains and displays some very fine and original architectural members, which must have been erected in the early part of the twelfth century, when the pointed-arch system was introduced here, at Canterbury, and a few other places. A portion of the nave, with its ailes, a fragment of the south transept, one lofty semicircular arch with three piers of a central tower, ruinous portions of the once-enriched west end, and the grand south porch only remain. These parts and features cannot fail to arrest the attention, and excite the curiosity of the zealous architectural antiquary, who sees and reads evidences of originality in design, science and skill in execution, fancy and art in ornamentation.* The more I have meditated on this sacred edifice, as a whole and in detail, the more am I impressed with the wish of seeing its history amply developed, and its architecture well elucidated. Hearne, in a series of architectural antiquities, was the first artist to attract public, or rather limited attention, to these interesting relics, by publishing three different engravings of the ruins: viz., a view of the fragment of its west front; another of the ruinous parts within the walls of the fallen tower at the south-west angle, and a distant view of the whole of the remaining building, from the valley, at a short distance to the north-west. The last view is so captivating to the artist's eye, that Turner was tempted to employ his fascinating pencil in delineating the same. Though unacquainted with these facts, and with very limited, very humble, powers, I was seduced to make a slight pencil sketch of the view in 1798, on my first examination of these ruins. Alas! how poor, how puerile is the last sketch

---

* There is preserved amongst the *Lansdowne MSS.* in the British Museum, a "Journal of a Tour through parts of Wiltshire, &c." (A.D. 1634) by three officers—probably a walk—in which they have recorded some interesting particulars of the Abbey Church, at Malmesbury. These remarks are printed in Brayley's "Graphic Illustrator."

compared to the other two! which I never look at but with emotions of pleasure, though alloyed with regret that I had not been placed, at that time, under the tutelage of such an artist as Hearne, or Turner. In after-life, I became acquainted with both; admired their professional works; respected, and even loved, the former for his amiability of disposition and suavity of manners; whilst I could not reconcile myself to be commonly courteous to the latter, from his chilling, forbidding tone and laconism of language and behaviour.

Besides the illustrations referred to, I may venture to direct the attention of such young architects and antiquaries as are not acquainted with the literary works devoted to Malmesbury Abbey, to the first volume of my "Architectural Antiquities," in which are fourteen quarto pages of letter-press, with precise references to authorities, and ten engraved illustrations of the building. In the same work are three prints, with descriptions, of the *Market Cross*, which Leland tells us was erected "by the men of the towne, in hominum memoria." The Society of Antiquaries of London published a series of engravings of the Abbey Church, from drawings by F. Nash, who was first introduced to public notice by prints from his early drawings in the Beauties of England, 1801. Unfortunately, there is not any literary information to accompany and explain either the history or the architecture of the church, and it is to be regretted that the drawings and engravings are not satisfactory.*

---

* Amongst instances of mismanagement and improvidence in appropriation of the Society's funds by former Councils of Antiquaries, was that of publishing large—very large—prints of certain English Cathedrals, also of the "Monumenta Vetusta," executed mostly by inexperienced apprentices to an engraver who was injudiciously employed by a Director of the Society, who exercised uncontrolled influence, not alone in the choice of subjects for publication, but in patronizing his favourites. Had £40. or £50. been paid for a good history and description of Malmesbury Abbey, and the plates printed in 4to. to match with the Archæologia, the work would have been more useful and satisfactory to the public, and more creditable to the Society. But then, and for many years since, that Society, like too many others, has suffered by cliques, by intrigue, by inefficient officers. These institutions, as well as the great national council of the nation, call on the members of the former, and the over-taxed people of the latter, for "a long pull, a strong pull, and a pull altogether." A well-written impartial history of the Society of Antiquaries is a desideratum in literature; not merely to show its rise, progress, and influence, but to be a warning to young associa-

In September, 1855, I revisited Malmesbury, after an absence of many years, and was much gratified in viewing the changed condition, the improvements, and the rational reforms which were manifested in the appearance of the streets, houses, shops, the aspect of the inhabitants, and the exterior and interior state of the grand fragment of the Abbey Church. This is now fitted for Christians to occupy during church hours; seems dry and wholesome to breathe in; and its firm and lasting architecture presents assurance of endurance for ages. Had the young architect employed to fit up and adorn this Protestant place of worship been then as familiar with the Christian architecture of the Anglo-Norman age as he now is, he would have performed his task with more credit to himself and gratification to the architectural antiquary. Not only is the inside rendered clean and pleasant, but the cemetery and surrounding space have been cleared of nuisances—pigstyes, stables, rick-yards, and other offensive desecrations. The adjoining abbey house, which was either a workhouse or occupied by poor families, appears like a rural mansion, with flower-gardens, shrubs, and other appendages of domestic comfort or luxury. Its position and scenic accompaniments are eminently picturesque. Considering the extent of ground formerly occupied by the abbey buildings and church, it is much to be desired that the whole of the debris and rubbish be taken away and the foundations and substructure laid bare, and thus displayed to the eye and judgment of the architectural antiquary.

The ruins, the desecration, the forlorn state of the once proud and commanding edifice, now before us, afford an awful lesson and warning to man,—to the philosopher, the politician, the religionist: each and all of whom may profit by the lesson involved in the history of this foundation, and its eventful climax. Limited in views, self-sufficient, and tyrannical, the rigid Roman Catholic, or his priest, impiously

---

tions. Favoritism should be sacredly eschewed; incompetent persons withheld from any and every office; frequent changes made in honorary offices; and competent committees appointed to check and control every paid official and each department of the executive. Whilst the Society of Antiquaries has been lamentably defective in all these essentials to healthy vigor and usefulness, the Zoological, Astronomical, Geological, and Geographical Societies have grown to dignified strength and to national importance.

fancied himself and his practices immaculate, and therefore demanded and arrogated supremacy and implicit obedience. Instead of working to till the soil and earn the food he ate, he devoted the greater part of his time and thoughts to religious ceremonies—to outward parade and to ostentatious acting. Instead of exerting his bodily strength to relieve the waggon from the slough, he prayed to his Jupiter, or other powerless god, to employ miraculous powers to extricate the load. Alas! how blind is poor human nature! how uncharitable in its estimation of the motives and principles of mutual obligation and forbearance! Comparing and contrasting the once rich and superb monasteries of this island, as they were in their zenith, with what they now are in uselessness and formless ruin, we cannot help deploring the spoliation and waste of edifices which were chiefly for pageantry—which were raised to seduce the imagination and to paralyze the judgment. The laity, the workers of the earth, were progressively inveigled to surrender all their rights and privileges of action, and even of thinking, to aggrandize a hierarchy—a priesthood of indomitable arrogance and presumption. As a natural and rational consequence they provoked a revolution, which swept away the evil that had produced delirium and moral death. Not only the workers of that evil suffered in the conflict, but their possessions were confiscated and placed in the possession of new proprietors who, in their turn, became enemies and hostile to the parties who had tyrannised over their rights and consciences. Hence we now see the results of misrule—the laws of retribution vindicated and executed in the wasteful ruins and the desecrated parade of ceremonials. The lesson is palpable and admonishing to the tyranny of a Czar, and of a Pope, who may profit by the example, if they honestly and wisely yield moral reform to prevent political and religious revolution.

THOMAS HOBBES, *born in Malmesbury April 5th,* 1588, *and died at Chatsworth 4th December,* 1679.

An eminent, a remarkable native of this town, demands a passing tribute of respect and a literary notice from me. "The Malmesbury Philosopher"—the man of original thinking—the acute intellect—the moral and religious reformer—who dared to speak out, and advocate new doctrines and opinions, which were regarded not only as heresy, but blasphemy, and hence was persecuted and prosecuted with vehemence and the most relentless tyranny. He rebelled against all religious despotism and intolerance, by writings and discourses which created hosts of bigoted critics. "Hobbes," says Mr. Mill, "is a great name in philosophy, on account of both what he taught, and the extraordinary impulse he communicated to the spirit of free enquiry in Europe." (*Fragment on Mackintosh*, page 19.)—"He may be considered the father of English Psychology, as well as (what every one must allow him to be) the first great English writer on the science of government." (*Penny Cyclopædia*, vol. xii., p. 255.) To this work the reader is referred for a dispassionate and honest account of the literary "leviathan" of Malmesbury. Fortunately, he met with a friend and patron in the contemporary Duke of Devonshire, who gave him a home and support. " Placed the greater part of his life in circumstances that would have made any other man, despite himself, a courtier,—the inmate of a noble house and tutor to a king,—amid the temptations of society, he steadily pursued philosophy, and, at the risk of losing great friends, and indeed with the sacrifice of royal favour, actually put forth and clung to opinions which were then most startling and obnoxious."—(Vide the same work.)

The extent of his writings, and the vast range of his studies, may be inferred by the number of his publications. These have recently been carefully edited and reprinted by the late estimable and zealous statesman and philanthropist, Sir Wm. Molesworth. That gentleman devoted many years to investigate and edit a new and comprehensive collection of his many literary works. They consist of his Latin and philosophical writings, five volumes octavo, and eleven more of his English compositions. As a real lover of literature, and of the author who formed and enlarged his mind, Sir William presented many copies of this edition to public institutions and libraries. He had also collected a mass of original materials and letters to form an extended biography of the author. It is hoped that these collections may be preserved in the British Museum, where they would be accessible to, and perhaps might yet be laid before, the reading public, by some worthy admirer of the late Sir William. I have sought in vain to ascertain the destination of these materials.

THOMAS HEARNE, *born* 1744; *died in London April* 27*th*, 1817.

The first artist who directed public attention to the picturesque ruins of Malmesbury Abbey was THOMAS HEARNE, who was a native of *Brinkworth*, a parish near that town. As that gentleman was also the first topographical artist that gave spirit, effect, and truly picturesque character to his local drawings—as the engravings published from his works may be said to have created a new feeling, an emulation in this department of art—and was amongst the earliest of my associates, after the commencement of the *Beauties of Wiltshire* and of *England*, I cannot neglect this opportunity of putting on record a brief compliment to his memory. Besides, I rank him amongst the Worthies of my own natal county. Hearne was sent to London in boyhood and articled to William Woollett, the justly admired landscape engraver, where he acquired that love for the picturesque and that partiality for topographical drawing which "grew with his growth and strengthened with his strength." Engaged to visit the Leeward Islands, as draftsman to the embassy under Sir R. Payne, he remained there some years, and on returning to London was soon profitably and successfully employed as a topographical artist. The commanding ruins of Malmesbury Abbey naturally excited his curiosity and gave occupation for his faithful pencil. With some truthful and beautiful views of them he induced Mr. William Byrne to join him in publishing a series of engravings under the title of "*The Antiquities of Great Britain.*" Amongst the Drawings made for this publication between the years 1771 and 1794 were views of the Abbey referred to, one of which, the fragment of the west front, was introduced as a frontispiece to the first volume. Two other views of Wiltshire antiquities were afterwards engraved for the same work; viz., the east end of Salisbury Cathedral, and a view of Stonehenge. The sale of this very beautiful work did not tempt the artists to devote either much energy or capital to excite publicity, and it was closed with seventy-two engravings. The engraver and the draftsman were well employed for life in their respective departments of art, and were much esteemed as artists and as members of that circle of society in which they were placed. Humble and simple in manners and habits,

Hearne enjoyed life in an eminent degree. For many years he occupied a first floor in Macclesfield Street, Soho, where I visited him, and also associated with him in the company of some of his brother artists, and with Mr. George Baker, one of the earliest collectors of drawings, proof prints, etchings, &c., with whom I ever became acquainted. Mr. Baker was a silkmercer in St. Paul's Churchyard, where his apartments were filled with the choice and valuable specimens he had collected. Proofs from Woollett's fine plates, from Hogarth's, and other engravers, with numerous drawings by Hearne, Alexander, and other similar artists, were objects of his domestic pride, whilst the authors of those works were his friends and associates.*

JOHN AUBREY, F.R.S., *" an eminent English antiquary," as designated by Watt in " Bibliotheca Britannica," was born at Easton Pearse, in the parish of Kington St. Michael, Wiltshire, March 12th, 1625, died, and was buried in the churchyard of St. Mary Magdalen, adjoining Trinity College, Oxford, in June 1717.*

I am thus particular in detail on all these points, as to the time and place of Aubrey's decease and burial, which had been doubtful, or erroneously stated by his biographers, until it was proved in the publication of my " Memoir " of him, in 1845. That volume contains a copious account of his own Auto-Biography, of his printed and manuscript writings, of his character, career, and vicissitudes in life, his connections and pursuits in college, and his later misfortunes and troubles. It also furnishes many anecdotes of eminent public persons with whom he corresponded and was familiar; and furnishes a picture of an age of lamentable national convulsions, fanaticism, and credulity. I am induced to point out these features of the volume, as only a small number of copies were printed, whence they are rare. Besides, this is the last opportunity I may have of stating certain facts and expressing my own opinions of a person who has engrossed much of my attention and partiality for many years. Remarkable coincidences between John Aubrey and myself have likewise ingratiated him deeply in my esti-

---

* Mr. Baker's library, and his drawings, proofs, &c., were sold by Sotheby in 1825, the first occupying three, and the second ten days' sale.

mation, and in my affections; whence a strong sympathy for his fortunes and misfortunes, for his character as an author and a gentleman, and for his fair fame in the annals of literature, has grown to its present ripeness. The same parish gave us birth, though at the distance of 146 years from each other: the same natural features of country, and similar personal manners and customs were impressed on the memories and feelings of both; whilst the vernacular language, or rather dialect and superstitions, were "familiar as household words." It is true, that he had the advantage of a regular classical education, both at schools and in college,—I never had the benefit of either; his parents and immediate relatives possessed landed and personal property; his uncles, on the father's and mother's side, were aldermen of the cities of London and Bristol, whilst mine were in trade, or cultivators of the soil: and herein all strict analogy fails. But his account of boy-days, his delight in seeing carpenters, smiths, upholsterers, and strangers come to his rustic home; his examination of, and remarks on flints, pebbles, and other objects of natural history, were quite in character with my own; as were his ambition to cultivate and deserve the acquaintance of his superiors in age, learning, and in public estimation. As he was pleased with old parchment manuscripts and ornamental capitals, so was I curious to understand and copy the strange wood-cuts in the spelling-books of Dyche and Fenning; and more especially the skilful and astonishing works (!) of my schoolmaster, Sparrow, in the engraving of ciphers and crests, on silver; and also the paintings of a swan, and a white horse, for signs at public-houses. My slates and copy-books were sadly disfigured by scratches and scrawlings. The latter portions of the lives of both were and are, however, palpably contrasted: he became embarrassed in circumstances, involved in harpy-like litigation with lawyers, lost his property, and was, at times, penniless and homeless. On the contrary, I have gradually, but almost imperceptibly, advanced in what is usually called success in life. I have encountered and overcome many of the vexations and troubles of worldly intercourse, and have succeeded in obtaining a moderate competence for old age, and have further been blessed with many domestic comforts and valuable friends.

I now proceed to lay before the reader such notices, opinions, and annotations on the life and times of John Aubrey as may, I hope will, induce him to seek further information about, and also peruse such of his writings as may tend to furnish rational amusement and substantial instruction.

Knowing that the real character, writings, and merits of Aubrey are not so popularly understood and appreciated as they deserve to be, I am eager and anxious to explain who he was, what he did to deserve the applause and esteem of posterity, and how far the modern reader and writer is indebted to him for facts, data, and information respecting persons and things of his age and times. He lived between 1625 and 1717, and was a scholar and a gentleman. His sphere of life and action embraced parts of Wiltshire, Oxfordshire, Kent, Surrey, Wales, and London. His intercourse was chiefly with the yeomanry, "rustiques," in early life; with the Oxonians, in the next stage; with lawyers, astrological "men of the town," afterwards; with money-lenders, black-legs, in another grade; and with philosophers, poets, wits, bon-vivants, artists, and with the two hostile parties of round-heads and royalists, in advanced age. With and from such personages much and various kinds of knowledge were to be obtained to improve and expand the mind. That Aubrey's was of a plastic nature is evinced by words from himself, and by deeds which he has left on record. In these words and in those records we can read his character; can see the impress of the times in which he lived; can behold the motives and actions of public men as they were influenced and exhibited by passing events, and by the rule or misrule of successive monarchs and their ministers.

In 1659, Aubrey thus expresses his partialities and lamentations. "I am heartily sorry I did not sit down to the *Antiquities* of these parts (Wiltshire) sooner; for since the time aforesaid, many things are irrecoverably lost. In former days the churches and great houses hereabouts did so abound with monuments and things remarkable, that it would have deterred an antiquary from undertaking it. In my remembrance much land hereabouts hath been inclosed, and every year more and more is taken in. Antiently the *Leghs* (now corruptly called Sleights), i. e., pastures, were noble large grounds, as yet the demesne lands at Castle Combe are. There was a world of people maintained by the plough, as yet in Northamptonshire, &c. There were no rates for the poor in my grandfather's dayes."

The tone and tendency of Aubrey's mind are strikingly shown in a memorandum on his first view of the vast ruins at AVEBURY. In January 1649, in the 24th year of his age, when in the company of some of the nobles and gentry of the county, being invited to join them at Lord Francis Seymour's, at Marlborough, he says, "These downes look as if they were sowen with great stones, very thick, and in a dusky evening they looke like a flock of sheep, and from whence they take their name (grey wethers): one might fancy it had been the scene where the giants fought with huge stones against the gods. . . . . . 'Twas here that our game began, and our chace at length led us through the village of *Aubury*, into the closes there where I was wonderfully surprised at the sight of those *vast stones of which I had never heard before*, as also of the mighty bank and graffe about it. I observed in the inclosures some segments of rude circles, made with these stones; whence I concluded they had been in the old time complete. I left my company awhile, entertaining myself with a more delightful indagation,* and then (cheered by the cry of the hounds) overtook the company and went with them to Kynnet, where was a good hunting dinner provided." Where is the hunter of the present day who would leave hounds and his excited companions to examine —hunt after—large masses of stones standing in fields, barkens, and hedges? But it is evident from this and other traits of character that Aubrey's more delighted and congenial sports were objects of antiquity, the never-tiring "highways and byeways of literature," and the history of his own species. In the same year he was collecting information respecting mysterious noises which disturbed the parliamentary commissioners at Woodstock. This notice of Aubury is the first that I have found recorded by any topographer or antiquary; and we learn from Aubrey's journals that he visited it again and again, and had the honour of conducting his king (Charles II.) up Silbury Hill and over the site of the Druid temple, when His Majesty commanded him to write an account of those objects.

---

* "Indagation: search, inquiry, examination."—Bayle, in Johnson's *Dictionary*.

Mr. Poulett Scrope, in his very interesting volume "The History of Castle Combe," characterises and compliments Aubrey "for shrewd power of observation, quaint notices of places and persons which we are never tired of quoting."

The late Rev. Dr. Ingram, President of Trinity College, Anglo-Saxon Professor of the University, author of "Memorials of Oxford," says, "Aubrey's life of the great mathematician, Oughtred, proves how much the world is indebted to him; but envy, malice, and sciolism must have their day. He was too laborious a man to be properly appreciated in an age of superficial acquirements and controversial excitement, two evils which generally combine to retard and obstruct intellectual vigour. I could say much on this head, but I forbear, lest, as Selden says, 'some conscious man may take it as a libel.'"

In testimony of the character of Aubrey, and particularly of his merits and value as a topographer of his and my own native county, I gladly and thankfully avail myself of the favourable comments and opinions of the Rev. J. E. Jackson, in an Address he read at the anniversary meeting of "The Wiltshire Archæological, &c., Society," at Devizes, Oct. 12th, 1853. "It is impossible to refer to the subject of Wiltshire history without mentioning Aubrey; and it would be ungrateful to omit him; for no man was more attached to his native county, and laboured more diligently, though in an odd way of his own, on its behalf. Though from position and education a gentleman, he was from an early period of his life so involved in litigation and trouble that he was never independent and never at rest. He was a barrister without anything to do; so spent his time in riding to and from Easton Piers, to another property he had near Salisbury, and in the enjoyment of visits and conversation at the houses of the gentry. He was an accomplished man, a good classical scholar, knew French and heraldry, could draw, and had a quaint way of expressing himself, which makes his descriptions amusing enough. He was a quick observer of things, but often in such a hurry to make them his own that he did not stop to observe them quite accurately. He was unmarried, but had, as he tells us, several hairbreadth escapes from matrimony. The history of these little adventures is not preserved to us, but they seem to have been, to him, causes of infinite trouble. Being at length reduced to poverty, he spent the latter years of his life no one can tell how; finding shelter, in adversity, under the roof of the Earl of Abingdon, at Lavington, or of the Longs of Draycot." The writer then proceeds to describe the Ashmolean Museum of Oxford, its present appearance, and the manuscripts which have been there deposited from Aubrey's time to the present, about 200 years.

I can safely and sincerely say, with my deeply-read friend, CHARLES KNIGHT,* "There are few books that I take up more willingly in a vacant half hour"—but how rarely has that been the case with either himself or me!—"than the scraps of biography which Aubrey, the antiquary, addressed to Anthony à Wood, and which were published, from the originals in the Ashmolean Museum, in 1813. These little fragments are so quaint and characteristic of the writer;—so sensible in some passages and so absurd in others;—so full of what may be called the Prose of Biography, with reference to the objects of historical and literary reverence,—and so encomiastic with regard to others whose memories have wholly perished in the popular view,—that I shall endeavour to look at them consecutively as singular examples of what a clever man thought of his contemporaries, and of others who were famous in his day, whether their opinions accord with, or are opposed to, our present estimate."

"Our common notion of John Aubrey used to be that he was a dreaming, credulous old gossip, with some literary pretensions, and nothing more. He believed in astrology, in omens, dreams, apparitions, voices, knockings. Is he without followers even at this hour? Anthony à Wood, who was under great obligations to his correspondence, calls him 'a shiftless person, roving and maggotty headed.' 'Roving' indeed he was; for he wandered up and down the land, when travelling was not quite so easy as now; and, according to the testimony of Gough, an antiquary after the sober fashion of the race, 'first brought us acquainted with the earliest monuments on the face of the country—the remains of Druidism, and of Roman, Saxon, and Danish fortifications.' 'Shiftless,' too, he might be called. He possessed an estate in Kent, which was destroyed by an irruption of the

---

* "Once upon a Time," 2 vols. 18mo. 1854, vol. i., p. 296.

sea; he became involved in lawsuits; he made an unhappy marriage; in a word, to make use of his own astrological solution of his misfortunes, he was 'born in an evil hour, Saturn directly opposing my ascendant.' But he was not 'shiftless' in the sense of one who had no proper business in life. He wanted little for his support, and as he had rich friends his dependence was not very burthensome to them. He lived about in country houses with kind squires with whom he took 'his diet and sweet otiums.' What could the man do when his estates were gone but to enjoy what he called 'a happy delitescency'—the obscurity of one who was never idle in noting down what he saw around him, for the use of others, or the benefit of those who were to come after him." I could gladly quote the whole of this article as a complimentary reference to, and mental portraiture of Aubrey, and as characterising the head and heart of the éloquent writer; but the reader will be well rewarded by perusing the whole of Mr. Knight's two little volumes.

The published and manuscript works of Aubrey are numerous and various. Considering the age and temper of the times in which he lived and wrote, it is not surprising that astrology was more popular than astronomy, and that its romance and mystic signs and phraseology were calculated to seduce the young Oxford student. His early associations were calculated to impose on his fancy before his judgment began to work. Hence we find, in his first printed work, the "*Miscellanies*," so much on irrational, visionary, fantastical, supernatural matters, that the more thinking and more philosophical persons of the present age cannot read them with patience and tranquil endurance. Such writers as Lilly, Dee, Wing, Ashmole, and others of corresponding natures and opinions, were more popular than Newton, Hobbes, Bacon, or Locke. When Aubrey was first at Oxford these Miscellanies treated on "day-fatality, omens, dreams, knockings, lucky and unlucky days," and many other similar absurd notions and subjects. Estimating Aubrey by this volume alone, we cannot wonder that such writers as Scott and Hamper should pronounce him credulous, dreamy, and visionary.

His *Autograph Memoir* is fortunately preserved, and contains so many graphic touches and traits of artistic skill, and of truthfulness, that almost every feature and lineament of personal character has been handed down to us. Besides, he tells us who drew and painted his portrait at different times of his life. That which has been preserved and given to the public in my "Memoir," cannot fail to impress the spectator decidedly in his favour. Though the horrible furze-bush of a wig not only oppresses and almost smothers the head and the face, we can see and read enough of manly intelligence, of urbanity, of simplicity, of courtesy, and of an expression calculated to propitiate the candid, honest stranger, in the assurance of an honest man and a friend. All the facial lines and forms are good, and were they divested of that "bushel of hair" which obscures and entirely eclipses the forehead, sides of the face, and all the skull, we should behold the head of an Englishman which would credit the species and honour the genus. Had he lived in these times of "Progress" and enlightenment, instead of those of plodding dullness and fanatical superstition, he would have appeared amongst the first class of planets in our intellectual hemisphere; for he had the elements of greatness in him.

Let us hear him relate some of his own "Sayings and Doings," and then endeavour to estimate and appreciate what he was, and what he might have been. "When a boy I was bred at Easton in eremetical solitude."—Such is the place now, though within four miles of a railroad station, and thriving market-town; Chippenham.—"I was very curious; my greatest delight to be with the artificers that came there; e. g., joyners, carpenters, cowpers, masons, and understood their trades; horis vacuis, I drew and painted. In 1634 (i. e., in his 8th year) was entered in my latin gramer by Mr. R. Latimer, a delicate little person of Leigh-de-la-Mere, a mile, fine walk; who had an easy way of teaching. At 8 I was a kind of engineer; and I fell then to drawing, beginning first with plain outlines and then to colours, being only my own instructor. I was wont, I remember, much to lament with myself that I lived not in a city; e. g., Bristole, where I might have access to watchmakers, locksmiths, &c. Not very much care for grammer. Apprehensive enough, but my memorie not tenacious; so that when a boy I was a promising morne enough: of an inventive and philosophicall head. My wit was always working, but not to verse. Exceeding mild of spirit; mightily susceptible of fascination; strong and early impulse of antiquities." Such evidences of early impressions, and isolated meditations, cannot fail to awaken reminiscences of my own early cogitations; and create an affection for the candid, honest confessor, who thus reveals himself, and his inward workings, to the sympathy and scrutiny of descendants for generations yet to come. But there are other touches of character yet to be exhibited. Losing his first schoolmaster, after half a year's attendance, he says, "I was afterwards under several dull ignorant teachers till 12 (1638), about which time I was sent to Blandford Schoole, in Dorset, W. Sutton, B.D., who was ill-natured. Here I recovered my health, and got my latin and greeke."

When writing the Memoir of Aubrey in 1844-5, and lamenting the loss of all traces to the time and place of his death, I felt very desirous of raising a Tablet in the church where he was buried, and likewise in that of his native parish: for the merits and memory of such worthy men should not be interred with their frail remains. Had my pecuniary sources been commensurate to the promptings of my nature, I should have carried my wishes into effect. I have also often wished to place a monumental tribute to the memory of my distressed parents and their progeny, but have been deterred from the same consideration. I had made inquiries and calculations of the expenses of both; and was mainly driven from my purpose and wishes by the unreasonable demands of the clergy of the two parishes. Both those gentlemen required what I considered an unreasonable sum, five guineas for each. This was merely the fee for the privilege of placing objects against the inner walls of churches, without any species of ornament to adorn them; and which might become sources of usefulness to future generations of beholders. That the clergy of a certain church should have some control and jurisdiction over the sacred edifice in which it is their duty to be frequently placed, and where it is equally their duty to inculcate lessons of charity, humanity, generosity, and all other human virtues, should manifest a greedy appetite for exacting the highest fees in their power, for interments, monumental memorials, &c., is to be much regretted. The avaricious demands for interments, and more particularly for placing fine monuments in such churches as those of Westminster, and St. Paul's, London, manifest not only a mercenary spirit, but is degrading to the Christian minister. Instead of demanding fees, on such occasions as those referred to, it would be more commendable and honourable were the clergy to court and encourage the appropriate and gratifying display of suitable and tasteful monuments in provincial as well as in city churches.

For some strictures on this subject, I refer the inquiring reader to my volume on "*Bath Abbey Church*," published in 1825.

CHARLTON HOUSE.—Previous to the tyrannic and ultimately substantial domination of Henry VIII., the monarchs and the barons appear to have ensconced themselves with their dependent retainers in large and doleful castles; but after the wars of "the Roses" had ceased, a new class of houses was erected, both in towns and in the provinces. The King and his Lords Treasurers seem to have vied with each other in raising stately mansions of large extent, of new and costly styles of architecture, and sumptuously adorning them with sculptural and pictorial ornamentation. The proud and arrogant Wolsey not merely surpassed all his compeers, but competed with his royal master. Hampton Court was calculated to rival Nonsuch, Sheene, Oatlands, Burleigh, &c., whilst Longleat, Wilton House and Longford Castle, in Wiltshire, emulated their palatial predecessors. That the royal treasurers were affluent and ambitious is evidenced by their mansions. Their numerous domestic establishments or households, and their domestic laws and regulations, tend to exemplify the epoch of the Tudor dynasty. We need no better proofs than are preserved in "the Household Books" of the monarchs and nobles of the age. Though Charlton House is not to be ranked with the palaces named, it is a fine and vigorous offshoot, and serves to mark a novelty in architectural design and advancement. Its windows are larger and more commanding, its chimney shafts and open parapets are more decorated, and the columnar parts and interior finishings have more decided features of Italian architecture. It has no castellated feature, but is truly domestic, and gives intimation of home-security, peace, and luxury. Commenced by Sir Henry Knyvett, in the time of King James I., it was laid out to bound the four sides of a large quadrangle, and intended to class, if not vie, with princely Longleat in the southern portion of the county. But the finances of the proprietor were not commensurate with his ambition, and he only raised the shell and parts of the edifice, leaving his successors to continue or finish the building. The west, or chief front, is represented in the "Architectural Antiquities," vol. ii., in which a short notice of it is given; but a fuller account will be found in vol. iii., "Beauties of Wiltshire," 1825. Another very cleverly engraved view of the east front of the house was drawn by T. Hearne, and engraved by W. Watts, for a volume of views of "Gentlemen's Seats," published by the last-named talented artist, who lived to the advanced age of 100, in 1851. This mansion extends over an area of 180 feet from north to south, by 128 in the opposite direction. The greater portion appears to have been raised from the designs of Matthew Brettingham for the Earl of Suffolk, who died in 1779. The hall, gallery, staircase, and many of the apartments are adorned with family and other portraits, also with historical pictures, and similar evidences of the taste and wealth of the collectors. The fifteenth earl, who died in 1820 at the age of 81, was very desirous of making Charlton House vie with the more fashionable and popular seats in the southern part of the county, and expended much money and devoted much zeal to attain these objects. When I met him at Charlton in 1802 he was preparing to cover-in the central court, make a noble staircase and gallery, and concentrate his pictures in these apartments. An account of some of these is given in my volume already noticed; but I would refer the lover of art to Dr. Waagen's "Treasures of Art in Great Britain," vol. iii., p. 54, for an interesting commentary on the Suffolk pictures. The reader will find notices of some of the portraits in the "Beauties" already referred to. A more ample and corrected account will be found in the third volume of "The Wiltshire Magazine," from the pen of the Reverend W. H. E. M<sup>c</sup>Knight, whose residence in the house, as tutor to some of the family, enabled him to become familiar with the pictures, the place, and the personal annals.

At LYDIARD TREGOZE is an old mansion of the St. Johns, and also the parish church, which may be regarded as the mausoleum of many branches of the family. The latter attracted my attention, and awakened my curiosity, more than any other church in this county when I first visited it at the beginning of the present century. The house, then occupied by the Rev. Thomas Collins, father of the Viscountess Bolingbroke, was shown to me by that gentleman, who also accompanied me to the adjoining church, which contained such a display of heraldic and genealogical hatchments, coats of arms fully emblazoned, painted glass, and family monuments, as both astonished and embarrassed me. As the work on which I was then engaged professed only to comment on what were deemed the "Beauties of Wiltshire," I was at a loss to know what to select from the numerous objects and matters here represented and alluded to. By referring to the third volume of "Beauties of Wiltshire," I find that thirteen pages are devoted to the church and its contents, to family history, and to the genealogical tables and monuments. The matter there published may be regarded as suggestions for detailed comment, rather than for history and biography.

Against the north wall of the chancel are three large framed panels, two of which form doors to fold against the third, which is fixed to the wall. On these are painted the armorial bearings, with portraits, views of tombs, &c., of the St. John family, with their descents, as drawn up "by Sir Richard St. George, Kn$^t$, Garter King at Arms, in the year 1615 and transcribed on these boards in 1694."

The most noted member of this family, an eminent statesman and writer, was *Henry St. John, Lord Viscount Bolingbroke,* who was buried in the church of Battersea, Surrey, where a monument is raised to his memory, stating that he died December 12th, 1751, aged 73. This nobleman's was an eventful and memorable life, as connected with the political and civil history of the country. He acted a dangerous part in the contests of party and monarchy, and was author of numerous literary works, which were published either anonymously or avowedly. Living on friendly terms with Swift, Gay, Pope, and other popular authors, flying his country, wedding a prostitute, joining and aiding the Pretender, and writing powerfully on persons in power, he was subjected to outlawry, and the confiscation of his title and estates. The annals of his life are given to the world by George Wingrove Cooke, Esq., 2 vols. 8vo. 1835. Dr. Goldsmith also wrote an able memoir of this extraordinary man, which accompanies an edition of his literary works, in 8 vols. 8vo. 1809, and asserts that "as a political writer few are his equal, and no one can exceed him." Pope has rendered the name of St. John popular and permanent by addressing his famed poem—Essay on Man—to him.

At a short distance west of Lydiard is the disfranchised borough of WOTTON-BASSET, whose mayor, burgesses, and resident householders, paying "scot and lot," or pot-wabblers, returned two members to Parliament from the time of Henry the Sixth. Like Malmesbury, and many other degraded boroughs, this was one of the politically corrupt of the county, and it consequently progressively degenerated in the scale of respectability and morality. The Reform Bill and Free Trade have produced palpable changes in these places, and still greater may be reasonably anticipated from the present political and improved state of society. Having witnessed the demoralizing and besotted condition of some boroughs, at the end of the last century, when "the Rights of Man" were scouted and ridiculed by some, but praised and courted by others, I cannot but hail with exultation and pride the changes that have come over the face of our glorious island. As contrasted with the present, I will venture to notice the almost semi-barbarous state of the burgesses of Wotton-Basset in the middle of the seventeenth century and at the end of the last. When I was there about sixty years back, there was preserved in the town hall a "ducking, or cucking stool," formerly employed to punish female scolds, and often to imperil their lives. This barbarous pastime—for the ceremony was viewed with vulgar and boisterous glee by some of the operators and spectators—was in accordance with the irrationality of the mayor and corporation of this once superstitious town, one of whose public acts is on record in a "Memorial to the House of Commons." Though without date, and printed on a sheet of coarse paper, it has every appearance of having been a faithful copy of a document presented to the lower house of Parliament. I presume it may be found in the archives of that House. A copy was given to me by a clergyman of Wotton-Basset, when I was there in 1798. It is printed in the third volume of "Beauties of Wiltshire," and again in the fifteenth volume of the "Beauties of England."

"*The Right of Common*" was one of the boons or privileges granted in former ages to the poor of many of the provincial towns and large villages in England. Like many other charitable and noble acts, it was preyed upon by human harpies, as displayed in the case alluded to. The petition states that "a free common of pasture, of above 2000 acres," had been encroached upon by Sir Francis Englefield, Knight, who imparked about 900 thereof, and held possession of the small remainder from the rightful owners of the whole. Complaints and appeals were made to the Knight, who refused to grant any redress, and who defended actions in different courts, whereby the inhabitants were put to great expense, and, as stated, almost ruined by "suits at law for the space of seven or eight years." As a final resource they memorialized the House, and in their appeal alledged that "the Lord in his mercy did send thunder and lightning from Heaven," whenever Sir Francis Englefield did send his cows into that part of the common which had been left unparked. The Knight's cows having been affrighted from the said pasture, the weather would "immediately become calme and faire." It was also asserted that the cattle of the townspeople were quiet and undisturbed by the tempests, &c. This petition was signed by the mayor and twenty-one of the inhabitants, "and many more would have signed, but being tenants of the lord of the manor, feared the consequences." Such a document, signed by the chief officer and inhabitants of a corporate town, and seriously addressed to the legislature of a kingdom, where Shakspeare and Milton had lived and published works that will live for centuries yet to come, must astonish the readers and writers of the present age. We cannot wonder at the credulity of Aubrey, who certainly associated with such men, though vastly their superior in intellectual powers and qualifications.

At HIGHWORTH, another small town at the eastern border of Wiltshire, I saw, at the time above alluded to, a *Stocks* for the confinement of "certain rogues and vagabonds," and a *Pillory* connected with the same, as fixtures in the market place. Although this town has not profited by an immediate junction with the modern rail-road, I presume that its public instruments of punishment have long disappeared, and that its ready communication with the metropolis has occasioned great changes here, as may be found in many other old towns.

CORSHAM HOUSE, or COURT.—The encouraging reception I experienced at BOWOOD (*ante*, p. 353) inspired me with a confidence I had not previously known. Hence I was induced to visit Corsham House, which, at the end of the last century, had become the most fashionable "show-house" in the vicinity of Bath: that nucleus and pink of provincial "bon-ton." Its large collection of pictures had gained fame, and was talked of and sought by connoisseurs, artists, and idlers of the neighbourhood, and even by others from the metropolis. Large additions and improvements had recently been made, and were then in progress, both in the house and its scenic appendages, and I became not a little anxious to witness the architectural and landscape novelties of the place. With excited feelings, and no little timidity, I approached the mansion, was introduced to Mr. and Mrs. Methuen, who, after hearing the nature of my mission, cordially and affably invited me to dine, sleep, and spend some time in the house. Though I cannot call up recollections of much detail of that remote time, I well remember that there was a large family circle, and that one or more strangers were generally at the table. Mr. Methuen was a plain country gentleman, kindly disposed, and seemed of a mild, amiable temper, whilst his lady emulated the metropolitan fashionables. In town she was amongst the chosen of the Almack coteries, and Methuen House, in Grosvenor Street, was famed for its balls, routs, masquerades, &c. I was present at one of the last, which was given to gratify the eldest son, Mr. Paul Methuen, who, on that occasion, personified three popular dramatic characters, one of which was Caleb Quotem. I assumed the dress and language of a barber (Dicky Gossip), and, with cards of my shop, was wondrously delighted with the motley group, as well as with the splendour of the scene and profusion of good things. The company did not break up before Sol had appeared above the tops of the city chimneys. The streets, however, were busy with old, tired watchmen returning from their drowsy beats, with chimney-sweeps and milkmaids; whilst market gardeners were eagerly pursuing their respective callings. Thenceforward I was a frequent guest at Corsham, and was induced to write and print a small volume, combining a history of the house and a Catalogue Raisonnée of 213 pictures. This volume is described in the second part of this Auto-Biography, in which the present section is referred to, though it was not then written. At Corsham I became acquainted with two professional gentlemen, who, for many years afterwards, were popularly distinguished in the annals of literature and art: Humphrey Repton, landscape gardener, a new title which he successfully assumed; and JOHN NASH, an architect. With these I continued on friendly terms till their respective deaths: the first in 1818, aged 66; and the second in 1835, aged 83. Both were employed by Mr. Methuen in their different professions to make Corsham House "the observed of all observers;" and both were frequent visitors. Mr. Nash's province was to alter and enlarge the mansion; not merely to adapt it for a large family, but with a view to display the paintings to advantage. Mr. Repton was engaged to lay out the grounds and lawn around the house. Both were born in the same year (1752); the first in Wales, the second in Suffolk; the one of humble, obscure parentage, the other of a respectable family, classing with the gentry of Bury St. Edmund's. Whilst Nash had to contend with difficulties and struggles in early life, Repton was benefited by good education and exciting associations, and was destined to succeed his father as an English merchant.* Our first news of Mr. Nash is of his being a miniature painter; next as scene-painter to a company of itinerant players in Wales, where my old friend, Mr. Pugin, joined him. We afterwards hear of him in London, living with a Mr. Edwards, a relation, in Bloomsbury Square, and of some adventures after his residence there. It is not surprising that a young man of his temperament and early associations was guilty of some irregularities and eccentricities. His daring and important schemes in Regent Street and Park, in Buckingham Palace, and other parts of London have been well known to all public persons of the metropolis, and have been more censured than praised by the periodical press. Nor have they escaped severe animadversion by many members of the houses of Parliament, and by most professional and amateur

---

* An interesting memoir, by Mr. Loudon, is given in his edition of Mr. Repton's professional works.

critics. Patronized and personally favoured by a prince and monarch who was reckless in his wanton expenditure of the public money, and in other wantonesses, we cannot contemplate the character of the architect without feelings of sorrow and terms of reprobation. A detailed history of the formation and buildings of Regent Street and Park, of Buckingham Palace, with its extraneous and useless marble arch, which alone cost more than £80,000., even up to its last strange migration to Hyde Park, would be a disgraceful exposure of cunning, of heedless disposal of public money, and of the lamentable irresponsibility of public officers, who are placed in official posts for which they are unfitted. The learned and talented author of the "Hand-book of London" states that the building of the new palace was the result of a "mere juggle on the part of the king and his architect." Yet with immense business, and consequent large income, the architect's habits and heedless expenditure exhausted his funds, and he died at his house in the Isle of Wight, leaving his second wife a widow, who became a pensioner on Sir John Soane and other friends.

The reader may refer for other facts to Cunningham's "Hand-book of London," under the heading Regent's Park and Street, Buckingham Palace, and the Opera House; also to "The Public Buildings of London," 2 vols. royal 8vo., 1825; the first volume of which I indiscreetly dedicated to the Architect's royal patron, George the Fourth.

That Mr. Nash and Mr. Repton had been personally acquainted before they were engaged at Corsham, is evident from the fact that the son of the latter (John Adey) was articled to the former, and had made drawings, if not the designs, for the mansion now referred to. From one of these an engraving was made for my "Beauties of Wiltshire," with the name of H. Repton, Esq. annexed.

A well-written history of the mansion at Corsham, of the pictures, and of the Methuen family, would form both an interesting and useful work. It would necessarily embrace accounts of the professional merits of architects between 1562, when the first house was erected, and of which the south front presents a fine characteristic example, and 1855, when large and prominent additions had recently been made for the present nobleman, by Thos. Bellamy, Esq. The last appears to have been occasioned by the unsound and flimsy manner in which Mr.

Nash's work had been performed. A judicious essay on the rise and progress of the Methuen family would necessarily embrace biographies of those persons who have been concerned and associated with the trade and commerce of the country, in its government and diplomacy, and in the landed property and civil policy of the state. In the *Beauties of Wiltshire*, vol. ii., will be found some notice of the family history, with personal anecdotes of Sir Paul Methuen, from information I obtained at Corsham House, in the beginning of this century. He died in 1757, in the 85th year of his age, and was buried in the Abbey Church of Westminster, where his father, " John Methuen, Esq., who died abroad in 1706," was also interred. The former was a man of high character, and much honoured by his monarch, George II., and particularly by his Queen, as well as by many foreign personages of distinction. His admonitory legacy to Mr. Methuen contains so much sound and valuable counsel to diplomatists, nobles, and the aristocracy of the country, that it cannot be too extensively known, nor too strictly followed. (See *Beauties of Wiltshire*, vol. ii., p. 300.)

In the Corsham House collection of old pictures, as in all the other galleries of the same class, though there are many works of genuine and of undoubted merit and value, there are likewise others that come before the eye of the acute and learned critic in " such questionable shapes," i.e., in drawing, colouring, and other indubitable qualities, that they excite mistrust and suspicion. It gives me pleasure to say, and also to tell my friend, Dr. Waagen, of Berlin, that although some of the Corsham pictures, which were there when both of us first knew the house, have been disposed of, there is still a large collection carefully preserved and in good condition. The learned professor, and author of a valuable work, " Treasures of Art of Great Britain," 3 vols. 8vo., 1854, did not visit this gallery when last at Bowood and at Charlton Park, having heard that the pictures of the former " had been dispersed."

HARTHAM PARK, in the vicinity of Corsham, was occupied by the Dowager Lady James, when I visited that seat in 1798. In giving a short notice of the place, in " the Beauties of Wiltshire," vol. iii., and in " the Beauties of England," vol. xv., I stated that the lady above-named was the person to whom Sterne wrote his famed "Letters to Eliza," and to whom that eccentric clergyman and author had addressed such glowing, amatory epistles. From recent and particular inquiries on this subject, I feel assured that "Eliza" was a different personage, and that instead of being one who left a spotless character behind, and bequeathed charities to the poor, "it might give pain to many worthy persons if the circumstances attending the latter part of her life were disclosed." By the publication of a volume called "The Table Talk of Samuel Rogers," the banker and poet, the above inuendo is partly explained by an anecdote, wherein Mr. Combes, author of Dr. Syntax and other popular works, is described as being detected in the bed-room of "Eliza" at Brighton. That the initials of Mr. and Mrs. J—, to whom several letters are addressed by Sterne, about the same time as those to Eliza, were Sir William James and his Lady, in after life, is very probable.

"THE WILTSHIRE ARCHÆOLOGICAL AND NATURAL HISTORY SOCIETY:" *its Origin, Progress, Meetings at Devizes, Salisbury, and Chippenham.—History of Wiltshire.*

Archæological ambulatory Societies are novelties of this age. They may date their origin in England to 1844, when a congress of lovers of the science—of the antiquities of their own country—assembled in Canterbury, where nearly two hundred gentlemen and ladies met in that truly historical city, and spent a week in visiting, discoursing on, and writing about those relics of former ages which belong to the place and its immediate vicinity. The event, the station, the class of persons who made up the group, combined to give excitement and zest to the young and to the aged. Though the Society of Antiquaries of London had been formed and known many years, had weekly meetings of its members, and had also published many volumes of Essays and Illustrations, its work and workings were thought to be aged and ineffective. Some of the younger members, after assembling together for a few months in London, agreed to make an excursion into Kent—see ancient buildings in their native places, and imbued (if I may say so) with realities, with a tangible character and expression, whereby they became objects to convey forcible truths and data for history. The scheme was tried and succeeded. Thenceforward, up to the summer of 1855, the original "Association," with an offshoot, or rival, and several others of local origin and application have been founded, and have very fortunately become unexpectedly popular. That devoted to Wiltshire, a county of such eminent attractions and interest, may be regarded as the latest member of the family. A short account of this, in its origin, progress, and prospects, cannot fail to interest the members and propitiate strangers. Being a favourite child of my own, I may be pardoned saying a few words in its praise. Whatever may be the present and future effects of the society, it cannot be irrelevant to give a brief notice of its origin. More than half a century has elapsed since I first revisited my native county with vague notions of writing something about its Beauties, i. e., its most eminent seats and other popular objects. Since that time I have traversed nearly the whole of the shire; examined all its noted antiquities, churches, monasteries, towns, and villages, and have written and published several volumes relating to the same. The whole of these are amply illustrated by engravings of varied merit, whilst I have given histories and descriptions of its towns, and some of its remarkable antiquities in Rees's Cyclopædia, in the Penny Cyclopædia, in the Architectural, the Cathedral, and the Picturesque Antiquities, in the Dictionary of Ancient Architecture, and in other miscellaneous publications. For these works I gradually collected many books, manuscripts, drawings, letters, &c. It had long been my wish to see these kept together, and preserved within the county, for the use and amusement of future topographers. Having much epistolary and personal intercourse with the late Sir R. C. Hoare, I suggested to him the desirableness of forming a county museum and library, stating that I would present the whole of my collection, if he would do the same with his; and expressing my belief that it would produce a beneficial effect and influence. This was before the estimable Baronet had obtained Mr. Cunnington's valuable collection; and before Mr. P. Crocker had been known to and by him. After completing the Cathedral and Architectural Antiquities, I wrote and printed a Catalogue of my Wiltshire materials, which I offered to sell for a moderate sum, if applied for a public object within the county. My friend, Mr. W. Cunnington of Devizes, grandson of the Wiltshire Antiquary of Heytesbury, became tempted by the proposal, and after some correspondence with myself and with several noblemen and gentlemen of the county it was agreed that they should be purchased for that town, as a nucleus of a topographical library and museum; and that efforts should be made to establish a county society. The whole were valued, by a gentleman long versed in books and general literature; and one hundred and fifty pounds were named as a reasonable sum. This was agreed to, and I promised to present to the society other models, books, drawings, &c., to the value of fifty pounds.

It is but justice, further to state, that this purchase and the formation of the Wiltshire Library and Society are mainly to be ascribed to the zeal, perseverance, and active exertions of Mr. Wm. Cunnington. I shall have occasion to speak again of that gentleman in a subsequent paragraph, in allusion to his valuable and interesting Museum of Wiltshire Geological specimens; and also of his much-respected grandfather, Mr. Cunnington, of Heytesbury.

"The Wiltshire Archæological and Natural History Society" was officially founded at Devizes, in September, 1853, when a meeting of ladies and gentlemen assembled to confirm laws which had been prepared by a committee, when officers were appointed, papers were read, and the company dined together. It was also resolved that another public meeting should be held at Salisbury in the following year. In September, 1854, the second congress met in that city, under the influential presidency of the Right Honourable Sidney Herbert, and with the cordial aid of the new bishop, the clergy, the mayor and corporation, and a very respectable and influential local committee. The city authorities granted the use of the council-house for the accommodation of the Society, for a temporary museum and place of meeting; whilst the Mayor, Mr. Lambert, presided at a public dinner. In the evening, papers were read, and a Soirée given in the council-house. On the second day the company devoted the morning to view the cathedral and other antiquities of the city; and at two o'clock they all assembled at the eminently classical mansion, *Wilton House,* to view its vast collection of works of art, and of archæology. Unfortunately a settled rain gave a gloom and chill to the scene; but the polite attentions of the learned host, and his amiable lady, diffused cheerfulness around, whilst the hospitable board exhibited not only plenty but abundance of those fine viands with wines and fruits which seem to please all classes and sects of persons. On the evening of the same day the newly-made prelate of the diocese invited the members of the Society to a Soirée in the spacious palace of Salisbury. Here a large party assembled to talk over and praise the many attractive objects of art concentrated in Wilton House: the beauties and wonders of the unique cathedral, which forms such a commanding feature in the palace garden. Nor were the other remarkable and interesting objects in and contiguous to the city left without inquiry, comment, and praises. Herein one of the attractive objects of this and other similar societies has been found; and herein we may descry a new feature of the present age, as contra-distinguished from that of the former and previous centuries, when the only places for occasional assemblies of provincials were periodical balls in town-halls and assembly-rooms. However attractive such may have been to persons who prefer dancing and gaming to the rational exercise of the mental faculties and the better qualities of the heart, we may be assured that the latter are the more likely to secure lasting happiness.

Such a reception and adhesion of members from Sarum gave assurance of success, and animated the committee to make additional exertion to secure further strength and popularity for the next meeting at Chippenham.* On the 11th, 12th, and 13th days of September, 1855, a company of nearly three hundred gentlemen and ladies of the county met together in this ancient town, when they were successively occupied and amused by a museum of varied objects of antiquity, geology, natural history, &c. Some papers were read, and the members with their friends dined at the Angel Inn, partaking of haunches of venison, presented by Lord Wellesley. Evening soirées at the Town Hall, visits to Lacock Abbey, Spye Park, Bowood, Castle Combe,

---

* Accounts of the Meetings at Devizes, and at Salisbury, with Addresses by the noble Patron, the Marquess of Lansdowne; the Right Honourable Sidney Herbert, the President, George Poulett Scrope, Esq., M.P., and the Rev. J. E. Jackson, are published in the Magazine of the Society.

Corsham House, Malmesbury Abbey, and other places, afforded much rational amusement, for three days.

The noble Patron of the society,—the Marquess of Lansdowne,—invited the members, with some of his lordship's friends, to visit and take refreshments at Bowood. This proved to be a most exciting and delectable treat, as that seat is not classed amongst the show-houses of the county, though the mansion and its artistic contents, with the park, pleasure-grounds and gardens, are of great beauty and interest. Fortunately for strangers, and indeed the whole company, (consisting of at least three hundred) the day was bright and cheering, and every face beamed with joy. Though I have witnessed fêtes and festivals, (at Frogmore, in Queen Charlotte's time, at Wanstead House, in Long Wellesley Long Pole's age of ox-roasting revelry, and at minor similar gatherings) I never was present at a scene so truly imposing and impressive; for buoyancy of heart and cheerfulness of countenance pervaded and gave zest and animation to every person. Let cynics and dullards reprobate feasting and the charms of social intercourse, they would not find many voters for them were they to resort to the ballot.*

At DRAYCOT HOUSE Lord Wellesley treated a large party, whilst Mr. Scrope had assembled another company at CASTLE COMBE, where they partook of handsome collations. A spacious tent was arranged on the lawn at the latter mansion. The picturesque scenery of this remarkable seat and village was much admired, as was the large parish Church, which had been recently restored to its original appearance and stability by its generous patron, who gave a lucid description of the building. The Reverend A. Fane further dilated on its architectural peculiarities, and the merits of the historian of the parish. The mayor of Salisbury likewise gratified the company with specimens of sacred music, on the Organ. In spite of rain, some of the members visited the ruins and site of the ancient baronial castle, likewise a kist-vaen in the vicinity, and a barrow, which had been opened in the morning. These objects, with the courteous and friendly recep-

---

* For an account of the house, scenery, and general characteristics of Bowood,—of its art treasures, noble possessors, and some of its eminent visitors, the reader is referred to a previous part of this volume, pp. 352 to 387.

tion of the host and his lady, rendered the afternoon gratifying to a numerous party.

Two memorable events and scenes belong to the Chippenham meeting: first, the news of the conquest of Sebastopol, which created boisterous rejoicings, and startled the serious and sedate antiquaries "out of their propriety of demeanour." The second was a large periodical cheese fair, when upwards of three hundred tons of that food were spread over the area of the new market-house and premises, and in the principal street of the town. What a contrast to Chippenham towards the end of the last century, when the royal mail cart, with a single horse and man, passed through this town in communication between London and the west of England! One of the guards was robbed within two miles of this place, and the thief was afterwards hung in chains. (See *ante*, p. 13.) At that time Chippenham was lampless, and almost lawless: its population was personally occupied in various processes of cloth-making,—for machinery, and spinning-jennies were alike unused. Such was the town more than seventy years ago, when I often saw the said mail cart, and also the suspended robber. I witnessed the first balloon that ever rose into the air at Bristol, which came to the earth at Derry-hill, near the memorable gibbet alluded to: such times and such events cannot be forgotten whilst life and memory last. To compare them with the vast changes which have been effected during many years, and to see friendly connections of long standing, induced me to renew my acquaintance with this town in 1855; besides, I was anxious to witness the progress and effects of the Wiltshire Society at a place where, at the end of the last century, topography and antiquity were words scarcely known by any of the inhabitants. But steam, gas, the electric telegraph, penny postage, and railroads have revolutionized the world, and rendered man almost a new creature. That enlightenment and progress have been made, and are making great strides in society must be apparent to all attentive observers; and that archæological literature has participated in the march, must be known to almost all classes of readers. To recognize their growth and effects, in Wiltshire, has been and will be a gratifying reward for the many exertions I have hitherto made to establish a *Topographical Association* in my native county.

## PLANS FOR A HISTORY OF WILTSHIRE.

The first person who projected and made collections for a topographical history of the county, I believe, was the amiable and zealous JOHN AUBREY, who, from boyhood to old age, directed his active mind to this subject. In the year 1659, he had attained the co-operation of such friends as the Rev. Thomas (afterwards bishop) Tanner, Thomas Gore, of Alderton, Sir John Erneley, William Yorke, Jeffrey Daniel, and others. Some of these parties had visited places and made collections, but Aubrey alone persevered to give substance and value to his new plan. In 1670 he printed and issued a prospectus; and to him we are indebted for anything of a substantial and useful nature. His miscellaneous manuscripts, deposited in the Ashmolean Museum, Oxford, manifest at once his sincerity of purpose, his zeal in the cause, and his habits and qualifications as a topographer and antiquary. Tanner, Ray, Dr. Plot, and others of his corresponding friends, urged him to publish the work, and he made a fair copy from the loose notes and papers, which he had deposited in the library of the Royal Society, London. It consists of two volumes, folio, closely and plainly written. The greater part of it was printed for "the Wiltshire Topographical Society," in 1847, and consists of much curious and interesting information relating to the county. I edited the work and interspersed it with many notes and explanations.* In 1845, I had previously written, for the same society, "A Memoir of John Aubrey," forming a goodly-sized quarto volume, and comprising a variety of topographical, biographical, archæological, and miscellaneous matter relating to the county, generally, and particularly allusive to the era of Aubrey's life and writings. Of these volumes only 250 copies were printed, for the members. †

In the year 1788, Mr. H. P. Wyndham, of Salisbury, printed a translation of the "Domesday Book for Wiltshire," in the Preface to which he appeals to the gentry of the county to aid him in a Topo-

---

\* Mr. Poulett Scrope, of Castle Combe, has a faithful copy of this manuscript which was made for the printed work just referred to.

† Copies of these volumes are amongst the Society's property at Devizes; but from the small numbers originally printed, they are become scarce.

graphical History. He suggests a subscription of twenty-five pounds from each person; recommends a committee, to consult and advise as to the best mode of obtaining funds, and co-operate in the execution of a work commensurate with the county and creditable to all parties. He also tendered one hundred pounds as an example, and as a proof of his sincerity and zeal in the cause. The then Earl of Radnor was a zealous advocate for the county history which Mr. Wyndham had proposed; and by an autograph letter from the former to the latter, which I saw in the library at Stourhead when I last visited it, his lordship said, " put my name down for a second £100, and if the subscription amounts to £1000, I will stand another hundred; and if it reaches to £2000, I will then add a fourth hundred." With a few such patrons, there would be no difficulty now either in securing sufficient materials, or authors with talents commensurate to the varied and remarkable topographical character of the district. Though much has been done for South Wiltshire—still susceptible of great improvement—the Northern portion yet remains an unworked field, for inquiry, research, and elucidation. Mr. Wyndham had manifested attachment to this species of literature, as well as qualifications to give good counsel, and also to write part of the work, by others which he had published on " The Topography of the Isle of Wight," and in " A Tour through Monmouthshire and South Wales." A second edition of the latter was printed in 1781, with many material additions to, and alterations from, the first edition.

The next move towards a COUNTY HISTORY was by SIR RICHARD COLT HOARE, who appears to have directed his attention towards topography and antiquities after visiting Italy and other parts of the Continent, and after publishing some works on places and objects seen in his tours. My first visit to Stourhead, was by an introduction to Sir Richard, who referred me to Robert Stearne Tighe, Esq., who was a neighbour, and who then appeared to be better qualified to furnish topographical information than the learned, amiable, and classical baronet. The latter, however, promised to present a drawing and an engraving of the pleasure-grounds at Stourhead for " the Beauties of Wiltshire"—the object of my inquiries. The second volume of that work I addressed to Sir Richard, in terms which satisfy my conscience after more than half a century's duration and vicissitudes. I refer to my intercourse with that estimable baronet and antiquary with pride and gratitude, for he continued in friendly correspondence with me to the end of his life, and patronized all my publications. For four or five years after our first acquaintance he had never intimated an intention of undertaking any topographical work on the county; nor had he then taken any part in Mr. Cunnington's researches amongst its barrows and other earthworks. The latter gentleman explored many of those, and had collected numerous and various relics of the ancient Britons, and of other tribes, who had settled in this part of the island. He had freely communicated the results of his researches to me, which were given to the public in the second volume of the work already referred to. Mr. Cunnington had corresponded and been acquainted with Sir Wm. A'Court, Mr. Henry Wansey, Mr. A. B. Lambert (his neighbours), and Mr. H. P. Wyndham, before he had been visited by Sir R. C. Hoare. He had also associated and corresponded with Mr. Wm. Smith, a surveyor and engineer, and who, as will be hereafter noticed, was diligently studying the stratification of the West of England. After Mr. Cunnington had obtained this new connection, and had formed a large museum of fossils and relics from the plains adjoining his house, the zealous baronet visited him at Heytesbury, and was naturally delighted and astonished to find in the provincial tradesman a gentleman of varied knowledge, of unassuming and humble conduct and manners, and who was capable of rendering essential aid on topography, archæology, and natural history. It is not surprising, that, thenceforward, Sir Richard courted the acquaintance and aid of the Heytesbury collector, or that he should have acquired a new impulse and zeal for the antiquities and topography of his native county. The patron had discovered a mine of archæological materials, which he zealously worked, and devoted the remainder of his life in preparing for the press the materials which Mr. Cunnington had amassed together, and of which the two folio volumes of "The History of Ancient Wiltshire" were the result. The Heytesbury museum was not purchased by Sir Richard until after the decease of Mr. Cunnington, in 1810, and after he had engaged *Mr. Philip Crocker* to make drawings of encampments, as well as of barrows and their contents. This young artist was admirably adapted for that task. He was employed, with one of his brothers, in filling up and finishing the Ordnance Surveys of the country around and comprising Salisbury Plain. From a love of antiquities he paid more than common attention to those of the Downs, and had very kindly furnished me with drawings and accounts of many of those objects for the work above referred to, and for another volume I wrote on Wiltshire, for the Beauties of England. I had long kept up an intimacy with Mr. Cunnington and Mr. Crocker, but my correspondence with them was interdicted by the baronet for some years, as far as related to antiquities. Though much hurt by this act, I had no ground for complaint; for, as he intended to publish accounts of the antiquities of Wiltshire, he was reasonably desirous that his work should contain not only the best and fullest information on the subjects embraced, but be the first to impart it to the public. The first volume of Ancient Wiltshire appears to have been finished in 1812, though its dedication is dated 1810. It is a pompous, ponderous, folio, with numerous engravings from drawings by Mr. Crocker. It was kindly dedicated to Mr. Cunnington, as "a tribute to justice and friendship; for you first projected the work and encouraged me to pursue it." In the preface to the second volume the baronet again acknowledges his obligations to the deceased originator of the work.

This second volume, devoted to North Wiltshire, was commenced in 1819, and finished in 1821, with the names and imprint of Lackington and his four partners. The first volume embraces the British, or primæval history, including Avebury, that most wondrous Celtic temple of Europe; whilst the second alludes to the Roman stations, roads, pavements, and other vestiges of that class of people. This is addressed to the Rev. Wm. Coxe, who had been an intimate associate with the author, since their union in Monmouthshire. It may be safely said, that the greater part of this second volume was the writing of Sir Richard, whilst the first is properly ascribed to Mr. Cunnington. Though I most cheerfully record my warm tribute of thanks to the memory of the generous and estimable patron and proprietor of these two splendid volumes, I cannot help regretting they had not been offered to the reading public in a moderately small size, and at a reasonable price. The same feelings and the same terms apply to the published work under the title of "*Modern Wiltshire*," which extends to six large folio volumes, and were published at the prices of eighty-one pounds, for the larger paper, and thirty-one pounds for the smaller. Of the *Ancient Wiltshire*, two sizes were printed: the larger at twenty pounds, and the smaller at twelve. At the time these volumes were published a sort of bibliomania prevailed amongst book collectors, some of whom gave exorbitant prices for volumes whose margins were of the widest and tallest guage, and were, consequently, the most ragged at the edges of the leaves. Fortunately this, like all other absurd and irrational fashions, has disappeared, whilst a cheap and popular literature is provided to instruct and rationalize the public mind.

From what has been here stated, as to the amount of labour and extent of patronage exhibited by Sir Richard C. Hoare, it is evident that he was partial to, and zealous in the pursuit of topography, and likewise desirous of promoting a comprehensive *History of Wiltshire*. I have now before me four different printed papers which he distributed through the county, appealing to local patriotism, and to the feelings and ambition of the landed gentry, the clergy, and indeed to all persons of property and laudable curiosity, to co-operate with him in his proposed work. The call was not responded to, and he commenced "*South Wiltshire*" in earnest, by a "History of the Hundreds of Mere, and Heytesbury," which were included in a large folio volume. (1822—4.) During its progress he engaged the Rev. John Offer to aid him, and also to commence the "Hundred of Branch and Dole," while Sir Richard was employed on those of "Everleigh, Ambresbury, and Underditch." Histories of the "Hundreds of Westbury and of Warminster" followed, and were succeeded by those of "Chalk, South Damerham, and Downton," which were prepared for the press by the amiable baronet, and by Lord Arundel. George Matcham, LL.D., W. H. Black, Charles Bowles, R. Harris, Henry Wansey, and J. G. Nichols were the other authors of these volumes, of which five were published, when the death of Sir Richard interrupted the progress of the work, in the year 1831. A sixth volume was intended to be devoted to Salisbury, which Mr. R. Benson, deputy Recorder of the city, had engaged to write. After much delay it was found that he had not prepared any of the work, and the executors of Sir Richard put the materials into the hands of Henry Hatcher, of Salisbury, who had previously written a brief history of that city, also another volume on the cathedral, and had translated the Itinerary of Richard of Cirencester. He commenced with zeal, and pursued it with untiring devotion till he had extended it to a bulk far beyond all anticipation (864 printed pages). In writing a short memoir of that learned and estimable man, which I was tempted to do at the commencement of this Biography, I stated that nearly the whole of the Salisbury volume was written by Mr. Hatcher, and that the Recorder's contribution was very small indeed. The work, as published, has the names of "Robert Benson, Esq., M.A., and Henry Hatcher, Esq.," as authors, in the title-page; is dedicated to George Matcham, Esq., and the preface is signed with the initials, R. B. The preface, however, has an appearance of strange mock-humility, by calling the work a "compilation," whereas it is as much entitled to the honour of originality and literary composition as Macaulay's History of England. I forbear to make further comment here, having explained the history of the whole work, and of the unfortunate "quarrels of the authors," in the memoir already referred to. In a copy of the "History of Salisbury," presented to me by Mr. Hatcher, will be found proof sheets of his intended title, dedication, and explanatory preface, as written by himself, but cancelled and superseded by other matter written by Mr. Benson, and sanctioned by one of the trustees. The volume thus given, with other Wiltshire books, are deposited in the library of the Wiltshire Archæological Society, at Devizes, where they may be inspected by the members of the society; and I will venture to say that this unique copy of the work will hereafter be regarded amongst the remarkable rarities, as well as "curiosities of literature."

There is a circumstance and peculiar feature in the history of Sir Richard Colt Hoare's career in South Wiltshire, which merits particular notice and praise. Having obtained the co-operation and promised assistance of several gentlemen whose partialities and pursuits were analagous to his own, he invited them to his delightful home and museum, to enjoy at once the pleasures of social intercourse, with those to be obtained from a choice and well-stored library. To these were connected pleasure-grounds, woods, and a lake of great extent, with scenic effects which could not fail of being eminently pleasing to almost every intellectual eye and mind. These literary and archæological unions continued for some years, and were sources of infinite delight to all who participated in them; not merely during the period of fruition, but in anticipating their advent of coming, and reminiscences after they had passed. One of the participants,—the Rev. Joseph Hunter,—whose profound knowledge of all branches of topography has been exhibited to the world in some folio volumes on portions of his native county, Yorkshire, has written a very vivid account of " The Stourhead Annual Gatherings," which may be seen in a volume of topographical papers published by "The Archæological Institute," recording the sixth annual meeting at Salisbury in 1849. In the same volume will be found topographical papers, by the gentlemen named, on the following subjects belonging to this county. " The Results of Archæological Investigations in Wiltshire," by Geo. Matcham, Esq.;—" On the Early English Settlements in South Britain," by Edwin Guest, Esq., with a map;—"An Examination of Silbury Hill," by the late Very Rev. J. Merewether, D.D., F.S.A., Dean of Hereford;—also another paper giving an Account of Barrows and other Earthworks, near Silbury Hill and Avebury, by the same zealous antiquary, and illustrated by thirty-five engraved illustrations. Other papers, with prints, will be found in the same interesting volume by the Rev. E. Duke, Charles Winston, Esq., Richard Westmacott, Jun., Esq., Edward Hawkins, Esq., the Rev. James Ingram, and Charles T. Newton, Esq., M.A. I must also refer to a paper by my old and respected friend, John Bowyer Nichols, in the second volume of the Wiltshire Magazine, for some useful information on the Stourhead topographic library and its contents.

At the commencement of these remarks on the Wiltshire Archæological Society, it was my intention of suggesting a *Plan for a History of the County*, differing in treatment from any previous local history by being more systematic and scientific than has been hitherto adopted. Being familiar with nearly every work of the kind which has hitherto been published, and having been intimate with most of the modern English topographers, I have had opportunities of knowing their respective qualifications and the real and comparative merits of their works. I have also had no small amount of experience, and have carefully noticed and marked the characteristics of their authors, as well as many readers of such publications. Whilst some works have attained deserved and eminent popularity, and have consequently been read and admired by many persons, others have been scarcely known beyond the limits of the locality which gave them birth, and then only occasionally referred to, not read. I will, however, notice works which have been both read and admired by experienced critics and by profound topographers. Of general county histories there have been but few; and these, from their prolixity, sizes, and prices, have been limited in sale, and only found in large libraries. Dorsetshire, Essex, Gloucestershire, Cheshire, Durham, Hertfordshire, Kent, Leicestershire, Norfolk, Northamptonshire, Surrey, and Yorkshire, are the counties which have been more elucidated and illustrated than any of the others. Some of these have been written by authors of high attainments and devotion to a favourite subject.

Dugdale attempted to furnish the reader with a history of Warwickshire; but could only accomplish a very small portion of the annals of that county. And we find that his successors, in the same walk, and during the century in which he wrote and published, produced volumes on Leicestershire, Nottinghamshire, Staffordshire, Rutlandshire, Kent, Berkshire, Oxfordshire, Devonshire, Cornwall, &c. In the eighteenth century many large and expensive folio volumes were produced on some of the above-named counties; but we search them in vain for that sort and extent of writing and illustration which the well-read topographical critic now seeks and expects to obtain. In my own time, and during the present century, we have had several works laid before the public, on counties, hundreds, parishes, towns, cities, and even country seats, also on castles, abbeys, and other single subjects. Many of these works contain much valuable and well-written matter, and are evidently the result of great labour, diligence, and talent: still I cannot point to one specimen of county history that will fully satisfy the wants and reasonable wishes of the critical topographer of the present enlightened and fastidious age. To obtain a comprehensive and discriminating History of Wiltshire, requires the united judgment and workmanship of three or more persons who have each made one particular class of science a favorite study, and thereby be well qualified to elucidate and illustrate that subject fully and completely. To avoid hobby-horseism is desirable.

A *good County History* is a desideratum in literature. It has never yet been written by one person; nor is it likely that it ever will be produced by one head and one hand. The variety of subjects such a work necessarily embraces—with the extent and diversity of materials which have to be consulted, analyzed, and investigated—demand much time, bodily labour, and mental exertion. To a decided love for the subject must be added, learning, industry, zeal, and a variety and amount of talent rarely to be met with in an individual. We have had many attempts to accomplish such a task, but without success. Hence it will be inferred that a complete topographical work embracing a whole county is only to be expected from the combination and exertions of a plurality of competent persons. With such, and with funds, a series of volumes might be produced of a quality, and in a style and manner, surpassing all preceding works of the class, and fitted to rank with Mr. Poulett Scrope's volume, already mentioned. In a preceding part of this Biography (p. 393) is a short notice of that publication, which may be regarded as a most satisfactory precedent and example of its kind. Calculated as it is to disabuse the general reader of prejudices against the common opinion of dullness and insipidity in archæological and topographical writings, it will show that the subject is full of flowers, and useful information.

Another volume of similar quality and treatment, also referred to in connection with that on Castle Combe, is now before me, with the title, "ÆDES HARTWELLIANÆ, or Notices of the Manor and Mansion of Hartwell." By Rear-Admiral W. H. Smyth, R.N. Printed for private circulation, 4to. 1851, with map and numerous illustrations. I am induced to notice this extraordinary Topographical volume from being written by a naval officer, whose studies, and pursuits on the ever-restless, ever-dangerous seas, might seem to disqualify him for writing on the history, topography, and local characteristics of a small tract of earth, almost devoid of water. But genius and zeal, when combined and devoted to any one pursuit, will triumph over difficulties and even dangers. In this unique work we find general and local history, archæology in various departments, geology, geography, astronomy, and other scientific objects, commented on and elucidated with remarkable perspicuity, precision, and satisfaction. The volume has been executed at the expense of John Lee, Esq., LL.D., whose mansion is a museum of art and archæology. Belonging to, and an active member of several literary and scientific societies, the estimable author has proved himself useful and valuable to all. Fortunately, he is united to a wife who not only participates in all his scientific and literary pursuits, but is enabled to render assistance in astronomical and other calculations and elucidations.

The young and even the aged topographer may be gratified and instructed by examining a volume relating to a county, or district in Ireland, which appears to have been published in 1837. Dissimilar in arrangement and treatment to any topographical work on England, I am induced to direct attention to its literary and graphic contents. It is a small quarto volume, full of useful information, compressed into a moderate space, by small type, and is illustrated by engravings of antiquities, plans, natural history, and topographical views. The title is, " Ordnance Survey of the County of Londonderry, by Colonel Colby, R.E.," 1837, pp. 337.

The Rev. Messrs. Blakeway and Owen's " History of Shrewsbury," (2 vols. 4to.) is not only replete with valuable and original information, but is arranged and treated with nice discrimination and judgment. Whilst the first of those gentlemen confined his researches and writings to historical and philological matters, the latter directed his attention and pen to descriptive anecdote and local commentary. Specimens of their treatment of archæological subjects are given in my " Architectural Antiquities " on Ludlow Castle, Buildwas Abbey, and Stokesay Castle, Shropshire.

I will venture to recommend that the contents, or subjects of a county history be arranged under the following heads, or divisions, instead of being placed in hundreds and parishes, as has been the usual custom: as this mode will enable an author to combine and unite his materials with more harmony and system than has hitherto been practised in any topographic work. Hence the substrata, or anatomy of a district, would constitute the basis or foundation, and thus commence with the most ancient of antiquities, beyond the first colonization of the island; for as my revered friend, Professor Buckland, once remarked to me, when speaking of Avebury, Stonehenge, and other monuments, usually called *the* primeval class, "even those are young when compared with the real antiquities of *our* science." "For yours," he said, "are of yesterday, ours of thousands of years; yet our studies and investigations have only commenced with the beginning of the present century, whilst yours have had a Leland, a Camden, a Dugdale, an Aubrey, a Stukeley, and many other scholars and learned men to clear the way and write dissertations and treatises on the history, arts, customs, &c., of the different races of people who colonized and occupied the British isles." These remarks, partly jocular, partly serious and sincere, were made at Taunton, in 1849, when I had the pleasure of meeting him with other members of the Somersetshire Archæological, &c., Society. At that time, and in that town, the learned and good-humoured professor gave us a vivid and graphic account of his own juvenile studies in geology, on the Mendip hills, and his subsequent ardent career in that sublime science.*

According to this plan, No. 1 will embrace *geological antiquities*, and, fortunately, the Wiltshire Society has amongst its members a gentleman fully competent to treat this subject in a style, and with a precision and demonstration that would reflect honour on himself, the Society, and the county. *Mr. Cunnington*, by extensive examination of the whole district, by diligent study, and intercourse with the most learned geologists, and by choice specimens which he has obtained, classed, and described, has such a text-book of documentary evidence as cannot fail of proving at once satisfactory to the man of science, and interesting to nearly every class of readers.

No. 2 would embrace, and refer to, what may be called superterraneous, which are now ranked as of the primeval period, i. e., earthworks on the surface, with the relics which they concealed and partly preserved. Accounts of the great boundary mounds, and other "dykes,"

---

* See an Account of this Meeting, and of the Doctor's sketch of an Auto-biography, in the Report of "The First General Meeting of the Somersetshire Archæological Society," held at Taunton, September 1849.

which prevail in this county, and of which so much has been published to the world, will be a comparatively easy task to condense, and bring into a focal point all the facts, with such inferences and deductions as a writer familiar with the subject is enabled to perform. For such a task, either of my friends, or both jointly, Mr. C. R. Smith, and Mr. Thomas Wright, honorary members of the Society, have shown themselves amply qualified by their many publications.

No. 3. This section I would devote to "*The Architectural Antiquities* of the County;"—including the Cathedral church, with other Christian edifices, also the monastic and parochial churches, castles, and ancient mansions.

No. 4. Civil divisions; appropriations of lands; manors; hundreds; parishes; tythings.

No. 5. Lords Lieutenants; military and municipal Officers, with their powers, prerogatives, and systems.

No. 6. Natural History of the County; may be safely entrusted to the Rev. J. C. Smith, whose papers on these subjects prove that he is well enabled to characterize and give interest to a discriminating essay on the ornithology, in particular, and the natural history, generally, of Wiltshire.

No. 7. Biographies of eminent persons, both natives of particular places, or those who, from having made it a home for a length of time, have identified themselves with, and may be ranked among, the Worthies of Wiltshire.

With such a Patron as the Wiltshire Archæological Society may boast and be proud of, in association with such a President, as the historian of Castle Combe,—with a zealous and able Topographer, the author of "the History, &c., of Doncaster Church," and editor of "the Wiltshire Magazine,"—we may reasonably hope and expect that a History of Wiltshire may be commenced with a guarantee of efficiency in literary qualifications, and with sanguine hope, that the abilities of the authors may find ample patronage to encourage them in so arduous an undertaking.

Should the members of this society think, with me, that the present is a favourable time to reconsider and adopt a plan for producing a County History, I would recommend some of them to assemble and compare notes and opinions on the subject. In combination there is strength; in co-operation much may be effected which would never be propounded, or scarcely hoped for, when the same persons are dispersed and inactive. Name a committee, with power to increase in numbers; mature a prospectus, or plan; circulate it freely and earnestly through the county; invite hints and adhesion, and appropriate the different departments to willing and competent parties; endeavour to ascertain and obtain access to original documents and materials; and I cannot allow myself to doubt that a fair and encouraging result will be the consequence.

FARLEIGH HUNGERFORD AND FARLEIGH CASTLE, WITH THEIR ASSOCIATIONS—GEOLOGY—WILLIAM SMITH—THE REV. BENJAMIN RICHARDSON—THE REV. JOSEPH TOWNSEND—LIEUT.-COLONEL HOULTON—DR. FRYER.

At the latter end of the last century, and beginning of the present, the truly romantic and rustic parish of Farleigh Hungerford, near Bath, was honoured and distinguished by a group of men of science who, though comparatively obscure and of humble habits and pursuits, have become eminent in the scientific annals of the country. The Rev. Benjamin Richardson was settled in the rectory of this parish in 1796, and in the following year I had the good fortune of being introduced to, and afterwards meeting, him at his parsonage, with the Rev. Joseph Townsend, of Pewsey; WILLIAM SMITH, who was employed as engineer to the Somerset Coal Canal, and who subsequently was honoured with the title of LL.D.; William Cunnington, of Heytesbury; the Rev. John Skinner, of Camerton; and Edward Fryer, M.D., editor of a memoir and of the literary works of James Barry, R.A., and professor of painting to the Royal Academy. Later in life, Colonel Houlton came into possession of the Farleigh estate, and expended much money on his mansion there, and on improvements in the parish. In such company, and at such a place, on different occasions, my time was most delectably spent. Every succeeding day was excitingly occupied in examinations, readings, discussions with my new friends on their new speculations, and varied novelties in fossilology, stratification, &c., whilst I occasionally visited some of the ancient buildings of the neighbourhood. The ruins of the once spacious and formidable castle, with its chapel and monuments; the village church; the remains of Hinton Abbey, with the early Anglo-Norman church at Lullington, were to my mind and eyes objects of curiosity and interest. Though I had not previously read or heard much on extraneous fossils, every specimen exhibited, and every comment made by my learned friends were new sources of pleasure to my latent fancy, and afterwards induced me to explore many quarries, heaps of stone, and new diggings among rocks and soils with avidity. Though the learned divines secured great deference and respect I remember that they listened attentively, and with polite courtesy, to the opinions and novel accounts which were brought forward by the other parties. The surveyor, however, seemed the main-spring, or moving power, in the newly-formed machine, as he was enabled to communicate new discoveries, or fresh matter, at every successive meeting of the parties. The very interesting brief " Memoirs of William Smith, LL.D., by his nephew and pupil, John Phillips, F.R.S., F.G.S., &c., 8vo., 1844," furnish a lucid account and exemplification of his travels over different parts of the island; of his keen examination of the prominent and even minute features of the different strata, and of such configurations of extraneous fossils as belonged to each varied specimen and its locality. Hence originated the new science of Geology, and to Mr. Smith is it indebted for its parentage and first nurture. In the volume referred to, are portraits of that gentleman, of Mr. Richardson, of Mr. Townsend, and of Francis, Duke of Bedford, forming interesting representations of the heads of persons whose zeal and talents were exemplarily employed in a new science which has proved so valuable and important to the country. In the portrait of Dr. Smith is recognized the plain, simple, unsophisticated, thinking man, whose amiability of heart and calm deliberative intellect rendered him the founder of a new science. He was aged 69 when the portrait was drawn by Fouran. In the year 1839 he had made arrangements to join the Scientific Association at Birmingham, and stopped on his way at Northampton, at the house of Mr. and Miss Baker, whose first studies in topography and antiquities commenced with their accompanying me to many places and objects in their native county, when I visited it for the Beauties of England, and afterwards for the

Architectural Antiquities. Illness arrested the progress of the good and estimable doctor, and terminated his worldly career in a few days. Dr. Smith was a native of Churchill, in Oxfordshire, and was born on the 23rd March, 1769.

Fortunately he found congenial spirits in the gentlemen before named, two of whom were men of classical and general learning, whilst the third possessed that practical acquaintance with the chalk formation and its concomitants which became useful in the speculations and cogitations of the other students. Sanctioned in my own opinions by those of one of the best topographers and archæologists of the country (the Rev. Joseph Hunter), I will quote a passage from his delightful little biographical brochure, entitled, "The Connection of Bath with the Literature and Science of England," 1827. "This city, in the vicinity of Farleigh, may justly be regarded as the cradle of English Geology, for that new science had its birth in this place, within our own time. Look into the Encyclopædias and Dictionaries published twenty years ago, and the word is not to be found, nor any of the innumerable terms which now form its novel vocabulary. Observe, too, how many persons in every part of the kingdom are now engaged in the study of this science, and you will see something of the importance in which it is now regarded. Smith observed, and in part systematized; but in theorizing, he was indebted to two gentlemen: the Rev. B. Richardson and Joseph Townsend, the latter of whom was one of the earliest writers on this science; and he also enriched our literature in the several departments of philosophy, travels, and practical divinity."

The REV. JOSEPH TOWNSEND was Rector of Pewsey when I first visited him in 1798, to which living he had been presented by his father, Mr. Chauncey Townsend, an eminent London merchant. He had previously visited Spain and many other parts of the continent, after a course of the usual studies and routine at Clare Hall, Cambridge. On returning to England, he first settled at Bath, where he became connected with a party of Wesleyan Dissenters, and preached in Lady Huntingdon's Chapel. To divert him from that sect, with its novel doctrines and fanaticism, the parent settled him in the Established Church, in which, fortunately, he continued to act as a zealous and respected pastor till his death, in 1816. As stated on a monument, by Westmacott, to his memory in Pewsey Church, he occupied that living fifty-three years, when he attained the "ripe old age" of 78. In this retirement he wrote and published many literary works on a great variety of subjects; yet, strange to say, I have sought in vain to find anything like a full biography of him in the dictionaries devoted to English memoirs. In the *Gentleman's Magazine* for 1816, are slight notices of his life and character; and in Warner's "Literary Recollections," 2 vols. 8vo., 1830, are related such traits and anecdotes as make us wish for a full-length picture of his life, acquirements, and works. He was a remarkable and estimable person, both for varied learning, and for readiness to benefit others who were desirous to acquire knowledge and impart it to the deserving. In the year 1847, I addressed a letter to my worthy friend and county-man, the Rev. John Ward, of Great Bedwin, near Pewsey, begging him to seek local information about Mr. Townsend. He promptly furnished a copy of an inscription to his memory in the chancel of the church. By this it appears that the Rector died November 6th, 1816, having been twice married, and had a family of six children by the first wife; that the second was widow of Admiral Sir John Clerke, and that she, as well as her husband, were interred within the church. Mr. Ward then remarks that the cross-roads of his part of Wiltshire "are very bad in the winter, and therefore not calculated to seduce me, or other persons, to travel over them voluntarily to explore churches and their monuments. Yet these highways," he continues, "were objects of solicitude to the former incumbent, who devoted much time and money to mend and render them safe, if not sound and good. From being unusually tall in stature, he thereby acquired the cognomen of Colossus of Roads." Jeremy Bentham thus characterises Mr. Townsend, in the tenth volume of his Works, page 92: "He seems to be a worthy creature, has been a good deal abroad, and has a great deal of knowledge; his studies have been a great deal in the same track as mine; he is a utilitarian, a naturalist, a chemist, a physician, and was once, what I had like to have been, a Methodist. There is a mixture of simplicity, candour, and a composed earnestness, tempered with good breeding, that has won upon me mightily." His "Travels in

Spain," in 3 vols. 8vo., were published in 1791, and again in 1795, and were praised by contemporary critics; whilst his "Physician's Vade Mecum" reached a tenth edition in 1807. His many other literary and scientific works tended to keep his name before the world, and augment his fame both at home and abroad. Not only in divinity, but in biblical criticism—in chemistry, agriculture, politics, science, and miscellaneous literature—his active and acute mind was ceaselessly employed.

The Rev. Richard Warner, the historian of Bath, and author of "Walks through Wales," and of several other works, states that "Mr. Townsend had more general knowledge and varied information than any man I ever knew." *

With LIEUT.-COLONEL HOULTON I became acquainted in 1802, in a tour I made, in that year, through the county of Devon. He was then seated in a delightful villa, called Mamhead Cottage, near Exeter, where, with a young and handsome wife, he seemed to be in a sort of terrestrial paradise, with every thing lovely and loveable about him. He was a fine specimen of the English gentleman, and had married a young heiress with a good fortune. He settled at first on his own estate at Grittleton, bequeathed to him by his uncle, Admiral Houlton, until, by his father's death, he succeeded to the property of Farleigh Hungerford, where he resided till his decease in 1839. Here he considerably enlarged an old house, and ornamented the exterior with Gothic windows, clustered chimney-shafts, pinnacles, and embattled parapets, &c. At Farleigh the amiable lord of the manor continued to live for many years, blessed with an excellent wife and large family, enjoying the respect and esteem of most of the neighbouring nobility and gentry. Moore, "the observed of all observers," was a frequent guest at Farleigh House, for the young ladies constituted an attractive and even fascinating party, not only by personal charms, but by accomplish-

---

* "Literary Recollections," vol. ii. p. 98. In the same volume are further remarks on the character, qualifications, and personal traits of Mr. Townsend. His collections are characterized by the same writer, as "being extensive, exquisitely beautiful, and scientifically arranged, and illustrating the strata of the earth and particularly of this island; the fruit of researches of a long and active life, which he briefly touched upon in the first volume of 'Moses,' his last and most eminent monument of united knowledge, genius, and industry."

ments in music, dancing, and singing. In the famed "Diary" of the fashionable Irish bard, we find the following passage characterizing the Houlton family as they appeared in April, 1834: "A pretty house, beautiful girls, hospitable host and hostess, excellent cook, good champagne and moselle, charming music: what more could a man wish?" I can only wish that the whole of the same writer's comments and characterizing notices of persons and events, as thus recorded in his *Diary*, had been as faithful in spirit and phraseology as that here quoted; and had they been prepared for the press by himself, his posthumous work would have escaped the severe criticism which has too justly been poured out against it.*

The REV. B. RICHARDSON had been Rector of Farleigh Hungerford from 1796 to 1832, and was justly respected for his many good qualities, as a minister and a man. By his attachment to such persons as previously named, he was often indulged with their company, whence he was induced to visit many parts of Wiltshire, Somersetshire, &c., to examine strata and collect specimens, and had amassed a large museum at the time of his decease. In a pleasing and interesting Vade Mecum on "the Literature of Bath," by G. Morehead, Esq., 1854, (p. 36) I find the following tribute to my much-respected friend of Farleigh, "who was thoroughly versed in the wonders of the creation, and who had so accurately examined all the formations for many miles around his own neighbourhood, that he could point out the very spots where the oolite prevailed, or the lias was ready to burst forth to the surface."

EDWARD FRYER, M.D., who was physician to the Duke of Sussex, had a house in Gower Street, London; and had been a staunch friend to the eccentric and querulous *James Barry*, the famed artist who executed the series of pictures in the great room of the Society of Arts, in the Adelphi, London. Dr. Fryer wrote a memoir of that artist, and

---

* For interesting accounts of the Castle of Farleigh, its Parish, the Lords of the Manor, the Houlton and Hungerford Pedigrees, &c., I can refer, with confidence and pleasure, to a "History of the Parish of Grittleton, by the Rev. J. E. Jackson," 4to., 1843; and to "A Guide to Farleigh Hungerford," by the same learned and zealous topographer, in 8vo., 1853. In the third volume of "The Beauties of Wiltshire," will be found an account of the castle, church, chapel, and mansion, written from materials furnished by the Colonel.

edited his Lectures, with a series of Letters, chiefly to and from his friend and generous patron, Edmund Burke, in 2 vols. 4to., 1809. The Doctor possessed an estate in the parish, called Farleigh Lodge Farm, which had descended to him from his father, and where he usually spent some time in the summer season. Near that house, in the year 1823, were discovered the ruins of a Roman Bath, described by Sir R. C. Hoare in the *Gentleman's Magazine* of that year.

The REV. JOHN SKINNER, of Camerton, in the county of Somerset, was one of the antiquaries who visited Farleigh at the time referred to. I am not sure that he paid particular attention to geology (then in an embryo state.) He was not only an enthusiast, but a theorist in Roman archæology, and had devoted much time and study to the castrametations, pavements, and other vestiges of that people, in his own immediate vicinity: and we know, by the manuscript collections which he bequeathed to the Bath Institution, that he had described and illustrated many of these. His theory, however, of placing the Camulodunum of Antoninus, at Camerton, near Bath, is visionary, and devoid of all plausibility.*

WILLIAM CUNNINGTON, of Heytesbury, though not a frequent visitor at Farleigh, may be properly classed with its local geological worthies. I observe, from some manuscript letters preserved by his family, that he corresponded both with Mr. Richardson and Mr. William Smith. By the same evidence it is also shown, that his first amusements and consequent studies were palæontology. Were it my province to write a detailed memoir of one of my earliest and best friends, it would be necessary to inquire into his early habits and pursuits, and the opportunities and incitements he had for study; but I must limit myself to a few leading facts and characteristics. As the name of Stukeley is intimately associated with Stonehenge, so is Cunnington with Wiltshire Archæology; both of which, as well as

---

* On the disputed subject of the true site of this distinguished Municipium of the Romans, I was enabled to bring forward much valuable evidence in the *Beauties of England,* "Essex," from the researches and papers of Mr. B. Strutt, of Colchester, who had published two valuable volumes on the history of that town. In a recent volume of the *Quarterly Review,* is a learned and discriminating Essay on the Anglo-Roman Colonization of Britain, and on the Station at Colchester.

the two antiquaries, belong to, and form parts of, the annals of our island. Though Stukeley was too sanguine and poetical in natural temperament to be implicitly followed or trusted, he was zealous, diligent, and unwearied in researches and inquiries. This is clearly evinced by his published works; but more particularly by his voluminous diaries, manuscripts, and drawings. The reading public have not done justice to his merits; whilst Fuller, Evelyn, Leland, and Camden have been well and fairly recognized and praised by the professional critic and by the most respected archæologists. My much-loved friend, Mr. Cunnington, has been properly commended by Sir Richard C. Hoare for his labours in exploring the barrows of Salisbury Plain, but the Baronet's language does not seem to come from the heart: it savours of condescension—a sort of lukewarm approval of the dependant, by his patron. An acute critic in the *Quarterly Review*, in his notice of the "Ancient Wiltshire," speaks of the dedication of that work to the Heytesbury Antiquary, as a piece of seeming mock humility. In my intercourse with Sir Richard, which was of much longer duration than his was with Mr. Cunnington, I often felt my literary pride and consequence wounded by the language and manner of the patron to the author. Horace Walpole manifested a similar hauteur towards poor Chatterton, and to other literary persons who came in contact with him.

That Mr. William Cunnington was a "native of Northamptonshire" is recorded on a tablet raised to his memory in Heytesbury Church, and that he died "on the 31st of December, 1820, aged 56," is also stated; but the place and time of his nativity are not put on record. I have sought in vain to verify these facts, by inquiring of his descendants, and also of the vicar of the parish of Gretton, where the names of Cunnington appear in the registers, but not that of William. I have met with no notice of his boy-days, nor have his early pursuits in life been chronicled. That he settled early at Heytesbury is generally admitted; and that he soon manifested a mind of capacity and energy is demonstrated by words and deeds which led to permanent distinction and fame. At the time I first visited him, in 1798, his warehouses assumed the appearance of one of those great establishments called a Bazaar. Active, energetic, and indefatigable, he overwrought his strength, and by devoting nights to study rather than to sleep, he both oppressed and injured his bodily and nervous system. He was therefore advised to detach himself from such labours, and seek change of air and scene by riding every day over the neighbouring Downs. Here his eye and fancy were attracted by the numerous barrows and artificial earthworks which abound in that primæval district. Tempted to explore some of these, by excavations, he was gratified and rewarded by the discovery of many relics indicative of times and people of far-distant ages. His mind was excited, his health materially benefited, and the discoveries became a matter of much speculation and provincial wonderment. At the time alluded to, I had the advantage and pleasure of spending three or four days with him, and was then taken to examine the castrametations in the vicinity of his home, and the variety of tumuli which abound between the western extremity of Salisbury Plain and Stonehenge. The scene seemed, to my eye and fancy, a sort of phantasmagoria— a dream—a romance. Imagination can recal, or reawaken some of the impressions then made, as well as the conversations and readings that ensued. We were both tyros in archæology and topography, and both were naturally curious and inquisitive. I had seen and known more of books than my friend; for at that time he had not examined Stukeley's volume on " Stonehenge," nor his " Itinerarium," nor Douglas's " Nenia Britannica "—books only known to, and appreciated by the initiated few. These works, and intercourse with such men as H. P. Wyndham, the Rev. W. Coxe, the Rev. Joseph Townsend, the Rev. Benjamin Richardson, W. Smith, P. Crocker, myself, and, afterwards with Sir Richard C. Hoare, induced Mr. Cunnington to prosecute his explorations, accumulate facts and materials, and ultimately become an efficient and experienced archæologist, and also a geologist of no mean account.

It should be borne in mind that the Society of Antiquaries of London was then in a very different state to what it has since become; that there were no Archæological Institutes and Societies; that the British Museum, and Record Offices were not readily accessible nor well organized; that there were not Camden and Arundel Societies; and that the antiquary was popularly regarded as a frivolous and visionary personage. To such men as Mr. Cunnington, Mr. Wyndham, Mr. Pennant, and Sir Richard Hoare, many of the present generation are under great and lasting obligations, and owe a debt which can only be liquidated by awarding to them just appreciation and praise.

In a letter, addressed by Mr. Cunnington to myself, in November, 1798, he mentions some researches and discoveries he had made on the Downs in the vicinity of his home, and of his intention to prosecute his work in the following summer. He laments the want of books, and of information as to the best modes of exploring the contents of barrows, and of other appearances on the surface of the primæval lands which exhibited traces of human occupancy. I procured for him Douglas's *Nenia Britannica*, as the best authority on, and elucidation of the subject, as containing admirable representations of the contents of barrows in the county of Kent, with remarks on their variety of deposit, and other valuable information. From that time, to the period of his death in 1810, my friend found abundant matter for excitement, for study, and for dissertation. By other letters, as well as by personal intercourse, at his own house in London and on the Downs, I am enabled to state that he continued every summer to promote and direct other local explorations, and to arrange and digest his materials during the winter. Hence he formed a collection and museum which excited the curiosity of his immediate neighbours, and of the nobility and gentry of the county. Amongst these were the Marquess and Marchioness of Bath, Mr. Aylmer Bourke Lambert, Mr. Thos. Davis, Mr. H. Penruddock Wyndham, M.P., Archdeacon Coxe, the Rev. W. L. Bowles, and the Rev. E. Duke. During his proceedings he indulged me with frequent accounts of his successive labours and discoveries, also of his correspondence with the gentlemen above-named, and with many others who were partial to the subject and felt interested in it, also in natural history, and other public literary matters. The names of some of these are enumerated in a note below, as calculated to show his connection and the tendency of his studies.*

---

\* The descendants of Mr. Cunnington have laudably, and with good feelings, preserved and classed, in two large folio volumes, a collection of more than THREE HUNDRED AUTOGRAPH LETTERS from the following persons, ranging from 1798 to 1809:—

A. B. Lambert, 53 letters; Sir R. C. Hoare, Bart., 99; H. P. Wyndham, M.P., 43;

I had published two volumes of the "Beauties of Wiltshire," for which Mr. Cunnington wrote accounts of some of his new discoveries: of the Roman villa at Pitmead; of the castrametations in the vicinity of Warminster; of fresh researches at Stonehenge, and on other topographical matters. In my new avocation of authorship, I found a valuable and generous friend in that gentleman, and, consequently, derived no small pleasure in frequent intercommunication, by books and letters, on various matters of archæological interest. Many of his own letters have, fortunately, been preserved. I have retained only twelve, but they are interesting in shewing how zealously, indefatigably, and conscientiously he pursued his labours, and recorded facts, whereby he accumulated a mass of useful and valuable information. They are also peculiarly gratifying to myself, and candid in the writer, particularly one of them, which contains good counsel and advice to a young author who was too apt then, as afterwards, to call things by their proper names, and not sophisticate their meaning by ambiguity or equivocal language. Party spirit was strong, and often led to great personal animosities, and to bitter enmities. Mr. Cunnington was a tory or aristocrat, and consequently fancied and asserted that the aristocracy, as a body, with nearly all its branches, were honest, uncorrupt, and almost guileless. I had, however, heard and *known* many instances quite the contrary, where princes, nobles, gentlemen, and even clergymen, were corrupt and idle pensioners, and otherwise worthless human beings. Hence we could not but differ in opinion on political subjects; but my good friend shewed me the folly and imprudence of speaking harshly and strongly of the higher classes of society; and I now read with admiration and gratitude the language of his wise and noble counsel.

---

Philip Crocker, 49; Archdeacon Coxe, 46; A. Crocker, 15; Lady Hippesley, 6; Lady Ilchester, 1; H. Johnson, M.D., 17; H. Hatcher, 3; Rev. R. Iremonger, 8; Rev. T. Lemon, 12; — Holloway, 5; Martin Williams, 11; Rev. Dr. Mayo, 2; Thos. Meade, 7; Wm. Owen, 5; James Parkinson, 6; Dr. Charles H. Parry, 1; the Rev. John Offer; the Rev. W. Richards; the Rev. B. Richardson; W. Smith, C.E.; the Rev. Joseph Townsend, 5; J. Britton, 25; W. Hindley; J. Heskell; Lord Arundell; Marchioness of Bath, 4; Matthew Boulton; J. Buckler; G. W. Brackenridge, 4; Timothy Cobb; Sir Wm. A'Court, Bart., 3; the Rev. E. Duke, 9; B. Barry; J. Bird; J. Brown; the Rev. Jas. Douglas, 16; Miss Dalrymple; J. S. Davis, M.D.; the Rev. Jas. Eyre; the Rev. R. Fenton, 8; Mrs. Fisher; the Rev. R. Graham.

As if "increase of appetite grew with what it fed on," Mr. Cunnington continued his pursuits amongst the artificial earthworks of Salisbury Plain for some successive years, thereby augmenting his collection and acquiring additional information. It does not appear, from the evidence I have seen, that he had meditated on publishing the results of his acquirements; nor was there any probability that a bookseller would speculate on a work involving such an outlay as would be required for drawings, engravings, paper, and printing. Mr. Coxe and Mr. Wyndham had been connected with publishers, and consequently had means of ascertaining their opinions. In 1804, Sir Richard C. Hoare had become acquainted with my friend, and then agreed to pay the expenses of further researches amongst the tumuli. A new field was opened, and the baronet entered upon his fresh career with zeal and liberality. On engaging to pay the further expenses of excavating, &c., the barrows, Sir Richard stipulated that Mr. Cunnington was not to communicate with me on these subjects! The more central, eastern, and northern portions of the Plain were next examined; and numerous objects were exhumed. About 1808, the well-known bookselling firm of Lackington and Co., of London, undertook to publish the large and expensive work on these Wiltshire Antiquities, the authorship and drawings for which were to be provided by Sir Richard, and the other expenses to be borne by the publishers. Hence originated the two ponderous volumes called "Ancient Wiltshire," commenced in 1810, and finished in 1821. At that time it was a fashion to covet and purchase large-paper books, uncut margins, very rare tomes, and for each of which extravagant prices were often given; but from the sizes and prices of such works as that now referred to, and others from the same house, it was found that the market was overstocked, and when the volumes of "Ancient Wiltshire" were completed, the booksellers declined to embark further capital in Sir Richard's "Modern Wiltshire," which he had commenced, and which he ultimately published at his own personal cost, incurring an expenditure of several thousand pounds.

Some idea of the extent of the manuscripts and drawings made by Mr. Cunnington for "Ancient Wiltshire," may be formed by a knowledge that they are arranged and bound in five large folio volumes of accounts, drawings, and views of barrows and their contents. Well might the learned and generous baronet compliment the industrious antiquary on his exertions, and for the judgment he manifested in such a collection. The young antiquary of the present age will grieve to learn that they are deposited, by bequest, as an heirloom in the mansion of Stourhead, where they are not easily accessible to the students and lovers of this class of ancient lore. In the same house is also such a collection of books, drawings, manuscripts, prints, and other materials of British topography as is not equalled in any public or private library in Europe. It comprises a large and invaluable series illustrative of the history and antiquities of Wiltshire, which the kind baronet gave me assurances were to be at the service of any gentleman or society who would undertake a complete history, or portions of a history, of the county. Amongst these collectanea are several large drawings of Salisbury Cathedral, by the justly-famed J. M. W. Turner, in his best style of that class of pictures. There is also a series of drawings of churches, of monuments, fonts, &c., by J. Buckler, F.S.A., bound in ten folio volumes; another of monastic buildings, by John Carter, F.S.A.; of Malmesbury and Lacock Abbeys; of ancient monuments, fonts, &c., by Thomas Trotter, with manuscript descriptions.

A good *Portrait* of Mr. Cunnington was painted by Samuel Woodford, R.A., which is preserved at Stourhead, and has been poorly engraved, by James Basire for the volumes of "Ancient Wiltshire."

On the south wall of the transept of the large and sadly-neglected Church of Heytesbury, a small marble tablet is placed to the memory of my estimable friend, with an inscription which truly and justly compliments him in saying, that by "his decease the literary world has lost a persevering antiquary and skilful geologist; the community of Heytesbury, a good neighbour and active fellow-citizen; the poor, a humane advocate and charitable protector; his own lamenting family, an affectionate husband and indulgent parent." On visiting that church in August, 1856, with the Wiltshire Archæological Society, I regretted to witness the defaced and almost obliterated inscription. It was remarked how desirable it would be to have it restored and protected, and it is earnestly hoped that such a laudable act will be speedily performed.

**FRANCIS BAILY,** D.C.L., F.R.S., *and member of many other societies, both British and Foreign. Born at Newbury, Berkshire, April 28th, 1774; died in Tavistock Place, London, August 30th, 1844; buried in the church of Thatcham, near Newbury, Berkshire.*

MR. F. BAILY'S RESIDENCE IN TAVISTOCK PLACE, LONDON.

Though not noticed among "The Curiosities of London," (of which my esteemed friend, Mr. John Timbs, has published a comparatively small, but very bulky volume, comprising a quantity of literary matter which would have formed at least ten of the volumes of novels of the last century) the house I have inhabited for about forty years, and that of my next-door neighbour, the late Mr. Baily, above referred to, are within twenty yards of each other, yet their entrance doors are at least five hundred apart. Thus, by a doorway in the garden-wall between the two houses, we might pass from one to the other in a minute; whereas, by the usual road-way, it would take about 600 steps, or gresses, as termed by William of Worcester, in measuring the streets and public buildings of Bristol in the fifteenth century. I mention this "Curiosity of London" to show that though I have been on visiting terms with the occupants of that house for a length of time, I do not know the name of persons who occupy the premises next to mine, the entrance doors of which are not twenty yards apart.

The accompanying two wood-cuts of Mr. Baily's house, belong to

JOHN BRITTON
LLD FSA
&c. &c. &c.

Engraved by F Storm from a Portrait by T. Phillips Esq R.A.
FOR
BRITTON'S AUTO BIOGRAPHY.
June 1849.

a small and amusing volume entitled "Things not generally known familiarly explained," by the same author, and show the mansion as placed in a garden and insulated from all other buildings. Within these walls Mr. Baily resided many years, wherein he had a good library, an observatory, and a room entirely appropriated to experiments. As mentioned by Mr. Timbs, in one of these, at the northeast angle, immediately behind the tree in the accompanying view, the astronomer "had contrived a pair of scales that enabled him, approximately, to weigh the vast Sphere; when he ascertained that it had within itself somewhere about 1,256,195,670,000,000,000,000,000 tons of matter."

EXPERIMENT ROOM IN MR. BAILY'S HOUSE.

Mr. Baily was a man of too much value and usefulness, in the annals of science and philosophy, to be named without emotion and admiration by those who knew his moral worth and importance in pursuits and works to which he devoted a long, active, and healthy life. From contiguity of residence and the friendly notice Mr. Baily indulged me with, I had many and frequent opportunities of seeing and hearing him in public and in private life, in scientific societies, at friendly unions, and in his domestic library and observatory.* I was also

---

* Scientific, artistic, and literary *Soirées* and *Conversaziones* were prevalent in London from the commencement of Sir Joseph Banks's Presidency of the Royal Society, and tended to promote personal and friendly intercourse between persons of similar pursuits and studies. The firm of Longman and Co., in Paternoster Row, and Miller, of Albe-

honoured by the presentation of several literary works and essays, which he wrote after settling in Tavistock Place, and from which I have derived much instruction. Thus circumstanced, I acquired some knowledge of the "sayings and doings" of the Royal, Astronomical, and Geographical Societies, in particular, as well as of the novelties which became subjects of public inquiry and comment relating to the scientific proceedings and publications of foreign and provincial societies and clubs. That of the Royal, however, was the chief, almost the only, one at which the learned men of London, at the beginning of this century, periodically and systematically assembled. Their routine of business, and subjects brought under notice, may be referred to rather as matters for history than of useful science: for it is a remarkable fact, a phenomenon of wonderment, that a knowledge of the circulation of the blood in the human body was a novelty and subject of controversy and speculation amongst doctors and most of the learned persons of that age.*

The Geological, Astronomical, and Geographical Societies, and also the British Association for the Advancement of Science, and several others, progressively started into life, attracted public notice, and called into action and energy the faculties and emulation of various classes of men of letters and science. Having myself taken an active part in the formation and promotion of some of these, I courted the advice and influence of my neighbour and friend. That of the Astronomical, however, engrossed his chief attention and solicitude, and I believe that it was projected and substantially formed by him. It is admitted by the members that he carefully watched its progress, attended all its meetings and committees, digested its laws, and successively acted as honorary secretary, treasurer, member of the committee, vice-president, and president. In short, it was a pet-child to the end of his life. In 1820 it was founded, and in 1831 obtained a

---

marle Street, assembled their literary friends and artists periodically at their respective houses, whose opinions they sought, and by whose advice they profited; whilst the presidents of some of the scientific societies called together the members of such institutions to meet patrons in the higher grades of society.

* See Aubrey's "Letters by Eminent Persons," Vol. iii., 277,—Account of Dr. William Harvey.

charter.* In this society's rooms we find an admirable *portrait* of *Mr. Baily*, by Thomas Phillips, R.A., which was subscribed for and presented by several of Mr. Baily's friends. After his decease a fine engraving of this portrait was executed by Mr. Lupton, at the expense of the Rev. R. Sheepshanks, and proofs were presented to the friends of the astronomer. A bust of Mr. Baily was executed by his namesake, E. H. Baily, R.A., for Miss Baily, sister of the former, who has presented it to the society.

Mr. Baily was a man of remarkable characteristics and qualifications; and at an early period of his life had attained sufficient wealth to enable him to prosecute the natural and acquired propensities of his disposition and ambition. He had been apprenticed to a tradesman in London, but found the occupation so incompatible with his innate tone of mind, that at the end of his bondage he visited North America, to see that country, and examine the habits, manners, and character of its inhabitants, for these were but little known to the untravelled English. The extent of those travels, the surface of the vast continent, the government of the people, with something of their political, religious, and commercial characteristics, were diligently and acutely examined by the young adventurer, who kept a detailed journal of such incidents as occurred, and of the opinions he formed during a progress over several hundred miles in the years 1796 and 1797. Since

---

* For brief accounts of the scientific, literary, and artistic societies, with the printing clubs of the United Kingdom, the reader is referred to a small volume by the Rev. Dr. Hume, 1847, with a supplement to 1853 by A. J. Evans. According to a statement in this volume the Astronomical Society had published, up to the year last named, twelve volumes of "Proceedings" and twenty volumes of "Transactions." The printed journals of most of the societies herein referred to, contain histories of their origin, progress, and rules; whilst the first, or precursor of all, the Royal, has been fully unfolded in two volumes by C. R. Weld, Esq., the assistant secretary to the Society. From this work we find that the early members made efforts to establish a conversazione or soirée; but it was reserved for Sir Joseph Banks to effect this object, during his forty-one years of presidentship. The Duke of Sussex, Sir Humphrey Davy, the Marquess of Northampton, and Lord Rosse gave it the most distinguished eclat by their periodical gathering of the members. The Earl de Grey, as president of the Royal Institute of British Architects, following such royal and noble examples, has assembled, at his splendid mansion in St. James's Square, a large and fashionable Soirée for many successive years.

his decease this journal has been printed at the expense of Miss Baily, sister of the author, after being carefully edited by Mr. A. De Morgan, an old and intimate friend of the astronomer. It forms a handsome octavo volume, with a preface by the learned editor, also the "Memoir of Francis Baily," by Sir John Herschel, Bart., and cannot fail to afford much gratification to every lover of astronomy, of science, and of laudable emulation.

A Catalogue Raisonné of the many scientific volumes and essays which were written and published by my friend abovenamed, would constitute at once a fertile topic, as well as commentary, on his life and merits; for they are evidences of devoted industry and of mental powers, as also of their practical tendencies. From youth, till the time of his lamented decease, Mr. Baily appears to have devoted his active and energetic mind to mathematics in all their intrinsic qualities, and thereby attained results which have proved of eminent service to the science in its national progress.

The number of Mr. Baily's volumes and papers, as enumerated by Sir John Herschel, in his Memoir, is ninety, which were produced between the years 1802 and 1842; the first being his "Tables for Purchasing and Renewing Leases," a third edition of which was issued in 1812, and is now very scarce. The last was a paper for the Astronomical Society, on "the Total Eclipse of the Sun on the 8th of July, 1842." To view and study that phenomenon, he made a journey to Pavia, where he witnessed it under the most favourable circumstances, with the most perfect instruments he could obtain; and has given a minute account of the whole "*central darkness; with an appearance very extraordinary, unprecedented, and singular.*"

Mr. Baily was a most exemplary man, and cannot be too much known or too highly extolled, as an eminent example to the rising generation. These facts and effects are too deeply impressed on my own memory and heart to be forgotten by the one, or not intensely felt by the other. Immediately on his decease, and with a zeal and affection which I need not be ashamed to avow, I was prompted to write a few remarks on his character and talents, with a view of putting them on record; but hearing that Sir John Herschel intended to produce a biographical essay for the Astronomical Society, and knowing the eminent qualifications of that distinguished astronomer, I forbore to continue the grateful task I had commenced. In November, 1844, Sir John read his memoir to a full meeting of the members of the society, when it excited unanimous approbation, united with corresponding sympathy for the individual commemorated. The essay was printed in the Monthly Transactions of the society, and separate copies were distributed amongst the personal friends of the deceased, and it has since appeared in the quarto *Memoirs*. It is barely justice to remark, that this biographical tribute is worthy of being classed amongst the best literary productions of the accomplished author and amiable man. It may be referred to as an admirable specimen of biography, at once honourable to the taste and talents of the writer, and conferring just and discriminating honours on the person commemorated. The main reasons for my venturing to write further on the subject must be ascribed to my affection for a most valued friend, a desire to record my own opinions and feelings, and to associate his name and memory with these reminiscences of a long and struggling life. If not the strongest, it has ever been a powerful incentive in me to covet and court the society of great and good men, to converse with them, and to conciliate their friendship.

Though an abstruse and diligent student all his life, and consequently much alone, and though he lived and died a bachelor, he enjoyed congenial company and the festive board, and was in the habit of frequently assembling at his own hospitable home, parties of six or eight (rarely more) of the most eminent men of science.

We have often read of distinguished literary and artistic clubs, and of famed convivial societies; but not so much of festive parties of confirmed students and men of profound science. These have usually been persons of secluded, abstracted habits, who have neglected and almost shunned the charms of society. Doctors Johnson and Goldsmith, with Burke, Garrick, and other members of the Literary Club, congregated around Reynolds's charmed table; and also conferred and reflected honour on the hospitable home of Mrs. Thrale, at Streatham. Dr. Johnson, in his Life of Swift, adverting to his intimacy with G. Wakefield, says, "At this man's table I enjoyed many cheerful and instructive hours, with companions such as are not often to be found assembled: with one who has lengthened, and one who has gladdened life,—with Dr. James, whose skill in physic will be long remembered; and with D. Garrick, whom I had hoped to gratify with this character of our common friend. But what are the hopes of man? I am disappointed by that stroke of death, which has eclipsed the gaiety of nations, and impoverished the stock of human happiness."

These social and intellectual conclaves are honourably commemorated in the interesting volumes of Boswell's "Johnson," whilst Goldsmith has introduced us to another group of "Worthies" in his "Retaliation." Had there been a Boswell or a Goldsmith to commemorate "the sayings and doings" of the Baily Club, as held at the Observatory-mansion, it might have obtained the fame of the clubs above referred to. Amongst the honoured names of these personages may be specified the following: Professor Airy, Rear-Admiral Sir Francis Beaufort, Rear-Admiral William H. Smyth, Col. Colby, Sir John F. W. Herschel, Bart., Lieut.-Col. Edward Sabine, Major-Gen. Sir Chas. W. Pasley, Dr. Peacock (Dean of Ely), The Rev. Dr. Whewell, (Master of Trinity College, Cambridge,) Lieutenant Stratford, R.N., The Rev. R. Sheepshanks, Dr. Roget, Professor Christie, Dr. Arnott, Dr. Robinson, Professor Buckland, Sir Robert Kane, Sir John Franklin, R.N., Professor Wheatstone, Thomas Galloway, George Bishop, A. De Morgan, G. B. Greenough, J. George Children, the Professors of Astronomy in Oxford, Cambridge, and Edinburgh, and many others, together with some of the eminent astronomers from the continent. With such companions, and the varied continuous conversation from six till eleven o'clock, devoid of religious and party topics, which rarely occurred, the mind was roused and stimulated. Not only the latest discoveries in every branch of science were brought under review, and tested by unrestrained criticism, but rendered permanent and popular by the approving testimony of such competent judges. Almost every phenomenon of the celestial bodies, abstruse points of mathematics, the real or supposed discoveries in the sun, moon, planets, and the terrestrial globe, constituted subjects of vivid conversation. Hence the opinions, theories, and speculations of the parties present, and of solitary astronomers of our national observatories, as well as those of foreign nations, were brought under review and commentary, to the gratification of the ever-inquiring astronomer, and to the astonishment of tyros like myself. I must own, that such company and converse not only humbled me in self-esteem, but gave me higher notions of the intellectual powers of man. Had I the graphic talents of a Boswell, to record some of the most remarkable conversations which occurred on those occasions, the reader would be better enabled to judge of and appreciate their importance, and the estimation in which I have regarded them.

The following sentences are from the pen of Mr. De Morgan, who had so many opportunities of knowing the personal character and qualifications of Mr. Baily; and I cheerfully accept and reprint them, as confirmatory of my own estimate.

"The energy of his character enabled him, while making his fortune, to place himself in the first rank of cultivators of one branch of science (mathematics), and after he had made his fortune to obtain like success in another (astronomy). The same resolution, which, with the ardour of twenty-five, would have led him over African deserts, for the promotion of one knowledge, sustained him, for the sake of another, through four years—to name only one labour of research, which involved more than twelve hundred hours of watching the oscillations of a pendulum. If any one had told Mr. Baily, at the time when the love of excitement and of scenery induced him to pass, not reckoning landings, about fifty days and nights in an open boat on the Ohio and the Mississippi, that the time would come when he would sit for as many hours as, put together, would make up all those days and nights, with his eye at a little telescope, watching and recording the slow travelling of an index passing over some wires, he would have treated the assertion with laughter, and would have held that his taste and views could never fall in with such a monotonous drudgery."—*Preface* to " Journal of a Tour," &c.

" What Mr. Baily's pursuits did for his own real good, must be referred to the memory of those who enjoyed his friendship; among whom there is surely not one who will venture to say positively that he ever *knew a better or a happier man.*"

As verifying this remark, I may refer to the last interview I had with my much-loved friend, and which was only a few days before he breathed his last. Prostrate on a sofa, his features were wasted and attenuated, the eyes sunken, the voice feeble and almost inaudible; but the following remark he expressed clearly and firmly:—" My life is nearly closed. I leave life with the same tranquillity and equanimity which I have generally felt and acted on in my personal intercourse with friends and strangers. I have been blessed with uninterrupted health, and excepting on one melancholy occasion (when run over by a galloping horse) have scarcely taken medicine. In short, I have had more than my share of terrestrial happiness, and leave it, as fulfilling an inscrutable law of animal nature, with thankfulness and resignation." The language, the person, the loss of such a friend and such a man, made an impression on the heart and mind which can never be erased.

To show the amiable and truly generous disposition of Mr. Baily, it was found that, by his last will, he had given handsome bequests to his immediate relations, and had also left complimentary and kind legacies to several of his more intimate friends. Amongst these I gratefully acknowledge a gift of one hundred pounds, free from legacy duty. I am induced to notice this gratifying and useful testimonial as a remarkable contrast to the conduct of three old and intimate friends, with whom I had associated for many years, and to whom I had rendered many civilities and devoted much of that time which was my only source of income. One left me one hundred pounds, to be given in " a piece of plate," which would be useless, and which one of his executors had ordered a friend to make, without consulting me. To forego this commission, I agreed to pay the silversmith ten pounds, and was further taxed by the payment of ten pounds for legacy duty! Another assumed *friend*, whom I had known and associated with more than thirty years, who had shown to myself and wife a will, engrossed and attested, in which he had bequeathed to us five thousand pounds; who, by a subsequent will, left several thousands to different persons and to public offices, but only five guineas for a mourning ring to myself, and an annuity of thirty pounds to my wife!! A third *friend*, whom I had known intimately for more than forty years, whom I had served and benefited in the early part of his career, who had advanced himself from poverty (as

I had done) to wealth (as I have not done), omitted to notice my name in his last will, which is at once remarkable for its length and for the vast fortune it disposes of!!!

In closing this desultory and defective biographical sketch, I cannot resist the impulse of making a passing remark on the monumental inscription placed in the church of a rural and almost obscure village where the corpse of Mr. Baily was interred. In spite of the sneers or rebukes of classical scholars and men of learning, I will venture to question the propriety of placing inscriptions in churches, particularly in provincial parishes, in Latin or Greek. As the object and usefulness of such record is to honour the dead, and to impart information to and excite emulation in the living, that cannot be so well and so laudably effected by any as by the native language.

For my reasons to justify this opinion, and for a very eloquent and admirable essay on such inscriptions, I refer to my volume on "A History, &c., of Bath Abbey Church," 8vo. and 4to., 1825.

---

The proof of the foregoing narrative was sent to the printer on the 2nd of December, 1856, with an intimation from Mr. Britton that he would rest for a day or two, and then write a few remarks relative to the two friends, Mr. Whittaker and Mr. Henry Neele, whose portraits were given with the first portion of the Biography. It was, however, the will of the Divine Disposer of events that he should not fulfil this intention. On the 4th of the same month he was taken ill with bronchitis, a disorder from which he had suffered severely during several previous winters.

From the first hour of his last and fatal illness he had an impression that he should not recover, although his wife and medical attendant had great reason to hope that he would again have strength to rally from the prostration consequent on this disorder.

At the end of four weeks, almost to the hour, he closed his eyes in death—passing from this world peacefully and resignedly. During his illness he at times suffered much bodily pain, which he bore patiently. His thoughts were quite abstracted from the concerns of this world—save on one occasion, when he expressed a wish to see his friend, Mr. J. H. Le Keux. When that gentleman kindly attended at his bedside, he requested him to give his best advice and counsel to his widow in the arrangement of his collection of prints, drawings, &c., preparatory to their sale.

The reader who shall glance through, even if he does not peruse, the two volumes of this Auto-Biography, will perceive that the life of John Britton was one of activity and perseverance, and of thorough devotion to those departments of topographical and archæological science to which, for more than half a century, he had dedicated his energies. What they will *not* see in the Biography, is the fact, of which all who knew him intimately had reiterated proofs—namely, that age had never blunted his sympathies, but that to the last his heart overflowed with genial kindness and benevolence. He was eminently one of those who are not content with merely accepting the opportunity to perform a kind office; it was rather his practice to seek out and make the opportunity when it did not present itself. Few men have been mourned by a larger circle of friends, and none have better merited their affectionate remembrance.

To Dr. Joseph Williams, of Tavistock Square, the widow and relatives of Mr. Britton owe a deep debt of gratitude for five years of the most kind, unremitting, and *generous* attention.

---

The following few remarks were intended to form part of the Preface to the present volume, and were written the evening before Mr. Britton was taken ill.

Every thing has a beginning and an end. All objects of nature and art—the creations of Omnipotence—the works of man, have a first formation and a dissolution. The vegetable world, and those of the animal and the animalculi, have a commencement—a birth, in accordance with the immutable laws of one potent Power, and terminate a short or protracted existence in obedience to their destined objects and ends. The human species is the most wonderful, most varied, most consummate of all created organized matter; for it is gradually, progressively, improving its intellectual powers, and thereby expanding and augmenting its useful and pleasurable attributes and deeds.

I can easily believe that there are subscribers to and readers of these self-memoirs who are as impatient to see the *finis* of the same as the writer now is, and has been for some months, he will say years, past; but the former are depending on and wholly at the mercy of the latter, who is often baffled and tyrannized over by circumstances, by accidents and incidents, which he can no more control, no more influence, than he can the capricious climate in which he lives and breathes, but which materially, imperiously, influences not only his spirits but his physical and mental powers and energies. Hence he becomes a slave, a feather to "skyey influences"—hence he has often been checked, paralyzed in the midst of health and joyousness by an insidious east wind, by a draught, or by damp in the atmosphere; which engenders disease in the head, lungs, and whole system, prostrating body and mind.

END OF THE AUTO-BIOGRAPHY.

WILLIAM ALEXANDER.

London, Published in Britton's Autobiography, 1849.

# INDEX TO AUTO-BIOGRAPHY.

ACKERMAN, Rudolph, printseller, 310, 311; lithography introduced by, 312; lines written and printed on the first lithographic stone, 313; "The Forget-Me-Not" published by, 313; Poetical Magazine published by, 315
Actors, managers, and musicians, testimonials to, 10
―――― and dramatic authors, distinguished, 126, 127
*Ædes Hartwellianæ*, by R.-Adm. Smyth, 457
Affectation of language and manners, absurdity of, 52
Agriculture in the author's native village, 29—32
Aikin, Arthur, editor of *Annual Review*, 269
―――― Dr., editor of the *Athenæum*, 270; the author acting as sub-editor, 270; Dr. T. Rees sub-editor, 278
Allen, Ralph, rewarded for improvements in mails, 13
Alexandre, M., ventriloquist, account of, 150, 322. *See* Vattemare
Allnut, John, splendid copy of Westminster, 311
Amateur theatricals, 91
Ambulator, by E. W. Brayley, 279
Ammonites, legend of, at Keynsham, 211
Amusement, places of, in and near London, 118—121
Anecdotes of the Rev. W. L. Bowles, Thos. Moore, and the Rev. George Crabbe, 369
Annual Register, Rivington's, 260; Robinson's, 262
―――― Review, edited by Aikin, 269; contributors to, 269; seventh volume by the Rev. T. Rees, 279
Annuals (The) origin of, 313
Anstey's "New Bath Guide," by J. Britton, 218
Anti-Corn-Law League, 12
Antiquaries, society of, its reform, 334
Archæological Society for Wilts, 392
―――――― Essay proposed as testimonial to the author, 17
―――――― Institute, 455
Archæology essential to topography, 335
Architects, testimonials and honours conferred upon, 8
"Architectural" and "Cathedral Antiquities" pirated, 5
Arno's Vale, (near Bristol) house of, 210
Artists, testimonials to, 9
Attic Miscellany, the author's contributions to the, 127
Attorneys, Ritson's strictures on, 87
Aubrey, John, Natural History of Wiltshire, 19; characteristics; memoir of, 28; his school-days, 47, 416, 425
Auctioneer, the trade, *note*, 274

Auctioneers of books and the fine arts:—Leigh & Sotheby, 322; S. Leigh Sotheby, 323; R. H. Evans, 323; James Christie, 323; G. H. Christie, 324; Peter Coxe, 324; King and Lochee, 325; Southgate, 326
Author:—Observations on Auto-Biography, 1; testimonial to, proposed, 15; public dinner to, 16; Auto-Biography adopted, 17; birth-place, attachment to, 25; description of native village, 27; birth and parentage, 37; brothers and sisters, 37, 39; schoolmasters, 42, 47—49; partiality for field sports, 43; accidents in youth, 44; early feat in horsemanship, 45; school-fellows, 50, 53; idle habits in boyhood, 55; view of house in which the author was born, 56; exterior view of ditto, 57; reminiscences of boyhood, 59; journey to London, 61; apprenticed to the wine and brandy trade, 62; book-stalls, early studies at, 66; industrious habits in apprenticeship, 67; view of wine-cellar in which he served his apprenticeship, 68; vicissitudes, privations and hardships, 73; an early love affair, 74; emancipation from apprenticeship, 74; pedestrian tour from London to Plympton, 74; return to London, 77; employed as cellarman at the London tavern, 78; change to Mrs. Lonsdale's, 79; engagement with Mr. Simpson, an attorney, 82; death of Mr. Simpson, 88; member of a spouting club, 92; engagement at Mr. Chapman's theatre, 97; first visit to a stage manager, 101; attacked with incipient fever, 124; marriage, 126; first appearance in literature, 127, 128; first literary essay, 131; the "Beauties of Wiltshire" proposed, 135; pedestrian tour previous to writing the "Beauties," 137—237; the "Beauties of England and Wales" undertaken in conjunction with Mr. Brayley, 238; pedestrian tour with Mr. Brayley, 239—242; "The Rights of Literature" vindicated, 246; connection with the house of Longman & Co., 247; with Vernor & Hood, 285; observations on the Slave Trade, *note*, 321; books, reading, study, 327; Chippenham revisited, 336; remarks on intoxication, 348; Bowood compared and contrasted, 352; introduction to Marquess of Lansdowne, 354; tribute to the Marchioness of Lansdowne, 367; anecdotes of the Rev. W. L. Bowles, Thomas Moore, and the Rev. George Crabbe, 369; last illness and death of the author, 482; his last-written sentences, 485
Authors, pensions and other public testimonials conferred on, 7; remuneration for their works, 245, 271; deserving of particular study, 248

Authorship, pleasures and honours, praised by M. F. Tupper, 343
Auto-Biographies of literary men, 2
Auto-Biography, remark on, by Dr. Johnson, 2; Richard Cumberland's opinions on, 3; Sir Egerton Brydges' remarks on, 4; Horace Smith on, 4

Babbage, Charles, 11, 152
Back, Sir George, 12
Badham, J. B., 9
Bailey, C., almshouses at Chippenham, 337
Baily, E. H., 366, 386, 477
Baily, Francis, 11; memoir of, 474; Astronomical Society projected by, 476; travels in America, 477; Sir J. Herschel's memoir of, 479; social and intellectual meetings at house of, 480; his energy of character exemplified, 481; tranquillity on approach of death, 482; his legacy to author, 482
Baker, George, 331
―――― Mr. 319
Baldwin, Charles, 261
―――― E., 10
―――― Robert, notice of, 260
―――― Archbishop, 290
Balfour, Clara Lucas, 248
Bancroft, Mr., 21
Bandinell, Rev. B., 203
Banim, John, 7
Banks, Sir Joseph, 107
Bannister, John, 96, 126, 315, 351, 400
Barbauld, Mrs., 283
Barker, Henry Ashton, celebrated artist, 212
―――― Thomas, 223, 294
―――― Thomas and Benjamin, painters, 223
Barnes, T., 308
Baron, Dr., 388
Barré, Colonel, his claims to the authorship of *Letters of Junius*, 19; notice of, 357
Barrett, Mr., 217
―――― William, 201
Barrow, Sir John, 11, 290
Barry, Charles, R.A., his letter on the testimonial to the author, 16; 152
Bartlett, W. H., 188, 205
Barton, Bernard, 7, 294
Baster, Mrs., 91
Bath, characteristic features of, 58, 216; the author's intercourse from boyhood, 50, 216; worthies of, 117, 220; an Account of, for Rees's *Cyclopedia, ib.*; the "History and Antiquities of Bath Abbey Church," *ib.*; notice of the church, 218; Dr. Harrington's epigrammatic distich on, *ib.*; *New Bath Guide* re-edited by the author, *ib.*; dedication to the booksellers, 219; Bath Institution, 220; valuable contributions to, 221; lectures by the author, *ib.*; Bath and Bristol contrasted, 222; Madame d'Arblay's opinion of Bath, 223; Thomas and Benjamin Barker, notice of, 223—225; Sir Thomas Lawrence at, 224; William and Prince Hoare, notice of, 225; Wm. Beckford's residence at, 226, 227; Lansdowne Tower erected by him, 228; *Beckford's Folly*, 229
Bath-Easton Villa, 235; poetical amusements at, 235, 236
Baud, Mr., 139
Baxter, Mr., notice of, 320
Baynton, Sir Edward, 361
Beaufort, Duke of, 34, 36

Beaumont, Sir Francis, 11
―――― Sir George, 365
Beauties of England and Wales projected, 238; published by Vernor and Hood, 285
Beauties of Wiltshire, origin of, 135
Beckford, Alderman, 8, 228
―――― William, notice of, 226; his residence at Bath, and death, 233
Beddoes, Dr., 201
Bedford, Duke of, 205, 299, 361
Beechey, Sir William, 9
Beeke, Dr., 206
Beilby and Knott, 157
Belcher, Sir Edward, 12
Bell, Sir Charles, 303
―――― John, 257, 310
Beloe, Rev. William, editor of the *British Critic*, 260
Belsham, Rev. Mr., 282
Belzoni, Giovanni, the *Patagonian Sampson*, appearance at Sadler's Wells theatre, 112, 113; his researches and discoveries in Egypt, 113, 114; notice of, 114, 115; pension granted to his widow, 115
Bennet, Mr., 294
Bensley, Thomas, 299
Bent, Mr. 276
Bentham, James, 305
―――― Jeremy, 358—361
―――― Sir Samuel, 9
―――― Mr., 319
Bentley, Richard, 287
Beresford, Viscount, 10
Betty, Master, 126
Bewick, Thomas, 131
"Bibliomania," by Rev. T. F. Dibdin, 105; the author affected by, 328
Bidder, G. P., 10
―――― Master, 126
Bindley, Mr., 319
Bird, Edw., Cunningham's memoir of, 207
Birkbeck, Dr., 149
Birmingham, riots at, 145; Dr. Priestley and William Hutton victims of the riots, 146; William Hutton, notice of, 147; J. Bisset, notice of, 148; lectures at, by the author, *ib.*; Sir Edward Thomason, notice of, 149; medal struck by Buonaparte, *ib.*; Thomas Wright Hill and family, 150; Music Hall, 151; Grammar School at, 152; Phipson's workshops, *ib.*; Follet Osler's glass manufactory, *ib.*; *British Association* held at, 153; extract from the author's lectures at, 154; letters from William Hamper to the author, 155; notice of Mr. Hamper, 156—158
Bishop, Sir H. R., 10
Bishopstone, Roman pavement at, 180
Bisset, J., author and poet, 148, 155, 237
Bitton, fine church at, 213; Rev. H. T. Ellacombe and H. A. Barker residents at, 212
Blackstone, Judge, 360
Bladon, Samuel, 273
Blakeway, Rev. J. B., and the Rev. Hugh Owen, authors of *A History of Shrewsbury*, 166, 171, 237, 458
Blenheim House, visited by the author, 141
Blessington, Countess of, 299
Bliss, Mr., bookseller of Oxford, 140, 237
―――― Dr., 28
―――― Philip, 203
Blomefield, Mr., 290
Bloomfield, Robert, 285
Blore, Edward, 194

Boddington, Mr., 365
Bohn, H. G., publisher, his new edition of the *Letters of Junius*, 20; his enterprise in business, 275; his large Catalogue, 280; sale of Walpole's *Anecdotes*, 289; his edition of *Dr. Syntax*, 315
Bolingbroke, Viscount, 436
Bolton, Miss, 321
Bonnycastle, 383
Books, reading, study, observations on, by the author, 327
—— Petrarch on the pleasures of, 327
—— M. F. Tupper in praise of, 329
Bookseller, lines on a stupid, 258
Booksellers, the patrons of authors, 219, 245
———— of Bath, dedication to, 219
———— trade sales of, 274
———— signs, 259
Booksellers and publishers, notices of:—
Ackerman, 310; Arch, 286; Baldwin, 260; Bell, 310; Bent, 276; Bladon, 273; Bohn, 20; Bowles, 284; Brown, 264; Cadell, T., 306; Cadell, W., 306; Cadell and Davies, 306; Cobbett, 294; Colburn, 317; Collins, 297; Cooke, 256; Crosby, 280; Curl, 297; Dilly, 285; Evans, 274; Fairburn, 128; Fellows, 285; Fisher, 131, 313; Forster, 286; Harris, 282; Harrison, 254; Hodgson, 277; Hogg, 257; Hone, 291; Hurst, J., 265; Hurst, Thos., 218, 265; Johnson, 282; Kearsley, 289; Kelly, 258; Knight, 8, 85, 256; Lackington, Allen, & Co., 103, 142, 248; Lane, 287; Law, 279; Lintot, 297; Longman, T., 264; Longman, T. N., 264; Longman and Rees, 265; Longman and Co., 266—273; Macklin, 294; Major, 288; Martin, 287; Mawman, 285; Miller, 290; Murray, 289; Newberry, 282; Orme, 266; Parsons, 274; Pickering, 303; Phillips, 283; Richardson, J., 286; Richardson, 319; Rivingtons, 259; Robinsons, 261; Scatchard & Letterman, 279; Sewell, 286; Sherwood, 274; Symonds, 273; Taylor, 304; Taylor & Hessey, 296; Tegg, 275; Vernor & Hood, 238, 285; Walker, 274, 276; Wheble, 329; Whittakers, 279; White, 294; Wilkes, 280; Wilkie, 277; Williams, 295
Booth, Henry, 9
—— Miss S, 321
Boswell, James, 3, 248
———— Henry, editor of *Antiquities*, 258
Boucher, Rev. John, his library, 323, 328
Bourne, J., 154
Bourrienne, M., 149
Bowdlers, the, 220
Bowles, Rev. William Lisle, 304, 364; notice of, 369; his promotions in the church, 370; his death 373
———— Rev. Dr., 369
———— Mrs., 373
———— Carrington, 284, 285
Bowood, seat of the Marquess of Lansdowne, compared and contrasted, 352; kind reception of the author at, 354; collection of portraits at, 356; manuscripts at, 358; letter of Dr. Popham on, 359; Dr. Bowring on, 359, 360; Jeremy Bentham's visit to, 361; distinguished visitors at, 364; gallery of paintings at, 365
Bowring, Dr. (Sir John), 7, 297; his observations on Bowood, 359, 360
Bowyer, Mr., 294
Boydell, Alderman, 224, 281, 294

Boys, Thomas, 394
Brackenridge, G. W., notice of, 211
Braham, John, 127
Brayley, E. W., the author's early studies with, 53; his song of the "Guinea Pig," 69; a *Prologue* by, 91; his *History of Surrey*, 119, 121; editor of the *Graphic Illustrator*, 190; co-editor with the author of the *British Atlas*, 221; extensive topographical tour in company with the author, 238; "Beauties of England and Wales" undertaken in conjunction with the author, 238; places visited prior to publication, 240; "History of Enamelling," for Rees's *Cyclopedia*, 268; "General Ambulator" by, 279; accounts of Bedfordshire, Berkshire, &c., in conjunction with author, 300
Brewster, Sir David, title and pension conferred on, 11; his opinion on the *Letters of Junius*, 20; his speech at the British Association, 153
Bridgewater, Earl of, 172, 303
———— Treatises, writers of the, 303
Bright, John, 11
Brislington church and Broomwell house, 211
Bristol, compared and contrasted between the years 1798 and 1852, and the author's early connection with it, 200; natives and literary characters, 201; History of the Church of St. Mary Redcliffe, 202; life of Chatterton, *ib.*; design for a medal on the restoration of Redcliffe church, 203; Seyer's charters, *ib.*; Eagles on the Rowley MSS., *ib.*; T. Proctor's inquiries about Redcliffe church, 204; the author engaged with W. Hosking and G. Godwin in restoring that church, *ib.*; "Nil Desperandum's" contribution, 205; the author's History of the Cathedral, *ib.*; peculiarities of the cathedral, 206; *Lectures on Architectural Antiquities* and the *Great Western Railway*, by the author, 207; death of the Rajah Rammohun Roy, 208; visit with the Archæological Institute, 209; "Arno's Vale," near Bristol, 210; view of the city from Brislington, 210, 211
Bristol, Lord, 361
British Association at Birmingham, and Sir David Brewster's speech, 153
*British Atlas*, by Britton & Brayley, 221
*British Gallery of Pictures*, published by Longman & Co., 270; artists engaged on, 271
Britten, William, 40
Britten, Thomas, 62
———— William, 41
———— Samuel, 41, 64
———— family, obscurity of its history: parish registers, 40
Brougham, H. Lord, 7, 21, 203, 272, 365
Brown, R., 11
———— Lancelot, 141
———— Christopher, 264
———— Capability, 361
———— Thomas, 264, 274
———— Charles, 274
Browne, W. R., 31
Bruce, Rev. Mr., 147
Brunel, Sir M. J., 10
———— J. K., 10
Brunton Miss, 321
Bryant, Elizabeth, 74
Brydges, Sir Egerton, his Auto-Biography, 2, 4, 248

Buchan's *Domestic Medicine*, popularity of, 67, 251
Buckingham, Duke of, his unpublished *Letters of Junius*, 20
—————— J. Silk, 12
Buckland, Rev. Dr., 11, 212, 303
Bull, Dr. John, 320
Bulwer, Sir E. L., 7, 21
Bunn, Alfred, 10
Bunsen, Chevalier, 21
Buonaparte's projected invasion of England, 149; medal struck to commemorate, 150
Burgess, George, 7
Burke, Edm., 90, 95, 107, 137, 145, 260, 383
Burney, Mr., 254
Busby, Dr., employed by Sir Richard Phillips, 255; anecdotes of the Dr. and his son, 255
Bust of the author proposed as public testimonial, 17
Butler, Rev. Dr., master of the Shrewsbury grammar-school, a friend of the author, 161, 166
—————— Samuel, 172
Byron, Lord, on religious hypocrisy, 8; 80, 245, 381, 386

Cadell, Thomas, Cadell, William, and Cadell and Davies, booksellers, notice of, 306
—————— Thomas, 257, 306
—————— Thomas, jun., 306
Calcott, E., 366
Callcott, Sir A. W., 9
Camden, William, 135
Campbell, Lord, 21
—————— Thomas, 4, 7, 230
Canning, George, 169, 290
Cannynges, William, 201
Canova, 366
Cantilupe, Bishop, 179
Capitalists and Commercial Men, testimonials to, 9
Caractacus, British prince, conquered and taken prisoner to Rome, 165
Carbury, Earl of, 173
Cardon, 271
Carey, David, 285
—————— George Saville, 320
—————— Rev. H. F., 297
Carleton, William, 7
Carlisle, Earl of, 11
Carlyle, Thomas, 297
Caroline, Queen, 384
Carpenter, Rev. Lant, 208
Carr, Sir John, action against Vernor and Hood for libel, 286
Carrington's "Dartmoor," quoted, 25
Carte, Thomas, 220
Carter, John, 176
Cartismandua, Queen, 165
Cartwright, Major, 185
Cary, Mr., 319
CASTLE COMBE, notice of, 387; manor-house of, 388; author's visit to Madam Scrope at, 388; History of, by G. P. Thomson-Scrope, 393; view of the market-cross of, 396; view of an altar-tomb in the church of, 397; font and base of a column in, 398; party at, 447
Catcott, George, 201
"Cathedral Antiquities," pirated, 5
Chalmers, Alexander, author of *Biographical Dictionary*, &c., notice of, 262, 263, 307

Chalmers, George, author of *Caledonia*, 336
—————— Rev. Thomas, 303
Chambers, Ephraim, author of the original *Cyclopædia*, 267
—————— Robert, 7
—————— Sir William, 353
—————— William, 7
Champion, J. O., his anecdotes on the hardships of an itinerant player's life, 117, 118
Chandler, Dr. S., 220
Chandos, Marquis of, 12
—————— testimonial, 12
Chantrey, Sir F., 9, 226, 366
Chapman, Mr., engagement of the author at his theatre, 97; the theatre destroyed by fire, 99
—————— Captain, 220
Characteristics of auto-biography, 3
Charlton house, 434
Chateaubriand, Viscount, a recipient of the literary fund, 244
Chatham, Earl of, 8
Chatterton, Thos., 126; brief notice of, 202
Chelwood parsonage, lines written in the garden of, 214
Chepstow, town and castle, visit to, 199
Cheyne, Dr., 220
Child's caul, the author born with one: superstitious prognostic therefrom, 41
Childs, Robert, 306
Chippenham, author's school-fellows there, 49, 54; visit to, after his apprenticeship, 75; notice of the town and residents, 336—339
Christie, G. H., 324
—————— James, sen., book-auctioneer, 323; sale-rooms of, 324
—————— James, jun., 325
—————— Rev. R. C., 398
Church Stretton, 163; courtesy of the Rev. J. Mainwaring, 164; mountain fortresses in the district of, 165
Clare, John, 297
Clarence, Duke of, 49
Clarendon, Earl of, 281
Clark, Rev. Richard, 320
Clarke, Mr., 274
—————— Francis, 153
—————— Henry, 9
—————— Jeremiah, 281
—————— Mr., his *Repertorium*, 324
—————— T. H., 205
Claverton, church, village, and scenery, 234
Clerkenwell in 1787, notice of, 61
Cliffe, C. F., his *Book of South Wales*, &c., 190, 198
Clive, R. H., 171
Clothiers' visits to author's native village, 33
Clowes and Sons, extensive printing establishment of, 277
Clubs and societies attended in youth, 73, 82, 83
Coachmakers' Hall, debating society, 89, 92
Cobb, James, 4
Cobbett, William, 2, 7, 248; notice of, 294
Cobden, Richard, testimonial to, and his letter acknowledging the bounty of the subscribers, 12
Cockrane, J. G., 294
Colbourne, William, 343
Colburn, Henry, 287, 317
Cole, R., 315
Coleridge, S. T., 2, 7, 186, 297, 370; Cottle's Reminiscences of, 201
Collard, Mr., 33

Collings, Mr., 219
Collins, Arthur, 297
——— Mr., 274
——— William, 366
Colman, Mr., 29
Colman, George, the younger, 54, 92; his *Squeeze for St. Paul's*, 96, 196, 320
Combe, James, 338
——— William, extraordinary and prolific author, 313; *Dr. Syntax's Tour* by, 315
Companies (Public) testimonials to directors and officers, 9
Comus (Milton's) acted at Ludlow castle, 172
Coneybeare, Rev. J. J., his *Essay on Epitaphs*, 217; History of Bath Abbey Church dedicated to his memory, 218
——— Rev. W. C., notice of, 211
Coningsby, Lord, 176
Cooke, Charles, 256, 257
——— E. W., 366, 391
——— G. F., eminent tragedian, 126; notorious drunkard, 351; dinner with the author, and its effects, 352
——— G. W., 21
——— John, notice of, 250, 256
Cooper, Sir Astley, 257
Cope, 366
Copeland, T., 84
Corbould, R., 254
Corney, 248
Cornwall, Barry, 297
Correspondence on the authorship of *Junius's Letters*, 21
Corresponding societies, 94
Corrie, Rev. Dr., 153
Corsham-house, 439
Costello, Miss, 119
Cosway, Richard, 310
Cottle's *Reminiscences of Coleridge, Southey*, &c., 201; joined Southey in an edition of Chatterton's works, 202
Cottingham, L. N., 178
Country and Town contrasted, 162
County histories, 456
——— history, treatment of a, 459
Courtier, Peter, 256; notice of, 279
Cowley, Abraham, 298
Cowper, William, 162
Coxe, Peter, auctioneer and poet, 324, 356
——— Mr., 135
——— Rev. William, 7, 245, 324, 328
Crabbe, Rev. George, 381; extract from his poem of *The Village*, 382; early struggles of, 383; patronized by Burke, 383; Chas. Knight's graphic sketch of, 383, 384; the author's introduction to, 384; his career and conduct at Trowbridge, 385; death of, 386; lines to the memory of, 387
Creed, Richard, 9
Crocker, Philip, 451
Croker, John Wilson, 3, 232
Croly, Rev. George, 297
Cromwell, Oliver, his supposed residence at Clerkenwell, 62
——— T., *History of Clerkenwell* by, 62, 82
Crosby, B., 280
Crotch, Master, 126
Crowe, E. Evans, 7
——— William, 364
——— Rev. W., 237
Cruelty of rustic labourers, 59
Cruikshank, George, artist, his designs, 111, 128, 129, 218, 291

Cruttwell, Rev. C., 240
Crutwell, Richard, 217
Cubitt, Thomas, 8
Cumberland, George, 239
——— Richard, his Auto-Biography, 2, 3; 245, 257, 327
Cunningham, Peter, secretary to the Testimonial to the author, 16, 119, 281
Cunningham, Allan, 207, 225, 288, 297
Cunnington, William, memoir of, 467—473
——— William, of Devizes, 445
Curll, Edward, 297
Curtis, John, 11
Cyclopædia, the original, compiled by Ephraim Chambers, 267; the *New*, edited by Dr. Abraham Rees, 268; the author's contributions to and reminiscences of, 268; artists engaged on, 269

Dacre, Mrs., 105
Dallas, Mr. 144
Dallaway, Rev. J., 288, 305
Dalton, Dr. John, 11
Daniel, George, 304
——— T., 220
D'Arblay, Madame, 223
"Dartmoor," poem by Carrington, quoted, 25
Davies, Rev. E., 7
——— John, 220
——— William, 306
Davenport, R. A., works written by, 93; his epigram on the *School of Eloquence*, 93; editor of Rivington's *Annual Register*, 248, 256, 260
Davy, Sir Humphrey, 11, 201
Dayes, Edward, 256
Debating societies frequented by the author, 73, 89, 92; their popularity offensive to Government, 94, 95
De Camp, Miss, 116
Dedications to booksellers, and Dr. Johnson's remarks on, 219
De la Beche, Sir H. T., 11
Delane, W. F. A., 11
De Loutherbourg's *Eidophusikon*, 97; description of it, 98, 99
Democrats, prosecution and trial of, 95, 181
Denman, Lord, 12
D'Eon, Chevalier, anecdotes of, 83
De Quincey, Thomas, 297
Derham, Mr., 249
Dewhurst, Mr., 270
Dibdin, Charles, sen., author of popular naval songs, notice of, 104—106
——— Charles, jun., notice of, 108—111
——— Rev. Thomas Frognall, notice of, 105, 248, 288, 304, 394
——— Thomas, 108, 109
——— Mr. and Mrs. Thomas, 101; a witty dialogue between, 102
——— family of, 91, 97, 100, 101, 102, 104, 105, 106, 108, 109, 110, 352
Dibdins (the three) notice of, 107—110
Dickens, Charles, 7, 111, 115, 121, 245, 315
Dighton, Mr., painter, caricaturist, and favourite comic singer, 101
Dilly, Charles, notice of, 285
Dinely, Sir John, anecdotes of, 84
Dinner (Public) to the author, 16; report of the speeches, 18
Dinners (Public) *see* Testimonials, 7—13
Directors of railway companies, testimonials to, 9
Dirty Dick of Leadenhall Street, 273

Disraeli, Benjamin, 12
——— Isaac, 115, 248
Dockray, R. B., 9
Dodsley, Robert, 260, 383
Domestic architecture, ancient, at Ludlow, 131; at Leominster, 175; at Hampton Court, 176; at Hereford, 179
Donaldson, Professor, his letter on the testimonial to the author, 8, 16
Donovan, Mr., 260, 269
Douce, F., 358
Dovaston, Mr., 166
Downton Castle, the seat of Richard Payne Knight, M.P., visit of the author to, 168, 169; his bequest to British Museum, 170
Drakard, John, 261
Drake, Dr., 245; his *Shakspere*, 302, 307
Draycot-house, in the author's boyhood, 48; party at, 447
Drayton, Michael, 298
Dryden, John, 219, 281
Du Bois, Edward, 4, 21; on Ritson's affected orthography, 88; his *Every Man his own Punster*, 102; his *Satirical Essay on Punning*, 102; his dancing at Sadler's Wells, 116; author of *My Pocket Book*, 286
Dugdale, Sir William, 156, 158, 252
Duncan, John S., his lines to the memory of the Rev. George Crabbe, 386, 387
Dunlop, William, 352
Dunning, John, 362
Dyce, Rev. Alexander, 304

Eagles, Thomas, on the "Rowley Controversy," 203; 210
Earlom, Mr., 62
Easthope, Sir John, 11
Eastlake, Sir Charles L., 9, 366
Easton, Mr., 286
Eating-houses, frequented by learned men, 83; eccentric visitors to one in Great Turnstile, *ib.*
Eccentric characters: Chevalier D'Eon, 83; Sir John Dinely, 84; Joseph Ritson, 87
Eden, Rev. John, 204
Egan, Pierce, 322
Eidophusikon, the author engaged at the exhibition of the, 97; description of the, by W. H. Pyne, 98
Elizabeth, Queen, 117
Ellacombe, Rev. H. T., vicar of Bitton, a friend to the author, 40, 212
Ellenborough, Lord, 292
Ellesmere, Earl of, 51
Elliott, Robert, a school-fellow of the author, 50; death of, 345
Ellis, Charles, author of a volume of poems, criticised and vindicated, 318
——— Agar, 365
——— George, 290
——— Sir Henry, 7, 358
Elm and Ash, 406
Eloquence, on the utility of, 89; school of, Old Change, satire on its members, 93
Elton, C. A., 297
Empson, Charles, 225
Encyclopædia Londinensis, notice and print of Salisbury cathedral, 279, 280
Enfield, Dr., 270, 283
Engineers, testimonials to, 10
English, E. F., 229
Erskine, Lord, 90, 181
Essex, Earl of, 175, 365

Essex, Mr., an early friend and adviser, 68; his son William, enamel painter, 69
Etheridge, George, 119
Etty, William, 9
European Magazine, notice of its editors, 286
Evans, Thomas, 274
——— R. H., 323
——— Mr., 69
Evelyn, John, 119
Everett and Co., 337
Examiner newspaper, its proprietors and its character, 316
Excise laws, their evil influence, 64
Exciseman's visits during apprenticeship to wine-trade, 64

Faden, Mr., 319
Fairburn, John, the author's first patron, and publisher of his early works, 128, 129
Falconer, Dr., 217, 220, 236, 270
Family ancestry and connexions of the author, 37
Farleigh Hungerford, and castle, 461
Farmer, Rev. Dr. R., 325
Farming, *see* Agriculture
Farquhar, Mr., 227
Farren, Mr., 91
Fellows, Sir Charles, 12
——— Mr., 285
Fellow-servants in apprenticeship, their general ignorance and vulgarity, 71
Feltham, John, author of *A Tour in the Isle of Man*, 236
Fenning, Elizabeth, 291
Ferrier, Dr., 21
Field, Barron, 4
Fielding, Henry, 220, 333
Field-sports, early lesson of the author in, 43
Finden, 289
First love, proofs of its engrossing influence, 74—77
Fisher, Henry, 131, 313
Fleet Street, distinguished residents in, 297
Fonblanque, A. M., 11
Fonthill, 20
Forbes, Sir Charles, 13
——— Professor, 11
Ford, Richard, 394
Forrest, Mr., 237, 239
Forster, C., notice of his publications, 286, 290
Fosbroke, Rev. T. D., 192, 193, 204, 237
Foster, glass-painter at Windsor, 139
——— John, 201
——— Mr., 139
Fox, Charles James, 8, 90, 95, 107, 239
——— W. J., 248
Fox (The) sagacity and cunning of, 35, 36 (*wood-cut*)
Foxley, seat of Uvedale Price, visit to, 188
——— village, 188
Franchi, Chevalier, 227
Francis, Sir Philip, his claims to the authorship of *Junius*, 19, 297, 357
Franklin, Dr., his Auto-Biography, 2, 107, 248, 259
Freeling, Sir Francis, 234
Frere, Hookham, 290
Fricker, Edith, 207
Friends, assumed, of the author, 482
Fry, Elizabeth, 12
Fryer, Edward, M.D., notice of, 466
Fuller, Thomas, quotations from, 329
Funerals, absurd ceremonials at, 87

Gaby, R. H., friend to the author, 75, 338; notice of, 344
Gagging Bills passed, 94; prosecution of distinguished democrats, 95
Gainsborough, Thomas, R.A., 98, 220; brief notice of, 225
Gale, Roger, 176
Gandy, Mr., 139
Garbett, Rev. T., 178
Gardening, controversy on, 136
Gardner, Mr., 253
Garrick, David, 220, 320
Garrow, Mr., 90
Gas, its first appearance in any theatre, 101
Geddes, Dr., 283
Genius, precocious, instances of, 126
Geography, map, and chart publishers: Cary, Faden, Smith, and Wyld, 319
*George Barnwell*, Lillo's once famous tragedy of, 71
George the Third, 94, 360; his visit to St. Paul's, and Colman's lines on, 96
——— the Fourth, 7
Gethan, Mr., 197
Gibbon, Edw., 245; his Auto-Biography, 2, 21
Gibson, John, 366
Gifford, William, 37, 245, 290, 295; quarrel with Peter Pindar, 275; trial with John Williams, 276
Gilbart, J. W., 9
Gildas, Mr., 220
Gill, Robert, 9
Gilpin, Rev. William, his works on the Wye, &c., 136, 190, 336
Gloucester, Duchess of, 361
Godwin, George, F.R.S., secretary to the testimonial to the author, 16, 23; succeeded Mr. Hosking at Redcliffe church, 204
——— William, 4, 95, 181, 251, 283
——— Mr., 217, 219
Goodrich castle (1798) court of (1831), 193, 194; visit of Architects' Institute to, 195
Goodrich, Mr., 229
Goodridge, H. E., 213; Lansdowne tower from his designs, 292
Goldsmid, Baron de, 9
Goldsmith, Dr., 274, 333, 354
Goodyere, Sir J. D., 85
Gore, Sir Thomas, 407
——— Mrs., 232
Gossett, Dr., 319
Gough, Lord, 10
——— Richard, a learned and enthusiastic topographer and antiquary, 117, 135, 300, 332, 334
Gould, Nathaniel, chairman of dinner to the author, 16
Government pensions, often misapplied, 6
——————————— to literary and scientific men (*see* Testimonials), 7—13
Graham, Sir James, 12
Grant and Griffiths, 282
Graves, Rev. R., author of *The Spiritual Quixote*, &c., 143, 217, 234, 235
Gray, J. E., 11
——— Thomas, 9
——— Thomas (poet) 190, 239
Great Western Railway, lectures on the, 209
Greatrakes, William, 357
Gregory, Dr., 283
Greig, Mr., 136
Grenville, Lord, 365
Greville, Colonel, 314
Grey, Sir George, 12

Greyhound, anecdote of a, 46
Griffith, Dr., editor of *Monthly Rev.* 259, 260
——— Moses, artist and servant, 336
Grignion, Mr., 254
Grimaldi, "Joe," 101; memoir of, by "Boz," 111; anecdote of the effect of his acting, 111, 112
Grittleton, parish of, 399
——— house, improvements, 399
Grose, Captain, 305
——— Francis, a celebrated antiquary, 336
Guidot, Mr. 220
Gunn, Rev. J., 305
Gurwood, Colonel, 7
Gutch, Rev. John, 140, 237

Hacker, C., 205
Haghe, L., 391
Hagley, the author's visit to, 159; Warner's description of, 159, 160
Hales, Mr., 220
Halifax, Lord, 219
Hall, Rev. Robert, 201
——— S. C., 160
——— Mr., 251
Hallam, Mr., 365
Hamilton, Duke of, 13
——— Mr., 361
——— Sir W. R., 11
Hamper, William, letters to the author from, 155; proposed History of Warwickshire by, 156; memoir of, 157; sale of his valuable collection of books, &c., 158
Hampton Court, Herefordshire, the author's visit to, 175; Stukeley's remarks on, 176
Hanhart, M. and N., 394
Harding, J. D., 391
Hardinge, Viscount, 10
Hardwick, Mr., 178
Hardy, Thomas, 95
Hare (The) its timidity and habits, 25, 46
Harford, C. J., advised the History of Redcliffe church, 202
Harlow, Mr., 366
Harper, Messrs., 280
Harrington, Dr., 217, 218, 223, 236
——— Sir John, 220
——— Sir Edward, 224
Harris, John, publisher, 282
——— Sir W. Snow, 11
Harrison, John, notice of his publications, 135, 251, 254, 256, 258
Hartham park, 442
Hatcher, H., author's memoir of, 18, 22, 307
Havell, Mr., 141
Hawkins, J. S., 305
Haydon, B. R., 9
Hayman, Frank, 118, 172
Hayter, Sir George, 9
Hayti, Christophe, King of, 321
Hazlewood, Joseph, 204
Hazlitt, William, 236, 295
Head, Sir Francis, his account of Clowes's printing-house, 277
Hearne, Thomas, 420; notice of, 424
Heath, Charles, 301
——— James, 254
Heraldic absurdities, 39
HEREFORD, visit to, 176; History of the Cathedral by the author, 179; fall of the western front, &c., 177; Wyatt's alterations and additions to, 178; Dr. Merewether, dean of, 178, 179; Cottingham's restoration of, 178; ancient map of the

world preserved in, 179; extract from the *Picturesque Antiquities of English Cities*, 179, 180; stone crosses at, 180
Herschel, Sir John, 11
—— Sir William, 220, 239
Hewlett, James, a celebrated painter of fruit and flowers, 50, 217, 225
Highworth, stocks and pillory at, 438
Hill, T. W., of Birmingham, 150
—— Arthur, of Bruce castle, Tottenham, 151
—— Edwin, controller of postage stamps, 151
—— Frederick, assistant secretary, General Post-Office, 151
—— Matthew, recorder of Birmingham, 151
—— Rowland, testimonial to his Post-Office reforms, 13; secretary to the General Post-Office, 151
—— Lord, 10
—— Dr. 267
—— Thomas, 266, 285
Hillier, Richard, the author's uncle, anecdotes and characteristics of, 43—46, 75
—— Samuel, the author's grandfather, characteristics of, 36, 42—44
—— Samuel, the author's uncle, characteristics of, 60, 64, 66, 75
—— family connections, 413
Hoadly, Bishop, 281
Hoare, Sir Richard Colt, 27; his opinion of topography, 332; his *Ancient* and *South Wiltshire*, 451
—— William, R.A., and Prince Hoare, natives of Bath, 225, 226
Hobbes, Thomas, notice of, 422
Hobhouse, Sir Benjamin, 108, 361, 385
Hodgson, Edm., auctioneer, notice of, 275
—— T, editor of *London Catalogue of Books*, 277
Hogg, Alexander, 251, 254; notice of his publications, 257
—— James, 7
Hogarth, William, 288, 365
Holbein, Hans, 176
Holcroft, Thomas, 116, 127, 181, 251, 283; his Auto-Biography, 2; persecuted by the Government for his opinions, 95; editor of *The Wit's Magazine*, 256
Holford, R., 319
Holland, Lord, 361, 365
Holloway, T., 139, 237, 239; engraver to the Literary Magazine and British Review, 286
Holmes, George, 310
Hood, Thomas, 4, 118, 286, 297; lines on a Child's Caul, 41; on Ham-house, 119
Hook, Theodore, 4, 7, 245; notice of, 295; his versatile talents, 296
Hone, William, 275; notice of his works and trial, 291—293
Honours conferred on military and naval officers, 6. See Testimonials, 7—13
Horn-book superseded in modern schools, 42
Horne, R. H., 248
Horner, Francis, 272
Hosking, William, engaged with the author to restore Redcliffe church, Bristol, 204
Houlton, Colonel, 400; notice of, 465
Howard, John, 8
—— Mr., 251
—— Henry, 269, 366
Howes, Mr., 274
Hudson, George, 10
Hughes, John Thomas, an early friend, his characteristics and singular career, 88—92; author of an amusing farce, 91

Hughes, Richard, 103
—— Sir Richard, 88
—— J. T., 89, 92, 94
Huish, Captain, 10
Hume, David, his Auto-Biography, 2
—— Joseph, M.P., letter to the author, 15
Hungerfords, the family of the, 405
Hunt, John and Leigh, projectors and editors of *The Examiner*, 4, 7, 245, 248, 316
—— F. Knight, 307
—— John, 4, 316, 317
—— Robert, artist, 317
Hunter, Rev. Joseph, a learned antiquary and topographer, 7, 220, 331, 332, 394, 463
Huntington, Wm., "S.S." his blasphemous hypocrisy, 80; anecdotes of his life, 81
Hurleston, T. E., 366
Hurst, John, 265
—— Thomas, 218
—— Thomas, bookseller, notice of, 265, 266
Hutton, William, his loss in the Birmingham riots, 145, 146; visited by the author, 147; his tour to the *Roman Wall*, 147; Auto-Biography of, 148; 2, 155, 187
—— Catharine, 143, 144
Hypochondriacism, a singular case of, 53
Hypocrisy in religion, illustrated in the author's early associates, 79; lines by Lord Byron on, 80

Ignorance in the author's native village, 29, 32, 39, 42, 54, 55, 57
Illness of the author, repeated attacks, 2, 22, 66, 67
Indentures of apprenticeship, their formal phraseology, 63
Ingram, Rev. James, of Oxford, 140
Intemperance and violence of the author's relatives, 43, 58
Interruptions to the author's progress with his work, 18, 22
Intoxication, observations on, 348; examples of, 348—351
Ireland, Samuel, his works, 135, 190
—— W.H., his Shaksperian forgeries, 144
Irving, G. V., 225
—— Washington, 242
Ivory, James, 7
Jackson, Rev. J. E., 213, 391, 405
—— John, 301, 366
—— Mr., 225
Jacob's Well, Barbican, spouting club at, 83, 92
Jacobins and Anti-Jacobins, their meetings and discussions, 94
James, Dr., 282
—— G. P. R., 21
Jameson, Mrs., 336, 356, 364, 365
Jamieson, Rev. Dr., 7
Jardine, Sir William, 294
Jeffrey, Lord, 7, 272
Jekyll, Mr., 362, 365
Jenyns, Mr., 294
Jenner, Dr., 13; vaccine inoculation, 388
Jephson, Dr., 13
Jerdan, William, 248; editor of *The Literary Gazette*, 318
Jerrold, Douglas, 231, 315
Jervas, Mr., 365
Johnson, Dr., on literary biographies, 2; his habit of frequenting an eating-house, 83; his remark on the Leasowes, 160; his rebuke on Dryden's dedications, 219; 248, 289; various editions of his *Dictionary*, 306

Johnson, J., patron of literary persons, 282
—— William, 274
Jones, John Gale, a political orator, 95, 320
—— Stephen, editor of *The European Magazine*, 286; works by, 301, 302
Joplin, T., 9
Journey to Plympton, in Devonshire, on a love-suit, 74—76; its doleful results, 77
Joyce, Jeremiah, notice of, 283
Junius's Letters, the author's *Essay* on their authorship, 19; his correspondence on the subject, 20; the Duke of Buckingham's unpublished Letters of, 20; Sir David Brewster's opinion of, 20; new edition of, by Henry G. Bohn, 20; Colonel Barré's claims to authorship of, 19, 357
Juvenile prodigies, notices of, 126

Kane, Sir Robert, 11
Keane, Lord, 10
Kearsley, George, 289
Kelly, Alderman T., 258
—— Michael, 126
—— Miss F., 321
Kemble, Charles, 126, 130
—— John P., 10, 100, 126, 131, 320, 351
Kenchester, a Roman station, 180
Key, family of, 253
Keynsham, ammonites at and legend of, 211
Keyse, Thomas, 120
Kidd, John, M.D., 303
—— Rev. T., 7
King, Edward, author of *Munimenta Antiqua*, his visit to the author, 335
King and Lochee, book auctioneers, 325, 328
Kington St. Michael, author's native place, described, 27, 55; collections for its history, 27; birth-place of John Aubrey, 28; house in which the author was born (*woodcuts*), 56, 57; departure for London, 60, 61; return after six years, eventful changes, 75
Kirby, Rev. William, 303
Kitchener, Dr., 327
Knight, Charles, public dinner to, 8; his account of Sir John Dineley, 84; 119, 147, 245; his *Thirty Years' Peace*, 250; *Pictorial London* by, 279; *British Almanac*, 281, 295; his remarks on Cobbett, 295; graphic sketch of Rev. G. Crabbe, 383, 384; 430
—— Richard Payne, M.P., 136; description of Downton castle, the seat of, 168; literary works by, 169; *On the Progress of Society*, 169; his gift to the British Museum, 170; 237
—— Price, and Repton, controversy on gardening by, 136
Knowles, J. Sheridan, 8
Konig, Frederick, 299
Kotzebue, M., 129, 130
Kyrle, John, the "Man of Ross," 191

Lackington. James, 103, 142, 248
Laing, William, 87
Lamb, Charles, 201, 297
Landor, Richard, 12
Landscape (The) a poem, 169, 361
Landseer, Charles, 366
—— Sir Edwin, 269, 366, 391
—— Thomas, 391
Lane, W., proprietor of Minerva Press, 287
—— G., editor of *British Press*, &c., 309
Langhorne, Henry, 124; notice of, 125; extract of a letter from, 126

Lansdowne, William, Marquess of, reception of the author by, 352; see Bowood, 352
—— Henry, Marquess of, 364, 380, 384, 385
—— Marchioness of, tribute to memory of, by the author, 367; Moore's traits of, 368; Lord John Russell's tribute to, 368
Lardner's *Cabinet Cyclopædia*, published by Longman and Co, 273
Las Casas, Comte, 149
Latimer, R., 47
Lawrence, Sir Thos., at Bath, 9, 170, 224, 366
Law and Literature, their asserted incompatibility, 86
—— students at debating societies, 89
Lawyers, titles and honours conferred on, 8
—— offices, engagements in, 82, 88
Laxton, William, 11
Layard, A. H., 12
Leasowes (The), the property of Shenstone, notice of, 160
Lectures by the author:—Birmingham, 148, 151; Bristol, 207; Bath, 221
—— Thelwall's political, &c., 184
Lee, Miss, 220
—— Rev. Dr., 134
Legal phraseology, its formality, 63
Leigh Delamere, anecdotes of, 402
—— and Sotheby, booksellers and auctioneers, 322, 328
—— Hanbury, 107
—— George, 322
Le Keux, J. H., 484
—— John and Henry, 194
Lely, Sir Peter, 176
Leman, Rev. T., 220; his present to the Bath Institution, 221; his essays on the Roman roads, 221
Leominster, visits to, by the author, 175
Leslie, C. R., 366
Letterman, Mr., 279
Lettsom, Dr. J. C., 355
Leveson, Sir Richard, 162
Lewis, John, 343
—— M. G., 4
Lichfield, Mrs., 91
Lillo, George, 71
Lind, Jenny, 10
Lindleys (the), 220
Linnel, Mr., 366
Lintot, Bernard, 297
Liston, John, 4
Literary men, memoirs of, 2; pensions, &c., conferred on, 7
—— piracy, 5, 69
—— Essay, testimonial to the author, 17
—— Fund, 107; applicants to, 244
—— works worthy of perusal, 248
—— Magazine and British Review, 286
—— Gazette, origin and editor of, 317
—— and scientific institutions established in London, 127
Literature, Royal Society of, ten honorary members pensioned by George IV., 7
—— rights of, vindicated by author, 246
Little Britain, booksellers resided there, 252
Llandaff, Edward, Bishop of, 387
Lloyd, Charles, 201
Local attachment, native place, 25
Locke, Joseph, 10
Lockhart, J. G., 245, 381
Lofft, Capel, 285
London: boyish aspirations, 60; first journey to, 61

London and Birmingham Railway, description of the, 154
—————— Magazine, 260
Londonderry, Ordnance survey of, 458
Long, Charles, 392
—————— Sir J. Tilney, 34, 343, 392; his seat at Draycot, 48; his daughter and her worthless husband, 49
Longman, Thomas, 259, 261, 264
—————— T. N., 264, 303
—————— and Co., the author's connection with, in various publications, 247; notice of the firm, 264—272; *Bibliotheca Anglo-Poetica* published by, 266; dinner parties of, 273; 287, 304, 307, 313, 376, 377
Lonsdale, Mark, author of burlettas, pantomimes, and songs, 100; his noted song of *Abraham Newland*, 100; memoir, 101
—————— Mrs., one of the author's employers in youth, her artful cajolery, 78, 79
—————— James, 315
Loudon, Mrs., 8
Loutherbourg, De, inventor and painter of the "Eidophusikon," 97
Love, Christopher, 37
Lovel, Robert, 201
Lowry, Mr., 269
Luckington, 409
Luckombe, Philip, 325, 326
Luders, C., 220
Ludlow, visited by the author, 170; *Early History of*, by Rev. J. B. Blakeway, 171; Rev. Hugh Owen's description of, 171, 172; castle of, 172; Milton's *Comus* first acted in the, 172; Butler's residence at, 173; a personal incident to author at, 173, 174
Luke, Sir Samuel, 173
Lumley, B., 10
Lydiard-Tregose, 435
Lyell, Sir Charles, 11, 395
Lynedoch, Lord, 10
Lysons, Daniel, 221
—————— Samuel, 220, 221, 307
—————— Messrs, 245
Lyte, Alderman Isaac, his almshouses at Kington St. Michael, 56
Lyttleton, Lord, 159

Mc Adam, Sir James, 10
Macaulay, Thomas B., 8, 21, 245
Macauley, Mrs., 220
Mc Connell, J. E., 10
Mc Creery, John, printer, and author of *The Press*, a poem, 287
Mac Culloch, J. R., 8, 245
Macdonald, Flora, 133
Mc Donnel, Sir E., 10
Mackay, Dr. Charles, 245
Mackenzie, Dr. R. S., 8, 21, 291
Mackintosh, Sir James, 8, 364
Macklin, Thomas, 224, 294
Maclise, Mr., 366
Mc Neill, Sir John, 10
Macready, W. C., 10
Madden, Sir F., 8
Magazines and Reviews noticed:—Annual Review, 269, 279; Athenæum, 270, 278; Attic Miscellany, 127; British Critic, 259; British Magazine, 255, 257; British Review, 286; Cobbett's Weekly Register, 294; Edinburgh Review, 272, 289; European Magazine, 286; Gentleman's Magazine, 300; Ladies' Magazine, 262; Ladies' Pocket Magazine, 256, 258; Literary Gazette, 317; Literary Magazine, 286; London Magazine, 296; Monthly Magazine, 255, 270, 283; Monthly Mirror, 285; Musical Magazine, 255; Musical World, 320; New Monthly Magazine, 317; Novelist's Magazine, 254; Pocket Magazine, 256; Poetical Magazine (Vernor & Hood's) 285; Poetical Magazine (Ackerman's) 315; Quarterly Review, 289, 290; Sporting Magazine, 127; Town and Country Magazine, 262; Wit's Magazine, 256
*Magna Britannia*, by Messrs. Lysons, 221
Maidford, 409
Mainwaring, Rev. J., 164, 237
Major, John, bookseller, notice of, 288, 289
Malcolm, J. P., author of *Londinum Redivivum*, anecdote of, 112
Malmesbury Abbey, 415
—————— Earl of, 365
Malthus, Rev. T. R., 8
Malton, Mr., 305
Man, the machinery, the physical and metaphysical economy of, 339; extract from Young's *Night Thoughts* on, 340
Manche, Thomas J., 203
Mann, John, 240
Mansfield, Lord, 360
Marble bust proposed as a testimonial to the author, 17
Markland, J. H., notice of, 234
Marmontel, M., 130
Marriage of the author, 2
Marsden, J. H., 304
Martin, B., his popular publications, 67, 287
—————— John, 9, 60, 299
Martineau, Miss, her *Introduction to the History of the Peace*, 245, 250
Mason, Mr., 190
Mathew, Rev. Theobald, 13
Mathews, Charles, comedian, 4, 91, 123, 126, 150, 322, 352
Mathias, Rev. T. J., 8
Mavor, Rev. W. F., notice of, 142
Mawman, Joseph, bookseller, 285
Mechi, Mr., his agricultural experiments, 411
Medal proposed as a testimonial to author, 17
—————— testimonial from the King of Prussia to the author, *see* engraving
Medical men, titles and other honours conferred on, 8
Melmoth, William, 220
Memory, its tenacity and power, 31, 59, 61
Mendham, Mr., wine-merchant, apprenticed to him, 62; his course of business, 64, 67; neglect of the author, monotony of apprenticeship, and its effects, 64, 66; emancipation, 66; view in his wine-cellars (*woodcut*) 68; his wife, servants, &c., 71—74; supplies the White Conduit-house, 120
Meredith, John, of Church Stretton, notice of, 163
Merewether, Rev. Dr., Dean of Hereford, 178; his work on the restoration of Hereford cathedral, 179
Methuen, Paul Cobb, 361, 439
Meyler, William, 143, 219
Meylor, Mr., 236
Meyrick, Sir S. R., notice of, 194
Michele, C. E., 11
Military and naval officers, testimonials, 6, 10
Mill, James, 272
Miller, Andrew, 306
—————— Lady, 220, 235

Miller, William, 290
Millers, Rev. George, 305
Millingen, James, 8
Millman, Lady, 203
——— Rev. H. H., 8
Milner, Rev. J., 305
Milton, John, 172
——— Mr., 254, 269
Minerva press, notice of the, 287
Miscellaneous testimonials, 13
Mitchell, Charles, 307
——— Sir F., 12
——— J., 10
——— Robert, 212
Mitford, Rev. J., 304, 369, 382
——— Miss, 8; her description of *Our Village*, 26; contrasted with the author's native village, 27; notice of, 279
Moffatt, Mr., 418
Molesworth, Sir William, 422
Molteno, Mr., 319
Monmouth, visit to, 195; the author's adventure there—"too civil by half," 196
Monotony of apprenticeship, 62; of a lawyer's office, 82
Montague, Basil, 304
Montefiore, Sir Moses, 13
Montgomery, James, 8
*Monthly Magazine* edited by Dr. Aikin, 270; published by Sir Richard Phillips, 283
Monumental inscriptions, remarks on, 483
Monuments, avaricious demands of clergy for erecting, 433
Moore, Thomas, 8, 245, 344, 364, 365, 368, 369, 373; memoir of, by Lord John Russell, 374; his Auto-Biography, 375; Lord Byron's apostrophe on, 376; extracts from his *Diary*, 377, 385; talents and accomplishments of, 378; his liabilities, and retreat to France, 379; death of, 380
More, Hannah, 202, 251
Morgan, Lady, 8
Morland, George, 365
Mornington, Earl of, 49
Morris, Thomas, 109
——— Valentine, 199
Moser, Mr., 286
Moyes, James, 298, 299
Mudie, Miss, 126
Mulready, W., R.A., 9; early works by, 133
Munden, Joseph, 126
Murchison, Sir R., 11
Murderer executed near the author's birthplace, 37
Murray, John, publisher, notice of, 289; 384
Musicians, managers, and actors, testimonials to, 10
*My Pocket Book*, trial concerning, 286

Napier, Sir Charles, 10
——— Sir Charles James, 10
Nares, Rev. Richard, 260
Nash, John, 158, 440
——— Joseph, 394
——— Richard, 223
Native place, attachment to, 25
Naval architects, testimonials to, 9
——— and military officers, testimonials, 6, 10
*Naval Songster*, compiled by the author, 128; addresses from, 128, 129
Neeld, Joseph, M.P., of Grittleton, 399, 400
Neele, Henry, extract from his *Lectures on English Poetry*, 106; 483

Neagle, Mr., 254
Nelson, Earl, 10
——— Viscount, 281
Newberry, Francis, publisher, notice of, 282
Newland, Abraham, song on, 100
Newport, George, 11
Newspaper press, *The Fourth Estate*, observations on the, 307, 308
Newspapers noticed:—Bell's Weekly Messenger, 310; British Press, 309; Dispatch, 296; Examiner, 316; Globe, 309; John Bull, 295; Times, 308
——— and Magazines in last century, 32
Newton St. Loe, remains of Roman villa, 213
——— Bishop, 172
——— Sir Isaac, 90, 107
——— Thomas, 107
——— Sir W., 9, 366
Nichols, John, printer and historian, 88, 271, 300, 301, 336
Nicholson, Peter, 305
Nicolas, Sir Harris, his edition of Ritson's Letters, 87, 88
Nightingale, John, author and editor of various works, 287
Northampton, Marquess of, letter to the author from, 15
*Novelist's Magazine*, by Harrison, 254

O'Brien, Charles, an eccentric character and author, 121; his *Magic Lantern*, 122
Occupation in boyhood, the author's, 55
O'Connell, Daniel, 12
*Odd Fellows' Song Book* by the author, 128
Officers of public companies, testimonials to, 9
O'Keefe, comic author, 92
Old age, Horace Smith on, 4, 5
Oliver, Dr., 220
Opie, John, 269
Origin of the present work explained, 1
Orme, Cosmo, 266
Ormerod, George, 156
Osler, Follet, 152
Ottley, W. Y., 269, 271
"Our Village," described by Miss Mitford, 26; contrasted with "My Village," 27
Ouseley, Sir William, 8
Owen, Rev. Hugh, 166, 171, 237
——— Richard, 11
Oxford, the author's first visit to, 139; further notice of, 140, 141

Paine, Thomas, 251
Palgrave, Sir F., 8, 21, 394
Palmer, John, his improved management of the Post-Office, and grant of £50,000 to, 13
Panton, T., a hypochondriac, anecdote of, 53
Papworth, Mr., architect, notice of, 311
Park, Thomas, 203
Parkes, David, his sympathy with the author, 166; his death, 167
Parker and Wix, solicitors, the author engaged in their office, 88—92
Parr, Rev. Dr., 260
Parents, anecdotes of the author's, 37, 38, 41, 55, 57, 58, 61, 78
Parris, E. T., 366
Parry, Dr., 217, 220, 236
——— Sir William E., 12
Parsons, bookseller, 250, 274
Passionate temperament of the author's maternal relatives, 38, 47, 61, 66

Paternoster Row, notice of, 250, 251; Dr. Thomas Rees's opinions and recollections of booksellers in, 252
Paterson's *Roads*, 282
Patronage in church and state, 6
Pedestrian journeys:—London to Wiltshire, on quitting apprenticeship, 75; thence to Plympton, to urge a love-suit, 76; return to London, 77; tour previous to writing the *Beauties of Wiltshire*, 137; in company with Mr. Brayley, for *Beauties of England and Wales*, 239—242
Pedigrees and armorial bearings, on, 39
Peel, Sir Robert, public dinner to, at Glasgow, 12; 21; his appreciation of literature and literary persons, 246
Pemberton, Charles, his Auto-Biography, 2; notice of, 127; 248
Pembroke, Earl of, 281, 361, 365
Pendergrass, Captain, 187
Penn, Admiral, 201, 203
—— John, 240
—— Granville, 203
Pennant, Thos., author of numerous works on topography, 336
Penrose, Rev. Dr., 140
Pensions and places conferred by Government on literary men and others, 7—13
Pepys, Mr., 119, 252
Perry, James, 308
Peter Pindar, *see* Wolcot
Petrarch, 327
Pettigrew, Dr., 355
Petty, Lord Henry, 364
Phillips, Sir Richard, publisher, 142, 148, 270; notice of, 283, 284
—— Charles, 297
—— Thomas, 127
—— T., R.A., 268, 269
—— Sir Thomas, 159
Phillipstall, Mons., his *Phantasmagoria*, 122
Phipson, William, of Birmingham, 152
Pickering, William, publisher, 303; authors engaged by, 304
Pickersgill, H. W., 366
Piero, the Fonthill dwarf, notice of, 230
Piersefield, walk through the park of, 198; anecdote of Valentine Morris, 199
Pindar, Peter, alias Dr. Wolcot, 275
Pinkerton, John, author, notice of, 272
Pinnock, William, author of *Catechisms*, 279
Piracy of the author's works, 5
Pistrucci, Benedetto, 9
Pizarro, the Life and Adventures of, compiled by the author, 129
—— Sheridan's play of, 129—131
Places of amusement in the early part of the present century, 118
Places and pensions, *see* Pensions
Plagiarisms, literary, 5, 21, 69
Planche, J. R., 10
Plate, service of, proposed as a testimonial to the author, 17
Plympton, pedestrian journey to, 74—77
Poaching in boyhood, its origin in idleness, 29
*Poets' Gallery*, notice of, 293
Political excitement at the close of the last century, 94; *Gagging Bills*, and persecution of distinguished democrats, 95
Politicians, testimonials to, 11
Polwhele, Rev. R., 143, 248
Poole, Thomas, 201
Pope, Alexander, 191, 239, 371
Popham, Rev. Dr., letter to the author, 359

Porter, Sir R. K., his picture of the Storming of Seringapatam, and other large paintings, 131, 132; presents his picture of the Battle of Agincourt to the city of London, 133; his early love of art, 133; notice of his mother and sisters, 134; his death, 135
Porteus, Bishop, 139
Portrait, proposed as a testimonial to the author, 17
Portsmouth, the author's visit to, 138
—— Duchess of, 176
Posthumous testimonials, statues, &c., 8
Post-Office, reforms in the, 13
Pote, Joseph, 295
Pottinger, Sir Henry, 12
Pownall, Governor, 220
Pratt, S. J. C., 142; Ramsey's notice of, 143; Catherine Hutton's remarks on, 144
—— Mr., 237
Precocious genius, instances of, 126
Press (The) testimonials to editors, &c., 10
—— the newspaper, observations on, 307
Price, Rev. Mr., of Oxford, 139
—— Uvedale, notice of, and his works, 188
—— Knight, and Repton, their controversy on gardening, 136
—— Dr., 282
Priestley, Rev. Dr., a victim at the Birmingham riots, 146; portrait of, drawn by the author, 146; 282, 286, 359
Prince, the German, 198
Printers, eminent, notices of:—Baldwin, Charles, 261; Baldwin, Charles, jun., 261; Bensley, Thos., 299; Mc Creery, J., 287; Moyes, James, 298; Nichols, John, 300; Nichols, J. B., 301; Spottiswoode, Andrew, 303; Strahan, Andrew, 302; Valpy, A. J., 301; Walter, John, 308; Woodfall, George, 253; Woodfall, H. S., 253
Prior, Matthew, 281
Private theatres and amateur performances, 90, 91
Prize essay proposed as a testimonial to the author, 17
Proctor, Thomas, letter of inquiry from, about Redcliffe church, Bristol, 203, 209
Prologues and Comic Tales, by Colman, O'Keefe, Peter Pindar, and others, 92
Prout, Dr. William, 303
Provis, John, his facts about the Great Western Railway, 208, 346
Prynne, Mr., 220
Public companies, testimonials to directors and officers of, 9
—— dinner to the author, 16
—— dinners and testimonials, 7—13
—— pensions frequently misapplied, 6
Publishers and authors, mutual dependence and obligations of, 244
Pye, H. J., 143
Pyne, W. H., author and artist, 312


Radcliffe, Mrs. 251
Radnor, Earl of, 361, 450
Raeburn, Sir H., 9
Rammohun Roy, the Rajah, 208
Ramsey, A., 143, 147
Ray, Mr., 249
Raymond, Mr., 255
Readings and music, popular assemblies, 321
Redcliffe church, Bristol, the author's connection with, 164; Essay on, 202; design for a medal on the restoration of, 203; 209

# INDEX.

Redding, Cyrus, 21; notices of Mr. Beckford, 230, 231, 233
Reed, I., editor of *European Mag.*, 286, 328
Rees, Rev. Dr. A., editor of the *Cylopædia*, 141, 245, 251, 256, 267, 278, 302
——— Dr. Thos., his anecdotes of authors, booksellers, and publishers, 253—277, 306; author of a volume on *South Wales*, 279
——— Owen, 264, 305, 376, 377
Religious hypocrisy, instances of, 79, 80
Repton on Corsham-house, *see* Nash
Revett, Mr., 305
*Review, The Quarterly*, originated by John Murray, 289; contributors to, 290; Southey's notice of the author, 247
Reynolds, F., 91
——— Sir J., 77, 137, 226, 324, 365, 377
——— J. H., 297
Richardson, John, one of the proprietors of the *Beauties of England and Wales*, 286
——— W., auctioneer, &c., 319
——— G., 305
——— Sir John, 12
——— John, 286
——— Mr., 319, 328
——— Samuel, 281
——— Rev. B., notice of, 466
Richer, Mr., Master, and Miss, admired tight-rope dancers, 115
Rickman, Mr., 152
Riding, hunting, and coursing, early lessons of the author in, 43—45
Ritson, Joseph, anecdotes of, 86, 87, 88
Rivington, Messrs, publishers, notice of, 259
Roads to the author's native village, 33
Robberds, J. W., 269
Robbins, Mr., 33
Roberts, David, 366
Robertson, Andrew, 9
——— Dr., 130, 245
Robinson, G., G., J. and J., notice of, 261
——— H. C., on the *Utility of Eloquence*, 89, 94
——— J. O., 307
——— Mr., 289
Rodney, Lord, 10
Rodwell, Mr., 299
Roebuck, J. A., 12
Rogers, Samuel, 365
Roget, Dr. P. M., 303
Roman wall, W. Hutton's tour to the, 147
Romney, Mr., 324, 365
Roscius, the young, 126
——— the female, 126
Roscoe, William, 8, 287
——— Robert, 304
Rose, George, 290
——— Stewart, 4
Rosoman, Mr., 72
Ross, Sir John, 13
——— Sir James C., 12
——— Sir W. C., 9
——— town of, Pope and Gilpin's praises of, 191; John Kyrle, "The Man of," 191; Rev. T. D. Fosbroke with author at, 192
Rowlandson, T., 311
Roy, General, 165
——— Rammohun, 208
Rundell, Philip, eminent goldsmith, 400
Russell, Lord John, 12, 365, 374, 380
——— Mr., 269
Rustic life improperly eulogized, 59
Rutland, Duke of, 13, 384
Rylance, Ralph, author, 287

Sadler, Robert, 338; letter from the author to, 339; his reply, 340; notice of, 341; his novel of *Wanley Penson*, 342; legacy to the author, 344; lines on War by, 363
Sadler's Wells Theatre, notice of, 103; performers and performances at, 104; remarkable incident at, 112; engagement of Belzoni at, 112
Salisbury Cathedral: view of north side; anecdote of, *note*, 280
Salt, Henry, 114, 115
Sanders, Prince, a negro impostor, 321
Sanderson, Sir James, 82
Satchwell, Mr., an early friend of author, 65
——— R. W., miniature painter, 65, 128
Saunders, C. A., 10
——— J., 109
Scatcherd, Mr., 279
——— and Letterman, 279
Schiavonetti, Signor, 131, 271
Schomburgh, Sir R. H., 13
School-days, and anecdotes of masters:—author's love of play, 41; first at a dame-school, 42; next at Foscot, 42; at Yatton Keynel, 47; at Draycot, 47; at Chippenham, 49; his school-mates there, 50—54; general reflections, 54
School of Eloquence, Old Change, epigram on, by R. A. Davenport, 92
Scientific persons, testimonials to, 11
Scotchmen in London, Ritson on, 87
Scott, Mr., 268
——— John, editor of *London Magazine*, his death, 261
——— G. L., 267
——— Miss, 322
——— Sir Walter, his Auto-Biography, 2; public testimonial to, 8; 245, 248, 272, 290, 353, 381
Scriven, E., 170, 289
Scrope, G. Poulett-Thomson, 392; author of *History of the Manor and Ancient Barony of Castle-Combe*, 393; other works by, 395
——— Rev. Dr. John, 388
——— Madam, 388; introduction to, 388
——— William, 353; his love of field-sports, 389; works on, 390; 398
Sedgwick, Rev. A., 11
Seppings, Sir R., 9
Severn (The) perilous passage and loss to the author in crossing, 199
Severn, Joseph, 366
Seward, Miss, 143
Sewell, John, 132, 286
Seyer, Rev. Samuel, his controversy with the author, 203
Shakspere, quotations from, 1, 33, 34, 63, 73, 96; Ireland's forgeries of, 144; 219, 289, 294, 304
Shaksperian theatre, and amateur performers, 89, 91
Sharpe, Thomas, of Coventry, 156, 159, 254
Shaw, Dr., 159
Shee, Sir Martin A., 9, 132, 377
Shelburne, Earl of, notice of, 355; patronage of to Judge Blackstone, 360
Shelley, Percy B., 4
Shenstone, William, 160
Sheridan, R. B., 53; notice of his play of *Pizarro*, 129, 130; anecdote of, 277
——— Thomas, 53
Sherwin, Dr., his present to the Bath Institution, 203, 220
Sherwood, William, 274

Shoberl, F., editor of the *Forget-Me-Not*, 311, 313
Shrewsbury, the author's visit to, 163; the *Wrekin*, 163; persons with whom the author became acquainted at, 166; remarks on the town, 167; history of, by Blakeway and Owen, 458
Shropshire, pedestrian tour through, 137
Siddons, Sarah, 130, 220, 351
——— Mr., 103, 104
Signs, booksellers', 259
Simms, Mr., 219
——— Miss, 91
Simpkin, W., 280
——— and Marshall, 280
Simpson, Mr., solicitor, one of the author's early employers, 82
Simpson, William, 391
Simson, W., 366
Singer, S. W., 304
Skelton, Joseph, 194
Skinner, Rev. J., his present to the Bath Institution, 221; notice of, 467
Slave-trade, a popular subject, 321
Smart, Sir George, 10
Smirke, Sir R., 8, 254
Smith, Horace, quotations from his *Greybeards Gossip*, 4, 59; 245; his notice of William Combe, 314
——— C. Roach, 8, 147
——— Dr., 220
——— Sir James E., 11
——— James, 4, 314
——— Prince, 89
——— Rev. J. Pye, 8
——— Sir Harry, 10
——— Sir Sidney, 10, 84, 108
——— Rev. Sidney, 272, 364
——— Timothy, 153
——— William, 11; notice of, 461
——— Mr., his *Book for a Rainy Day*, 115
——— engraver, 254
——— of the Strand, 319
Smollett, Dr. Tobias, 219, 222, 233
Smyth, Admiral, 393
Snelling, T., 298
Soane, Sir J., 8, 305; purchases the Belzonian sarcophagus, 113; Hogarth's *Election*, 325
Societies, Royal, Antiquarian, &c., 318
Solicitors, Ritson's strictures on, 87
Somerville, Mrs., 8
Sotheby, Samuel Leigh, book-auctioneer, 323
South, Sir James, 11
Southampton, Earl of, 219
Southern, Henry, 297
Southey, Robert, LL.D., 8; native of Bristol, 41; Cottle's *Reminiscences* of, 201; editor of Chatterton's works, 202; the marriage-register of, 207; testimonial to, 207; his notice of the author in the *Quarterly Review*, 247; 269, 290
Southgate, Mr., 326
Spackman, Mr., 224
Sparrow, Wm., one of the author's schoolmasters, 48; death of, 347
Spencer, Earl, 65
*Sporting Magazine*, the author's contributions to the, 127
Spottiswoode, Andrew, 303
Spouting clubs attended in youth, 83, 92, 95
St. Paul's Cathedral, George the Third's visit to, 96; Colman's lines on, 96
——— Churchyard, booksellers in, 250
Stanfield, Mr., 366

Stanton St. Quintin, 405
Statesmen, testimonials to, 11
Stationers' Hall, notice of, 280; Leigh Hunt on the portraits in, 281
Statues and public monuments, *see* Testimonials, 7—13
Steele, Sir Richard, 281
Steevens, George, 328
Stephenson, George, 10
——— Robert, 10
Sterne, Lawrence, alleged plagiarisms from Burton's *Melancholy*, 21; 219, 289, 333
Stevens, Alexander, 95
——— G. A., 97
Stevenson, Sir John, 10
Stone, Frank, 366
Storer, James, 136
Stothard, Mr., 394
Stourhead, annual gatherings at, 455
Stowe, John, 252
Stowe, unpublished *Letters of Junius* at, 20
Strahan, A., "King's printer," notice of, 302
Strand, booksellers and publishers residing in the, 306—323
Stratford-upon-Avon, author's visit to, 144
Stratton, one of author's schoolmasters, 48
——— Miss, her remarks on the Stage, 116
Strype, John, 252
Stuart, Lord Dudley, 12
——— Daniel, 309
——— Mr., 305
Studies during apprenticeship, 53, 63
Stukeley, Dr., 172
Stump, William, 47, 416
Subscriptions, public, *see* Testimonials, 7—13
Sudeley, Lord, 107
Suffolk, Earl of, 365
Superstition in the author's native village, 37, 41, 57
Sussex, Duke of, 321
Sutherland, Duke of, 51
Swedenborg, Baron, 62
Symonds, H. D., 259; notice of, 273
——— Dr., 172
——— Sir W., 9
*Syntax, Dr., in Search of the Picturesque*, popularity of, 315; notice of Wm. Combe, the author of, 313, 314


Talfourd, Mr. Justice, 8; his literary pursuits, 86
Tanner, Bishop, 27
Tapsell, William, a sincere friend of the author, 122; misfortunes of, 125
*Taste, on the Principles of*, by Richard P. Knight, 169
Taylor, John, 4, 143
——— Josiah, bookseller, the author's connexion with, 247, 305
——— Mr., 157
——— Mrs., 297
——— Miss Jane, 297
——— Wm., of Norwich, 248; notice of, 269
——— & Hessey, publishers of the *London Magazine*, 296; contributors to, 297
Tegg, Thomas, bookseller, notice of, 275
Temple of Flora, St. George's Fields, 121
Tennant, Sir J. E., 12
Tennyson, Alfred, 8
Testimonial from the public to the author, 15
Testimonials to literary and scientific men, artists, &c., tabular view of, 7—13
——— miscellaneous, 13

Tetbury, mop at, 414
Thackeray, W. M., 245, 246, 315
Theatrical associates in youth, 91
*The Fourth Estate*, by F. Knight Hunt, 307
Thelwall, John, lecturer and orator, 95; a native of Bath, 180; his trial and acquittal, 181—183; 237
Thirlwall, Rev. C., 8
Thomason, Sir Edward, at Birmingham, 12, 149; a resident at Bath, 233
Thompson, Peter, 127
Thomson, Geo. Poulett, M.P., notice of, 392
——— James, 333
Thorpe, Benjamin, 8
——— John, 338
Thorwaldsen, Bentel, 8, 366
Thrale, Mrs., 223
Thunder-storms, superstitions in connection with, 37
Thurlow, Lord, 181, 383
Thurston, John, artist, 131
Tierney, Mr., 365
*Times*, (The) influence and popularity of, 308
Timperley, C. H., 263
Tintern Abbey, visit to, and adventure at, 197
Titles, honours, &c., tabular view of, 7—13
Todd, Rev. H. J., 8, 172, 331, 393
Tomkins, Mr., 271
Tonson, Jacob, 306
Tooke, J. Horne, his trial and acquittal, 95
——— W., 304
Tootal, Edward, 10
Topographers, learned, 335, 336
*Topographical Literature, &c., an Essay on*, by the author, 332
Topography and topographers, 135
——— its capabilities and attributes, 331; Sir R. C. Hoare's opinion of, 332; Rev. Jos. Hunter on, 332; Richard Gough on, 332; Thomas Warton on, 333
Torrington, Viscount, 10
"Touting," an instance of, 173; a stage-struck heroine, 174
Towers, Rev. Dr., his works, and personal anecdotes of him, 70
Townsend, Joseph, 362
——— Rev. Joseph, 220, 359, 364; notice of, 463—465
Tracton, Lord, 361
Travellers, testimonials to, 12
Travelling in the last century, 27, 61
Trelech, the inn and its accommodation, 196; large stones at, 197
Tresham, Henry, 271
Trotter, Dr., 351
Trusler, Rev. Dr., works, and personal anecdotes of, 69; sermons, in *script type*, 70
Tupper, M. F., in praise of authorship, 243; books eulogized by, 329; the author's opinion of, 243
Turnbull, Rev. T. S., 150
Turner, Charles, 321
——— & Cooke's *Southern Coast*, 287
——— Dawson, his letter to the author on the testimonial to him, 15
——— J. M. W., notice of, 256
——— Sharon, 8
*Twelfth-Night Characters*, compiled by the author, 129
Twiss, Horace, 4
Tyranny of the Government at the close of the last century, 94
Tyson, W., antiquary and topographer, 209
Tytler, P. F., 8

*Union of Architecture, Sculpture, and Painting*, by the author, 113
Upham, Mr., 217
Uwins, Thomas, 9, 315
Valpy, A. J., 301
——— Dr., 301
Vanbrugh, Sir John, 141
Vandyke, 176
Varley, John, 175
Vattemare, *see* Alexandre, 150, 322
Vernon, Robert, 13
Vernor and Hood project the *Beauties of England and Wales*, 238; the author's personal connections with, 285; Sir John Carr's action against, 286
Village life and scenery: *Our Village*, by Miss Mitford, 26; the author's village, 27—29; anecdotes of rural life, 32—35
Vincent, Mr., 229
Vivian, G., lord of manor of Claverton, 235

Wade, John, his new edition of the *Letters of Junius*, 20, 330
Waghorn, Lieutenant, 13
Wakefield, Gilbert, 282
Waldegrave, the Ladies, 361
Wales, Prince of, 108
Walker, John, engraver, 136
——— John, publisher, 274; publisher of the works of Peter Pindar, 276
——— Rev. A. J., notice of, 180
——— Rev. J., 28, 140
——— Miss, notice of, 180
Walpole, Horace, 119, 288
Walter, John, his perseverance in advancing *The Times*, 308
Walton, Mr., 297
——— Izaac, 288, 297, 391
War, lines on, by Robert Sadler, 363
Warburton, Bishop, 220
Warner, Rev. Richard, his *Walks in Wales*, 136; sketch of Hagley, from his *Northern Tour*, 159; his residence at Newton St. Loe, and the author's interview with, 213; lines written in the garden of Chelwood parsonage, 214; *Literary Recollections* by, 215; Whitaker's criticisms on his writings, 216; his *Bath Guide*, 217; notice of the Rev. Richard Greaves, 235
Warton, Rev. Joseph, 305
——— Thomas, 96, 331, 333, 393
Wathen, James, author and traveller, anecdotes of, 180, 186—188
Watkins, Dr., 70
Watson, Bishop, 282
——— Caroline, 143
——— Sir W., 220
Watt, James, 8
——— editor of *Bibliotheca Brit.*, 142, 313
Watts, Dr. Isaac, 249, 333
Webbe, William, 158
Wedgewoods, the, 201
Weld, Mr., 318
Wellbeloved, Rev. C., 269
Wellesley, W. P. T. L., 49, 392
Wells, Somerset, youthful adventure at, 75
West, Benjamin, P.R.A., 133; at Windsor, 139; 237, 317
——— James, 358
Westmacott, Sir R., 4, 366
Westminster Abbey, splendid copy of the History of, 311
Whately, Rev. R., 8, 387

Wheatley, F., 310
Wheble, John, printer and bookseller, 127; his urgency for the author to begin the *Beauties of Wiltshire*, 135; his renewal of the project, 330; his arrest by order of the House of Commons, 338
———— Philip Carteret, 358
Whewell, Rev. William, 303
Whish, Rev. W. R., 203
Whitaker, Rev. John, topograper and critic, the author's visit to, 215, 260; notice of, 335 (*portrait*); 483
———— Rev. Dr., 331, 336, 393
White, B. and J., booksellers, 294
———— Rev. Gilbert, 331
———— 'Squire, 55
Whittaker, Messrs., booksellers, 279
Whittington, Rev. G. D., 305
Wickenden, Joseph,
Wiffin, J. H., librarian to the Duke of Bedford, 299
Wilberforce, Rev. S., 8
———— William, 321
Wilkes, John, publisher of the *Encyclopædia Londinensis*, 280
———— Alderman, 330
Wilkie, Messrs., booksellers, 277
———— Sir David, 9, 366, 391
Wilkinson, Sir G., 113
———— John, 323
Wilks, T. E., 111
———— Washington, his *History of the Half Century* recommended, 250
Williams, D., founder of Literary Fund, 107
———— Rev. D., 109
———— D. E., 224
———— Edward, bookseller, 295
———— Edward Pote, 295
———— John, 276
———— Joseph, M.D., 484
———— P. H., 8, 90, 94, 95, 107, 181
Willis, Professor, 178
Willmott, Rev. R. A., 279
Wilson, Andrew, 324
———— George, 12
———— James, 11
———— artist, 365
Wiltshire Archæological and Nat. Hist. Society founded, 392; G. P. Scrope's *Inaugural Address*, 392; origin and progress of, 443; meeting at Devizes, 445; at Salisbury, 445; at Chippenham, 446
———— Beauties of, suggested by Mr. Wheble, 135; works consulted, 136; pedestrian tour preparatory to writing the work, 137; its origin, 330
———— North, its characteristics in the author's boyhood, 30
———— Ancient and Modern, 453

Wiltshire Society in London, the, 384; the Austins and Queen Caroline, 384; Moore's speech at, 385
———— plans for a history of, 449—455
———— Mr., 225
Windsor, the author's first visit to, and publications on, 136
Wine and brandy-trade, author apprenticed to, 64; characteristics of the business, 65, 78
*Wine and Walnuts*, extracts from, 98
*Wit's Magazine*, edited by T. Holcroft, 256
Wodderspoon, John, 245; his volume of autographs, 307
Wolcot, Dr. (*Peter Pindar*) 92, 97, 143, 251, 258; notice of his writings and quarrel with William Gifford, 275; his outwitting a publisher, 276
Wolferston, Pipe, 156
Wolstoncraft, Mary, 283
Wolverhampton, visited by the author, 161; Rev. R. Warner's description of, 161; the church of St. Peter at, 162
Wood, Anthony à, 28, 47
———— Mr., 220
———— Rev. William, 269
Woodfall, G. and H. S., notices of, 253
Woodstock, visited by author, 141; passes a day with Dr. Mavor at, 141
Wordsworth, William, 8, 201
Worthington, engraver, 289
Wotton Basset, 437
Wrekin (The) a demi-mountain, notice of, 163
Wright, George, his imitations and musical powers, 122
———— Lieutenant, 76
———— Mr., political publisher, 275
———— Thomas, 304
Wyatt, James, 176, 178
Wyattville, Sir J., 8, 139
Wycombe, Lord, 362
Wye, the river, notice of, 189; reference to works on, 190
Wyld, Ann, 104
———— James, geographer, 319
Wyndcliffe, on the Wye, view from, 198
Wyndham, Penruddock, 27, 135
Wynn, Peter, 235
Wyon, W., 9
Wyse, Right Hon. Thomas, on the testimonial to the author, 16

Yatton-Keynel, John Aubrey and the author at school there, 47; schoolmaster at, 48
Yearsley, Ann, 201
York, Duke of, 244
Young, Charles, 91, 126
———— Edward, 340


THE END.

NORWICH: PRINTED BY CHARLES MUSKETT, OLD HAYMARKET.

# SUBSCRIBERS

TO

### The Britton Testimonial,

AS PRINTED AT THE CLOSE OF THE

## AUTHOR'S AUTO-BIOGRAPHY.
## 1856.

---

### Ten Guineas and upwards.

HER MOST GRACIOUS MAJESTY VICTORIA, QUEEN OF GREAT BRITAIN.
HIS ROYAL HIGHNESS PRINCE ALBERT.
HIS MAJESTY THE KING OF PRUSSIA.
HIS MAJESTY THE KING OF THE BELGIANS.

His Grace the Duke of Sutherland.
The Most Honourable the Marquess of Lansdowne.
The Right Honourable Lord Londesborough.
The Right Honourable Lord Broughton de Gyfford.
Charles Barclay, Esq.
Beriah Botfield, Esq., M.A., F.R.S., &c.
A. Burgess, Esq., C.E., £15. 15s.
Thomas Cubitt, Esq., Clapham Park, and The Denbies, £21.
William Cubitt, Esq., M.P., Alderman of London, £21.
Andrew Cuthell, Esq., Architect.
William Dixon, Esq., £17. 10s.
The Baron de Goldsmid.
Hudson Gurney, Esq., F.R. & A.S., £21.
Thomas Grissell, Esq., F.R. & S.A., Norbury Park.
John Jackson, Esq., Yeoman, Rochdale.
William S. Jones, Esq., £12.
Sir Francis Graham Moon, Bart., Ex-Lord Mayor of London.
John Bowyer Nichols, Esq., F.S.A.
Thomas Proctor, Esq., Walls Court, £21.
Dr. William Roots.
J. Scott Russell, Esq., C.E., F.R.S., &c.
Alderman Salomons, Lord Mayor of London, Tunbridge Wells.
William Tite, Esq., Architect, M.P., F.R. & A.S., £15. 15s.
The Reverend Thomas Smith Turnbull, £21.
The Rev. Dr. Webb, Master of Clare Hall, Cambridge.

---

### Five Guineas.

*The misused and questionable title of Esquire has been omitted in the following lists.*

Nil Desperandum. (Bristol?)
The Right Hon. the Earl Amherst.
Sir Edmund Antrobus, Bart.
Henry Ashton Barker,
Sir Charles Barry, Architect, R.A.
The Right Hon. Lord Beresford.
The Right Hon. Lady Beresford.
Henry George Bohn.
Geo. Weare Brackenridge, F.S.A.
Sir David Brewster, F.R.S.
Henry Broadley, M.P.
Thomas Brown.
I. K. Brunel, C.E.
D. Burton, Architect, F.R.S.
J. B. Byron.
W. Chadwick.
George H. Christie.
C. R. Cockerell, Professor of Architecture, Royal Academy.
Lewis Cubitt, Architect.

## SUBSCRIBERS TO THE BRITTON TESTIMONIAL.

Mrs. Lewis Cubitt.
Sir Thomas Deane, Architect.
J. W. Freshfield, M.P.
Nathaniel Gould, F.S.A.
William Grane.
Thomas A. Green, F.S.A.
The Right Hon. the Earl de Grey.
His Grace the Duke of Hamilton.
Philip Hardwick, Architect, R.A.
The Right Hon. Sidney Herbert, M.P.
W. Herbert, Architect.
Charles Hill, F.S.A.
Sir Hugh Richard Hoare, Bart.
Henry Merrick Hoare.
Robert Stayner Holford, M.P.
A. Beresford Hope, M.P.
Henry Thomas Hope.
John Howell.
The Rev. J. E. Jackson, M.A.
J. Kenyon.
R. J. P. King.
Charles Knight.
John Lee, D.C.L., F.R. & A.S.
Henry Lee. Architect.
The Architectural and Archæological Society of Liverpool.
The London Institution.
The Right Hon. Lord Methuen.
Samuel Mullen.
John Neeld, M.P.
Joseph Neeld, M.P.
The Most Hon. the Marquess of Northampton.
Thomas Page, C.E.
James Pennethorne, Architect.
The Lord Chief Baron Pollock.
The Right Hon. Sir John Romilly.
Thomas Ryland, Jun.
George G. Scott, Architect.
George Powlett Scrope, M.P., &c.
Sydney Smirke, Architect.
S. Leigh Sotheby.
T. H. S. Sotheron-Estcourt, M.P.
William Spence, F.S.A.
Richd. J. Spiers, Ex-Mayor of Oxford.
R. Stevenson, M.P., C.E., F.R.S.
Sir R. G. Throckmorton, Bart,
William Tooke, F.R.S.
Thomas Turton, D.D., Bishop of Ely.
George Vivian.
James Wadmore.
George F. White, Architect.
B. G. Windus.
James Yates, F.R.S.

## Three Guineas.

B. Alchin.
Miss Baily.
Sir John Boileau, Bart., F.R. and A.S.
W. J. Booth, Architect.
Chevalier Bunsen, D.C.L., Oxford and Cambridge.
W. Chapman.
Dominic Colnaghi
T. D. Donaldson, Professor of Architecture in University College.
J. Walter King Eyton, F.S.A.
A. T. Gilbert, D.D., Bishop of Chichester.
Sir Stephen Glynne, Bart.
Wm. Hosking, C.E., Architect.
Henry Charles Hoare.
W. H. Ince, Architect.
W. S. Inman, Architect.
Miss Kerr.
Sir Edward Bulwer Lytton, Bart., M.P.
Henry Lawson.
James H. Markland, LL.D., F.R. & A.S.
R. Maugham.
The Rev. John Mitford.
The Rev. W. H. E. McKnight.
Sir Oswald Moseley, Bart., F.G.S.
T. R. Musgrave.
Charles Muskett.
The Rev. John Parkes.
R. K. Penson, Architect.
George Petrie.
R. B. Phillips.
John Phillips, F.G.S.
The Rev. Dr. Plumptre.
A. Rainy.
The Rev. Dr. Thomas Rees.
Bingham Richards.
David Roberts, R.A.
Sir Cusack P. Roney.
J. B. Swete.
William W. Salmon.
Henry Shaw, F.S.A.
The Rev. J. M. Traherne, F.R. & A.S.
Dawson Turner, F.S.A.
John Thompson.
His Excellency M. Van de Weyer.
Samuel Ware, Architect.
R. Weston.
Joseph White
C. F. Wickes, Architect.

## Two Guineas.

George Ackerman.
John Adamson, F.S.A.
The Right Hon. the Earl of Albemarle.
Jabez Allies, F.S.A.
Society of Antiquaries, Newcastle.
The Rev. T. B. Ashley.
Arthur Ashpitel, Architect, F.S.A.
J. P. Atkins.
E. M. Atkins.
Francis Attwood.
The Rev. Edward Awdry.
Miss Baker.
William Beattie, M.D.
George Beadnell.

## SUBSCRIBERS TO THE BRITTON TESTIMONIAL.

Thomas A. Beddoes.
George Bell.
Thomas Bell, F.R.A.
James Bennett.
George Bishop, F.R.S., &c.
W. H. Blaauw, F.S.A.
M. H. Bloxham, F.S.A.
The Rev. Joseph Bosworth, LL.D.
Sir John Bowring, LL.D.
Dr. Bradley.
John Braham.
The Rev. E. and Mrs. A. E. Bray.
R. Britton.
Wm. Brockedon, F.R.S.
Thomas Brook.
J. S. Buckingham.
John Buller.
Thos. Bullock, Jun.
The Ven. Archdeacon Berney.
B. B. Cabbell, M.P.
J. G. Children, F.R. & A.S.
John Chilcott.
Mons. Claudet.
Thomas Clark.
Charles Clarke, Bristol.
Thomas Clark, Guildford.
John Cochrane.
The Right Hon. Lord Colborne.
R. Cole, F.S.A.
Henry Cole.
Jacob Cole.
W. Wilkie Collins.
James Commins.
John Conolly, M.D.
Bolton Corney, F.S.A.
Rev. W. Copplestone.
George R. Corner, F.S.A.
William Cotton, M.A., F.S.A.
Thomas Coventry, F.A.S.
F. Crace, F.S.A.
J. Crace.
Edward Cresy, F.S.A., Architect.
The Rev. Dr. Cromwell, F.S.A.
Peter Cunningham, F.S.A.
William Cunnington, F.G.S.
Mrs. Cunnington.
The Hon. & Rev. H. C. Cust, F.S.A.
James Darnill.
George Davey.
B. R. Davies.
O. Delepierre, LL.D.
J. C. Denham.
J. Dickinson, F.R.S.
R. B. Dockray, C.E.
Wm. Donaldson.
W. J. Donthorne.
John Doyle.
P. B. Duncan, F.S.A.
W. Dunnage.
J. Elger, Architect.
The Rev. H. T. Ellacombe, F.S.A.
Joseph Ellis.
Joseph Ellis, Jun., Brighton.
Charles Ellis.
The Right Hon. the Earl of Ellesmere.
The Very Rev. the Dean of Ely, D.D., F.R.S.
Charles Empson.

William Ewart, M.P.
F. W. Fairholt, F.S.A.
The Ven. Archdeacon Fane.
William Figg.
Robert Fitch, F.G.S.
Charles Fowler, Architect.
The Ven. Archdeacon Freer, F.S.A.
Charles Frost, F.S.A.
J. R. Gardener, Architect.
Sills Gibbons.
Mrs. Gibbons.
The Rev. Dr. Giles.
Capt. Gladstone, M.P.
J. H. Monk, D.D., Bishop of Gloucester.
J. H. Glover, F.S.A.
Charles Godwin.
George Godwin.
George Godwin, Jun., Architect, F.R.S., F.S.A.
Henry Godwin.
J. E. Gray, LL.D., F.R.S.
Thomas A. Green, F.S.A.
B. W. Greenfield.
George Gwilt, Architect, F.S.A.
Charles Hacker, Architect.
Sir Benjamin Hall, Bart., M.P.
S. C. Hall, F.S.A.
Henry Hallam, F.R.S., F.S.A., &c.
The Rev. R. Hart.
J. D. Harding
The Right Hon. the Earl of Harrowby.
E. Haycock, Architect.
Christopher Heady.
M. D. Hill, Commissioner.
S. J. Hill.
J. Hill.
S. Hill, Architect.
John Hogarth.
Thomas Hogdson.
A. Holden.
James Hopgood.
Thomas Howse.
R. Hudson, F.R.A., F.S.A.
John Hughes.
The Rev. J. H. Hughes, M.A.
The Rev. Dr. Hume.
E. Hunt.
The Rev. Joseph Hunter, F.S.A.
Robert Hunter, F.S.A.
Miss Innes.
David Irving, LL.D.
The Rev. D. James, F.S.A.
T. Jaques.
Edward Johnson.
W. S. Jones.
J. H. Le Keux.
J. Lilly.
The Very Rev. the Dean of Llandaff.
Charles E. Long, F.S.A.
William Long.
Thomas Longman.
Joseph Longmore.
Mrs. Lowden.
M. A. Lower, M.A., F.S.A.
Thomas Lupton.
Sir James Mc Adam, C.E.
Charles Mackay, LL.D.

## SUBSCRIBERS TO THE BRITTON TESTIMONIAL.

The Ven. Archdeacon Macdonald.
Sir Frederick Madden, F.S.A.
The Rev. E. L. Magoon, D.C.L., New York.
J. H. Markland, LL.D., F.R.S.
R. Marshall.
Serjeant Merewether.
The Rev. Thomas Meyler.
Charles Mitchell.
The Rev. John Mitford.
The Rev. Henry Moseley, D.D.
E. Moxon.
Richard Mullings.
Sir Roderic Murchison, F.R.S., &c.
J. Gough Nichols, F.S.A.
Miss Nichols.
James Noyes.
John Noyes.
George Ormerod, F.R. & A.S.
William Osmond.
William Parke.
E. T. Parris.
J. Parrott.
John Partridge.
Rev. A. B. Perkins.
T. J. Pettigrew, F.R.S., F.S.A.
Sir Thomas Phillips, Bart., F.S.A.
T. W. Phillips.
J. L. Phillips.
The Rev. A. Phillips, D.D.
H. W. Pickersgill, R.A.
J. W. Pile.
Lewis Pocock, F.S.A.
William Pocock, Architect.
James Ponsford, Architect.
William Powell.
George Pownall.
Thomas Poynder.
Edward Pretty, F.S.A.
James Prior, F.S.A.
Cyrus Redding.
The Rev. Dr. Thomas Rees.
Lovell Reeve.
G. Repton, Architect.
John A. Repton, F.S.A.
Thomas Reseigh.
C. J. Richardson, Architect, F.S.A.
H. Crabb Robinson, F.S.A.
Dr. Roget.
Sir William C. Ross.
Matthew E. Rowe.
Richard Rowland.
W. K. Hamilton, D.D., Bp. of Salisbury.
Joseph Sams.
Thos. B. Saunders.
The Rev. H. M. Scarth.
Edward. Sharpe, Architect.
Richard Sims.
S. W. Simms.
George Simpson.
S. W. Singer.
Charles Roach Smith.
The Rev. J. J. Smith.
Lieut.-Col. Hamilton Smith, R.M.
John Russell Smith.
Smith and Elder.
S. J. Smith, Architect.
John Smith.
H. S. Smith.
Rear-Admiral Smyth, F.R.S., F.S.A., &c.
Sion College.
Spalding and Hodge.
Charles Spence.
G. J. Squibb.
C. Stanfield, R.A.
The Right Hon. the Earl Stanhope.
Thomas Stevenson, F.S.A.
Sir John Stoddart, LL.D.
Sir John E. Swinburne, Bart.
The Rev. E. Taggart, F.S.A.
Arthur Taylor, F.S.A.
George L. Taylor, Architect, F.S.A.
R. Taylor, F.R.S., &c.
John Taylor.
James Taylor.
Martin Taylor.
James Thomson.
John Thompson, Artist.
Peter Thompson.
John Timbs.
Thomas Tooke, F.R.S., F.S.A.
W. C. Towers.
Martin F. Tupper.
The Rev. W. H. Turner.
W. H. Tymms.
J. Van Voorst.
James Walker, C.E.
Miss Walker.
William Wansey, F.S.A.
The Rev. J. Ward.
Samuel Warren.
T. S. Watson.
Albert Way, F.S.A.
The Rev. John Webb, F.S.A.
F. Webb.
The Rev. Dr. Wellesley.
The Very Rev. the Dean of Wells.
Robert B. Wheler.
Mrs. W. White.
E. P. Williams.
George A. Williams.
Joseph L. Williams.
Dr. Joseph Williams.
G. Willis.
Thomas J. Willson, Architect.
Effingham Wilson.
The Rev. J. Wilson, D.D. Master of Trinity College, Oxford.
C. R. Sumner, D.D., Bishop of Winchester.
John Wodderspoon.
Wolverhampton Library.
James Wyld.
Edward Wyndham, F.S.A.
J. Ashton Yates.
Mrs. Yates.
John A. Yatman.

### The Britton Testimonial.

---

# AN ACCOUNT

## OF

# A PUBLIC DINNER

### GIVEN TO

## JOHN BRITTON, F.S.A.

AT THE CASTLE HOTEL, RICHMOND,

ON THE 74TH ANNIVERSARY OF HIS BIRTH, JULY 7, 1845,

### With the Toasts & Speeches on the Occasion,

*A List of Subscribers;*

AND AN

## EXPLANATORY PREFACE,

### BY T. E. JONES.

---

PRINTED FOR THE SUBSCRIBERS TO THE TESTIMONIAL.

1846.

LONDON:
JAQUES AND SON, PRINTERS, KENTON STREET,
BRUNSWICK SQUARE.

# CONTENTS.

|  | Page |
|---|---|
| RESOLUTIONS OF COMMITTEE | iv |
| PREFACE, explanatory of the origin and object of a Subscription to present Mr. Britton with a PUBLIC TESTIMONIAL, for his long and useful services in Archæological Literature | v |
| PUBLIC DINNER given to him at Richmond, June 7, 1845; with a List of the Gentlemen present; and the TOASTS and SPEECHES on that occasion | 1-23 |

## TOASTS.

| | Proposed by | Replied to by | |
|---|---|---|---|
| 1. THE QUEEN | The Chairman | .. .. | 1 |
| 2. THE QUEEN DOWAGER, PRINCE ALBERT, and the rest of the ROYAL FAMILY. | The Chairman | .. .. | 1 |
| 3. JOHN BRITTON, Esq. | The Chairman | Mr. Britton | 2 |
| 4. The SOCIETY OF ANTIQUARIES | Mr. W. Tooke | The Rev. Dr. Ingram | 9 |
| 5. The CHAIRMAN | The Dean of Hereford | The Chairman | 11 |
| 6. The CHURCH OF ENGLAND; and the DEAN OF HEREFORD | The Chairman | The Dean of Hereford | 13 |
| 7. The HONORARY SECRETARIES; GEO. GODWIN, Esq. and P. CUNNINGHAM, Esq. | The Rev. Dr. Rees | Mr. Godwin | 15 |
| 8. The INSTITUTE OF BRITISH ARCHITECTS; and WM. TITE, Esq. | Dr. Conolly | Mr. Tite | 17 |
| 9. The FREEMASONS; and WM. CUBITT, Esq. | Mr. Godwin | Mr. W. Cubitt | 20 |
| 10. The ROYAL ACADEMY; and D. ROBERTS, Esq., R.A. | The Chairman | Mr. D. Roberts | 22 |
| Speech of Mr. S. C. HALL | | | 23 |

\*\*\* The following Toasts appeared in the Programme, but were unavoidably omitted, owing to the length of time occupied by the preceding Speeches:—

| | | | |
|---|---|---|---|
| 11. The INSTITUTE OF CIVIL ENGINEERS; and PROFESSOR HOSKING | Mr. Grissell | Mr. Hosking. | |
| 12. BRITISH LITERATURE; and W. JERDAN, Esq. | Mr. B. H. Smart | Mr. Jerdan. | |
| LIST OF SUBSCRIBERS | | | 25 |

# BRITTON TESTIMONIAL.

AT a MEETING of the Committee, held on the 13th of December, 1845, it was

RESOLVED,—That the Subscriptions be appropriated to the preparation of a BIBLIOGRAPHICAL MEMOIR OF MR. BRITTON'S LITERARY LIFE, to be printed in three sizes; and copies to be presented to the Subscribers, of a size and value proportionate to the amount of their respective contributions. Also, that Mr. Britton be requested to prepare such a work at his earliest convenience, and to superintend the printing and embellishments.

RESOLVED,—That the Portrait of Mr. Britton, painted by Mr. John Wood, now submitted to the Committee, be engraved by Mr. Wagstaff, for distribution amongst the Subscribers.

A Report, by Mr. T. E. Jones, of the proceedings at the Public Dinner at Richmond, on the 7th of July last, was presented to the Committee, and ordered to be printed.

### Subscriptions

CONTINUE TO BE RECEIVED BY

*The Treasurer,* N. GOULD, ESQ., 4, Tavistock Square;

*The Honorary Secretaries,* { GEO. GODWIN, JUN., ESQ., 11, Pelham Crescent, Brompton; P. CUNNINGHAM, ESQ., Audit Office, Somerset Place;

And by Messrs. DIXON & CO., Bankers, 25, Chancery Lane.

## PREFACE.

HAVING been removed by Mr. Britton in my youth from the mechanical and dull routine of an uncongenial occupation, and since guided and stimulated by him in the pursuit of literary avocations, I have felt more than ordinarily gratified by the Public Testimonial to his literary and personal merits, projected by several of his old and attached friends, on his retirement from the profession of literature.

At the festival at Richmond I had the pleasure of participating in the enthusiasm with which this project was recognized and advocated; and being anxious that a lasting record should be preserved of the proceedings on that occasion, I placed at the disposal of the Committee my short-hand notes of the speeches made by the Chairman, by Mr. Britton, and by other gentlemen who addressed the company. The Committee concur in the desire that each Subscriber should possess a Report of that meeting; and, by the courtesy of the Honorary Secretaries and Mr. Britton, I have been enabled to precede it by the following narrative of the circumstances connected with the subject, together with extracts from letters written by some of the Subscribers. The respective parties who proposed and responded to the toasts drunk at the Dinner have revised my notes, and thereby given to them greater accuracy than they would otherwise have possessed.

*Public Testimonials* of respect and esteem have been often paid to *public* men. These, however, have generally been limited to statesmen, military and naval officers, men of science, or those who, as chairmen or secretaries of thriving railway or other joint-stock companies, have promoted the pecuniary objects of their friends and admirers. It is true that each and all of these persons have generally deserved, in their respective spheres, the honours thus conferred; but do not *literary men* deserve the same, and is it not impossible to do otherwise than observe the comparative indifference with which the claims of such have hitherto been regarded. Few, indeed, have been the public acknowledgments and rewards paid to them during the present century; and most of those acknowledgments have been merely social, friendly meetings, of a festive nature, to hail and compliment, in the person of the author, the merit of his works. In this way James Hogg, the Ettrick Shepherd, and others have been greeted; and recently, Mr. Charles Dickens, not only in England, but in America, and more lately still, Mr. Charles Knight, have received similar demonstrations of well-merited respect. The honour of the Baronetage was, indeed, conferred upon Sir Walter Scott, as that of Knighthood has been upon Sir Henry Ellis, Sir Harris Nicolas, Sir Frederic Madden, Sir Francis Palgrave, and others. But these are rare instances. More rare still are those of more substantial compliments paid to literary men, in certain annuities, generously bestowed by the Sovereign, or the Ministers of the Crown, or through the medium of the Royal Society of Literature. Of the former class, the pensions granted to Thomas Moore, to Mrs. Somerville, to Lady Shee, and to Mrs. Hood, are among the most gratifying; and it is to be lamented, that the Society referred to was prevented granting to other deserving individuals, annuities similar to those which it bestowed, in the year 1824, on Coleridge, Malthus, Mathias, the Rev. E. Davies, the Rev. Dr. Jamieson, Sir William Ouseley, Millingen, Roscoe, the Rev. H. J. Todd, and Sharon Turner; the last of whom only is living.

The too frequent apathy to the merits of the *Author* proves, in the words of Mr. Britton, that " the *Literary profession* has not yet attained a rank commensurate to its real influence and usefulness;" and, to continue the quotation, that " it is quite time it should be fairly recognized as one of the liberal professions of this age and country.

Medicine, Law, and Divinity, have," he adds, " their respective schools, colleges, diplomas, and ranks; and their numerous practitioners are incited to study and emulation, by the titles and rewards which often crown their successful career. Literature, on the contrary, has no such school or college; nor is there any national endowment, or distinctive honorary title, to inspire or reward the man of letters. He rarely acquires fortune, or even a respectable competency by his labours: he is still more rarely complimented by a title or a pension from the monarch or the state; and it but seldom, very seldom, happens that the strictly literary man enjoys in old age the ' *otium cum dignitate*' of life."\*

It must be obvious that public tributes to the merits of living authors have advantages far greater than those tardy favors bestowed only when they have no power to soothe, or to console their object. Posthumous honours are poor rewards for living privations. " They may please and gratify relations and friends, but can do nothing for the individual; whereas every fair tribute of respect, and every compliment conferred on living merit, even in the later stages of existence, tend to make those stages consolatory and pleasant.† They become a sort of substitute for departed friends: they sweeten the daily draught of life, and counteract or neutralize the poison of envy, which

---

\* Preface to " *The History of Toddington,*" 4to. 1840. In quoting this and similar passages from the works of Mr. Britton, I am influenced, not merely by their application to the subject of my own remarks, and a desire to show his sentiments thereon, but further by the conviction, that the volumes in which they originally appeared are unknown to many of the subscribers to this Testimonial, and must, in a very few years, become extremely rare.

† The late MR. THOS. HOOD lived but a very short time after Sir Robert Peel had conferred on him and his surviving widow, a pension of one hundred pounds per year; but his last and painful days of hopeless sickness, were materially soothed, and even cheered, by the consciousness that his wife and children would derive essential aid from the Prime Minister's generous grant. The correspondence between the kind donor, and the witty but suffering author, is alike honourably characteristic of both, and I regret that it is not in my power to gratify the reader by copies of their letters.

is thrown into the cup of every person of eminence in art, science, or literature."*

A desire publicly to recognize Mr. Britton's varied services in the cause of Architecture and Archæology has, I am well assured, frequently been felt by many of his friends; but it was not till the month of February, 1845, that some members of the *Institute of British Architects*, and that of the *Civil Engineers*, and of the *Builders' Society*, resolved on taking active measures to accomplish the desired object. A Committee was immediately formed: Mr. George Godwin, and Mr. P. Cunningham readily undertook to officiate as Honorary Secretaries, and a printed circular was addressed to many eminent persons engaged in architectural and antiquarian pursuits, as well as to some of Mr. Britton's personal friends and associates, soliciting their co-operation. How amply that proposal was responded to is shewn by the Subscription List, appended to this Report.

Among the first to encourage and promote the plan may be named the Marquess of Northampton, whose affability and courtesy to all persons engaged in science, literature, and art, have conferred honour upon himself, and demands the gratitude of every one engaged in these branches of knowledge and accomplishment. His Lordship addressed Mr. Britton on the subject as follows:

> "As I look on your works, especially your *Architectural Antiquities* and your *English Cathedrals*, as having contributed very much to produce the anxiety now manifested to preserve the venerable edifices of our forefathers, it will give me much pleasure to have my name among those friends who are desirous to give you a Testimonial of their regard.
> Your's very truly,
> NORTHAMPTON."

The letters of the Duke of Hamilton, Earl de Grey, the Bishop of Ely, Mr. Hume, the Rev. Dr. Ingram, Professors Hosking, Donaldson, and Cockerell, the Rev. T. S. Turnbull, and many other eminent individuals

---

* Preface to "*The History, &c. of Worcester Cathedral*," 4to. 1835.

were also truly gratifying to the author's feelings. Extracts from some of them are here quoted.

THOMAS L. DONALDSON, ESQ., *Professor of Architecture, University College.* 15*th April,* 1845.

"MY DEAR SIR,—I concur most heartily in the idea of a Testimonial to the Father of British Antiquities; and I shall be most happy to promote it to the utmost of my power. I will mention the subject at the meeting of the Royal Institute of British Architects, this evening. My pen and my voice have ever concurred to assert the extent of the obligations we are all under to you; and I doubt not that the Testimonial will worthily convey the full impression of your high merits, as an antiquary and lover of the arts."

Sincerely yours,
T. L. DONALDSON.

The following is from JOSEPH HUME, ESQ., M.P., &c.

DEAR SIR,—" I have much pleasure in adding my name to the list of your friends, in connection with the intended Testimonial. It is not the amount of money to be subscribed, but the proofs of sympathy from so many distinguished men, in all situations of life, that I should value, as evidence of the high respect paid to you and your valuable and persevering labours in elucidation of the Architectural Antiquities of England; and if a long life of labour has not brought that pecuniary return which your talents deserved, you have the satisfaction of knowing that, in the opinion of some of the best judges in the country, you have deserved a more full and ample reward than the present expression of approval can afford. I had long ago expressed my sense of your devotion to the elucidation of the Antiquities of this country, and of your claims to public attention, by examining you before a *Select* Committee on Public Monuments and public places, and it was my intention to propose that you should be employed by the Government to go round the kingdom, and place on record your opinion of all the ancient buildings which your publications had not comprehended; with the view of measures being taken by the Government to preserve those that should be considered valuable, as the French Government has done, since Guizot's Orders in 1837. I brought that subject before Parliament, and named you as the man who, of all persons I knew, could and would do justice to the confidence of such a commission; and I shall always regret that the Government did not then adopt measures to carry out my suggestions. That you may enjoy the satisfaction, during the remaining part of your life, of having done great good in your time, and that you have the good opinion of so many of your fellow men, is the hope and wish of

Your's sincerely,

JOSEPH HUME."

As a pleasing feature of the project, a *Public Dinner* to Mr. Britton was suggested; and the time and place judiciously chosen for it by the Committee, were the 7th of July, 1845, (the seventy-fourth anniversary of his birth,) and the Castle Hotel, Richmond, his favourite summer retreat.

The Marquess of Northampton being unable to preside at this meeting, Thomas Wyse, Esq., M.P., promptly consented to do so; and in his letters to the Honorary Secretaries, (one of which will be found in a future page,) he evinced an anxious desire to be present, and to urge in an assembly of Mr. Britton's friends, the merits of those exertions, which, but a short time previously, he had referred to in his place in the House of Commons.* By an arrangement of the Government, a legislative measure, which called impera-

---

* The following letter will be read with interest, as commemorating Mr. Britton's share in the motion made in Parliament by Mr. Wyse, for the formation of a *Museum of National Antiquities*. That motion was unsuccessful, but it has since been intimated that the Trustees of the British Museum intend to carry out the plan. The exertions of Mr. Wyse were mainly instrumental in leading to this result, and therefore deserve honourable notice.

"17, *Wilton Place, March* 5, 1845.

"MY DEAR SIR,—Pray accept my warm thanks, not only for your acceptable and highly instructive present,—for which, had not the urgent business of this week prevented, you should have had my acknowledgments sooner,—but still more for that zealous and honest sympathy, which you testify now, as in the first years of life, for the promotion of all that can raise or preserve the true glory (the arts and civilization) of the country. It does you honour beyond what my words can confer, the truly generous and munificent

tively for the attendance of Mr. Wyse in Parliament, on the day fixed for the meeting at Richmond, deprived Mr. Britton and the visitors on that occasion, of his aid and sympathy as Chairman. In his unavoidable absence, the duties of the post were performed by Mr. Gould, the Treasurer to the Testimonial, with much zeal, animation, and tact. So far as the proceedings at the Dinner can be indicated by an accurate verbal report, every subscriber not present may now become acquainted with them; but much of their interest is necessarily lost in that feeble process, which, in the words I remember to have heard from the late John Thelwall, " preserves only the dry bones of the skeleton, from whence the animated soul has fled."\* Those who had the gratification to be present, will long remember the enthusiasm of that memorable evening.

---

manner in which you are ready to give evidence of this noble disposition; and ought to be an incentive to younger men to follow you in the same useful course. I gladly accept your offer of a Petition from yourself, and of exertions to originate another from the Artists. No man is more entitled to appeal to his own knowledge and experience, or to offer recommendations for the establishment of the projected institution than yourself. I shall be happy in the course of the discussion to have the means of fortifying my own opinions by so high an authority as *yours*. I purpose next week to renew my notice, and to fix the debate for as *early* a period as possible *after* Easter. Till then I shall be too much occupied with the Art-Union Committee and Report, to attend to it.

"The motion will be for an Address to the Crown, to provide an Institution, which shall combine—

" 1. *A Museum of the National Antiquities of the United Kingdom,* from the earliest period, arranged chronologically.

" 2. *Archives and Library of National Antiquities,* in connection with Art (Fine and Industrial).

" 3. A Commission or Board for the preservation of National Monuments.

" Each will require the other, but each will derive assistance from the others. You may petition for any one or all of them.

I am, Dear Sir,
Very truly, your's,
THOMAS WYSE."

" P.S. Messrs. Barry, Eastlake, Pugin, &c. are all in favour of this plan."

---

\* *Lectures on Oratory,* London Mechanics' Institution, 1833-4.

In reference to the appropriation of the subscriptions, as a permanent token of respect and admiration, various plans were successively considered and rejected. The first proposal was, either to present Mr. Britton with the sum subscribed, or with its value in a piece of plate. He, however, promptly and decidedly declined the former, and equally objected to the latter, unless it should present some appropriate novelty of form and character—such, for instance, as a model, in silver, of the north porch, or the chapter-house of Salisbury Cathedral, or other similar object. At the same time, he expressed a desire that the amount should rather be applied to some *Literary Work*, which, connected with his own writings, might augment the general fund of useful knowledge. He considered that an original and elaborate essay, produced from the subscription, and avowed and recognized as its result, would constitute a far more gratifying Testimonial to his exertions, than any other plan that might be proposed; whilst, being printed, at the cost of the subscribers, every one of them might receive a copy, as an acknowledgment, and a lasting memento of his own share in its production. To carry out these views, Mr. Britton proposed that a premium of one hundred guineas should be offered for the best " Essay on the study of *Archæological Literature*, more particularly that branch devoted to the *Ancient Architecture of Great Britain:*" the Essay selected as the most meritorious to be printed, and distributed, as mentioned.

It was suggested by some members of the Committee, that, by investing the subscriptions, an *annual* or *biennial Prize*, for an architectural or archæological essay or drawing, might be offered in perpetuity, as a desirable means of recording their sense of Mr. Britton's labours:—others proposed to have his *portrait* painted and engraved;—and some preferred having a *medal* struck, bearing his profile on the one side, and a suitable device or inscription, on the other. The whole of these plans however, were early relinquished, in consequence of a letter from Mr. Britton to the Committee, in May, 1845, in which he observed:—" Admitting that I should regard either of these propositions as a gratifying compliment, I presume that the Committee will *adopt that preferred by the recipient,* especially if it be thought likely to promote the study of Archæology. The friends I have consulted on this subject think, with me, that the periodical prize is objectionable; and that the proposed Essay on Archæological Literature is the most eligible and appropriate."

Mr. Britton's desire that the object of the Testimonial should be of a LITERARY nature was strengthened on more mature consideration; but, as it appeared impracticable to ensure such a production in the way of competition, he undertook to devote his own leisure to the preparation of a work appropriate to the occasion, and to expend the subscriptions in its printing and embellishment.

In deciding on the character of the work he proposed to write Mr. Britton was chiefly influenced by the following letters from his much-esteemed friend, Mr. Dawson Turner, the Author of many literary works on Antiquities, &c.

"*April* 10*th,* 1845.

MY DEAR SIR,—" I am delighted at the tribute about to be paid to your deserts, and hope that, though not resident in London, I may be allowed to have my name inserted among the subscribers, and for the larger sum. No man living deserves such a mark of respect more richly than yourself, and the unselfish mode in which you propose to receive it, does you the highest honour. I should only have proposed one alteration had I been present; and I wish I could now carry it,—that *instead of an Archæological Essay,* we should have a full HISTORY OF YOUR LITERARY LIFE, *as exemplified by your works, with extracts from them, and a detailed account of each.* We should so, indeed, raise a glorious and imperishable monument to your memory; and I am mistaken if there are many among the subscribers who would not willingly double their subscriptions for such an object.

In another letter of *June* 14*th,* the same valued friend and correspondent writes as follows:—

" As to the Literary Essay in your honour, my opinion is unchanged. It ought to be an account of your works; a full one, with copious extracts; and I wish, but fear I wish in vain, that I may be able to present myself at Richmond, on the 7th of July, and urge it. In such an Essay you would speak of the events of your life; of your friends and patrons, now most of them dead; of the artists you employed; of the eminent persons you were brought in the way of, and of the difficulties, pleasures, and annoyances that attended, soothed, and embittered your career; and you would intersperse the narrative with a thousand anecdotes. You would thus make a charming book of materials that would otherwise perish with you; and you would do invaluable good in your generation by the example you would hold out."

---

The Committee have concurred in the foregoing view, and Mr. Britton has commenced a volume, in which he proposes to illustrate the topics suggested by Mr. Dawson Turner; and it may be presumed that a most interesting record of his own labours, and the progress of Archæological Literature during the last half century, will be the result. It will constitute, in fact, "*The Literary Life of the Author of the Architectural Antiquities,*" and whilst it imparts an account of the origin, progress, and characteristics of his various publications and writings, it will include incidental anecdotes of contemporary literature, and of authors, artists, publishers, and other persons, in connection therewith. With respect to this intended work, Mr. Britton remarks: "A similar account of the life and works of Camden, of Dugdale, of Stukeley, or of Bacon, would have afforded much valuable information; not merely as related to themselves and their literary works, but as part and parcel of the annals of their respective times and associations. As professional authors, entirely or mainly dependant on their writings for subsistence, the names of Dryden, Smollett, De Foe, Johnson, Goldsmith, Coleridge, Holcroft, Aikin, Southey, Hutton, Butler, Gifford, Galt, and Cunningham, are conspicuous and estimable in the annals of fame. Some of these have honoured themselves, and gratified their admirers, by auto-biographical sketches, which are acknowledged to rank among the most interesting productions of their pens. Those of Hume,

Franklin, Coleridge, Gifford, Gibbon, and Holcroft, are well calculated to stimulate the ambition of genius, and incite that laudable aspiration which leads to fame. To some of those I have been indebted for excitements, and that ardent desire of attaining literary knowledge and distinction, which have progressively originated the numerous publications I have produced."

Though not personally acquainted with the state of Topographical Literature and the publishing trade, thirty years ago, I have obtained some knowledge of both by Reviews, Catalogues, and other sources: and more particularly by the descriptions which Mr. Britton has put on record in Prefaces to and on the wrappers of his numerous publications. From these I learn that the purchasers and patrons of such works were then not only liberal, but amounted to a large number: and included many distinguished noblemen, merchants, and men of different grades in life. Had such an appeal as the present been made then, the List hereto annexed would have embraced the names of many whose libraries have since been disposed of, and whose places are occupied by a class of persons differently disposed and circumstanced. Mr. Britton has a list of above one hundred names of distinguished collectors and correspondents, who manifested much partiality for topographical and antiquarian publications, but who are now numbered with the dead.—" *Sic transit gloria mundi.*"

The volume now contemplated, will necessarily comprise much information analagous to that which might have been expected in an *Essay on Archæological Literature;* and, as it will be accompanied by an engraved Portrait of the Author, by Mr. C. E. Wagstaff, from a skilful picture expressly executed for the purpose, by Mr. John Wood, the subscribers will receive the combined advantages of *two* of the plans originally proposed. A selection of the engravings that have illustrated Mr. Britton's works will be appended, in order to elucidate the general style of their embellishments. It will be printed in royal octavo; and a few copies will be worked in quarto for the subscribers of Three Pounds and upwards. Twenty-five copies, in imperial quarto, will be printed for Princes and other illustrious and distinguished individuals; and it is proposed to forward copies to certain National Libraries of England, France, Prussia, &c.

The Committee, in sanctioning the above plan, have been actuated by a desire to comply with the wishes of Mr. Britton, and to arrive at a conclusion satisfactory to himself and his friends, that no person desirous of possessing it, or doing honour to the subject, may hereafter have cause of complaint.

I cannot conclude these hasty and imperfect remarks better than by resorting to the language of a liberal gentleman to whose critical inspection the proofs of the preceding pages have been submitted, and by whose remarks they are materially improved. In speaking of the Author and his projected volume, he writes, " To himself the composition of such a work cannot but be a delightful task. It will be, in fact, to live over again the portion of his existence most useful to the public,—most honourable to himself,—most abounding in agreeable recollections. It will bring him once more, as it were, into contact with the companions, and friends, and patrons of his better days, ' the loved, the honoured, and the dead;' and he may be more flattered himself that what he will be able to record of them will be of general interest. Regarded in a more enlarged point of view, the book may be considered little less than a History of British Archæology for the last half-century, and what will probably be justly considered as its highest merit, it may serve as a stimulus to rising genius, while it testifies how active exertions and unsparing diligence, supported by a spotless character, may not only triumph over difficulties, but produce that singularly honourable result so lately witnessed at Richmond."

T. E. JONES.

*London, 1st January,* 1846.

# REPORT

OF THE PROCEEDINGS AND SPEECHES AT A DINNER GIVEN TO

## JOHN BRITTON, ESQ., F.S.A.

AT THE CASTLE HOTEL, RICHMOND, JULY 7, 1845,

(THE 74TH ANNIVERSARY OF HIS BIRTH-DAY.)

**NATHANIEL GOULD, ESQ., IN THE CHAIR.**

*Eighty-two Gentlemen were present.*

The cloth having been removed,

THE CHAIRMAN said,—Gentlemen, The first Toast I have to propose is one which precedes all others on occasions of this sort: The merits of the Queen as a Sovereign, a Mother, and a Wife, are so well known to us all, that I need only request that you will heartily drink the health of "HER MAJESTY THE QUEEN." (Drank with much enthusiasm.)

THE CHAIRMAN.—The next Toast is one which would not call for marked observation, but for a particular circumstance to which I shall hereafter allude. It is,—"THE QUEEN DOWAGER, PRINCE ALBERT, and the rest of THE ROYAL FAMILY." I cannot allow this to pass without observing that Prince Albert is connected in mind with the objects of our meeting, and the pursuits of many of the gentlemen present; in the great attention he pays to the progress of the arts and sciences, the taste and virtû of the present day. Hardly a week elapses, during the great London season, without his attending some one of those Societies of Science and Literature which adorn the country and age in which we live; and though he be not actually our King, nor by birth an Englishman, he does, in a royal way, connect his thoughts and his actions, his wishes and his desires, not only with those of our Queen, but also with those of the British public. (*Cheers.*) We observe him constantly attending his duties as President of the Royal Commission of the Fine Arts; and I can only say, on the subject of attention to Her Majesty, that I have repeatedly met him on horseback with the Queen at an early hour; even after an attendance at the opera the preceding night;—this very morning, I so met him in Hyde Park, enjoying the brilliant day-spring with Her Majesty, in all the appearance of affection and comfort,—of attached union and social enjoyment, free from the glare of Royalty and the burden of State; and thus shews himself to be the faithful and affectionate husband. The Queen Dowager has endeared herself to us by Her Majesty's amiable qualities as a Woman, as a Queen, as a Wife, and as a Widow. The Prince of Wales is yet a " Child of Hope." Let us then drink the healths of " the Queen Dowager, Prince Albert, and the rest of the Royal Family." (Drank with much cheering.)

THE CHAIRMAN.—After having done honour to those toasts which are both customary and dear to us, I come to one which may be called " *the Order of the Day*;" that, indeed, upon which hangs the object of our meeting, the centralization of our wishes, and the enthusiasm of our feelings,—in fact, the Toast of the day. (*Cheers.*) I see by those cheers that you anticipate me; I need then hardly say, that I allude to the Gentleman on my right hand.

Gentlemen; I must pause to beg of you to pardon me for the apparent presumption of taking the Chair on so peculiar an occasion. I assure you that I sought it not,—it is not that I did not endeavour to avoid it; but " some have greatness thrust upon them,"—and that is my case. Mr. Wyse, your intended Chairman, has been kept away by imperious calls in the House of Commons, and it was but yesterday that I was called upon to take this Chair, which I so unworthily fill; but which I own is a task of gratifying duty.

Personally unknown as I am to a great majority of the gentlemen present, they are not unknown to me; the trumpet of fame has made many of their names familiar to me, as well as notorious to the world; and it was only at the earnest request of the Committee that I ventured to accept this post, among so many men better qualified. I hope, therefore, that you will excuse all errors of omission or commission, " take the will for the deed," and make the best of me as you find me. (*Cheers.*)

Gentlemen,—Mr. Britton is not a new acquaintance; he has been associated with several gentlemen now present, Commissioners of an extensive district, for a period of more than thirty-two years, in a post of trust and responsibility; and I have never found, I have never known, I have never heard, that in his onerous and confidential occupations, he has done less than his duty, to the satisfaction of the said Commissioners, to the benefit of the trust, and to the credit of himself.

Mr. Britton's life is public property. (*Cheers.*) He is not ashamed of its being known, that the first days of little Britton exhibited no great capabilities of body, or promises of greatness of mind. He is not ashamed of its being known to his present companions and friends, the scientific and learned of the day; that he had but few of the advantages of learning in his reach; that whilst in humble life, he *made* his own opportunities of acquiring knowledge; and that he is truly the *Architect and Builder* of his own Fame and Fortune. I am happy to know that some here to day are companions of his early life, and to see one gentleman who has been associated with him in his various works of literature and usefulness for nearly half a century. Mr. Britton has travelled far and wide; and mentally he has travelled much farther. Not satisfied with elucidating the history of the architecture of his own country, as existing in those ancient monuments of Stonehenge and Avebury; the palaces of our monarchs; the cathedrals of our church; the mansions of our nobility: not satisfied with "the Beauties of England," he has given us the Architectural Antiquities of Normandy, whence much of our own has been derived. He has not only studied but exemplified all that he has seen, and has skilfully illustrated every thing that he has touched.

But, Gentlemen, it is not because of these labours and these beauties of his that we have assembled to day; but to acknowledge to him that his labours have not been simply vast or beautiful, but that they have been instructive and useful. (*Cheers.*) The improved system of Architecture which is extant in this our day, is shown by the view from this window; it must be acknowledged by the youngest amongst us; that our very cottages assert it. And let us but look back to the period of our youth, when a dwelling house was little better than a large packing case; and we see at once how great and rapid is the progress that has been made. Mr. Britton's works have led the way to much of this improvement; and if not a practical Architect himself, he has been the cause of Architecture in others. But I am talking to Gentlemen who know those things much better than myself. Had it been Naval Architecture or Ship-Building, I should have been more at home. But, I say, Gentlemen, that when we consider the *usefulness* of Mr. Britton's works, we cannot but regard it as a misfortune that no Minister has thought it worth his notice to distinguish this usefulness, and bestow some mark, some token of respect, on the author of it.

We have met here together to show Mr. Britton that the value and the utility of his works, if forgotten or overlooked by Ministers, have not been so overlooked by his contemporaries and friends; to acknowledge to him that he has been of service to the science of Architecture, which improves the every day comfort of our dwellings, and the gratification of our senses; that, in fact, he has been a man of worth and value in his day.

Gentlemen, when I look at the man on my right hand, and see only a mildness of countenance, and nothing to make me think him a great man or a bold man, I am the more astonished at the greatness of his labours and the boldness of his darings. I see by this List now in my hand, that he has ventured on publications to an extent, and in a style of elegance, correctness, and expense, that prove him to have been actuated more for the public good than his private advantage; and this List, large as it is, is not so large as it might have been made. However, it shows that he himself, assisted by a Gentleman now present, to whom I have already alluded, Mr. Brayley, (*cheers,*) has published 66 Volumes, (besides numerous Essays,) containing 17,122 printed pages, embellished with 1866 Engravings. You who know what it is to write twenty pages for printing can appreciate these labours; and those of you acquainted with ornamental works can understand the labour of superintending such engravings, drawn to scale and critically correct, as all those in Mr. Britton's publications are allowed to be; but, as a commercial man, I myself can appreciate the amount and the risk of £50,328 which have been expended in producing these works. (*Continued cheering.*)

Gentlemen, all this is matter of fact and record to most of us. Many a time have I thought, and many a time have I spoken about a meeting of this kind; and many others have thought and spoken as I have; but until this day it has not been accomplished. It is not every man, however prominent in his day, that introduces any thing good or any thing useful to society. But Mr. Britton has led the way, and has introduced something both good and useful in his numerous and splendid works on Topography and Architecture. But I fear that I may be travelling out of the record. This meeting is to give proof to Mr. Britton that we have appreciated in him qualities of mind and manner, perseverance and assiduity, hardly to be surpassed, even if they may be equalled.

Here he is, Gentlemen, still among us, still in possession of all his faculties; and I should be sorry indeed should his health require it, but he might now honourably retire into the green pastures by the water courses, and be comfortable. I was not aware of it, Gentlemen, but I am now told that this is his birth-day, (*cheers,*) and I learn from himself that he is in his 75th year; an *ancient Britton* indeed, born in 1771; but who would believe it, on looking at him? Gentlemen, does not this "green old age" prove that the wear and tear of virtuous mental labour tells far less than the ravages of wild and abused youth. I should like to see the apprenticed companions of those days, when *he* would steal from his master's vaults to glean knowledge at a book-stall, whilst they were spending their time and their earnings in idleness or intoxication, and mark how *they* bear their age, if they now exist.

Gentlemen, this meeting is but the beginning of what we intend to do, and whatever the Testimonial may be which the Committee may decide to present to Mr. Britton, I know that it will be given with respect, with sincerity, and with good feeling. I have only one regret, which is, that he has no son, who might, with his name, hand down also his mildness, his perseverance, his boldness, and his usefulness, to another period; and who might say, "That was my Father, he was useful in his day, and " in his day his usefulness was acknowledged; his name was Britton, and " born and bred a Britton, I glory in the name."

Gentlemen, I have done, and now propose to you, with all the honours of royalty, the health of JOHN BRITTON, Esq. (Drunk with much cheering.)

MR. BRITTON.—Mr. Chairman and Gentlemen, or rather, if I may be allowed to depart from customary phraseology, I will say, *Friends,* kind and indulgent Friends, I cannot express the gratification, the conflicting emotions, I feel, at this testimony of your kindness; at the unanimous and enthusiastic manner you have received the health which has been proposed so admirably, and with so much good taste, by our excellent Chairman. I had intended to have said much on the present occasion, and to have explained some circumstances, to illustrate, and, I hope, to justify, the encomiums which the Chairman has just bestowed on myself and my literary works. But when I tell you that I have been very unwell for some days past, and am still weak and depressed; that I feel Old Age creeping upon me, and that his admonitions are unequivocal, and not to be evaded; I trust you will excuse me, if I fail in those physical and mental exertions which are necessary to express my own wishes, and justify your expectations. (*Cheers.*) You must, therefore, take the will for the deed, and draw upon your own imaginations and kind interpretations for any deficiency of matter or manner in myself. You all know my personal and public history; it has been imparted to the world, from time to time, in auto-biographical and introductory notices to my various literary works.* I have told you in the

* In particular I would refer to Prefaces to the third volume of " the Beauties of Wiltshire,"—to " the History of Worcester Cathedral,"—" Dictionary of the Architec-

List which has been alluded to by the Chairman, the extent, the number, and certain other peculiarities of the publications I have brought before the world; and I may say, without arrogance, that they are not only numerous, but of a class and style of execution, previously unknown in literature. (*Cheers.*) I hope to be exonerated from any degree of vanity, when I assert, that most of those works will bear the test of the most critical examination; because they have been the result of great labour, diligent inquiry, and scrupulous investigation. I must, however, admit, that I have produced these works under disadvantageous circumstances: for never having had instruction at any academy, school, or college, I was compelled to seek diligently and diffidently, in various ways, and through different channels, to acquire some knowledge of that class, or department of Literature, which accident had led me to cultivate. I avow these things with sincerity and honesty, to show what can be attained by perseverance and industry. (*Cheers.*) When I consider my literary career, I am led to remember that I was not only uneducated, in the ordinary sense of the word, but in early life,—indeed, up to the age of sixteen, or later,—unacquainted with either an English Grammar, or a Dictionary. With very small funds, I was induced to purchase some books of that description; for, though eager to read, and desirous of obtaining knowledge, I was impeded by my ignorance of the meaning of many words, as well as with their proper arrangement in sentences. Amongst the first books I obtained, were De Foe's, Smollett's, and Fielding's novels. Though these excited my curiosity, and afforded much amusement, I do not forget the difficulty and embarrassment I felt in understanding them. In Bailey's *Dictionary* I found a key which opened my eyes and my mind, and let in a new world of words, and of ideas. You may form some notion of the difficulties I had to contend with, when I tell you that, in the early period of my life, I was for nearly six years occupied in a wine cellar, buried alive: where, however, by an energy and industry which belonged to my natural disposition, I contrived to do as much work in six hours as my fellow-apprentice did in ten: so that I had much time left for reading and study; and thus acquired a little knowledge, which, once implanted, and once stimulated, led me onwards; first, to undertake certain small and trifling works, and afterwards others, larger and more arduous, in succession: until, at length, I have accomplished the number of volumes, essays, and embellishments, which have been detailed to you by our admirable Chairman. (*Cheers.*)

When I sat down to make out that brief List of publications, I was

---

ture and Archæology of the Middle Ages,"—" The Fine Arts of the English School,"— " History of Toddington:"—Introduction to the " Beauties of England and Wales." &c. &c.

unconscious of their number,—of their extent,—and of their cost. Yet I must confess, that I am not ashamed to refer to them for integrity of intention and accuracy in detail, though I must unequivocally admit there is not one of them satisfactory to my fastidious disposition. It was my intention to have said something more relating to my literary pursuits and productions; for these are subjects which seem to belong to the time and subject of this meeting. Your object is to compliment Literature through one of its professors; and if time would permit, I could furnish many curious, and, I believe, interesting particulars of the progress and characteristics of both, during the last half century. In those pursuits, and in my continued exertions through life, I have experienced the sympathy and support of many professional critics: I have, however, met with some of different temperament. Three of them, particularly, have been harsh, illiberal, and inveterate in their personal hostility; and have systematically endeavoured to depreciate and degrade my works. Instead of crushing me, or driving me from the field of enterprise and exertion, their vindictive writings have served only to stimulate me to further and more earnest efforts to attain success, and thereby impeach their judgment. (*Cheers.*) I am happy to say I have surmounted their hostility, and can now regard with pity, and pardon those unhappy men whose chief occupation and delight is calumny and condemnation.

Aware that there are other toasts to be proposed, and Gentlemen present who will respond to them, not only with ability, but with intimate knowledge of their respective subjects, and who I am sure will be rewarded with your attention, it is my duty and desire to be very brief. The Chairman has already told you that I have this day completed my seventy-fourth year. I have met some of my friends in this delightful place, on previous anniversaries for seven years past; but I little anticipated such a meeting as the present. When I see the assemblage of friends now around me, I feel it to be one of the greatest possible rewards for the works I have accomplished, and the difficulties and obstacles I have surmounted; and I am deeply impressed with sentiments and feelings which I cannot adequately explain. (*Great cheering.*) When my friends first suggested a public subscription, and a public dinner, with the ulterior object of offering me some *testimonial* of their approbation of my labours and their results, I paused; but, at length, acquiesced. I however said, that I had no desire to receive an ostentatious and useless piece of Plate; and fortunately that I was not in need of a pecuniary compliment. I suggested, on the contrary, that the money raised might be appropriated to some *Literary* work; as my public career, my fame, and most of my happiness, had been derived from Literature. On this subject different opinions have been started, and different plans proposed; but, though I am not perfectly satisfied with either, I cannot doubt that the

Committee, which has conducted the matter thus far, will devise some application of the amount, which, whilst it may be permanently gratifying to myself, will also satisfy every Subscriber. (*Cheers.*) To that Committee, as well as to all those friends who have kindly and generously come forward in the present cause, I tender my warmest,—my most fervent thanks. I must particularly allude with gratitude to Mr. GODWIN and Mr. CUNNINGHAM, the Honorary Secretaries, who have undertaken a laborious task, and have accomplished that task in a manner creditable to themselves; to the cause of Literature; and to that of Friendship. From peculiar circumstances, we are not gratified and honoured by the company of the Marquess of Lansdowne, the Marquess of Northampton, Earl de Grey, Lord Beresford, and other noblemen, as well as several Members of the House of Commons, all of whom have manifested friendship to me on many occasions; and most of whom, but for the urgent pressure of Parliamentary business, would have been present on this occasion. Their letters, however, to myself and to the Secretaries, evince the warmest interest in the cause for which we meet.

It was my intention to have referred to, and quoted certain passages from my published writings, expressive of opinions, and illustrative of facts, which might elucidate something of my own literary life, and, at the same time, furnish useful information to my younger auditors. I feel, however, my physical energies fail, and I also feel reluctant to occupy an undue portion of the short space which can be devoted to the object of this evening. The remarks of the Gentlemen who will have to address you, I trust and expect will be more amusing and instructive than any thing I can impart in an unpremeditated and embarrassed manner. (*Cheers.*)

Respecting my own literary works, which I know will hereafter be duly appreciated, as well as my natural disposition and character, I am willing to submit them to the impartial and unerring decision of Time; and conclude with the sentiment of the dramatic poet,—

> " 'Tis not in mortals to command success,
> But we'll do more, Sempronius, we'll deserve it."

In conclusion, (for I dread being tedious or irrelevant,) I thank, sincerely thank you, for the compliments you have paid me; and assure you, those thanks are uttered with real and heart-felt cordiality. May you all live long and happy; may the young aspire to usefulness and eminence; and may the old feel, like myself, delighted, honoured, and gratified, by the sympathy, and amenities of friendship, in the latter days of life. (*Enthusiastic applause.*)

## MR. TOOKE'S SPEECH.

W. TOOKE, ESQ., F.R.S.—Mr. Chairman and Gentlemen, Sensible of my inadequacy to do justice to the toast which has been intrusted to me to propose, but relying equally on your indulgence, and on the undoubted claim on your respect of the subject of it, I have undertaken with pleasure the duty of calling your attention to the merits of a distinguished literary body, many of whose members have honoured us with their presence on this occasion:— "THE SOCIETY OF ANTIQUARIES."

This tribute of respect is peculiarly appropriate to the occasion of our meeting, and enables me to advert to the activity and ability with which my friend, Mr. Britton, with ordinary, and even limited means, but with extraordinary perseverance, and unbounded zeal, has, with credit to himself, and advantage to the cause of antiquarian literature, come in aid of the objects of the Society whose interesting labours you are now solicited to acknowledge.

My acquaintance with Mr. Britton dates back to a period of nearly half a century, and was hereditarily transmitted to me by one more capable of appreciating his merits;—my honoured father. Since then it has been my pride and pleasure to continue in habits of friendship with Mr. Britton, and to witness his indefatigable exertions in the pursuit and development of the Architectural Antiquities of England; the whole circle of which he has sedulously investigated and illustrated, from the rude but solemn vestiges of Stonehenge, to that lighter and less enduring specimen of modern caprice, the Pavilion, at Brighton.

Immersed myself in pursuits at variance with these more pleasing subjects, I feel incapable of accomplishing the wish I should otherwise entertain, of filling up this outline of Mr. Britton's services, by referring to the various publications by means of which he has so greatly advanced and ornamented the science to which he is attached. My incapacity, however, will be amply supplied by the more certain knowledge of those by whom I am surrounded. To them, as to myself, Mr. Britton has endeared himself, as well by public usefulness, as by private worth; and he has well earned the distinction he has thus acquired, by the energy of mind which has sustained him, under difficulties and discouragements of no common nature.

Having borne this just but feeble testimony to the merits of our friend Mr. Britton, I must return to the immediate subject of the toast, by observing, that among the many learned antiquaries present, we are honoured with the company of one, particularly distinguished for his erudition in one of the most interesting departments of our national literature; I allude to the learned

Professor of Anglo-Saxon Literature, at Oxford, the REV. DR. INGRAM. (*Cheers.*) Gentlemen, I beg leave to propose, " DR. INGRAM and THE SOCIETY OF ANTIQUARIES."

THE REV. DR. INGRAM.—Gentlemen, In rising to return thanks for the honour conferred on me by the mention of my name in conjunction with the venerable Society of Antiquaries, I have to regret that the commendation of so valuable a Society has not fallen into more able hands; I feel encouragement, nevertheless, when I find myself supported on all sides by so many zealous and efficient Members of that learned body now assembled in this room. I do not, however, mean to imply, that the laudable pursuits of that ancient institution require my feeble advocacy and support. Such advances have been made in our time in general science, in literature, and in art, and particularly in Archæology, that the volumes printed by the Society of Antiquaries for some years past, may well bear a comparison with those of any preceding period since its formation. Their works, therefore, will, I trust, long survive, and support themselves by their intrinsic excellence. Much may be done by united efforts: but all divisions and altercations tend to embarrass and impede the most strenuous exertions. The eloquence and the *harmony* displayed on this occasion, are such as may afford us a subject of congratulation; and the present age may well be proud, if man might be proud of any thing, of the progress which has been made in modern times in all the arts and conveniences of life. As a proof of this, let us look only at the scene around us; and when we consider the splendid construction of this room, viewed either within or without, combined with the elegance of yonder bridge, (*Richmond Bridge, visible from the windows of the Castle Inn,*) and the picturesque and varied prospect beyond; and then observe assembled here the studious antiquary, together with the merchant, the architect, and the artist, to do honour to a private individual, who has distinguished himself by his literary industry and exertions, and by the illustration of our national antiquities; who would not rejoice to witness such a demonstration of the popular taste? Mr. Britton's lot and mine have been in different directions; but our pursuits have been congenial. We have corresponded together, and we have never lost sight of each other; we are natives of the same county; and I have always been happy to employ what little leisure I could obtain, during about half a century that I have known him, in promoting objects similar to his own; and I was, therefore, glad to avail myself of the present opportunity of doing justice to his claims by my personal attendance here. I beg leave again to thank you for the compliment you have just paid me, and on the part of the Society of Antiquaries, to acknowledge the cordiality with which this toast has been received. (*Cheers.*)

## THE DEAN OF HEREFORD'S SPEECH.

THE DEAN OF HEREFORD.—Gentlemen, Although I find myself called upon to address you at this late period of the evening, I cannot hesitate to undertake a duty which I feel to be one of considerable importance in the present proceedings. I have been deeply impressed with the manifestations of delight which have been shewn in connection with the principal cause of our assembling here;—such, indeed, as I have never seen surpassed; though still not greater than the object of them has deserved. I must revert, however, to my more immediate purpose, and proceed to perform a duty which is peculiarly gratifying to me; and I am quite certain when I name the gentleman to whom that duty refers, you will all admit how much indebted to him we are. I am sure we all appreciate his kindness, and the very distinguished manner in which he has conducted the business of this evening. Situated as we are in this great land, and feeling as we do the advantages of being Englishmen;—advantages which, though they cannot be enumerated, are to be *felt* every moment of our lives,—living in a country " whose merchants are princes,"—we must all delight to perceive the proceedings of that class especially marked by a kindness of feeling towards their fellow-men, which should enter to a great extent into the sentiments of all who have to perform the responsibilities of wealth; and which we, none of us, in proportion to our several stations, should forget. When we see one of the class I have alluded to, presiding over us this evening, and consider the admirable manner in which he has performed the duties of his distinguished position, we may well congratulate ourselves on such a demonstration. That seat was to have been taken by a member of Parliament; but although he has been detained elsewhere by the performance of the labours which are required of him by his country, we have no reason to regret his absence, on account of the duties of the post he would have filled;—still, I should have been glad to have seen that gentleman in the chair—tasteful and talented as he is, and a warm supporter of the arts—without any disparagement to the gentleman on my right hand; and not the less so because he is not a member of the church to which I belong. However differing in opinion from him, I could have sat on his left hand with pleasure, as brethren should sit by the side of their brethren, in so good and honourable a cause. (*Cheers.*)

Our most respected president, in his modesty, his genuine modesty, has begged that, in the remarks which he has made, you should take the will for the deed; but in the manner in which he has discharged the duties of the evening, we have had satisfactory evidence both of the *will*, and of the *deed*. (*Cheers.*)

I have had it intimated to me, I must confess, that in the course of the evening I may be required to trespass on your attention again; it is, therefore, unnecessary for me to say more now. The few remarks I have made were, indeed, hardly needed. " Good wine," it is said, " needs no bush ;" and our excellent chairman's talents and tact need no eulogium. The toast I have the honour of proposing to you is, "OUR PRESIDENT OF THE EVENING."

THE CHAIRMAN.—Gentlemen, I would rather not have trespassed on you again so soon, but as I am compelled to rise to return you my sincere thanks for the honour you have done me by so hearty a response to the toast which has been proposed, I will not waste your time by affecting either the modesty of surprise, or the cant of being unused to public speaking.

I have already said, that I came into this chair not by presumption, but from necessity; and my small services to an old friend on such an occasion could only be required to be rendered. I am, indeed, sorry that Mr. Wyse is not in this chair; and, amongst other reasons, for that to which the worthy Dean has just alluded, of shewing that in meetings of this kind, men of all professions can join; that we get together, free from particular opinions or disputed questions in religion; encouraging rather the general principles of liberality, friendship and sociality. I assure you that it is pleasant to me to see here together in harmony, so many men distinguished in literature and science; men of different pursuits, of different branches of study, of various opinions on politics and religion. I am happy to recognize many with whom I am personally acquainted, and more only known to me by reputation; I find friends with whom in matters of business I have been long connected; near me, on my left, sits the designer of our Royal Exchange; nearly opposite, one of those gentlemen to whom our public docks are indebted for valuable services; and wherever I cast my eye are those to whom we owe either the designs or the erection of the public works recently arisen, or now rising and adorning our metropolis. These circumstances add much to the value I set upon the kind and flattering manner in which you have drunk my health.

Gentlemen, Mr. Britton is honoured by the presence of many, high in academic learning, and full of collegiate honours; but the meeting of this evening shews, that, whilst we honour both the institutions from whence they come, and, in those gentlemen, the honours they have achieved, there is no aristocracy in science : that the advantages of collegiate or expensive education are not essential to success; for the best education may be abused, and the highest prospects and promises marred, by a want of application and assiduity and many among the gentlemen now present prove in themselves, that self determination and self-dependance are sufficient to raise men to the foremost ranks of those who, in their age and country, can be useful to society. But I have observed, that however successful a man may have been without the benefit of a collegiate education, he is most frequently, when he has acquired the power, found desirous of giving his sons the advantages of that education which had been denied to himself; putting them as it were on the railway of learning, to get quickly to the most desirable points. To the young gentlemen who have been brought up to Civil Engineering, of whom some are present, it must be most gratifying to see what increasing fields for action are continually opening to them; that science has indeed become not merely a matter of study, but of widely extended, useful application; and that a remuneration for the cost of their learning is of easier attainment, and *ultimate* independance more certain than in almost any other profession.

The present day is truly the day of science; and we can only hope that whilst its progress has hitherto been marked by great advantages to the interests of society at large, it may not induce improvident speculation, or engender vanity, vain glory, quackery, and atheism. I find that I have not kept the promise I made on rising; excuse my prolixity, and allow me to wish you all health, and all and each success in the various departments of learning or science you have espoused. (*Cheers.*)

Gentlemen, I must now propose to you the health of a reverend friend on my left, the Dean of Hereford, and therewith, " the Church of England;" and having spoken so much already, I shall not trouble you long in doing it. When I consider the state of Architecture in this country at the time when our Christian Church was planted, and reflect on the introduction and progress of religious buildings, I cannot fail to observe the close connection it has ever had with the Church. In fact, its dignity and power was maintained and upheld through the middle ages entirely by our church architects; and to them we owe nearly all that has been worth preserving. Indeed, it is to Religion, in whatever form or wherever found, that Architecture owes its origin and its improvement. Whether we look at our own surprising monument of Stonehenge, the various memorials of the Celts of Brittany, or travel to the Caves of Elephanta, the Pyramids of Egypt, the wonders of Thebes, or the Barrows of South America;—or descending at a subsequent period to the Temples of Greece;— and even at this time to some of our recently-erected churches, we shall see that Religion has been both the parent and nurse of Architecture. However, I shall say no more, but simply propose the health of " THE VERY REVEREND THE DEAN OF HEREFORD, AND THE CHURCH."

The Dean of Hereford.—Gentlemen, I can without affectation say, I feel much embarrassment at the kind manner in which you have connected my name with the Church of England: but whenever I am called upon to respond to expressions of regard to the Church of England, no consideration would induce me to abstain from doing so. If in any man fidelity and straightforwardness may be expected, surely it is in a clergyman that you would look for such demeanour. I am a minister of that church; and was so ordained on deliberate consideration, and conviction. I have ate the bread of the church, and enjoyed her distinctions, and as long as I do so, am bound to maintain her principles, and to honour those who honour her. I cannot respect that man's principles, if they can be so called, who does not, in all his actions, consult the spirit of that church whose minister he is; or of him who admits the possibility of subscribing to the Articles of the Church of England in one sense, and holding them in another. I cannot regard such a course as consistent with honesty or duty. I am aware, that in these days much controversy has prevailed on such matters; and I must deprecate the pressing of even *revived proprieties*, if the people are not prepared to receive and appreciate them; but let it not be forgotten that the conscientious clergyman has no easy course to pursue;—and as a Cathedral Clergyman, I could instance facts which would be much to the point. But it may be said that this is no place for such discussion; and therefore, having declared my adhesion to that church which you have been pleased to distinguish, and to couple with my name; and having expressed my gratitude to you for the manner in which you have received that proposal; I must add, that it is very gratifying to me to be present on this occasion, and in this place. Not far from hence I spent the most pleasant, and in one sense the most careless, though not inactive, period of my life; for I was a Curate within three or four miles of this place many years ago, and at that time there were few things connected with the locality that I was not interested in. In this neighbourhood I first put into practical experiment the predilection I had long cherished for Ecclesiastical Architecture; and in proportion to such a predilection must be my estimation of Mr. Britton's services in that cause. I may add, that the noble work of restoration of the venerable cathedral church of Hereford, in which we are engaged, and of the history of which edifice Mr. Britton has published an interesting volume, entails upon me additional obligation to make such just acknowledgment.

I have long since learnt to ascribe to our talented guest the high honour, not only of perpetuating the memory of many exquisite works of art, since destroyed, but of making generally known the gems of British Architecture, and thereby reviving a taste for the graceful symmetry and magnificence of our ancient Ecclesiastical Edifices. I feel bound to say, and I do so gladly and cordially, that Mr. Britton has thus been a benefactor to the church and to his country; and happy am I to enjoy this opportunity of acknowledging how sincerely I estimate his high merit. At the same time I tender to you my grateful acknowledgments of the honour you have conferred on me, in receiving my name as you have done, in connection with that establishment which I so much revere and love.

THE REVEREND DR. REES.—I rise, Mr. Chairman, to discharge, through you, a very pleasing debt of gratitude to two gentlemen to whom we are all eminently indebted. Had it not been for the lateness of the hour at which I have to address you, it would have afforded me peculiar pleasure to advert to the cause of our meeting at this time and place. It has been to me a source of very great satisfaction to witness the tribute of respect that has been this day paid to a gentleman whom I have had the happiness of knowing for nearly half a century; a gentleman with whose progress in literature and science, through life, I have had continual opportunities of being acquainted; and one whose personal merits, and the usefulness of whose works have been long familiar to me. Mr. Britton has had the singular merit of not only being active and industrious himself, but has also been, in a very eminent degree, the cause of activity and industry in others. He was the first whose taste perceived the want, and whose spirit and enterprise led to the production, of an improved class of pictorial illustrations for works on Topography and Antiquities. The artistic talents which he has been the means of calling into exercise, have received their due recompense; for, as the Chairman has informed us, no less a sum than £50,000 has been expended in remunerating those professional labours. Mr. Britton's works cannot fail to have improved the public mind with regard to architecture; and we know that he has improved the taste and knowledge of our architects, by directing their attention to the interesting models to be found among the architectural antiquities of our island. But I must now revert to the subject with which I began, and call upon you to express our obligations to MR. GODWIN and MR. CUNNINGHAM, the gentlemen who have acted as Honorary Secretaries in our present object, for their kind and valuable assistance to the Committee who are conducting the Testimonial to Mr. Britton. I do this with much pleasure, and I am sure you must all be happy to express the gratitude we feel to those gentlemen.

MR. GODWIN.—Mr. Chairman and Gentlemen, Before I thank you for the kind manner in which you have acknowledged the small services of my colleague and myself, I will, in pursuance of my duty as Secretary, read a letter from Mr. Wyse, to show that his absence has not proceeded from want of desire to be present. The letter is as follows:—

"House of Commons, July 4th, 1845.

"MY DEAR SIR.—I have just learned from Sir James Graham, in answer to my question in the House this evening, that it is the intention of the Government to take the *Colleges Bill*, (Ireland,) the *first* of the orders of the day, on Monday. The bill being still in committee, demands the close and uninterrupted attendance of every Irish member, and I especially, from the long solicitude I have felt on the subject, feel myself more particularly *bound* to watch over its progress. This will compel me, *most reluctantly*, to sacrifice the honour and gratification I had anticipated in presiding over the dinner intended to be given to my friend, Mr. Britton. I cannot tell you or him how much I feel this disappointment; I had hoped it would have afforded the opportunity I have so long desired, of expressing my own sense of the many obligations which our national antiquities owe to his zeal and intelligence, and have been the organ in so doing, of what I believe to be the sentiment of every one acquainted with his long and most meritorious and useful labours.

"I also desire to be afforded an occasion, and none could present itself more favourable to the purpose, of calling the attention of the supporters and appreciators of our early arts to the want, which we all feel and deplore, of institutions for their preservation. The issue of my late motion in the House of Commons is proof of how much remains to be done, to place us in this respect in the position which we ought to occupy. The interest which the public takes is not, I trust, to be measured by the apathy of public men, and I cannot but believe I should have found an echo amongst the gentlemen whom I had hoped to meet, to my strong feelings on the subject.

"Though compelled by this *mal a-propos* to give up the pleasure to which I had looked, I hope you will not less believe I most warmly sympathize in the object of your meeting, and hope I may be afforded, on some future occasion, the means of enlarging these expressions of regard and respect to the object of these honours—Mr. Britton.

I am, dear Sir, your's, very truly,

THOMAS WYSE."

The same cause, Sir, has kept Mr. Hume away, who has stated in a letter that he " was desirous to show that respect to Mr. Britton, which his long and valuable services merit." I have also received letters regretting their inability to attend from the Marquess of Northampton, Earl De Grey, Mr. Cockerell, R.A., Mr. Barry, R.A., Mr. Uwins, R.A., Mr. Pickersgill, R.A., Mr. Neeld, M.P., Mr. Donaldson, Mr. Ludlow Bruges, M.P., Mr. Baily, R.A., and fifty others. The first-mentioned distinguished and amiable nobleman says in a letter to Mr. Britton: " I must conclude by wishing that you may long live to remember it, as a satisfactory proof of the sense of your countrymen of your important services to the knowledge of mediæval architecture."

As regards the office of Secretary, I accepted it as a duty, and as a slight acknowledgment of the advantage I, in common with other architects, have derived from Mr. Britton's works. Every lover of our ancient architectural glories, every man studying to acquire the power humbly to imitate them, is much indebted to him. By placing faithful representations of these buildings before the public, and rendering topographical literature agreeable as well as instructive, he has led them to appreciate these structures, and has mainly induced the present improved state of feeling on the subject. What should we know of many buildings now destroyed, if they had not been faithfully depicted and described, and how many more would have been destroyed but for the preservative spirit inculcated?

> " Out upon time, who for ever will leave,
> But enough of the past for the future to grieve,
> O'er that which has been, and o'er that which must be:
> What we have seen our sons shall see;
> Remnants of things that have passed away,
> Fragments of stone reared by creatures of clay!"

How much then we owe to those who have ravished these noble works from the grasp of time, and induced a general desire to preserve them! I should have felt gratitude for this even as a stranger, but having had the gratification of a long connection with Mr. Britton, and having always found him a warm friend and a good man, there was still stronger reason why I should give all the aid in my power to the present endeavour to gratify him. This is but the beginning of the end,—which end is to present to Mr. Britton some permanent Testimonial of respect and esteem; and until that be effected, you may still command my services, and I venture to say, those of my colleague, Mr. Cunningham, who is unexpectedly prevented from being present this evening.

Dr. Conolly.—Mr. Chairman and Gentlemen, I beg in the first place to propitiate your indulgence, by assuring you that I shall not detain you long, or attempt a lecture on the particular subject which I have to introduce to you;—which is, " the Institute of British Architects," in connection with the name of Mr. Tite.

I should, indeed, be most presumptuous, if I pretended to possess much knowledge of the subject. I can only join with you in the gratification we must all feel at the progress which the architecture of this country has made, and is making; as manifested in our public buildings, our great commercial edifices, and in our domestic structures; and above all, I regard with pleasure the improvement in that kind of architecture which is destined for the comfort and accommodation of the poorer classes of society; and which, indeed, has grown up entirely in our own day. There is also a branch of architecture—the ecclesiastical branch—in which it is impossible not to observe the change that has lately been effected. All these improvements show how much architecture is associated with the grandeur and the comfort of our country, and with the highest aspirations of man. And here, Gentlemen, I shall beg your attention to a matter connected with our ecclesiastical architecture, and in relation to my excellent and esteemed friend, Mr. Britton. There is probably no gentleman present who has not, at some time or other, felt his interest excited respecting the tomb and burial-place of Shakspeare. The church of Stratford-upon-Avon, Gentlemen, the mausoleum of England's Bard, the *chancel* of that church, wherein he lies interred, the shrine which contains the bones of that great man, were all, ten years ago, absolutely falling into decay: the remains of the poet rested, as they do now, in one of the most picturesque churches in England—situated in a large church-yard on the banks of the Avon, associated for ever with his name—yet the beautiful carving of the walls of that building was obliterated with whitewash; the roof was hidden by a ceiling of plaster; oak carving was covered thick with yellow paint; the pavement was broken and uneven; and the monument of Shakspeare was quite neglected: the tomb-stones of his family were going fast to ruin: and even the inscription on the grave-stone of his beloved daughter was partially effaced, to make room for the name of some person of another family. This was the state of things ten years ago. I had the great felicity to rouse the attention of the inhabitants of Stratford to the subject, and to teach them the duty of preserving this venerable pile. In doing so, I had the pleasure of meeting Mr. Britton, who entered into the subject with his characteristic zeal, and, by his inestimable aid, with the directions which he gave us, we were enabled to restore that chancel, and to preserve the church from inevitable ruin: for, after the chancel was restored, more money was raised, and the whole church, from one end to the other, is now renovated and preserved, I trust for many ages to come. (*Much cheering.*)

On such an occasion as the present, I could not omit alluding to this subject. I will only trouble you with a very few words more. I am delighted to hear that the " Institute of British Architects" has been extremely beneficial, by concentrating the talents of nearly all the architects of the country, and by encouraging every thing which tends to elevate the dignity of architecture, and the position of its professors. I am gratified to hear that such is the character of this Institution, and I am sure you will unite with me in connecting the toast of "THE INSTITUTE OF BRITISH ARCHITECTS" with the health of so eminent a member of it as MR. TITE.

W. TITE, ESQ., F.R.S.—Gentlemen, I beg to thank you for the honour you have just done me, and for the association of my name with the Institute of British Architects: I rejoice to be present at this meeting, and in their name and my own to bear testimony to the value and importance of Mr. Britton's labours. At the present time, in England, it is delightful to see the skill and elegance with which the beautiful and appropriate forms of Gothic architecture are applied to the various purposes of life. That style has been deeply studied, its various periods and phases distinctly defined, a fondness for its character, almost as a national feeling, has risen up in this country, and I cannot but acknowledge that these advantages have been mainly derived from the public spirit and good taste of our friend and guest on this occasion. To prove the truth of this assertion, I need not go back to the time of our great architect, Wren,—who, with all his skill and learning, yet ignorant on this subject, could find nothing in the beauties of its detail, but " idle jetties and crinkum-crankum work,"— because at a much later period, and even in our own time, this very neighbourhood could show how little was understood of Gothic Architecture, when the puerilities and absurdities of Strawberry Hill could be applauded even to the very echo. This neighbourhood also could show, in the now destroyed palace of Kew, how little acquaintance with our national architecture was possessed even by the " tasteful Wyatt." This ignorance has ceased; and in the works of Britton, and the school of illustrators he has founded, the amateur has been furnished with the means of correcting and informing his taste, and the architect with models for his imitation and study. I shall be happy to see the Committee carry out effectually the further purposes of this meeting; and I trust they will do so in such a manner as may best express our gratitude and respect to the author of the Architectural and Cathedral Antiquities.

With reference to the Institution with which you have been pleased to associate my name, though I regret that more of its members are not present, to do justice to the cause for which we assemble, and to recognize the truth of what I have stated, yet I think I may venture to say, that the Institute feels most grateful to Mr. Britton; and, therefore, as one of the Vice-Presidents, on their part I beg to offer him their thanks and congratulations.

MR. GODWIN.—I am deputed to propose a toast which cannot fail to interest a meeting like the present, although from the lateness of the hour I fear to address you at any length. The toast is, "THE ANCIENT FRATERNITY OF FREEMASONS." The freemasons of to-day are known only in connection with good dinners and great charity; but in former times, as you well know, they occupied a different position. It seems clear, that the greater number of the magnificent works produced in the middle ages were erected by bands of men, having in some degree a religious character, and protected by certain enactments,—who were in reality "free-masons," and the progenitors of the present lodges. This fact accounts for several phenomena observable in tracing the history of Architecture, which I feel assured would interest you if there were time for comment. There are at this table several of the most eminent builders of the day,—Mr. William Cubitt, Mr. Grissell, Mr. Herbert, Mr. Elger, and others,—who each in himself represents a large fraternity of free-masons. They are men who have built miles of sewers, covered New London with squares, streets, and terraces, and Old England with interminable railways; and this makes the toast more fitting still, especially as several of them are high in the mysteries of Freemasonry. I do not know that they can still sing—

> "High honour to masons the craft daily brings;
> We're brothers of princes, and fellows of kings:"

but I do know that they practise charity and the virtues, and if they do not teach Euclid, they still inculcate morality. In order that I may bear witness to this, at least in one case, I will couple with this toast the name of MR. WILLIAM CUBITT, not simply as a distinguished member of the craft, but as an old and warm friend of Mr. Britton. (*Cheers.*)

W. CUBITT, ESQ.—Mr. Chairman and Gentlemen, The prevailing characteristic of a Freemason's heart is charity; as a Freemason, and acting on that principle, I shall not permit myself to dwell long at this late hour, lest by so doing, I should inflict a penalty on those kind friends who may be already somewhat fatigued. This is, however, an occasion on which much ought to be said; and called up as the representative of Freemasonry, and being in my own person a practical, and I may almost say an operative mason, it would be unbecoming in me to be altogether silent, when the ancient edifices of the country and their illustrator are the theme. It would also be utterly inconsistent with the strong feeling I entertain of what is due to Mr. Britton, whose great literary works we are here met to commemorate.

The Freemasons of the present day have been spoken of by our talented friend, Mr. Godwin, as traditionally and historically connected with the building of those interesting monuments of the middle ages, which Mr. Britton has devoted the best years of a long and active life to illustrate. You must not expect me to say much about Freemasonry: it does not need my advocacy, nor does it permit me here to unveil its mysteries. I may say, as in truth I can say, that it is ancient and honourable; and if any of the gentlemen now assembled desire to know more of the matter, there are others as well as myself, who will be happy to introduce them where, on proper conditions, they may become members of a craft which would confer honour on them, as I have no doubt they would do honour to it. With regard to Mr. Britton, I am under no restriction in speaking, save the narrow limits of my own feeble powers; and glad should I be if I knew how to say half which might truly and accurately be stated, in addition to a vast deal which has been so well said this evening, in honourable testimony of his private and public character. Whenever and wherever our ancient and magnificent cathedrals shall become the theme of discussion and admiration, there Mr. Britton's useful and beautiful publications will have their meed of praise: the man who had a mind sufficiently comprehensive to conceive a project so great as that which he entered on, and who with untiring energies, assiduously exerted through half a century, was enabled to achieve his task, deserves the approbation and esteem of all lovers of architecture and of literature; and I feel assured, that his name will descend to distant ages, in connection with those venerable structures which he has so ably and effectively elucidated. It is true that all these wondrous buildings must fall to ruin by the lapse of time, yet the records which he has caused to be made of them, will still be preserved in the well-stored library. His publications will be found to represent them in all their picturesque and varied beauty, as well as in all their minute, and elaborate details; so that if either from extreme age, or from any other cause, the country were bereft of them, those works will enable some future generation to reconstruct their fac-similies. Mr. Britton has done this great work for the country, to the honour of our age, and to the honour of the Freemasons who constructed these monuments; and in so doing he has inscribed his own name on the very buildings themselves, and while doing that which will serve to illustrate and perpetuate the history and character of such numerous, vast, and important edifices, he has unintentionally, but inevitably, made them the monuments of his own important and arduous achievements. (*Applause.*)

Gentlemen, I thank you most sincerely for associating my name, in the way you have been pleased to do, as an old and warm friend of Mr. Britton. I feel it to be no small honour to be thus designated, and am proud of a friendship which I have long enjoyed; and while I selfishly hope that he may long be spared, let me offer my best wishes that you, Gentlemen, may all have a continuance of kindly intercourse with him. (*Cheers.*)

THE CHAIRMAN.—Gentlemen, There is a toast which, though I propose it last, is far from being the least in our estimation. To such a meeting as this, composed of so many literary and scientific men, the Fine Arts must be dear.

We are all well aware that literature and science owe much to Painting and Engraving;—even our friend Britton's scientific accounts and delighting descriptions are greatly improved by the assistance of the Arts;—for where language fails, engraving often succeeds.

Letter-press alone, could never impart a just idea of the " Beauties of England," whether in the " human face divine," the scenery of our country, the seats of our nobility, or the architecture of our cathedrals. The Fine Arts then must not be forgotten by us; and therefore I give you " THE ROYAL ACADEMY and MR. DAVID ROBERTS."

DAVID ROBERTS, ESQ., R.A.—Mr. Chairman and Gentlemen, In the name of the Royal Academy, and of gentlemen connected with the arts, it affords me sincere pleasure to join with those literary and scientific friends I see around me, in paying a just and merited compliment to one to whom the arts, as well as literature and the world at large, owe a debt of gratitude. The numerous works given to the public, by our venerable guest, during a long life, must have tended much—not only to diffuse a taste for what is beautiful in our magnificent monastic remains—but to direct attention to the preservation of that which has been hitherto much neglected. The accuracy and artistic feeling displayed, for the first time in this or any other country, in the treatment of the subjects delineated in those works, is only equalled by the exquisite beauty of the engravings.

The anxiety, labour, and cost of producing such a series of splendid works, no mere *pecuniary* return can ever repay. It must, therefore, be peculiarly gratifying to find around him this day those friends who, like myself, are here, not only to pay him that respect he merits, but to repay a debt we all owe him: and for myself, I may be pardoned the vanity of stating, on an occasion of this kind, that as far as I am known by my works, my devotion to that particular walk, or line in which I am best known, although it may not have been originated, was yet greatly perfected and confirmed by an early acquaintance with the architectural productions of my much-respected friend, John Britton. *(Cheers.)*

At the close of the evening, S. C. HALL, ESQ., F.S.A., briefly addressed the Chair.

He expressed his exceeding satisfaction at meeting so many persons, distinguished in literature, science, and art, assembled to do honour to a gentleman whose high reputation had been widely spread by his successful exertions, almost equally bestowed upon the cause of the man of science, the artist, and the man of letters. It was a too frequent, and far too well founded charge, that such men as Mr. Britton were left to receive the thanks of posterity; obtaining no substantial reward while they lived, and earning reputation only when they had ceased to be stimulated by its influence, and were " deaf to the voice of the charmer." The gathering to-day of so many personal friends, and public admirers of the character and talents of Mr. Britton, could not but assure him, that towards the close of a long, assiduous, and serviceable career, he enjoyed that respect and regard which ever became the best recompense of useful and good men,—whose labours had been exerted, not for private advantage only, but for the service of mankind. The meeting of to-day, therefore, was one which forestalled posthumous fame; which in tendering homage to worth, gave it when it could be felt and appreciated, and not too late to stimulate to renewed activity. The present assembly was not beneficial as regarded Mr. Britton alone; it was an honour in which every person present had his share; and no doubt among those who had there met together, there were some, perhaps not a few, who were justified in anticipating similar expressions of esteem and respect, when, after lives of useful labour, they were, like Mr. Britton, looking forward to a period of rest. Thus, then, the proceedings on this occasion might have a higher and more important effect than was at the moment anticipated:—who could say how far it might operate in encouraging others to energy equal to that which Mr. Britton had displayed for more than half a century; prompting to similar useful exertions, by assuring the reward, which in his case had been realised, of thorough appreciation on the part of his compeers,—his fellow-labourers in the broad fields of Literature, Science, and Art,—and a grateful recognition of ample services for the good and the improvement of mankind.

Mr. Hall added, that he, like Mr. Britton, (although in a far humbler and more limited degree,) had exercised the irksome, difficult, always onerous, and rarely grateful, duty of public Criticism, and could therefore sympathise with his veteran friend in the annoyances to which its due discharge had occasionally subjected him. It was a duty that often produced adversaries, but seldom created friends; if, however, Mr. Britton had, at times, known what it was to feel infinitely more pain than he had given by censuring the works of others, and had suffered for his advocacy of truth, he had, at all events, the satisfaction of knowing there were many who comprehended whilst they duly appreciated his motives, and by whom his intentions were understood. The results of to-day were a sufficient set-off against a host of annoyances, which he who resolves to discharge an allotted task honestly and fearlessly, must be always ready to bear.

# GENTLEMEN AT THE DINNER,
## July 7, 1845.

### NATHANIEL GOULD, ESQ., IN THE CHAIR.

— ABRAHAM, ESQ., Architect.
DR. ALLNATT, F.S.A.
JOSEPH BLUNT, ESQ.
WM. J. BOOTH, ESQ., Architect.
E. W. BRAYLEY, ESQ., F.S.A.
JOHN BRITTON, ESQ., F.S.A.
THOMAS BROWN, ESQ.
DECIMUS BURTON, ESQ., Architect, F.S.A.
WM. CHADWICK, ESQ.
WM. CHAPMAN, ESQ.
J. CHUBB, ESQ.
M. CHUBB, ESQ.
J. CONOLLY, ESQ., M.D.
R. COOKE, ESQ.
G. R. CORNER, ESQ., F.S.A.
R. S. COX, ESQ.
JOHN CRANAGE, ESQ.
F. CREW, ESQ.
WM. CUBITT, ESQ.
JAS. DARNILL, ESQ.
B. R. DAVIES, ESQ.
ROBERT DICKSON, ESQ., M.D.
W. J. DONTHORN, ESQ., Architect, F.S.A.
WM. DUNNAGE, ESQ.
J. ELGER, ESQ., Architect.
CHARLES FOWLER, ESQ., Architect.
JOHN S. GASKOIN, ESQ.
SILLS GIBBONS, ESQ.
GEO. GODWIN, ESQ., Architect.
GEO. GODWIN, JUN., ESQ., Architect, F.R.S., F.S.A., *Hon. Sec.*
THOS. GRISSELL, ESQ.
WM. GRANE, ESQ.
WM. GUNSTON, ESQ.
S. C. HALL, ESQ., F.S.A.
EDWARD HALL, ESQ.
J. D. HARDING, ESQ.
WM. HERBERT, ESQ.
THE DEAN OF HEREFORD.
J. HOPGOOD, ESQ.
WM. HOSKING, ESQ., Architect, C.E.
THE REV. J. INGRAM, D.D., F.S.A.
J. INGRAM, ESQ.
MR. C. JAQUES, JUN.
WM. JERDAN, ESQ.
MR. T. E. JONES.
H. E. KENDALL, JUN., ESQ., Arch., F.S.A.
THE REV. DR. KNAPP.
— LOCKHART, ESQ.
GEO. MAIR, ESQ., Architect.
CHAS. MARTIN, ESQ.
R. MAUGHAM, ESQ.
E. R. MORAN, ESQ.
R. MULLINGS, ESQ.
J. B. NICHOLS, ESQ., F.S.A.
J. PARROTT, ESQ.
LEWIS POCOCK, ESQ., F.S.A.
JAMES PONSFORD, ESQ.
A. RAINY, ESQ.
THE REV. DR. REES, F.S.A.
MR. JOHN REES.
MR. WM. REID.
— REMINGTON, ESQ.
DAVID ROBERTS, ESQ., R.A.
T. H. SEALY, ESQ.
B. H. SMART, ESQ.
JOHN SMITH, ESQ.
J. SMITH, JUN., ESQ.
CAPT. SMYTH, R.N., F.R.S.
LIEUT. STRATFORD, R.N., F.R.S.
WM. STRONG. ESQ.
THE REV. E. TAGART, F.S.A.
ARTHUR TAYLOR, ESQ.
G. L. TAYLOR, ESQ., Architect, F.S.A.
JOHN THOMPSON, ESQ.
JOHN TIMBS, ESQ.
WILLIAM TITE, ESQ., Architect, F.R.S.
WILLIAM TOOKE, ESQ., F.R.S.
WM. WANSEY, ESQ., F.S.A.
RICHARD SAMUEL WHITE, ESQ.
CHAS. F. WHITING, ESQ.
E. P. WILLIAMS, ESQ.

www.ingramcontent.com/pod-product-compliance
Lightning Source LLC
Chambersburg PA
CBHW062122160426
43191CB00013B/2174

*9 781535 811767*